Introducing Autodesk Maya

This book is your perfect hands-on guide to start animating quickly. Using approachable, real-world exercises, you'll master the fundamentals of this animation software by following full-color screenshots step by step. Each chapter opens with a quick discussion of concepts and learning objectives, and then launches into hands-on tutorials that give you firsthand experience and a good start. You'll learn the basics of modeling, texturing, animating, and visual effects. Whether you're a complete beginner or migrating from another 3D application, this task-based book provides the solid grounding you need in Autodesk Maya.

Key Features

- Model with polygons, meshes, and more
- Add motion with simple and complex animations
- Add color and textures to visualize materials and surfaces
- Render scenes with great lighting and camera placement

Introducing Autodesk Maya

Dariush Derakhshani

CRC Press
Taylor & Francis Group
Boca Raton London New York

CRC Press is an imprint of the
Taylor & Francis Group, an **informa** business

First edition published 2025
by CRC Press
2385 NW Executive Center Drive, Suite 320, Boca Raton FL 33431

and by CRC Press
4 Park Square, Milton Park, Abingdon, Oxon, OX14 4RN

CRC Press is an imprint of Taylor & Francis Group, LLC

ISBN: 978-1-138-59055-7 (hbk)
ISBN: 978-1-138-59054-0 (pbk)
ISBN: 978-0-429-49095-8 (ebk)

DOI: 10.1201/9780429490958

Typeset in Times
by codeMantra

Access the Support Material: https://www.routledge.com/9781138590540

For Product Safety Concerns and Information please contact our EU representative GPSR@taylorandfrancis.com Taylor & Francis Verlag GmbH, Kaufingerstraße 24, 80331 München, Germany.
Batch No. RP133797

Contents

About the Author

Dariush Derakhshani is a Visual Effects Supervisor, Animation Producer, and an award-winning CG animator and author of several Maya books, including the best-selling series *Introducing Maya: 3D for Beginners and Maya: Secrets of the Pros*. Dariush has been an animator and supervisor on commercials and feature films for over 25 years at such places as ReelFX/Radium, Digital Domain, CaféFX, Cobalt FX, and Sight Effects. Dariush has an MFA in Film, TV, and Computer Animation from USC Film School and has been teaching Maya and animation classes in Los Angeles for over 25 years for schools like USC, California Institute of the Arts, Rutgers, and Drexel. Dariush has been publishing tutorials, articles, and books on Maya for the past 24 years in such publications as Post, PostPerspective, CGW, 3D World, DigitalMediaNet. com, and AWN.com. He is a member of the Visual Effects Society, is a VES Award nominee, has won several Telly Awards and the London Advertising Award for commercial effects, the Bronze Plaque from the Columbus Film Festival, and a graduate fellowship from Paramount Pictures, and shares other accolades from the London International Advertising Festival and the AICP (American Independent Commercial Producers).

Introduction

Welcome to Introducing Autodesk Maya and the world of computer-generated imagery (CGI). Whether you're new to 3D graphics or venturing into Autodesk's powerhouse animation software from another 3D application, you'll find this book a perfect primer. This book introduces you to the Autodesk® Maya® software and shows how you can work with Maya to create your art, whether it's animated or static in design.

Twenty years ago, the first edition of this book was written out of the author's desire for solid, comprehensive, and yet open-ended teaching material about Maya for his classes. This book exposes you to all the facets of Maya by introducing and explaining its tools and functions to help you understand how Maya operates. In addition, you'll find hands-on examples and tutorials that give you first-hand experience with the toolsets. Working through these will help you develop skills as well as knowledge. These tutorials expose you to various ways of accomplishing tasks with this intricate and comprehensive artistic tool.

Finally, this book explains workflow. You'll learn not only how specific tasks are accomplished but why—that is, how they fit into the larger process of producing three-dimensional (3D) animation. By doing that, these chapters should give you the confidence to venture deeper into the Maya feature set on your own or by using any of the other Maya learning tools and books as a guide.

It can be frustrating to learn a powerful tool such as Maya, so it's important to remember to pace yourself. The number-one complaint of readers of books like this is a sense that either the pace is too fast or the steps are too complicated or overwhelming. That's a tough nut to crack, to be sure, and no two readers are the same. But this book offers you the chance to run things at your own pace. The exercises and steps may seem challenging at times, but keep in mind that the more you try—even the more you fail at some attempts—the more you'll learn about how to operate Maya. Experience is the key to learning workflows in any software program, and with experience comes failure and aggravation. Nevertheless, try and try again, and you'll see that further attempts will be easier and more fruitful.

Above all, this book aims to inspire you to use Maya as a creative tool to achieve and explore your own artistic vision.

What You'll Learn from This Book

Introducing Autodesk Maya is updated from the previous versions of the book and updated to incorporate Arnold for Maya rendering as well as some new modeling workflows.

The book aims to show you how Maya works and introduce you to every part of the toolset to give you a glimpse of the possibilities available with Maya as a primer to get you started.

You'll learn the basic concepts underlying animation and 3D and how to work with the Maya interface. You'll then learn the basic methods of modeling—creating objects that appear to exist in 3D space and that can be animated. You'll also explore shading and texturing—the techniques of applying surfaces to the objects you create—and you'll learn how to create lights and shadows in a scene. Animation is an enormously rich topic, but the practice and theory provided here will give you a solid footing. Next, you'll learn how to control the process of rendering, turning your images into files that can be viewed.

After you've finished this book and its exercises, you'll have experience in almost everything Maya offers, giving you a solid foundation on which to base the rest of your Maya and computer-generated imagery experience.

The goal of this book is to get you familiar enough with all the parts of Maya so you can work on your own and start a long and healthy education with a powerful and flexible tool.

You will, however, learn the most from yourself.

Who Should Read This Book

Anyone who is curious about learning Maya or who is migrating from another 3D software package can learn something from this book. Even if you're highly experienced in another 3D package such as the open-source Blender or Autodesk® 3ds Max® or Cinema 4D®, you'll find this book helpful in showing you how Maya operates so you can migrate your existing skill set quickly and efficiently. By being exposed to everything Maya has to offer, you'll better understand how you can use its toolset to create or improve your art and work.

If you already have cursory or even intermediate experience with Maya, culled from time-spent learning at home, you can fill many holes with the information available in this book as well as expand your experience. Self-education is a powerful tool, and the more you expose yourself to different sources, opinions, and methods, the better educated you'll be.

In addition, this book is invaluable for teachers in the computer graphics (CG) field. This book was written to cater to those who want to pick up the fundamentals of Maya as well as those who want to teach classes based on a solid body of course material. You won't find a better basis for a class when you combine this book with your own curriculum.

How to Use This Book

To begin reading this book, open it to some pages and read.

Introducing Autodesk Maya approaches the subject in a linear fashion that tracks how most animation productions are undertaken. But the book has numerous cross-references to make sure the chapters make sense no matter in which order you want to tackle them. You can open this book to any chapter and work through the tutorials and examples laid out for the Maya task being covered. Feel free to browse the chapters and jump into anything that strikes your fancy. However, if you're completely new to CG, you may want to take the chapters in order.

Although you can learn a lot just by reading the explanations and studying the illustrations, it's best to read this book while you're using Maya so that you can try the exercises for yourself as you read them. If you don't already have Maya, you can download an educational license if you are a qualifying student or faculty member at `www.students.autodesk.com/` or a 30-day trial version of the software at `www.autodesk.com/maya`. This book refers to a companion web page (`https://www.routledge.com/9781138590540`), containing all the example and support files you'll need for the exercises in the text to help you through some of the tutorials, which is a valuable educational aid. You will also find helpful Maya videos on the author's Youtube channel @Koosh3d. You can use the example files to check the progress of your work, or you can use them as a starting point if you want to skip ahead with an exercise. The latter can save the more experienced reader tons of time. You'll also find it valuable to examine these files in depth to see how scenes are set up and how some of the concepts introduced in the book are implemented. Because Maya is a complex, professional software application, the exercises are both realistically ambitious and simple enough for new users to complete. Take them one step at a time and find your own pace, accepting aggravations and failures as part of the process. Take your time; you're not working on a deadline—yet.

How This Book is Organized

Chapter 1, "Introduction to Computer Graphics and 3D," introduces you to common CG concepts to give you a basic overview of how CG happens and how Maya relates to the overall process. In addition, it describes basic animation concepts to better build a foundation for further study.

Chapter 2, "Jumping into Basic Animation Head First," creates a simple animation to introduce you to the Maya interface and workflow and give you a taste of how things work right away. By animating the planets in our solar system, you'll learn basic concepts of creating and animating in Maya and how to use its powerful object structure.

Chapter 3, "The Autodesk® Maya® Interface," presents the entire Maya interface and shows you how it's used in production. Beginning with a roadmap of the screen, this chapter also explains how Maya defines and organizes objects in a scene while you are set to the task of building a decorative box model.

Chapter 4, "Beginning Polygonal Modeling," is an introduction to modeling concepts and workflows. It shows you how to start modeling using polygonal geometry to create various objects, from a cartoon hand to a catapult, using some of the new tools incorporated into Autodesk Maya 2015.

Chapter 5, "Modeling with NURBS Surfaces and Deformers," takes your lesson in modeling a step further. It shows you how to model with deformers and surfacing techniques, using NURBS to create a glass candle jar to later light and render in a scene. You'll also learn how to create NURBS surfaces directly into polygon meshes easily.

Chapter 6, "Practical Experience!," rounds out your modeling lessons with a comprehensive exercise showing you how to model a child's toy airplane using polygons. This chapter also exposes you to the powerful File Referencing workflow available in Maya.

Chapter 7, "Autodesk® Maya® Shading and Texturing," shows you how to assign textures and shaders to your models. Using a toy wagon model, you'll learn how to texture it to look like a real toy wagon as well as lay out its UVs for proper texture placement. Then, you'll create detailed photo-realistic textures based on photos for the decorative box and toy plane models. You'll also learn how to use toon shading to achieve a cartoon look for your renders.

Chapter 8, "Introduction to Animation," covers the basics of how to animate a bouncing ball using keyframes and then moves on to creating and coordinating more complex animation—throwing an axe and firing a catapult. You'll also learn how to import objects into an existing animation and transfer animation from one object to another, a common exercise in professional productions. In addition, you'll learn how to use the Graph Editor to edit and finesse your animation as well as animate objects along paths.

Chapter 9, "More Animation!," expands on Chapter 8 to show you how to use the Maya skeleton and kinematics system to create a simple walk cycle. This chapter also covers how to animate objects by using relationships between them. A thrilling exercise shows you how to rig a hand for easier animation and then a locomotive model for automated animation, some of the most productive uses of Maya.

Chapter 10, "Autodesk® Maya® Lighting," begins by showing you how to light a 3D scene as you learn how to light the toy plane and box that you modeled and textured earlier in the book. It also shows you how to use the tools to create and edit Maya lights for illumination, shadows, and special lighting effects. The mental ray for Maya Physical Sun and Sky feature is explored in this chapter as an introduction to some sophisticated techniques for mental ray lighting.

Chapter 11, "Autodesk® Maya® and Arnold Rendering," explains how to create image files from your Maya scene and how to achieve the best look for your animation using proper cameras and rendering settings. You'll also learn about the Maya renderer, the Vector renderer, and using HDRI and image-based lighting through Arnold for Maya, as well as raytracing, motion blur, and depth of field. You'll have a chance to render the toy airplane and decorative box to round out your skills.

Chapter 12, "Autodesk® Maya® Dynamics and Effects," introduces you to the powerful Maya dynamics animation system as well as nParticle technology. You'll animate pool balls colliding with one another using rigid body dynamics, and you'll fire the catapult. Using nParticle animation, you'll also create steam to add to your locomotive scene. You will then be exposed to nCloth to create a tablecloth and a flag. This chapter also shows you how to use Paint Effects to create animated flowers and grass within minutes.

Hardware and Software Considerations

Because computer hardware is a quickly moving target and Maya now runs on three distinct operating systems (Windows 10/11, Linux, and Mac OS X), specifying which hardware components will work with Maya is something of a challenge. Fortunately, Autodesk has a "qualified hardware" page on its website that describes the latest hardware to be qualified to work with Maya for each operating system, as well as whether you're running the 32-bit or 64-bit version. Go to the following site for the most up-to-date information on system requirements:

www.autodesk.com/maya

Although you can find specific hardware recommendations on these web pages, some general statements can be made about what constitutes a good platform on which to run Maya. First, be sure to get a fast processor; Maya eats through CPU cycles like crazy, so a fast processor is important. Second, you need lots of RAM (memory) to run Maya—at least 8 GB, but 16 GB or more is better to have, especially if you're working with large scene files and are on a 64-bit system. Third, if you expect to interact well with your Maya scenes, a powerful video card is a must; although Maya will mosey along with a poor graphics card, screen redraws will be slow with complex scenes, which can quickly become frustrating. You may want to consider a workstation graphics card for the best compatibility (rather than a consumer-grade gaming video card). Several companies make entry-level through top-performing workstation cards to fit any budget. A large hard disk is also important—most computers these days come with huge drives anyway.

Fortunately, computer hardware is so fast that even laptop computers can now run Maya well. In addition, even hardware that is not officially supported by Autodesk can often run Maya—just remember that you won't be able to get technical support if your system doesn't meet the company's qualifications.

Free Autodesk Software for Students and Educators

The Autodesk Education Community is an online resource with more than 5 million members that enables educators and students to download—for free (see website for terms and conditions)—the same software used by professionals worldwide. You can also access additional tools and materials to help you design, visualize, and simulate ideas. Connect with other learners to stay current with the latest industry trends and get the most out of your designs. Get started today at https://www.autodesk.com/education.

The Next Step

By the time you finish *Introducing Autodesk® Maya®*, you'll have some solid skills for using Maya. This primer should get you ready to move into more detailed work in Maya, whichever direction you choose to take your journey.

You can contact the author through www.koosh3d.com, Youtube @Koosh3d, and Facebook at www.facebook.com/IntroMaya. You may also go to the book's web page for the project files from the book at https://www.routledge.com/9781138590540.

1

Introduction to Computer Graphics and 3D

Learning Outcomes

In this chapter, you will be able to

Develop an appreciation for the computer graphics process

Discern between different types of digital image files

Recognize key terms and principles in film and animation

A Preview of the CG Process

Try not to view this experience as learning a software package but as learning a way of working to an end. It's hard to relax when you're trying to cram tons of information into your brain. Try not to make this experience about how this software application works, but about how you work with this tool.

CG is the abbreviation for *computer graphics*, and both terms are used interchangeably.

The process of creating in CG requires that you either model or arrange prebuilt objects in a scene, give them color and light, possibly animate them, and then render them through a virtual camera to make an image, much like with real cinematography.

> A large community on the Web provides free and for-purchase models and textures that you can use in your scenes. Sites such as www.turbosquid.com, www.textures.com, and www.archive3d.net can cut out a lot of the time you might spend creating all the models or textures for a scene.

After you build your scene in 3D using models, lights, and a camera, the computer *renders* the scene, converting it to a 2D image. Through setup and rendering, CG is born—and, with a little luck, a CG artist is also born.

A CG animation production can be compared to the film/TV industry's typical workflow which consists of three broad stages: preproduction, production, and postproduction. In film and TV, *preproduction* is the process in which the script and storyboards are written, costumes and sets are designed and built, actors are cast and rehearse, the crew is hired, and the equipment is rented and set up. In the *production* phase, scenes are taped or filmed in the most efficient order. *Postproduction*

(often simply called *post*) describes everything that happens afterward: the scenes are edited into a story; a musical score, sound effects, and additional dialogue are added; and visual effects may also be added.

Preproduction for a CG animation means gathering reference materials, motion tests, layout drawings, model sketches, and such to make the actual CG production as straightforward as possible. Production begins when you start creating models of characters, sets, and props from the storyboards, model sheets, and concept art. Then these *assets* are animated, and finally, shots are then lit and ready for rendering. Postproduction for a CG project is where all of a CG film's elements are brought together and assembled into the final form through editing, adding sound, and so on.

The CG Production Workflow

Modeling almost always begins the CG process, which then can lead to texturing and then on to rigging (animation setup) and animation (or vice versa). Lighting usually follows next, with rendering pulling up the rear as the last step. (Of course, the process isn't completely linear; you'll often go back and forth adjusting models, lights, and textures along the way, and even editing and manipulating renders with photo-image editors and compositing programs like Adobe Photoshop or After Effects or even programs that allow you to paint directly on 3D models such as Adobe Substance Painter.)

Modeling, the topic of Chapters 4–6, is usually the first step in creating CG. Downloading or purchasing models from the Internet can often cut down the amount of time you spend on your project, if you don't prefer modeling or texturing.

Knowing how an object is used in a scene gives you its criteria for modeling. Creating a highly detailed model for a faraway shot will waste your time and expand rendering times needlessly.

> Because your computer stores everything in the scene as vector math as opposed to pixels (called raster), the term *geometry* refers to all the surfaces and models in a scene.

When the models are complete, it's a good idea to begin *texturing* and *shading*, the process of applying colors and material textures to an object to make it renderable. In Figure 1.1, an elephant model is shown, with textures applied to its lower body.

DOI: 10.1201/9780429490958-2

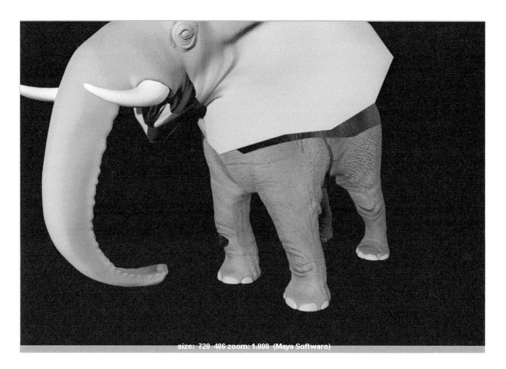

FIGURE 1.1   Texturing adds detail to an otherwise flat model.

Because applied textures may look different after animating and lighting the scene, it's wise to leave final adjustments for later. You'll learn more about texturing and shading in Chapter 7, "Autodesk Maya Shading and Texturing."

Next comes the process of animating. *Animation* shows *change over time*. All animation, from paper flipbooks to film to Maya, is based on the principle of *persistence of vision* that when we see a series of rapidly changing images (called *frames*), we perceive the changing of the image to be in continuous motion.

You know when something doesn't look right, and so will the people watching your animation. So, to animate something properly, you will need to do quite a lot of setup beyond just modeling and texturing. In character animation, for example, you'll need to create and attach an *armature*, or skeleton, to manipulate the character and to make it move like a puppet. I cover animation techniques in Maya in Chapter 8, "Introduction to Animation," and Chapter 9, "More Animation!"

Next, there is lighting. *CG is fundamentally all about light.* Without light, we wouldn't see anything; simulating light is one of the most influential steps in CG. During the lighting step, you set up virtual lights in your scene to illuminate your objects and actions, as you'll learn in Chapter 10, "Autodesk Maya Lighting." Before long, you'll start modeling and texturing differently—that is, working with the final lighting of the scene in mind.

When you're done lighting, you move to rendering; your computer takes your scene and makes all the computations it needs to render your scene into images. Rendering time depends on how much geometry is used in the scene as well as on the number of lights, the size of your textures, and the quality and size of your output: the more efficient your scene,

the shorter the rendering times. The more experience you gain, the more efficient your eye will become.

Digital Images

When you're finished with your animation, you'll probably want as many people as possible to see it (and like it!). Here is a primer on the types of digital images and how they are discerned.

As mentioned, each image file holds the color information in *channels*. All color images have red, green, and blue color channels. Some images have a fourth channel called the *alpha* channel (a.k.a. *matte* channel), which defines what portions of the image are transparent (see-through) or opaque (solid). You can read more about alpha channels in Chapter 7.

First, most image files store the color of each pixel as three values representing red, green, and blue (a.k.a. RGB). The image type depends on how much storage is allotted to each pixel (the *color depth*).

Grayscale

The image is black and white with varying degrees of gray (typically 256 shades). These are good for use as texture maps such as bump and displacement maps.

8-Bit Image File (a.k.a. 24-Bit Color Display)

Each color channel is given 8 bits for a range of 256 shades of each red, green, and blue channel, for a total of 16 million colors in the image.

16-Bit Image

Used in television and film work with such file types as Extended Dynamic Range Image File Format (EXR) and Tagged Image File Format (TIFF), a 16-bit image file holds 16 bits of information for each color channel, resulting in an impressive number of color levels and ranges.

32-Bit Image

32-bit image files, such as the High Dynamic Range (HDR) and OpenEXR formats, give you an incredible amount of range in each color channel. EXR files, in particular, are a standard at many film studios and television productions because of their impressive image range and quality.

Some images also have a fourth channel in addition to the RGB called Alpha (a.k.a. RGBA) that can give the image transparency.

File Formats

Several image file formats are available today. The main difference between file formats is how the image is stored. Some formats compress the file to reduce its size. However, as the degree of compression increases, the color quality of the image decreases.

The popular formats to render from Maya are TIFF and EXR. These file formats maintain a good color image, include an alpha channel, and are either uncompressed or barely compressed (lossless compression) for high quality. Note that some image file types such as TIFF may have 8, 16, or even 32 bits of color depth, while some other file types such as JPEG, (or JPG) can have only 8-bit color depth.

To see an animation rendered in a file sequence of TIFFs or JPEGs, for example, you must play them back using a frame player, such as FCheck (which is included with Maya) or compile them into a movie file using a program such as Adobe After Effects.

Animations can also be output directly to movie files such as AVI or QuickTime. These usually large files are self-contained and hold all the images necessary for the animation that they play back as frames. Movie files can also be compressed, but they suffer from quality loss the more they're compressed.

Maya can render directly to a movie format, saving you from having to render a large sequence of files, though it's always best to render a sequence of files that can be compiled into a movie file later using a program such as Adobe After Effects, Adobe Premiere Pro, or QuickTime Pro.

Resolution, Aspect Ratio, and Frame Rate

Resolution denotes the size of an image by the number of horizontal and vertical pixels, usually expressed as #×# (for example, 1,280×720). The higher the resolution, the finer the image detail will be, and the larger the files. Full HD, for example, is defined as 1,920×1,080. *Aspect ratio* is the ratio of the screen's width to its height. Finally, the number of frames played back per second determines the *frame rate* of the animation. This is denoted as *frames per second* (fps). Most digital movie files are output at 24 fps to mimic the frame rate of movies.

You should have your frame rate set properly before animating to match the frame rate you intend to use for playing the animation back. Playing back a 24 fps animation at 30 fps will show a slower-moving animation. Conversely, playing a 30 fps animation at 24 fps will create a faster-moving animation that will either skip some frames or end later than it should. Most animations are created for 24 fps, which is Maya's default setting.

3D Coordinate Space, World Axis, and Local Axis

Space is defined in three axes—X, Y, and Z—representing width, height, and depth. The three axes form a numeric grid in which a particular point is defined by *coordinates* set forth as (#,#,#), corresponding to (X,Y,Z), respectively. At the zero point of these axes is the *origin*. This is at (0,0,0) and is the intersection of all three axes. The 3D space defined by these three axes is called the *World axis*, in which the XYZ axes are *fixed references*. The axis in *World Space* is always fixed and is represented in Maya by the XYZ axis icon in the lower-left corner of the Perspective window.

Because objects can be oriented in all sorts of directions within the World axis, it's necessary for each object to have its own width, height, and depth axis independent of the World axis. This is called the *Local axis*. The *Local axis* is the XYZ-coordinate space that is attached to every object in Maya. When that object rotates or moves, its Local axis rotates and moves with it. This is necessary to make animating an object easier as it moves and orients around in the World axis. Figure 1.2 shows an example of a Local axis in action, where you can see a large yellow planet and its moon rotating around the central Sun.

Basic Animation Concepts

The following sections define the key terms you'll come across numerous times on your journey into animation and CG.

Frames, Keyframes, and In-Betweens

Each drawing of an animation—or, in the case of CG, a single rendered image—is called a *frame*. The term *frame* also refers to a unit of time in animation whose exact chronological length depends on how fast the animation will eventually play back (frame rate).

Keyframes are frames in which the animator creates a pose or other such state of being for an object or character. Animation is created when an object travels or changes from

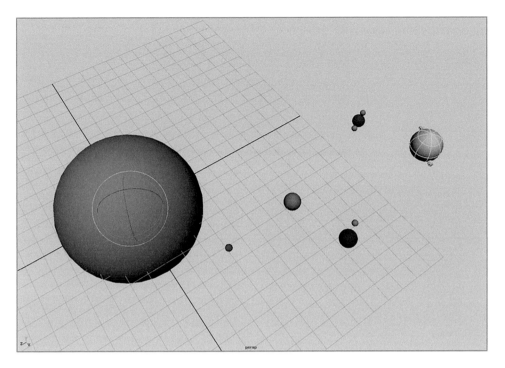

FIGURE 1.2   The Sun at the origin, with Earth and other planets orbiting the World axis while rotating on their own axes.

one keyframe to another. In CG, a keyframe can be set on almost any aspect of an object—its color, position, size, and so on. Maya then interpolates the *in-between* frames between the keyframes set by the animator. Figure 1.3 illustrates a keyframe sequence in Maya.

Weight

Weight is an implied, if not critical, concept in design and animation. How you show an object in motion greatly affects its weight and therefore its believability. Weight in animation is a perception of mass. An object's movement, how it reacts in motion, and how it reacts to other objects together convey the feeling of weight. Otherwise, the animation will look bogus—or, as they say, "cartoonish."

Weight can be created with a variety of techniques developed by traditional animators over the years. Each technique distorts the shape of the object or character in some way to make it look as if it's moving. The following are a few animation principles to keep in mind:

Squash and Stretch

This technique makes a character, for example, respond to gravity, movement, and inertia by squashing it down and stretching it up when it moves. For example, a cartoon character will squeeze down when it's about to jump up, stretch out a bit while it's flying in the air, and squash back down when it lands.

Ease-In and Ease-Out

Objects never really stop suddenly; everything comes to rest in its own time, slowing before coming to a complete stop in most cases. This is referred to as *ease-out*. Objects don't immediately start moving either; they accelerate a bit before reaching full speed; this is referred to as *ease-in*. The bouncing-ball tutorial in Chapter 8 illustrates ease-in and ease-out.

Follow-Through and Anticipation

Sometimes you have to exaggerate the weight of an object in animation, especially in cartoons. You can exaggerate a character's weight, for instance, by using well-designed follow-through and anticipation.

You should create a bit of movement in your character or object *before* it moves. *Anticipation* is a technique in which a character or object winds up before it moves, like a spring that coils inward before it bounces.

Likewise, objects ending an action typically have a *follow-through*. Think about the movement of gymnasts. When they land, they need to bend a bit at the knees and waist to stabilize their landing. In the same way, a cape on a jumping character will continue to move even after the character lands.

The axe tutorial in Chapter 8 will give you a chance to implement these two concepts.

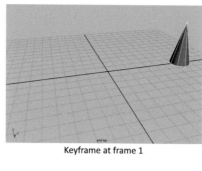

Keyframe at frame 1

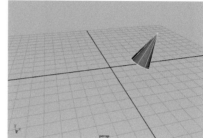

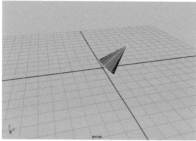

Frame 5

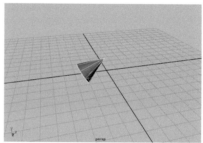

Frame 10

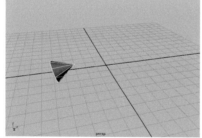

Frame 15

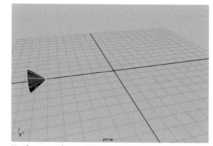

Frame 20

Frame 25

Keyframe at frame 30

FIGURE 1.3 In the first Frame of this sequence, a keyframe is set on the position, rotation, and scale of the cone. On Frame 30, the same properties are again keyframed. Maya calculates all the movements in between.

Summary

In this chapter, you learned the basic process of working in CG, called a _workflow_. In addition, you were introduced to some fundamentals of digital images and animation principles.

Now that you have a foundation in CG and 3D terminology and core concepts, you're ready to tackle the software. Maya is a capable, intricate program. The more you understand how _you_ work artistically, the better use you'll make of this exceptional tool. Have fun!

2

Jumping into Basic Animation Head First

Learning Outcomes

In this chapter, you will be able to

Gain a working understanding of the user interface and how to navigate in three-dimensional space

Learn project structure in Maya and how to create projects in Maya

Create, name, and manipulate simple objects with the Move, Rotate, and Scale tools

Make and apply simple shaders to scene geometry through the Hypershade

Add keyframes to objects to create animation

Adjust pivot points

Create and edit hierarchies by using groups

Output your animation through playblasting

You Put the *U* in User Interface

Fire up your computer, and let's get going. This section will introduce you to getting around the Maya user interface (UI).

The overall goal of this chapter is to expose you to Maya UI basics as well as important scene creation and editing tools. You'll find more details on the interface in Chapter 3, "The Autodesk Maya Interface."

KEYBOARD AND SYMBOL CONVENTIONS USED IN THIS BOOK

The following terms are used throughout this book:

Click and LMB + Click

These actions refer to a mouse click with the primary (left) mouse button.

RMB + Click

This refers to a mouse click with the right mouse button.

MMB + Click

This refers to a mouse click with the middle mouse button.

Shift + Click

This indicates you should hold down the Shift key as you click with the primary (left) mouse button.

Shift + Select

This indicates you should hold down the Shift key as you select the next object for multiple selections.

The ❑ Symbol

This, next to a menu command, indicates you should click the box (❑) next to the menu command to open the options for that command.

DOI: 10.1201/9780429490958-3

Home Screen

By default, when you launch Maya, it presents you with the Home Screen, giving you access to recent files and projects. Simply click the blue Go to Maya button in the top-right corner to proceed to the Maya interface. You can disable the Home Screen by clicking the *Show Home Screen on startup* check box in the lower-left corner of the Home Screen. You can always access the Home Screen by clicking the House icon in the upper left of the Maya UI or through the WIndows menu in Maya's main interface. We have disabled the Home Screen throughout this book.

A Quick Screen Roadmap

Once you are out of the Home Screen, let's get to the basics of how Maya is laid out (see Figure 2.1). Running across the top of the screen, right under the application title bar, are the UI elements: the main menu bar, the Status line, and the Shelf. On Mac OS X, note that the main menu bar runs across the top of the screen, above the application title bar.

Figure 2.1 shows the major parts of the UI. In the middle of the interface is the *workspace*, which is host to your *panels* (or Scene windows) and their menu options (known as *views* or *viewports* in some other 3D packages). This is where most of your focus will be.

Click inside the large Perspective view panel (named *persp*) with the mouse to activate the panel, highlighting its border slightly. Press the spacebar to display a four-panel layout, which gives you top, front, and side views, as well as the perspective view. Press the spacebar in any of the panels to

display a large view of that panel, and press the spacebar again to return to the four-panel layout.

To the right of the panels is the Attribute Editor/Channel Box/Modeling Toolkit. This is where most of the information (attributes) about a selected object is displayed and edited. Also, this is where you access the Modeling Toolkit suite of polygon tools. Simply click any of the tabs to access these functions. Furthermore, pressing Ctrl+A toggles between the Attribute Editor and the Channel Box.

In short, the Attribute Editor gives you access to all of an object's attributes, whereas the Channel Box is a quicker display of the most commonly animated attributes of the selected object.

Letter Keys and Syntax in Maya

Maya is case-sensitive (meaning it distinguishes between lowercase and uppercase letters). The conventions of this book are to always print an uppercase letter to denote which key you must press. So, when I ask you to press the E key, for example, you should simply press the E key on your keyboard (thereby entering a lowercase *e*). When an uppercase letter is called for, the book tells you to press Shift+E, thereby entering the uppercase letter *E* into Maya. Also, make sure your Caps Lock key is turned off.

Mouse Controls

Maya requires the use of a three-button mouse, even on a Mac. The clickable scroll wheel found on most mice can be used as the third button by pressing down to click with the wheel.

FIGURE 2.1   The initial Maya screen.

SHORTCUTS TO NAVIGATING

Here's a rundown of how to navigate Maya. Keep in mind that the Option key is used on a Mac in place of the Alt key on a PC.

Alt + MMB + Click

Tracking moves left, right, up, or down in two dimensions; hold down the Alt key, press and hold the middle mouse button (MMB), and drag the mouse.

Alt + RMB + Click

This dollies into or out of a view, essentially zooming the view in and out. Hold down the Alt key, press and hold the right mouse button (RMB), and drag the mouse.

Scroll Wheel

The scroll wheel acts as a middle mouse button when pressed and can also dolly into or out of a view just like the Alt+RMB+click combination when scrolling the wheel.

Alt + Click

This rotates or orbits the camera around in a Perspective window. To orbit, hold down the Alt key and the left mouse button (LMB). You cannot tumble your view in an orthographic panel (Front, Side, and Top).

The ViewCube

The ViewCube is a navigational aid that should initially be visible in the upper-right corner of the panel when you launch Maya. The ViewCube lets you easily change your current panel's view.

Mouse over parts of the ViewCube and a blue highlight appears at the top edges, all outer corners, and each face of the cube. By clicking an area of the ViewCube (shown here), you can switch to other views for that panel. Clicking the outer corners gets you back to the perspective view. You can toggle the ViewCube on or off in the UI by choosing Display ➢ Heads Up Display ➢ ViewCube. The ViewCube is turned off and generally not used in this book.

Mac Keys

The Option key on a Mac serves the same function as the Alt key on a PC. Although a few Ctrl key combinations in Windows are accessed via the Command key on a Mac, Mac users can use the Mac's Ctrl key for their key combinations just like PC users do.

In Maya, you press and hold the Alt key on a PC (or the Option key on a Mac) along with the appropriate mouse button to move in the view panel.

- The left mouse button (LMB) acts as the primary selection button and allows you to orbit around objects when used with the Alt key.
- The right mouse button (RMB) activates numerous shortcut menus and lets you zoom when used with the Alt key.

- The middle mouse button (MMB) used with the Alt key lets you move within the Maya interface panels, and the mouse's wheel can be used to zoom in and out as well.

Making Selections

Selecting objects in a view panel is as easy as clicking them. As you select an object, its attributes appear in the Attribute

Editor or Channel Box on the right. To select multiple objects, simply hold the Shift key as you click objects to add to your current selection. If you press Ctrl+LMB (press the Ctrl key and click) on an active object, you'll deselect it. To clear all of your current selections, click anywhere in the empty areas of the view panel.

> Remember, when you press Shift+click to select, Maya adds to the current selection. When you press Ctrl+click, Maya deselects the object you clicked.

Manipulating Objects

When you select an object and enable one of the transformation tools (tools that allow you to move, rotate, or scale an object), you'll see a manipulator appear at or around the selected object. Figure 2.2 shows the three distinct and most common manipulators for all objects in Maya (Move, Rotate, and Scale) as well as the Universal Manipulator. You use these manipulators to adjust attributes of the objects visually and in real time.

To activate a transform tool, select an object and then click one of the transform tool icons in the Tool Box, shown in Figure 2.3.

> Press 4 for Wireframe mode; press 5 for Shaded mode.

Try This

Let's put some of this into action.

1. Press 4 for wireframe mode. Choose Create ➤ Polygon Primitives ➤ Sphere. Drag in a view panel anywhere on its grid to create a wireframe sphere and then size it to your liking. If this does not happen and instead a sphere simply appears in your window, a default setting has previously been changed, which is okay. In this case, turn on Interactive Creation if it was previously turned off. Click Create ➤ Polygon Primitives and make sure the check box next to Interactive Creation at the bottom of the menu is checked.

   In one of the view panels, press the 4 key on your keyboard, and the display of the sphere will become wireframe. This is called *Wireframe mode*. Press the 5 key to return to *Shaded mode*. You should also see an in-view message at the top of your view stating "wireframe display is now on. Press 5 to display objects in shaded mode." Please note that sometimes settings are different, and you may see your initial views in wireframe mode.

You can turn off in-view messages by toggling off the In-View Messages check box under Display ➤ Heads Up Display.

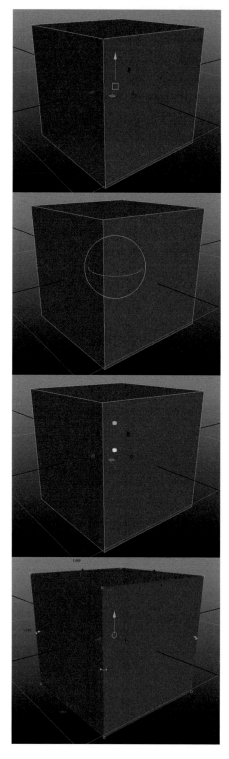

FIGURE 2.2 The Maya manipulators.

FIGURE 2.3   The transform tools in the Tool Box.

2. With the sphere selected, select the Move tool () from the Tool Box. The first manipulator shown earlier in Figure 2.2 should appear in the middle of the sphere. The three arrows represent the three axes of possible movement for the object. Red is for the X-axis, green is for the Y-axis, and blue is for the Z-axis. Cyan is for free movement in both axes of the active panel view. Clicking any one of the three arrows lets you move the object only on that particular axis. The square in the middle of the manipulator lets you move the object freely around the plane of the view panel, regardless of the axis. The three squares represent planar movement in two of the three axes at a time, for example, moving on the XY plane or the YZ plane.

3. Next, select the Rotate tool ( ) from the Tool Box, and you'll see the second manipulator from Figure 2.2. The three colored circles represent the three axes of rotation for the object—red for X, green for Y, and blue for Z. Select a circle to rotate the object on that axis. The yellow circle surrounding the three-axis circles lets you freely rotate the object on all three axes.

4. Try selecting the Scale tool ( ) to see the third manipulator from Figure 2.2. By selecting one of the axis handles and dragging the mouse, you can scale the object in a nonuniform manner in that axis. The middle cyan box scales the object uniformly on all three axes.

5. Try selecting the Universal Manipulator, which is not shown in the Tool Box but is found by choosing Modify ➤ Transformation Tools ➤ Universal Manipulator. Its icon ( ) appears under the

Tool Box after you select it from the menu. This tool acts in place of all three manipulators you just tried. Grabbing the familiar arrows translates the sphere. Selecting any of the curved arrows in the middle of the edges of the manipulator box lets you rotate the sphere in that axis. Finally, selecting and dragging the cyan boxes in the corners of the manipulator box lets you scale the sphere. If you hold down the Ctrl key as you drag, you can scale the sphere in just one axis.

Go ahead and click around the interface some more. Create more primitive objects and tool around a bit. Move around the view panels and see how it feels. Give the tires a good kick.

Enough chatting—let's jump into the solar system exercise.

Project: The Solar System

This project will familiarize you with the fundamentals of navigating Maya, object creation, hierarchy, and pivots, all of which are important concepts for scene manipulation and animation within Maya. In this exercise, you'll gain experience with UI elements while setting up a Maya project in which you create and manipulate objects. You will animate a simple simulation of your working solar system, making and adjusting hierarchies for animation and setting keyframes.

Starting with the Sun in the center, the planets in order are Mercury, Venus, Earth, Mars, Jupiter, Saturn, Uranus, Neptune, and Pluto. (Yes, yes, I know Pluto isn't classified as a planet anymore.) All these planets orbit the Sun in ellipses, but you'll give them circular orbits for this exercise. Most planets have a number of moons that orbit them, and a few, including Saturn, have large rings that circle them. For this exercise, you will create only two moons for any planet that has more than two moons, like Jupiter.

The more you run this exercise, the clearer the scene manipulation and hierarchy structure will become to you. Art is a marriage of inspiration, hard work, and practice.

Creating a Project

Projects are the way Maya manages a scene's assets. A file and folder structure keeps your files organized according to projects. You will want to create a new project for this new exercise.

The top level of this organization is the *project folder*. Within the project folder are numerous file folders that hold your files. When you set your workspace to a project folder (or when you create a new project), Maya will know where to look for elements and folders for that project. The two most important types are the Scenes and Images folders. The Scenes folder stores your scene files, which contain all the information for your scene. The Images folder stores images you've rendered from your scene.

NAMING OBJECTS AND KEEPING THE SCENE ORGANIZED

In Maya and most other CG packages, keeping things organized is important to workflow. When you pick up a disorganized scene, it is time-consuming to figure out exactly how everything works together. Get into the habit of naming your objects and keeping a clean scene or you'll be bombarded by dirty looks from other artists when they have to handle your cluttered scenes.

The scene files discussed in this chapter are included in the book's download page, available at https://www.routledge.com/9781138590540. They are in a project layout explained in the following text. Copy the scene files on the web page for this project into your own project folders after you create the project.

To create a new project for this assignment, follow these steps:

1. Choose File ➤ Project Window to open the Project Window and then click the New button.

2. In the Current Project field in the Project Window, enter **Solar_System** as the name for your project. In the Location box, type the location where you want to store your projects.

   The default location for Windows is the current user's My Documents folder usually found here: `My Documents\maya\projects`; for Macs, the default location is Home (`/Users/<yourname>`) in the `Documents/maya/projects/default` folder. If you prefer, you can put projects in a folder on a secondary or external hard drive to keep them separate from your operating system; this allows for easier backup and is generally a safer environment.

3. If you're using a Windows system, create a folder on your hard drive called **Projects** using Windows Explorer. If you're using a Mac, select a drive in the Finder and create a folder on the drive called **Projects**. In the Project Window, click the folder icon next to the Location field and select `D:\Projects` (Windows) or `<Hard Drive Name>/Projects` (Mac) for the location. Maya will fill in all the other fields for you with defaults. Click Accept to create the necessary folders in your specified location. Figure 2.4 shows the completed Project Window in Mac OS X; except for the drive name, the values are the same on Windows.

After you create projects, you can switch between them by choosing File ➤ Set Project and selecting the new project. Maya will then use that project's folders until you switch to or create another project. You may also select a recent project by choosing File ➤ Recent Projects.

DON'T FORGET TO ALWAYS SET YOUR PROJECT FIRST!

Once you have created a project, you should make sure to set your project before continuing with your work, which you can do through the File Menu or selecting it from the Home Screen. The exercises in this book are based on projects, and you'll need to set your project whenever you start a new exercise. Otherwise, the scene may not load properly, or your files may not save to the proper locations for that project. Don't say I didn't warn you!

The Production Process: Creating and Animating the Objects

In this project, you'll first create the Sun, the planets, and their moons; then, you'll animate their respective orbits and rotations.

USE CUBES INSTEAD OF SPHERES

Make the planets with cubes instead to make it easier to see them spin.

Creating the Sun and the Planets

The first thing you'll do is create the Sun and the planets. Follow these steps:

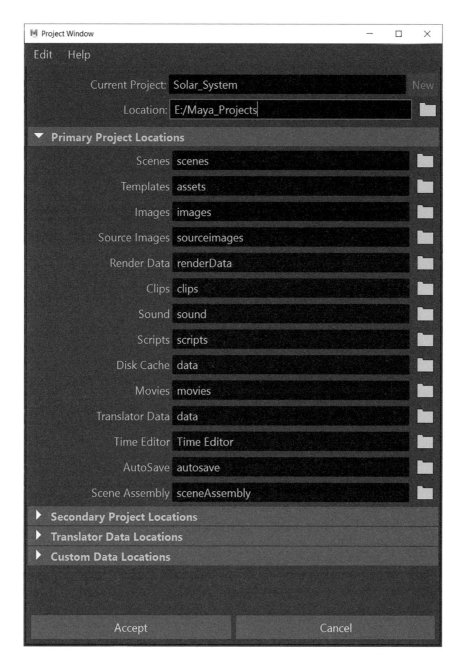

FIGURE 2.4 The completed Project Window for the Solar System project.

1. Choose File ➢ New Scene (or press Ctrl+N). Maya asks if you want to save your current scene. Save the file if you need to or click Don't Save to discard the scene.

2. By default, the screen should begin in an expanded perspective view. Press the spacebar to enable the four-panel view. When you're in the four-panel view, press the spacebar with the cursor inside the top view panel to select and maximize it.

3. To create the Sun, you need to create a primitive sphere. A *primitive* is a basic 3D shape. First, let's turn off a default feature called Interactive Creation. Uncheck Create ➢ Polygon Primitives ➢ Interactive Creation to toggle it off, as shown in Figure 2.5.

Interactive Creation lets you create a primitive by clicking and dragging to specify its size and position. You'll find this option when you choose Create ➢ NURBS Primitives or Create ➢ Polygon Primitives. When this option, at the bottom of each of those menus, is unselected or off, the created primitive appears at the origin in 3D space at a uniform scale of 1.0.

4. With Interactive Creation now turned off, choose Create ➢ Polygon Primitives ➢ Sphere. Doing so places a polygon sphere exactly at the origin that is,

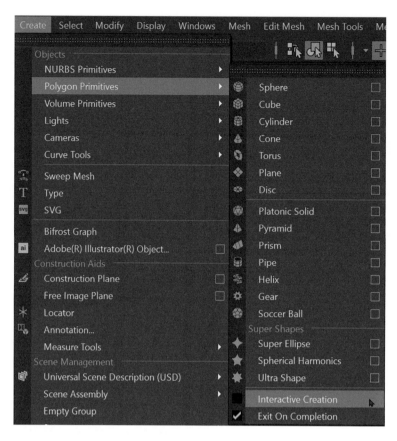

FIGURE 2.5   Turning off Interactive Creation.

at a position of 0,0,0 for X,Y,Z. This is good, because the origin of the workspace will be the center of the solar system, too. The sphere will be selected, and some of its attributes will show on the right of the UI in the Attribute Editor.

5. Press Ctrl+A to toggle off the Attribute Editor and toggle on the Channel Box in its place.

6. Select the word *pSphere1* in the Channel Box (shown in Figure 2.6) and enter **Sun** to rename it. If you don't see the Channel Box in your Maya window, press Ctrl+A to toggle the view from the Attribute Editor to the Channel Box.

   Naming your objects right after creation is a good habit to develop and is particularly important if anyone needs to alter your scene file; proper naming will keep them from getting frustrated when they work on your scene.

Always keep in mind that Maya is case-sensitive. An object named *sun* is different from an object named *Sun*.

6. Choose the Scale tool in the Tool Box to activate the Scale manipulator, and uniformly scale the Sun sphere up to about four times its creation scale of 1. For more precision, you can select the sphere and

enter a value of **4** in all three entry fields (the white window next to the attribute) for the Scale X, Scale Y, and Scale Z channels in the Channel Box shown in Figure 2.7.

7. After you enter the final value, press Enter, and the sphere will grow to four times its original size. Entering exact values in the Channel Box is a way to scale the sphere precisely; using the manipulator isn't as precise.

Creating the Planets

Next, you'll create the primitive spheres for the planets. Leave Interactive Creation off, and follow these steps:

1. Create a polygon sphere for Mercury just as you did before, by choosing Create ➢ Polygon Primitives ➢ Sphere. A new sphere appears at the origin. Click its name in the Channel Box and change it to **Mercury**.

2. Choose the Move tool from the Tool Box to activate the Move manipulator and move Mercury a few grid units away from the Sun sphere in the positive X direction. (Click the red arrow and drag it to the right.) Leave about 2 grid units between the Mercury sphere and the Sun sphere.

3. Because Mercury is the second-smallest planet and is tiny compared to the Sun, scale it down to 1/20th

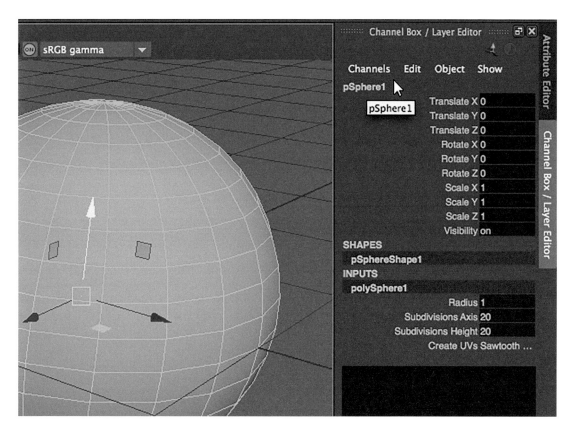

FIGURE 2.6   Renaming the sphere in the Channel Box.

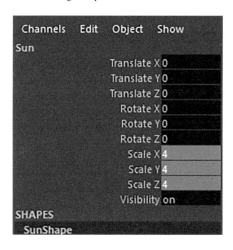

FIGURE 2.7   The Sun sphere's Scale values in the Channel Box.

the size of the Sun sphere, or type **0.2** in all three axes of Scale in the Channel Box.

4. Repeat steps 1 through 3 to create the rest of the planets and line them up, placing each one farther out along the X-axis with about two grid units of space between them. If you run out of grid, simply select Display ➢ Grid ❐, set the Length and Width value in the Grid Options window to 36 or more, and click Apply and Close.

5. Scale each planet sphere proportionally as shown in the chart on the right. Make sure to name each planet in the Channel Box (as in step 1 for Mercury)

for each new planet sphere you create, using the chart below as a reference.

Planet	Sphere Sizes
Venus	0.5
Earth	0.5
Mars	0.4
Jupiter	1.0
Saturn	0.9
Uranus	0.7
Neptune	0.7
Pluto	0.15

These proportions aren't exactly real, but they will do nicely here. Figure 2.8 shows how your solar system should look now.

No, Pluto isn't actually a planet anymore, but for nostalgia's sake, we'll include it here in our solar system. Poor Pluto!

Using Snaps

Now is the perfect time to start using *snaps*. Table 2.1 shows some common snap icons. These icons run across the top of the UI just below the main menu bar, as shown here.

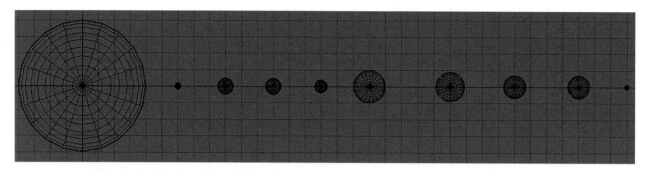

FIGURE 2.8   All the spheres are lined up in place.

You use snaps to snap objects into place with precision, by placing them by their pivot points directly onto grid points, onto other object pivots, onto curve points, and so on. Here you'll reposition all the planets slightly to center them on the nearest grid line intersection:

1. Select the first planet, Mercury. Choose the Move tool from the Tool Box and toggle on grid snaps by

   clicking the Snap To Grids icon (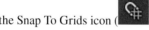).

2. The center of the Move manipulator changes from a square to a circle, signaling that some form of snapping is active. Grab the manipulator in the middle by this circle and move it slightly to the left or right to snap it onto the closest grid intersection on the X-axis.

3. Select the remaining planets and snap them all to the closest grid intersection on the X-axis, making sure to keep about two grid spaces between them. Because the Sun sphere was created at the origin and you haven't moved it, you don't need to snap it onto an intersection.

Making Saturn's Ring

Now, let's create the ring for Saturn. To do so, follow these steps:

TABLE 2.1

Snap Icons

Snap Icon	Name	Description
	Snap To Grids	Snaps objects to intersections of the view's grid
	Snap To Curves	Snaps objects along a curve
	Snap To Points	Snaps objects to object points such as CVs or vertices
	Snap To Projected Center	Snaps an object to the center of another object
	Snap To View Planes	Snaps objects to view planes

1. Press the spacebar in the top view to maximize it. Choose Create ➢ Polygon Primitives ➢ Torus to place a donut shape at the origin (Interactive Creation is still off). Use the Move tool to snap the ring to the same grid intersection as Saturn. This ensures that both the planet and its ring are on the same pivot point and share the same center.

2. Select the torus shape you've created and name it **Ring** in the Channel Box.

3. While the torus shape is still selected in the top view, press the spacebar to display the four-panel layout. Place the mouse cursor in the perspective view and press the spacebar to maximize the Perspective window.

4. Press the F key to focus the perspective display on the ring and on Saturn. Pressing F centers and zooms in the panel on just the selected objects. Remember, this is a lowercase F.

5. Press 5 to get into Shaded mode, if not already.

6. From the Tool Box, select the Scale tool and scale the torus down to 0 or close to 0 on the Y-axis (the torus's height, in this case) to flatten it.

   You need to edit the attributes of the ring to increase the inside radius of the donut shape and create a gap between the planet and the ring.

7. Press Ctrl+A (Ctrl or Cmd+A will work on a Mac) to toggle the Attribute Editor if it's not on and then click the polyTorus1 tab to select its creation node (see Figure 2.9).

8. Increase the Radius attribute to about 1.5 and decrease the Section Radius attribute to about 0.4 to get the desired effect.

Now all your planets are complete, and you can move on to the moons.

Saving Your Work

Save your work, unless you like to live on the edge. Power failures and other unforeseen circumstances (such as your pet jumping onto your keyboard) may not happen often, but they do happen. Because you created this as a new project,

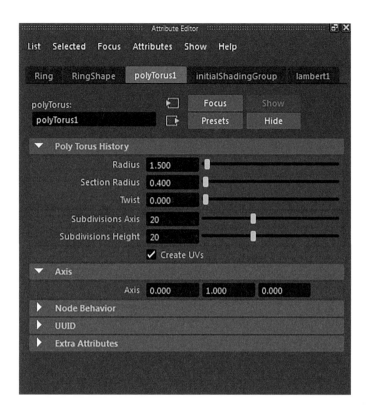

FIGURE 2.9 Changing the creation attributes of the polygon torus in the Attribute Editor.

the Save File window will direct you to the Scenes folder of that project. Save your scene as **planets** in the .ma (Maya ASCII) format.

The file Planets _ v1.ma in the Scenes folder of the Solar_System project, available on the book's web page, shows what the scene should look like at this point.

SAVING MULTIPLE VERSIONS OF YOUR WORK

Maya software's Incremental and Save feature essentially makes a backup of your scene file every time you save your scene with File ➤ Increment and Save instead of File ➤ Save. Every time you use Increment and Save, Maya will create a new scene file appended with a new incremental number (for example, planets.0001. ma, planets.0002.ma, etc.) in your Scenes folder.

The scene files for the projects in this book use a slightly different naming system than the names generated by Incremental and Save, so there is no risk of files overwriting each other.

The AutoSave feature automatically saves your file at a set interval of time. To enable AutoSave, choose Windows ➤ Settings/Preferences ➤ Preferences. In the Categories column on the left, choose Settings ➤ Files/ Projects. You can enable AutoSave as well as set its time interval and save location under the AutoSave heading.

Creating the Moons

For the planets with moons, create a new polygon sphere for each moon. For simplicity's sake, create only two moons for any planet. The first moon will be Earth's. Use the top view to follow these steps:

1. Create a polygon sphere and scale it to about half the size of Earth using the Scale tool. Visually estimate the size of the moon.
2. Move the sphere to within half a unit of Earth, using the Move tool by the X-axis. There's no need to snap it to a grid point, so toggle off the Snap To Grids icon (   ). Name the moon **earthMoon**. Notice there are no spaces in the names. Maya doesn't use spaces in anything.
3. Repeat steps 1 and 2 for the remaining moons, placing them each within half a grid unit from their respective planets. When placing two moons, place them on opposite sides of the planet. Make sure to name your moons.
4. After you've finished with all the moons, their placements, and their sizes, you should have a scene similar to Figure 2.10 in perspective view. If you don't, it's clear Maya doesn't like you.

Applying a Simple Shader

To help distinguish one gray planet from another, let's attach simple shaders (a.k.a. materials) to each of the planets to give them color. Shaders, in short, are materials that give an

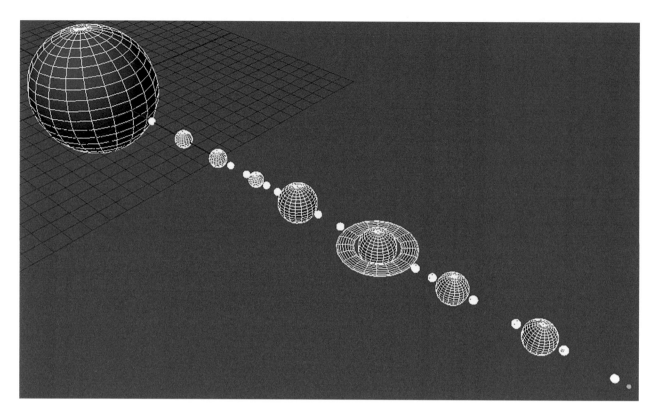

FIGURE 2.10   The planets and moons in position in perspective view.

object its particular look, whether it is color or a tactile texture. Follow these steps:

1. Choose Windows ➤ Rendering Editors ➤ Hypershade to open the Hypershade window. With this window, you create the look of your objects by assigning colors, surface properties, and so on. Youll notice four default (or initial) shader icons already loaded, as well as a new material youll create in the next step (see Figure 2.11).

HYPERSHADE WINDOW LAYOUT

The Hypershade is customizable, so your initial Hypershade window layout may not exactly match the ones shown in this book. For example, in Figure 2.11 (which should match the initial view you see when you launch Maya for the first time), you can see there is a section called Material Viewer showing a thumbnail image of a sphere shape in the upper-right corner of the Hypershade. The Material Viewer has been turned off for the majority of this book, but it can be accessed through the Hypershade's Window menu. This window will be explained further in Chapter 3.

2. In the Create panel on the lower left of the Hypershade window, click the Lambert icon (Figure 2.11) to create a new Lambert shader node. A new node called lambert2 appears in the top-left panel (called the Browser) as well as in the work area as a gray icon (lambert2) connected to a blue icon (lambert2SG). This is where the Hypershade lists all the materials in the scene. In the top-right panel, called the Material Viewer, the Hypershade shows a preview of the selected material. A selected material's more important attributes are listed in the Property Editor directly below the Material Viewer. Click the Lambert icon in the Create panel eight more times to create a total of nine new Lambert shading groups (lambert2 through lambert10). This adds quite a few icons in the work area, some of them right on top of each other, that you can ignore for now.

3. In the Hypershade's Browser (upper part of the window), click the first of the new Lambert nodes (select lambert2, *do not select lambert1*) to display its attributes in the Property Editor. (The material's complete list of attributes is shown in the Attribute Editor in the main Maya UI window.) At the top of the Property Editor, rename lambert2 to **Mercury_ Color** to identify this material as the one you'll use for Mercury.

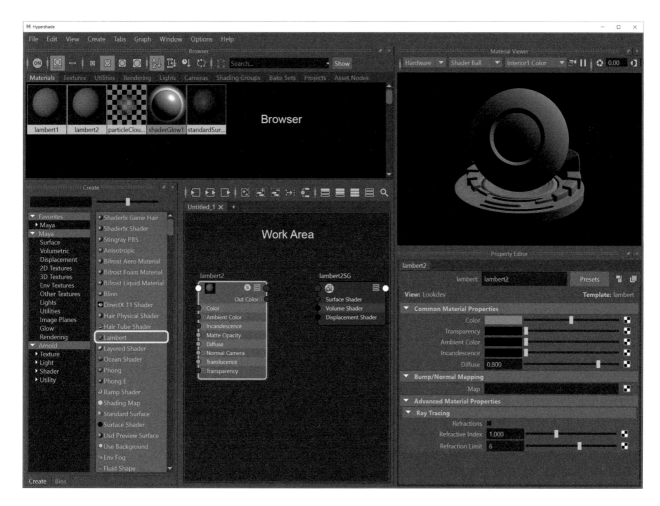

FIGURE 2.11 The Hypershade window.

4. Name each of the remaining planets' materials in the Hypershade's Property Editor (Venus_Color, Earth_Color, Mars_Color, Jupiter_Color, Saturn_Color, ranus_Color, Neptune_Color, and Pluto_Color) and save your work. Since there are no spaces in Maya, using an underscore (_) works well as a replacement for a space.

After you've created and named all the materials (a.k.a. shaders), you can assign appropriate colors to each of the shaders according to the planets that they represent.

1. Click Mercury_Color's lambert icon in the Hypershade to display its properties (see Figure 2.12).
2. To change the color of the shader, click the gray box next to the Color attribute. This opens the Color Chooser window, where you can choose a new color by using the color wheel or by adjusting values with the Hue, Saturation, Value (a.k.a. HSV) sliders. Go with an orange color, such as in Figure 2.13 (take note of the HSV values, and see that Color Management is checked, otherwise your HSV values will differ

from those shown in the figure). If you are on a Mac with Catalina or a later version of Mac's Operating System OSX, you may get a security warning popup. Follow the directions to enable Color picker, by adding Maya application in "System Preferences- ➢ Security & Privacy- ➢ Accessibility.

3. Change the remainder of the shaders as follows:

Mercury	Orange-brown
Venus	Beige-yellow
Earth	Blue
Mars	Red-orange
Jupiter	Yellow-green
Saturn	Pale yellow
Uranus	Cyan
Neptune	Aqua blue
Pluto	Bright gray

Figure 2.14 shows the materials.

4. Next, let's apply the materials to the planets. Select a planet in the Perspective window, and RMB+click

FIGURE 2.12   Mercury's material in the Hypershade Property Editor.

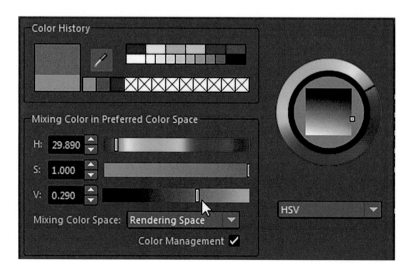

FIGURE 2.13   The Color Chooser window.

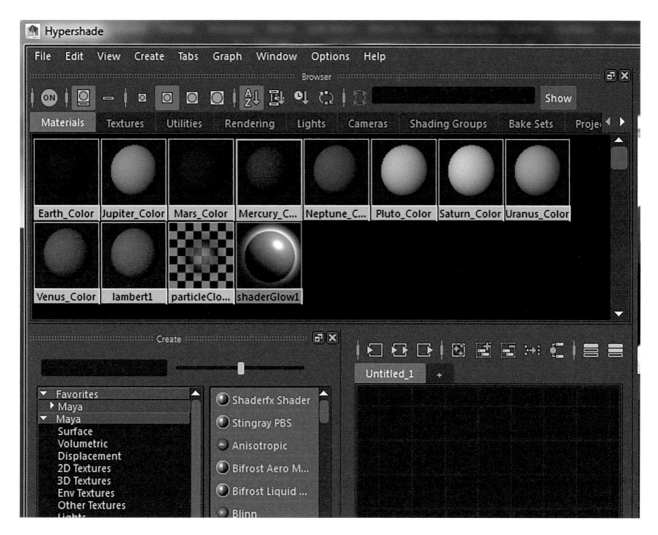

FIGURE 2.14 The Hypershade window with all the colored planet materials.

its corresponding material in the Hypershade window to open a *marking menu*. Marking menus is a fast UI workflow to allow you to select commands and options as you work in your panels without having to access the main menu bar.

5. Still holding the right mouse button, drag up to highlight Assign Material To Selection and release the button to select it. You can also use the middle mouse button to drag the material from the Hypershade window to its planet. Leave the moons set to the default gray color. When you're finished, you should have a scene similar to Figure 2.15.

A marking menu is a context-sensitive menu that appears when you RMB+click an object or a shader. For example, clicking a polygon cube in a scene brings up a marking menu where you can select the cube's vertices, faces, edges, and so on, and where you can quickly access some often-used options and tools. The kind of marking menu that appears depends on the node you are RMB+clicking.

Now that you're finished, you're ready to animate. Save this file; if you use Incremental and Save as recommended earlier, your file will get an incrementally increasing number appended to the original file name.

Creating the Animation

To begin this phase of the project, load the file `Planets_v2.ma` in the Scenes folder of the Solar_System project on the web page to your hard drive, or continue with your own scene file.

The animation you'll do for the planet's self-rotation is straightforward. You'll rotate the planets around their own axes for their self-rotation, and then you'll animate the moons around the planets for their lunar orbits. Finally, you'll make the planets and their moons orbit the Sun.

This exercise focuses on hierarchy and pivot points. A *pivot point* is an object's center of balance of sorts. Every object or node created in Maya has a pivot point, especially primitives like you're creating here. That pivot point is usually at the center of the primitive and moves along with the object if it's moved.

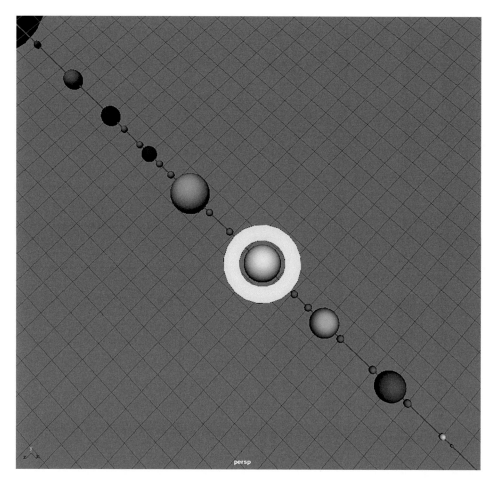

FIGURE 2.15   The shaded planets in perspective view.

Now, you need to set up the animation settings for your scene file:

1. Press F4 to open the Animation menu set, or select it from the drop-down menu shown earlier in this chapter. *Menu sets* are groupings of menu headings in the main menu bar. They're organized according to the type of task at hand. You'll see the several menu headings change.

2. At the bottom of the main Maya UI, you'll notice a slider bar (the Range slider) directly below the strip of numbers counting off the frames (the Time slider) in the scene. Using the Range slider, you'll set the length of your animation to go from 1 to 240. Enter **1** in the Animation Start Frame box (Figure 2.16). Enter a value of **240** in the Animation End Frame box, as shown in Figure 2.16.

3. To the right of the Range slider, click the Animation

   Preferences icon (![icon]), click Settings (Figure 2.17), and make sure Time is set to Film (24 fps).

Choose Windows ➤ Settings/Preferences ➤ Preferences to open the Preferences window. Under Settings ➤ Undo, make sure Undo is on and set Queue to Infinite, allowing you to press Ctrl+Z as many times as needed. To close the Preferences window, click Save.

Mercury's Rotation

Now you're ready to animate Mercury's rotation. Follow these steps:

1. Select Mercury, and press E to activate the Rotate tool. The E key is the hotkey to invoke the Rotate tool in Maya. Remember, it's a lowercase E. Press F to focus on Mercury in the perspective view, or zoom in on it manually.

2. Make sure you're on frame 1 of your animation range by clicking and dragging the Scrub bar (refer to the earlier Figure 2.16) to place it at the desired frame.

FIGURE 2.16 The Time and Range sliders.

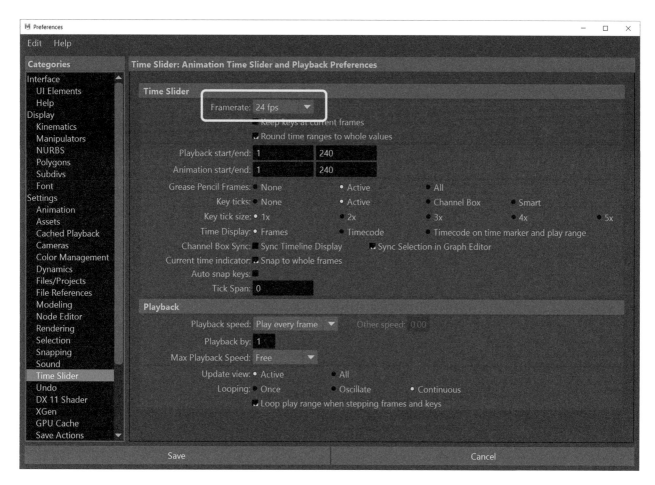

FIGURE 2.17 Set Time to 24 fps on the Time Slider tab of the Preferences window.

You can also manually type the frame value of **1** in the Current Frame box.

3. For Mercury, you'll set your initial keyframe for the Y-axis rotation. RMB+click the attribute name for Rotate Y in the Channel Box to select it and bring up a context menu, as shown in Figure 2.18. Select Key Selected from the context menu. This places a keyframe for a rotation of 0 just in the Y-axis at frame 1 for the Mercury sphere. A small box in the Rotate Y attribute turns red to indicate that a keyframe exists for that attribute.

Conversely, instead of RMB+clicking Rotate Y in the Channel Box, you could also set a keyframe through the main menu bar (in the Animation menu set) by selecting Key ➢ Set Key. However, this method will set a keyframe for *all* attributes of the Mercury sphere, which is not efficient and may give different results as you follow along with this exercise. You should ideally try to set keyframes only on attributes you need.

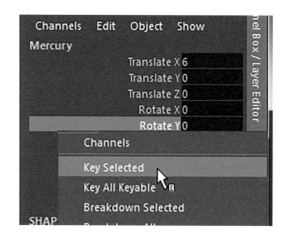

FIGURE 2.18 Setting the initial keyframe for Mercury's Y-axis rotation.

4. Using the Scrub bar in the Time slider, go to frame 240. Grab the Rotation manipulator handle by the Y-axis (the green circle) and turn it clockwise a few times to

rotate the sphere clockwise. You'll notice that you can rotate the object only so far in one direction before it seems to reset to its original rotation. Rotate it as far as it will go and release the mouse button. Then, click the manipulator again and drag to rotate the sphere as many times as necessary until you're satisfied with its spin.

5. RMB+click the Rotate Y attribute in the Channel Box and choose Key Selected again. This sets a keyframe for your new Y-axis rotation at frame 240 for the Mercury sphere.

6. To play back your animation, you can scrub your Time slider. Click in the Time slider on the Scrub bar, hold down the left mouse button, and move your cursor from side to side to scrub in real time. You'll see Mercury rotating in your active view panel, if you set your two keyframes as described.

You have the self-rotation for Mercury worked out. Mercury has no moon, so let's get Mercury orbiting the Sun.

Grouping Mercury for a New Pivot Point

You've learned that every object in Maya is created with a pivot point around which it rotates and scales and which acts as the placement for its X-, Y-, and Z-coordinates. To orbit Mercury around the Sun sphere, the sphere must revolve around a pivot point that is placed in the middle of the Sun sphere. If the pivot point for Mercury is already at the center of itself, how can you revolve it around the Sun sphere?

One idea is to move its current pivot point from the center of itself to the center of the Sun sphere. That would, however, negate Mercury's own rotation, and it would no longer spin around its own center, so you can't do that. You need to create a new pivot point for this object. This way, you have the original pivot point at Mercury's center so it can self-rotate, and you have a second pivot point at the Sun sphere so that Mercury can revolve around that point around the Sun sphere. You'll accomplish this by creating a new *parent node* above Mercury in the hierarchy. What does that mean?

To explain, I'll take time in the following section to introduce the concept of Maya object structure: nodes and hierarchies. Save your progress so far and open a new blank scene. After this explanation, you'll resume the solar system exercise.

Hierarchy and Maya Object Structure

On top of everything you see in Maya (its interface) is a layer you don't see: the code. The layer of code keeps the objects in Maya organized through a network of nodes. How you relate these nodes to each other defines how you've built your scene. So, having a solid understanding of how Maya defines objects and how they interact is essential to an efficient and successful animation process.

Understanding Nodes

At its core, Maya relies on packets of information called *nodes*, and each node carries with it a group of attributes that in combination define an object. These attributes can be spatial coordinates, geometric descriptors, color values, and so on. You can define, animate, and interconnect any or all of these attributes individually or in concert, which gives you amazing control over a scene.

Nodes that define the shape of a surface or a primitive are called *creation nodes* or *shape nodes*. These nodes carry the information that defines how that object is created. For example, a sphere's creation node has an attribute for its radius. Changing that attribute changes the radius of the sphere at its base level, making it a bigger or smaller sphere. This is different from scaling the sphere as you've done with the planets so far. Shape nodes are low on the hierarchy chain and are always child nodes of *transform nodes*. The sphere applies attributes from its creation node first and then moves down the chain to apply attributes from other nodes (such as position, rotation, or scale).

The most visible and used nodes are the transform nodes, also known as directed acyclic graph nodes. These nodes contain all the transformation attributes for an object or a group of objects below it. *Transformations* are the values for translation (position), rotation, and scale. These nodes also hold hierarchy information about any other children or parent nodes to which they're attached. When you move or scale an object, you adjust attributes in this node.

Parents and Children

A *parent node* is simply a node that passes its transformations down the hierarchy chain to its children. A *child node* inherits the transforms of all the parents above it. So, by using hierarchies for the solar system exercise, you'll create a nested hierarchy of parents and children to animate the orbital rotation of the nine planets and some of their moons.

With the proper hierarchy, the animation of the planet (the parent) orbiting the Sun automatically translates to the moon (the child). In effect, the planet takes the moon with it as it goes around the Sun.

Child nodes have their own transformations that can be coupled with any inherited transformations from their parent, and these transformations affect them and any of their children down the line.

You're about to experience this firsthand as you continue the solar system exercise. The more you hear about these concepts in different contexts, the easier they will be to master.

Figure 2.19 shows the Outliner and Hypergraph views with a simple hierarchy of objects for your reference. The Outliner and Hypergraph show you the objects in your scene in an outline and flowchart format, respectively. Both of these windows allow you to access the different levels of nodes (the hierarchy) in a scene and are discussed further in Chapter 3.

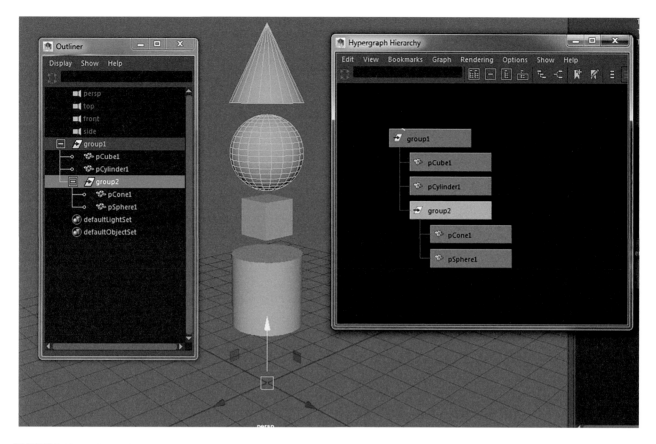

FIGURE 2.19   A simple hierarchy in both the Outliner and Hypergraph windows.

A top parent node called group1 holds its children pCube1, pCylinder1, and the nested group node group2. The node group2 is the parent node of pCone1 and pSphere1.

The Solar System, Resumed

If you still feel a little unsure about nodes and hierarchies, take the time to reread the previous section. You'll practice these concepts as you resume the solar system exercise. By the time you've finished this exercise, you'll have a strong sense of how hierarchies work in Maya, although you should feel free to repeat the entire exercise if you think that will help you master hierarchies. Understanding nodes and hierarchies is absolutely critical to animating in Maya, and perhaps most CG applications.

If you're new to CG animation, take your time with the following section.

Animating Mercury's Orbit around the Sun

Load your scene from where you last saved it. When you left off, you had created the self-rotation animation for Mercury and were about to create a second pivot point for the planet to orbit around the Sun sphere by creating a new parent node for the Mercury sphere.

To create a new pivot point by making a new parent node, follow these steps:

1. With Mercury selected, press E for the Rotate tool and then choose Edit ≻ Group from the main menu bar (you can also press Ctrl+G). The Channel Box displays attributes for a new node called group1. Notice that nothing about the Mercury sphere changed, except that the Rotation manipulator handle seems to have jumped from where it was centered on Mercury all the way back to the origin, where the zero points of the X-, Y-, and Z-axes collide. Figure 2.20 shows the new Mercury group (called group1) and its pivot location.

   You just created a new Maya object (called a group node) by grouping Mercury to itself, *which has its own pivot point* which is placed by default at the origin. With this new group node object that is now Mercury's parent, you effectively have a second pivot point for animating. Because an object's manipulator always appears at the object's pivot point when it's selected, what seemed to be Mercury's Rotate manipulator jumped to the origin when the new group node was created. But be assured that Mercury still has its own pivot point at its center, and that you're looking at the pivot point location for Mercury's new parent node. The fact the parent node's pivot is by default at the origin, that is fortunate for you because that happens to be

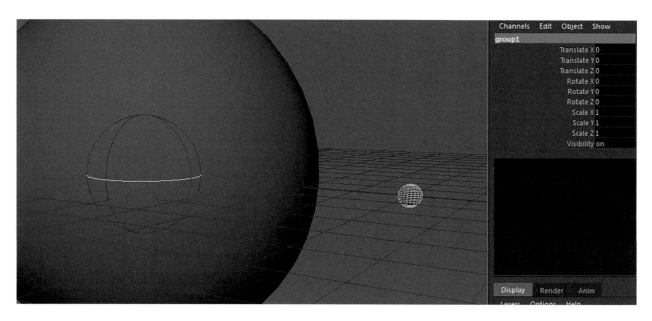

FIGURE 2.20 Grouping Mercury to itself creates a new pivot point at the origin.

the center of the Sun sphere—exactly where you need it to be for Mercury to orbit the Sun sphere properly.

2. Without unselecting anything in Maya, click the group1 name in the Channel Box (remember you can switch back and forth between the Channel Box and the Attribute Editor with Ctrl-A), and change the name of this new group to **Mercury_Orbit**. It's important to make the distinction between node names so you never get confused. Now you know that the Mercury node is the planet sphere itself, whereas Mercury_Orbit is the name of the new parent node that you'll animate to orbit Mercury around the Sun sphere.

3. Click anywhere in an empty space in your view window to unselect Mercury_Orbit. Try selecting it again by clicking the Mercury sphere. Notice that when you click Mercury, you select only the planet and not the new parent node Mercury_Orbit, the group that has its pivot point at the center of the Sun sphere. This happens because you're in Object mode. To select the group Mercury_Orbit, select the Mercury_Orbit directly in the Outliner, as shown in Figure 2.21. Selecting objects as well as group nodes is typically best done using the Outliner.

4. Go back to frame 1 of your animation. Set a keyframe for Mercury_Orbit's Rotate Y attribute by RMB+clicking its name in the Channel Box and then choosing Key Selected.

5. Go to frame 240, grab Mercury_Orbit's Rotate manipulator handle by the green Y-axis, and spin it around the Sun twice in either direction. (It doesn't matter if you go clockwise or counterclockwise.) You can also enter **720** in the Rotate Y attribute field in the Channel Box (or **-720** to go in the other direction).

6. Set a keyframe at frame 240 for Mercury_Orbit's Rotate Y attribute, as you did in step 4. Scrub your animation to play it back.

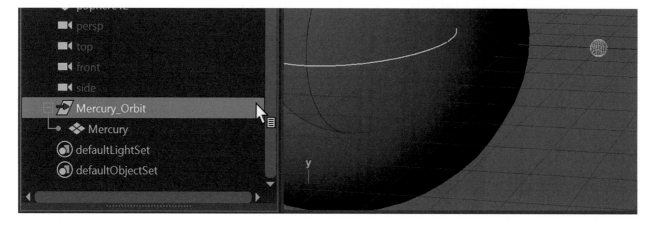

FIGURE 2.21 Selecting the Mercury_Orbit group node in the Outliner.

Does that make good sense? You'll have the chance to do this a few more times as you animate the other planets and their moons. However, if you still find yourself a little fuzzy on this concept (which is perfectly normal), repeat the steps to animate Mercury in a new scene file if need be. One down, eight to go.

Creating Venus

For your next planet, Venus, follow the same procedure as for Mercury's self-rotation (steps 1–6 in the "Mercury's Rotation" section) and animate it so that it rotates around itself, just like Mercury. Then, effectively create a new pivot point you can use to animate the orbit around the Sun, by grouping Venus to itself to create a new parent node (as you did for Mercury_Orbit in steps 1 and 2 in the previous section) and call the new parent node **Venus_Orbit**. Lastly, animate Venus_Orbit to revolve around the Sun sphere just as you did with Mercury_Orbit in steps 3–6.

Earth and the Moon

Now you need to animate the third planet, Earth, in much the same way, except that this time there will be the added complication of a moon. (Earth? Hey, I can see my house from here!)

To animate Earth and the moon, follow these steps:

1. Select Earth and give it its self-rotation animation as you did for Mercury.

2. Select the moon and give it its own self-rotation animation by spinning it around itself and keyframing it as you've just done with Earth.

3. To spin the moon around Earth, you'll do as you did earlier in this chapter to orbit a planet around the Sun: first, group the moon to itself by choosing Edit ➤ Group; then, name the new parent node **Moon_Orbit**.

This time, however, you need the pivot point to be at the center of Earth and not at the center of the Sun object, where it is currently. Follow these steps:

1. Turn on the grid snap ( ) and press the D key to be able to move the pivot point of that new group node. The moon orbit's manipulator changes from a rotation handle to the Pivot Point manipulator. This manipulator acts just like the Move manipulator, but instead of moving the object, it moves the object's pivot point. Just don't rotate the pivot using this Pivot Point manipulator, use just the move handles.

2. Grab the yellow circle in the middle of the manipulator and move the Moon_Orbit pivot point to snap it to the grid point located at the center of Earth (see Figure 2.22).

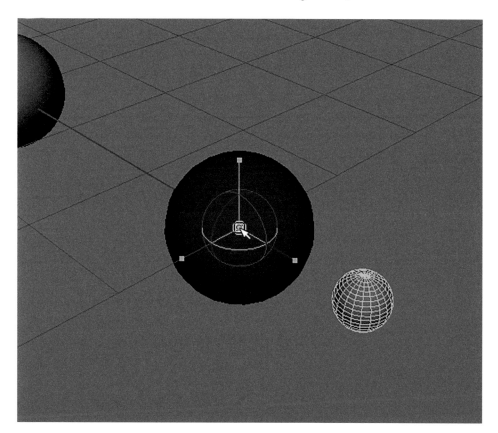

FIGURE 2.22 Moving the Moon_Orbit group node's pivot point to the center of Earth.

3. Now press the D key again to exit the Pivot Point manipulator and return to the Rotation manipulator for Moon_Orbit. At frame 1, set a keyframe for the moon's Y-axis rotation. Then, at frame 240, rotate the moon around the Y-axis and set a keyframe. Return to frame 1.

Grouping the Moon with Earth

To animate Earth's orbit of the Sun, you need to make sure the moon will also follow Earth around the Sun sphere. Instead of just selecting Earth and grouping it to itself as you've done for the other two planets that have no moon, you need to include the Moon_Orbit group node in this new group with the Earth. Follow these steps:

1. Select the Earth sphere in the view panel or in the Outliner. Ctrl+click the Moon_Orbit group in the Outliner to make sure you get the parent node of the moon, and then choose Edit ➤ Group to create a new parent group node that parents both the Moon_Orbit and the Earth sphere. Name this new parent node **Earth_Orbit**. Remember, when you click on just the Earth and/or the moon in the view panel, the parent node Earth_Orbit won't be selected. That is the group that contains both these objects and has its pivot point at the center of the Sun, where we need it. If you do indeed have the Earth_Orbit node selected, its manipulator should be in the middle of the Sun sphere. I'll deliberately illustrate this mistake and its consequences when you animate Pluto a little later.

2. Set a keyframe for Earth_Orbit's Rotate Y attribute at frame 1, again by RMB+clicking Rotate Y in the Channel Box and selecting Key Selected.

3. Go to frame 240, spin Earth and the moon around the Sun sphere a few times in whichever direction and for however many revolutions you want, and set a keyframe at frame 240.

Now the first three planets are going around themselves and around the Sun, with a moon for Earth. If you haven't been saving your work, save or Increment and Save it now. Just don't save over the unanimated version from earlier.

Creating the Other Planets' Moons

Repeat this grouping procedure from the previous section Earth and the Moon for the remaining planets to create their moon orbit parent nodes (make sure to name the parent nodes as you go along, for example, mars_moon_orbit, saturn_moon_orbit, etc.), but leave out Pluto for now (poor Pluto!). Make sure to center the pivot point for each of the new moon's parent nodes on its respective planet like we did in the Earth and the Moon section for Earth's moon.

If you find that one of your moons is left behind by its planet or that it no longer revolves around the planet, you most likely made an error when grouping the moon and planet. Undo (Ctrl+Z) until you're at the point right before you grouped them and try again. If that still doesn't work, start over from the earlier version of the file you saved just before you began animating it. Repetition is actually helpful when learning hierarchies in Maya, anyway. You'll learn how to fix it in the section "Using the Outliner" later in this chapter.

Auto Keyframe

Let's use the Auto Keyframe feature when animating the remaining planets and moons to simplify keyframing. Auto Keyframe automatically sets a keyframe for any *attribute that changes from a previously set keyframe*. For example, an initial keyframe for an attribute such as Y-axis rotation needs to be set at some point in the animation. The next time the Y-axis rotation is changed when at a different frame in the timeline, Maya will set a keyframe at that frame for that attribute automatically.

To turn on Auto Keyframe, click the Auto Keyframe icon (), which is to the right of the Range slider in the lower right of the main UI. When the icon is red, the Auto Keyframe is active.

To use Auto Keyframe to animate Mars' moon to orbit Mars, follow these steps:

1. Turn on Auto Keyframe so that its icon is red.

2. Start at frame 1. Select the moon orbit parent of Mars (mars_moon_orbit) and set a keyframe for its Y-axis orbit by highlighting Rotate Y in the Channel Box and selecting Key Selected. Again, make sure the mars_moon_orbit parent node's pivot is centered on the Mars sphere.

3. Go to frame 240. Revolve the moon around Mars several times in a direction of your choosing. Maya automatically sets a frame for Y rotation at frame 240. Save your file.

4. You can repeat this process to animate the rest of the planets and their moons.

Using the Outliner

As you've seen, the Outliner is an outline listing of all the objects and nodes in your scene. For an in-depth look at the Outliner, see Chapter 3. For now, let's look at how to use the Outliner to illustrate the hierarchies for the planets and moons. When all is good and proper, the Outliner should look like Figure 2.23. Choose Windows ➤ Outliner (if its not already docked to the left side of the main screen, which is default) to

FIGURE 2.23   The Outliner view of the planet hierarchies.

mars_moon_orbit, and mars_moon2_orbit (the top nodes of the moons that circle the planet Mars) and grouped them all together, placing that pivot point at the center of the Sun. You called this node Mars_Orbit. This is the *parent node* because it's the topmost node for this group. Wherever this parent node goes, the child nodes that are under it will follow.

Hierarchies such as this are a cornerstone of Maya animation. It's imperative that you're comfortable with how they work and how to work with them. If you find yourself scratching your head even a little, try the exercise again. A proper foundation is critical. Remember, this learning 3D thing isn't easy, but patience and repetition help a lot.

Correcting Hierarchy Problems Using the Outliner

One of the most common problems you'll run into with this project is a planet revolving around the Sun without its moon. To illustrate how to fix it using the Outliner, as opposed to undoing and redoing it as suggested earlier, the following steps will force you to make this error with Pluto. Usually, people learn more from mistakes than from doing things correctly.

Go to Pluto, start the same animation procedure as outlined earlier, and then follow these steps to force an error:

1. Create Pluto's own self-rotation by spinning it around itself and keyframing as before.
2. Do the same for Pluto's moon's self-rotation.
3. Group the moon to itself and grid snap the pivot point at the center of Pluto to create the moon's orbit of Pluto.
   When Pluto's moon (pluto_moon) is orbiting Pluto, you're ready to group the moon's orbit and Pluto together to create an orbit of the Sun sphere for both.
4. Here is where you make your mistake. In Object mode, select the sphere for Pluto's moon and select the sphere for Pluto. Your error is that you're in Object mode instead of switching to Hierarchy mode.
5. Choose Edit ➤ Group to group them together and call that new node **Pluto_Orbit** (following the naming convention you used for the others).
6. Animate Pluto_Orbit revolving around the Sun.
7. Play back the animation.

Notice that the moon is no longer orbiting the planet. This is because you didn't include pluto_moon_orbit in your group Pluto_Orbit. The animation of the moon going around Pluto is stored in that node, and because it's no longer attached to Pluto_Orbit, there's no moon orbit of Pluto.

Figure 2.24 shows the hierarchy of Pluto and how it's different from that of the other planets: the moon's orbit node has been left out of the group. (Earth has been expanded as a contrasting example.)

Using the Outliner, you can easily fix this problem. Place the pluto_moon_orbit node under the Pluto_Orbit node. Go to frame 1 of the animation, grab the pluto_moon_orbit node in the Outliner, and use the middle mouse button to drag it to the Pluto_Orbit node so that it has a white dashed line around it to show a connection, as in Figure 2.25 (left). The proper grouping is shown in Figure 2.25 (right).

open the Outliner window. If you havent yet properly named everything, including the moons, take this opportunity to do so by double-clicking a name in the Outliner and entering a new name.

Let's look at the planet Mars and its layout in the Outliner to better understand the hierarchy for all the planets. All the other planets should be laid out exactly like Mars (except the planets that have just one or no moon).

At the bottom of the hierarchy are Mars's two moons, mars_moon and mars_moon2. Each of those moons is spinning on its own pivot point. You grouped each moon to itself to create the mars_moon_orbit and mars_moon2_orbit nodes, and placed their pivot points at the center of Mars to animate their orbits around Mars.

Mars is spinning on its own pivot point, but it needs another pivot point to be able to orbit the Sun. Because you had to make the moons go with it around the Sun, you selected Mars,

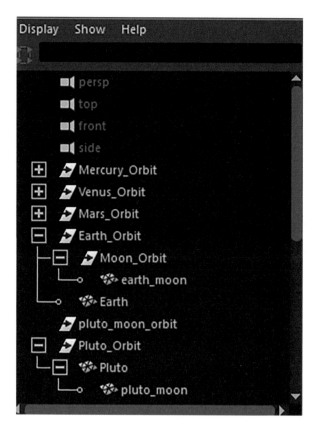

You've just grouped pluto_moon_orbit under Pluto_Orbit, a practice known as *parenting*. Now you need to parent pluto_moon under pluto_moon_orbit as well. Use the MMB to drag pluto_moon onto pluto_moon_orbit. When you play back the animation, you'll see that the moon is revolving around the planet and that Pluto and the moon are orbiting the Sun sphere. Now that you've corrected Pluto's layout in the Outliner, it's similar to the layouts for the other properly working planets.

The file `Planets_v3.mb` in the Scenes folder of the Solar_System project on the book's web page will give you an idea of how this project should look. The first five planet systems are grouped and animated as a reference, leaving the final four for you to finish.

You can add objects to a group by MMB+dragging their listing onto the desired parent node in the Outliner. You can also remove objects from a group by MMB+dragging them out of the parent node to a different place in the Outliner.

FIGURE 2.24 Pluto's incorrect hierarchy.

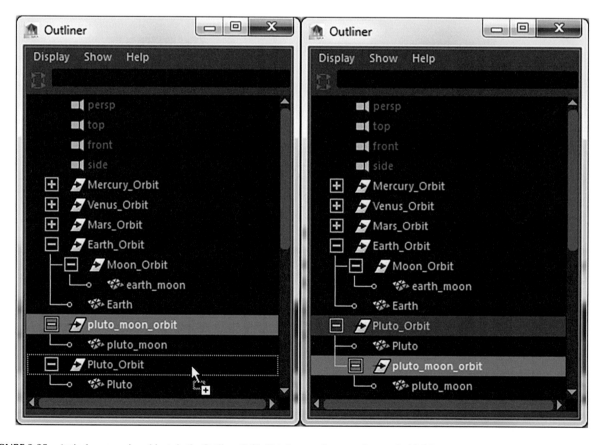

FIGURE 2.25 Actively regrouping objects in the Outliner (left). Pluto's moon is grouped properly (right).

Grouping Terminology

Grouping terminology can be confusing. Grouping Node A under Node B makes Node A *a child* of Node B. Node B is now the *parent of* Node A. Furthermore, any transformation or movement applied to the parent Node B will be *inherited* by the child Node A.

When you group Node A and Node B, both nodes become *siblings* under a newly created parent node, Node C. This new node is created just to be the parent of Nodes A and B and is otherwise known as a *null node.* To group objects, select them and choose Edit ➤ Group. Parenting nodes together places the first selected node under the second selected node. For example, if you select Node A, Shift+select Node B, and then choose Edit ➤ Parent, Node A will group under Node B and become its child. This is the same procedure as MMB+ dragging Node B to Node A in the Outliner, as you did with Pluto's moon and Pluto itself.

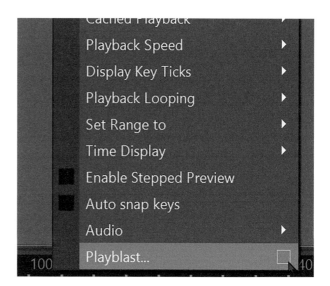

FIGURE 2.26   Selecting Playblast Option Box.

Outputting Your Work: Playblasting

What's the use of animating all this work and not being able to show it? There are several ways of outputting your work in Maya, most of which involve rendering to images. One faster way of outputting your animation in a simple shaded view is called *playblasting.* Playblasting creates a sequence of images that playback on your computer at the proper frame rate. Only if your PC is slow or if you're playblasting a large sequence of frames will your playback degrade. In this case, playblasting 240 frames shouldn't be a problem.

A *playblast,* as it's called in Maya, outputs the view panel's view into an image sequence, QuickTime, or AVI movie. You can also save the image sequence or movie file to disk if you like. Playblasting is done mainly to test the look and animation of a scene, especially when its playback is slow within Maya.

When you have your solar system animated, output a playblast by following these steps:

1. With your animation completed, click on the perspective panel to make it active in the four-panel layout (you can even maximize the Perspective window). Press 5 to enter Shaded mode.

2. RMB+click anywhere in the Time slider, and select Playblast ❑ from the context menu, as shown in Figure 2.26. The option box is shown for the Playblast options in Figure 2.27.

3. In the Playblast options, set Format to qt if you have Quicktime installed or otherwise choose AVI with the IYUV codec option as shown in Figure 2.27 for Windows systems. For a Mac, select the avfoundation for Format to get a QuickTime file. Set Display Size to From Window. Check the Save To File option, and give your playblast a name. Set the Scale to **1.0**.

However, for some Windows users qt is not an option, so you should select avi instead. As mentioned, Mac users should see avfoundation as an option instead of QT for QuickTime output.

4. If you checked the qt option, Maya runs through the animation and creates a QuickTime movie file (or an AVI movie file if you selected the avi option) that is based on the Shaded-mode appearance of the currently active view panel (which should be the Perspective panel). Because you also checked the Save To File option, the movie file is saved to disk. You can also click the Browse button to store the playblast video file anywhere you like. Click the Playblast button.

5. When Maya runs through the animation, Windows Media Player or QuickTime automatically opens and plays the movie file of the animation at the proper speed of 24 fps, as shown in Figure 2.28. Now you can share your animation with others without having to open Maya and play it back in the scene.

Summary

In this chapter, you learned how to start working in Maya by learning how to navigate the UI. Then, you began working by creating a new project, creating basic objects such as primitives, and placing objects in the scene. You learned how to place pivot points for objects and how to use snaps to place points precisely. You gained some experience with the Channel Box and Attribute Editor to set an object's attributes.

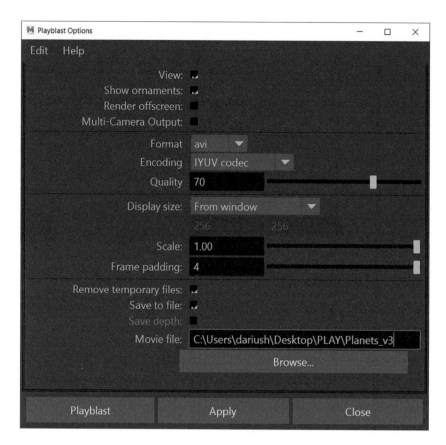

FIGURE 2.27 The option box for creating a playblast preview.

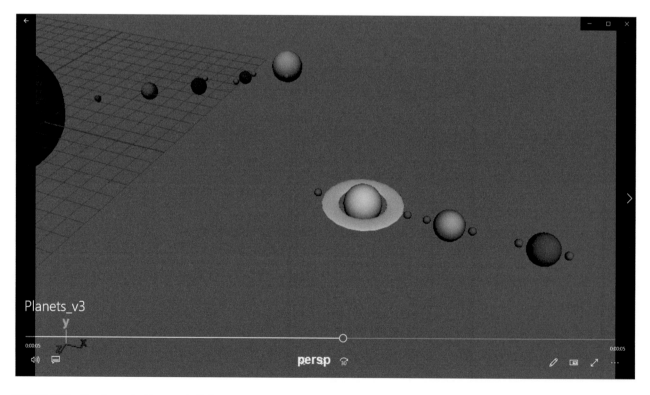

FIGURE 2.28 Creating a playblast movie file is easy.

You then went on to create simple shaders for your objects and set keyframes to animate a solar system. You explored object hierarchy and grouping conventions to organize your scene better, and finally, you learned how to output a basic playblast video file of your completed animation.

The planet animation you created is based on a system of layering simple actions on top of each other to achieve a more elaborate result. Much of your time in actual animation, as opposed to setup or modeling, will be spent adjusting the small things. These small things give the scene life and character. You'll find that finishing 85% of a scene will take about 15% of the time. The remaining 85% of the time goes into perfecting the final 15% of the scene.

3

The Autodesk® Maya® Interface

Learning Outcomes

In this chapter, you will be able to

Recognize and use Maya user interface elements

Understand how Maya view panels and windows work

Use manipulators to transform objects in three-dimensional space

Create and use reference planes for modeling from pictures

Use polygon modeling techniques

Extrude
Bevel
Edge loops
Multi-Cut tool
Component editing—edges, faces, and vertices

Use the Layer Editor to organize your scene

Render test frames to preview your work

Gain confidence in using the Attribute Editor

Better manage your scenes and object hierarchies with the Outliner

Navigating in Maya

The key to being a good digital artist or animator isn't knowing *where* to find all the tools and buttons but knowing *how* to find the features you need. The purpose of this chapter is to help you get to know Maya and how it operates, building on your experience so far.

Explore the interface. Using your mouse, check out the menus and the tools. Just be careful not to change any settings; the rest of this book and its projects assume your Maya settings are all at their defaults. If you do change some settings inadvertently, reverting to the defaults is easy. Choose Windows ➤ Settings/Preferences ➤ Preferences. In the Preferences window, choose Edit ➤ Restore Default Settings. Now all the settings and interface elements are restored to their default states.

Exploring the Maya Layout

Let's take another look at the initial Maya screen in Figure 3.1—this time with the four-panel layout and Attribute Editor and not the Full Perspective window and Channel Box that you saw in the previous chapter.

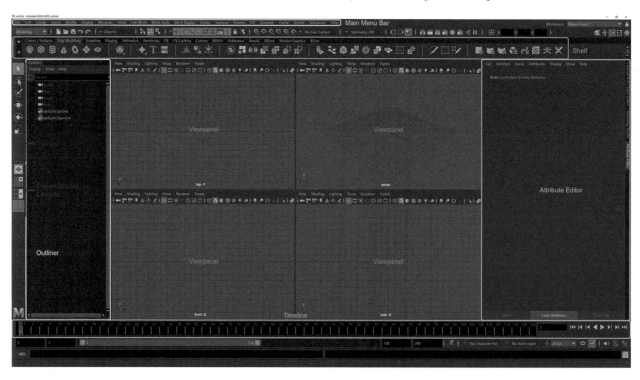

FIGURE 3.1 The initial Maya screen.

DOI: 10.1201/9780429490958-4

The *main menu bar*, *Status line*, and *Shelf* all run across the top of the screen. The Tool Box runs vertically on the left side of the screen. It contains icons for your transform tools (such as Move, Rotate, and Scale) as well as quick-view selections to allow you to customize your panel layouts quickly. The Attribute Editor, Channel Box/Layer Editor, and Modeling Toolkit (the Attribute Editor is currently displayed in Figure 3.1) run down the right side of the screen. Finally, listed from the top down, the Time slider, the Range slider, the Character Set menu, the Auto Keyframe button, and the Animation Preferences button, some of which you've already used, run across the bottom of the screen.

REMINDER: MAYA MOUSE CONTROLS

In Maya, holding the Alt key on a PC or the Option key on a Mac along with the appropriate button allows you to move in the view panel. The left mouse button (LMB) acts as the primary selection button and lets you orbit around objects when used with the Alt key. The right mouse button (RMB) activates numerous context menus and lets you zoom in with the Alt key. The middle mouse button (MMB) with the Alt key lets you move within the Maya interface, and the mouse's wheel can also be used to zoom in and out.

The Main Menu Bar

In Maya, menu choices are context-sensitive; they depend on what you're doing. The main menu bar is shown in Figure 3.2. By switching menu sets, you change your menu choices and hence your available tool set. The menu sets in Maya are Modeling, Rigging, Animation, FX, and Rendering.

Menu Sets

The Menu Set drop-down is the first thing on the Status line, as shown in Figure 3.3.

No matter which menu set you're working in, the first seven menu items are constant: File, Edit, Create, Select, Modify, Display, and Windows, as is the last menu entry, Help.

Some plug-ins can also add menu items to the main menu bar. If the plug-in is turned off, that menu item is removed. So, don't panic if you don't see the same main menu bar pictured throughout this book.

ADVANCED TIP: FLOATING MENUS

In Maya, you can *tear off* menus to create separate floating boxes that you can place anywhere in the workspace, as shown here. This makes accessing menu commands easier, especially when you need to use the same command repeatedly. To tear off a menu, click the dashed line at the top of the menu and drag the menu where you want it.

FIGURE 3.3   The Menu Set drop-down menu.

FIGURE 3.2   The main menu bar is where the magic happens.

Submenus and the Option Box

You'll notice two different demarcations to the right of some menu items (Figure 3.4): arrows and boxes (called *option boxes*). Clicking an arrow opens a submenu that contains more specific commands. Clicking an option box (☐) opens a dialog box in which you can set the options for that particular tool.

Marking Menus

Marking menus are a fast user interface (UI) workflow to allow you to select commands and options without accessing the main menu bar, as you did in the Hypershade in Chapter 2's solar system exercise. For example, RMB+clicking on a polygon object in your scene gives you the marking menu shown in Figure 3.5. With this particular marking menu, you can select vertices on that object by moving your mouse to highlight the vertex box, as shown in Figure 3.6 (top), which then enables you to select any vertex or vertices as shown in Figure 3.6 (bottom). Notice that when you are in vertex selection mode, the wireframe of the object turns light blue and the vertices turn pink.

Work Panels and Navigation

The main focus of Maya is its work windows (called *viewports* or *panels*), which are the perspective and orthographic views. You use these windows to create, manipulate, and view 3D objects, particles, and animations.

Perspective/Orthographic Panels

The default Maya layout usually begins with a full-screen perspective view, as shown in Figure 3.7.

By pressing and releasing the spacebar in the full-size view panel, you switch your view to the four-panel layout shown in Figure 3.8. Pressing the spacebar again in a view panel returns your active view panel to a full-screen view of that panel. If pressing the spacebar does not toggle to the four-panel view for whatever reason, you can also use the preset display layout icons shown in Figure 3.9.

Orthographic views (top, front, and side) are commonly used for modeling because they're best at conveying exact dimensions and size relationships.

FIGURE 3.4 Submenus and the all-important option box.

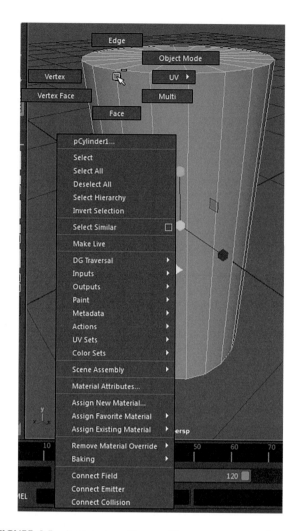

FIGURE 3.5 A context-sensitive marking menu appears when you RMB+click an object.

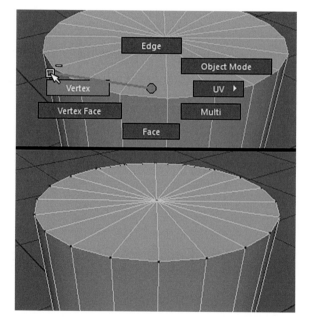

FIGURE 3.6 By using a marking menu, you can easily select components of an object without using the Status line's icons (top). Vertex selection mode (bottom).

SHORTCUTS TO VIEWING

Here's a summary of the most important keyboard shortcuts. Keep in mind that the Option key is used on a Macintosh in place of the Alt key on a PC. See Chapter 2 for more details.

Alt + MMB + Click
> Tracks around a window.

Alt + RMB + Click
> Dollies into or out of a view.

Scroll Wheel
> Dollies into or out of a view.

Alt + LMB + Click
> Rotates or orbits the camera around in a Perspective window.

Alt + Ctrl + Click and Drag
> Dollies your view into the screen area specified in your mouse drag.

Macintosh Keys
> The Option key on a Mac is used as the Alt key on a PC.

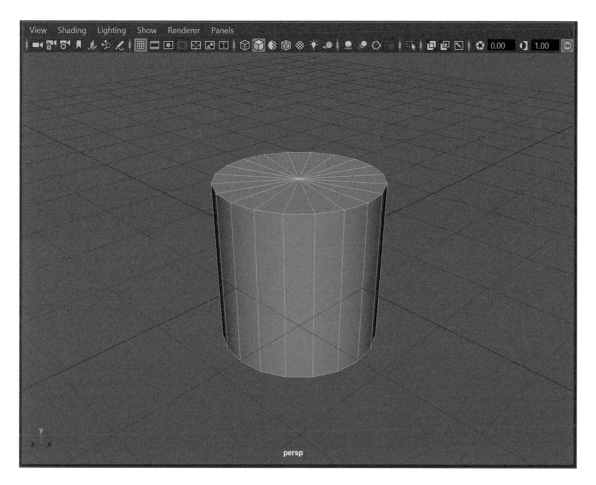

FIGURE 3.7   The full perspective view panel.

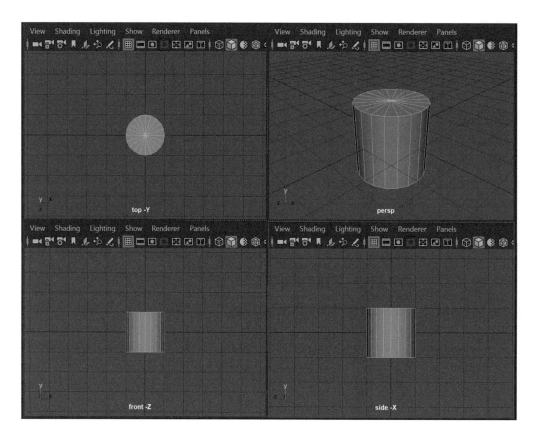

FIGURE 3.8   The four-panel layout.

FIGURE 3.9   Panel layouts.

Wireframe and Shaded Modes

When you're working in the windows, you can view your 3D objects either as wireframe models (as in Figure 3.10 top) or as solid, hardware-rendered models called *Shaded mode* (see Figure 3.10 bottom). When you press 4 or 5, notice that a text helper opens to tell you your current viewing mode. These messages are called *in-view messages* and can be helpful as you learn the Maya workflow. You can toggle these messages on or off by choosing, in the main menu bar, Display ➤ Heads Up Display ➤ In-View Messages.

You can cycle through the modes of display by pressing 4, 5, 6, and 7. Wireframe mode is 4, Shaded mode is 5 and shows you a solid view of the objects, Texture Shaded mode is 6 and shows any textures that are applied to the objects, and Lighted mode is 7 and shows a hardware preview of the objects as they're lit in the scene. Table 3.1 gives a quick reference for toggling display levels.

Pressing 5 for Shaded mode lets you see your objects as solid forms and volumes. Pressing 6 for Texture mode is good for the rudimentary alignment of textures. Pressing 7 for Lighted mode is useful for spotting proper lighting direction and object highlights when you first begin lighting a scene. Lighted mode (press 7) will make objects appear black when there are no lights in the scene. Figure 3.10 (bottom) shows Lighted mode with a single light in the scene.

You can also use the view panel's row of icons to toggle view modes for that panel, as shown here.

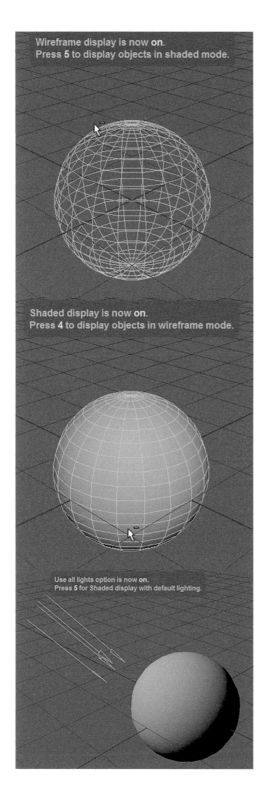

Wireframe display is now **on**.
Press **5** to display objects in shaded mode.

Shaded display is now **on**.
Press **4** to display objects in wireframe mode.

Use all lights option is now on.
Press **5** for Shaded display with default lighting.

FIGURE 3.10 Wireframe display of a selected sphere (top), a Shaded display of the selected sphere (middle), and a Lighted display (bottom).

TABLE 3.1

Levels of Display Detail

Key	Function
4	Toggles into Wireframe mode
5	Toggles into Shaded mode
6	Toggles into Textured mode
7	Toggles into Lighted mode

Other display commands you'll find useful while working in the Modeling windows are found under the panel's (a.k.a. viewport's) View menu shown in Figure 3.11. Look At Selection centers on the selected object or objects. Frame All (hotkey = A) moves the view in or out to display all the objects in the scene, and Frame Selection (hotkey = F) centers on and moves the view in or out to fully frame the selected object or objects in the panel.

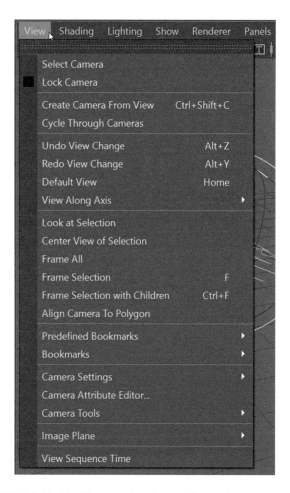

FIGURE 3.11 The View menu in a view panel's menu bar.

The Manipulators

Manipulators are onscreen handles that you use to manipulate the selected object with tools such as Move or Rotate, as you saw in the solar system exercise. Figure 3.12 shows three distinct and common manipulators for all objects in Maya (keep in mind the following hotkeys are lowercase letters—see the Caps and Hotkeys Note): Move (press W), Rotate (press E), and Scale (press R). In addition, the fourth manipulator shown in Figure 3.12 is the Universal Manipulator, which allows you to move, rotate, or scale an object all within one manipulator (select Modify ➤ Transformation Tools ➤ Universal Manipulator or press Ctrl + T).

You can access the manipulators using either the icons from the Tool Box on the left of the UI or the hotkeys shown in Table 3.2.

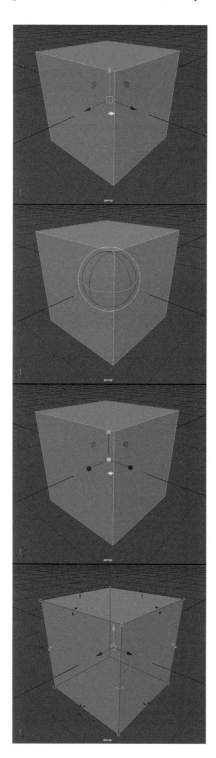

FIGURE 3.12 Using manipulators.

CAPS AND HOTKEYS

Keyboard shortcuts in Maya are *case-sensitive* because in many cases, pressing a single letter key has a different effect than pressing Shift+that letter (which makes the letter uppercase). This book shows all single letters as capitals in the text (the same way they appear on your keyboard). The Shift key is included in the text only when it's part of an uppercase shortcut. So, if you find yourself wondering why pressing a hotkey isn't working, make sure you aren't pressing Shift or that the Caps Lock isn't enabled.

Try This

In a new scene, choose Create ➤ Polygon Primitives ➤ Sphere, drag in a view panel on its grid to create a sphere, and then size it however you like. If you have Interactive Creation already turned off for Polygon primitives, a sphere simply appears at the origin. Press the 5 key in one of the view panels for Shaded mode. In the previous chapter, you tried the manipulators on a sphere to get a feel for how they work. In Chapter 2 you may have noticed the feedback feature on the Universal Manipulator. Select Modify ➤ Transformation Tools ➤ Universal Manipulator, and you'll notice the Universal Manipulator icon appear just below the Tool Box (Symmetry: Off) Manipulate the sphere in the view panel and take a look.

The Universal Manipulator interactively shows you the movement, rotation, or scale as you manipulate the sphere. Notice the coordinates that come up and change as you move the sphere. When you rotate using this manipulator, you see the degree of change. Notice the scale values in dark gray on the three outside edges of the manipulator box; they change when you scale the sphere.

TABLE 3.2

Manipulator Hotkeys

Key	Function
W	Activates the Move tool
E	Activates the Rotate tool
R	Activates the Scale tool
Q	Select tool; also deselects any Translation tools

You can scale any manipulator handle. Press the plus key (+) to increase a manipulator's size, and press the minus key (–) to decrease it.

Soft Selection

Soft selection is a way to select part of an object (like a vertex) and manipulate it so that neighboring vertices are affected as well, but in decreasing amounts. Soft selection is best described by seeing it in action.

1. In a new scene, create a polygonal sphere at the origin.
2. RMB + click and hold on the sphere to bring up a *marking menu*. Select vertices as shown in Figure 3.13.
3. Your display now shows the sphere as light blue and pink points indicating where the vertices are. (I cover vertices in detail in the next chapter.) Manipulating vertices allows you to alter the shape of a polygonal mesh. Click any single vertex to select it.
4. Press W for the Move tool and move the vertex away from the sphere, as shown in Figure 3.14. Doing so creates a spike on the sphere.
5. This time, let's go into the options for the Move tool. Select Modify ➢ Transformation Tools ➢ Move Tool ❏ to open the Tool Settings window, shown in Figure 3.15 as it's docked to the Maya window, however, it may open as a separate window. If you need to expand the window while it's docked, click and drag the vertical bar on the right of the Tool Settings window to see the full width of the panel.
6. Scroll down to the Soft Selection heading and toggle on Soft Select, as shown in Figure 3.16.

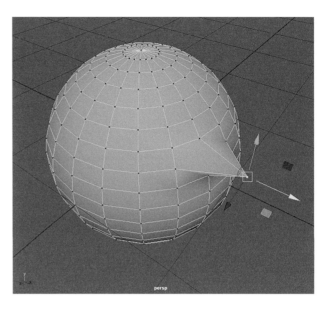

FIGURE 3.14   Pull a vertex to make a spike.

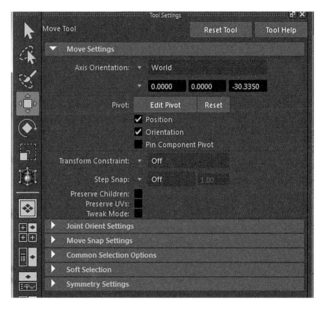

FIGURE 3.15   The option box for the Move tool opens Tool Settings, shown docked.

7. In the perspective view panel, RMB + click the sphere again for the Marking Menu and select Vertex. Select a different vertex on the sphere. When you do, a color gradient from yellow to red to black appears on your model. This gradient (a.k.a. a heatmap) shows you the influence of your soft selection. Figure 3.17 shows you the falloff region on the sphere.
8. The area of influence is too large for this sphere, so set the Falloff Radius from 5.0 to 1.0 and move that vertex away from the sphere. This time, instead of a spike forming on the sphere, a much larger, but smooth, bulb forms out of the sphere, as shown in Figure 3.18, which is similar to the Maya tool called Soft Modification Tool (not covered here).

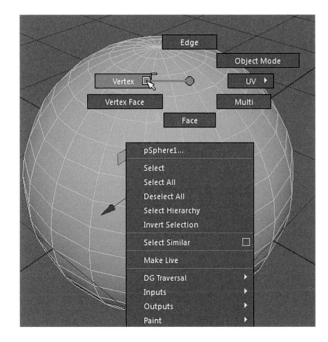

FIGURE 3.13   Selecting vertices.

FIGURE 3.16 Click Soft Select.

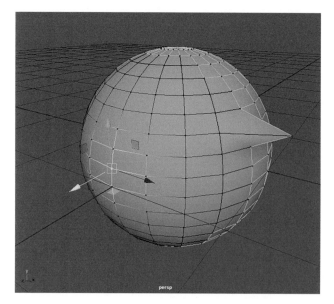

FIGURE 3.17 Soft Select shows you the falloff gradient.

9. You can further adjust the size of the falloff area by adjusting the Falloff Radius attribute in the Tool Settings. Be sure to turn off Soft Select and close the Tool Settings window.

Using soft selection on a transform tool such as Move allows you to make organic changes to your mesh easily. The hotkey

for toggling Soft Selection on and off is B and if you hold the B key down and drag your mouse left or right, it will adjust the Falloff Radius of the soft selection interactively.

Symmetry

Using the Symmetry transformation option makes symmetrical edits to a mesh. Follow these steps to experience Symmetry with the Move tool:

1. Create a polygonal sphere at the origin in a new scene.
2. Invoke the Move tool options by double-clicking the Move tool icon in the Tool Box on the left of the UI, shown in Figure 3.19. The options will open just as if you selected the option box through the menu.
3. At the bottom of the Tool Settings window (a.k.a. option box), in the Symmetry Settings section, as shown previously at the bottom of Figure 3.16, click the Symmetry pulldown menu's down arrow (next to the box that says Off) and select an axis for symmetry. Select Object Z for now.

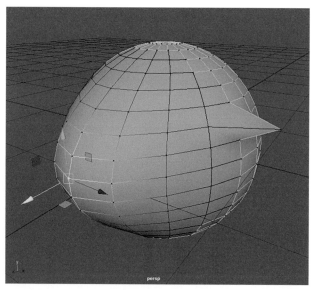

FIGURE 3.18 Use soft selection to pull out a bulb rather than a spike.

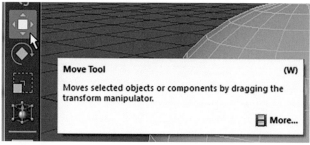

FIGURE 3.19 Hovering over the icon will give you some information about that tool. Double-clicking the icon will open the options for that tool.

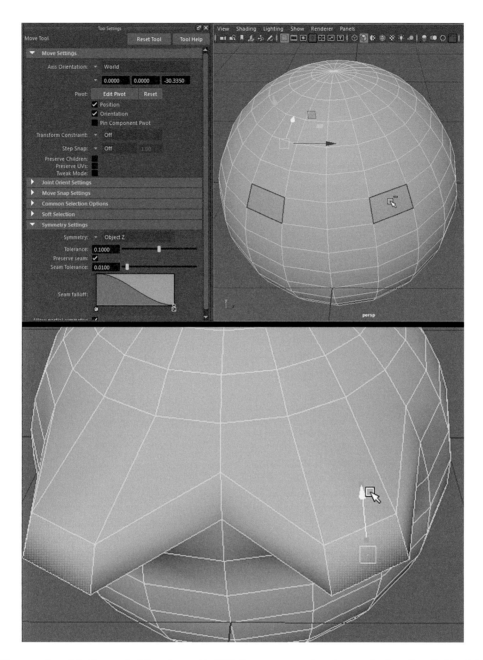

FIGURE 3.20 The user selected the face on the left and moved it. With Symmetry turned on, the opposite face along the Z-axis is also selected and moved.

4. Enter component selection mode by RMB+clicking the sphere and choosing Faces from the marking menu that appears.

5. Move your cursor over a face, and it turns blue; a face on the opposite side of the sphere turns blue as well. Select a face on one side of the sphere, and a face on the opposite side of the sphere is also selected (Figure 3.20, top). Now when you try to move that selected face, the opposite face moves as well in the opposite direction, as shown in Figure 3.20 (bottom).

6. Make sure to turn off Symmetry when you're done.

These symmetry controls are more easily accessed at the top middle of the main UI as shown here.

Building a Decorative Box

Let's get back to making things and explore the interface as we go along. In this exercise, you'll build a decorative box, as shown in Figure 3.21. You will learn to use reference images for modeling, model polygons with Bevel and Extrude tools, and then add edges with Edge Loop and Multi-Cut. Through the process, the Layer Editor helps you stay organized, and you can hide objects from view. This box will be a fairly simple model to make, but you'll use it extensively in Chapters 7, 10, and 11 when working with texture, light, and rendering.

Notice that the box has intricately carved grooves and surface features. You'll build the box to fit the reference and then rely on texture maps created in Chapter 7, "Autodesk® Maya® Shading and Texturing," to create the details on the surface of

FIGURE 3.21   A photo of the decorative box.

the box. You'll begin by creating *reference planes* in the next section.

Begin by downloading the Decorative_Box project folder from the book's web page to your local hard drive. Then set your Maya project to the Decorative_Box by selecting File ➤ Set Project. Navigate to the location of the Decorative_Box folder on your hard drive, select it, and click Set.

Creating Reference Planes

You can use image references from photos or drawings to model your objects in Maya quite easily. These references are basically photos or drawings of your intended model, usually from three different views of the model (front, side, and top).

We will be going through creating reference planes in an old-school and less efficient way, for now, to get you better familiar with working in Maya and using its interface. A faster way to create these reference planes will be explained later by using Free Image Planes for another modeling exercise in Chapter 6.

The image reference photos of the decorative box have already been created and proportioned properly. (You will see a more thorough review of this process for an exercise in Chapter 6, "Practical Experience.") You can find the images for the box in the Sourceimages folder of the Decorative_Box project folders. Table 3.3 lists their names, along with their statistics.

The idea here is to map these photos to polygon planes created in Maya. Again, we are going the long way at first for more exposure to Maya's workflow and interface, and we will visit a more efficient method later in Chapter 6.

First, press Ctrl + A to toggle off the Attribute Editor and display the Channel Box, if it isn't already. Next, be sure Interactive Creation is turned off under Create ➤ Polygon Primitives (Figure 3.22) and then create the reference planes in steps 1–3 with their ratios shown in Table 3.4.

TABLE 3.3

Reference Views and Image Sizes

Filename	View	Image Size	Aspect Ratio
boxFrontRef.jpg	Front	1,749 × 2,023	0.865:1
boxSideRef.jpg	Side	1,862 × 2,046	0.910:1
boxTopRef.jpg	Top	1,782 × 1,791	1.005:1

FIGURE 3.22   Make sure Interactive Creation is toggled off.

TABLE 3.4

Reference Planes and Sizes

Reference Plane	Width	Height
Front	0.865	1
Side	0.910	1
Top	1.005	1

1. In the front view panel, create a polygonal plane by choosing Create ➤ Polygon Primitives ➤ Plane ❑. This plane is for the front image, so in the option box, set Axis to Z, Width to **0.865**, and Height to **1.0**. Make sure the check box for Preserve Aspect Ratio is deselected, as shown in Figure 3.23. Setting Axis to Z will place the plane properly in the front view. Click Apply to create the plane and keep the option box open.

2. Switch to the side view panel. Create a second plane, this time with a width of **0.910** and a height of **1**. Set Axis to X and make sure Preserve Aspect Ratio is unchecked. Click Apply to create the plane.

3. Switch to the top view panel. Create a third plane with a width of **1.005** and a height of **1** and set Axis to Y. Make sure the Preserve Aspect Ratio box is still

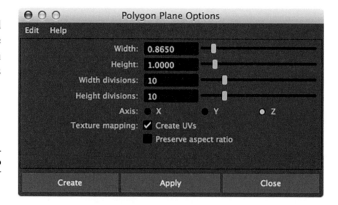

FIGURE 3.23   Option box for creating a plane for the front view.

unchecked and click Create to create the plane and close the option box. Your planes should look like those shown in Figure 3.24.

4. Select the front image plane. In the Channel Box, double-click pPlane1 and rename it to **frontPlane**. Select the side plane and rename it from pPlane2 to **sidePlane**. Rename the top plane from pPlane3 to **topPlane**.

5. You still need to place and scale these planes to align them. Take a look at Figure 3.25 to size your reference planes and place them as shown. There are two ways to position these planes. You can manually scale and move them to visually match what you see

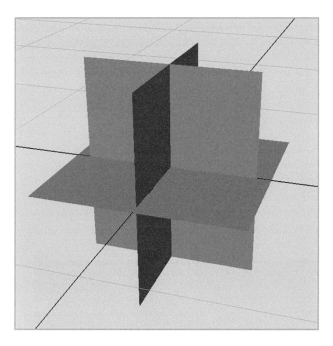

FIGURE 3.24   The three view planes are ready and waiting at the origin.

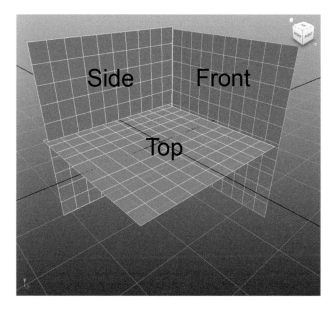

FIGURE 3.25   Arrange the reference planes for the box model.

TABLE 3.5

Reference Planes: Scale and Position

Reference Plane	XYZ Scale	XYZ Position
Front	4.711, 4.711, 4.711	0.134, 0.017, −2.167
Side	4.856, 4.856, 4.856	−1.979, 0, 0
Top	4.28, 4.28, 4.28	0, 0, 0.133

in Figure 3.25, or you can enter the exact values for scale and translation as shown in Table 3.5 using the Channel Box or Attribute Editor (I discuss these windows next before continuing with the box exercise).

6. Save your work using the main menu bar by choosing File ➢ Save Scene As. Name your work, remembering to use version numbers to keep track of your progress, or using File ➢ Increment and Save instead.

You can compare your progress to `boxModel01.mb` in the Scenes folder of the Decorative_Box project on the book's web page.

The Channel Box/Attribute Editor Explained

To the right of the panels is the Attribute Editor/Channel Box. This is where you'll find (and edit) most of the information, or attributes, about a selected object. Pressing Ctrl + A toggles between the Attribute Editor and the Channel Box.

The Channel Box lists an *object's channels*—that is, the attributes of an object that are most commonly animated. When an object is selected in one of the main views, its name appears at the top of the Channel Box, and its channels are listed. You can edit all the channel values and rename the object itself here.

Toggle on the Attribute Editor by pressing Ctrl + A. This window gives you access to all of a selected object's attributes, whereas the Channel Box displays only the most commonly animated attributes.

Tabs running across the top of the Attribute Editor give you access to the other nodes related to that object, as shown in Figure 3.26.

You can click and drag the top of the Attribute Editor to undock it from the main UI. Once you have it in its own window, pressing Ctrl + A will open the Attribute Editor in its own window from then on. However, you can dock the Attribute Editor to the main UI by dragging it back over to the Channel Box area. After that, pressing Ctrl+A will toggle between the Channel Box and Attribute Editor again.

To lock the UI from any unintentional docking issues which can be annoying, in the main Maya menu, choose Windows ➢ Workspaces ➢ Disable Docking/Undocking.

Mapping the Box's Reference Planes with Hypershade

Now you'll import the three reference JPEG (JPG) images from the Sourceimages folder into Maya through the Hypershade window. Click Windows ➢ Rendering Editors ➢ Hypershade

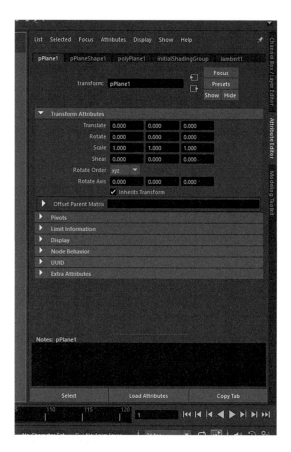

FIGURE 3.26 The Attribute Editor docked to the main UI.

to open this highly powerful texturing window. In the top-left panel (called the Browser), click the Textures tab (highlighted in Figure 3.27). This tab will be empty at first, but once you add the reference JPEGs, their icons will show here.

In a file browser (Windows Explorer in Windows or the Finder in Mac OS X) window, navigate to the Sourceimages folder of the Decorative_Box project from the companion web page. One by one, select `boxFrontRef.jpg`, `box-LeftRef.jpg`, and `boxTopRef.jpg` and drag them individually into the bottom panel (called the Work Area) of the Hypershade window, as shown in Figure 3.27.

Once you have imported the JPEG images, the Hypershade displays them in the Work Area. You use the Alt+LMB, RMB, or MMB key combinations to pan and zoom in the Hypershade window, like in other Maya views. Keep in mind: once imported into Maya, do not move, rename, or delete texture images for the risk of losing connection to them in Maya (though it is easy to reconnect the file paths if the files have been moved or renamed). It's generally best to have your images named and in their proper locations before bringing them into Maya. Usually, texture images are placed in the source images folder of any given project.

Now, back to the Hypershade window: The Hypershade Browser panel has tabs along the top. Since you already clicked the Textures tab highlighted in Figure 3.27, you will see the three JPEGs up there as well. Return to the Materials tab to display your scene's materials, a.k.a. shaders. There will be three defaults that are always in every Maya scene (lambert1, particleCloud1, and shaderGlow1), *which you should just leave alone.*

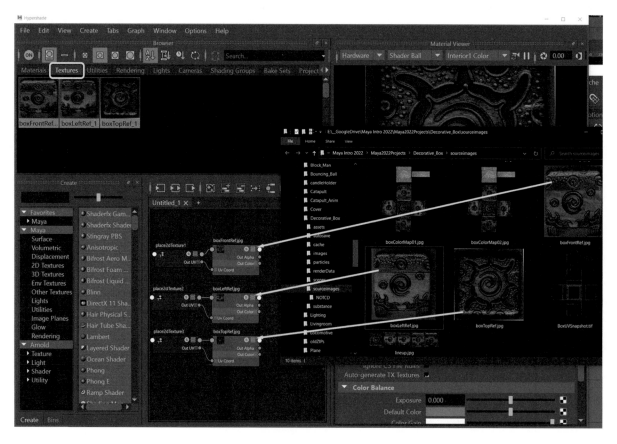

FIGURE 3.27 Drag the JPEGs one by one into the Hypershade window's Work Area.

The bottom-middle panel is the Work Area and is just that: a work area for you to create and edit materials for your scene. The top section (the Browser) displays all the texture and shader nodes available in your scene, again, separated by tabs.

Any time you need to apply a new material to an object in your scene, you need to create a new shader. Therefore, for this example, you need to create three new shaders to assign to the reference plane objects that will each get one of the three reference images. You can load the scene file to boxModel01.mb in the Scenes folder of the Decorative_Box project from the companion web page or continue with your own scene.

1. Create three Lambert shaders in the Hypershade by clicking three individual times on the Lambert button in the Create panel on the left side of the Hypershade window, as shown in Figure 3.28. Notice that the new Lambert shaders appear up in the Browser as well as annoyingly stacked on top of each other in the Work Area. Click and drag the icons to arrange them a little nicer to read with the shaders (Lamberts) on the right and the image icons on the left as shown.

2. If you don't see any of the icons you want to work with in the Work Area, just MMB + click and drag any of the thumbnail icons from the Browser to place them in the Work Area. Figure 3.29 shows bringing one of the reference images into the work area.

3. Select the lambert2 node, and you'll see some of its attributes in the panel on the right side of the Hypershade, called the Property Editor. You will also see a sample render of that shader above the Property Editor in the Material Viewer window, as shown in Figure 3.30.

4. The nodes you see in the Work Area have colored dots on the left side, called Input Sockets. On the right, the dots are called Output Sockets. These sockets allow you to easily connect textures to shaders. Click the green Output Socket next to Out Color for the boxFrontRef.jpg node, and a rubber band pulls out. Drag the rubber band to the red Input Socket of the lambert2 node, as shown in Figure 3.31. This will make that JPEG image be the color of the lambert2 shader. Rename that Lambert material to **frontImage**.

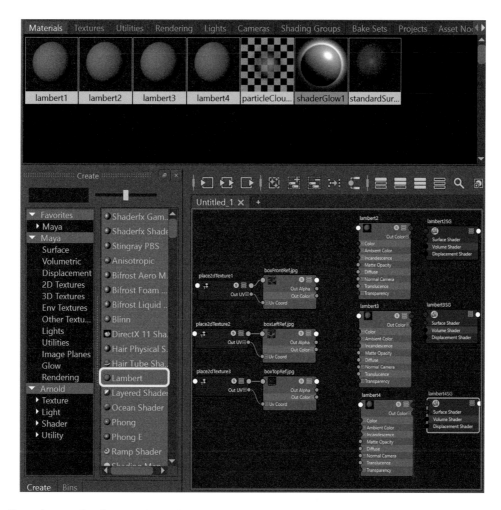

FIGURE 3.28 Create three new Lambert materials and arrange the icons.

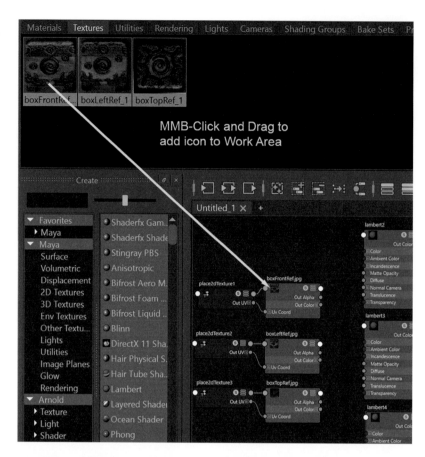

FIGURE 3.29   MMB + click and drag any thumbnail icon to bring it into the Work Area.

FIGURE 3.30   The Property Editor in the Hypershade with the Material Viewer above it displays information about the selected node.

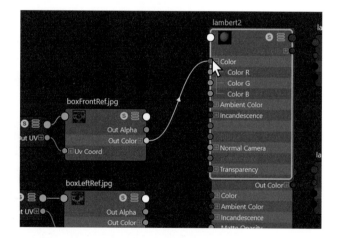

FIGURE 3.31   Connect the Out Color socket of the reference image to the Color input of the lambert2 shader.

5. Repeat step 4 two times to connect and rename the materials for the front and side views. Make sure you label the materials properly; it's tough to tell the side and front images apart.

6. To assign the materials to each plane, simply MMB + drag each shader's thumbnail icon (or node) from the Hypershade to its respective reference plane in the perspective view panel (called persp). Press 6

FIGURE 3.32 The images are applied to the planes.

for Texture mode in the Perspective window, as shown in Figure 3.32. Close the Hypershade.

7. Choose File ➢ Save Scene As or Increment and Save to save a new version of your work.

You can compare your progress to `boxModel02.mb` in the Scenes folder of the Decorative_Box project at the companion web page.

The Hypershade Explained

Just as the Outliner window lists the objects in your scene, the Hypershade window lists the textures and shaders. Shaders are assigned to objects to give them their visual appearance—their look and feel.

The Hypershade (Window ➢ Rendering Editors ➢ Hypershade) displays shaders and textures in a graphical flow-chart layout (see Figure 3.33). The Hypershade window has a few main areas: the *Create* panel the *Bins* panel, the *Browser* panel, the Material viewer, the Property Editor, and the *Work Area*. The Window menu at the Hypershade's menu bar allows you to turn on and off any of these panels. You can also tear them off, or dock them into the Hypershade by clicking the top of any panel and dragging it around in the Hypershade.

The Create Panel

Figure 3.33 shows the Create Panel on the left side of the window. The Create panel gives you access to creating a variety of render nodes (shaders and textures, for example) by clicking them. Once you click an icon in the Create panel, it will show up in the Browser panel above as well as in the Work Area. The Bins tab at the bottom of the Create Panel adds a level of organization by letting you store sets of shaders in different bins to sort them. The list of categories on the left of the Create Panel allows you to filter by type of material you want to create such as a Maya material or an Arnold material, etc.

The Browser Panel

After you create a render node, it appears in the Browser area as a thumbnail icon. Clicking an icon opens its settings in the Property Editor on the right of the Hypershade window as well as showing it in the main UI's Attribute Editor. You use the MMB to drag any icon from the Browser to the Work Area, where you can work on making or editing shading networks.

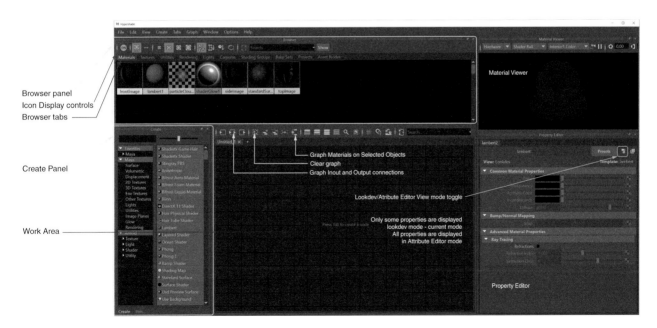

FIGURE 3.33 The Hypershade's default layout.

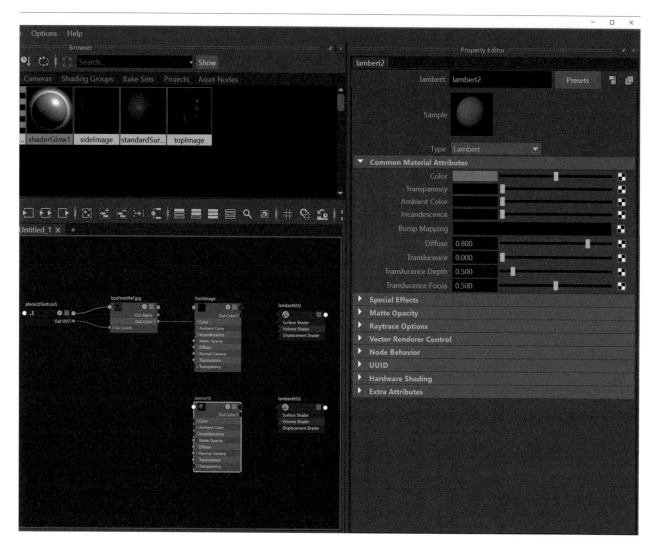

FIGURE 3.34   The Hypershade with Attribute Editor mode and the Material Viewer turned off.

The Work Area

The Work Area is a free-form workspace where you can connect render nodes to form-shading networks that you can assign to your objects for rendering. You can add nodes to the workspace by MMB + clicking and dragging them from the Browser panel of the Hypershade window.

The Material Viewer

The Material Viewer panel gives you an icon representing how your currently selected material looks. This panel by default sits above the Property Editor. It is usually turned off throughout the figures in this book past this chapter to save space. It is turned on and off through the Window menu in the Hypershade.

The Property Editor

The Property Editor panel gives you access to the settings of any selected node in the Hypershade. This panel has two view

options: Lookdev display (shown in Figure 3.33) and Attribute Editor display (as shown in Figure 3.34, where the Material Viewer is also turned off). Lookdev display shows you only the more important settings, a.k.a. properties. The Attribute Editor view shows all the attributes and is almost identical to the main Attribute Editor window in the main Maya UI. You will primarily use the layout shown in Figure 3.34 throughout this book, where the Material Viewer panel has been turned off to maximize space. You can turn off panels by clicking the "X" Close icon in the upper right of any panel.

You can turn any of the panels on and off by accessing the Window menu in the Hypershade, as shown in Figure 3.35, to turn them back on as floating windows. Drag the floating panel to inside the Hypershade to dock it as you prefer.

Organizing Workflow with the Layer Editor

Now that you have the polygon reference planes set up and mapped, you'll create *display layers* to help organize the scene before you actually start modeling. You can load the scene file

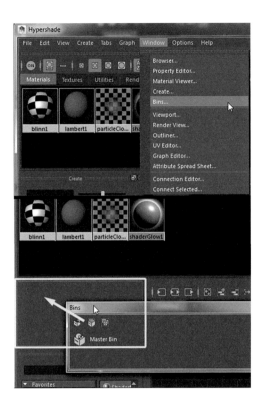

FIGURE 3.35 Turning parts of the Hypershade on (top) and docking them to the Hypershade (bottom).

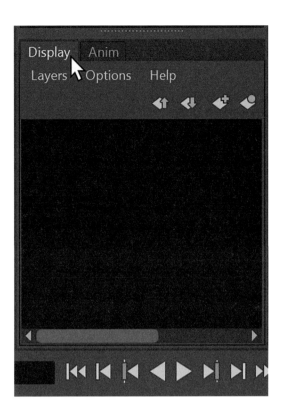

FIGURE 3.36 The Display tab in the Layer Editor.

`boxModel02.mb` in the Scenes folder of the Decorative_Box project from the companion web page or continue with your own scene.

1. Select the three reference planes and toggle off the Attribute Editor to show the Channel Box. Under the Channel Box is the Layer Editor. Click the Display tab, as shown in Figure 3.36.

2. With the planes selected still, click the Create A New Layer And Assign Selected Objects icon at the top of the Layer Editor, as shown in Figure 3.37. Doing so creates a new layer for these three reference planes.

3. In the Layer Editor, double-click the name layer1 to open the Edit Layer window. Rename the layer to **referenceLayer**, as shown in Figure 3.38.

4. Toggle the display of this layer by toggling the V icon, shown in Figure 3.39.

5. Save another version. You can compare your progress to `boxModel03.mb` in the Scenes folder of the Decorative_Box project.

Display layers allow you to easily turn on and off the display of the reference planes as you model the decorative box. Become familiar with this feature early because it will be a valuable asset when you animate complicated scenes.

To add items to an already created layer, select the objects; then RMB + click the desired layer and choose Add Selected Objects. You can also use the layers to select groups of objects by choosing Layers ➢ Select Objects In Selected Layers or

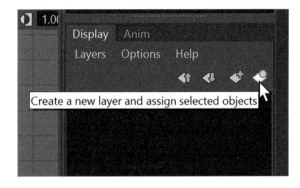

FIGURE 3.37 Click to create a new display layer and add the selected objects automatically.

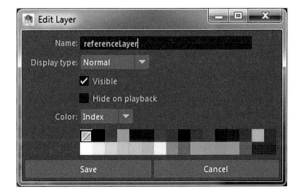

FIGURE 3.38 Name the new display layer.

FIGURE 3.39 Toggle the visibility of the reference layer.

by RMB + clicking the layer and choosing Select Objects. To change the name and color of a layer, double-click the layer to open the Edit Layer window, as shown earlier in Figure 3.38.

Modeling the Decorative Box

Make sure you are in Texture mode (press 6) so you can see the reference plane and the images on them in the perspective view panel. Also, be sure to toggle on visibility of the references' display layer. In Chapter 4, I'll cover in more detail the modeling tools you'll use.

You can load the scene file `boxModel03.mb` in the Scenes folder of the Decorative_Box project from the companion web page or continue with your own scene. To model the box to fit the references, follow these steps:

1. With Interactive Creation turned off, select Create ➤ Polygonal Primitives ➤ Cube. Position and size the cube to roughly match the size of the reference planes for the decorative box.

2. To make it easier to see the reference planes and their images in relation to the box you just created, in the menu bar of the perspective (persp) view panel, select Shading ➤ X-Ray, as shown in Figure 3.40. Now you can see the box and the reference images at the same time.

3. Scale and position the cube to match the size of the main part of the box, as shown in Figure 3.41. Don't bother sizing the box to include the little feet on the bottom of the box. Use X-Ray mode in the Side, Front, and Top modeling panels in Maya to line up the cube as best as you can. This will be the base model for the decorative box.

4. Switch off X-Ray mode in your views (in the persp view panel's menu bar, select Shading ➤ X-Ray). Let's work on the rounded bevel on top of the box, where the lid is. Select the poly cube, open the Attribute Editor (Ctrl + A), and click the pCubeShape1 tab to access the shape node attributes.

5. Under Object Display ➤ Drawing Overrides, check Enable Overrides to enable it. Deselect Shading to

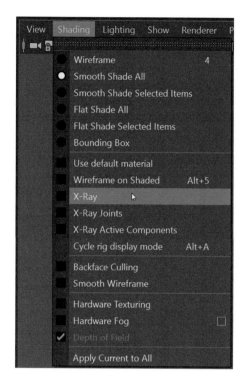

FIGURE 3.40 Set the display to X-Ray mode so you can see how the poly cube and the decorative box line up.

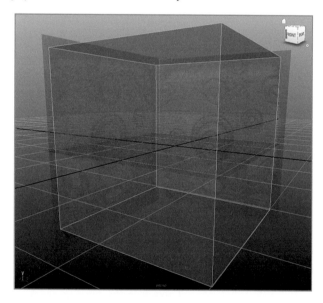

FIGURE 3.41 Size the cube to fit the box references.

display the poly cube as a wireframe while the reference planes remain displayed as textured planes. This way, you can more easily match the cube to the decorative box (see Figure 3.42).

6. RMB + click the box and select Edge from the marking menu, as shown in Figure 3.43.

7. Select the top four edges of the cube and switch to the front view, as shown in Figure 3.44. Using the front view, you'll shape the top of the cube.

8. Make sure you are in the Modeling menu set; then select Edit Mesh ➤ Bevel and a pop-up menu with

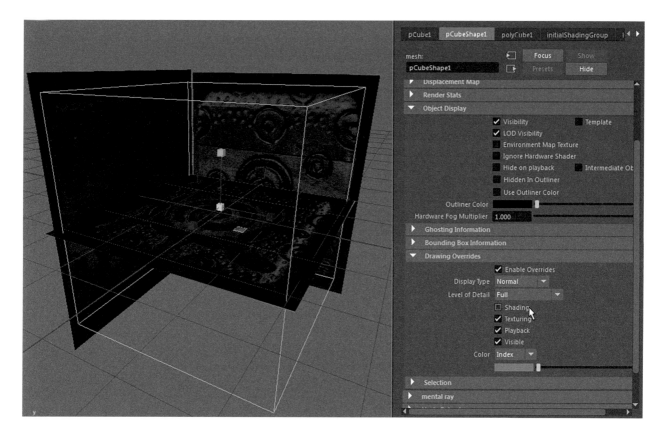

FIGURE 3.42   Display the cube as a wireframe.

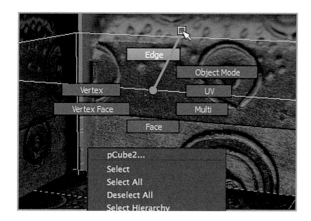

FIGURE 3.43   Select Edge from the marking menu.

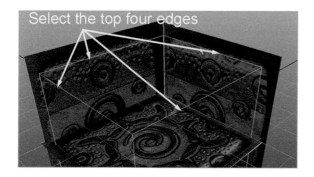

FIGURE 3.44   Select the top four edges.

FIGURE 3.45   Default bevel.

various Bevel settings opens. Don't worry about the settings; you'll adjust them after the fact. You should now have something like Figure 3.45 if your bevel options were at the defaults. Because you created a bevel operation on the cube, Maya has created a new node connected to the cube. You will access this bevel node to adjust the bevel settings on the cube.

9. RMB + click the cube, select Object Mode from the marking menu, and then select the cube. Toggle on the Attribute Editor and select the new polyBevel1

tab. Using the front view panel, set Fraction so that it lines up with the rounded top of the box, at about **0.26**. Set Segments to **12**. Make sure Auto Fit, Offset As Fraction, and World Space are all checked (see Figure 3.46).

10. In the side view panel, move the bottom-corner vertices on the cube to line up the bottom corners of the box to the reference image.

11. In the front view panel, move the bottom-corner vertices to match the bottom of the box in the image (see Figure 3.47). Don't worry about the curvature in the middle of the box or the feet just yet. Save your work.

12. Let's take a quick look at how this box will look rendered now. Click anywhere in the persp view panel to

make it the active panel. In the Status line (the group of icons at the top of the screen), click the Render The Current Frame icon, as shown in Figure 3.48. The Render View window will open and will show a black frame. This is because there are no lights in the scene, and the default renderer is set to Arnold.

13. In the main menu bar, select Arnold ➢ Lights ➢ Skydome Light to create an even lighting throughout the scene. We will cover more of lighting and Arnold later in the book.

14. Click the Render The Current Frame icon (Figure 3.48) again, but this time the box will render along with the reference planes against a white background as shown in Figure 3.49.

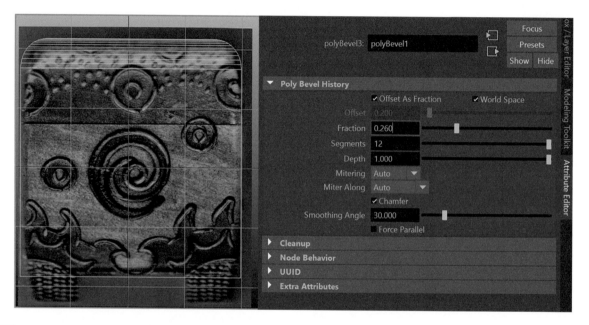

FIGURE 3.46 Set the bevel to fit the rounded top of the box in the front view panel.

FIGURE 3.47 Taper the bottom of the cube.

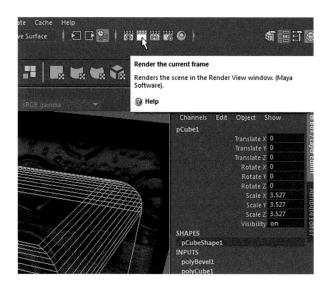

FIGURE 3.48   Render a frame of the box from the Status line.

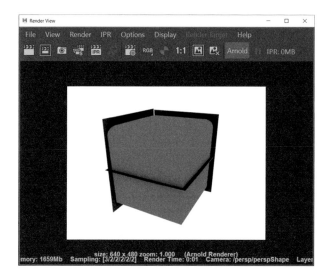

FIGURE 3.49   The model thus far is rendered using Arnold.

15. Save your work. You can compare your progress to boxModel04.mb in the Scenes folder of the Decorative_Box project from the companion web page.

When you rendered your work in step 15, the Render View opened to show you a gray-shaded box with the reference planes barely showing, as you can see in Figure 3.49.

Status Line Explained

Here are some details about the Status Line before we continue with the box modeling exercise. The Status line (see Figure 3.50) contains several important and often-used icons.

The Status line begins with a drop-down menu that gives you access to the menu sets in Maya. You'll notice that intermittently throughout the Status line are white vertical line breaks with either a box or an arrow in the middle. Clicking a break opens or closes sections of the Status line.

Some of the most often-used icons are identified here.

Scene File Icons

The tools in the first section of the Status line deal with file operations; they are Start A New Scene ( ), Open An Existing Scene ( ), or Save Your Current Scene ( ).

Selection Modes

Selection modes allow you to select different levels of an object's hierarchy (see Table 3.6). For example, using a selection mode, you can select an entire group of objects, only one of the objects in that group, or even components (vertices, faces, and so on) on the surface of that object, depending on the selection mode you're in.

To switch between the two most often-used modes—Object and Component—press the F8 key. You can also select among the Component and Object modes from the marking menu when you RMB + click an object.

TABLE 3.6

Selection Modes

Icon	Name	Description
	Hierarchy and Combinations mode	Lets you select groups of objects
	Object mode	Lets you select objects such as geometry, cameras, lights, and so on
	Component mode	Lets you select an object's components, such as vertices, faces, UVs, and so on

FIGURE 3.50   The Status line.

You'll work with these selection mask filters throughout the book, but you will likely access them through marking menus as you have already done to select vertices and edges of a polygonal object. For a quick preview, hover your cursor over each of the icons to see a tooltip that gives the icon's name and describes its function.

Snapping Functions, or Snaps

The icons with the magnets are called *snaps*. They allow you to snap your cursor or object to specific points in the scene, as you saw in the solar system exercise. You can snap to other objects, to CVs or vertices (   ), and to grid intersections (   ) and other locations by toggling these icons. Table 3.7 shows the various snaps.

The Channel Box/Layer Editor Icons

These last five buttons on the Status line (Figure 3.51) toggle between the Attribute Editor, Channel Box, and Modeling

TABLE 3.7

Snap Icons

Icon	Name	Description
	Snap To Points	This icon lets you snap objects to object points such as CVs or vertices.
	Snap To Grids	This icon lets you snap objects to intersections of the view's grid.
	Snap To Curves	This icon lets you snap objects along a curve.
	Snap To Projected Center	This icon lets you snap to the center of a selected object.
	Snap To View Planes	This icon lets you snap objects to view planes.
	Make The Selected Object Live	This icon has nothing to do with snapping but is grouped with the Snap To icons. It lets you create objects such as curves directly on a surface.

Toolkit view on the right side of the UI as well as accessing Character Controls. Clicking the first icon (   ) shows or toggles the Modeling Toolkit. The second icon (   ) toggles on the Character Controls (not covered in this book).

FIGURE 3.51   Attribute Editor/Channel Box/Tool Settings icons.

The third icon (   ) toggles between the Attribute Editor and the Channel Box, which is the last icon (   ). Toggling between the Attribute Editor and Channel box is also accomplished by pressing Ctrl + A.

The second to last icon (   ) displays or hides the Tool Settings window along the left side of the UI, as you've seen with soft selections when you double-clicked on the Move Tool earlier.

Editing the Decorative Box Model Using the Shelf

Back to work on the box model. You will use the Shelf in the UI to access some of the commands for the next series of steps as you continue working on the box. The Shelf runs directly under the Status line and contains an assortment of tools and commands in separate tabs, as shown in Figure 3.52.

You can load the scene file boxModel04.mb in the Scenes folder of the Decorative_Box project from the companion web page or continue with your own scene.

In the following steps, you will add surface detail to the model so you can more adequately adjust its shape:

1. Orient the persp view panel so you can see the bottom of the box and then select the box model. In the Shelf, click the Poly Modeling tab. Double-click the Multi-Cut tool (as shown in Figure 3.53). The Tool Settings (a.k.a. Options Box) will open showing you the Multi-Cut tool's settings (Figure 3.54).

2. Your cursor will change to a knife icon (may also give you a cross shape). Click and drag along the back edge, as shown in Figure 3.55, to select a point near the bottom-left edge of the box that corresponds with where the box's feet begin. The readout should show 75% or so.

FIGURE 3.52   The Shelf.

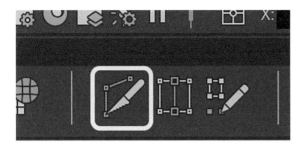

FIGURE 3.53 The Multi-Cut Tool icon in the Shelf.

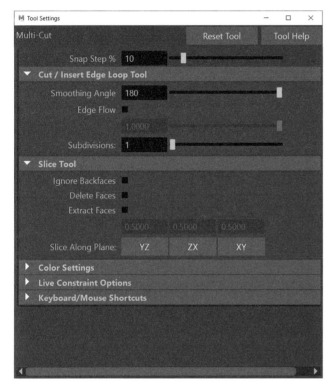

FIGURE 3.54 The Multi-Cut Tool settings.

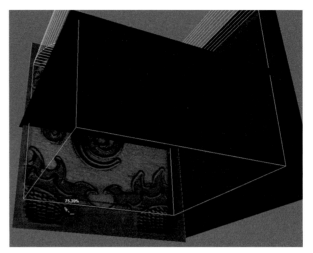

FIGURE 3.55 Select the first point for the Multi-Cut.

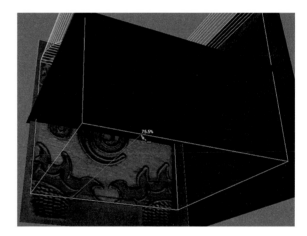

FIGURE 3.56 Create a new edge line along the bottom of the box.

3. Click and drag a second point on the opposite edge on the bottom of the box (at about 75% again) to create a new edge line, as shown in Figure 3.56. Click the RMB to commit the new edge line. This creates surface detail along the bottom of the box for you to model the feet for the box. This methodology is explained in detail in Chapter 4.

4. Using the same procedures in steps 1–3, create three more edge lines for a total of four separate cuts in the bottom face of the cube that line up with the legs of the box, as shown in Figure 3.57. The preceding three steps have created a surface detail called *faces* that allow you to create the feet for the box.

5. Click the Select Tool icon in the Tool Box to the left of the UI (shown in Figure 3.58) to exit the Multi-Cut tool. Your cursor returns to the regular Maya cursor.

6. RMB+click the box and select Face from the marking menu (Figure 3.59). As you hover your mouse over the parts of the box, the new faces in the four corners of the box you just created will be highlighted in red. Shift + click the four corner faces to select all four faces, as shown in Figure 3.60.

7. With the four faces selected, go into the Shelf and select the Extrude icon shown in Figure 3.61. This tool is also accessible through the menu Edit Mesh ➤ Extrude.

8. Your manipulator will change, as shown in Figure 3.62. Grab the Z-axis move handle and drag it down to "pull" the feet out of the bottom of the box as shown.

9. By moving vertices, taper the feet to match the reference images in the front and side view panels; see Figure 3.63.

10. Save your work. You can compare your progress to boxModel05.mb in the Scenes folder of the Decorative_Box project.

FIGURE 3.57   Cut the bottom face four times to create divisions for the box's feet.

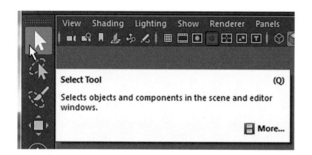

FIGURE 3.58   The Select tool in the Tool Box.

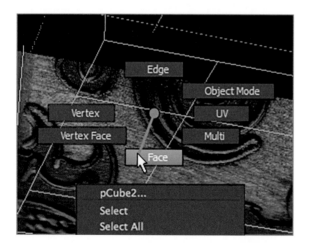

FIGURE 3.59   Select Face from the marking menu.

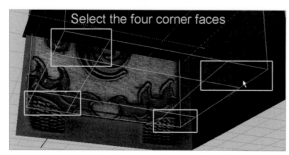

FIGURE 3.60   Select the four corner faces.

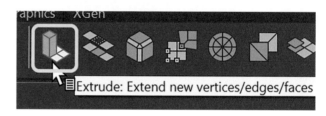

FIGURE 3.61   The Extrude icon in the Shelf.

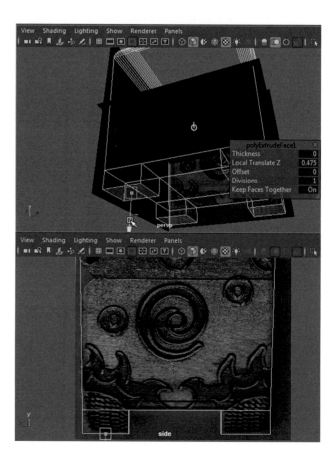

FIGURE 3.62   Extrude the feet.

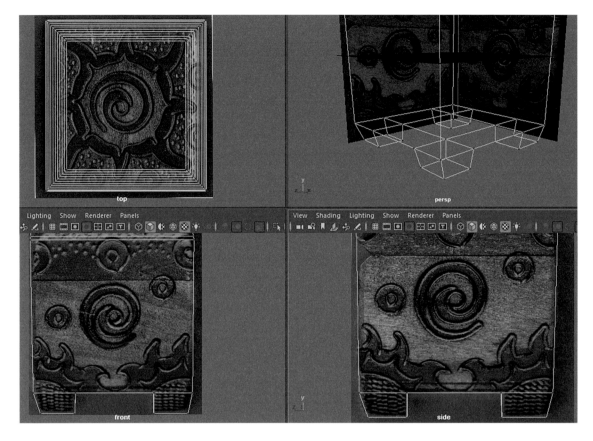

FIGURE 3.63 Move the vertices on the feet to line them up with the reference images.

The Shelf and Tool Box Explained

Here is a brief explanation of the tools and icons in the Shelf and Tool Box before we continue with the box modeling exercise.

The Shelf

The *Shelf*, shown earlier in Figure 3.52, is an area where you keep icons for tools. It's divided into tabs that define functions for the tool icons in the Shelf. Don't worry too much about the Shelf right now; it may be better to use the commands from the menus first before turning to icons and shelves.

The Tool Box

The Tool Box, shown in Figure 3.64, displays the most commonly used tools. Table 3.8 lists the icons and their functions.

In addition to the common commands, the Tool Box displays several choices for screen layouts that let you change the interface with a single click. Experiment with the layouts by clicking any of the three screen layout presets in the Tool Box shown as the first 3 icons in Figure 3.65. The fourth icon in Figure 3.65 toggles on and off the Outliner, which shows you an inventory of the objects in your scene, as we have already seen. The icon is blue when the Outliner is on, and gray when off.

FIGURE 3.64 The Tool Box.

TABLE 3.8

Tool Box Icons

Icon	Name	Description
	Select	Lets you select objects
	Lasso Select	Allows for a free-form selection using a lasso marquee
	Paint Selection Tool	Enables the Paint Selection tool
	Translate (Move)	Moves the selection
	Rotate	Rotates the selection
	Scale	Scales the selection
	Last Tool Used	Shows the last tool that was used (shown as Multi-Cut Tool here, sometimes shown blank)

Continuing the Decorative Box Model

Back to work! You'll be spending more time getting the box in shape. You can load the scene file `boxModel05.mb` in the Scenes folder of the Decorative_Box project or continue with your own scene. In the following steps, you will add more

FIGURE 3.65 Toggles display of the Outliner.

faces and edges to the model surface (a.k.a. mesh) so you can add detail to the shape:

1. The middle of the box has a bit of a curve; you will need to create a new edge line that runs across the middle of the box so you can bow out the sides in the middle. In the Layer Editor, toggle off visibility for the reference images by clicking the **V** icon for reference planes. Now you can see just the model of the box.

2. Select the box, and in the Polygons tab of the Shelf, double-click the Multi-Cut Tool icon ( ). Click and drag your Multi-Cut cursor ( ) along the box's first edge to place a point in the middle of that edge (at about 50%), as shown in Figure 3.66.

3. Place a new split point in the middle of the next edge of the box (working from left to right), creating an edge line along one side of the box. Continue to place two more split points in the middle of each remaining edge to create a horizontal cut line in the middle of the box, as shown in Figure 3.67. Your last point will display the word *close* next to your cursor. Press Enter, and you now have a horizontal split along the middle of the box.

4. Click the Select Tool icon in the Tool Box to the left of the UI ( ) to exit the Multi-Cut tool. Your cursor returns to the regular Maya cursor. Turn on the referencePlanes layer to show the image references.

5. RMB+click the box and choose Vertex from the marking menu. Move the new vertices in the middle of the box to bow out the box slightly. Move the rest

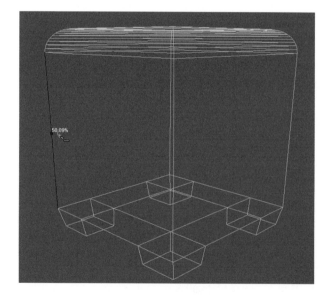

FIGURE 3.66 Insert the first point of a Multi-Cut at about 50% along this first edge.

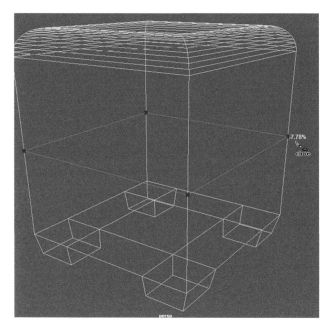

FIGURE 3.67   Create a horizontal edge line all the way around the box.

of the vertices to match the model to the box images in the side and front view panels (see Figure 3.68).

6. Save your work. You can compare your progress to boxModel06.mb in the Scenes folder of the Decorative_Box project.

FIGURE 3.68   Adjust the cube to fit the reference images.

Time Slider and Help Line Explained

In this section, you will examine the bottom part of the UI where the Help line and Time slider live before completing the box modeling exercise in the next section.

Time Slider/Range Slider

Running horizontally across the bottom of the screen are the Time slider and the Range slider, as shown in Figure 3.69. The Time slider displays the range of frames available in your animation and gives you a gray bar, known as the *Current Time indicator*. You can click it and then drag it back and forth in a scrubbing motion to move through time in your sequence. (When instructed in this book to *scrub* to a certain point in your animation, use this indicator to do so.)

The text box to the right of the Time slider gives you your current frame, but you can also use the text box to enter the frame you want to access. Immediately next to the current time readout is a set of DVD/DVR-type playback controls that you can use to play back your animation.

Below the Time slider is the Range slider, which you use to adjust the range of animation playback for your Time slider. The text boxes on either side of this slider give you readouts for the start and end frames of the scene and of the range selected.

You can adjust any of these settings by typing in these text boxes or by lengthening or shortening the slider with the handles on either end of the bar. When you change the range, you change only the viewable frame range of the scene; you don't adjust any of the animation. Adjusting the Range Slider lets you zoom into sections of the timeline, which makes adjusting keyframes and timing much easier, especially in long animations.

Command Line/Help Line

Maya Embedded Language (MEL) is the user-accessible programming language of Maya. Use the Command line (see Figure 3.70) to enter single MEL commands directly from the keyboard in the white text box portion of the bar.

Below the Command line is the Help line. This bar provides a quick reference for almost everything on the screen. It also prompts you for the next step in a particular function or the next required input for a task's completion. The Help line is useful when you're not really sure about the next step in a command, such as which object to select next. You'll be surprised by how much you'll learn about tool functions by reading the prompts displayed here.

Finishing the Decorative Box Model

Now that you have the overall shape of the box finished, you need to add a few finishing details to the box. You will round out the edges of the box so they are not sharp, as well as add a line around the top of the box for the lid's seam and hinges. You can load the scene file boxModel06.mb in the Scenes folder of the Decorative_Box project or continue with your own scene.

Scrub Bar · Current frame · Playback controls · Animation start frame · Range bar handles · Scene end frame · Frame rate · Auto Keyframe · Character set selection menu · Animation Preferences

FIGURE 3.69   The Time and Range sliders.

Help Line · Command Line · Command Feedback · Script Editor Button

FIGURE 3.70   The Command line and the Help line.

To make a model more dynamic, you can round or *bevel* the edges to heighten the realism of the model when it is lit and rendered.

1. Let's turn off the image reference planes again, but this time, let's do it a different way. Open the Outliner window by choosing Windows ➢ Outliner or pressing the Outliner icon ( ) in the Tool Box. You are already somewhat familiar with the Outliner from the solar system exercise in the previous chapter. Select frontPlane, sidePlane, and topPlane in the Outliner and hide them by selecting Display ➢ Hide ➢ Hide Selection or by pressing H. This way, you can individually hide any object in your scene. Notice that when an object is hidden, its Outliner entry is grayed out (Figure 3.71).

2. Select the box and open the Attribute Editor. Under the Object Display ➢ Drawing Overrides headings, uncheck the Enable Overrides box, as shown in Figure 3.72, to display the box in Shaded mode again. This will help you see how the bevel works.

3. You will bevel the edges of the box throughout to soften the crisp corners of the cube that the real box doesn't have. RMB + click the box and choose Edge from the marking menu. Shift+select all the outer edges of the cube, as shown in Figure 3.73.

4. With those edges selected, select Edit Mesh ➢ Bevel ❏. Set everything to the defaults, but change Segments from 1 to **3**. Click Bevel, and your box should resemble the one shown in Figure 3.74.

5. Select the cube and delete its history by selecting Edit ➢ Delete By Type ➢ History. This process essentially cleans up the model and the procedures it has undergone. You'll learn about History in the following chapters.

6. You have one final detail to tend to on the lid. You need to add the hinge area you can see in the side view panel's reference image. Select the reference planes in the Outliner (pPlane1, pPlane2, and pPlane3) and press H to unhide them (you can also choose Display➢ Show ➢ Show Selection). Make

FIGURE 3.71   Hiding objects using the Outliner.

sure you're in Texture Shaded mode in your views (press 6) to see the box images.

7. Select the box. Turn its display back to wireframe by going into the Attribute Editor and, in the pCube-Shape1 tab, turning on Enable Overrides under the Object Display ➢ Drawing Overrides heading.

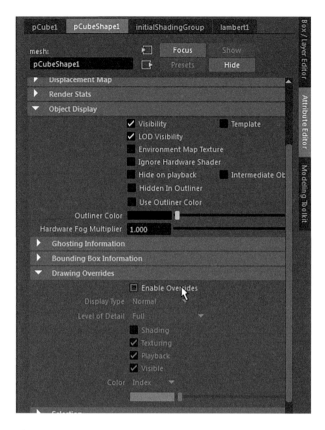

FIGURE 3.72   Uncheck the box for Enable Drawing Overrides in the Attribute Editor to display the box in Shaded mode again.

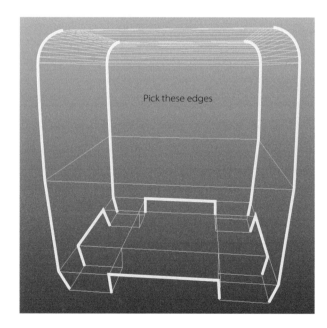

FIGURE 3.73   Select all of these edges for beveling.

8. Select Mesh Tools ➢ Insert Edge Loop. This tool is like the Multi-Cut tool in that it inserts new edges into a model. Your cursor will change to a solid triangle. Click the upper edge of the box and drag a

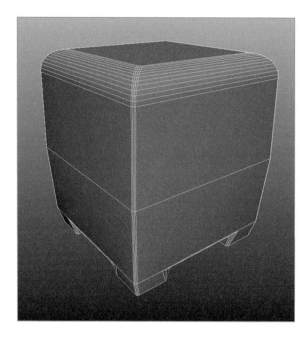

FIGURE 3.74   The beveled edges of the box.

dashed line to line up with the lid's seam in the box reference images, as shown in Figure 3.75. Once it's placed and you release the mouse button, the edge line will be completed, and the dashed line will turn solid.

9. In the side view panel, insert four more horizontal edge loops for a total of five edge loops, as shown in Figure 3.76. This gives you edges with which to create the wedge cutout where the box is hinged, and that gives you a little indentation where the lid meets the box. You won't create a separate lid because you won't animate the box to open or close, and you don't need to see the inside.

10. In the side view panel, select the appropriate vertices (see Figure 3.77) and move them to create the wedge-shaped indentation as shown.

11. Choose Select ➢ Select Edge Loop Tool. Select the middle edge loop you created earlier for the indent where the lid meets the box, as shown in Figure 3.78. Press R to scale the edge loop slightly inward, as shown.

12. Hide the reference planes again through the Layer Editor and turn Shading back on for the cube in the Attribute Editor. Figure 3.79 (left) shows the completed box. But there's still a little snag. Notice the dark area where the lid meets the box, where you just created the slightly indented seam line. This is because of Normals. It makes the lid look as if it's angled inward.

13. Select the box and choose Mesh Display ➢ Set Normal Angle. In the Set Normal Angle window that pops open, set Angle to the default of **30** and click Apply And Close. Doing so fixes the darkening, as

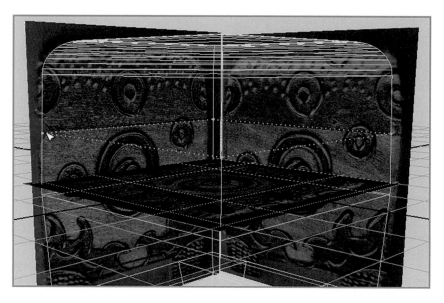

FIGURE 3.75   Insert an edge loop to line up with the seam in the real box.

Insert these five edges

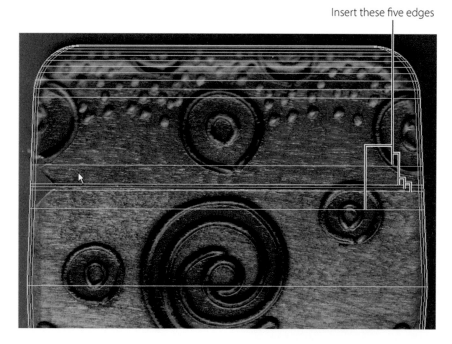

FIGURE 3.76   Insert these five edge loops for the lid of the box.

FIGURE 3.77   Move the vertices to create the hinge area in the back of the box.

Select this edge loop

FIGURE 3.78 Select this edge loop and scale it to create an indent line where the lid meets the box.

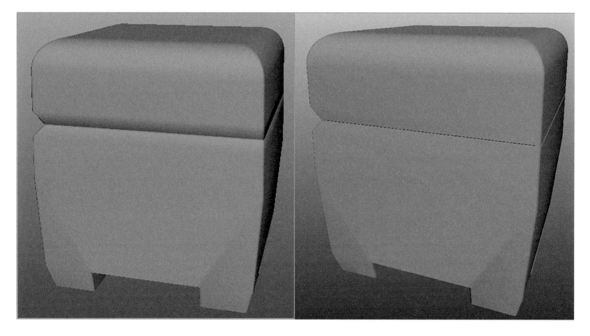

FIGURE 3.79 The completed box needs one more adjustment (left). The box now looks better after adjusting Normals (right).

shown in Figure 3.79 (right). For more on Normals, see the "Normals" sidebar. Select the box and delete its history by choosing Edit ➤ Delete By Type ➤ History.

14. Save your work, grab someone you love, and give them a hug.

You're finished with the modeling portion of this decorative box, and you've gotten to know the interface much better. In later chapters, you'll texture, light, and render the box with photorealism in mind. You can load `boxModel07.mb` from the Scenes folder in the Decorative_Box project to compare your work.

NORMALS

Normals are imaginary lines that are perpendicular to a mesh's poly face and that define sides for that face. They also help determine how a renderer, such as Arnold or V-Ray shades the surface. In some cases when you're modeling, you may notice an action that causes part of your model to display a darkened area as you saw in the decorative box in Figure 3.79. By manually setting a Normal angle for the box as you did in step 13 of the exercise, you override the display anomaly. You'll learn more about Normals in Chapter 7.

The Attribute Editor and Outliner Explained

You have worked with the Attribute Editor and Outliner several times already. Here's a brief overview of these all-important windows in the workflow in Maya.

The Attribute Editor Window

To use the Attribute Editor, select Windows ➢ Attribute Editor (Ctrl + A). The Attribute Editor window is arguably the most important window in Maya. As you've already seen, objects are defined by a series of attributes, and you edit and even set keyframes for these attributes using the Attribute Editor. Some attributes listed in the Attribute Editor are also shown in the Channel Box. These attributes, despite being shown in two places, are the same.

The Attribute Editor has tabs that correspond to the object's node structure. You learned a little about the Maya object structure in the previous chapter.

You'll see an area for writing notes at the bottom of the Attribute Editor. This is handy because you can put reminders here of important events, such as how you set up an object or even a birthday or an anniversary. If you drag the horizontal bar, you can adjust the size of the notes space, as shown in Figure 3.80.

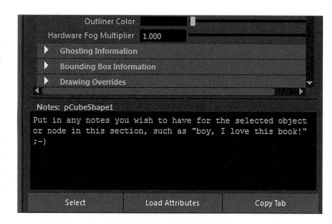

FIGURE 3.80 You can keep notes with an object's attributes in the Attribute Editor.

The Outliner

The Outliner is perfect for organizing, grouping objects, renaming nodes, and so forth, as you've already seen.

To use the Outliner, select Windows ➢ Outliner (see Figure 3.81). It displays all the objects in your scene as an outline. You can select any object in a scene by clicking its name.

The objects are listed by order of creation within the scene, but you can easily reorganize them by MMB + clicking and dragging an object to a new location in the window. This is a fantastic way to keep your scene organized. In addition, you can easily rename an object by double-clicking its Outliner entry and typing a new name.

A separator bar in the Outliner lets you split the display into two separate outline views. By clicking and dragging this bar up or down, you can see either end of a long list, with both ends having independent scrolling control.

Introducing the Modeling Toolkit

As you've seen in the interface, alongside the right of the UI where the Attribute Editor and Channel Box reside is a tab called Modeling Toolkit, shown in Figure 3.82. This suite of tools makes polygon modeling more efficient since the most often-used tools are centralized in one place. In addition, the Modeling Toolkit, when activated, allows for faster and easier component selection and editing.

In the Modeling Toolkit, the top half centers around making selections, while the bottom half lists important polygon workflow tools such as Bevel and Extrude. All of the Modeling Toolkit tools work slightly differently than the standard Maya tools of the same name; however, the results of the executed

FIGURE 3.81 The Outliner.

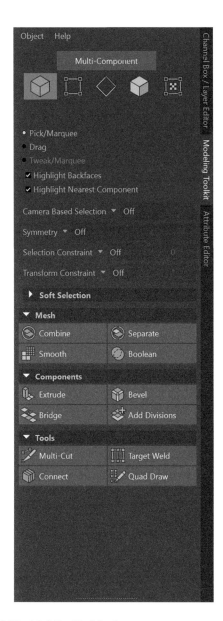

FIGURE 3.82 Modeling Toolkit tab.

tool are identical. This tool set is explored in depth and put to good use in Chapter 4.

Summary

In this chapter, you learned more about the UI and the primary windows used in Maya as you worked on modeling the decorative box. The UI combines mouse and keyboard input as well as plenty of menu and tool icons that you can select and use to accomplish your tasks.

You'll be quizzed in 10 minutes. Do you have it all memorized? Don't worry if you haven't absorbed all the information in this chapter. Now that you've had some exposure to the Maya UI, you'll be familiar with the various windows when you really get to work. You can always come back to this chapter to refresh your memory. Remember, you should learn the Maya program using its default settings. When in doubt, remember to access the Maya Help system (F1 keyboard shortcut or the Help menu in the main menu bar).

4

Beginning Polygonal Modeling

Learning Outcomes

In this chapter, you will be able to

Decide how to plan your model

Edit polygon geometry in traditional Maya as well as Modeling Toolkit workflows

Navigate the Modeling Toolkit interface

Work with the Modeling Toolkit selection workflow

Extrude, bevel, and wedge polygons

Use edge loops to create detail

Create curves and use the Revolve function to convert them to polygon meshes

Adjust grouping and hierarchies in a complex model

Planning Your Model

When you dissect the components of an object into primitive shapes, you can then translate and re-create the object in 3D terms.

First, you should take reference pictures from many angles, get dimensions, and even write down a description of the object. The more perspectives from which you see your subject, the better you'll understand and be able to interpret your model.

You must also decide the purpose of your model and determine the level of detail at which it will be seen in your CG scene. Consider the two scenes in Figure 4.1. If you need to create a park bench for a far shot (left), it will be a waste of time and effort to model all the details such as the grooves in the armrest. However, if your bench is shown in a close-up (the images on the right), you'll need those details.

If you aren't certain how much detail you'll need, it's better to create a higher level of detail rather than skimping. You can more easily pare down details than create it later.

Keep in mind that you can also add detail to the look of your model in the texturing phase of production, as you'll see with the decorative box later in the book. (Chapter 7, "Autodesk® Maya® Shading and Texturing," covers texturing.)

Choosing a Method

Polygon modeling involves tearing and extruding from larger pieces to form a desired shape. This method is much more preferred by most digital artists in most fields.

NURBS modeling is great for organic shapes because smooth lines, or *curves*, are the basis of all NURBS surfaces, but this modeling is not used much outside of mechanical/automotive/architectural design anymore. This is because NURBS tend to be more wieldy in comparison to polygonal modeling since NURBS are more difficult to create a complete model without several surfaces that must be perfectly stitched together, a process not covered by this book. Basic NURBS modeling techniques, however, are covered in the next chapter.

FIGURE 4.1   The level of detail you need to include in a model depends on how it will be seen in the animation.

DOI: 10.1201/9780429490958-5

An Overview of Polygons

Polygons consist of *faces*. A single polygon *face* is a flat surface made when three or more points called *vertices* are connected. The position of each *vertex* defines the shape and size of the face, usually a triangle. The line that connects one vertex to another is called an *edge*. Some polygonal faces have four vertices instead of three, creating a square face called a *quad*.

Polygonal faces are attached along their polygonal edges to make up a more complex surface that constitutes your model (as shown with the polygonal sphere in Figure 4.2). A camping tent is a perfect example. The intersections of the poles are the faces' vertices. The poles are the edges of the faces, and the cloth draped over the tent's frame is the resultant surface.

Polygon models are the simplest for a computer to render. They're used for gaming applications, which need to render the models as the game is running. Gaming artists create models with a small number of polygons, called *low-count poly models*, which a PC or game console can render in real-time. Higher-resolution polygon models are frequently used in television and film work.

Using Primitives

Primitives are the simplest objects you can generate in Maya (or in any 3D application). They are simple geometric shapes—polygons or NURBS. Typically, primitives are used to sculpt models because you can define the level of detail of the primitive's surface; they offer great sculpting versatility through vertex manipulation.

To get a better sense of how to begin a modeling assignment, you may find it helpful to analyze your modeling subjects into forms and shapes that fit in with Maya primitives. Figure 4.3 shows all of the primitives (except super shapes) in Maya, including NURBS, polygons, and volume primitives. Quite different from geometry primitives, volume primitives are used for lighting and atmosphere effects, such as fog or haze, and don't really play a part in modeling.

Polygon Basics

Polygon modeling is popular because its resulting models are usually one piece of geometry with many facets. You can, therefore, deform polygon models without fear of patches coming apart, as can happen with NURBS. Polygons, however, have a finite detail limitation and can look jagged up close or when scaled up. One solution to this problem in the Maya software is the Smooth tool, which smoothes your mesh into a more organic shape by increasing its polygon count and rounding off areas. You'll be using the Smooth tool later in this chapter.

A popular method of polygonal modeling called *box modeling* involves creating a base object (a.k.a. a primitive) such as a simple cube and then pulling and pushing faces to draw angles to create more faces. With NURBS you typically need to start by creating curves like outlines or shapes.

A second method for creating poly surfaces uses the same curves that NURBS surfaces use or even converts a completed NURBS surface model to polygons. A third method is to create poly surfaces directly with the Polygon tool, which allows you to outline the shape of each face, which is less often used.

Creating Polygonal Primitives

With a poly mesh, detail is defined by *subdivisions*, which are the number of rows and columns of poly faces that run up, down, and across. The more subdivisions you have, the greater definition and detail you can create with the mesh.

Choosing Create ➢ Polygon Primitives gives you access to the poly primitives. Opening the option box for any of them gives you access to their creation options. To see an example, choose Create ➢ Polygon Primitives ➢ Sphere ❑ to open the option box.

To get started, first make sure History is turned on (as shown here) in the status bar along the top of the user interface (UI) or there will be no creation node; then, click Create to make

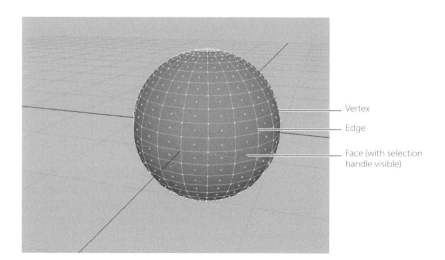

FIGURE 4.2   A polygonal sphere and its components.

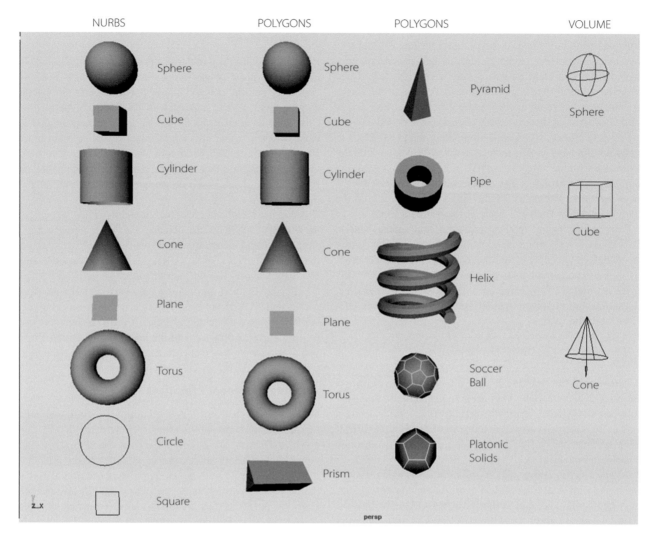

FIGURE 4.3   The primary Maya primitives.

the poly sphere. If you don't see that icon in the Status Line, click to expand it with the vertical lines also shown here. It is turned on by default, so you should be ok regardless.

Open the Attribute Editor and switch to the sphere's creation node, called polySphere1. In the creation node polySphere1, you'll find the Subdivisions Axis and Subdivisions Height sliders (in the option box, these are called Axis and Height Divisions), which you can use to change the surface detail retroactively.

The Polygon Tool

You can use the Polygon tool to create a single polygon face by laying down its vertices (switch to the Modeling menu set and then choose Mesh Tools ➤ Create Polygon). When you select this tool, you can draw a polygon face in any shape and any number of sides by clicking to place each point or vertex. Aside from creating a polygon primitive by choosing Create ➤ Polygon Primitives, this is the simplest way to create a polygon shape. Figure 4.4 shows some simple and complex single faces you can create with the Polygon tool.

After you've laid down all your vertices, press Enter to create the poly face and exit the tool. For complex shapes, you may want to create more than just a single face so that you can manipulate the shape. For example, you may want to fold it.

Try This

The poly shown in Figure 4.5 was created with the Polygon tool and has only one face. Therefore, adjusting or deforming the surface is impossible. In addition, since the polygon has more than four sides, it is called an NGon and is generally avoided. Faces in polygon models generally stay to three (tris) or four sides (quads), so this is currently an undesired polygon. To fix this NGon and be able to fold this

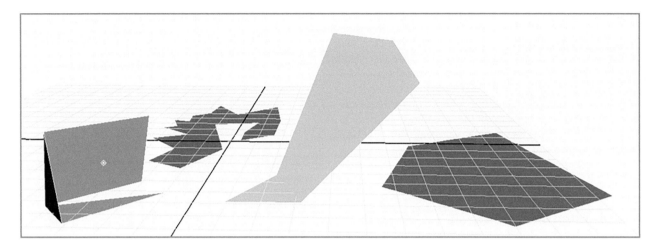

FIGURE 4.4   Polygon faces created with the Polygon tool.

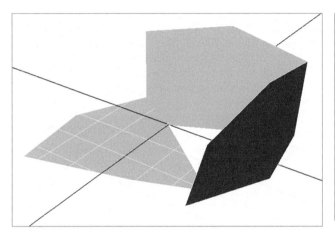

FIGURE 4.5   A single-faced polygon with a complex shape and too many sides—an NGon.

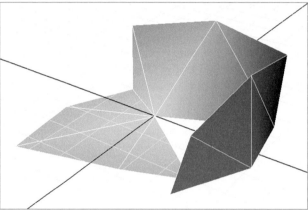

FIGURE 4.6   Creating a more desirable mesh by triangulating the faces.

object, you need more faces and the edges between them. First, make your own intricate poly shape with the Polygon tool by clicking vertices down in the different views to get vertices in all three axes.

With the surface selected, choose Mesh ➤ Triangulate (under the Remesh section of the menu). The custom shape now has more faces and edges and is easier to edit but was still simple to create. If you need a uniquely shaped poly, you could start with this tool and then triangulate your surface into several faces, as shown in Figure 4.6.

Faces that have too many edges (a.k.a. Ngons) may cause you trouble later in the workflow, particularly in further manipulation of the mesh containing any Ngons and also when rendering. It's recommended to always work with polygons with three (tri) or four (quad) sides, with quads being preferred as you become more experienced with modeling.

Poly Editing Tools

Here's a brief preview of what to expect in the world of poly editing. You should experiment with each tool on a primitive sphere as it's introduced, so saddle up to your Maya window and try each tool as you read along.

Later in this chapter, you'll deploy these new skills. You'll create a cute toy airplane to exercise your modeling skills in Chapter 6, "Practical Experience!" For most of the work in this chapter, you'll use the Polygons menu.

Open the Edit Mesh menu, tear it off, and place it somewhere on your screen so you can get a good look at the tools and functions, which are separated into sections according to function type. For example, tools that work on vertices are found in the Edit Mesh menu's Vertex section. It's important to note these sections because some tools have the same name and may be repeated more than once in the menu but function differently when applied to vertices, faces, or edges. For tools repeated like this, I will call out the section name in the text to help.

Modeling Toolkit

Modeling Toolkit integrates component-level selection and editing tools (such as selecting vertices, edges, and faces, and extruding them, for example) for a more streamlined modeling workflow. Modeling Toolkit can make tedious modeling chores much easier, especially for advanced modeling techniques. I will be covering some of the Modeling Toolkit workflow and how it's integrated into Maya alongside traditional workflows to give you a comparison and allow you to decide which workflow suits you. You'll take a look at the Modeling Toolkit and its interface later in this chapter.

The Poly Extrusion Tools

The most used poly editing tools have to do with extrusion. You can use Extrude to pull out a face, edge, or vertex of a polygon surface to create additions to that surface. In the Modeling menu set, you access the Extrude tool in the menu Edit Mesh ➤ Extrude. You can also extrude a component (face, edge, or vertex) by simply holding Shift while you Move that component. We will start by using the menu commands and use Shift+Move later in this chapter. When choosing extrude, Maya automatically distinguishes between edge, face, or vertex extrusion based on which of those components you've already selected. Follow these steps:

1. Select a face or multiple faces of a polygon and choose Edit Mesh ➤ Extrude. The regular manipulator changes to a special manipulator, as shown in the left image in Figure 4.7.

2. Grab the Z-axis move handle (the blue arrow) and drag it away from the sphere, as shown in the center of Figure 4.7.

3. Use the scale handles (the boxes) to scale the faces of the extrusion. The cyan circle rotates the face. The image at the right in Figure 4.7 shows the faces extruded, rotated, and scaled.

4. Choose the Extrude command again without deselecting the faces, and you extrude even more, keeping the original extrusion shape and building on top of that.

5. Select the edges of the poly surface instead of the faces and choose Edit Mesh ➤ Extrude to extrude flat surfaces from the edges selected. The special manipulator works the same way as Extrude does for poly faces.

The faces you select will pull out from the sphere, and new faces are created on the sides of the extrusion(s). The Extrude tool is an exceptionally powerful tool in that it allows you to easily create additions to any poly surface in any direction. Later in this chapter, you'll use it to make a simple cartoony hand.

You can also use the direction and shape of a curve to extrude faces. Create a curve in the shape you want your extrusion to take, select the curve, Shift+select the faces, and choose Extrude ❑. Taper decreases or increases the size of the face as it extrudes. Twist rotates the face as it extrudes, and Divisions increase the smoothness of the resulting extrusion. Choose Selected for the Curve setting. When you have your settings for those attributes, click the Extrude button (see Figure 4.8).

Although it seems to be strange behavior, the Twist and Taper values are taken into account in the extrusion. You can edit these values when you uncheck Selected, or you can reselect this option after you enter values for Twist and Taper. If your faces aren't extruding to the shape of the curve, increase the number of divisions.

Modeling Toolkit and Extrusions

Modeling Toolkit makes selecting and editing polygonal components more streamlined, accelerating some workflows by incorporating tools into one place for ease of access as well as by reducing how often you have to exit one tool or mode and enter another one. Since a lot of what Modeling Toolkit does centers around component selections, let's start there first.

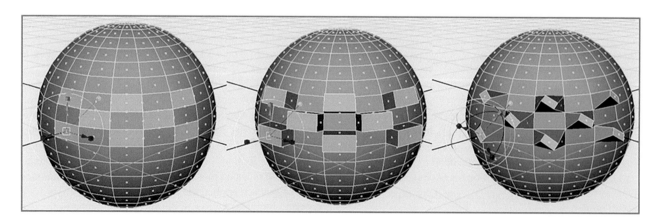

FIGURE 4.7 Extruding several faces at once on a sphere. The left image shows the selected faces, the middle image shows those faces extruded, and the right image shows those faces extruded with a rotation and smaller scale.

Beginning Polygonal Modeling

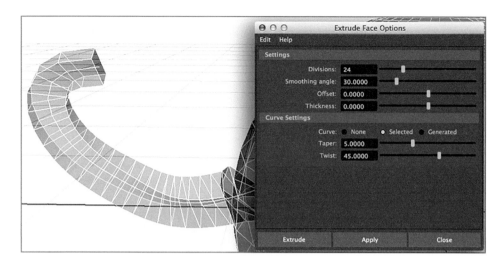

FIGURE 4.8 Extruding a face along a path curve.

Modeling Toolkit Interface

By default, the Modeling Toolkit plug-in should be enabled, which places the Modeling Toolkit menu on the main menu bar. If you don't see Modeling Toolkit, simply choose Windows ➤ Setting/Preferences ➤ Plug-In Manager. About halfway down the list, you should see ModelingToolkit.dll (or ModelingToolkit.bundle on a Mac). Check Loaded and Auto Load, as shown in Figure 4.9.

FIGURE 4.9 Loading the Modeling Toolkit plug-in, if needed.

Modeling Toolkit also places an icon on your status bar, next to the XYZ input fields, shown next to the cursor and already turned on in Figure 4.10. When the Modeling Toolkit icon is turned on, the Modeling Toolkit is automatically invoked whenever you enter component selection mode. Click the icon to turn Modeling Toolkit on if it isn't already.

In addition, Modeling Toolkit places a tab in the Channel Box, called Modeling Toolkit, to make displaying its toolset easier, as shown in Figure 4.11. You will notice toward the top of the Modeling Toolkit panel four icons for selecting, moving, rotating, and scaling. These operate in the same way as transformation tools; however, they enable the Modeling Toolkit functionality. You'll see this in action throughout the book and introduced next.

Modeling Toolkit Extrusion

Now that you have a little background on how the Modeling Toolkit integrates with Maya, let's use it in comparison to the Maya Extrude tool you just used on a sphere.

1. Make sure the Modeling Toolkit icon (　) in the status bar is active to see the Modeling Toolkit tab alongside the Attribute Editor and Channel Box/Layer Editor tabs.

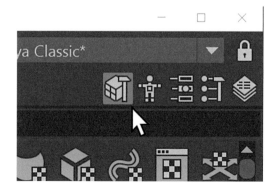

FIGURE 4.10 The Modeling Toolkit icon button.

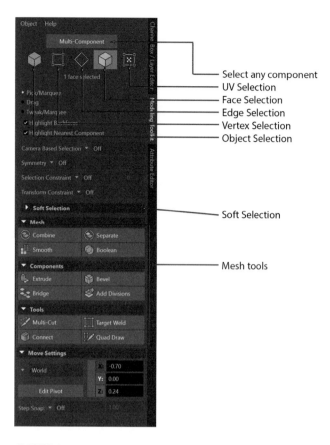

FIGURE 4.11   The Modeling Toolkit panel.

2. Create a polygon sphere and press 5 for Shaded mode.

3. Right-click the sphere in your scene and select Face from the marking menu for face selection mode. This is the easiest way to select components in Maya, which also works the same while using the Modeling Toolkit.

4. Hold down Shift to select two faces side-by-side on the sphere.

5. In the Modeling Toolkit panel, click Extrude under the Components heading, as shown in Figure 4.12. A floating options panel appears next to the selected faces.

6. In the floating panel, your cursor will change to a double-headed horizontal arrow as you hover over each of the attributes (such as Offset or Divisions). Hover over Thickness and click and drag left or right to set the amount of extrusion (Figure 4.13).

7. You can also enter numbers directly. In the floating panel, click in the Divisions text box and set the number to **3**. This will give you multiple sections along your extrusion. You can also click and drag in the floating panel to set the Divisions number interactively as you did with Thickness.

8. Click and drag on Offset in the floating panel to make the extruded faces bigger or smaller. You may also enter a value for Offset in the floating panel, since clicking and dragging is pretty sensitive. Figure 4.14 shows an extrusion of 0.29 with a Divisions of 3 and an Offset of 0.04.

9. Finally, click the Keep Faces Together text box to toggle the option on and off in the floating panel to see how the extrusion changes. Figure 4.15 shows the same extrusion as Figure 4.14, but with Keep Faces Together turned off. Whatever options you set will be used the next time you extrude in the Modeling Toolkit. Simply turn off the Extrude button to exit the tool and commit the changes.

All of these extrusion options and settings are available in the Maya Extrude tool but are a little more streamlined in the Modeling Toolkit workflow. Experiment to see how you like to work. You will be using a combination of traditional Maya and Modeling Toolkit workflows throughout this chapter and other parts of the book.

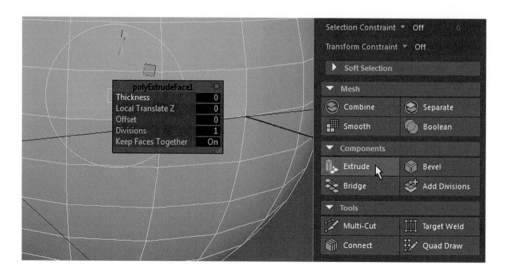

FIGURE 4.12   Click Extrude in the Modeling Toolkit panel.

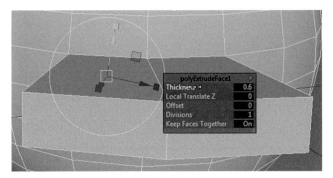

FIGURE 4.13 Click and drag the Thickness value to set the extrusion amount.

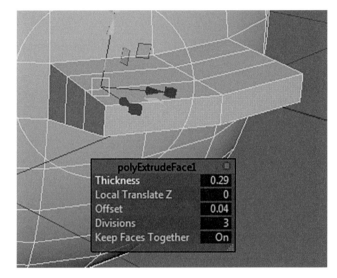

FIGURE 4.14 Modeling Toolkit extrusion in action.

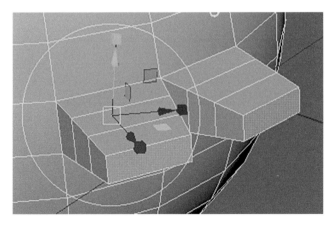

FIGURE 4.15 Keep Faces Together is turned off.

The Wedge Tool

Similar to extruding faces, Wedge pulls out a poly face, but it does so in an arc instead of a straight line. For this tool, you need to select a face and an edge of the selected face for a pivot axis of the corner. Here's how to do this.

RMB+click a mesh and select Multi from the marking menu, which lets you select any type of component. Select a face, then Shift+select one of the face's edges, and finally choose Edit Mesh ➢ Wedge (under the Face section of the menu).

A floating panel appears, and you can select the degree of turn in the Wedge Angle setting (90° is the default) as well as the number of faces used to create the wedge (by changing the Divisions value), as shown in Figure 4.16.

The Wedge tool is useful for items such as elbows, knees, archways, and so on.

The Poke Tool

Poke is great for creating detailed sections of a mesh (poly surface) and bumps or indentations. To use the Poke tool to add detail to a face, select a face and then choose Edit Mesh ➢ Poke.

A vertex is added to the middle of the face, and the Move manipulator appears on the screen for that new vertex, as shown in Figure 4.17. This lets you move the point to where you need it on the face. You can add bumps and depressions to your surface as well as create regions of extra detail. By selectively adding detail, you can subdivide specific areas of a polygon for extra detailed work, leaving lower poly counts in less-detailed areas for an efficient model.

The Bevel Tool

Use the Bevel tool to round sharp corners and edges and to help catch light and generally make a model's edges look more polished. With the Bevel tool, you must select an edge or multiple edges and then use them to create multiple new faces to round that edge or corner.

Create a poly cube and stretch it out like a brick shape as in Figure 4.18. Select an edge along the top of the cube and choose Edit Mesh ➢ Bevel (under the Components section of the menu). The Fraction value in the floating panel sets the distance from the edge to the center of where the new face will be. This basically determines the size of the beveled corner.

FIGURE 4.16 Executing a Wedge operation on the face of a sphere.

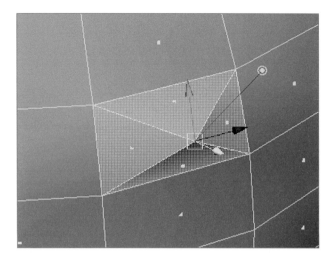

FIGURE 4.17   Poke helps create areas of detail in your model.

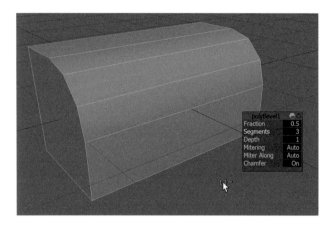

FIGURE 4.18   Increase Segments to create a rounder corner.

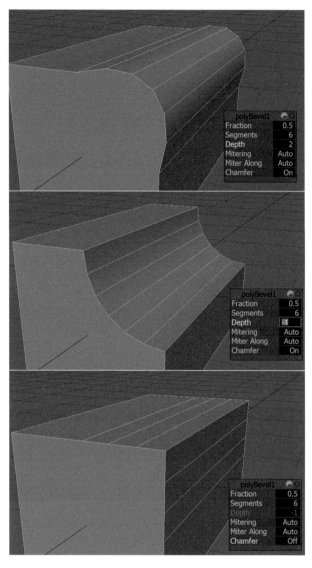

FIGURE 4.19   A poly bevel's Depth above 1 creates a bulge (top), lower than 0 creates a channel (middle). Bottom image shows Chamfer set to Off.

The Segments number defines how many segments are created for the bevel: the more segments, the smoother the beveled edge (see Figure 4.18). Leaving Segments at 1 creates a sharp corner.

The setting of the Depth slider specifies the roundness of the corner. Setting the number ABOVE 1.0 will make the beveled edge bulge out, as shown in Figure 4.19 (top), while a value of 0 creates a flat edge while negative numbers create a channel as seen in Figure 4.19 (middle). Remember to set the Segments value higher for a smoother bevel. The Chamfer setting when Off gives extra edges from the Bevel but does not adjust the geometry's shape as shown in Figure 4.19 (bottom).

You can invoke the bevel tool through the Modeling Toolkit as well. Simply turn on Modeling Toolkit (⬚) and click the Bevel icon instead of choosing Edit Mesh ➢ Bevel as you did before, and you'll access the same Bevel tool, as shown in Figure 4.20.

In addition, Bevel responds to the type of selection you make. So far, you have beveled edges. This time, create a new cube and select the top face. In Modeling Toolkit, click Bevel and set Fraction to 0.2 and Segments to 6 with a Depth of −1.0 in the floating panel. The tool will bevel all four edges around the selected top face (Figure 4.21).

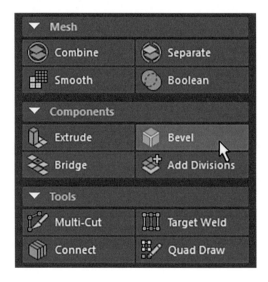

FIGURE 4.20   Bevel icon in Modeling Toolkit.

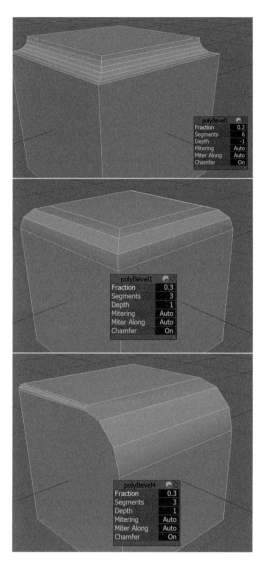

FIGURE 4.21 Here you have beveled the top face of a cube, instead of just a single edge (top). A cube with all four top edges beveled at once (middle) compared to the same cube with the top edges beveled one by one (bottom).

Use the Bevel tool to round polygonal edges and add polish to your models. To get uniform bevels around a model, it's best to select all the involved edges to create a single bevel as opposed to selecting each edge and beveling it individually. Figure 4.21 (middle) shows a cube's top side with a uniform bevel because all four top edges were beveled together, while Figure 4.21 (bottom) shows how uneven the bevel becomes when beveling each edge individually around the top of the cube.

Having even a *slightly* rounded edge on a model—a box, for example—greatly enhances the look of that box when it's lighted and rendered because the edges catch much more light, helping define the shape of the box. A perfectly sharp corner with no bevel doesn't catch any light, making the model look less realistic.

Putting the Tools to Use: Making a Cartoon Hand

Starting with a simple polygonal cube, you'll create a basic cartoon hand using a mix of Maya and Modeling Toolkit workflows.

Download the entire Poly_Hand project from the web page. Set your project to this folder and follow these steps:

1. With Interactive Creation turned off, create a polygonal cube. Open the Attribute Editor and, in the polyCube1 tab, set Subdivisions Width to **3**, Subdivisions Height to **1**, and Subdivisions Depth to **1**. If you don't have that tab in the Attribute Editor, click Undo to remove the cube, turn on History, and re-create the cube.

2. Scale the cube to X=4, Y=1.3, and Z=4.5 so that it looks like Figure 4.22.

3. If the Modeling Toolkit is off, turn it on with its icon

   (![icon]) in the status bar. RMB+click the cube and choose Face from the marking menu.

4. Select the front face in the corner closest to you. You'll extrude the face to make the first part of the index finger. Before you extrude, though, rotate the face a bit in the Y-axis, away from the rest of the hand, to angle the extrusion toward where the thumb would be, as shown in Figure 4.23 (left).

5. In the Modeling Toolkit panel, click the Extrude button. In the floating panel, set Divisions to **2**, Thickness to **3.7**, and Offset to **−0.1**. You can press W to exit the Extrude tool (and consequently enter the Move tool). Figure 4.23 (right) shows the full index finger with a slight rotation away from the hand from the previous step.

   Save your work and compare it to the scene file `poly_hand_v1.mb` in the Poly_Hand project on the web page.

6. Repeat steps 4 and 5 for the remaining two fingers using the extrusion Thickness values shown in

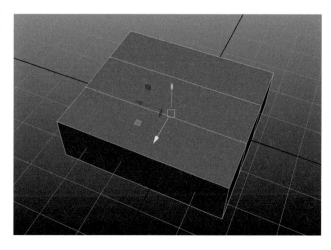

FIGURE 4.22 The poly cube in position to make the hand.

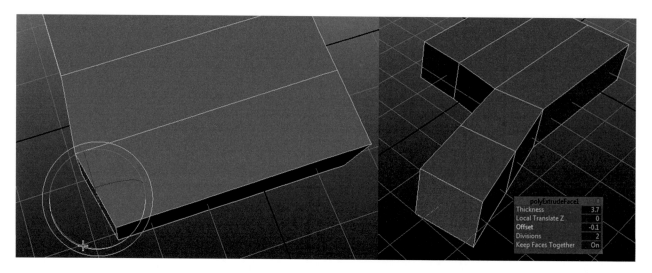

FIGURE 4.23 Rotate the face (left) and then extrude the index finger (right).

Table 4.1. Remember to rotate the initial face of each finger slightly away from the previous finger before extruding so that the extrusions will have small gaps between them, as shown in Figure 4.24. Otherwise, the fingers will extrude right up against each other, like a glove with the fingers glued together.

Use Table 4.1 as a guide for the length of the extrusion for the two fingers.

When you're finished with the three fingers, select the hand. In the Perspective panel, press 2 to give you a smooth preview of the hand. With a polygonal object, pressing the 1, 2, and 3 keys previews the smoothness your model will have when it's smoothed (a polygonal modeling operation about to be discussed). Pressing 2 also shows the original shape of

TABLE 4.1

Extrusion Length Guide

Finger	Extrude Local Z Value
Middle	4.2
Pinkie	3.0

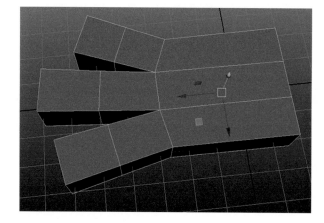

FIGURE 4.24 Three fingers.

the hand as a wireframe cage (see Figure 4.25, left) as a reference.

With the hand still selected, press 3. The original wireframe cage disappears, as shown in Figure 4.25 (right). This doesn't actually alter the geometry or create more faces for the smoothing, but if you render using Arnold (you'll need to add a light first), your hand will look smooth! This keeps the actual geometry more efficient in the scene, adding the extra overhead of smoothing to the renderer. More on smoothing later in this chapter. Press 1 to exit the smooth preview and return to the original model view. The scene file `poly_hand_v2.mb` shows the hand with the three fingers created.

7. Let's work on the thumb. You need to insert some new divisions on the body of the hand to extrude a thumb. With the hand selected, choose Mesh Tools ➤ Insert Edge Loop and click the side edge of the hand, as shown in Figure 4.26. A dotted line appears. Drag along the edge you clicked to place the insertion and release the mouse button to place the new loop of edges.

8. Insert a second loop of edges at the middle of the hand, as shown in Figure 4.27. Press W to exit the Insert Edge Loop tool.

9. Rotate and then scale down the face shown in Figure 4.28 in the Z-axis to get ready to extrude the thumb.

10. In the Modeling Toolkit, click Extrude and, in the floating panel, set Thickness to **3**, Offset to **−0.1**, and Divisions to **2**, as with the other three fingers (see Figure 4.29).

11. Select the three faces at the base of the hand (where it would meet an imaginary wrist) and scale them down in the X-axis and up in the Y-axis to create a flare, as shown in Figure 4.30.

12. If you press 3 to preview the hand smoothed, it will lose a good amount of its detail and become too soft.

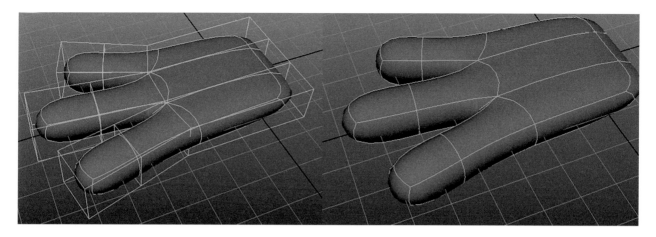

FIGURE 4.25 A smoothed preview of the hand, with the original shape shown as a cage (left) and a full smooth preview without the cage (right).

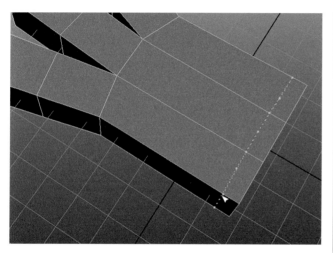

FIGURE 4.26 Insert an edge loop at the base of the hand.

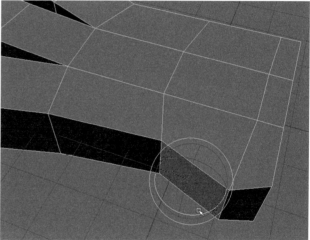

FIGURE 4.28 Scale and rotate the thumb's face to get it ready to extrude.

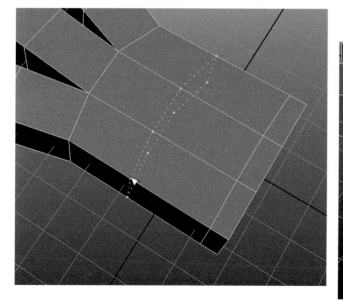

FIGURE 4.27 Insert a second loop of edges up toward the middle of the hand.

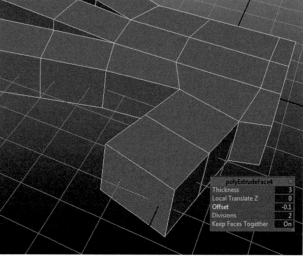

FIGURE 4.29 Extrude the thumb.

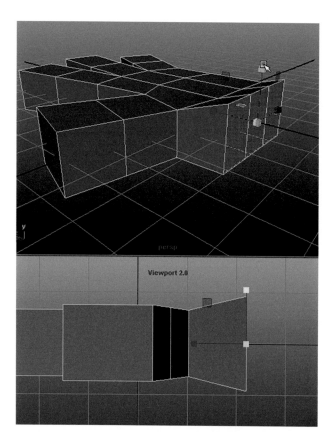

FIGURE 4.30   Create a flare at the base of the hand.

Let's keep some of the angles of the hand by beveling the edges all around the hand. Select the outer edges all around the hand, as shown in Figure 4.31, in X-Ray view (which you invoke in a view panel by selecting in its menu bar Shading ➤ X-Ray). Make sure to get all the edges around the outside of the hand, fingers, and thumb.

13. In the Modeling Toolkit, click Bevel and in the floating panel set Fraction to **0.5** and Segments to **1**. Figure 4.32 shows the beveled hand (left) and again with Smooth Preview (right) enabled (by pressing 3).

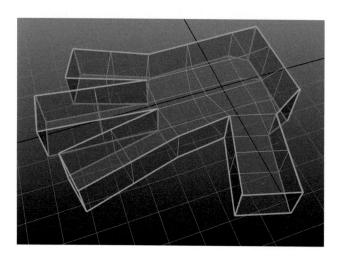

FIGURE 4.31   Select all the edges outlining the entire hand.

14. While in Smooth Preview, select the ring of faces around the base of the thumb and scale them down a bit to accentuate the flare of the thumb, as shown in Figure 4.33. Make any additional adjustments to your liking by manipulating faces and vertices.

15. Exit Smooth Preview (press 1). To add more detail to the hand, you'll raise the knuckles. You need to create new vertices for the knuckles where each finger meets the hand. In the Modeling Toolkit panel, click the Multi-Cut icon (Multi-Cut). Click and drag along the edge of the hand, right below where the index finger attaches to the hand, until the yellow readout reads about 65%. Release the mouse button to lay down the first point of the Multi-Cut operation.

16. Now click the opposite edge across at about 34%, as shown in Figure 4.34 (left). You'll notice an orange line stretch across denoting where a new edge will be placed.

17. Click across the remaining knuckle faces to lay down a cut line across the top of the hand, as shown in Figure 4.34 (right).

18. RMB+click to commit, and the tool will add three new edges (and hence three new faces) along the back of the hand for the knuckles. Select each of those new faces and choose Edit Mesh ➤ Poke (under the Face section) to subdivide them into five triangles, with a vertex in the center. A special manipulator appears when you invoke the Poke command. Use the Z translate handle to pull up those middle vertices to make knuckles (see Figure 4.35).

19. Now that you have a cartoony hand, you can smooth out the mesh to make it less boxy. When pressing 3 for the Smooth Preview, while the hand may render smoothed, we want to actually smooth the geometry for more faces, to be able to rig and animate it, for instance. In Object mode, select the hand and press 3 to see a preview of what the hand will look like after it is smoothed. Press 1 to exit the smooth preview. Choose Mesh ➤ Smooth ❒; in the option box, under Exponential Controls, select Maya Catmull-Clark for the Subdivision Type, set Division Levels to **2**, and leave the other options at their defaults (see Figure 4.36). The smoothed hand shows all of its history nodes in Figure 4.37.

20. Click Smooth. Your cartoon hand should take on a smoother, rounder look. This time, however, you've altered the geometry and actually made the mesh smoother and given it a higher density of polygons. Notice all the nodes listed under Inputs in the Channel Box in Figure 4.36 (right). This is because History has been on for the entire duration of this exercise. At any time, you can select one of those nodes and edit something—the extrusion of the pinkie, for example, though you may get some undesired results adjusting parameters earlier in the history of an object.

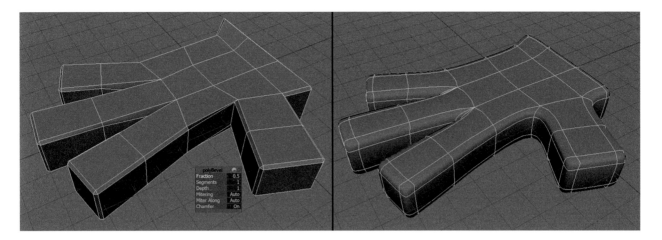

FIGURE 4.32 Beveling all around the hand (left) and shown with Smooth Preview (right).

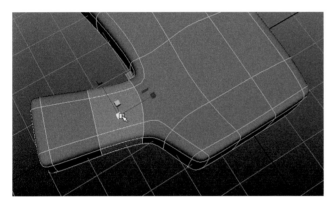

FIGURE 4.33 Scale down these faces to flare the thumb a bit more.

To verify that you've been working correctly, you can load the finished hand file (with its history intact), which is called `poly_hand_v3.mb`, available from the book's web page. If you don't need any of the history anymore, then with the hand selected, choose Edit ➤ Delete By Type ➤ History to get rid of all those extra nodes. Deleting History on models is typically done before a model is set up for animation (a.k.a. rigging).

Creating Areas of Detail on a Poly Mesh

As you saw with the cartoon hand, it became necessary to add more faces to parts of the surface to create various details, such as with the knuckles. Maya provides several ways to add surface detail or increase a poly's subdivisions, as you've begun to see in the cartoon hand exercise. Let's take a deeper look at these and more tools for adding detail to a mesh.

The Add Divisions Tool

You can use the Add Divisions tool to increase the number of faces of a poly surface by evenly dividing either all faces or just those selected. Select the poly surface face or faces and choose Edit Mesh ➤ Add Divisions (under the Components section of the menu). You can also click the Add Divisions icon in the Modeling Toolkit (Add Divisions).

The tool is context-sensitive to your current selection, so when you have faces selected, you will add divisions to those faces. When you have edges selected, the tool will split the edges adding vertices. In the option box, you can adjust the number of times the faces are divided by moving the Division Levels slider. With Add Divisions set to Exponentially under

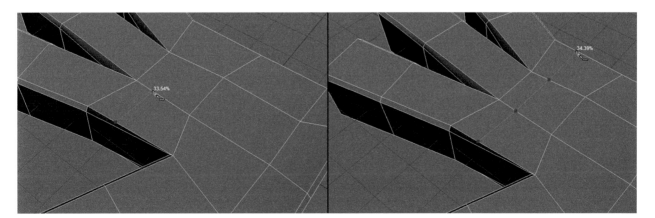

FIGURE 4.34 Use the Multi-Cut tool to lay down edges for the knuckles.

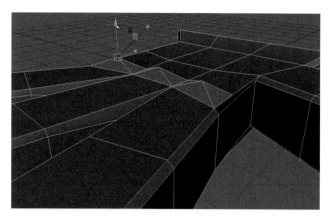

FIGURE 4.35   Use the Poke tool to raise the knuckles.

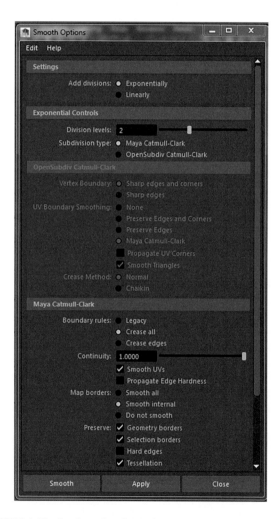

FIGURE 4.36   Set the options for the Smooth operation.

the Settings heading, the Mode drop-down menu gives you the choice to subdivide your faces into quads (four-sided faces, as on the left of Figure 4.38) or triangles (three-sided faces, as on the right in Figure 4.38). Quads traditionally make the most sense.

You can also select a poly edge to divide. Running this tool on edges divides the selected edges into separate edges along

the same face, giving you more vertices along that edge. It doesn't divide the face; rather, you can use it to change the shape of the face by moving the new vertices or edge segments, as shown in Figure 4.39. Just make sure to select Add Divisions when you have edges selected.

You use the Add Divisions tool to create regions of detail on a poly surface.

Multi-Cut Tool

As you saw when creating more faces and edges for the hand's knuckles in the previous exercise, the Multi-Cut tool allows you to lay down edges along faces fairly easily. You access the Multi-Cut tool in Modeling Toolkit, under the Tools heading. You can also make multiple cuts on the same face, as shown in Figure 4.40.

You can also access the Multi-Cut tool through the main menu Mesh Tools ➤ Multi-Cut.

Insert Edge Loop Tool

This handy tool adds edges to a poly selection, much like the Multi-Cut tool, but it does so more quickly by working along the entire poly surface, along common vertices. The Insert Edge Loop tool automatically runs a new edge along the poly surface perpendicular to the subdivision line you click, without requiring you to click multiple times as with the Modeling Toolkit Multi-Cut tool. It also generally creates a cleaner geometry, maintaining a good polygon flow, whereas Multi-Cut could easily create faces with more than four sides (NGon). While this is not a big deal now as you are learning modeling with Maya, you'll eventually want to keep away from NGons as much as feasible in a model.

Now, you've used this tool in the decorative box in Chapter 3, "The Autodesk Maya Interface," and earlier in this chapter on the cartoon hand and you will continue using it throughout this book. You'll find it indispensable in creating polygonal models because it creates subdivisions quickly and cleanly.

For instance, subdividing a polygonal cube is quicker and cleaner than using the Multi-Cut tool. With a poly cube selected, choose Mesh Tools ➤ Insert Edge Loop. Click an edge, and the tool places an edge running perpendicular from that point to the next edge across the surface and across to the next edge, as shown in Figure 4.41. If you click and drag along an edge, you can interactively position the new split edges.

Offset Edge Loop Tool

Much like the Insert Edge Loop tool, the Offset Edge Loop tool (Mesh Tools ➤ Offset Edge Loop) inserts not one, but two edge loop rings of edges across the surface of a poly. Edges are placed on both sides of a selected edge, equally spaced apart. For example, create a polygon sphere and select one of the vertical edges, as shown in Figure 4.42. Maya displays two dashed lines on both sides of the selected edge. Drag the mouse to place the offset edge loops; release the mouse button to create the two new edge loops.

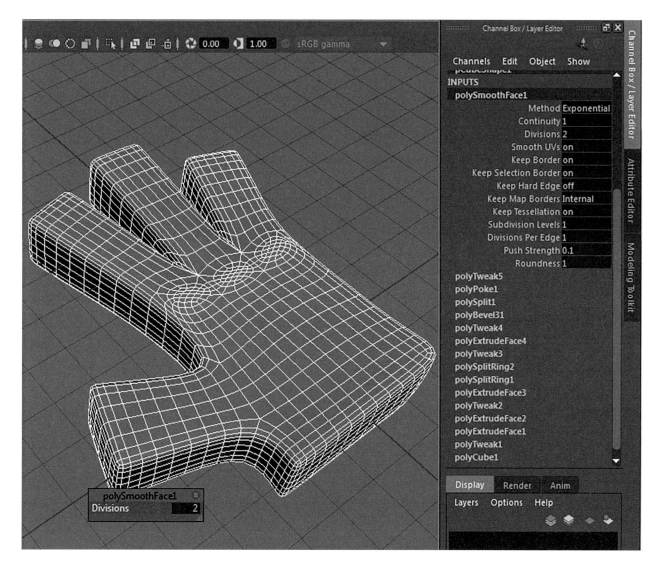

FIGURE 4.37 The smoothed hand is shown with all its history nodes.

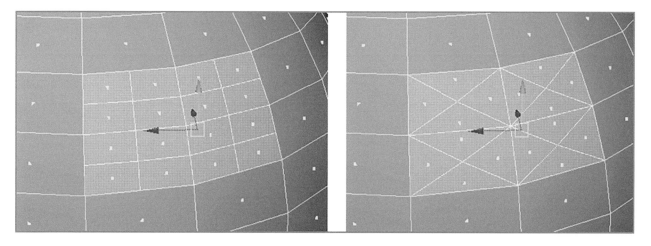

FIGURE 4.38 The Mode drop-down menu of the Add Divisions tool lets you subdivide faces into quads or triangles.

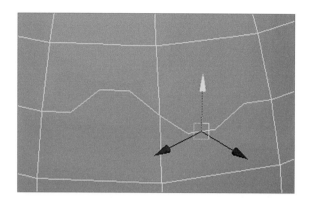

FIGURE 4.39 Dividing edges.

The Offset Edge Loop tool is perfect for adding detail symmetrically on a surface quickly.

Connect Tool

Similar to the Insert Edge Loop tool is the Modeling Toolkit Connect function. Simply select an edge and click the Connect button in the Modeling Toolkit panel. This will create edges going around the object perpendicular to the selected edge. The Slide attribute places the perpendicular cut along the selected edge, which is slightly less interactive than Insert Edge Loop. However, the Segments attribute allows you to insert more than one ring of edges, while Pinch spaces those extra segments evenly (Figure 4.43). You can also select Mesh Tools ➤ Connect in the main menu bar.

Drag Selection and Bridge Tool

One of Modeling Toolkit's nicest features is its drag selection mode. This allows you to essentially click and drag your cursor over the components you want to be selected with your cursor instead of having to click every component, almost like a painting.

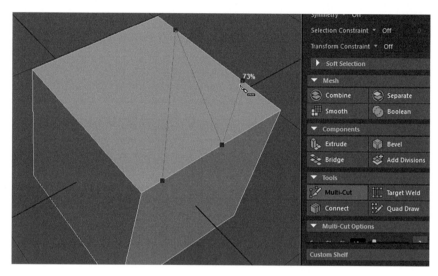

FIGURE 4.40 The Multi-Cut tool.

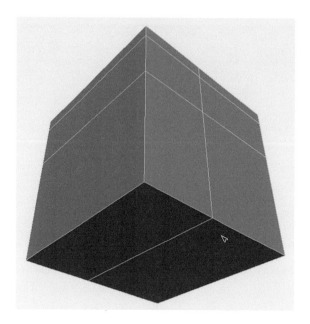

FIGURE 4.41 Using the Insert Edge Loop tool.

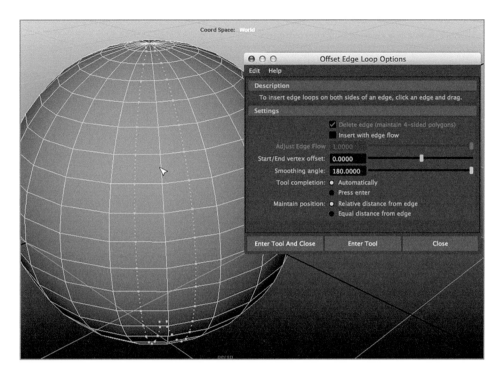

FIGURE 4.42   The Offset Edge Loop tool and its options.

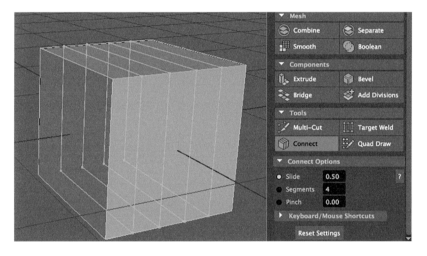

FIGURE 4.43   The Connect tool creates edges much like Insert Edge Loop.

Try This

1. Create a cube in an empty scene and set Subdivisions Width to **1**, Subdivisions Height to **4**, and Subdivisions Depth to **5**, as shown in Figure 4.44. Figure 4.44 is shown in X-Ray mode (which is enabled in the Perspective panel's menu bar by choosing Shading ➢ X-Ray).

2. You are going to delete a square shape out of the front and back of the box. Exit X-Ray view mode if you are currently in X-Ray (view panel menu: Shading ➢ X-Ray).

3. Make sure the Modeling Toolkit panel is open. Enter into face selection mode through the marking menu.

4. In the Modeling Toolkit panel, select the Drag option under the transformation icons, as shown in Figure 4.45. Your selection cursor changes to a circle. Click one of the inside faces and drag along a six-face square in the middle of the front of the cube, also in Figure 4.45. The Drag option makes it easier to select those faces by just dragging your mouse over them.

5. Orbit your view to see the back of the box, hold down Shift, and Drag+select the same six-face square on the back of the box.

6. Press Delete on your keyboard to delete the 12 selected faces, leaving you with a hollow box, as shown in Figure 4.46.

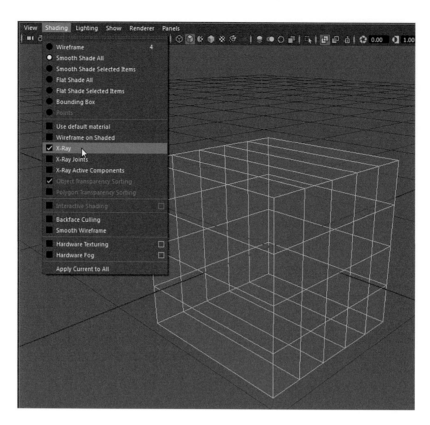

FIGURE 4.44 Create a subdivided box.

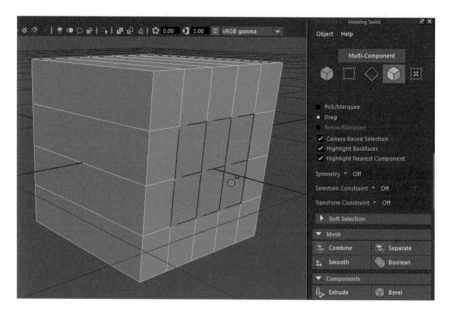

FIGURE 4.45 Drag+select a six-face square on the front of the box.

7. Now you're going to "fill in" the box to make a square-shaped tube. Switch to edge selection. Double-click on one of the front edges as shown in Figure 4.47 (top left). When you double-click when selecting an edge, Maya will select the entire *loop* of edges (edges that are contiguous), or in this case, it selects the entire *boundary* of edges that are contiguous around the hole we just made. Double-clicking to select loops or boundaries of edges saves a lot of time.

8. Now Shift+double-click on one of the back edges as shown in Figure 4.47 (top right) to select that boundary of edges to add to your selection. Now we have the front and back boundary edges of the hole selected.

9. In the Modeling Toolkit panel, click Bridge (or through Edit Mesh ➤ Bridge), and new faces will appear connecting the selected edges (Figure 4.48). In the floating panel, Divisions allow you to add more segments to the tunnel we just made.

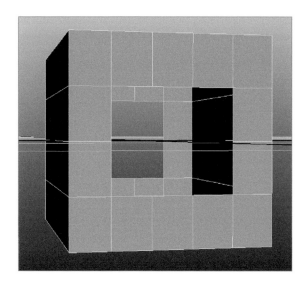

FIGURE 4.46 Delete the square shapes out of the box.

Symmetry Selections

One way to model efficiently is using the ability to select components in symmetry, meaning the components you select on one side of a surface are automatically selected on the other side, making modeling appreciably faster. Let's see how Symmetry works in the following steps.

Try This

1. Create a polygon sphere in a new scene. Press 5 for Shaded view and set the Symmetry pulldown menu at the top of the UI to Object Z as shown in Figure 4.49 (left). You can also access Symmetry in the Modeling Toolkit by clicking the word *Symmetry* to get the same pulldown menu.

2. Switch to Face selection and as you hover over the sphere, you'll notice Maya wants to select a pair of

faces (Figure 4.49 top right) along the Z-axis. Select one face (it will select two symmetrically).

3. Let's use Extrude! Press W for the Move tool and hold Shift (you'll see "extrude" appear on the cursor) as you move the one face away from the sphere and you will see an extrusion form symmetrically on both sides of the sphere on the Z-axis as in Figure 4.49 (bottom right).

4. This type of symmetry relies on the middle of the given object along the chosen axis (in this case, Z). However, to define your own center line, set Symmetry to Topology, and then select an edge on the sphere that you want to be the centerline for the symmetry. In Figure 4.50 (left), we've chosen an edge on the side of the same sphere.

5. Now when you select components, like faces as in Figure 4.50 (right), you can see the symmetry is centered around the previously chosen edge.

As you saw with extrusion, if you engage any poly editing function, it will act on the symmetrically selected components, whether they are faces, edges, or vertices.

Keep in mind that for Symmetry to work properly, your mesh needs to be symmetrical itself. With uneven topology, where one side has a different number of faces than the other, Symmetry selections may not work correctly.

Combine, Merge, and the Target Weld Tool

The Combine function is important in cleaning up your model and creating *a unified single mesh* out of any parts that form it. When modeling, you'll sometimes use several different

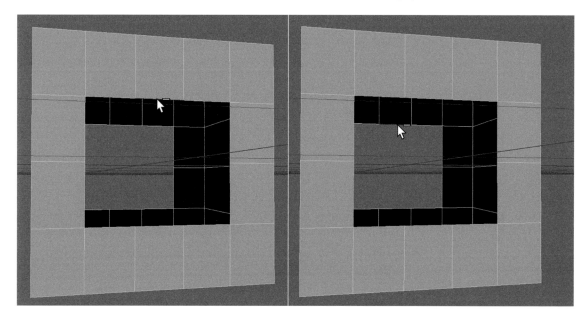

FIGURE 4.47 Select a boundary of edges for the front and back of the cube.

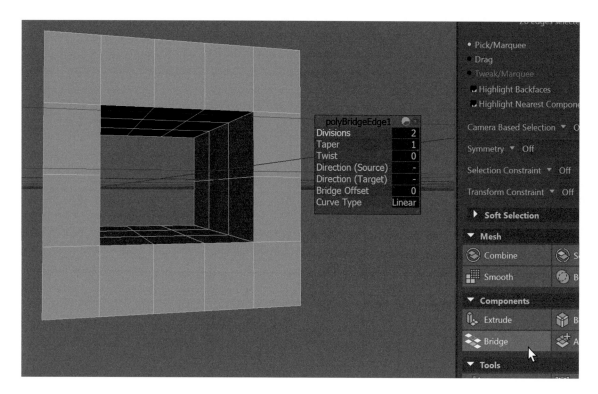

FIGURE 4.48 Bridge the boundary edges together to form a tunnel.

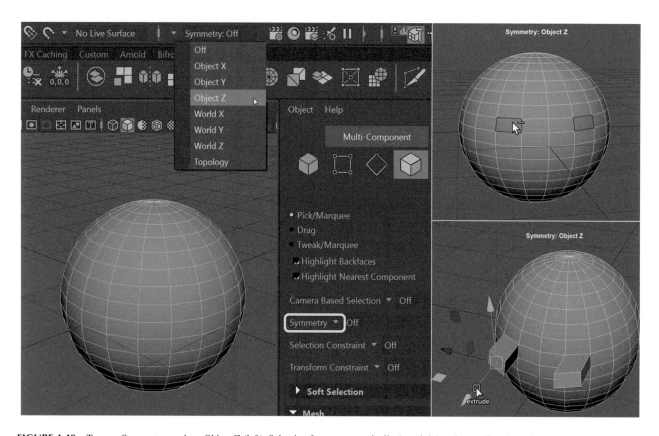

FIGURE 4.49 Turn on Symmetry mode to Object Z (left). Selecting faces symmetrically (top right) and extruding them (bottom right).

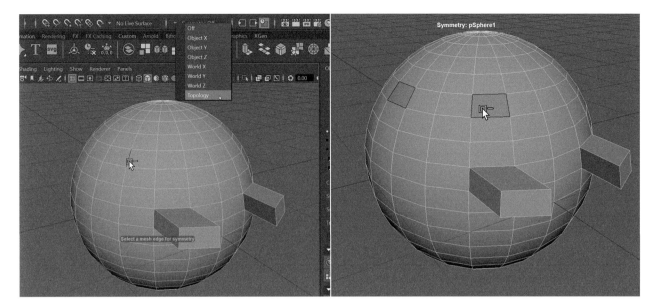

FIGURE 4.50 Set Symmetry to Topology and select an edge (left). Symmetry now centers on the chosen edge (right).

polygon meshes and surfaces to generate your final shape. Using Combine, you can create a single polygonal object out of the pieces, which can save system resources and simplify your scene.

Frequently, when you're modeling a mesh, you'll need to fold over pieces and weld parts together, especially when you combine meshes into a single mesh. Doing so often leaves you with several vertices occupying the same space. Merging them simplifies the model and makes the mesh much nicer to work with, from rigging to rendering. The Merge tool fuses multiple vertices at the same point into one vertex on the model. The Target Weld tool from the Modeling Toolkit is a more interactive way to fuse vertices together. You'll take a look at both in order to compare the workflows.

In the following simple example, you'll create two boxes that connect to each other along a common edge, and then you'll combine and merge them into one seamless polygonal mesh. To begin, follow these steps:

1. In a new scene, create a poly cube. While holding down Shift, move the cube to create a copy and place them apart from each other, as shown in Figure 4.51.

2. Select the bottom edge of the cube on the right that faces the other cube and while holding Shift, move the edge out a little to create a new face, as shown in Figure 4.52. This will be a flange connecting the two cubes. It isn't important how far you pull the edge out; you'll connect the two cubes by moving the vertices manually.

3. Select the first corner vertex on the newly extruded face and snap it into place on the corner vertex of the other cube, as shown in Figure 4.53 (top). Remember, you can click the Snap To Points icon ( ) to snap the vertex onto the cube's corner.

4. Snap the other vertex to the opposite corner so that the cubes are connected with a flange along a common edge, as shown in Figure 4.53 (bottom).

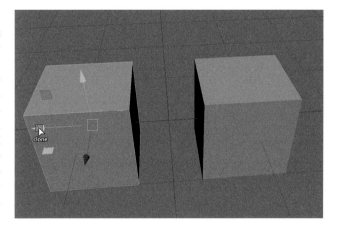

FIGURE 4.51 Copy a cube and place the two cubes close to each other.

Even though the cubes seem to be connected at a common edge, they're still two separate polygonal meshes. You can easily select and move just one of the stacked vertices and disconnect the connective face of the two cubes. You need to merge the stacked vertices of the cubes into a single vertex. However, the Merge function won't fuse vertices from two separate meshes together; you must first combine the cubes into a single poly mesh. The following steps continue this task.

5. Select the two cubes (one has the extra flange on the bottom, of course) and choose Mesh ➢ Combine. Doing so makes a single poly mesh out of the two cubes. You will now be able to use the Merge function in the following steps.

6. Even though the cubes are now one mesh, you still have two vertices at each of the connecting corners of the cube on the left, which can cause all sorts of issues moving forward, especially with rigging and smoothing the model. Click the vertex in the front corner of the newly combined boxes and pull the

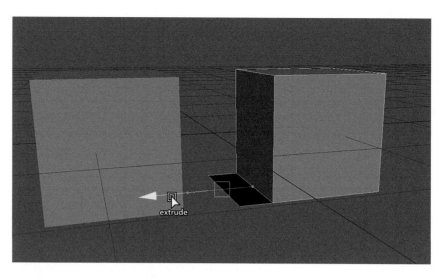

FIGURE 4.52   Extrude the bottom edge to create a flange.

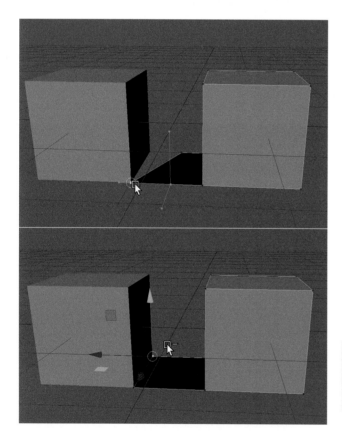

FIGURE 4.53   Snap the first corner vertex to the newly extruded face (top) and then the second corner vertex (bottom).

vertex back as shown in Figure 4.54 (left), which will disconnect the flange at one end. (Click the vertex to

select just one. Don't use a marquee selection, which will select both vertices at once.)

7. Let's start at the back corner. To merge the vertices at that corner, select both the vertices that are on top of each other at the far corner by using a marquee selection and then choose Edit Mesh ➣ Merge to fuse the two vertices. As you can see in Figure 4.54 (right), clicking the back corner vertex and moving it reshapes both cubes since the corner is now fused together.

8. Now, for the front corner where you peeled back the vertex to create a gap in step 6, you'll use the Target Weld tool instead. In this case, you do not need the two vertices sitting on top of each other or even close together as with the Merge tool. Choose Mesh Tools ➣ Target Weld. Click the corner vertex on the flange on the cube on the right and then drag your cursor to highlight the corner vertex on the box on the left, as shown in Figure 4.55. Now the near corner of this mesh is fused into a single vertex.

To separate a combined mesh back into its component meshes, choose Mesh ➣ Separate. You can't use Separate if the mesh you've combined has merged vertices.

You'll notice fewer errors and issues with clean models when you animate, light, and render them. Combining meshes makes them easier to deal with, and the Merge function and the Target Weld tool cut down on unwanted vertices.

If the Merge function isn't working on vertices in your model, make sure the model is a single mesh, and if not, use the Combine function.

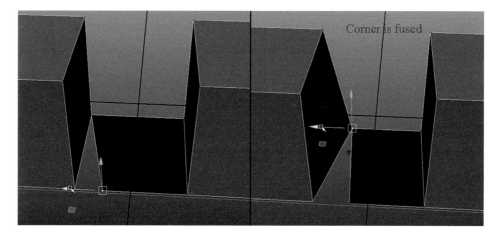

FIGURE 4.54   There are still two different vertices at the corner, and the boxes aren't really connected (left). Once merged, the back corner is now connected properly (right).

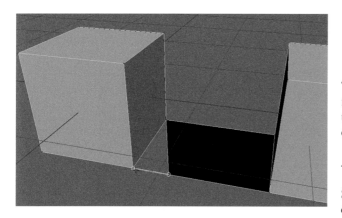

FIGURE 4.55   Target Weld tool in action.

The Slide Edge Tool

If you need to move an edge on a model, selecting the edge or edges and using the Move tool will change the shape of the mesh. Let's see how this works:

1. Choose Create ➢ Polygon Primitives ➢ Cone ❏ and set Height Divisions to 2, as shown in Figure 4.56 (left).
2. RMB+click and select Edges and then double-click the middle row of horizontal edges to select the entire loop. Move the loop of selected edges down, and the cone turns into a pointy witch hat, as shown in Figure 4.55 (middle).
3. Press Z for undo to return the object to its original cone shape. Now, with the same loop of edges selected, choose Mesh Tools ➢ Slide Edge and MMB+drag one of the vertical edges (the vertical edge you MMB+click+drag will turn red) of the cone to slide the selected loop of edges up and down the cone without changing its shape. You can also use the keyboard hotkeys for Slide by holding down

Shift+Ctrl while you Move the edge loop as shown in Figure 4.55 (right), where the word slide appears on the Move manipulator.

The Slide Edge tool is perfect for moving edges on a complex mesh surface without altering the shape of that surface, and using the Shift+Ctrl+Move shortcut makes for a fast way to customize your mesh.

The Duplicate Face Tool

Select one or more faces and choose Edit Mesh ➢ Duplicate to create a copy of the selected faces. You can use the manipulator that appears to move, scale, or rotate your copied faces, which are now their own objects.

The Extract Tool

The Extract tool is similar to the Extrude tool, but it doesn't create any extra faces. Select the faces and choose Edit Mesh ➢ Extract to pull the faces off the surface (see Figure 4.57). If the Separate Extracted Faces option is enabled in the option box, the extracted face will be a separate poly object; otherwise, it will remain part of the original.

This tool is useful for creating a new mesh from part of the original mesh you are extracting from. You can also use the Extract tool to create a hole in an object and still keep the original faces. When you use this tool with the Multi-Cut tool to make custom edges, you can create cutouts of almost any shape. You'll see this functionality of creating custom-shaped holes with the Split Mesh With Projected Curve function in a moment.

The Smooth Tool

The Smooth tool (choose Mesh ➢ Smooth) evenly subdivides the poly surface or selected faces, creating several more faces to smooth and round out the original poly object,

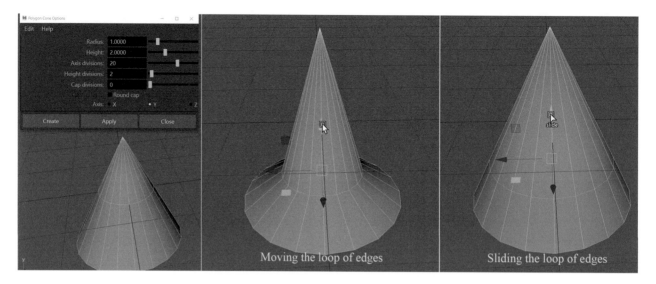

FIGURE 4.56 Create a cone (left). The middle image shows what happens to the cone when you move the middle loop of edges as opposed to using the Slide Edge tool, as shown on the right.

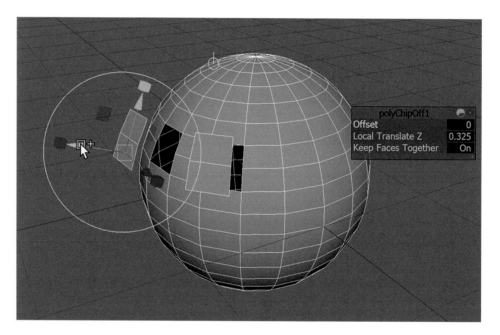

FIGURE 4.57 Pull off the faces.

as you saw earlier in this chapter with the cartoony hand model exercise.

Creating a Hole in a Mesh Surface Using Split Mesh With Projected Curve

Sometimes you need to cut a hole in a mesh to create an opening or window of sorts. You can simply select faces on that mesh and delete them to create a simple, face-shaped hole. However, if you need a more intricate, custom-shaped hole, you'll need to first use Split Mesh With Projected Curve to make a custom shape.

1. Create a polygon sphere in a new scene.
2. Now you'll create a curve directly on the sphere to outline the hole's shape. With the sphere selected,

click the Make the Selected Object Live icon ( ) in the status bar next to the snapping icons. The text box next to this icon will change from No Live Surface to pSphere1 and will turn blue (pSphere1). Making an object live will enable you to perform some functions directly on that mesh.

3. Choose Create ➤ Curve Tools ➤ EP Curve Tool. Click the sphere and a little X appears. Click again, and a line begins to appear on the sphere. Click a number of points to create an interesting shape, and because the sphere is live, these curve points will be placed on top of the sphere, as shown in Figure 4.58

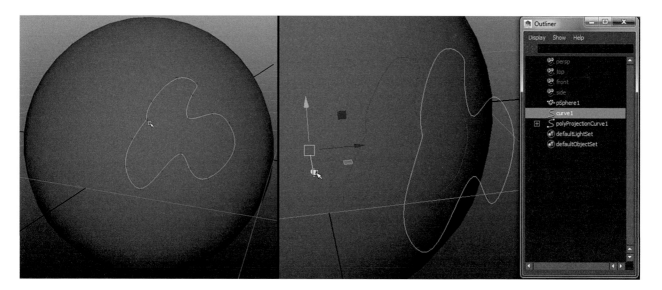

FIGURE 4.58 Draw an EP curve directly on the sphere (left). The projected curve (shown on the sphere in pink) adjusts if you move the original curve (shown away from the sphere in green).

(top). You can simply snap the final EP you draw on top of the first EP you drew with point snaps (   ) to close the curve shape. In the Outliner, the line is called `curve1`. You can learn more about creating curves in Chapter 5, "Modeling with NURBS Surfaces and Deformers."

4. You need to project this curved shape onto the sphere because it is still a separate object despite you creating it on top of the sphere. Disable Make Live by clicking its icon (   ) again.

5. Next, select the sphere and then the curved line. Choose Edit Mesh ➤ Project Curve On Mesh. Now if you select `curve1` in the Outliner (Figure 4.58, right) and move it around in your scene, the projected curve on the sphere (shown in your scene as pink) will adjust, staying on the sphere as shown in Figure 4.58 (right).

6. Now you can use this projected curve to outline a new set of edges on your sphere! In the Outliner, select the sphere and the projected curve (`poly-ProjectionCurve1`) and choose Edit Mesh ➤ Split Mesh With Projected Curve.

7. Maya creates a new sphere that is subdivided with the new edges you drew, as you can see in the Outliner in Figure 4.59 (left). You can delete the original sphere and curve you drew (`pSphere1` and `curve1`), as well as the projected curve (`polyProjection-Curve1`), leaving you with `pSphere2`.

8. Now simply delete the faces inside that shape, and you have your custom hole, as shown in Figure 4.59 (right)!

Keep in mind creating custom holes like this in your mesh will likely create Ngons, which are polygons with more than four sides. Ngons are explained in the "Modeling a Catapult" exercise.

Projecting a line shape onto a mesh surface will allow you to not only cut holes as in this exercise but also easily create custom lengths of edges for modeling use.

Sculpting Tools

With the sculpting tools, you paint on a polygon surface to move the vertices in and out, essentially to mold the surface, as you will see with the candle modeling exercise in Chapter 5. In that chapter, you will use this tool to add detail to a polygon model. Once you have played with the Sculpt Geometry tool in Chapter 5, try loading the `poly _ hand _ v3.mb` model and sculpting some detail into the cartoon hand.

To access the different sculpting tools, select your poly object, choose Mesh Tools ➤ Sculpting Tools, and select the tool to use. Make sure to click ❏ for the options box so you can adjust each tool setting as you play around. Tear off the Sculpting Tools menu to access each of the different tools; then play around with sculpting a sphere to get a hang of it (see Figure 4.60).

I won't cover these tools in any length in this book; however, you will see how the sculpting tools work in the next chapter. Create a poly with a large number of subdivisions so you'll have a smoother result when using the sculpting tools.

Modeling a Catapult

You're going to create a catapult in this exercise using these polygon techniques. You'll use some sketches as a reference for the model. Since this is a more involved object than a hand, it's much better to start with good plans. This, of course, involves some research, web surfing, image gathering, or sketching to get a feel for what it truly is you're trying to make.

To begin, create a new project for all the files called Catapult or copy the Catapult project from the companion website to your hard drive. If you do not create a new project, set your current project to the copied Catapult project on your drive. Choose File ➤ Set Project and select the Catapult project

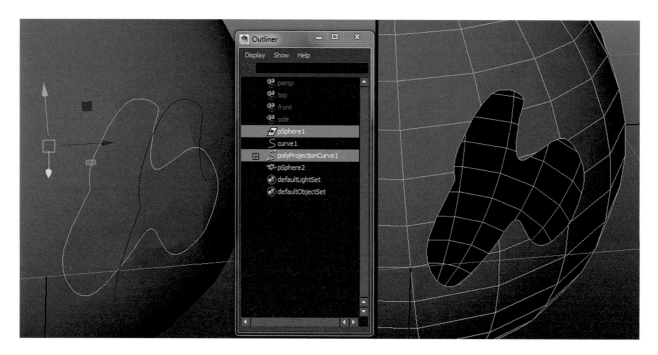

FIGURE 4.59   Splitting the sphere with its projected curve (left) and then deleting those faces to make a custom hole (right).

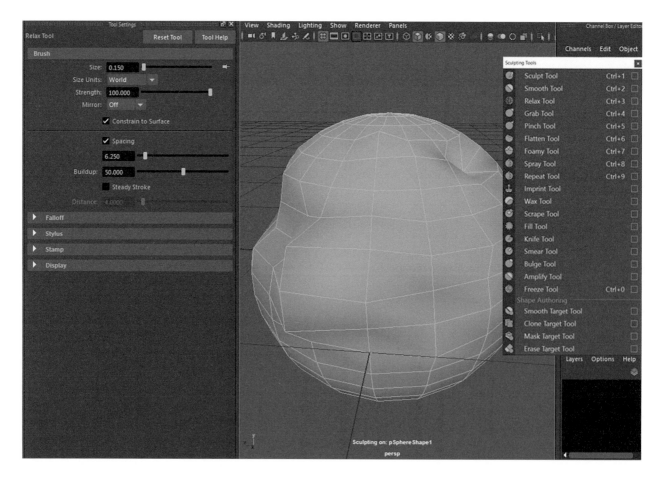

FIGURE 4.60   The Sculpt Geometry tool deforms the surface.

downloaded from the companion website. Remember that you can enable Incremental Save to make backups at any point in the exercise.

Now, let's use a design already sketched out for reference. To begin, study the design sketches included in the Sourceimages folder of the project. These sketches set up the intent rather easily.

In Chapter 8, "Introduction to Animation," you'll animate the catapult. When building any model, it's important to keep the animation in mind, especially for grouping related objects in the scene hierarchy so that they will move as you intend. Creating a good scene hierarchy will be crucial to a smooth animation workflow, so throughout this exercise, you'll use the Outliner to keep the catapult's component pieces organized as you create them.

The Production Process

The trick with a complex object model is to approach it part by part. Deconstruct the major elements of the original into distinct shapes that you can approach one by one. The catapult can be broken down into five distinct objects, each with its own subobjects.

- Base
- Wheels
- Fulcrum assembly
- Winch assembly
- Arm assembly

You will model each part separately based on the sketch in Figure 4.61 and the detailed schematic in Figure 4.62.

The Base

The base consists of simple polygonal cubes representing timber and arranged to connect to each other. Keep in mind that in this exercise Interactive Creation for primitives is turned off (select Create ➢ Polygon Primitives and make sure Interactive Creation is unchecked). Also, in the Perspective view, choose Shading ➢ Wireframe On Shaded to turn on the wireframe lines while in Shaded mode to match the figures in this exercise.

Creating the Base Objects

To begin the catapult base, follow these steps:

1. Choose Create ➢ Polygon Primitives ➢ Cube to lay down your first cube. This will be for the two long, broad boards running alongside.

2. Scale the cube to 2.0 in X, 0.8 in Y, and 19.5 in Z. Move it off the center of the grid about 2 units to the right.

3. Now you'll add some detail to the simple cube by beveling the sides, using either the Modeling Toolkit or the traditional Bevel tool. Either select the four edges running on top of the board or the top face. In the main menu bar, select Edit Mesh ➢ Bevel. Set Fraction to **0.1** and Segments to **2**. Figure 4.63 shows the resulting board.

4. Select the remaining edges on the board, bevel them to a fraction of **0.5**, and set Segments to **2**. See Figure 4.64.

Beveling the edges of your models can be an important detail. Light will pick up edges much better when they are beveled, even slightly. Perfect 90-degree corners can look too much like CG models and not real objects.

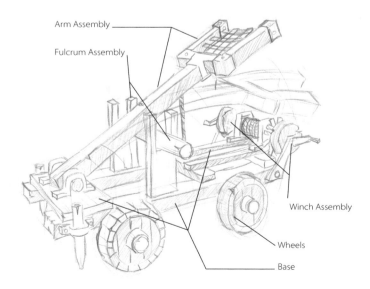

FIGURE 4.61 A sketch of the catapult to model.

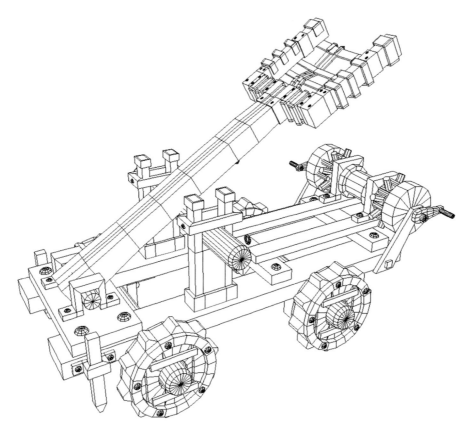

FIGURE 4.62 A schematic diagram of the finished model to illustrate the goal.

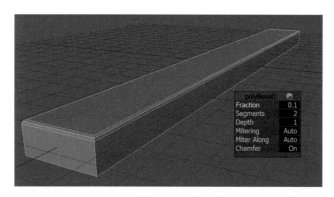

FIGURE 4.63 Create a bevel for the baseboard object.

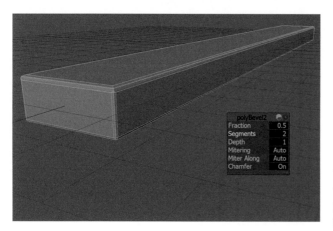

FIGURE 4.64 Beveling the bottom edges.

5. Select the board and Shift+Move a copy about four units to the left. You should now have something similar to Figure 4.65 (top).

6. Now for the cross braces and platform. Create a poly cube and scale it to 7.25 in X, 0.6 in Y, and 3.25 in Z. Place this platform on top of the two beams, at the end of the catapult's base.

7. With the first board that you beveled, you had a different bevel for the top edges than for the bottom and sides. For this board, you'll have the same bevel width for all its edges. Select the cube in object mode (not the edges as before) and choose Edit Mesh ➤ Bevel or click the Bevel icon in the Modeling Toolkit. Set Fraction to **0.2** and Segments to **2**. Figure 4.65 (bottom) shows the platform board in place and beveled.

8. Create a cube for the first of the top two cross braces and scale it 6.5 in X, 0.6 in Y, and 1.2 in Z. Place it on top of the beams at the head of the base and bevel this cube exactly as in the previous step.

9. Shift+Move to duplicate and move the copy about a third of the way down toward the end (Figure 4.66).

Using Booleans

You're going to add some detail as you go along, namely, the large screws that hold the timber together. The screws will basically be slotted screw heads placed at the intersection of

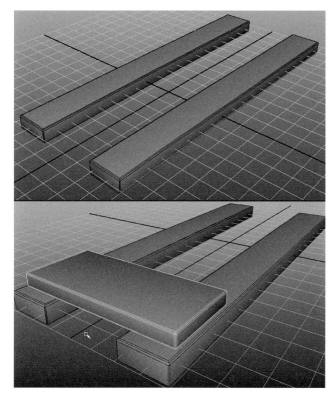

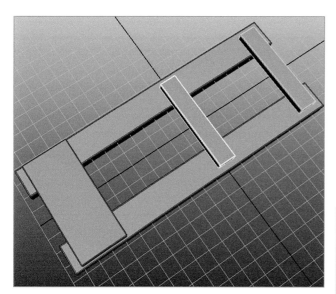

FIGURE 4.65 The long boards at the base (top) and the platform board in place (bottom).

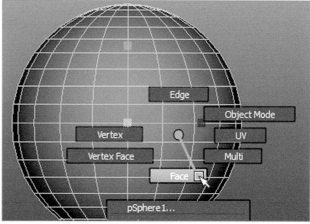

FIGURE 4.66 Cross bracing the base.

the pieces. In this section, you will use Booleans to help create the screw heads.

Booleans are impressive operations that allow you to, among other things, cut holes or shapes in a mesh fairly easily. Basically, a Boolean is a geometric operation that creates a shape from the addition of two shapes (Union), the subtraction of one shape from another (Difference), or the common intersection of two shapes (Intersection).

Be forewarned, however, that Boolean operations can be problematic. Sometimes you get a result that is wrong—or, even worse, the entire mesh disappears and you have to undo. Use Booleans sparingly and only on a mesh that is clean and prepared. You've cleaned and prepped your panel mesh, so there should be no problems. (Actually, there will be a problem, but that's half the fun of learning, so let's get on with it.)

First, you need to create the rounded screw head.

1. Create a polygonal sphere (Create ➤ Polygon Primitives ➤ Sphere) and move it from the origin off to the side in the X-axis of the base model. Scale the sphere down to 0.15 in XYZ.

2. With the sphere still selected, switch to the front view and press F to frame. RMB+click the sphere and select Face from the marking menu (Figure 4.67). Select the bottom half of the sphere's faces and press Delete on your keyboard to make a hemisphere (Figure 4.68).

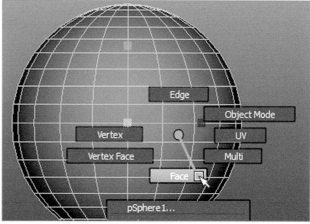

FIGURE 4.67 Use the marking menu to set the selection to Face.

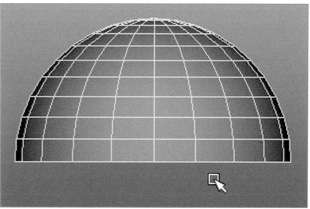

FIGURE 4.68 Delete the bottom half of the faces.

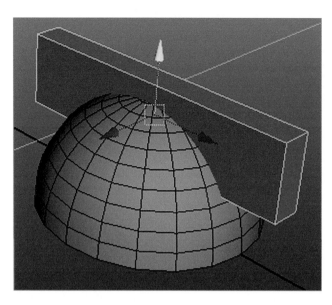

FIGURE 4.69   Place the scaled cube over the screw head.

3. RMB+click the hemisphere and select Object Mode from the marking menu; this exits face selection mode. Create a poly cube and scale it to 0.4, 0.1, 0.04. Place it over the hemisphere as shown in Figure 4.69.

Now you have both objects that you need for a Boolean operation, and they are placed properly to create a slot in the top of the screw head.

FIGURE 4.70   Selecting a Difference Boolean.

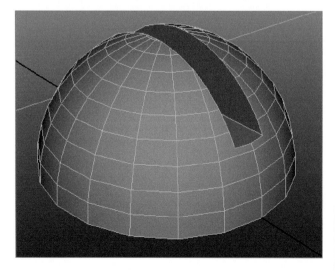

FIGURE 4.71   The screw head is now slotted.

4. Select the hemisphere first and then the cube that was set into it. Select Mesh ➤ Booleans ➤ Difference (Figure 4.70). The cube disappears, and the screw head is left with a slot in the top. However, the screw head appears hollow. In the floating menu of the Boolean operation, set the Classification attribute to Edge from Normal, and your screw head will become solid, as shown in Figure 4.71.

Ngons!

If you take a good close look at the screw head, especially where the slot is, you will notice faces that have more than four sides, which makes them Ngons. As I noted earlier in this chapter, faces that have more than four edges may be problematic with further modeling or rendering. This simple screw head most likely will not pose any problems in the application here, but let's go over how to prevent any problems early on. You will select the potential problem faces (those around the slot) and triangulate them.

1. Select all the faces around the slot, as shown in Figure 4.72 (left). Choose Mesh ➤ Triangulate. This is the easiest and fastest way to subdivide these faces from being Ngons without having to use the Multi-Cut tool to manually fix them. Although it may not look as clean as before (Figure 4.72, right), the geometry is clean and will not be a potential problem like Ngons may be.

2. Select the screw head and choose Edit ➤ Delete By Type ➤ History. This cleans out any history on the object now that you're satisfied with it.

3. Notice that the screw head's pivot point is at the origin. With the object selected, choose Modify ➤ Center Pivot.

4. Name the object **ScrewHead** and position it at one of the intersections of the boards you've built so far.

5. Using Shift+Move, duplicate that first screw head and place the copies one by one at all the other intersections on the base, as shown in Figure 4.73. These are pretty big screws, huh? For this simple catapult, they'll do fine. The workflow to make more realistic screws is the same if you want to make this again with more realism and scale.

6. Now take the objects in the scene and group them into a logical order, as shown in the Outliner in Figure 4.73.

Save your file and compare it to `catapult _ v1.mb` in the Catapult project from the companion website to see what the completed base should look like.

> The time you spend keeping your scene objects organized now will pay off later when you animate the catapult in Chapter 8.

FIGURE 4.72 Select the faces around the slot (left) and triangulate them (right).

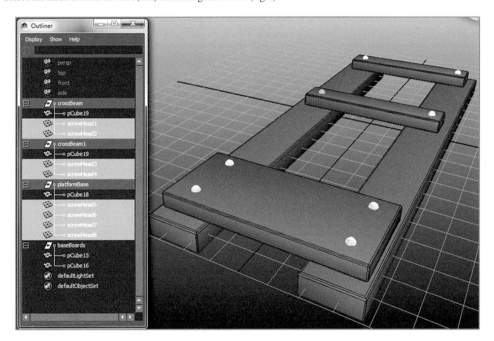

FIGURE 4.73 Place the screw heads on the base and organize your scene.

The Winch Baseboards

Next to the model for the base are the bars that hold the winch assembly to the base. Refer to the sketch of the catapult (Figure 4.60, earlier) to refresh yourself on the layout of the catapult and its pieces. Follow these steps:

1. Create two long, narrow, beveled poly cubes for the baseboards of the winch and position them across the top two side braces. Put a couple of screws on the middle crossbeam (see Figure 4.74).

2. For the brackets that hold down the winch, create a small poly cube and move it off to the side of the base to get it out of the way. Scale the cube to 0.5, 0.3, 0.45. Select the side face and click the Extrude button in the Modeling Toolkit panel. Use **0.8** for the Thickness attribute, as shown in Figure 4.75. Going through the Extrude command versus Shift+Moving the face to extrude it allows you to more accurately enter the above values for the extrusion.

3. Select the top face of the original cube and use the Modeling Toolkit to extrude it to a Thickness setting

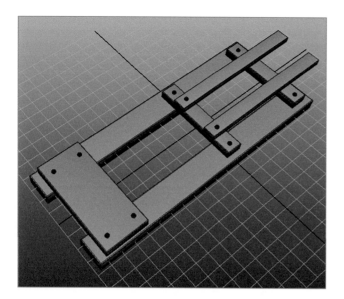

FIGURE 4.74   Adding the winch baseboards.

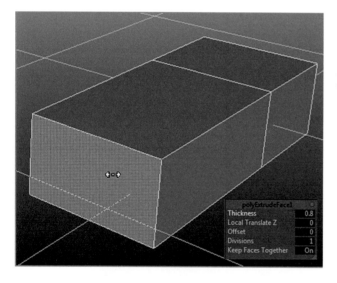

FIGURE 4.75   Use the Modeling Toolkit to extrude the face.

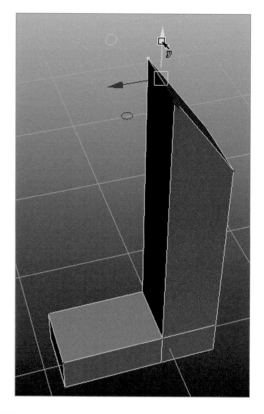

FIGURE 4.76   Extrude the top to create an *L* shape; then move the vertices up to angle the top of the *L*.

of **1.54** to take it up to an *L* shape. Select the two inside vertices on the top of the *L* and move them up to create about a 45-degree angle at the tip, as shown in Figure 4.76.

4. Select that angled face and select Extrude in the Modeling Toolkit or choose Edit Mesh ➤ Extrude for an extrusion. Click the cyan-colored switch icon above the Extrude manipulator (shown next to the cursor in Figure 4.77, left). This will switch the extrusion axis (Figure 4.77, center) so you can pull the faces out straight and not angled up. Then grab the Z Move manipulator and manually pull the extrusion out about 0.75 units.

5. Press E to exit the Extrude tool and enter Rotate. Select the end face and rotate it to make it flat vertically and scale it down in Y-axis to prevent it from

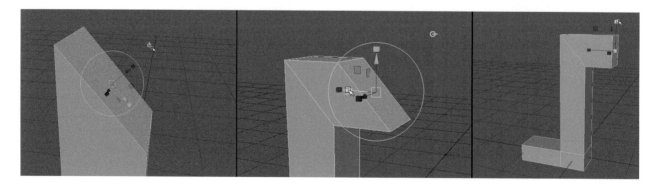

FIGURE 4.77   Click the switch icon (left) to switch the axis of extrusion (center). Rotate and scale the face to square it (right).

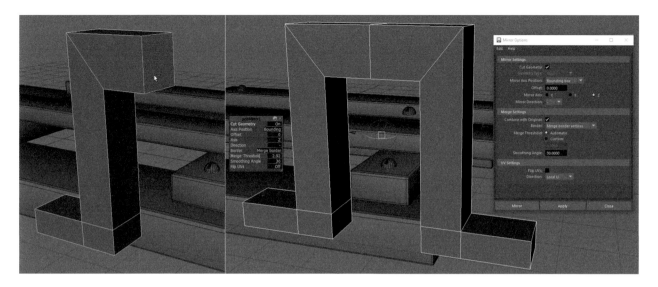

FIGURE 4.78 Delete the face (left) and set the Mirror Geometry options (right).

flaring upward (Figure 4.77, right). It is important to make the face vertical because it affects step 6.

6. This shape forms half of the braces you need. To create the other half, select the face shown in Figure 4.78 (left) and delete it (press Delete). Enter Object mode, select the mesh, and choose Mesh ➤ Mirror ❑. Set Mirror Aix Position to Bounding box. Set Mirror Axis to Z and make sure Mirror Direction is set to – (negative). Leave the remaining options as shown in Figure 4.78 (right). Click Mirror, and you will have a full bracket.

If your face is not rotated to be vertical in the previous step, you may see a gap between the two sides of the bracket. In this case, select the vertices on both sides of this gap and use Edit Mesh ➤ Merge to Center to seal the bracket into one piece.

7. Name the object **bracket** and move it on top of one of the baseboards for the winch; then place a duplicated screw head on the flanges of the bracket. Group the bracket and screw heads together by selecting them and choosing Edit ➤ Group; call the group **bracketGroup**.

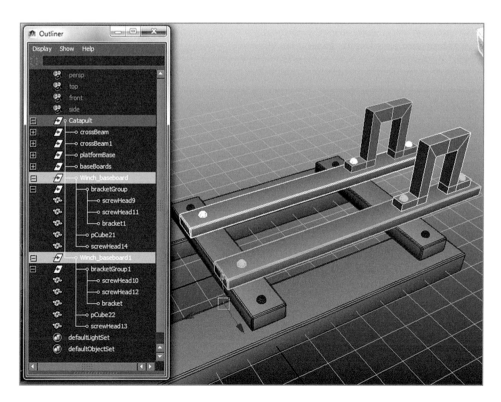

FIGURE 4.79 The winch's base completed.

FIGURE 4.80 MMB+dragging the duplicated bracketGroup to another location in the Outliner removes the group from the Winch_baseboard1 group.

8. Duplicate bracketGroup and move the copy to the other baseboard, as shown in Figure 4.79. Organize your scene as shown in the Outliner in Figure 4.79.

The Ground Spikes

The last items you need for the base are the spikes that secure the base into the ground at the foot of the catapult. Follow these steps:

1. Duplicate one of the bracket groups and name it **bracketGroupCOPY**. Remove the group from its current hierarchy (the Winch_baseboard1 group) by MMB+dragging it to another location in the Outliner (see Figure 4.80). Center its pivot (Modify ➤ Center Pivot).

2. Move the bracket to the other side of the base. Rotate it on its side, scale it to about half its size in all three axes, and place it as shown in Figure 4.81 (left). Select the top vertices and move them closer to the base, as shown in Figure 4.81 (right).

3. Now for the spike itself. Create a poly cube and position and scale it to fit through the bracket. Scale the spike cube to about 3.5 in the Y-axis. Select the bottom face of the spike cube and choose Edit Mesh ➤ Extrude or use the Modeling Toolkit. In the floating panel, set Thickness to **0.5** and Offset to **0.15**, as shown in Figure 4.82. You may have to adjust the scale of the cube and or the Offset value of the extrusion to get your spike to resemble the one in the book since the exact scaling of the cube you just created may be different than what I've done here.

4. Bevel the spike if you'd like. Then select spike and bracketGroupCOPY and group them together, calling the new group **stakeGroup**; center its pivot.

5. Duplicate the stake group and move and rotate it 180° in the Y-axis to fit to the other side of the

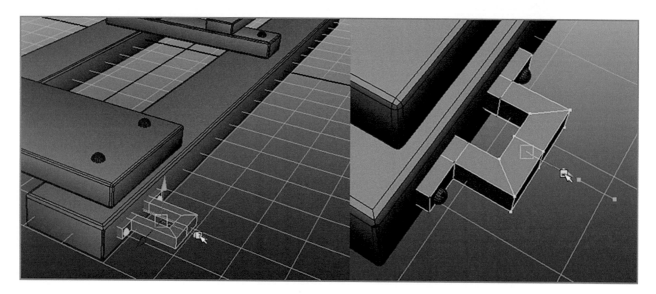

FIGURE 4.81 Position and scale the bracket assembly for the ground spikes (left). Move the vertices to reduce the depth (right).

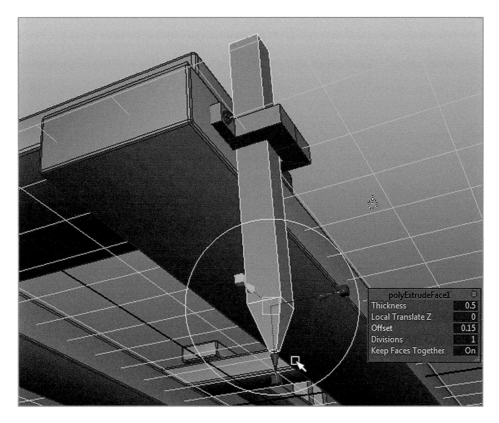

FIGURE 4.82 Creating the spike.

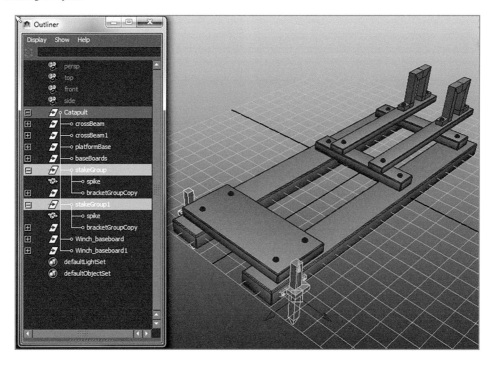

FIGURE 4.83 The completed base.

base. Organize everything into a parent Catapult group (see Figure 4.83) and save your scene as a new version.

The scene file `catapult_v2.mb` in the Catapult project from the companion website has the completed base for comparison.

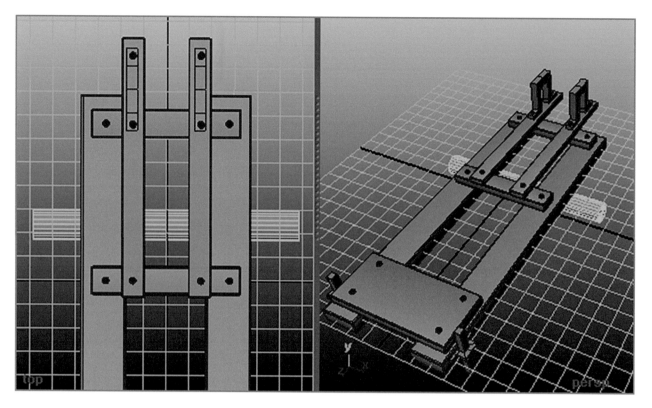

FIGURE 4.84 Place the rear axle.

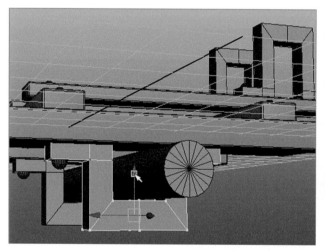

FIGURE 4.85 Make the bracket fit snugly around the axle

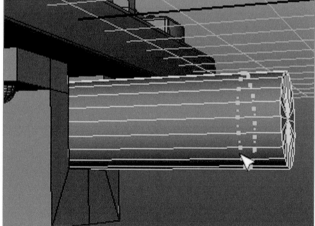

FIGURE 4.86 Insert an edge loop on the axle.

The Wheels

What's a catapult if you can't move it around to vanquish your enemies? So now, you will create the wheels. Follow these steps:

1. First is the axle. Create a polygon cylinder (Create ➤ Polygon Primitives ➤ Cylinder) and then scale, rotate, and place it as shown in Figure 4.84 to be the rear axle.

2. Duplicate one of the stake assembly's bracket groups (bracketGroupCOPY) two times; then move and scale

each of the two copies to hold the axle on either side. Move down the top vertices of the bracket to make the bracket fit snugly around the axle as needed, as in Figure 4.85. Remember to move the duplicated brackets out of their existing hierarchy in the stakeGroups. Group both the axle brackets together and name the group **Axle_Brackets**. You are not grouping the brackets with the axle cylinder. Keep them separate. You'll organize the hierarchy better a little later.

3. To make the axle a little more interesting, let's add a taper at the ends. You will insert new edges around the ends by using Insert Edge Loop, which

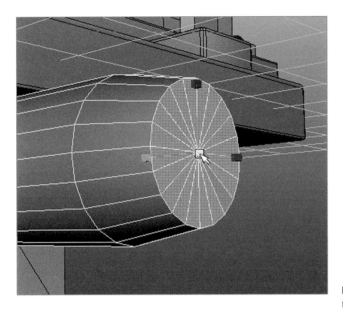

FIGURE 4.87 Scale the faces to taper the axle.

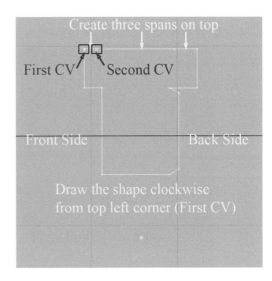

FIGURE 4.88 The profile curve for the wheel is drawn clockwise in the front view panel.

will be much faster than the Multi-Cut tool in this case. Select the rear axle cylinder and choose Mesh Tools ➢ Insert Edge Loop. Your cursor turns into a triangle. Select one of the horizontal edges on the cylinder toward one end, as shown in Figure 4.86. A dashed line will appear running vertically around the cylinder. Drag the cursor to place the dashed line as shown in Figure 4.86 and release the mouse button to commit the new edges to that location. Repeat the procedure for the other side.

4. Select the end cap faces and scale them down on each side of the axle cylinder, as shown in Figure 4.87, to create tapered ends. Name the cylinder **rearAxle**. Now you're ready for the rear wheels.

5. To model a wheel, first you'll use NURBS curves to lay out a profile to revolve. Make sure to be in the Front view panel. Choose Create ➢ Curve Tools ➢ CV Curve Tool ❐ and select 1 Linear for Curve Degree. Since the wheel's profile will have no smooth curves, you can create a linear CV curve like that in Figure 4.88, laying down CVs clockwise starting in the top-left corner, as shown, and snap the last CV to the first one; otherwise, your wheel may become inside out and flat black in step 7. This is something that can easily be fixed in step 7 as well. It's important for the design to create three spans for the top part of the curve. Place the pivot point (hold down the D key or press Insert on a PC or Home on a Mac) about three-quarters of a unit below the curve, as also shown in Figure 4.88. This curve will be the profile of the front of the wheel.

6. Place the profile curve above the rear axle. To make sure the pivot point for the profile lines up with the center of the axle, turn on Snap To Points (a.k.a. Point Snap) () and press and hold down D to

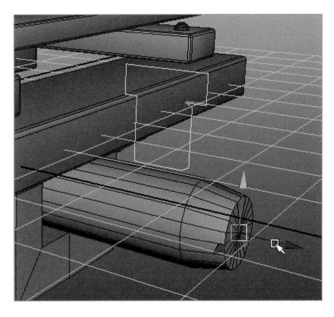

FIGURE 4.89 The profile curve is in place for the rear wheel.

FIGURE 4.90 Selecting the Revolve surface operation.

move the pivot. Snap the pivot to the center of the axle, as shown in Figure 4.89. Turn off Point Snap.

7. Select the curve and revolve it by choosing Surfaces ➢ Revolve ❐ (Figure 4.90). In the option box,

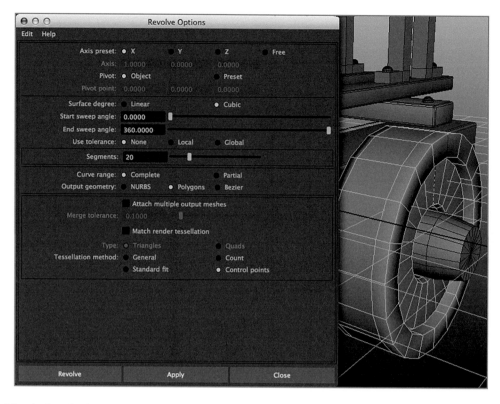

FIGURE 4.91   The wheel revolved.

set Axis Preset to X to make it revolve correctly. Change Segments from the default 8 to **20** to give a smoother wheel. Set Output Geometry to Polygons and set Tessellation Method to Control Points. This will create the edges of the faces along the CV points on the curve. Click Revolve, and there it is (Figure 4.91).

If for some reason your wheel object displays as black, this means the surface is inside out (the normals are reversed). With the wheel object selected, in the Modeling menu set, select Mesh Display ➤ Reverse under the Normals menu heading.

8. Select the wheel object and bevel it. With the wheel still selected, delete the history and the original NURBS curve since you won't need either again.

9. Add some detail to the wheel. Duplicate a screw head and remove the copy from whatever group it was in by MMB+dragging it out of the current group in the Outliner. Arrange a few of the screw heads around the front face of the wheel.

10. Add a couple of braces on the front of the wheel above and below the wheel's middle hole with two thin, stretched, and beveled poly cubes, with screws on either side (as shown in Figure 4.92). Again, make sure to remove the duplicated screw heads from whatever group you got them from.

11. Select all the objects of the wheel, group them together by pressing Ctrl+G, and call the group **wheel**. Center the wheel group's pivot point by choosing Modify ➤ Center Pivot.

12. Adding studs to the wheel makes for better traction when moving the catapult through mud and also for a cooler-looking catapult. To create all the studs at once, grab every other middle face along the outside of the wheel and extrude them with a Thickness of **−0.3** and an Offset of **0.1**, as shown in Figure 4.93. If your studs are extruding inward into the wheel, then simply use a Thickness value of 0.3 instead of −0.3. You can also use Shift+Move to extrude the faces to a thickness by eye.

13. Copy the wheel group and rotate it 180° in the Y-axis to create the other rear wheel for the other side. Position it on the other side of the rear axle.

14. Group the two wheels with the rear axle and call the new group node **Rear_Wheel**.

15. Select the Rear_Wheel node and the Axle_Brackets group node and duplicate them by choosing Edit ➤ Duplicate or by pressing the hotkey Ctrl+D. Move the objects to the foot of the catapult for the front wheels. Rename the wheel group node **Front_Wheel**.

16. Add the new axle bracket and wheel group nodes to the Catapult top node by MMB+dragging them onto the Catapult node in the Outliner; save your scene. Figure 4.94 shows the positions and Outliner hierarchy of the wheels.

The file `catapult_v3.mb` in the Catapult project from the companion website reflects the finished wheels and base.

FIGURE 4.92 Adding detail to the wheel.

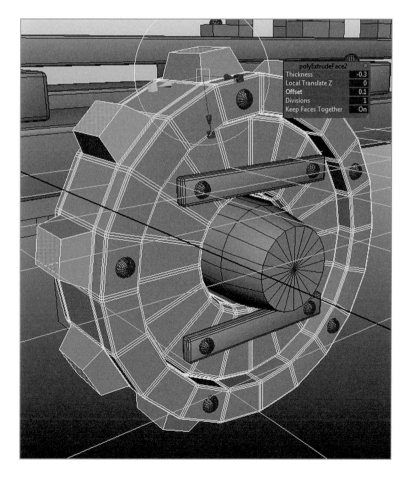

FIGURE 4.93 Extrude studs for the wheel.

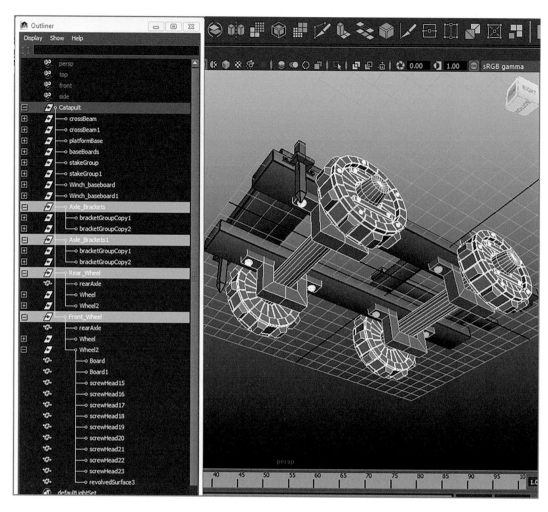

FIGURE 4.94   The wheels and brackets are positioned, and the hierarchy is organized.

The Winch Assembly

To be able to pull the catapult arm down to cock it to fire a projectile, you'll need the winch assembly to wind a rope that connects to the arm to wind it down into the firing position. Since animating a rope can be a rather involved and advanced technique, the catapult will not actually be built with a rope. To build the winch assembly, follow these steps:

1. The first part of the winch is the pulley around which the rope winds. In the front view panel, create a profile curve for extrusion as you did with the wheel that looks more or less like the profile curve in Figure 4.95, drawn clockwise starting with the left side of the profile curve. In this figure, the first CV of the profile curve is on the left end of the curve. Place the pivot point of the curve at that first CV. Revolve the curve around the X-axis with only 12 segments (as opposed to the wheel's 20). Center its pivot, and you have the pulley.

    If your pulley object is black, its surface is likely inside out (reversed normals), depending on how you created the profile curve in this step. In this case, select the pulley object and select Mesh Display ➢ Reverse under the Normals menu heading.

2. Position the pulley at the rear of the catapult, placing the brackets in the grooves (see Figure 4.96).

3. Now you'll need some sort of geared wheel and handle to crank the pulley. Create a poly cylinder and rotate it so it's on its side like one of the wheels. Scale it to a squat disk with scale values of **1.4** in the X- and Z-axes and **0.4** in the Y-axis. Select the disk and bevel it.

4. Off on the side of your scene, create another poly cylinder, and rotate it to its side as well. Scale it to be a long, thin stick. You'll use this as the first of eight gear teeth for the wheel. Position it at the top of the wheel, as shown in Figure 4.97. Click the Snap To Points icon in the Status line (   ) and snap the pivot point (press D to move the pivot) to the center of the wheel. Turn off Snap To Points. The keyboard shortcut for Snap to Points is holding down V to enable the point-snapping function.

5. Instead of duplicating the gear tooth and positioning it seven more times individually, you'll use the array capabilities of the Duplicate Special tool. Select the tooth and choose Edit ➢ Duplicate Special ❐. In the option box, set Rotate to **45** in the X-axis, and set

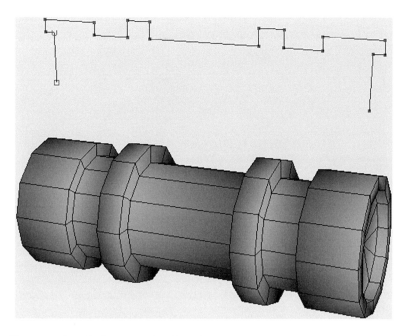

FIGURE 4.95   Create a profile curve and revolve it to create the object shown below the profile curve.

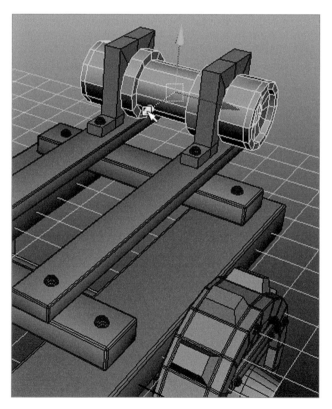

FIGURE 4.96   Place the pulley.

FIGURE 4.97   Making a gear wheel.

Number Of Copies to **7**. Since the pivot for the tooth is at the center of the wheel, as soon as you click the Duplicate Special button, Maya places seven copies around the wheel at 45° intervals (Figure 4.98).

6. Now for the handle. Create a poly cube with enough segments for you to adjust vertices and faces to match the handle shown in Figure 4.99. Create cylinders for the crank axle and handle and place them as shown.

Group all the parts together and snap the pivot point to the center of the gear wheel disk. Name the group **handle**. You can bevel the handle if you want.

7. Group the geometry together, call the object **Turn_Wheel**, and center its pivot. Place it at the end of the pulley. Place a copy (rotated 180°) on the other side of the pulley. Figure 4.100 shows the placement.

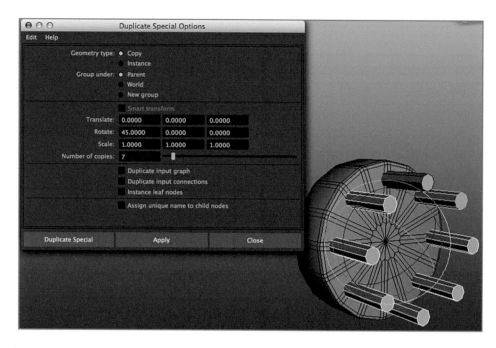

FIGURE 4.98 Eight gear teeth in place.

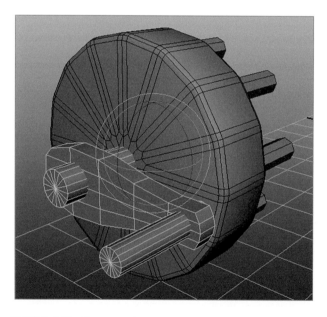

FIGURE 4.99 Use two cylinders and a poly cube to create the handle shapes.

8. Now you'll need gear teeth on the pulley cylinder shape. Create a poly cylinder to be a long, thin tube like the gear teeth and position it at the end of the pulley. Place it so that it is in between two of the turning wheel gear teeth. Place the pivot at the center of the pulley using Snap To Points.

9. Duplicate the new tooth seven times around the pulley at 45-degree intervals with Duplicate Special.

10. Make a copy of each of those eight teeth and move the copies to the other side of the pulley for the other gear. Group the pulley and turning wheels together and name the object **Winch**, as shown in Figure 4.101. Center the pivot.

11. Using a couple of poly cubes that you shape by moving vertices, make a winch arm on either side to brace the winch to the catapult. Bevel the shapes when you are happy with their shapes. Place the braces between the crank handle and the turning wheel on both sides, and bolt them to the catapult's base, as shown in Figure 4.102. Group them and add them to the hierarchy as shown. Save your scene file.

To verify your work up to this point, compare it to `cata-pult_v4.mb` in the Catapult project from the companion website.

The Arm

OK, now I'm kicking you out of the nest to fly on your own! Try creating the arm (see Figure 4.103), without step-by-step instruction, using all the techniques you've learned and the following hints and diagrams:

- Create an intricate-looking arm with face extrusions. That's all you'll need for the arm geometry. Follow Figure 4.104 for subdivision positions to make the extrusions work correctly.

- Duplicate and place screw heads around the basket assembly, as shown in Figure 4.105.

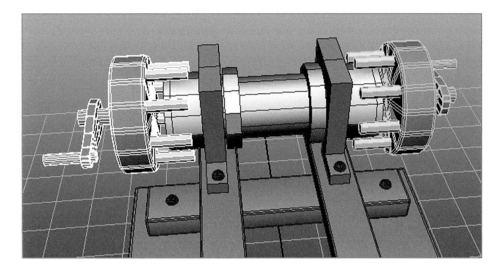

FIGURE 4.100 Place the turn wheels.

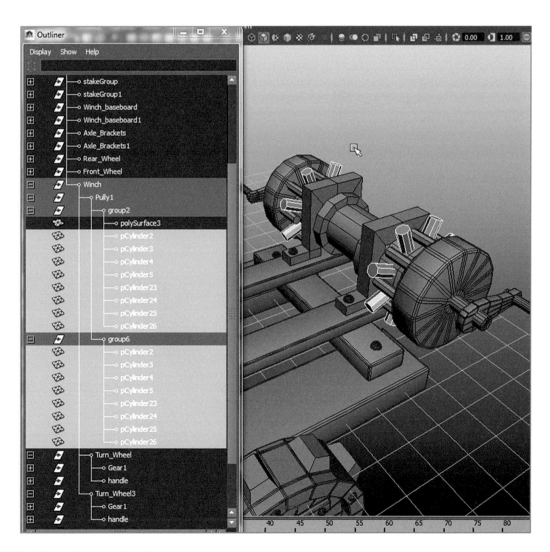

FIGURE 4.101 The winch gears and handles.

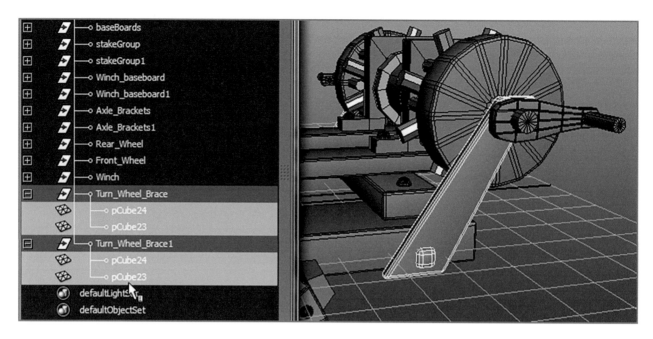

FIGURE 4.102   The assembled winch.

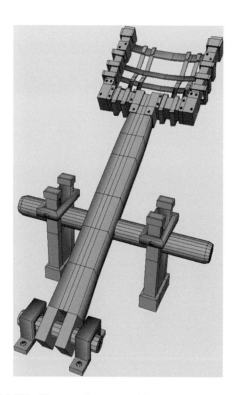

FIGURE 4.103   The catapult arm assembly.

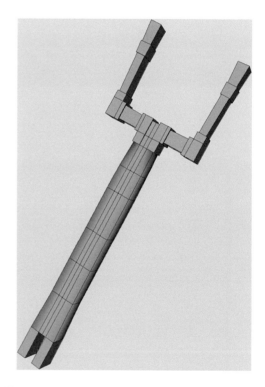

FIGURE 4.104   Follow the subdivisions on your model.

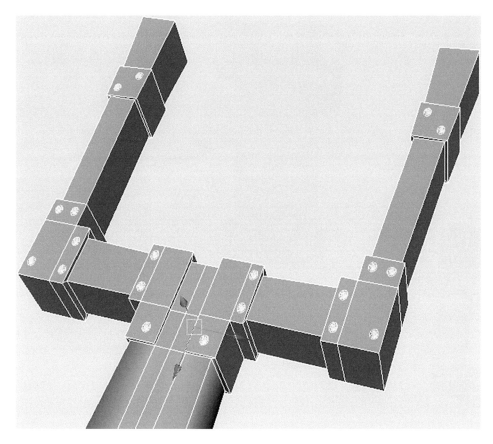

FIGURE 4.105   Place screw heads around the basket arms.

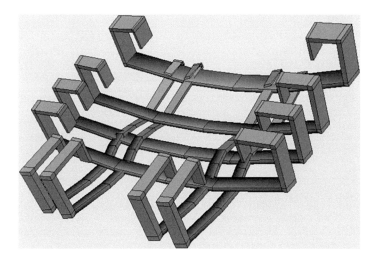

FIGURE 4.106   Basket straps.

FIGURE 4.107   Follow the subdivisions on the arm stand.

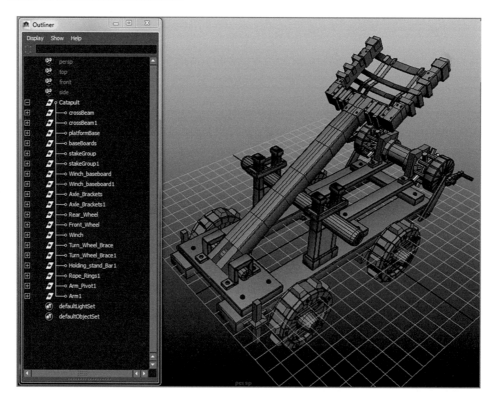

FIGURE 4.108   The completed catapult.

- Create the straps for the basket with poly cubes. It's easier than it looks. You'll just need to create and extrude the cubes with enough subdivisions to allow you to bend them to weave them together, as shown in Figure 4.106. The ends of the straps wrap around the arm's basket with extrusions.

- Create the hinge for the arm with a couple of duplicated brackets and a cylinder.

- Create the arm's stand with multiple extrusions from a cube. Follow the subdivisions in Figure 4.107 for reference.
- Bevel the parts you feel could use some nice edging, including the arm and stand pieces.
- Group the objects together and add their groups to the `Catapult` node.

When you've finished, save your scene file and compare it to `catapult_v5.mb` in the Catapult project from the companion website. Figure 4.108 shows the finished catapult.

Summary

In this chapter, you learned about the basic modeling workflows with Maya and the Modeling Toolkit and how best to approach a model. This chapter dealt with polygon modeling and covered several polygon creation and editing tools, as well as several polygon subdivision tools. You put those tools to good use by building a cartoon hand and smoothing it out, as well as making a model of an old-fashioned catapult using traditional Maya workflows as well as new Modeling Toolkit workflows. The latter exercise stressed the importance of putting a model together step-by-step and understanding how elements join together to form a whole in a proper hierarchy. You'll have a chance to make another model of that kind in Chapter 6, when you create a toy airplane that is then used later in the book to be lighted and rendered.

Complex models become much easier to create when you recognize how to deconstruct them into their base components. You can divide even simple objects into more easily managed segments from which you can create a model.

The art of modeling with polygons is like anything else in Maya: Your technique and workflow will improve with practice and time. It's less important to know all the tricks of the trade than it is to know how to approach a model and fit it into a wireframe mesh.

5

Modeling with NURBS Surfaces and Deformers

Learning Outcomes

In this chapter, you will be able to

Use the surfacing techniques (Loft, Set Planar, and Revolve) to create surfaces

Convert NURBS geometry into polygons

Create polygon meshes directly from NURBS techniques

Model a pair of glass candle holders and convert them to polygons

Create CV curves and use Revolve to create a poly mesh

Attach and Detach curves

Use the Sculpt Geometry tool to sculpt a mesh surface

Use the Soft Modification Deformer

Use nonlinear deformers to adjust existing geometry

Create edits to existing models using lattices

Animate an object to deform through a lattice

NURBS for Organic Curves

NURBS is an acronym for *Non-Uniform Rational B-Spline*. That's good to know for cocktail parties. Impress your friends! NURBS modeling excels at creating curved shapes and lines, so it's most often used for organic forms such as animals and people, as well as highly detailed cars. These organic shapes are typically created with a quilt of NURBS surfaces, called *patches*. Patch modeling can be powerful for creating complex shapes such as characters, but it can also be quite difficult and

will not be covered in this book. I will, however, touch on the basics of NURBS surface modeling in this chapter.

In essence, Bézier curves are created with a starting and ending *control vertex* (CV) and usually, two or more CVs in between that provide a smooth curvature. As each CV is laid down, the curve or spline tries to go from the previous CV to the next one in the smoothest possible manner.

As shown in Figure 5.1, CVs control the curvature. The *hulls* connect the CVs and are useful for selecting multiple rows of CVs at a time. The starting CV appears in the Autodesk® Maya® software as a closed box. The second CV, which defines the curve's direction, is an open box, so you can easily see the direction in which a curve has been created. The curve ends, of course, on the endpoint CV. The start and end CVs are the only CVs that are always actually on the curve itself.

NURBS Modeling

NURBS surfaces are defined by curves called *isoparms*, which are created with CVs. The surface is created between these isoparms to form *spans* that follow the surface curvature defined by the isoparms, as in Figure 5.2. The more spans, the greater the detail and control over the surface.

It can be easier to get a smooth deformation on a NURBS surface with few CVs than on a polygon. Achieving the same smooth look on a polygon would take much more surface detail, i.e., more vertices and faces. As you can see in Figure 5.3, NURBS modeling yields a smoother deformation, whereas polygons can become jagged at the edges.

You can convert NURBS to polygons at any time, but converting polygons back to NURBS can be tricky.

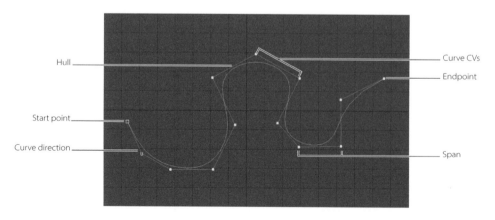

FIGURE 5.1 A Bézier curve and its components.

DOI: 10.1201/9780429490958-6

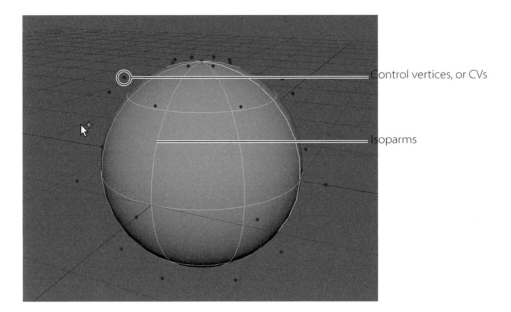

FIGURE 5.2 NURBS surfaces are created between isoparms. You can sculpt them by moving their CVs.

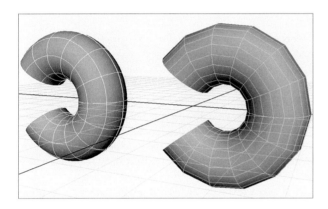

FIGURE 5.3 A NURBS cylinder (left) and a polygonal cylinder (right) bent into a *C* shape. The NURBS cylinder remains smooth, and the polygon cylinder shows its edges.

Try This

Open a new scene (choose File ➤ New Scene). In the new scene, you'll create a few curves on the ground plane grid in the perspective (persp) panel. Maximize the persp view by moving your cursor to it and pressing the spacebar. Choose Create ➤ Curve Tools ➤ CV Curve Tool. Your cursor turns into a cross. Lay down a series of points to define a curved line on the grid. Notice how the Bézier curve is created between the CVs as they're laid down.

Spans are isoparms that run horizontally in a NURBS surface; *sections* are isoparms that run vertically in the object.

NURBS surfaces are created by connecting (or *spanning*) curves. Typical NURBS modeling pipelines first involve creating curves that define the edges, outline, paths, and/or boundaries of surfaces.

A surface's shape is defined by its isoparms. These surface curves, or curves that reside solely on a surface, show the outline of a shape much as the chicken wire does in a wire mesh sculpture. CVs on the isoparms define and govern the shape of these isoparms just as they would regular curves. Adjusting a NURBS surface involves manipulating the CVs of the object.

Levels of Detail

NURBS is a type of surface in Maya that lets you adjust its detail level at any time to become more or less defined as needed. Pressing 1, 2, or 3 toggles between detail levels for any selected NURBS object from low quality at 1 to high quality at 3. Though similar, this is not the same as pressing 1, 2, or 3 for a polygon object, which shows a smooth preview of the poly mesh.

NURBS Surfacing Techniques

The easiest way to create a NURBS surface is to create a NURBS primitive, and then you can sculpt the primitive surface by moving its CVs. But you can also make surfaces in several ways without using a primitive. All these methods involve using NURBS curves to define a boundary, shape, or path of the surface and then using one of the methods described in the following sections to create the surfaces.

The following sections will give you an overview of surfacing techniques before we move on to using some of them to create a new model later in this chapter.

Lofting

The most common surfacing method is *lofting*, which takes at least two curves and creates a surface span between each selected curve in the order in which they're selected. Figure 5.4 shows the result of lofting a few curves together.

To create the loft in Figure 5.4, follow these steps:

1. Switch to the Modeling menu set (press F2).
2. Draw the two curves.
3. Select the curves in the order in which you want the surface to be generated.
4. Choose Surfaces ➢ Loft, or click the Loft icon in the Curves/Surfaces shelf ( ).

When you define more curves for the loft, Maya can create more complex shapes. The more CVs for each curve, the more isoparms you have and the more detail in the surface. Lofting works best when curves are drawn as cross-sectional slices of the object to be modeled.

Lofting is used to make a variety of surfaces, which may be as simple as tabletops or as complex as human faces.

Revolved Surface

A *revolved surface* requires only one curve that is turned around a point in space to create a surface, like a woodworker

FIGURE 5.5   A profile curve is drawn in the outline of a wine glass in the Y-axis (left image) and the revolved surface (right image).

shaping a table leg on a lathe. First, you draw a *profile curve* to create a profile of the desired object, and then you revolve this curve (anywhere from 0° to 360°) around a single point in the scene to sweep a surface.

The profile revolves around the object's pivot point, which is typically placed at the origin but can be easily moved. Figure 5.5 (left) shows the profile curve for a wine glass. The curve is then revolved around the Y-axis a full 360° to create the wine glass. Figure 5.5 (right) is the complete revolved surface with the profile revolved around the Y-axis.

To create a revolved surface, draw and select your profile curve and then choose Surfaces ➢ Revolve.

A revolved surface is useful for creating objects such as bottles, furniture legs, and baseball bats—anything that is symmetrical around an axis.

Extruded Surface

This is a little like the Polygon Extrude you've used in the previous chapter; in that it draws out a shape. However, with a NURBS *extruded surface*, you first need two curves: a profile curve and a path curve. First, you draw the profile curve to create the profile shape of the desired surface. Then you draw out the curve from one end of the path curve to its other end, creating spans of a surface along that travel. The higher the CV count on each curve, the more detail the surface will have. An extruded surface can also take the profile curve and simply stretch it to a specified distance straight along one direction or axis, doing away with the profile curve. Figure 5.6 shows the profile and path curves, and Figure 5.7 shows the resulting surface after the profile is extruded along the path.

To create an extruded surface, follow these steps:

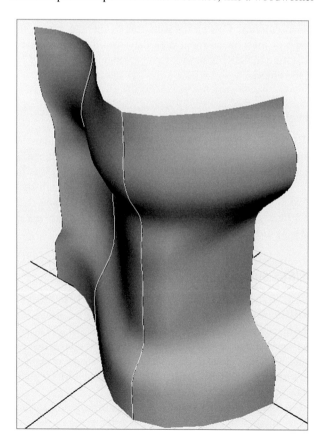

FIGURE 5.4   A loft created with four curves that are selected in order from left to right.

1. Draw both curves, a profile and a path curve.
2. First select the profile curve.

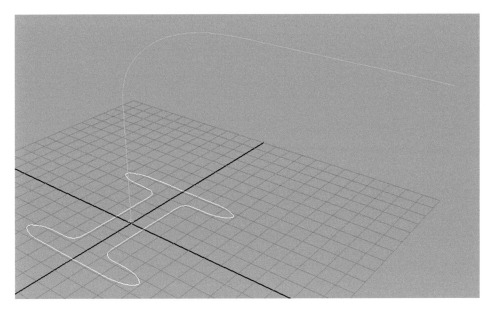

FIGURE 5.6   The profile curve is drawn in the shape of an *I*, and the path curve comes up and bends toward the camera.

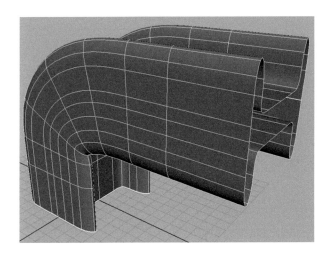

FIGURE 5.7   After extrusion, the surface becomes a bent I-beam.

3. Shift+click the path curve.
4. Choose Surfaces ➢ Extrude.

An extruded surface is used to make items such as winding tunnels, coiled garden hoses, springs, and curtains.

Planar Surface

A *planar surface* uses one perfectly flat curve to make a two-dimensional cap in the shape of that curve. It's almost like laying down a NURBS plane (a flat, square NURBS primitive) and carving out the shape of the curve like a cookie cutter. The resulting surface is a perfectly flat, cutout shape.

To experiment with a planar surface, follow these steps:

1. Draw a curve and make sure the last CV is snapped on to the first CV so it looks like a closed shape as shown in Figure 5.8 (top left). If the curve is either open or not flat, the surface will not materialize.

2. Select the curve and choose Surfaces ➢ Planar for a planar surface to be created with default values as in Figure 5.8 (top right).
3. Delete that NURBS surface and draw a second curve inside the first one. Make sure it's closed as in Figure 5.8 (bottom left).
4. Select the first, outside curve, then select the smaller inside curve and choose Surfaces ➢ Planar to now create a surface. This time the smaller shape is cut-out of the larger shape as seen in Figure 5.8 (bottom right).

A planar surface is great for flat lettering, for pieces of a marionette doll or paper cutout, or for capping the ends of a hollow extrusion. It's usually best to create the planar surface as a polygon mesh, a technique you'll see later in this chapter in the "Using NURBS Surfacing to Create Polygons" section.

If you try creating a planar surface using a curve and notice that Maya doesn't allow it, make sure the curve is closed and that the curve is perfectly flat. If any of the CVs aren't on the same plane as the others, the planar surface won't work.

Beveled Surface

With the Bevel Surface function, you take an open or closed curve and extrude its outline to create a side surface. It creates a bevel on one or both corners of the resulting surface to create an edge that can be made smooth or sharp (see Figure 5.9). The many options in the Bevel tool allow you to control the size of the bevel and depth of extrusion, giving you great flexibility.

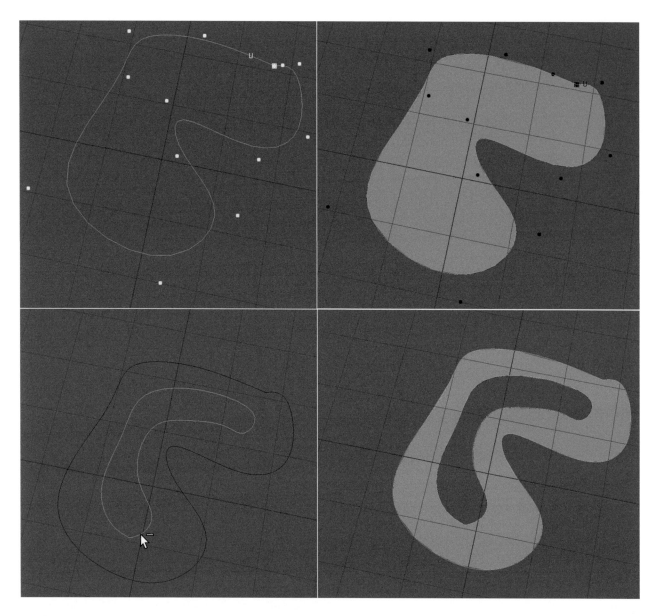

FIGURE 5.8   Create a closed curve (top left); the resulting planar surface (top right); two curves are created (bottom left); a planar surface based on a curve within a curve to create a cutout in the main shape (bottom right).

When a bevel is created, you can easily cap the bevel with planar surfaces.

To create a bevel, draw and then select your curve and choose Surfaces ➢ Bevel.

Maya also offers a Bevel Plus surface, which has more creation options for advanced bevels. A beveled surface is great for creating three-dimensional (3D) lettering, for creating items such as bottle caps or buttons, and for rounding out an object's edges.

Boundary Surface

A *boundary surface* is so named because it's created within the boundaries of three or four surrounding curves. For example, you draw two vertical curves opposite each other to define the two side edges of the surface. Then you draw two horizontal curves to define the upper and lower edges. These curves can have depth; they need not be flat for the boundary surface to work, unlike a planar surface. Although you can select the curves in any order, it's best to select them in opposing pairs. In Figure 5.10, four curves are created and arranged to form the edges of a surface. First, you would select the vertical pair of curves because they're opposing pairs; then, you would select the second two horizontal curves before choosing Surfaces ➢ Boundary.

A boundary surface is useful for creating shapes such as car hoods, fenders, and other formed panels, especially when created as a polygon mesh.

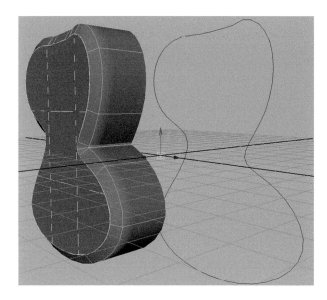

FIGURE 5.9 A curve before and after it's beveled. The beveled surface has been given a planar cap.

Using NURBS Surfacing to Create Polygons

You can easily create swatches of polygon surfaces instead of NURBS surfaces by using any of these NURBS surfacing tools, which may be much more desirable than a NURBS surface. To create a polygonal surface instead of a NURBS surface, open the option box (□) for any particular NURBS tool.

Try This

> Draw two CV curves as you did at the beginning of this chapter, both with the same number of CVs. Choose Surfaces ➤ Loft □ and click the Polygons option for Output Geometry. Set Type to Quads and leave the Tessellation method as Standard fit. Set the Chord height ratio to 0.95 and the 3D delta to 0.07, as shown in Figure 5.11. Click Apply.

The creation options that appear at the bottom of the option window affect the tessellation of the resulting surface; that is, you use them to specify the level of detail and the number of faces with which the surface is created.

The Standard Fit Tessellation method uses the fewest faces to create the surface without compromising overall integrity. The sliders adjust the resulting number of faces in order to fit the finer curvature of the input curves, particularly Chord Height Ratio and 3D delta.

The Chord Height Ratio determines the amount of curve in a particular region and calculates how many more faces to use to give an adequate representation of that curved area with polygons. Values approaching 1.0 create more faces and better detail with surfaces that have multiple or very intense curves.

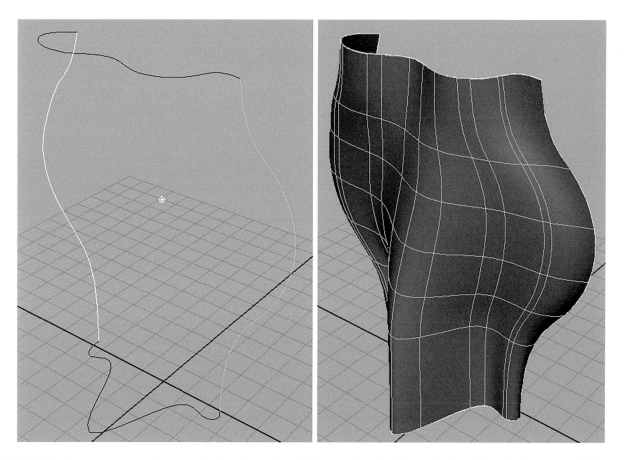

FIGURE 5.10 Four curves arranged to create the edges for a surface (left); the resulting boundary surface formed from the four curves (right).

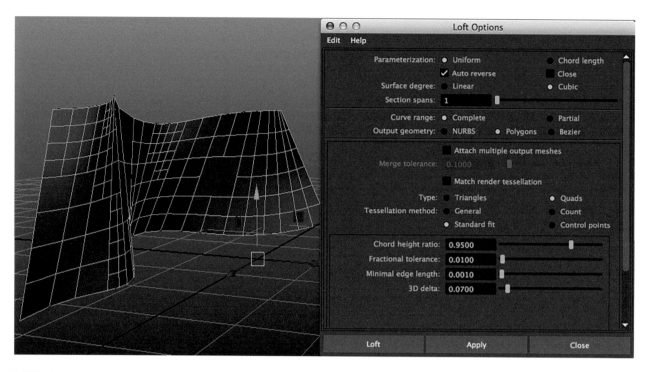

FIGURE 5.11 Create two curves and loft between them to make a polygon mesh.

So curvaceous shapes will generally need a Chord Height Ratio of 0.94–0.97 or so to create a smoother mesh from the curve shape. Lower 3D Delta values will fit smaller faces around tight curves and lower the Fractional Tolerance settings, giving you a smoother surface and a greater number of faces.

Construction History

History has to do with how objects react to change. Leaving History on when creating objects allows you to adjust the original parameters that created that object. For example, the loft you just created will update whenever the curves you used to create the loft move or change shape.

Try This

Select the new poly surface you just lofted in the previous "Try This" and open the Attribute Editor. Select the nurbsTessellate1 tab and open the Advanced Tessellation Options heading. In the Standard Fit Options heading, experiment with changing the Chord Height Ratio and Delta values to see how the poly surface re-creates itself.

Also, try selecting the CVs of the original curves (RMB+click one of the two curves you made and select Control Vertex from the marking menu). Adjust the curve, and the surface will re-create itself because of surface history.

You may need to toggle History on before you create the objects if you want History to be on for the objects. It is usually on by default.

In the status line, the History icon ( ) toggles History on and off. Why wouldn't you want History turned on for everything? After a long day of modeling, having History on for every single object can slow down your scene file, adding unnecessary bloat to your workflow. But it isn't typically a problem on most surface types unless the scene is huge, so you should leave it on while you're still modeling.

If you no longer want a surface or an object to retain its History, you can selectively delete it from the surface. Select the surface and choose Edit ➤ Delete By Type ➤ History. You can also rid the entire scene of History by choosing Edit ➤ Delete All By Type ➤ History. Just don't get them mixed up!

Other Tessellation Methods

Standard Fit will probably do the best job in most situations; however, here are the other tessellation methods you can use:

- The General Tessellation method creates a specific number of lines, evenly dividing the horizontal (U) and vertical (V) into rows of polygon faces.

- The Control Points method tessellates the surface according to the number of points on the input curves. As the number of CVs and spans on the curves increase, so does the number of divisions of polygons.
- The Count method simply relies on how many faces you tell it to make—the higher the count, the higher the tessellation on the surface. Experiment with the options to get the best poly surface results.

Converting a NURBS Model to Polygons

Some people prefer to model on NURBS curves and either create poly surfaces or convert to polygons after the entire model is done with NURBS surfaces. Ultimately, you'll find your own workflow preference, but it helps greatly if you're comfortable using all surfacing methods. In the following section, you'll convert a NURBS model to polygons.

Try This

Convert a NURBS-modeled axe into a poly model like one that might be needed in a game.

Open `axe_model_v1.mb` in the Scenes folder of the Axe project from the companion web page. The toughest part of this simple process is getting the poly model to follow all the curves in the axe with fidelity, so you'll have to convert parts of the axe differently. Follow these steps:

1. Grab the handle and choose Modify ➤ Convert ➤ NURBS To Polygons ❐. Use the default presets, but if need be, reestablish default settings by choosing Edit ➤ Reset Settings in the Option Box. Click Apply, and a poly version of the axe handle appears on top of the NURBS version and you can see that it converts well to polygons using default settings. Move it eight units to the right to get it out of the way. You'll move the other parts of the same eight units as well to assemble the poly axe properly.

2. Select the back part of the axe head. All those surfaces are grouped together to make selection easy. The default settings will work for this part as well, so click Apply and move the resulting model eight units to the left.

3. The front of the axe head holds a lot of different arcs, so you'll have to create it with finer controls. Change Fractional Tolerance from 0.01 to 0.0005. This yields more polygons but finer-curved surfaces. Figure 5.12 shows the result.

Sculpting NURBS

Imagine that you can create a NURBS surface and sculpt it using your cursor the way hands mold the surface of wet clay.

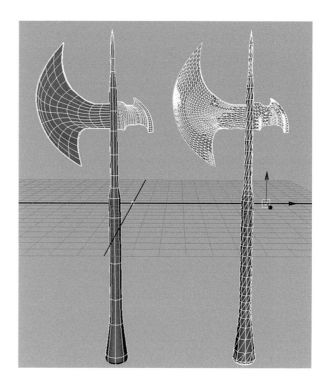

FIGURE 5.12 A faithful high-poly conversion (on the right) of a NURBS axe (on the left).

As you saw with the Sculpt Geometry tool in Chapter 4, you can push and pull vertices easily by virtually painting on the surface. You can sculpt NURBS surfaces much the same way by accessing Surfaces ➤ Sculpt Geometry Tool ❐.

If you plan to sculpt a more detailed surface, be sure to create a surface with plenty of surface spans and sections. You'll try this tool a little bit in the next section.

Creating a Pair of Glass Candle Holders

Let's put some of this information to good use and build a pair of glass candle jars. You will use these glass jars in Chapters 7, 10, and 11 to create shaders (materials), light them, and render them. Copy the project folder `candleHolder` from the book's companion web page and set your project to it.

Creating the Objects

You'll start with a profile curve for a Revolve surface:

1. Click Create ➤ Curve Tools ➤ CV Curve tool and turn on grid snaps (   ) in the status bar.

2. In the front view panel, click the origin to snap the first CV to (0,0,0). Snap the second and third CVs to the grid points on the left. Click the fourth CV slightly higher than the third CV to create a sharp curve. Figure 5.13 marks the first four CVs.

Continue laying down CVs to match the shape shown in Figure 5.13. This will be the profile curve for the body of the jar, which will give the glass

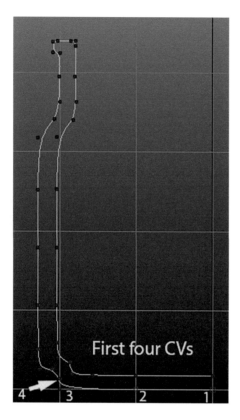

FIGURE 5.13 Starting with the first four CVs and then going clockwise around, complete your curve to match this shape.

thickness, which will be important for rendering glass later.

3. In the Modeling menu set, select Surfaces ➢ Revolve ❒. Make sure Axis Preset is Y and set Output Geometry to Polygons. Set Type to Quads. To get smooth curves in the mesh, increase Chord Height Ratio to **0.97** or use **0.935** for a less dense model instead. (See the "Making Less Dense Candle Geometry" sidebar for more information before moving on to the next steps.) Lower 3D Delta to **0.06**. Click Revolve to make the jar's body (Figure 5.14).

MAKING LESS DENSE CANDLE GEOMETRY

The geometry you are now creating for the candle is pretty smooth and therefore will make a larger file and tax your system just a little more. You can create all the revolved surfaces in step 3 and future steps by using a Chord Height Ratio value of 0.935 instead of 0.97. This will create significantly fewer polygons to tax your system if your machine is running slow. However, the candle may not look quite as detailed as you are creating in this and future chapters where you light and render the candle.

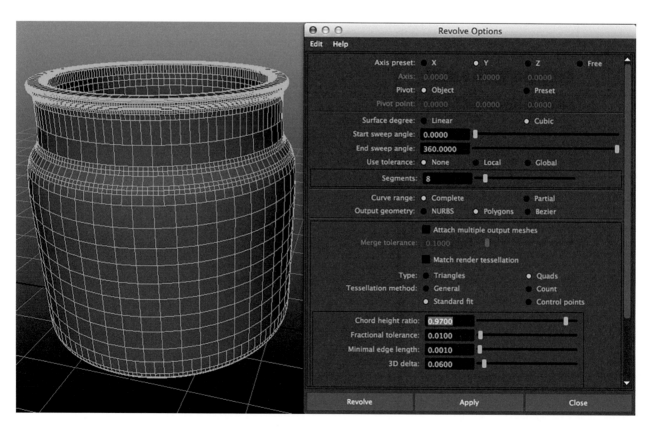

FIGURE 5.14 Revolve the surface with these settings.

4. Now for the lid. In the front view panel, click the Show menu in the view panel's menu bar and toggle off Polygons, as shown in Figure 5.15. This will disable polygon display in the front view panel to make it easy to work on the next profile curve for the lid.

5. The lid will have two parts: the main glass lid and a plastic stopper that goes around the bottom of the glass part where it inserts into the jar. Create a curve to match Figure 5.16. Notice where the first few CVs are created and follow counterclockwise to lay down all the CVs as shown, fitting it to the top of the jar's curve we just created.

FIGURE 5.15   Turn off polygons in the front view panel.

6. Now let's make a profile curve for the plastic sealer that goes around the base of the lid. In the front view panel, create another curve to match the shape in Figure 5.17 sandwiched in-between the jar's curve and the lid's curve.

7. Now, the plastic sealer is open-ended, so you need to close that curve to get a solid geometry when you revolve it. In Object mode, select the curve and choose Curves ➤ Open/Close. The end will close, but it will elongate. Select the end CVs and move them back to line up with the glass lid's curve, as shown in Figure 5.18.

8. Now for the fun part! Go into the persp view panel where you can still see polygons, select the plastic sealer's profile curve, and choose Surfaces ➤ Revolve just as you did last time, with the same settings originally shown in step 3 and Figure 5.14. Figure 5.19 (left) shows the plastic sealer. Repeat the Revolve process for the lid's profile curve to create the lid as in Figure 5.19 (right).

9. What's a candle jar without a candle? You need the candle in the jar to form right up against the glass, so you'll use part of the same profile curve you used for the jar. Select the original jar body profile curve, and in the Outliner, change its name to **glassProfile**. With it still selected, choose Edit ➤ Duplicate (or press Ctrl+D to copy the curve). Rename that curve from glassProfile to **candleProfile**. Feel free to turn on or off the Polygon view in the persp view panel to make it easier to see the curves as needed like you did in step 4 earlier.

10. Select the glassProfile curve again and press Ctrl+H to hide it from view. Its entry in the Outliner will turn gray. RMB+click the duplicated curve (candleProfile) and select Curve Point from the marking menu. Click the curve and drag the little red point that appears on the curve up the inside wall to the

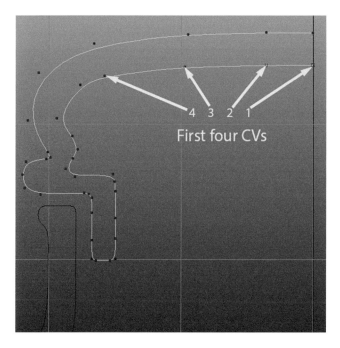

FIGURE 5.16   Start with the first CVs shown and follow the line counterclockwise to create this profile for the glass lid.

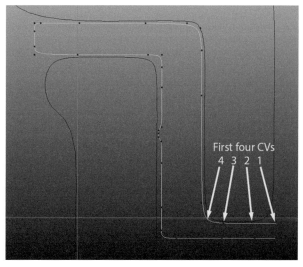

FIGURE 5.17   Profile curve for the plastic sealer for the lid.

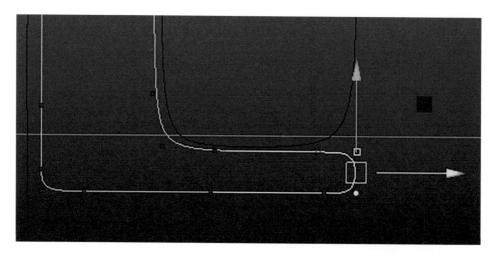

FIGURE 5.18   Close the curve and adjust the CVs to reshape the profile for the plastic stopper.

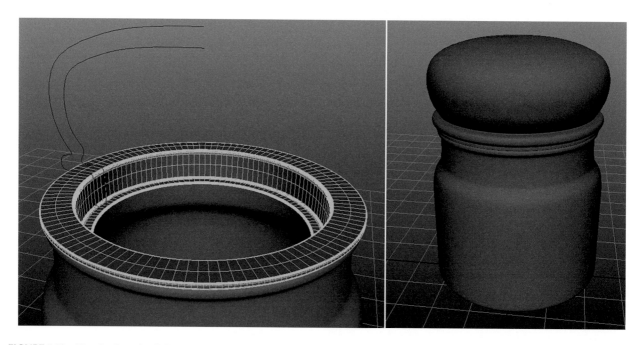

FIGURE 5.19   The plastic sealer (left) and the completed jar (right).

right below where it begins to curve in, as shown in Figure 5.20. Release the mouse, and the point turns yellow. You are going to break the curve at this point.

11. Choose Curves ➢ Detach to cut the curve at that point. The top of the curve should be green now and the bottom white. Select just the top part of the curve and press Delete to delete it. Figure 5.21 (left) shows the remaining curve you'll use to create the candle.

12. Draw a straight-line curve as shown in the front view panel to match Figure 5.21 (right). It's okay if the first CV isn't exactly on the candle's profile curve; close is good enough.

13. Now select both the straight-line curve and the candleProfile curve and choose Curves ➢ Attach □. Set Attach Method to Connect, set Multiple Knots to

Remove, and uncheck Keep Originals, as shown in Figure 5.22. Click Attach, and the two curves will connect as shown to make the candle's profile curve.

14. With that candle curve selected, choose Surfaces ➢ Revolve with the same settings as in step 3 to create the candle.

You can edit the shape of any of these curves you've created, and because of History, the surfaces you created with Revolve will adjust to match the new profiles if you move their CVs to adjust the curve shape. To turn the glass profile curve (glassProfile) back on, select it in the Outliner and press Shift+H. You can easily edit the shape of the object to your liking now. Once you are done, simply delete the profile curves if you don't need them anymore.

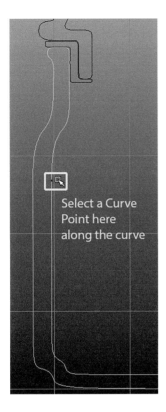

FIGURE 5.20 Selecting a point on curve.

If the mesh also disappears, you can simply hide the curves with Ctrl-H to get them out of the way instead. This may be preferred to give you more latitude to change these shapes with the original profile curves at a later time. Keep in mind, however, if you hide the original curves, that if the mesh or the

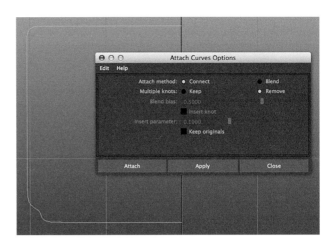

FIGURE 5.22 Attach the curves to complete the candle's profile.

curves move, the geometry may change due to History. As a final option, if the mesh goes away if you delete the original profile curve, you will first need to delete History on the mesh (Edit ➤ Delete By Type ➤ History) and then you can delete the profile curve. For the purposes of this exercise, it's better to delete the curves to avoid any undesirable results down the line.

Once you delete (or hide) the profile curves, name the objects. Group the lid objects together (name it **jarLid**) and group the glass jar and candle together (name it **jarCandle**), as shown in Figure 5.23. Finally, in the front view panel, select Show ➤ Polygons (in the view panel's menu bar) to turn on the display of polygons in that view panel.

You can find the candle jar in `candleModel_v01.mb` in the `scenes` folder of the candleHolder project. This file still retains the original profile curves for you.

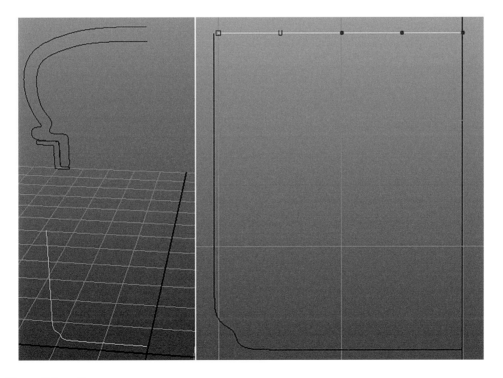

FIGURE 5.21 The candle's profile curve.

FIGURE 5.23 The final candle's hierarchy.

candleModel_ v02.mb has the completed jar without the original profile curves and with the objects properly named and grouped. This file uses the smoother geometry called for in step 3 (with a Chord Height Ratio value of 0.97) and therefore is also a larger file than if you created the jar with a lower Chord Height Ratio value.

> A curve point is a point directly on a curve. You cannot move a curve point like you can a CV to adjust the shape of the curve. Curve points are used mostly for attach and detach functions.

Detailing the Objects

Now let's add a little detail to the candle inside the jar using the Sculpt geometry tool. Continue with your own file, or open candleModel _ v02.mb in the scenes folder of the candleHolder project.

1. Select the outer glass jar and press Ctrl+H to hide it. In the Outliner, select the jarLid group and press Ctrl+H to hide the lid and plastic sealer, too.

2. In the Modeling menu set, choose Mesh Tools ➣ Sculpting Tools ➣ Sculpt Tool ❑. It's especially important to open the option box for this tool.

 In the Sculpt Tool options, set Brush Size to 0.25. Your cursor changes to the Artisan brush, a gray circle, as shown in Figure 5.24.

3. If you click the candle with the brush, it will push in the geometry quite a bit. Undo anything you may have done with this tool. If the geometry pulls out instead

of pushing in, turn on the Invert check box in the tool options. In the options, set Strength to 0.2, this will limit the amount of influence each brush stroke will have on moving the geometry. This ensures that the sculpting is layered slowly; each successive brush stroke will push the geometry slowly further. Feel free to reduce the Strength value for more finesse in your sculpting. You could also adjust the Buildup value to 3.0 instead of adjusting Strength. This attribute controls the maximum amount you affect the geometry with each stroke. Adjusting Strength, however, allows for more finesse.

 Sculpt the top of the candle slightly to create an uneven surface. Figure 5.24 shows the resulting uneven candle top. Try not to sculpt the sides of the candle; this may cause the sides to bulge out and then penetrate the glass jar. Try working only on the top of the candle for a melted look.

4. In the options, toggle on the Invert setting to allow the Sculpt tool to pull up the geometry. Slowly raise the middle top of the candle to create a place for the wick, as shown in Figure 5.25.

5. Press W to exit the Sculpt tool and then close Tool Options. With Interactive Creation turned off, create a polygon cylinder with Height Divisions of 8 and Cap Divisions of 4. Scale and place the cylinder to be the wick of the candle, as shown in Figure 5.26 (left).

6. Select vertices and move and rotate them around to give the cylinder a more interesting shape. Then use the Sculpt tool to misshape the cylinder as if the wick has already been burned, as shown in Figure 5.26 (right). Press 3 to see a smooth preview of the wick as you work.

> In addition, the Smooth tool (Mesh Tools ➣ Sculpting Tools ➣ Smooth Tool) blends the pushed-in and pulled-out areas of the surface to yield a smoother result. In general, if you plan to sculpt a detailed surface, be sure to create the mesh with plenty of faces.

7. Once you are happy with the wick, smooth the wick's geometry by choosing Mesh ➣ Smooth ❑. Set Division Levels to **1** and click Smooth.

8. Select the wick and erase the history on it by choosing Edit ➣ Delete By Type ➣ History. Name the object **wick** and place it into the jarCandle group, as shown in Figure 5.27.

9. In the Outliner, select the jarLid group and press Shift+H to unhide it. Also, select the glassJar object (under the jarCandle group) to unhide that as well. Then group both jarLid and jarCandle groups together into a new group called **candleGroup**.

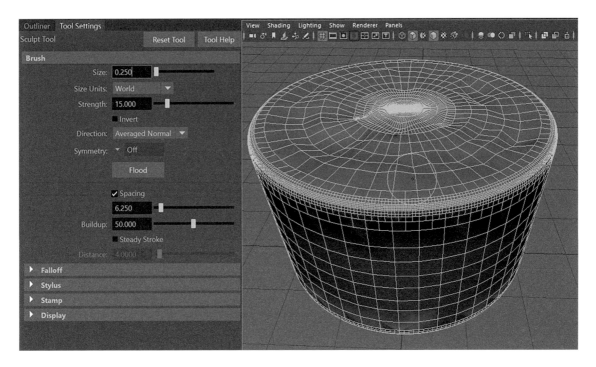

FIGURE 5.24 The Sculpt tool lets you mold your surface by painting on it. Here, the brush is set to push in the surface of the sphere as you paint.

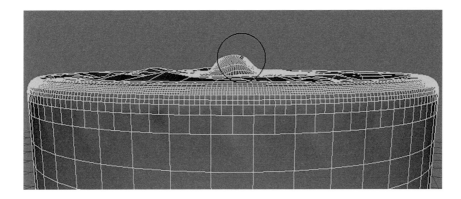

FIGURE 5.25 Raise the top center a little for a place to put the candle's wick.

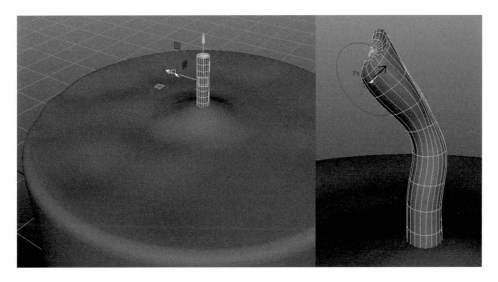

FIGURE 5.26 Place a cylinder as the candle's wick (left) and use the Sculpt tool and manual vertex manipulation to shape it into an already burned wick as shown (right).

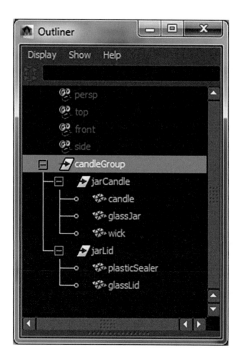

FIGURE 5.27   Group the wick into the hierarchy.

You can check your work against the file `candleModel_v03.mb` in the `scenes` folder of the candleHolder project. With the glass candle jar holder complete, you'll be able to use it later to create a glass and candle wax shader in Chapter 7 and then render the object with reflections and refractions in Chapter 11. Nice job! Go grab a cookie.

Modeling with Simple Deformers

In many ways, deformers are the Swiss Army knives of Maya animation, except that you can't open a bottle with them. *Deformers* are handy for creating and editing modeled shapes in Maya. These tools allow you to change the shape of an object easily. Rather than using CVs or vertices to distort or bend an object manually, you can use a deformer to affect the entire object. Popular deformers, such as Bend and Flare, can be powerful tools for adjusting your models quickly and evenly, as you're about to see.

Nonlinear deformers, such as Bend and Flare, create simple shape adjustments for the attached geometry, such as bending the object. You can also use deformers in animation to create effects or deformations in your objects. You'll explore this later in the book.

Using the Soft Modification Deformer

First, let's try using the Soft Modification tool. Choose Modify ➢ Transformation Tools ➢ Soft Modification Tool, and its

icon ( ) appears below the Tool Box. This tool allows you to select an area on a surface or model and make any adjustments in an interesting way. These adjustments taper off away

from the initial place of selection, giving you an easy way to soft-modify an area of a model, much like lifting up a tablecloth from the middle. This is like the Soft Selection function we covered in Chapter 3, though Soft Modification gives you a handle object (which shows up in the Outliner) that you can manipulate and animate at any time, whereas Soft Selection does not.

To try the Soft Modification tool, follow these steps:

1. In a new scene create a Polygon plane by choosing Create ➢ Polygon Primitives ➢ Plane ❑. Set both the Width Divisions and Height Divisions sliders to 10 and click Create.

2. Click and drag a plane on the grid if Interactive Creation is turned on; otherwise, a plane appears at the origin of your grid. Select the Scale tool and scale the plane up to about the size of the grid.

3. Select Modify ➢ Transformation Tools ➢ Soft Modification Tool and click the plane somewhere just off the middle. Doing so creates an *S* and a special manipulator to allow you to move, rotate, or scale this soft selection (see Figure 5.28). You also see a yellow-to-red-to-black gradient around the S manipulator. This shows you the area and degree of influence, where yellow moves the most and black the least.

4. Grab the cone handle and drag it up to move the soft selection up. Notice that the plane lifts up in that area only, gradually falling off.

5. Grabbing the cube handle scales the soft selection, and dragging the circle rotates it. After you've finished making your soft adjustments, make sure to press W for the Move tool and to exit the Soft Modification tool. Otherwise, you will create new soft modification handles every time you click the mesh.

You can go back to any soft modification by selecting the *S* on the surface for later editing or selecting it from the Outliner. You can place as many soft selections as you need on a surface. Figure 5.29 shows the soft modification adjusting the plane.

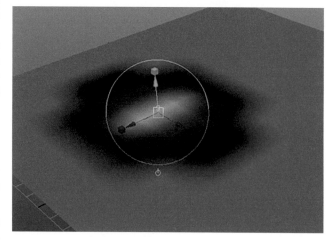

FIGURE 5.28   Creating and manipulating a soft modification.

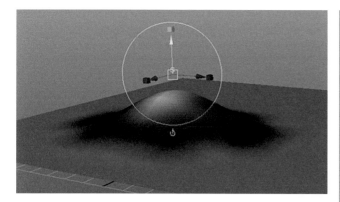

FIGURE 5.29   Lifting an area of the Polygon plane.

Modeling Using the Bend Deformer

Let's apply a deformer. In a new Maya scene, you'll create a polygonal cylinder and bend it to get a quick idea of how deformers work. Follow these steps:

1. Choose Create ➤ Polygon Primitives and turn on Interactive Creation. Then, choose Create ➤ Polygon Primitives ➤ Cylinder. Click and drag to create the base. Make it a few units in diameter; the exact sizing isn't important here. Click and drag to make the height of the cylinder 7 or 8 units. Make sure your create options are set to the defaults so that they're consistent with these directions.

To make sure the settings are at their defaults, open the command's option box and click the Reset Settings or Reset Tool button.

2. With the cylinder selected, make sure you're still in the Modeling menu set and choose Deform ➤ Nonlinear ➤ Bend, under the Create section. Your cylinder turns magenta if you are in wireframe display mode, and a thin line appears at the center of the cylinder, running lengthwise. Figure 5.30 shows the deformer and its Channel Box attributes. Depending on your settings, your deformer may be created in a different axis than the one pictured. You can reset the deformer's options as needed. Click bend1 in the Channel Box to expand the deformer's attributes as shown in the figure.

3. Click Curvature and enter a value of **60**. Notice that the cylinder takes on an odd shape, as shown in Figure 5.31. The Bend deformer itself is bending nicely, but the geometry isn't. Also, the geometry is offset and weird-looking because there aren't enough divisions in the geometry to allow for a proper bend.

4. Select the cylinder, and click polyCylinder1 in the Channel Box to expand the shape node's attributes. Enter a value of **12** for the Subdivisions

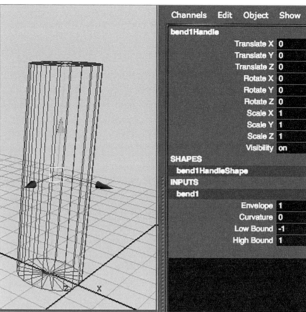

FIGURE 5.30   Creating the Bend deformer.

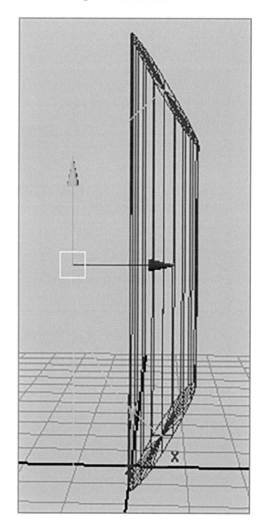

FIGURE 5.31   Notice the problem with this cylinder.

Height attribute (see Figure 5.32), and your cylinder will bend with the deformer properly, as shown in Figure 5.33.

5. Try adjusting the Bend deformer's Low Bound and High Bound attributes. This allows you to bend one part of the cylinder without affecting the other. For example, set the Bend deformer's High Bound option to **0.25** instead of 1. This causes the top half of the cylinder to bend only one-quarter of the way up and continue straight from there.

Experiment with moving the Bend deformer, and see how doing so affects the geometry of the cylinder. The deformer's position plays an important role in how it shapes an object's geometry.

Adjusting an Existing Axe Model

In this exercise, you'll take a NURBS model of an axe and fine-tune the back end of the axe head. In the existing model, the back end of the axe head is blunt, as you can see in Figure 5.34. You'll need to sharpen the blunt end with a nonlinear deformer. Open the AxeHead_v01.ma file in the scenes folder of the Axe project from the companion web page, and follow these steps:

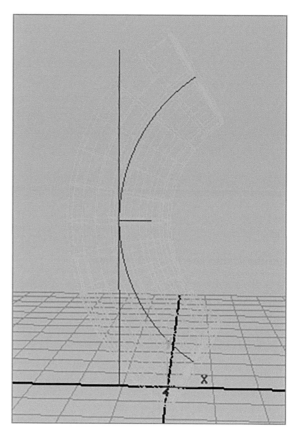

FIGURE 5.33 The cylinder bends properly now that it has the right number of divisions.

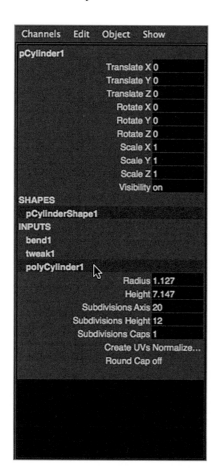

FIGURE 5.32 Increase Subdivisions Height to 12.

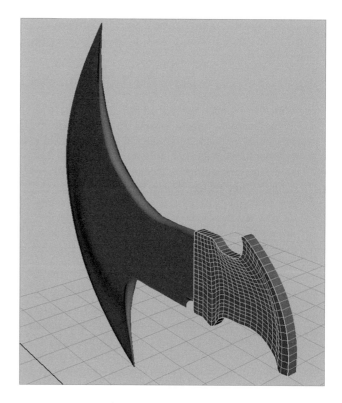

FIGURE 5.34 The axe head is blunt.

1. Select the top group of the axe head's back end. To do so, open the Outliner and select `axeHead_Back` (see Figure 5.35).
2. Press F4 to switch to the Modeling menu set, if you're not already.
3. Create a Flare deformer by choosing Deform ➢ Nonlinear ➢ Flare, under the Create section. The Flare deformer appears as a cylindrical object (see Figure 5.36).

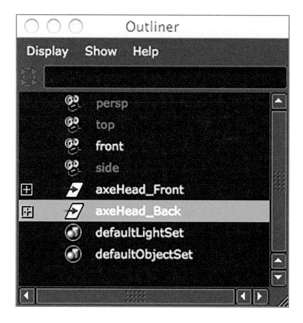

FIGURE 5.35 Select the back of the axe head.

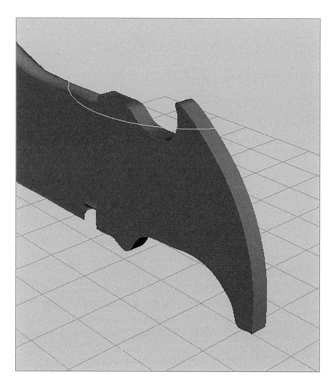

FIGURE 5.36 The Flare deformer appears as a cylinder.

4. Rotate the deformer 90° in the Z-axis, as shown in Figure 5.37.
5. Open the Attribute Editor (Ctrl+A), click the flare1 tab to access the Flare controls, and enter the following values:

Attribute	Value
Start Flare Z	0.020
High Bound	0.50

These values taper in the end of that part of the axe head, as shown in Figure 5.38. This is a much easier way of sharpening the blunt end than adjusting the individual CVs of the NURBS surfaces.

Deformers use History to distort the geometry to which they're attached. You can animate any of the attributes that control the deformer shapes, but in this case, you're using the deformer as a means to adjust a model. When you get the desired shape, you can discard the deformer. However, simply selecting and deleting the deformer will reset the geometry to its original blunt shape. You need to pick the `axeHead_Back` geometry group (not the deformer) and delete its History by choosing Edit ➢ Delete By Type ➢ History.

The Lattice Deformer

When a model requires more intricate editing with a deformer, you'll need to use a lattice. A *lattice* is a scaffold that fits around your geometry. The lattice object controls the shape of the geometry. When a lattice point is moved, the lattice smoothly deforms the underlying geometry. The more lattice points, the greater control you have. The more divisions the geometry has, the more smoothly the geometry will deform.

Lattices are especially useful when you need to edit a relatively complex poly mesh or NURBS surface that is too dense to edit efficiently directly with CVs or vertices. With a lattice, you don't have to move the individual surface points.

Lattices can work on any surface type, and a single lattice can affect multiple surfaces simultaneously. You can also move an object through a lattice (or vice versa) to animate a deformation effect, such as a golf ball sliding through a garden hose.

Creating an Alien Hand

Make sure you're in the Modeling menu set. To adjust an existing model or surface, select the models or applicable groups to deform, and choose Deform ➢ Lattice, under the Create section. Figure 5.39 shows a polygonal hand model with a default lattice applied. The top node of the hand has been selected and the lattice applied.

Your objective is to create an alien hand by thinning and elongating the hand and each of the fingers—we all know aliens have long, gawky fingers! Because it would take a lot of time and effort to achieve this by moving the vertices of the poly mesh itself, using lattices here is ideal.

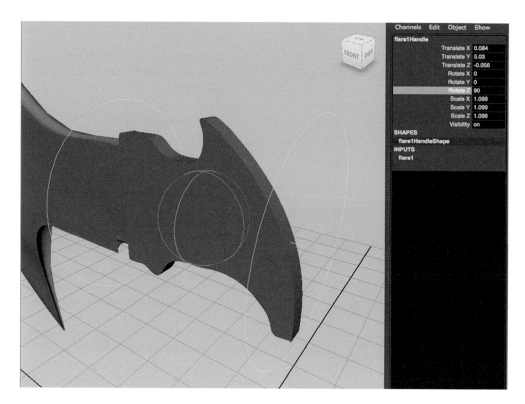

FIGURE 5.37   Rotate the deformer 90° in the Z-axis.

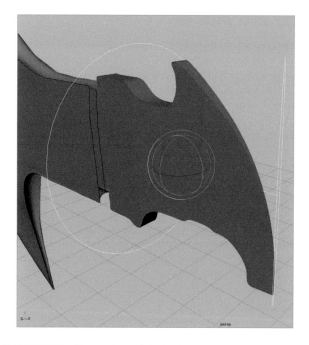

FIGURE 5.38   Sharpen the axe's back edge.

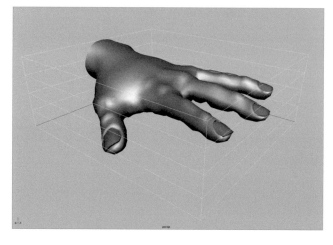

FIGURE 5.39   A lattice is applied to the polygonal hand model.

To elongate and thin the entire hand, load the scene file `detailed_poly_hand.ma` from the Poly_Hand project from the companion web page, and follow these steps:

1. Select the top node of the hand (`poly_hand`) in the Outliner and choose Deform ➢ Lattice, under the Create section of the menu. Doing so creates a default lattice that affects the entire hand, finger-nails, and all. Although you can change the lattice settings in the option box upon creation, you'll edit the lattice after it's applied to the hand.

2. The lattice is selected after it's created. Open the Attribute Editor and click the ffd1LatticeShape tab. The three attributes of interest here are S Divisions, T Divisions, and U Divisions. These sliders con-trol how many divisions the lattice uses to deform its geometry. Set S Divisions to **3**, T Divisions to **2**, and U Divisions to **3** for the result shown in Figure 5.40.

- A 3×2×3 lattice refers to the number of division lines in the lattice as opposed to the number of sections; otherwise, this would be a 2×1×2 lattice!

3. With the lattice selected, press F8 to switch to Component mode or RMB+Click on the lattice and select Lattice Point from the Marking Menu to display the lattice's points. You'll use these points to change the overall shape of the hand. Select the lattice points on the thumb side of the hand and move them to squeeze in that half of the hand. Notice how only that zone of the model is affected by that part of the lattice.

4. Toggle back to Object mode (press F8 again) and scale the entire lattice to be thinner in the Z-axis and longer in the X-axis. The entire hand is deformed in accordance with how the lattice is scaled (see Figure 5.41).

   Now that you've altered the hand, you have no need for this lattice. If you delete the lattice, the hand will snap back to its original shape. You need to delete the construction history on the hand to get rid of the lattice, as you did with the axe head exercise earlier in this chapter.

5. Select the top node of the hand and choose Edit ➢ Delete By Type ➢ History.

Creating Alien Fingers

The next step is to elongate the individual fingers and widen the knuckles. Let's begin with the index finger. Follow these steps:

1. Select the top node of the hand and create a new lattice as before. It forms around the entire hand.

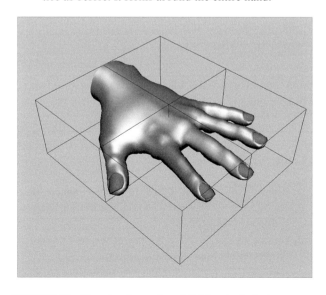

FIGURE 5.40 Changing the number of divisions in the lattice.

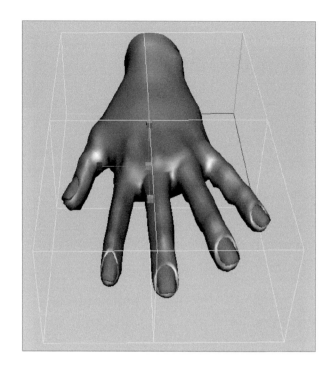

FIGURE 5.41 Lengthen the hand using the deformer.

Although you can divide the lattice so that its divisions line up with the fingers, it's much easier and more interactive to scale and position the entire lattice so it fits around the index finger only.

Simply moving and scaling the selected lattice will deform the hand geometry. You don't want to do this. Instead, you need to select the lattice and its base node. This lets you change the lattice without affecting the hand.

2. In the Outliner, select both the ffd1Lattice and ffd-1Base nodes (see Figure 5.42).

3. Scale, rotate, and transform the lattice to fit around the index finger, as shown in Figure 5.43.

4. Deselect the base, and set the lattice S Divisions to **7**, T Divisions to **2**, and U Divisions to **3**.

5. Adjust the lattice to lengthen the finger by pulling the lattice points (see Figure 5.44). Pick the lattice points around each of the knuckles individually and scale them sideways to widen them.

6. To delete the lattice and keep the changes to the finger, select the top node of the hand and delete its History.

7. Repeat this entire procedure for the rest of the fingers to finish your alien hand. (Try to creep out your younger sister with it.)

8. To get rid of all the lattices and keep the alien shape, select the hand meshes and choose Edit ➢ Delete By Type ➢ History.

The alien hand in Figure 5.45 was created by adjusting the polygonal hand from this exercise using only lattices.

FIGURE 5.42   Select the lattice and base nodes.

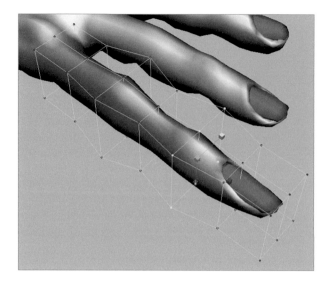

FIGURE 5.44   Flare out the knuckles.

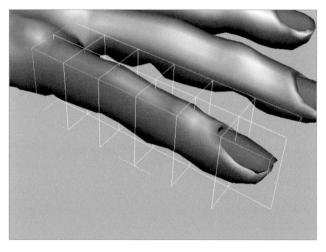

FIGURE 5.43   Position the lattice and its base to fit around the index finger.

As you can see, lattices give you powerful editing capabilities without the complication of dealing with surface points directly. Lattices can help you reshape an entire complex model quickly or adjust minor details on parts of a larger whole.

In Chapter 8, "Introduction to Animation," you'll animate an object using another type of deformer. You'll also learn how to deform an object along a path.

Animating through a Lattice

Lattices don't only work on polygons; they can be used on any geometry in Maya and at any stage in your workflow to create or adjust models. You can also use lattices to create animated

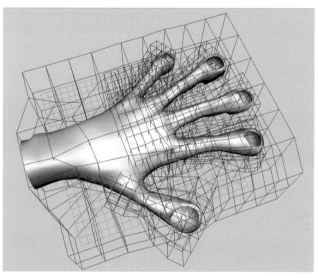

FIGURE 5.45   The human hand model is transformed into an alien hand by using lattices to deform the geometry.

effects. For example, you can create the effect of a balloon squeezing through a pipe by animating the balloon geometry through a lattice.

In the following exercise, you'll create a NURBS sphere with 8 sections and 16 spans and an open-ended NURBS cylinder that has no end caps:

1. Choose Create ➣ NURBS Primitives ➣ Sphere ❒, set Number Of Sections to **8** and Number Of Spans to **16**, and create the sphere.

2. Choose Create ➣ NURBS Primitives ➣ Cylinder ❒ and check None for the Caps option. Scale and arrange the sphere balloon and cylinder pipe as shown in Figure 5.46.

3. Select the balloon and create a lattice for it (see Figure 5.47). (This time, go into the Animation menu

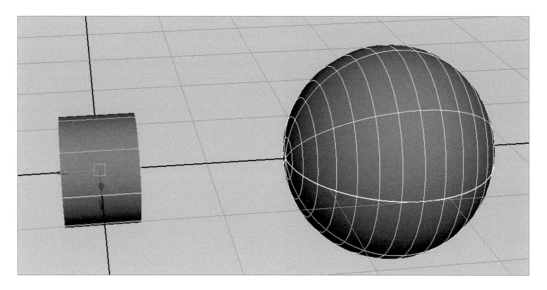

FIGURE 5.46 Arrange the balloon and pipe.

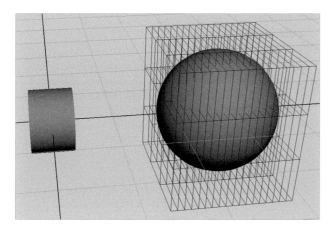

FIGURE 5.47 Create a lattice for the sphere.

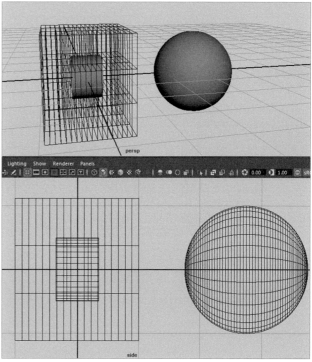

FIGURE 5.48 Relocate the lattice to the cylinder.

set and choose Anim Deform ➢ Lattice.) Set the S, T, and U Divisions to **4**, **19**, and **4**, respectively. You set this number of lattice divisions to create a smoother deformation when the sphere goes through the pipe.

4. Select the lattice and its base in the Outliner (ffd-1Lattice and ffd1Base nodes) and move the middle of the lattice so it fits over the length of the pipe (see Figure 5.48).

5. Deselect the lattice base and choose Component mode for the lattice. Select the appropriate points and shape the lattice so the middle of the lattice fits into the cylinder (see Figure 5.49).

6. Select the sphere and move it back and forth through the pipe and lattice. Notice how it squeezes to fit through. If you look closely, you'll see that the sphere starts to squeeze a little before it enters the pipe. You'll also see parts of the sphere sticking out of the very ends of the pipe. This effect, in which geometry passes through itself or another surface, is called

interpenetration. You can avoid this by using a more highly segmented sphere and lattice. If you try this exercise with a lower-segmented sphere and/or lattice, you'll notice the interpenetrations even more. Figure 5.50 shows the balloon squeezing through the pipe.

In a similar fashion, you can create a lattice along a curved path and have an object travel through it. You'll try this in Chapter 8.

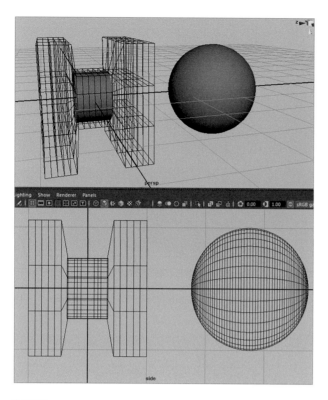

FIGURE 5.49   Squeeze in the lattice points to fit the cylinder.

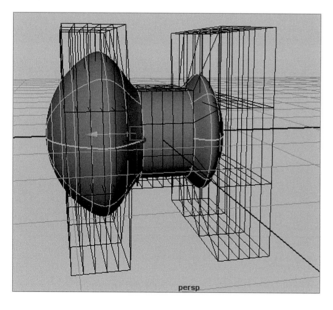

FIGURE 5.50   Squeezing the balloon through the pipe using a lattice deformer.

Summary

In this chapter, you tackled NURBS modeling by going through the usual surfacing tools, from lofting to revolving. Then you explored the implications of surface History and how surfaces adjust to changes when History is enabled. You then put those lessons to work on creating a pair of glass candle holders.

This chapter also covered various modeling techniques to help you break away from typical ways of thinking. You learned how to use a lattice to adjust a polygon hand model into an alien hand, as well as how to animate a balloon pushing through a pipe. Different workflows give you the flexibility to choose your own modeling style. To make good choices, however, you'll need to practice.

Keep at it; model everything you can get your hands and eyes on. As you're doing that, stay on top of how you organize your nodes and keep everything named and organized.

For further practice, use this chapter as a reference to create some of the following models using NURBS surfaces and lattices to aid in shaping polygons:

Bathroom Sink

Snap a few digital stills of your bathroom sink or find some pictures on the Internet. A sink will give you a great chance to explore NURBS surfacing, making pristine curves and smooth surfaces. It may be a bit involved, but it's not overwhelming.

Cartoon Head

Use Maya Artisan and the Sculpt Geometry tool to turn an ordinary sphere into a cartoonish head. It's fun to use Sculpt Geometry to model. Try to make the head using only Artisan.

Computer Mouse

A PC or Mac mouse makes a great simple NURBS model.

6

Practical Experience!

Learning Outcomes

In this chapter, you will be able to

Use bevels and extrusions efficiently

Manipulate curves to create poly meshes with Revolves and Loft Surfaces

Create a shape with a path extrusion

Use reference images to shape your models

See how to set up views with grid lines to align reference images for modeling

See how images are lined up to make reference images for modeling

Work in the Hypershade to assign image maps to objects in the scene

Use a Boolean operation to cut holes in a mesh

Evaluating the Toy Plane

Download the entire Plane project folder structure from the book's companion web page to your computer's hard drive and set your project to that location.

Figure 6.1 shows a bathtub toy airplane that you'll be modeling first in this chapter. There's certainly enough detail in this object to make it a good exercise, but it won't be difficult to complete. You can always return to this exercise to add more of your own detail or even redesign it for more challenges, which is something I highly recommend.

Study the photos (Figures 6.1–6.3) carefully to get an understanding of the components that make up this object. You will model the parts individually instead of attacking the entire shape as a single object. This way of thinking helps complex objects become easier to understand and model. The plane consists of the body, landing pontoons, engine/propeller, stabilizer wings, and main wings, as shown in Figure 6.1. In Chapter 3's decorative box exercise, you used reference planes to give you an accurate guide to build the box, and you'll do the same with the individual parts of the plane.

Building the Landing Pontoons

Let's start with the landing pontoons. You need to model only one and then make a duplicate and mirror it for the other side. Download the Plane project from the companion website, and make sure to set your project to the Plane project now on your hard drive.

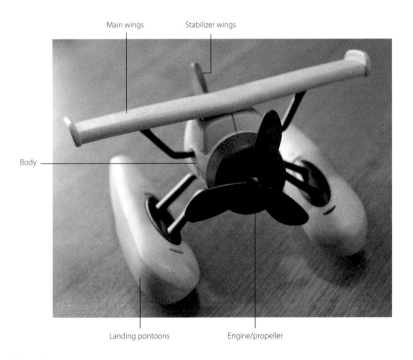

FIGURE 6.1   The toy plane is cute!

DOI: 10.1201/9780429490958-7

FIGURE 6.2   The side photo of the plane.

FIGURE 6.3   The top photo of the plane.

Reference Images

First, you need to assemble the reference planes to make the model easier to build. Figure 6.4 shows the top, side, and front views of a pontoon scaled and lined up in Adobe Photoshop. I copied and pasted the individual photos into a larger image, and then used grid lines to line up the proportions of the pontoon. Keep in mind that when you take a photo, in most cases there will be *perspective shift*, or *parallax*, in the image. Because of that shift, the different views of the same object will never exactly line up. Once each individual photo is scaled and lined up like in Figure 6.4, you can output each image as its own file to bring into Maya for top, side, and front reference.

Now, you'll import the images and create the model reference planes on which to work. As opposed to the reference planes using polygon planes, we made for the Decorative Box exercise in Chapter 3, this time we will be using Free Image Planes to make it much simpler.

Creating Reference Planes for the Images

The reference images of the toy airplane have already been created for you. You can find them in the source images folder of the Plane project on the companion website. They're shown in Table 6.1.

You'll need to create three planes for each of the three views with which to model the pontoons, using the following steps:

1. In a new scene, choose Create ➢ Free Image Plane for the front reference image of the pontoon. This places a green square plane in the scene as shown in Figure 6.5 (top). In the Attribute Editor, click the folder icon next to Image Name and navigate to the source images folder of the Plane project you downloaded. Select the file pontoonFrontReference.jpg

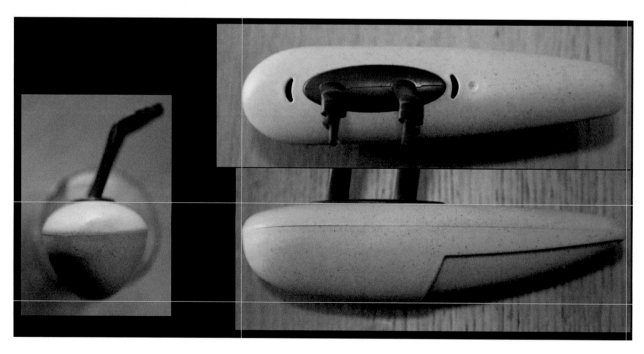

FIGURE 6.4   The reference photos of the pontoon are lined up.

TABLE 6.1

Reference Views and Sizes

Filename	View	Image Size	Aspect Ratio
pontoonTopReference.jpg	Top	1,600×650	1:0.406
pontoonSideReference.jpg	Side	1,600×650	1:0.406
pontoonFrontReference.jpg	Front	1,600×650	1:0.406

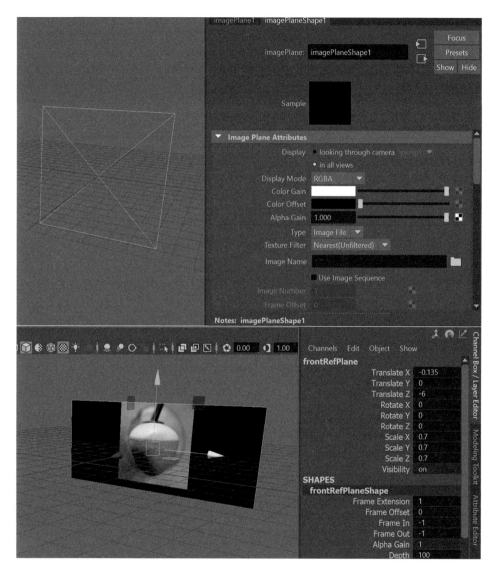

FIGURE 6.5 Creating a Free Image Plane for the front view of the pontoon.

and it appears on the Free Image Plane. Notice that the Free Image Plane adjusted its shape to fit the image of the pontoon automatically.

2. Scale the Free Image Plane to 0.7 units in all three axes and move it back −6 units in Translate Z and −1.35 units in Translate X to place the plane as shown in Figure 6.5 (bottom). Name this plane **frontRefPlane**.

3. Create a second Free Image Plane. Rotate it at 90° in the Y-axis. This will be the side reference view. In the Attribute Editor, click the folder icon for Image Name and select the pontoonSideReference.jpg file in the source images folder of the Plane project.

4. Scale this side view plane to 0.75 in all three axes and name it **sideRefPlane** (Figure 6.6).

5. Create a third Free Image Plane and rotate it to −90° in the X-Axis to lay it flat to the ground plane and then to 90° in the Y-Axis. This will be the top view reference and align it with the side and front reference views. Scale the plane to 0.75 in all three axes.

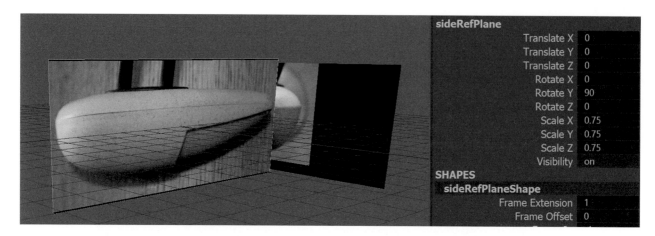

FIGURE 6.6 The side Free Image Planes is placed.

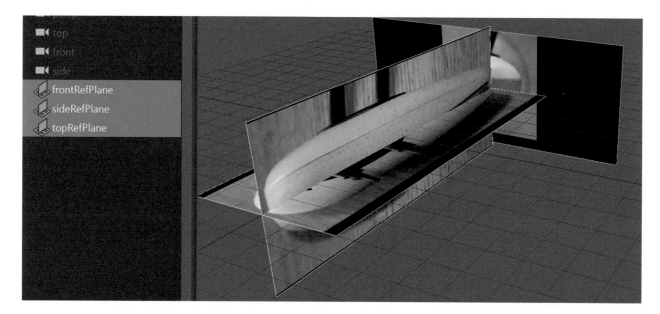

FIGURE 6.7 All three Free Image Planes are placed.

6. In the Attribute Editor, click the folder icon for Image Name and select the `pontoonTopReference.jpg` file in the source images folder of the Plane project. Name this plane **topRefPlane**. Figure 6.7 shows all three planes in place.

Managing the Reference Planes

Now that all three image planes have been created with the proper placements for this model, let's make it easier to manage them.

1. Select all three Free Image Planes and group them together (Ctrl-G). Name the group **pontoonRefPlanesGroup**.

2. Create a display layer for the planes to make it easy to manage them. To do so, select pontoon-RefPlanesGroup and, in the Layer Editor below the Channel Box, click the Create A New Layer And Assign Selected Objects icon ( ) (shown in Figure 6.8).

FIGURE 6.8 The Layer Editor.

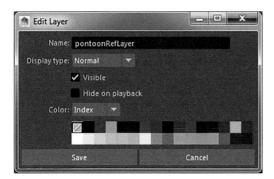

FIGURE 6.9   Name the new layer.

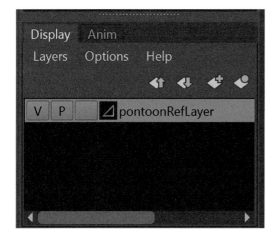

FIGURE 6.10   The new layer in Layer Editor.

3. Double-click the new layer and name it **pontoon-RefLayer** in the window that pops up (see Figure 6.9). Your Layer Editor should resemble the one shown in Figure 6.10. For more on the Layer Editor, see Chapter 3.

To toggle the display of the reference planes to get them out of the way, you can simply toggle the box to the extreme left of the layer name, currently checked with a *V* for "visible" in Figure 6.10. Keep it visible for now.

Save your work. You can download the scene file pontoonModel _ v01.ma from the Scenes folder of the Plane project from the companion website to check your work or skip to this point.

Just be sure to set your project to the Plane project on your hard drive after downloading the entire project from the website. Otherwise, the images for the reference planes may not show up.

To remain in step with this chapter, make sure Interactive Creation is turned off when you create any new primitives.

Blocking Out the Pontoon

The pontoon will start with a poly cube in the following steps:

1. In the Layer Editor, click the empty area to the right of the Visibility toggle box for the pontoonRefLayer layer twice so you see an R appear, as shown in Figure 6.11. This action sets that layer as a reference layer and makes the objects in the layer unselectable in the view panels. If you try clicking any of the three reference planes, nothing will happen, making it easier to model on top of. Clicking it once more will return the layer to normal. Keep it set to R.

2. Create a poly cube. In the top view panel's menu (not the main Maya menu bar), select Shading ➤ X-Ray (Figure 6.12) to allow you to see through the shaded box but not block your reference image. Place and scale the cube over the pontoon; then RMB+click the mesh and select Vertex from the marking menu (to enter vertex mode) to move the corner vertices to roughly match the shape of the pontoon, as shown in Figure 6.13.

3. Switch to the side view panel and enable X-Ray mode (Shading ➤ X-Ray). Move the corner vertices to get a

FIGURE 6.11   Set the reference planes layer to Reference to make it unselectable in the view panels.

FIGURE 6.12   Set your view panel shading display to X-Ray.

FIGURE 6.13 Shape a cube over the body of the pontoon in the top view panel.

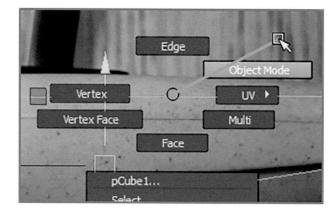

FIGURE 6.15 Select Object Mode in the marking menu.

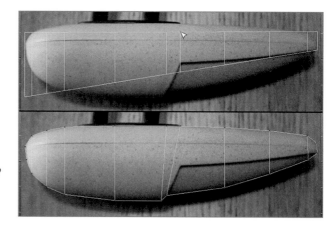

FIGURE 6.16 Insert nine edge loops along the pontoon's side (top) and then move vertices to better match the shape in the side view panel (bottom).

rough shape of the pontoon from the side, as shown in Figure 6.14.

4. Switch to Object mode (RMB+click the cube and select Object Mode from the marking menu, as shown in Figure 6.15). This is the fastest way to switch selection modes.

5. Make sure you are in the Modeling menu set and select the pontoon. Choose Mesh Tools ➢ Insert Edge Loop. Insert nine edge loops along the pontoon, as shown in Figure 6.16 (top).

6. Using the marking menu, RMB+click on the mesh to switch back to vertex selection. While in the side view panel, move the vertices of the new edge loops to better match the shape of the pontoon's side, as shown later in Figure 6.20 (bottom). Don't worry about the dark gray arms that attach the pontoon to the body of the plane; shape your cube only to the yellow pontoon for now.

7. Switch to the top view panel and move the vertices to better match the shape from the top, as shown in Figure 6.17.

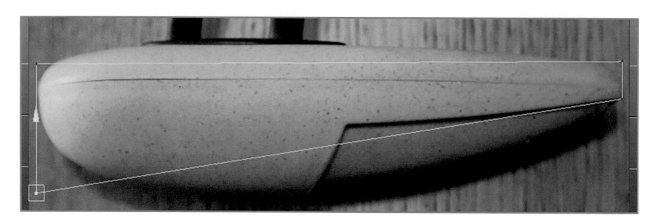

FIGURE 6.14 Shape the pontoon in the side view.

FIGURE 6.17 Move vertices in the top view panel to better match the pontoon's shape.

8. In the side view panel, insert three edge loops (Mesh Tools ➢ Insert Edge Loop), as shown in Figure 6.18. Save your work as the next version to avoid writing over your older work.

Shaping the Pontoon

The scene file `pontoonModel_v02.ma` in the Scenes folder of the Plane project will bring you to this point. Now, let's shape the pontoon some more.

1. In the persp view, rotate your view (a.k.a. tumble) to see the bottom of the pontoon. Make sure X Ray is off so you can see the pontoon as a solid object. In the Layer Editor, toggle the shading mode of the pontoonRefLayer by clicking the R toggle until it displays a *T*. The planes turn to a gray wireframe when selected (as shown in Figure 6.19) and disappear when not selected.

2. Switch to edge selection mode. One by one from front to back, select the bottom row of edges on the pontoon's underside, and scale them in the X-axis *only* to taper the belly of the shape, as shown in Figure 6.20. You can shape it to your liking, without worrying about much accuracy of the photo references. You can refer to Figures 6.2 and 6.3 for a better look at the two pontoons' shape.

3. In the pers view panel, select the vertices one at a time on the section up from the very bottom that you just adjusted in the previous step and shape them slightly to continue the taper of the belly to your liking. Figure 6.21 shows the pontoon so far.

4. Now tumble your view in the persp view panel to see the top of the pontoon. Select the top row of edges and scale them in a little bit to taper the top slightly, as shown in Figure 6.22.

5. The shape of the pontoon can differ from the reference planes a bit; you're trying to get the overall proportion/shape from the photos. You can continue to shape the pontoon to your liking. Once you are happy with it, select the pontoon and press 3 in the persp view panel to see a smooth preview. It looks much more like the actual pontoon when you see it in Smooth Preview (Figure 6.23). Press 1 to exit Smooth Preview for the pontoon. Save your work as a new version number!

Attaching the Arms

The scene file `pontoonModel_v03.ma` in the Scenes folder of the Plane project will bring you to this point.

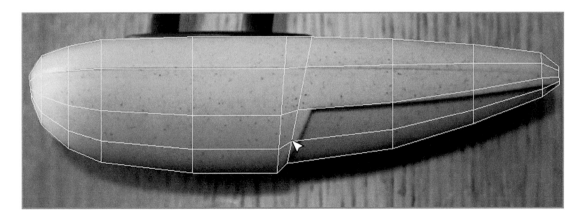

FIGURE 6.18 Insert three edge loops as shown in the side view panel.

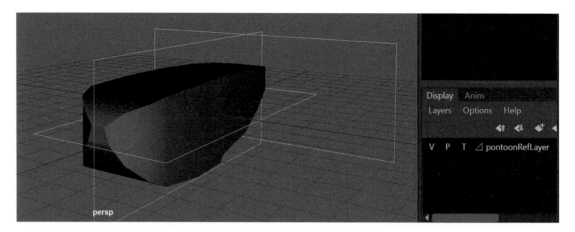

FIGURE 6.19   The reference planes layer in Template mode shows a gray wireframe when the planes are selected.

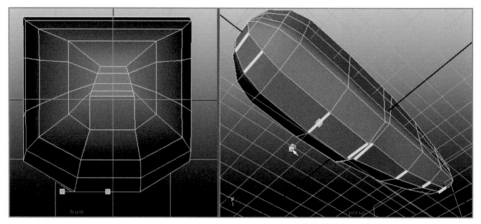

Taper these edges

FIGURE 6.20   Shape the bottom of the pontoon to your fancy by scaling down the bottom row of edges one at a time in the X-axis.

Remember that the reference planes are not visible right now because their Display Layer is set to T for Template. Now let's tackle the gray arms that will eventually attach the pontoon to the plane's body. You'll also start using the Modeling Toolkit in the following steps:

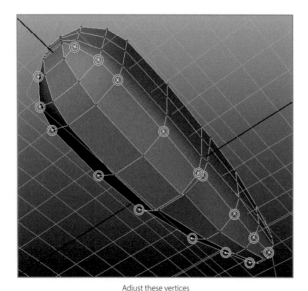

Adjust these vertices

FIGURE 6.21   Keep shaping the pontoon, now by moving the vertices that are one segment higher than the bottom edges you just adjusted.

1. In the top view panel, create a cube. Click the Channel Box/Layer Editor tab on the right of the user interface (UI) to show the Channel Box if it isn't already displayed (see Figure 6.24). With the new cube selected, click the polyCube2 entry (your cube may have a slightly different number, like poly-Cube3 or so), which will show you attributes for the cube's subdivisions. Set Subdivisions Width to **2**, Subdivisions Height to **2**, and Subdivisions Depth to **6**, as shown in Figure 6.24.

2. Turn the display toggle of the pontoonRefLayer back to R to now see the images. Press 4 for wireframe view mode, and move, rotate, and scale the cube to fit the gray base of the attaching arms in the top view panel. Move its vertices to better match the shape, as shown in Figure 6.25. Note that this base shape is purposely not centered on the pontoon. Name the

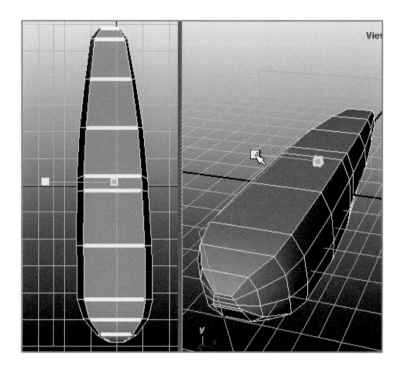

FIGURE 6.22   Taper the top edges to your liking.

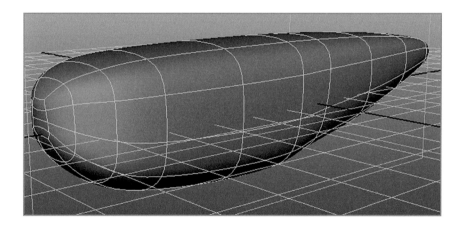

FIGURE 6.23   The base pontoon in Smooth Preview.

cube **pontoonArmBase**. Also, select the body of the pontoon and name it **pontoon**.

3. Press 5 for shaded mode and turn off X-Ray mode if it's on in the persp view panel (Shading ➢ X-Ray). Move the pontoonArmBase cube and scale it down in the Y-axis to have just the top sticking through the pontoon. Adjust the top vertices and/or edges to curve the top to fit the top of the pontoon, as shown in Figure 6.26. Toggle off the view of the reference images in the Layer Editor.

4. Click the Show/Hide Modeling Toolkit icon (   ) in the upper right of the Maya UI, as shown in Figure 6.27 or the Modeling Toolkit tab, to display the

Modeling Toolkit. The right side of the UI now displays the suite of tools in the toolkit, and the Modeling Toolkit tab appears alongside the Channel Box/Layer Editor and Attribute Editor tabs if it didn't before.

5. Click the Edge Selection icon at the top of the toolkit (   ). Select the outside row of edges all the way around the top, as shown in Figure 6.28 (top). Then click the Bevel button in the Modeling Toolkit. Enter a Segments value of **2** and a Fraction value of **0.60**, as shown in Figure 6.28 (bottom).

6. In the top view, turn on the reference image planes through the Layer Editor, press 4 for wireframe mode, and adjust the highlighted vertices to better

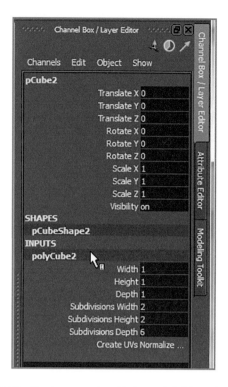

FIGURE 6.24 Create a new cube with these subdivision values.

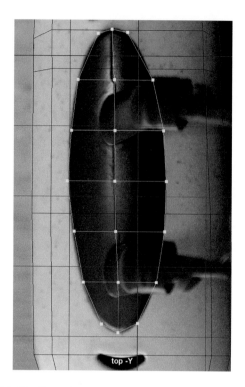

FIGURE 6.25 Shape the cube to fit the base of the attaching arms.

FIGURE 6.26 Scale and position the cube. Adjust the top vertices to better match the pontoon's curvature.

align with the arms coming out of the base, as shown in Figure 6.29 (left). Then in the main menu bar, choose Mesh Tools ➢ Offset Edge Loop and select the middle vertical loop of edges on top of the arm base to place two edge loops on either side, as shown in Figure 6.29 (middle). Press W to exit the tool and enter the Move tool. Select the highlighted vertices and adjust them to fit the base of the arms, as shown in Figure 6.29 (right).

7. In the Modeling Toolkit, click the Face Selection icon ( ). Select the faces shown in Figure 6.30 (top) and Shift+Move the faces to extrude them straight up just a tiny bit as shown in Figure 6.30 (bottom). Keep these faces selected.

8. We are going to set the height of the extrusions manually. With those faces still selected, in the Attribute Editor's polyExtrudeFace1 tab, set the Translate

FIGURE 6.27 Show the Modeling Toolkit, if it's not already shown.

Y value to **3.5** and Divisions to **6**, as shown in Figure 6.31.

9. In the front view panel, select vertices and move them to create an angle to the right for the arm. At the top of the arm, select the top two rows of vertices and move and rotate them to create a bend, as shown in Figure 6.32.

10. Click the Channel Box/Layer Editor tab to switch out of the Modeling Toolkit view, and in the Layer Editor, turn off the visibility of the pontoonRefLayer. Turn off X-Ray view in your views.

11. Select both the pontoon and the arm base and press Ctrl+G to group them. Name the group **left-PontoonGroup**. Press 3 to see the pontoon in Smooth Preview, as shown in Figure 6.33. Save your work. There's just one detail to add at the bottom of the pontoon.

12. With the pontoon selected, press 1 to exit Smooth Preview. Go back into the Modeling Toolkit by clicking its tab. Enter Face Selection ( ) and select the nine faces in the back-bottom part of the pontoon, as shown in Figure 6.34 (top). Click the Extrude button in the Modeling Toolkit and set Divisions to **3**, Thickness to **−0.17**, and Offset to **0.11**, as shown in Figure 6.34 (bottom). Click W to exit the tool. This creates a little indent at the back of the pontoon, and the Divisions value of 3 will keep the edges sharper when you eventually smooth the model.

13. In the Outliner, select the pontoonRefPlanesGroup and delete it. In the Layer Editor, RMB+click the

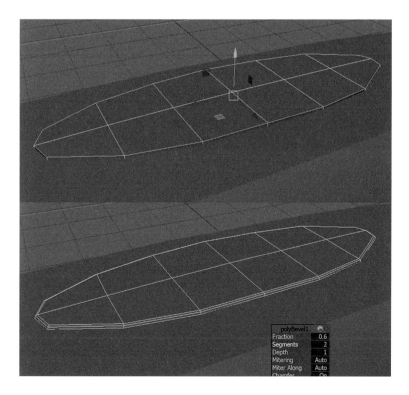

FIGURE 6.28 Select the top outside edges (top) and bevel them.

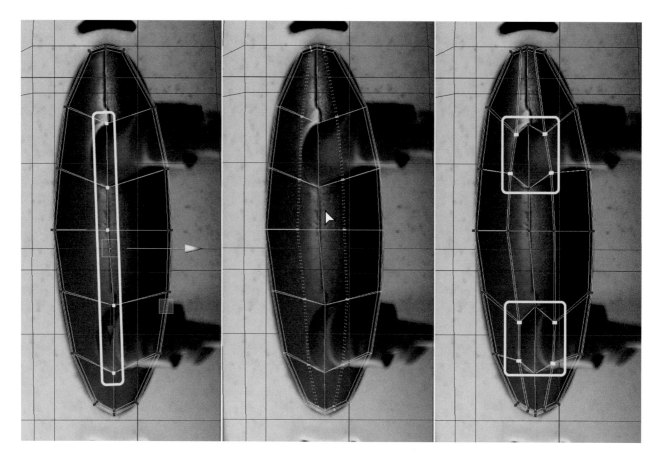

FIGURE 6.29   Line up the vertices to where the arms come out of the base (left) and then use the Offset Edge Loop to place edge loops as shown (middle). Finally, adjust the selected vertices to fit around the arm at the base (right).

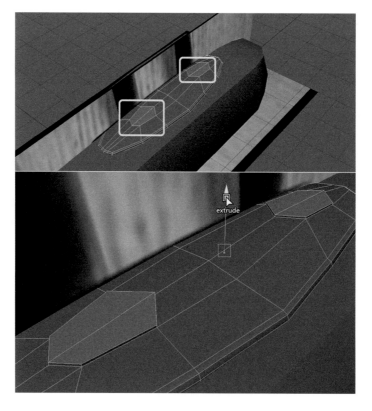

FIGURE 6.30   Select these faces (top) and extrude them a tiny bit with Shift+Move (bottom).

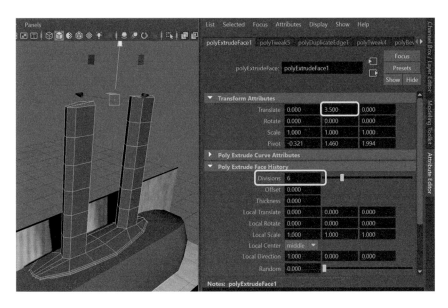

FIGURE 6.31   Set the height and add divisions to the extrusion.

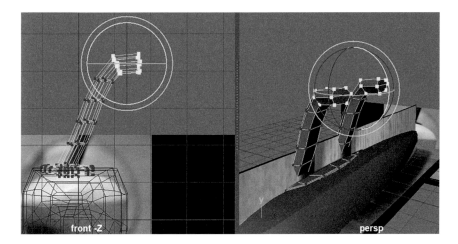

FIGURE 6.32   Create an angle to the arm and a bend at the tip.

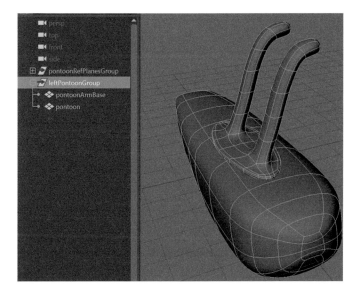

FIGURE 6.33   The left side pontoon is almost done and shown here in a smooth preview.

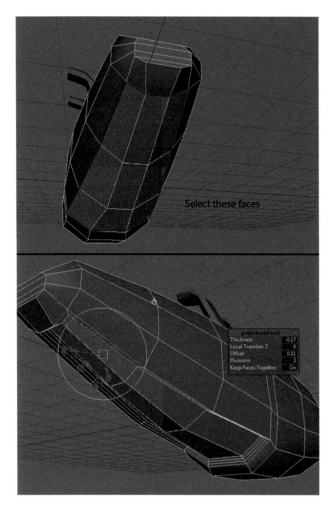

Select these faces

FIGURE 6.34   Select these nine faces (left) and create an inset in the bottom back of the pontoon using Extrude (right).

pontoonRefLayer and select Delete Layer. You are doing this so that when you assemble the final plane, you will not import unwanted reference planes, display layers, or shaders along with the pontoon. It's best to keep a clean workflow!

You're done with the pontoon! Go celebrate with some cookies. Save your work! You will undoubtedly adjust this model later when you attach it to the plane's body, as well as smooth the geometry. You can compare your work to the scene file pontoonModel_v04.ma in the Scenes folder of the Plane project.

Oh, What a Body! Modeling the Body of the Plane

With one of the pontoons finished, you can move on to model the body of the plane in much the same way you modeled the pontoon. If you like a challenge and can use the practice, use the steps at the beginning of this chapter where you created

three Free Image Planes for the pontoon, to now create three new reference view planes for the body of the plane in a new Maya scene. In the Sourceimages folder of the Plane project, you will find bodyBackReference.jpg, bodyBottomReference.jpg, and bodySideReference.jpg to use as the images. They are all sized 1,600×1,200 with an aspect ratio of 1:0.750. Just make sure to line up the Free Image Planes and uniformly scale them as needed. Group them together and make sure the reference planes end up about 14 units in length to better fit the scale of the pontoon you already made.

You can skip creating the reference planes and get right to modeling by loading the scene file bodyModel_v01.ma in the Scenes folder of the Plane project. This file has the reference view planes already set up and ready with the proper grouping and scale. Who loves you?

Blocking Out the Shape

In this section, you'll block out the shape of the body; follow these steps:

1. Create a cube at the origin. This time instead of using X-Ray shading to see through the model to the reference images, you'll force the body geometry to show as wireframe even in Shaded mode. With the cube selected, open the Attribute Editor, click the pCube1 tab, and then click the Display heading. Click the Drawing Overrides heading, check the box Enable Overrides, and then uncheck the Shading box, as shown in Figure 6.35.

   Your cube should display as a wireframe, even though your reference planes display Textured view.

2. Using the top and side views, scale and place the cube over the body of the plane. You want a little overlap between the body and the gray engine at the front of the plane, as shown in Figure 6.36.

3. In the side view panel, insert eight vertical edge loops (Mesh Tools ➤ Insert Edge Loop), as shown in Figure 6.37 (top). Still in the side view, adjust the vertices to shape the cube to the plane, as shown in Figure 6.37 (bottom).

4. In the top view, insert a horizontal edge loop at the widest part of the plane, as shown in Figure 6.38 (left). Then place a vertical edge loop straight up the middle of the plane, as shown in Figure 6.38 (middle). Finally, adjust the vertices to fit the shape of the plane, as shown in Figure 6.38 (right). Name the object **body**.

5. Go into the persp view panel, and with the body selected, press 3 for a smooth preview. As we did in step 1, in the Attribute Editor for the body object, in the body tab, under Display ➤ Drawing Overrides, turn off Enable Overrides to see the mesh in Shaded mode once again. It's looking pretty good.

6. In the side view panel, notice the very back end of the body is too rounded when you compare it to the side of the plane, as in Figure 6.39 (left). Press 1 to exit Smooth Preview, and it lines back up again. The

FIGURE 6.35 Create a drawing override to make the cube display as a wireframe all the time.

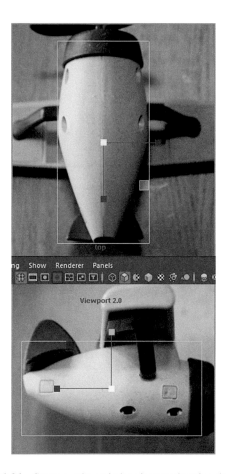

FIGURE 6.36 Create a cube and place it properly using the top and side views.

smoothing rounds that corner too much. To avoid that, you need to add two more edge loops, as shown in Figure 6.39 (middle), to preserve detail when smoothed. Press 3 again, and the back-end lines up nicer in a smooth preview, as shown in Figure 6.39 (right).

7. Turn off the image reference planes' layer (body-RefLayer) in the Layer Editor.

8. Press 1 to exit Smooth Preview. Display the Modeling Toolkit by clicking its tab in the Channel Box area.

   If the Modeling Toolkit tab is not present, you need to click the Show Modeling Toolkit icon ( ) in the upper right of the UI (as previously shown in Figure 6.27).

9. Enable Face Selection by clicking its icon ( ) in the Modeling Toolkit, and select the six faces at the back of the body, as shown in Figure 6.40 (left). Then click the Extrude button and set Divisions to **3**, Thickness to **−0.10**, and Offset to **0.20**. This creates a little inset at the back of the plane similar to the

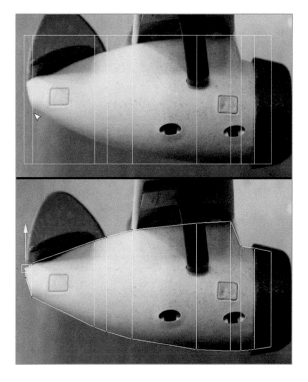

FIGURE 6.37 Insert these edge loops (top) and then adjust the vertices to shape the cube to the plane (bottom).

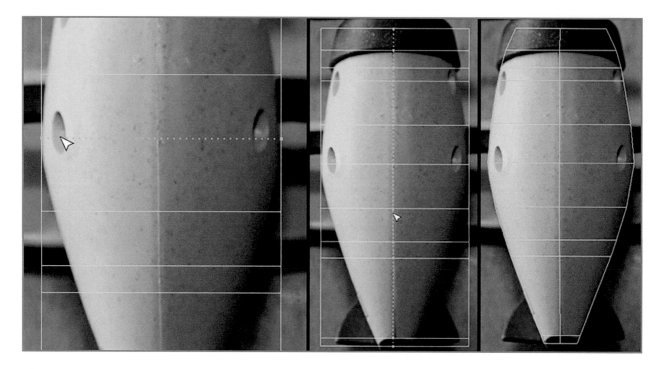

FIGURE 6.38   Place a horizontal edge loop (left) and then a vertical edge loop up the center (middle). Then move vertices to shape the body in the top view (right).

Too rounded here   Insert these edge loops

FIGURE 6.39   The end of the body gets too smooth (left), so add these two edge loops (middle), and when you smooth preview again, the end fits better (right).

toy's back end as seen in Figure 6.40 (right). Click the Extrude button again to exit the tool.

10. With the body selected, press 3 for a smooth preview, and you'll likely notice a little bit of pinching around the inset you just created as in Figure 6.41 (left). Stay in smooth preview. Enter Vertex Selection by clicking the [icon] icon in the Modeling Toolkit and move a pair of vertices, as shown in Figure 6.41 (right), to alleviate the pinching. Repeat for the other side. Press 1 to exit Smooth Preview for the body's model.

Now you're done with the body of the plane. You can check your work against the scene file `bodyModel_v02.ma` in the Scenes folder of the Plane project.

The Rear Stabilizers

You'll create these back stabilizer wings as a new model directly in the body scene. Continue with your file or use `bodyModel_v02.ma` to start modeling the rear stabilizer wings.

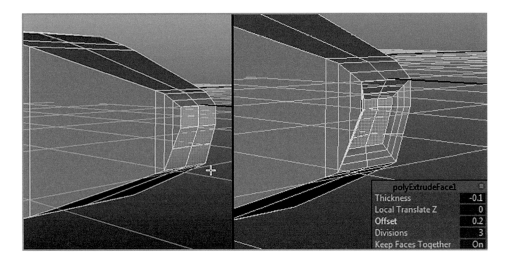

FIGURE 6.40 Select these faces (left) and then extrude them to create an inset (right).

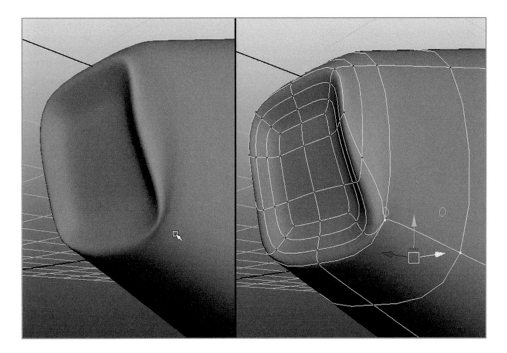

FIGURE 6.41 There is a pinch in the back (left), so adjust a few vertices to fix it (right).

1. Turn visibility on for bodyRefLayer in the Layer Editor (click the toggle to display a *V*). Select the body geometry and turn on Enable Overrides again to make it display as wireframe (found in the Attribute Editor's body tab (as opposed to the bodyShape tab) under Display ➢Drawing Overrides) as you did in step 1 of the previous section, "Blocking Out the Shape."

2. Create a poly cube in the side view panel; using the side and front view panels, move, rotate, and scale the cube to roughly fit the vertical stabilizer wing in the reference photo, as shown in Figure 6.42 (top left and top right).

3. Using the Insert Edge Loop tool, insert five new edge loops vertically, as shown in Figure 6.42 (bottom left), and use the vertices to adjust the shape of the wing, as shown in Figure 6.42 (bottom right).

4. Insert a vertical edge loop, as shown in Figure 6.43 (top left), to align with the side wing that comes out from the vertical wing.

5. Now you need to insert some edge loops to let you extrude the horizontal side wings that come out of the vertical wing to make an upside-down *T* for the stabilizers. If you use the Insert Edge Loop tool, the edge loops will be curved like the arch of the shape so far, as shown in Figure 6.43 (top middle). Instead,

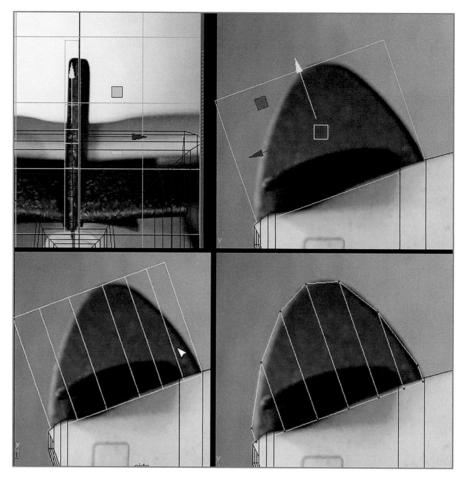

FIGURE 6.42   Create and place a cube for the vertical wing (top). Insert edge loops (bottom left) and adjust the shape (bottom right).

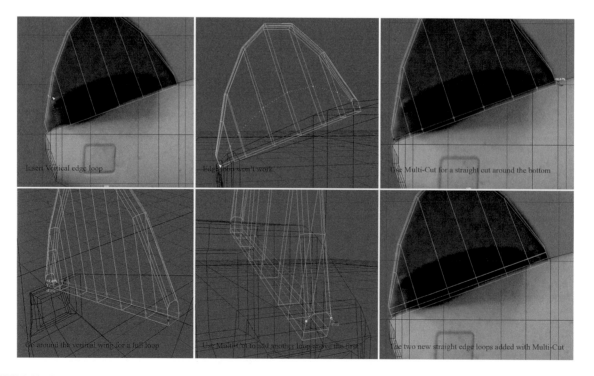

FIGURE 6.43   Insert a vertical edge loop (left) and then use Multi-Cut to insert a pair of horizontal edges that loop around (middle and right).

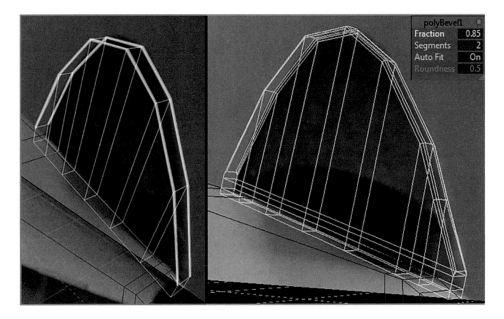

FIGURE 6.44   Select these edges (left) and bevel them (right).

select the vertical wing object, and choose Mesh Tools ➤ Multi-Cut.

In the side view panel, click to place the first vertex of the multi-cut as shown in Figure 6.43 (top right) and then click on the opposite side of the vertical wing to insert edges across the bottom of the vertical wing, again as in Figure 6.43 (top right).

In the perspective panel, swing your view around so you can complete the multi-cut around to the other side of the vertical wing, clicking finally on the original yellow point where we started the multi-cut. The cursor will display the word "close" as shown in Figure 6.43 (lower left).

6. Use the tool again as in step 5 to place a parallel cut a little further up the vertical wing, as shown in Figure 6.43 (lower middle). Figure 6.43 (lower right) shows a side view of both added row of edges inserted with the Multi-Cut tool.

7. In the Modeling Toolkit, enable Edge Selection ( ). In the persp view panel, if you double-click one of the upper edges on the vertical wing's top arch, it will select an entire edge loop on the top arch of the wing shape. Do this twice to select the edge loops on both sides of the arch of the wing, as shown in Figure 6.44 (left).

8. Click the Bevel button in the Modeling Toolkit and set Segments to **2** and Fraction to **0.85**, as shown in Figure 6.44 (right). Press W to exit the tool.

9. In the persp view panel, select the five faces shown at the base of the vertical wing where the side wings are. Make sure to select five on each side of the vertical wing, as shown in Figure 6.45.

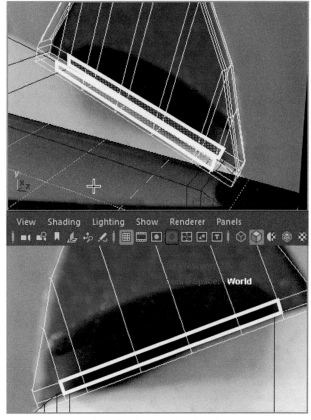

Select five faces on both sides

FIGURE 6.45   Select these five faces on both sides of the vertical wing.

10. In the Modeling Toolkit, click Extrude and set Divisions to **3**, Thickness to **1.5**, and Offset to **0.03** for a slight taper at the end, as shown in Figure 6.46

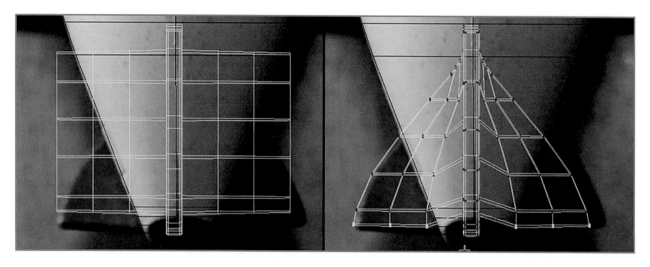

FIGURE 6.46   Extrude the side wings (left) and shape them to create a nice shape, even though it won't line up on one side (right).

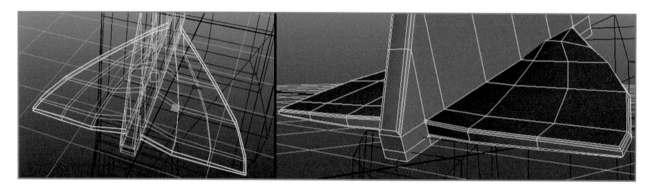

FIGURE 6.47   Select the edges around the side wings (left) and bevel them (right).

(left). Press W for the Move tool and then use the top view to adjust vertices to loosely match the shape of these side wings for the stabilizers, as shown in Figure 6.46 (right). As you can see, the image used for reference is not centered well. But you should keep your geometry symmetrical, even though it won't line up well on the right side of the plane in the image.

11. Turn off the visibility of the bodyRefLayer in the Layer Editor. For the stabilizer wings, uncheck Enable Overrides in the Attribute Editor to show the wings in Shaded mode. Also, in the persp view's panel menu bar, select Shading ➢ Wireframe On Shaded to display the wireframe on top of the shaded models.

12. Select the outer loop of edges around the side wings, as shown in Figure 6.47 (left), and click Bevel in Modeling Toolkit with a Segments value of **2** and a Fraction value of **1.5**, as shown in Figure 6.47 (right).

13. At the front of the vertical wing, select the vertices shown in Figure 6.48 and scale them closer together in the X-axis to taper the front blade of that wing a bit. Select the tail wing object and call it **tail**.

14. Select the plane's body geometry and uncheck Enable Overrides (in the Attribute Editor's body tab under Display ➢ Drawing Overrides) so you can see the entire plane in Shaded mode. Press 3 to see it in a smooth preview. Press 1 to get out of smooth preview of the meshes.

Save your work! You can check your work against the scene file `bodyModel_v03.ma` in the Scenes folder of the Plane project.

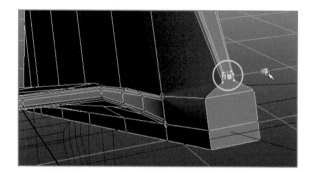

FIGURE 6.48   Select these vertices and squeeze them together in the X-axis.

You Spin Me Right Round—The Engine and Propeller

Now for the propeller! In the same scene as the body, you'll create the engine and propellers at the front of the plane. Begin with your current scene, or use `bodyModel _ v03.ma`. To begin with the engine, follow along here:

1. In the Layer Editor, make sure the bodyRefLayer is visible and the R toggle is off so you can see and select the plane images. You need only the side reference image now, so select the other two image reference planes and press Ctrl+H to hide them. In the Outliner, their entries (bodyBottomRefPlane and bodyBackRefPlane) show up as gray. To unhide them, you would select them in the Outliner and press Shift+H. Leave them hidden for now.

2. Select the body and press 3 for a smooth preview.

3. In the side view, create a CV (control vertex) curve to match the top half profile of the engine, as shown in Figure 6.49. You'll use this curve to revolve a surface.

4. In the persp view, select the profile curve and choose Display ➢ NURBS ➢ CVs to show the CVs of the curve. Click the Snap To Points icon in the status bar

   () at the top of the Maya UI.

5. Press and hold D to engage the Pivot Move tool and move the pivot of the curve to snap to the bottom CV in the middle of the engine, as shown in Figure 6.50. This will ensure a good revolve. Turn off the point snap and then with the curve selected, choose Display ➢ NURBS ➢ CVs to turn off the CVs on the curve.

6. Then, with the curve selected, choose Surfaces ➢ Revolve ☐. Set Axis preset to **Z**, Segments to **8**, Output Geometry to Polygons, and Type to Quads; leave the Tessellation method on Standard Fit. Set the Chord Height ratio to **0.925** and the 3D delta hTto **0.10**. Click Revolve to make the engine fit around the front of the plane, as shown in Figure 6.51.

7. The engine may not be perfectly centered on the plane body, so move it to center it on the body. Then choose Edit ➢ Delete By Type ➢ History to erase the history on that shape. Select the profile curve and delete it. Select the engine geometry you just created and name it **engine**.

Engine Detail

Now for some detail inside the engine.

1. Choose Create ➢ Polygon Primitives ➢ Cylinder ☐ and set Axis Divisions to **16**, Height Divisions to **11**, and Cap Divisions to **1**. Set Axis to Y and leave the rest at the defaults. Click Create and place the cylinder in front of the engine. Scale it to **0.125** in X and Z, and set the Y-axis scale to **0.4**, as shown in Figure 6.52.

First three CVs

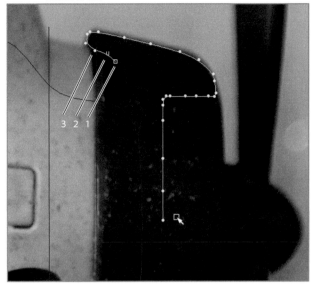

FIGURE 6.49   Draw a profile curve for the shape of the engine.

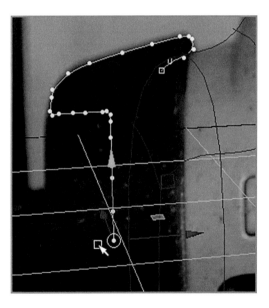

FIGURE 6.50   Snap the pivot to the bottom CV.

2. In the Modeling Toolkit, enter Face Selection; in the side view, select every other ring of faces, as shown in Figure 6.53 (left). Click the Extrude button with a Thickness value of **0.03** and a Divisions value of **1**, as shown in Figure 6.53 (right).

3. Select the cylinder in Object mode, move it back into the engine, and place it as shown in Figure 6.54.

4. Turn on Snap To Points ( ) and press and hold D to move the pivot. Snap the pivot point of the cylinder to the center of the engine, as shown in Figure 6.55.

5. Choose Edit ➢ Duplicate Special ☐. Set Rotate to **36** in the Z-axis and Number Of Copies to **9** and click

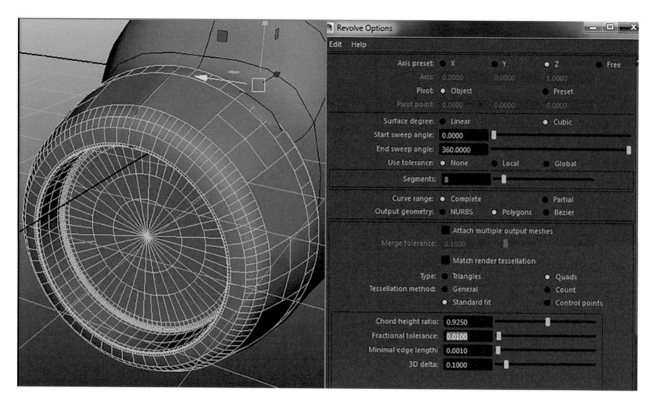

FIGURE 6.51   Revolve the curve to make the engine geometry.

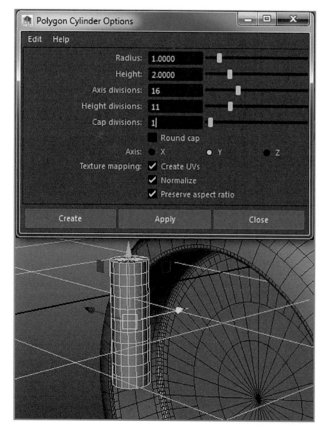

FIGURE 6.52   Create this cylinder and place it in front of the engine.

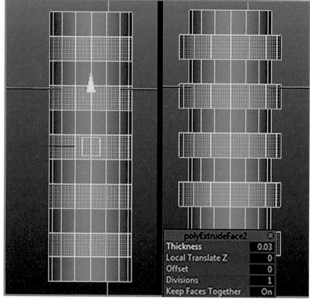

FIGURE 6.53   Select every other ring of faces (left) and extrude them (right).

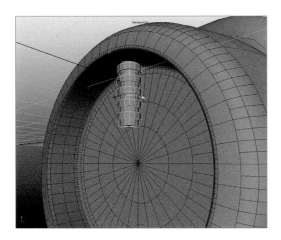

FIGURE 6.54   Place the cylinder into the engine.

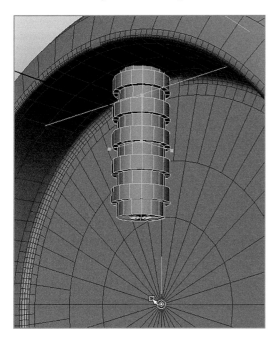

FIGURE 6.55   Snap the pivot to the engine's center.

Apply, as shown in Figure 6.56. This creates a ring of these cylinders inside the engine.

The Propeller Blades

Follow these steps to create the propeller blades:

1. Create a polygon cone. In the Channel Box, click polyCone1 and set Subdivisions Axis to **6** and Subdivisions Height to **3**. Scale the cone to **0.72** in all three axes and rotate and place it against the inside of the engine. Select the sharp tip's vertex and push it back to make the cone blunt, as shown in Figure 6.57.

2. In the Modeling menu set, insert an edge loop toward the middle of the cone, as shown in Figure 6.58. Select every other of the new faces on the cone and click the Extrude button in the Modeling Toolkit. Set Divisions to **1**, Thickness to **3.2**, and Offset to **0** to create the blades of the propeller, as shown in Figure 6.59. Click Extrude to turn off the tool.

3. The blades sure do look weird; they are angled away from the engine. With the three faces at the ends of the blades still selected, move them back in the Y-axis to make them flush with the engine. The blades will go through the engine geometry a little bit, and that's okay for now.

4. On each of the three blades, insert an edge loop about where the blade intersects with the engine geometry, as shown in Figure 6.60 (left), and then scale the new edge loops to be much larger, as in Figure 6.60 (right).

5. If you press 3 for a smooth preview, the propellers look pretty good. Select them and move them out so the blades don't penetrate the engine geometry.

6. Stay in smooth preview for the body (but not the engine; the engine will not need smoothing later) and

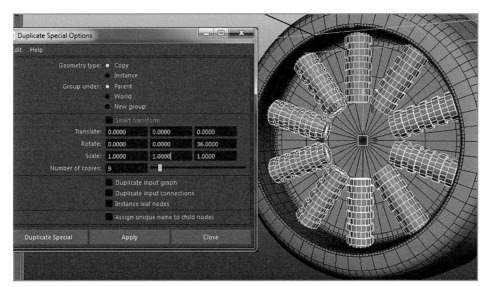

FIGURE 6.56   Create a ring of cylinders inside the engine.

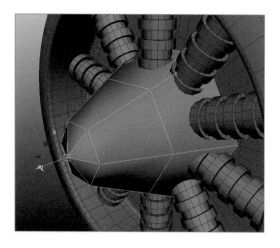

FIGURE 6.57   Place a cone in the engine and shorten the tip to make it blunt.

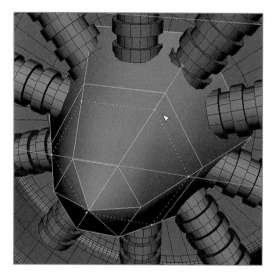

FIGURE 6.58   Insert an edge loop.

work around the body of the plane. Move vertices on the body where it meets the engine to make sure that the body is not penetrating the engine.

Now you're done with the body and need to move to the wings. Save your work and compare it to the scene file body-Model _ v04.ma in the Scenes folder of the Plane project. Note that this file has the plane body and propeller and stabilizer wings already set in smooth preview.

The Plane's Wings

How can you fly without wings? Here you'll create the wings in the existing plane body scene file and get them to attach to the body.

Modeling the Wing

Continue with your own model or use bodyModel_v04.ma to continue.

1. Turn the visibility on for the bodyRefLayer. Then, in the Outliner, select the two hidden gray reference planes grouped under bodyRefPlanesGroup (click the plus sign to reveal them in the Outliner). Press Shift+H to unhide them in your view panels.

2. Select all the parts of the plane you have made so far and press Ctrl+H to hide them.

3. In the persp view, press 6 for Texture mode to see the reference image of the toy plane again. Create a cube and, in the Attribute Editor, in the pCube tab, check Enable Overrides under Display ≻ Drawing Overrides. Turn off Shading as you've done before to make the cube display as a wireframe. Using the

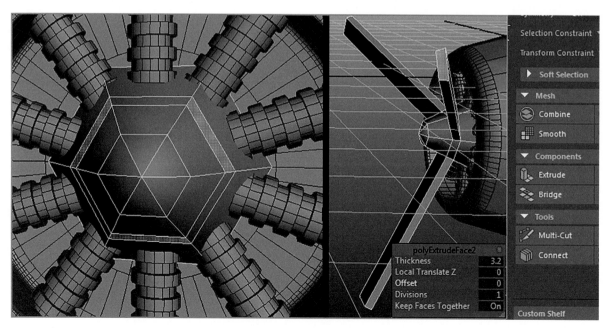

FIGURE 6.59   Select every other face (left) and extrude them to create the propeller blades (right).

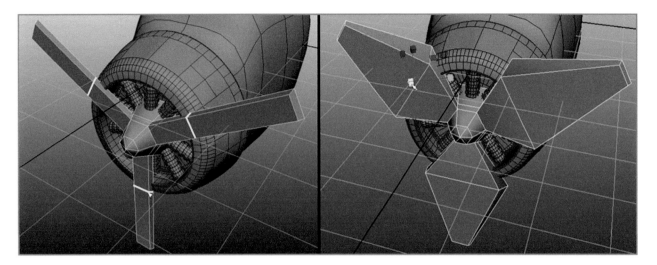

FIGURE 6.60 Insert an edge loop on each of the three blades (left) and then scale the new edge loops to be much bigger (right).

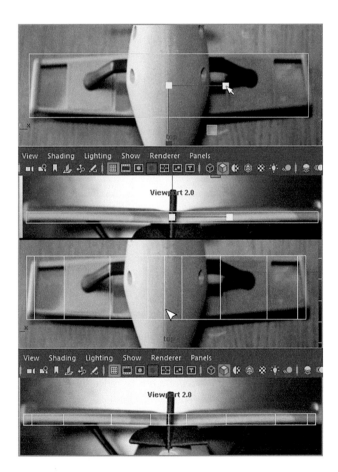

FIGURE 6.61 Create a cube and place it as shown to start the left side of the wing (top). Insert the edge loops as shown (bottom).

top views, size and orient the cube to fit over the wing, as shown in Figure 6.61 (top). Since there is some perspective shift in the photos, the placements will be rough and will not line up in the side view at all, and that's okay. Insert edge loops, as shown in Figure 6.61 (bottom), to create more segments.

4. Now you'll need to shape the wing. This time, let's use a feature called Symmetry. In the top view, RMB+click the body and enter vertex mode. At the top of the Maya UI, click the little arrow to the left of the drop-down menu Symmetry: Off and choose Object X.

As a side note, you can also access Symmetry through Modify ➢ Transformation Tools ➢ Move Tool ❐, or you can double-click the Move tool icon ( ) in the Tool Box.

5. With Symmetry enabled in Object X, any time you select vertices on one side of the wing, the opposite side's vertices in the object's X-axis will be selected as well as shown in Figure 6.62. This way you can shape one side of the wing, and the other side will shape itself to match.

6. Use the top view to shape the left side of the wing, and as you do so, the right side will shape itself.

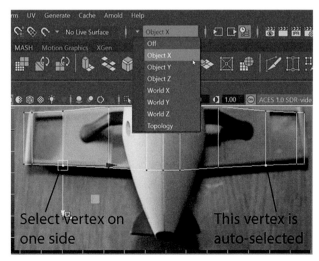

FIGURE 6.62 Using Symmetry lets you shape one side of the wing and reflect that shape to the other side automatically.

Select this face
and extrude

Symmetry
will select
and extrude
this face
automatically

FIGURE 6.63   Shape the vertices on one side, and Symmetry will shape the other side (top). Extrude the top face (middle). Then select and extrude the bottom end face (bottom).

Don't worry if the shape of the wing does not match the image; remember that the image is not perfectly symmetrical. This is okay. Figure 6.62 shows the wing shaped using the Symmetry feature.

7. In the front view and with Symmetry still on, shape the wing on the left to the image, as shown in Figure 6.63 (top).

8. RMB+click the body and choose Faces for face selection mode. At the end of the wing on the left, select the top face at the very end. Symmetry will automatically select the other side's top-end face as well.

9. Then in the Modeling Toolkit, click the Extrude button. Set Divisions to **3**, Thickness to **0.35**, and Offset to **0.05**. Both ends will extrude up, as shown in Figure 6.63 (middle).

10. Select the bottom face at the end of the wing on the left side. Again, in the Modeling Toolkit, click the Extrude button. Set Divisions to **2**, Thickness to **0.15**, and Offset to **0.05**. This will extrude the ends of the wings, as shown in Figure 6.63 (bottom).

11. At the top of the Maya UI (or through the Move Tool options), turn off Symmetry. Turn off the display of the reference image layer (bodyRefLayer). From here on, you'll shape the plane without the reference images. Select the top back edge that runs across the wing, as shown in Figure 6.64 (top), and move the edges down to taper the back of the wing down.

12. Select the wing and in the Attribute Editor uncheck Enable Overrides to show the wing in Shaded mode again. Press 5 for Shaded mode in the persp view. Insert an edge loop two-thirds of the way up the side of the wing, as shown in Figure 6.64 (bottom). This will help retain the shape of the wing when you smooth the mesh later.

13. At the top of the Maya UI, turn on Symmetry in Object X.

14. RMB+click the wing and enter edge selection. Shape the tip of the wing as shown in Figure 6.65. Symmetry will take care of the opposite side. Then add an edge loop as shown. You will have to add an edge loop to the wing tip on the other side; Symmetry will not work with the Insert Edge Loop tool.

15. Make any personal adjustments you'd like and press 3 to smooth preview the wing. Once you're happy with the shape, press 1 to exit Smooth Preview and choose Mesh ➢ Smooth ❑. Make sure the settings are at default in the option box by selecting Edit ➢ Reset Settings and then click Smooth.

16. Orbit your camera to look at the underside of the wing. On the underside of the wing, select the faces, as shown in Figure 6.66. In the Modeling Toolkit, click the Extrude button. Set Divisions to **2**, Thickness to **−0.16**, and Offset to **0.10**, as in Figure 6.66 (bottom). Press W for the Move tool and to exit Extrude.

17. Now select the outer edges of those four new indents in the underside of the wing, as shown in Figure 6.67 (top). In the Modeling Toolkit, bevel them with a Segments value of **2** and a Fraction value of **0.60**, as shown in Figure 6.67 (bottom). Turn off Bevel. Save!

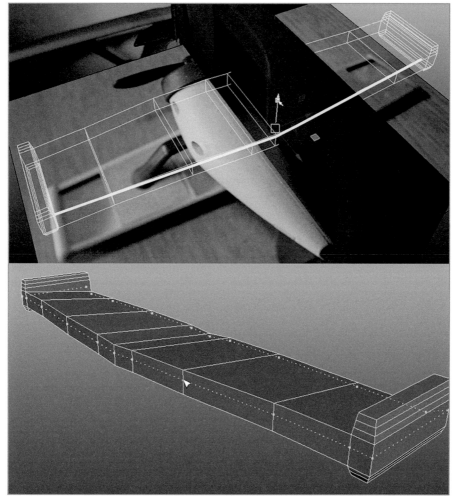

Select the edges on the top back of the wing

FIGURE 6.64 Select the topside back edges of the wing and move them down to taper the wing (top). Insert an edge loop two-thirds up the side of the wing (bottom).

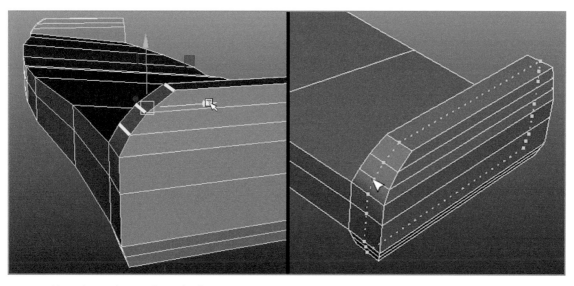

Move these edges to shape the tip

FIGURE 6.65 Shape the tip of the wing to curve it back a bit (left) and then add an edge loop at the wing tip for both sides of the wing (right).

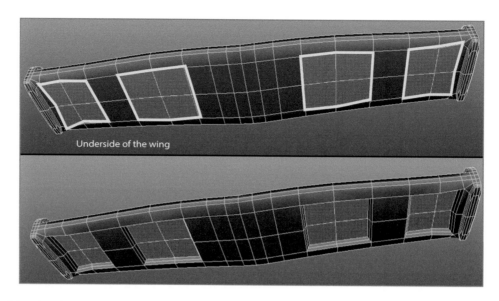

FIGURE 6.66   Select these faces under the wing (top) and extrude to create indents in the wing's underside (bottom).

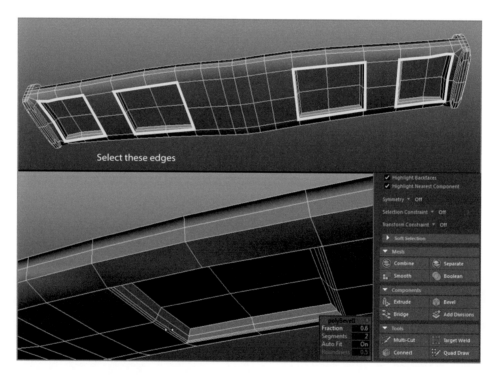

FIGURE 6.67   Select these edges (top) and bevel them (bottom).

Organizing the Scene and Smoothing the Geometry

Now let's take a moment to clean up and organize the scene and smooth the rest of the geometry:

1. Open the Outliner and select all the hidden objects that appear in gray text. Press Shift+H to unhide them. You should now see the plane, back stabilizer wings, and propellers in a smooth preview.

2. In the Outliner, select all the pCylinder objects you created inside the engine and press Ctrl+G to group them. Call the group **insideEngine**.

3. Select the propeller and name it **props**. Select the wing and call it **wings**. Figure 6.68 shows the Outliner with the proper names.

4. Select all the parts of the plane and press 1 to exit Smooth Preview for all the objects.

5. Select the body, propellers, and tail wings, as shown in Figure 6.69 (top left), and choose Mesh ➢ Smooth ❑. Check to make sure you are set to Exponentially for Add Divisions, select Maya Catmull-Clark for Subdivision Type, and set Division Levels to **2**, as shown in Figure 6.69 (right). Click Apply to smooth the plane, as shown in Figure 6.69 (bottom left).

FIGURE 6.68 The Outliner shows the organized scene.

6. Select all the geometry and choose Edit ➤ Delete By Type ➤ History to get rid of all the construction history.

7. Since you don't need the reference images anymore, delete the reference plane's top group (bodyRefPlanes-Group). RMB+click the bodyRefLayer in the Layer Editor and select Delete Layer. And in the Hypershade (Windows ➤ Rendering Editors ➤ Hypershade), click Edit ➤ Delete Unused Nodes. Save!

Adding the Wing Supports

Now you just need to connect the wings to the plane using the following steps:

1. The wings sit a little low and penetrate the top of the plane's body a little bit. Select the wing object and move it up to sit on top of the body. Rotate it a bit in the X-axis to align it with the angle of the top of the plane's body better.

2. Let's smooth the wing a little more. With the wing selected, choose Mesh ➤ Smooth, set Division Levels back to **1**, and click Smooth. Select the smoothed wing and delete the history (Edit ➤ Delete By Type ➤ History).

3. Now let's make the support connecting the wing to the sides of the plane. Maximize the front view (press the spacebar). Choose Create ➤ Curve Tools ➤ CV Curve Tool and create a curve starting at the body of the plane up to the underside of the left side wing, as shown in Figure 6.70.

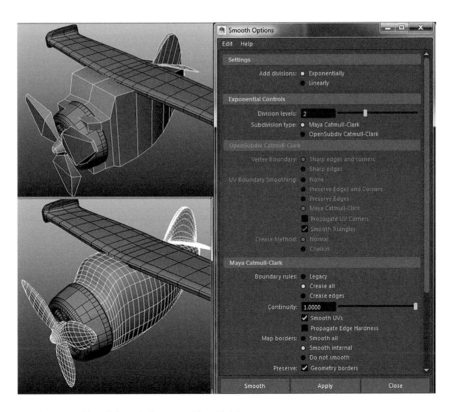

FIGURE 6.69 The plane before smoothing (left) and after smoothing (right).

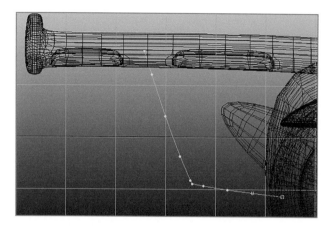

FIGURE 6.70 Create this curve for the wing support.

FIGURE 6.71 Create an oval shape and place it at the start of the curve.

6. In the persp view panel's menu, click Show and check Polygons back on. Stay in wireframe view (press 4).

7. Select the oval and the curve and select Surfaces ➢ Extrude ❐. Set Style to Tube, Result Position to At Path, Output Geometry to Polygons, Type to Quads, and make sure Chord Height Ratio is set to 0.9 as shown in Figure 6.72 and then click Extrude. Press 5 to see it in Shaded mode and assess how you like it. You can adjust the shape or size of the oval as well as the shape of the CV curve line to customize the resulting support shape that connects the wing to the body.

8. If you are happy with the shape of the support, select the original oval and the CV curve and delete them. Select the support arm geometry and name it **supportArm** in the Outliner.

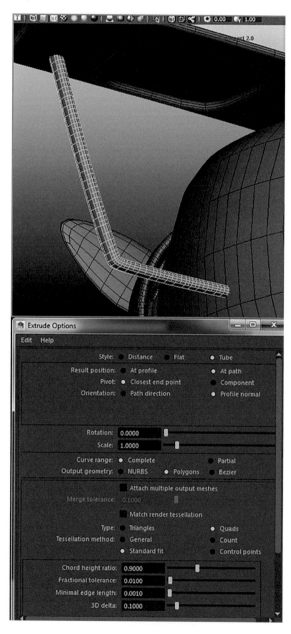

FIGURE 6.72 Extrude to create the support for the wing.

4. In the persp view's menu, select Show and uncheck Polygons to turn off polygon view in the view panel. This shows you the curve you just made by itself. Select the curve and select Display ➢ NURBS ➢ CVs to show the CV points on the curve.

5. Next, create a circle (Create ➢NURBS Primitives ➢ Circle). Scale it to a small oval and place it at the start of the CV curve line you just made, which is just inside the body of the plane. You can use Snap To Points to place the oval exactly at the start of the curve, as shown in Figure 6.71.

9. Now you need another for the other side of the plane. With supportArm selected, press Ctrl+D to duplicate it in place. In the Channel Box, enter an X-Scale value of **−1.0** to create a mirror of the original arm. Since the pivot point of the original supportArm is in the center, scaling it in X-axis to −1 should place it perfectly on the other side of the plane.

10. Move the arms a little toward the back of the plane so the part that meets the wing is centered on the wing, as shown in Figure 6.73.

11. Select both support arms and choose Modify ➢ Freeze Transformations. Name them **wingSupport1** and **wingSupport2**.

12. Select the wing supports and the wing itself, group them together, and call the group **wingGroup**. Move wingGroup a little closer to the front of the plane to line up the wing, as shown in Figure 6.74.

13. Select the insideEngine and wingGroup groups and all the other parts of the plane and group them together. Call the group **planeGroup**.

Save your work and compare it to the scene file `bodyModel_v05.ma` in the Scenes folder of the Plane project.

Assembling the Plane

You have all the parts finished, so let's assemble the plane into a complete scene and make any finishing touches. In your current body model or the `bodyModel_v05.ma` scene, you just need to import the pontoons and you're done.

1. Choose File ➢ Import. In the file dialog, on the right side, make sure Use Namespaces is checked. Navigate to the latest pontoon model you created or to the `pontoonModel_v04.ma` file in the Scenes folder of the Plane project on the website.

2. A single pontoon will appear, unsmoothed, in the middle of the scene. In the Outliner, its name will be something like pontoonModel_v04:leftPontoonGroup. The name before the colon is the filename from which you imported the model. The part of the name on the right is the node name.

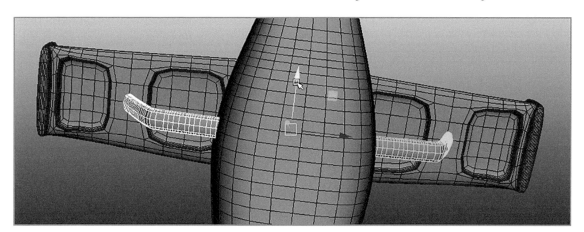

FIGURE 6.73   The support arms in place!

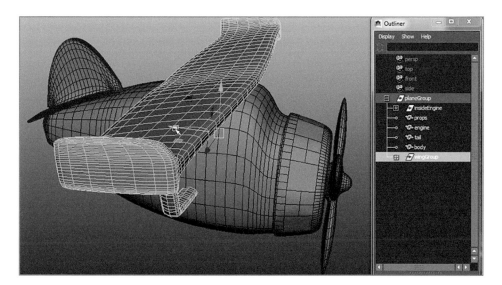

FIGURE 6.74   Place the wing assembly.

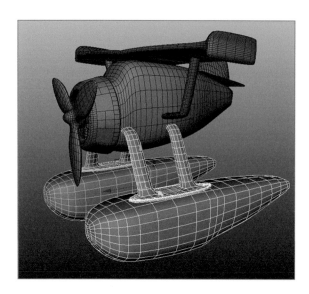

FIGURE 6.75 Place the pontoon, duplicate it, and place the duplicate on the other side.

3. Select the two pieces of geometry that make up the pontoon (not the top group) and choose Mesh ➢ Smooth ❑. Set Division Levels to **1** and click Smooth.

4. Select the top node of the newly smoothed pontoon assembly (pontoonModel_v04:leftPontoonGroup) and rename it to **leftPontoonGroup** in the Outliner. Then move it into place (as shown in Figure 6.75) and orient it properly by rotating it 180° in the Y-axis.

5. Duplicate the pontoon group (leftPontoonGroup) by pressing Ctrl+D and set the copy's X-axis scale to **−1.0**. Call the new group **rightPontoonGroup** and move it to the other side of the plane body. Figure 6.75 shows the proper placement for both pontoons.

6. Select the geometry for both pontoons (not the top nodes) and choose Edit ➢ Delete By Type ➢ History.

7. With the geometry still selected, choose Modify ➢ Freeze Transformations.

8. Using the Outliner, place both pontoon groups into the planeGroup by MMB+dragging them onto the planeGroup node.

9. Now you'll adjust how the pontoons look on the plane. In the Outliner, select the two top nodes of the pontoons. Select Deform ➢ Lattice ❑. Set Divisions to **4, 3, 2** and click Create. This places a single lattice box around both the pontoons.

10. You want to spread the pontoons to make a wider base for the place. RMB+click the lattice itself and choose Lattice Point. Select the eight lattice points shown in Figure 6.76 (left) and move them away from the plane and up closer to the wing, as shown in Figure 6.76 (right).

11. Repeat for the other pontoon's lattice points to make the stance of the pontoons wider and closer to the wing. If your pontoon geometry is different from the one shown or the ones in the sample scene file `pontoonModel_v04.ma`, you may need to adjust your lattice differently. You may also choose to skip this step because it's a minor tweak. The proportions look nicer now!

12. Select the pontoon group nodes (Figure 6.77) and delete their history to get rid of the lattice (Edit ➢ Delete By Type ➢ History).

Figure 6.77 shows the completed plane and its hierarchy. You can check your work against the scene file `bodyModel_v06.ma` in the Scenes folder of the Plane project. In the following chapters, you will add textures and lighting to render the plane as a plastic bathtub toy.

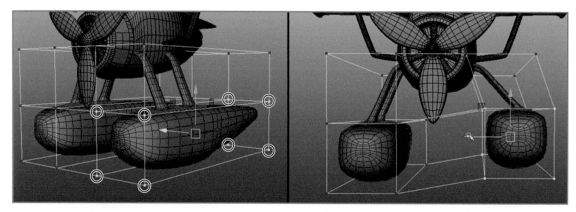

Select these eight lattice points

FIGURE 6.76 Select these eight lattice points and move the pontoon away from the plane body and up closer to the wing (left).

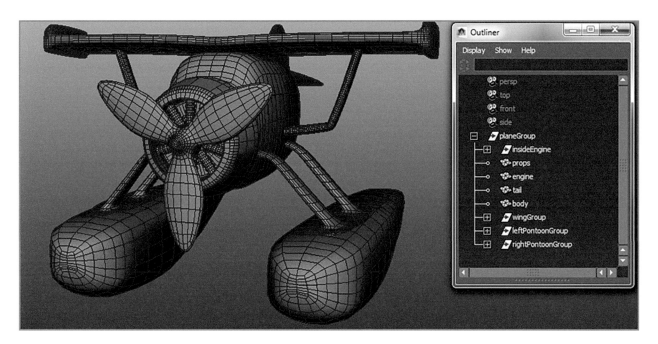

FIGURE 6.77   The pontoons are adjusted, and the plane is ready to fly!

Summary

In this chapter, you flexed your knowledge from the previous chapters and concentrated on creating a model of a toy airplane. You used many of the tools discussed in the previous chapters, from extruding to adding edge loops to using bevels.

Creating a model can be a lot of hard and sometimes tedious work, but when you start seeing it take shape, the excitement begins to build. From the basic shaping of the plane's parts to the details of assembling the plane, you worked hard in this chapter to create the toy plane.

You can take the procedures you used in this chapter to build your own toy design. The important lesson to take away from this chapter is how in depth you can get with a model and how a lengthy modeling process takes shape. Along the way, don't forget to name your pieces and group everything in a sensible fashion.

7

Autodesk® Maya® Shading and Texturing

Learning Outcomes

In this chapter, you will be able to

- Differentiate between different shader types
- Create and edit shader networks in the Hypershade window
- Apply shaders and textures to a model
- Set up UVs on a model for the best texture placement
- Understand the steps to set up texture images to fit a model's UV layout
- Tweak UVs to align texture details
- Use Maya's toon shading to create a cartoon look

Maya Shading

When you create any objects, Maya assigns the same default shader to them called Lambert1, which has a neutral gray color. All objects start their life in Maya attached to this Lambert1 shader. The shader allows your objects to render and display properly. If no shader is attached to a surface, an object can't be seen when rendered. In the Maya viewports, it will appear wireframe all the time, or as flat green, even in the Shaded view.

Shading is the proper term for applying a renderable color, surface bumps, transparency, reflection, shine, or similar attributes to an object in Maya. It's closely related to, but distinct from, *texturing*, which is what you do when you apply a map or other node to an *attribute of a shader* to create some sort of surface detail. For example, adding a scanned photo of a brick wall to the Color attribute of a shader is considered applying texture. Adding another scanned photo of the bumps and contours of the same brick wall to the Bump Mapping attribute is also considered applying a texture. Nevertheless, because textures are often applied to shaders, the entire process of shading is sometimes informally referred to as *texturing*. Applying textures to shaders is also called *texture mapping* or simply *mapping*.

Shaders are based on nodes. Each node holds the attributes that define the shader. You create shader networks of interconnected shading nodes, akin to the hierarchies and groups of models.

As you learn about shading in this chapter, you'll deal at length with the Hypershade window. See Chapter 2, "Jumping into Basic Animation Headfirst," and Chapter 3, "The Autodesk® Maya® Interface," for the layout of this window and for a hands-on introduction. You can access the Hypershade window by choosing Windows ➤ Rendering Editors ➤ Hypershade. Shading in Maya is almost always done hand in hand with lighting.

Maya Native Shader Types

Open the Hypershade window by choosing Windows ➤ Rendering Editors ➤ Hypershade or pressing the Hypershade icon in the Task Bar at the top of the Maya user interface (UI) (![icon]). In the left column of the Hypershade window called Create, you'll see a listing of Maya's native shading nodes (Figure 7.1), split into categories. The first category displays surface nodes, a.k.a. material nodes or shader types. Of these shader types, a few are common to other 3D packages (Lambert, Phong, Blinn, for example).

The way light bounces off an object defines how you see that object. The surface of the object may have pigments that affect the wavelength of light that reflects off it, giving the surface color. Other features of that object's surface also dictate how light is reflected. You can adjust the settings for a shader's look

FIGURE 7.1 The Maya shading nodes and categories.

DOI: 10.1201/9780429490958-8

either through the Hypershade's Property Editor on the right of the window, or through the usual Attribute Editor in the main Maya UI.

Most light, after it hits a surface, *diffuses* across an area of that surface showing off the object's color. It may also reflect a hot spot called a *specular* highlight (basically, a reflection of a light's source). The shaders in Maya differ in how they deal with specular and diffuse parameters according to the specific math that drives them. As you learn about the shader types, think of the things around you and what shader type would best fit them. Some Maya shaders, such as the Hair Tube shader and the Use Background shader, are specific to creating special effects.

With the powerful Arnold renderer being included with Maya, Maya's native shaders will seem out-of-date with the newer shaders that Arnold offers. We will work with Arnold's shaders in a future chapter in this book, but since it's important to learn CG fundamentals first, and the native shaders are still useful, I'll begin by covering Maya's native shading types as an introduction to shaders and how they work.

The Lambert Shader Type

The default shader type is *Lambert*, an evenly diffused shading type found in dull or matte surfaces. A sheet of regular paper, for example, can be a Lambert surface.

A Lambert surface diffuses and scatters light evenly across its surface in all directions, as you can see in Figure 7.2.

The Phong Shader Type

Phong shading brings to a surface's rendering the notions of specular highlight and reflectivity. A Phong surface reflects light with a sharp hot spot, creating a specular highlight that drops off sharply, as shown in Figure 7.3. You'll find that

FIGURE 7.3   A Phong shader.

glossy objects such as plastics, glass, and most metals take well to Phong shading.

The Blinn Shader Type

The *Blinn* shading method brings to the surface a highly accurate specular lighting model that offers superior control over the specular's appearance (see Figure 7.4). A Blinn surface reflects light with a hot spot, creating a specular that diffuses somewhat more gradually than a Phong. The result is a shader that is good for use on shiny surfaces and metallic surfaces.

FIGURE 7.2   A Lambert shader.

FIGURE 7.4   A Blinn shader.

FIGURE 7.5   A Phong E shader.

FIGURE 7.6   An Anisotropic shader.

The Phong E Shader Type

The Phong E shader type expands the Phong shading model to include more control over the specular highlight. A Phong E surface reflects light much like a regular Phong does, but it has more detailed control over the specular settings to adjust the glossiness of the surface (see Figure 7.5). This creates a surface with a specular that drops off more gradually and yet remains sharper than a Blinn. Phong E also has greater color control over the specular than do Phong and Blinn, giving you more options for metallic reflections.

The Anisotropic Shader Type

The Anisotropic shader is good to use on surfaces that are deformed, such as a foil wrapper or warped plastic (see Figure 7.6).

Anisotropic refers to something whose properties differ according to direction. An anisotropic surface reflects light unevenly and creates an irregular-shaped specular highlight that is good for representing surfaces with directional grooves, like CDs. This creates a specular highlight that is uneven across the surface, changing according to the direction you specify on the surface, as opposed to a Blinn or Phong where the specular is circular.

The Layered Shader Type

A *Layered* shader allows the stacking of shaders to create complex shading effects, which is useful for creating objects composed of multiple materials (see Figure 7.7). By using the Layered shader to texture different materials on different parts of the object, you can avoid using excess geometry.

You control Layered shaders by using transparency maps to define which areas show which layers of the shader. You drag

FIGURE 7.7   A Layered shader.

material nodes into the top area of the Attribute Editor and stack them from left to right, with the leftmost shader being the topmost layer assigned to the surface, like a candy shell around a chocolate.

Layered shaders are valuable resources to control compound and complex shaders. They're also perfect for putting labels on objects or adding dirt to aged surfaces.

The Ramp Shader Type

A *ramp texture* is a gradient image map that can be attached to almost any attribute of a shader as a *texture*. Ramps can create transitions between colors and can even be used to control particles. (See Chapter 12, "Autodcsk® Maya® Dynamics and Effects.") When used as a texture, a ramp can be connected to any attribute of a shader to create graduating color scales, transparency effects, increasing glow effects, and so on.

Now a *Ramp shader* (as opposed to the ramp texture discussed earlier) is a self-contained shader node that automatically has several ramp textures (a.k.a. gradients) already attached to several attributes. This makes for a simplified editing environment for the shader because all the colors and handles are accessible through the Ramp shader's Property Editor in the Hypershade window, as shown in Figure 7.8. The Attribute Editor in the main UI will display much the same information, slightly differently than the Property Editor.

Once you start using Ramp Shaders, to create a new color in any of the horizontal ramps, click in the swatch to create a new ramp position. Edit its color through its Selected Color swatch.

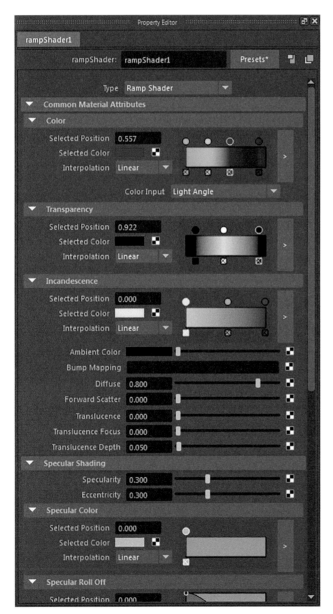

FIGURE 7.8 A Ramp shader in the Property Editor.

You can move the position by grabbing the circle right above the ramp and dragging left or right. To delete a color, click the box beneath it.

These ramp textures are automatically attached to the Color, Transparency, Incandescence, Specular Color, Reflectivity, and Environment attributes of a Ramp shader. In addition, a special curve ramp is attached to the Specular Roll Off attribute to give you more precise control over how the specular highlight diminishes over the surface.

Bifrost Materials

You can see three icons marked Bifrost Materials in the Create panel, toward the top. Bifrost is a liquid simulation engine in Maya that typically uses its own materials. Since I do not cover the advanced workflow behind Bifrost in this book, I will leave these materials out of this book.

Shaderfx and Stingray PBS Shader Types

These shaders sit at the top of the Create panel in the Hypershade. Shaderfx is an editing tool for creating shader networks for game engines. Stingray is Autodesk's own game engine. Because these are advanced shaders specific to games, their functions will not be covered in this introductory book. However, in short, they will allow you to create materials and looks for your game assets in Maya and let you import those looks directly into the appropriate game engine without needing to re-create the materials in the engine itself.

Shader Attributes

Shaders are composed of nodes just like other Maya objects. Within these nodes, attributes define what shaders do. Here is a brief rundown of the common shader attributes with which you'll be working. In the Hypershade, click on Lambert 1 and follow along in the main Maya window's Attribute Editor (the Hypershade's Property Editor is fine to use, but may display the following attributes in a different order):

Color
    An RGB (red, green, blue) or hue, saturation, and value (HSV) value defines what color the shader is when it receives a neutral color light. For more on RGB and HSV, see the "RGB and HSV" sidebar in this chapter.

RGB AND HSV

Computers represent color as sets of numeric values corresponding to the red, green, and blue channels of the image. An 8-bit image ranges from 0 to 255, so for each primary color, you have 256 possible levels. With three channels, you have 256×256×256 (16.7 million) possible combinations of each primary color mixed to form the final color. Each RGB channel defines how much of that color is present in the displayed color.

Color value can also be set on the HSV channels. The hue value defines the actual tint (from red to green to violet) of the color. The saturation defines *how much* of that tint is present in the color. Finally, value defines the brightness of the color, from black to white. The higher the value, the brighter the color will be.

Transparency

The higher the Transparency value, the less opaque and more see-through the object becomes. Although usually expressed in a black-to-white gradient, with black being opaque or solid and white being totally clear, transparency can have color. In a color transparency, the shader's color shifts because only some of its RGB values are transparent, as opposed to the whole.

Ambient Color

This color affects the overall color attribute of a shader because this adds a flat ambient color irrespective of lighting in the scene. The default is black, which keeps the darker areas of a surface dark. The lighter the ambient color, the lighter those areas become. A bright Ambient Color setting flattens out an object, as shown in Figure 7.9.

Incandescence

This attribute is the ability to self-illuminate. Objects that seem to give off or have their own

light, such as an office's fluorescent light fixture, can be given an Incandescence value. Incandescence doesn't, however, light objects around it in regular renders, nor does it create a glow. Also, incandescence tends to flatten the object into more of a solid color (see Figure 7.10).

Bump Mapping

This attribute creates a textured feel for the surface by adding highlights and shadows to the render to make the surface appear bumpy or physically textured. It doesn't alter the surface of the geometry, although it makes the surface appear to have ridges, marks, scratches, and so forth. The more intense the variation in tones of a bump map, the greater the bump. Bump maps are frequently used to make surfaces look more real because nothing in reality has a perfectly smooth surface. Using bumps very close-up may create problems; bumps are generally good for adding inexpensive detail to a model that isn't in extreme close-up (see Figure 7.11).

Bump maps on geometry don't work well when seen up close. Those cases require displacement maps. I'll cover displacement maps in Chapter 11.

Diffuse

This value governs how much light is reflected from the surface in all directions. When light strikes a surface, light disperses across the surface and helps illuminate it. The higher this value, the brighter its object is when lit. The lower the Diffuse value, the

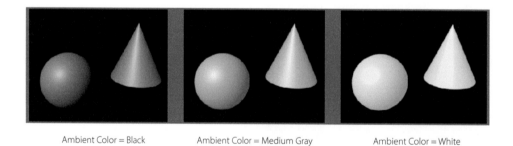

Ambient Color = Black   Ambient Color = Medium Gray   Ambient Color = White

FIGURE 7.9　Ambient color values flatten an object.

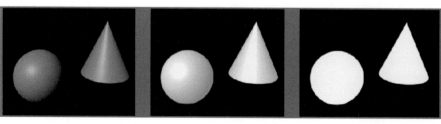

Incandescence = 0   Incandescence = 0.5   Incandescence = 1

FIGURE 7.10　Incandescence values.

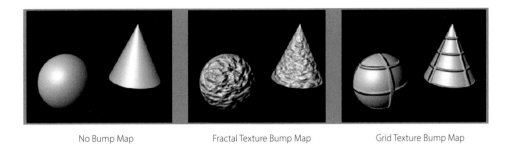

No Bump Map   Fractal Texture Bump Map   Grid Texture Bump Map

FIGURE 7.11   The effects of a bump map.

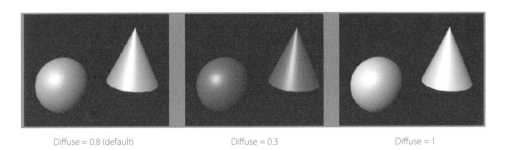

Diffuse = 0.8 (default)   Diffuse = 0.3   Diffuse = 1

FIGURE 7.12   How a Diffuse value affects a shader's look.

more light is "absorbed" into the surface, yielding a darker result (see Figure 7.12).

Translucence and Translucence Focus

The Translucence and Translucence Focus attributes give the material the ability to transmit light through its surface, like a piece of canvas in front of a light. At a value of 1 for Translucence, all light shines through the object; at 0, none does. The Translucence Focus attribute specifies how much of that light is scattered. A light material such as paper should have a high translucence focus, and thicker surfaces should have low focus rates.

Glow Intensity

Found in the Special Effects section of the Attribute Editor, the Glow Intensity attribute adds a glow to the object, as if it were emitting light into a foggy area (see Figure 7.13). However, especially with advanced renderers like Arnold, making an object glow is typically done in an image editor on the image after rendering, as opposed to inside of Maya itself.

Matte Opacity

Objects rendered through Maya generate a solid *matte*. Where there is a solid object, the matte is white; where there is nothing, the matte is black. In compositing programs, which bring together elements created independently into a single composite scene, mattes (also known as the alpha channel) help to separate rendered CG from their backgrounds. Turning down the slider decreases the brightness of the object's matte, making it appear more transparent. For more information about mattes, see the sidebar "Image Mattes" in this chapter, and see Chapter 11.

Raytrace Options

With raytracing, you can achieve true reflections and refractions in your scene even with Maya's older, native shaders. This subset of attributes allows you to set the shader's raytracing abilities. See Chapter 11 for more on raytracing.

Some attributes are available only with certain shader types. The following are the attributes for the Phong, Phong E, and Blinn shaders because they can be shiny and reflective:

Glow = 0   Glow = 0.5   Glow = 1

FIGURE 7.13   Adding a simple glow.

Specular Color

    This sets the color of the highlights on a shiny surface. Black produces no specular, and white creates a bright one.

Reflectivity

    This sets the amount of reflection visible in the surface. The higher the value, the more reflective the object will render. Increasing this value increases the visibility of the Reflected Color attribute or of true reflections in the scene when raytraced.

Reflected Color

    This gives the surface a reflection. Texture maps can be assigned to this attribute to give the object a fake reflection of whatever is in the image file or texture without a raytraced render. Using raytracing to get true reflections, however, is the only way to generate reflections of other objects in the scene, and is the basis for most contemporary renderers such as Arnold.

Cosine Power

    Available only with a Phong shader, this attribute changes the size of the shiny highlights (a.k.a. specular) on the surface. The higher the number, the smaller the highlight looks.

IMAGE MATTES

Image files are stored with a red, a green, and a blue channel that keep the amount of each color in each pixel of the image. Some image formats, including Tag Image File Format (TIFF) and Portable Network Graphics (PNG), can also have an alpha channel, known as a *matte channel* or *image matte*. This is a grayscale channel that controls the opacity of an image. Completely white parts of the matte make those parts of the image opaque (solid), whereas black parts make those parts of the image fully transparent. Gray in the matte channel makes those parts of the image partly transparent. These mattes are used in *compositing*—bringing together elements created separately into a single composite scene. See Chapter 11 for an example of how an alpha channel works.

Roughness, Highlight Size, Whiteness

    These control the specular highlight on a Phong E surface only. They control specular focus, amount of specular, and highlight color, respectively.

Shading and Texturing the Toy Plane

In the following section, you'll add some of Maya's native shaders to the toy plane from Chapter 6, "Practical Experience!" The plane is fairly straightforward to shade. Use `body-Model _ v06.ma` from the plane project from the companion website. You have just two colors on the body of the plane. You'll start by making shaders in the Hypershade.

1. With either your scene file or `bodyModel _ v06.ma` loaded, open the Hypershade (Windows ➢ Rendering Editors ➢ Hypershade). You need to re-create a plastic look for the toy plane. Create two Blinn shaders by clicking Blinn in the Create column in the Hypershade twice, as shown in Figure 7.14. Name the first shader **gray** and the second shader **yellow**.

    The toy plane is yellow and gray, but it has some flakes of dark gray in both colors. Figure 7.15 is a close-up photo of a yellow pontoon to showcase the dark "noise" in the plastic color. You will mimic that with a texture node called Noise.

2. On the left side of the Create Panel in the Hypershade under Favorites, click 2D Textures to display the 2D (two dimensional) texture nodes. Then click Noise to create a new noise texture, and a noise1 node appears in the Hypershade's work area (Figure 7.16 right). Click the Textures tab at the top of the Hypershade

FIGURE 7.14 Create two Blinn shaders.

FIGURE 7.15 A close-up of a yellow pontoon shows flakes of dark gray in the plastic color.

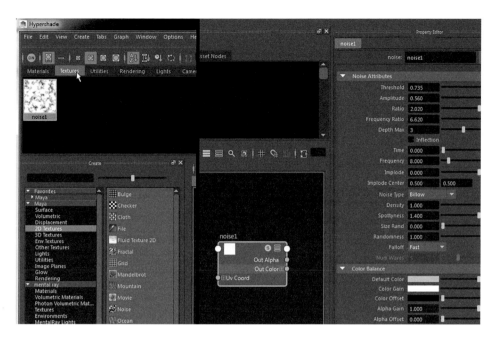

FIGURE 7.16 Click to create a new noise texture node and find it in the Textures tab (left). The noise1 icon in the Work Area of the Hypershade next to the Property Editor showing its attributes (right).

to display the noise texture there as well, as shown in Figure 7.16 (left). If you do not see the noise1 texture node in the work area of, then MMB+drag the noise1 icon from the top of the Hypershade to the work area in the lower right of the Hypershade. Having the icon in the work area (as shown in Figure 7.16, right) allows you to make shader connections easier. More on this later.

3. It doesn't look like much now, but you will adjust the attributes on this noise texture to simulate the dark flakes in the plastic. With the noise texture node still selected, in the Property Editor (or the Attribute Editor, if you prefer) set the attribute values, as shown in Table 7.1, leaving the remaining attributes at their default values.

Now, in the Color Balance heading, click the white color swatch next to the Color Gain attribute and set that color to a mustard yellow using the HSV values of **46.0**, **0.756**, **0.472**, as shown in Figure 7.17. Click in the top of the Hypershade's Property Editor and rename the node from noise1 to **noiseYellow**. This color will give you the yellow you need for that plastic.

4. Next, you'll duplicate the yellow noise node to make a blue-gray version for the gray plastic parts of the plane. In the Hypershade, select noiseYellow and choose Edit ➢ Duplicate ➢ Shading Network. Name the duplicate texture node **noiseGray**. The duplicated texture will appear on the Textures tab at the top of the Hypershade. If you don't see it there already, MMB+drag the noiseGray texture node down to the Work Area next to the yellow one you've already created.

TABLE 7.1

Noise Texture Values

Attribute	Value
Threshold	0.735
Amplitude	0.56
Ratio	2.02
Frequency ratio	6.62
Spottyness	1.4

FIGURE 7.17 Setting the noise texture values.

5. In the Color Balance heading for the noiseGray node, set the Color Gain HSV values to **231**, **0.56**, **0.20** to change it from mustard yellow to blue-gray for this texture node.

6. Switch to the Materials tab and select the gray shader in the Hypershade to display it in the Property Editor. MMB+drag the grayNoise node from the Work Area to the Color attribute of the gray shader in the Attribute Editor, as shown in Figure 7.18. This will set the gray noise texture you just made to be the color of the gray plastic material.

7. Select the yellow Blinn shader and then MMB+drag the noiseYellow node from the Work Area to the Color attribute. This connects the yellow color to the yellow Blinn shader.

8. Now let's assign the shaders to the parts of the plane. In the persp viewport, select the wings, body, and two pontoons and assign the yellow Blinn shader to them by RMB+clicking and holding the mouse button in the Hypershade and selecting Assign Material To Selection, as shown in Figure 7.19.

9. Select the remaining parts of the plane and assign the gray Blinn shader to them, as shown in Figure 7.20.

Now let's see what it looks like! First let's make sure we are in Maya's native renderer and not Arnold, as is the default in Maya, especially if you started this project with your own blank scene as opposed to loading a scene file provided you. Click the Render Settings icon in the Status line as shown below.

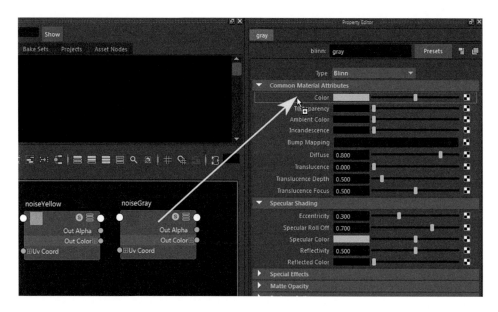

FIGURE 7.18   MMB+drag the gray noise texture to the Color attribute of the gray Blinn shader.

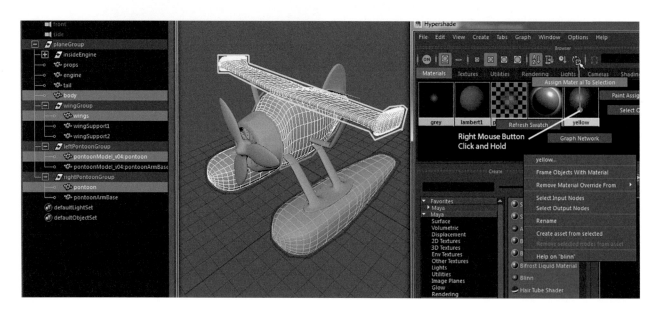

FIGURE 7.19   Select these parts of the plane and assign the yellow Blinn to them.

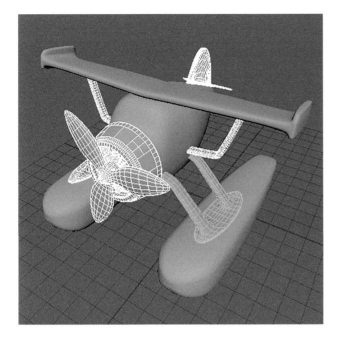

FIGURE 7.20 Select the remaining parts of the plane and assign the gray Blinn shader to them.

Maya will use default lights and render an image (Figure 7.21) with the basic shaders you just created using the basic native renderer. Not bad. Feel free to adjust the colors or the attributes of the noise textures to your liking. Once you start lighting the scene in Chapter 10, you will adjust the shaders to make the toy plane look like better plastic using Arnold rendering. For now, you're done! You can check your work against the scene file `planeShading _ v01.ma` in the Scenes folder of the Plane project.

You can embellish a model a lot at the texturing level. The more you explore and experience shaders and modeling, the better you'll be at juggling modeling with texturing to get the most effective solution. For example, you can use more elaborate noise patterns to mimic the flakes in the plane's plastic, as opposed to using the simple pattern you created with a noise texture. That is a more involved workflow, which you will tackle later in this chapter with UVs and texture maps.

You'll begin UV layout and texturing a toy red wagon later in this chapter and then go into more detailed texturing with the decorative box, which you'll then light and render in mental ray. For even more practice, try loading the catapult model from Chapter 4, "Beginning Polygonal Modeling," and texturing it from top to bottom.

At the top of the Render Settings window, click the Render Using drop-down menu and select Maya Software as shown below. The scenes provided in this book are already set to Maya Software rendering.

In the persp viewport, render a view of your plane by clicking the Render Current frame icon on the Status line (🎞️). Since you haven't created any lights in the scene,

Textures and Surfaces

Texture nodes generate maps to connect to an attribute of a shader. There are two types of textures: procedural and bit-mapped (sometimes called maps). *Procedural* textures use Maya attributes to generate an effect, such as a ramp gradient, checkerboard, or fractal noise texture. You can adjust each of these procedural textures by changing their attribute values.

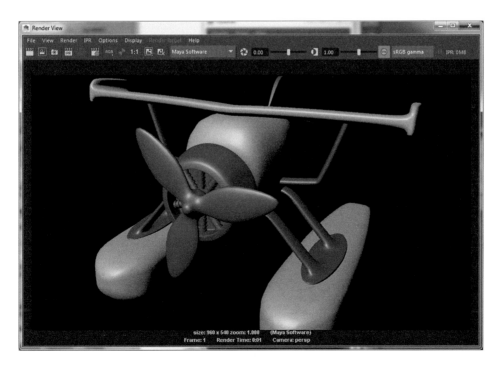

FIGURE 7.21 The plane renders with yellow and gray Blinn shaders to look a little like plastic.

A *map*, on the other hand, is a saved image file that is imported into the scene through a file texture node. These files are pregenerated through whatever imaging programs you have and include digital pictures and scanned photos. You need to place all texture nodes onto their surfaces through the shader. You can map them directly onto the UV values of the surface or project them.

UV Mapping

UV mapping places the texture directly on the surface and uses the surface coordinates (called UVs) for its positioning. In this case, you must do some work to set up the UVs on the surface to make sure the created images line up properly. What follows is a brief summary of how UV mapping works. You'll get hands-on experience with UV layout with the red wagon and decorative box exercises later in this chapter.

Just as 3D space is based on coordinates in XYZ, surfaces have coordinates denoted by U and V values along a 2D coordinate system for width and height. The UV value helps a texture position itself on the surface. The U and V values range from 0 to 1, with (0,0) UV being the origin point of the surface.

Maya creates UVs for primitive surfaces automatically, but frequently you need to edit UVs for proper texture placement, particularly on polygonal meshes after you've edited them. In some instances, placing textures on a poly mesh requires projecting the textures onto the mesh because the poly UVs may not line up as expected after the mesh has been edited. See the next section, "Using Projections."

If the placement of your texture or image isn't quite right, simply use the 2D placement node of the texture node to position it properly. See the section "Texture Nodes" later in this chapter for more information.

Using Projections

UV placement is by far the preferred way of placing textures on a surface, but sometimes textures need to be projected onto the surface, disregarding UVs entirely. A *projection* is what it sounds like. The file image, ramp, or other texture being used can be *beamed* onto the object in several ways.

You can create any texture node as either a normal UV map or as a projected texture. In the Create Render Node window, simply clicking a texture icon creates it as a normal mapped texture. To create the texture as a projection, however, you must RMB+click the icon and select Create As Projection (see Figure 7.22).

When you create a projected texture, a new node is attached to the texture node. This projection node controls the method of projection with an attached 3D placement node. Select the projection node to set the type of projection in the Hypershade's Property Editor or the Attribute Editor (see Figure 7.23).

Setting the projection type will allow you to project an image or a texture without having it warp and distort, depending on the model you're mapping. For example, a planar projection on a sphere will warp the edges of the image as they stretch into infinity on the sides of the sphere.

FIGURE 7.22 Selecting the type of map layout.

Try This

In a new scene, create a NURBS sphere and a NURBS cone and place them side-by-side. Create a Blinn shader and assign it to both objects. In the Blinn shader's Attribute Editor, set its Color attribute to a checkerboard pattern, as shown in Figure 7.24.

Now, try removing the color map from the Blinn shader you just made. In the Blinn shader's Attribute Editor, RMB+click on the word *Color*; then choose Break Connection from the context menu. Doing so severs the connection to the checker texture map node and resets the color to gray. Now, re-create a new checker texture map for the color, but this time create it as a projection by RMB+clicking the Checker texture icon in the Create Render Node window. In the illustration on the left in Figure 7.25, you see the perspective view in Texture mode (press the 6 key) with the two objects and the planar projection placement node.

Try moving the planar placement object around in the scene to see how the texture maps itself to the objects. The illustration on the right of Figure 7.25 shows the rendered objects.

Try the other projection types to see how they affect the texture being mapped.

Projection placement nodes control how the projection maps its image or texture onto the surface. Using a sphere with a spherical projected checker, with U and V wrap turned off on the checkerboard texture, you can see how manipulating the place3dTexture node affects the texture.

FIGURE 7.23 The projection node in the Hypershade's Property Editor (left) as well as the Attribute Editor (right).

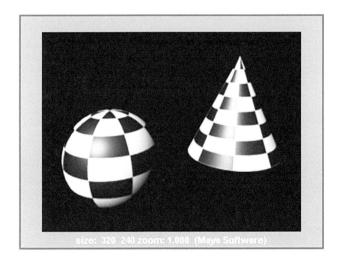

FIGURE 7.24 Assign a checkerboard pattern to the sphere and cone with Normal checked.

In addition to the Move, Rotate, and Scale tools, you can use the special manipulator (press T to activate or click the Show Manipulator Tool icon in the toolbar) to adjust the placement as you watch it update on your object, as shown in Figure 7.26, with a Spherical projection.

Drag the handles on the special manipulator to change the coverage of the projection, orientation, size, and so forth. All projection types have special manipulators. Figure 7.27 shows the manipulator for a Planar projection wrapping the checkerboard pattern in a thin band all the way around the sphere.

To summarize, projection textures depend on a projector node to position the texture onto the geometry. If the object assigned to a projected texture is moving, consider grouping the projection placement node to the object itself in the Outliner.

We will focus on UV mapping later in this chapter, but it's good to know that projections are available for those instances where projecting is more useful than UVs.

Texture Nodes

You can create several texture nodes in Maya. This section covers the more important ones. All texture nodes, however, have common attributes that affect their final look. In the Hypershade, click to create any node from the 2D Textures section in the Create panel (in this case, a checker) and take a look at its attributes in the Hypershade's Property Editor (see Figure 7.28). The Color Balance and Effects headings affect the color of the texture (as you saw with the noise textures from the plane exercise).

Color Balance

This set of attributes adjusts the overall brightness and color balance of your texture. Use these attributes to tint or brighten a texture without having to change all the individual attributes of the shader.

Effects

You can invert the texture's color space by clicking the Invert check box. This changes black to white

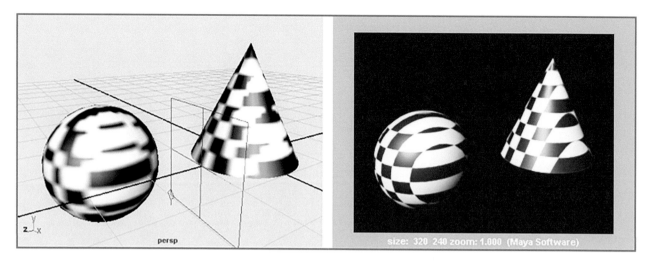

FIGURE 7.25   A planar projection checkerboard in the viewport (left) and rendered (right).

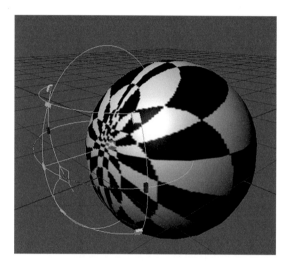

FIGURE 7.26   The spherical projection's manipulator tool.

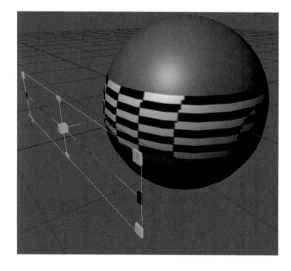

FIGURE 7.27   The manipulator wrapping the checkerboard texture around the sphere (left of image, perspective view; right of image, rendered view).

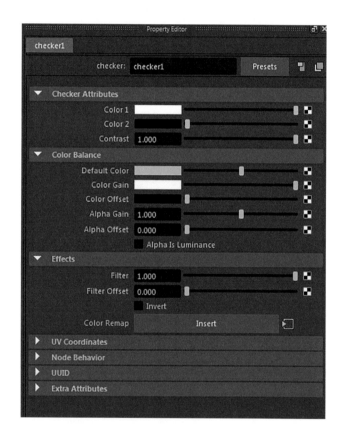

FIGURE 7.28   Some common attributes for all texture nodes.

and white to black in addition to inverting the RGB values of colors.

You can map textures to almost any shader attribute for detail. Even the tiniest amount of texture on a surface's bump, specular, or color can increase its realism or contribute to a better look.

Place2dTexture Nodes

When you create most textures (2D textures to be exact), you will see a purple Place2dTexture node alongside the actual

FIGURE 7.29   A purple 2D placement node in the Hypershade and Property Editor for a checker texture node.

texture as seen in Figure 7.29, be it a checker or a file or a fractal, etc. 2D texture nodes come with a 2D placement node to control their repetition, rotation, size, offset, and so on. You can immediately access this node in the Attribute Editor by clicking its tab, or in the Hypershade, select the texture node from the Textures tab (in this case a checker) and click the Input And Output Connections icon in the Hypershade. Then click the place2dTexture node and examine its attributes in the Property Editor. Adjust the setting in this node of your 2D texture in the Attribute Editor, or Property Editor, as shown in Figure 7.29, to position it within the Shader network.

The Repeat UV setting controls how many times the texture is repeated. For example, increasing the Repeat UV values for a checker map will increase the number of checkers you will see. The higher the wrap values, the smaller the texture appears, but the more times it appears on the surface.

The Wrap U and Wrap V check boxes allow the texture to wrap around the edges of their limits to repeat. When these checkboxes are turned off, the texture appears only once, and the rest of the surface is the color of the Default Color attribute found in the texture node.

The Mirror U and Mirror V settings allow the texture to mirror itself when it repeats. The Coverage, Translate Frame, and Rotate Frame settings control where the image is mapped. They're useful for positioning a digital image or a scanned picture.

Ramp Texture

Now, let's look at some of the more popular texture nodes. In the Hypershade, click on the 2D Textures and 3D Textures entries in the Create pane of the Hypershade to filter seeing only their nodes on the right side of the Create pane (as shown in Figure 7.30) to more easily follow along the following descriptions of some popular texture nodes, starting with the Ramp Texture.

A *ramp* is a gradient in which one color transitions into the next color. A ramp is useful for many things, but mostly it's perfect for making color gradients. Initially, the ramp texture will show as a simple black-to-white gradient (from left to right), as shown in Figure 7.31 (top).

FIGURE 7.30   Viewing the 2D and 3D texture nodes in the Create pane of the Hypershade window.

But it's easy to create gradients using any colors. Simply use the round handles on top of the ramp to select that color and to move it left and right on the ramp. The square handle at the bottom deletes the color. To create a new color, click inside the ramp. Figure 7.31 (bottom) shows a multicolored ramp. Clicking the right arrow button to the right of the ramp shown in Figure 7.31 (bottom) will open a larger ramp window to work with if you need extra precision. Note that Figure 7.31 (bottom) is from the Attribute Editor and not the Hypershade Property Editor.

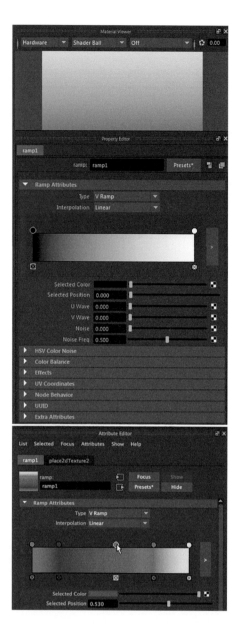

FIGURE 7.31 The default ramp texture in the Property Editor (top). Adding and changing colors in a ramp is easy to do (bottom).

> The ramp *texture* is different from the Ramp *shader*. The Ramp shader automatically has several ramp textures mapped to some of its attributes.

The Type setting allows you to create a gradient running along the U or V direction of the surface (for example, up/down vs. left right), as well as to make circular, radial, diagonal, and other types of gradients. The Interpolation setting controls how the colors grade from one to the next. Experiment with them to see how they work.

The U Wave and V Wave attributes let you add a squiggle to the U or V coordinate of the ramp, and the Noise and Noise Freq (frequency) attributes specify randomness for the placement of the ramp colors throughout the surface.

Using the HSV Color Noise attributes, you can specify random noise patterns of hue, saturation, and value to add some interest to your texture. The HSV Color Noise options are great for making your shader just a bit different to enhance its look.

Fractal, Noise, and Mountain Textures

The Fractal, Noise, and Mountain textures are used to create a random noise pattern to add to an object's color, transparency, or any other shader attribute. For example, when creating a surface, you'll almost always want to add a little dirt or a few surface blemishes to the shader to make the object look less CG. These textures are commonly used for creating bump maps.

Bulge, Cloth, Checker, Grid, and Water Textures

The Bulge, Cloth, Checker, Grid, and Water textures help create surface features when used on a shader's Bump Mapping attribute. Each creates an interesting pattern to add to a surface to create tactile detail, but you can also use them to create color or specular irregularities.

When used as a texture for a bump, Grid is useful for creating the spacing between tiles, Cloth is perfect for clothing, and Checker is good for rubber grips. Placing a Water texture on a slight reflection makes for a nice poolside reflection in patio furniture.

The File Node

You use the file node to import image files into Maya for texturing. For instance, if you want to texture a CG face with a digital picture of your own face, you can use the file node to import a Maya-supported image file.

Importing an Image File as a Texture

To attach an image to the Color attribute of a Lambert shader, for example, follow these steps:

1. Create a Lambert shader in the Hypershade. (Phong, Blinn, or any of the shaders will do.)

2. Click the Map button (⬛) next to the Color attribute of the new Lambert shader to map a texture to it. RMB+click the File button in the Create Render Node window that pops up and select Create Texture. The Attribute Editor shows the attributes for the file node (with an image already loaded); see Figure 7.32.

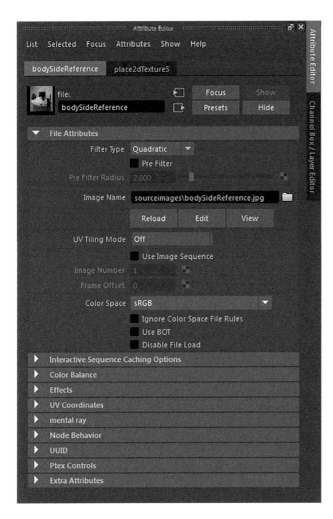

FIGURE 7.32   The file texture node.

3. Next to the Image Name attribute, click the Folder icon to open the file browser to select an image. Find the image file of choice on your computer. (It's best to put images to use as textures in the project's Sourceimages folder. As a matter of fact, the file browser defaults directly to the Sourceimages folder of your current project.) Double-click the file to load it.

4. After you import the image file, it connects to the Color attribute of that shader and also automatically connects the alpha to transparency if there is an alpha channel in the image. You can position it as you please by using its place2dTexture node or by manipulating the projection node if you created the file texture node as a projection.

You can attach an image file to any attribute of a shader that is *mappable*, meaning it's able to accept a texture node. Frequently, image files are used for the color of a shader as well as for bump and transparency maps. You can replace the image file by double-clicking the file texture node in the Hypershade and choosing another image file with the file browser.

ATTRIBUTE EDITOR VS. PROPERTY EDITOR

You can choose to view and edit material (shader) and texture nodes in either the Hypershade's Property Editor or the Attribute Editor in the main UI. I prefer the Attribute Editor as it gives you a small preview icon of your material or texture in the upper-left corner. However, using the Property Editor right in the Hypershade is fast and convenient. You can use one or the other as you choose as you continue with the steps in this book. Please note, however, that the Property Editor has two view modes controlled by the icon ( ) in the upper right of the Property Editor in the Hypershade. LookDev mode shows only some of the more important attributes, while regular mode shows all the attributes, just like the Attribute Editor in the main UI.

Using Photoshop Files: The PSD File Node

Maya can also use Adobe Photoshop Photoshop Document (PSD) files as image files in creating shading networks, though this is generally not preferred in terms of scene efficiency and image file sizes. The advantage of using PSD files which can be larger files, is that you can specify the layers within the Photoshop file for different attributes of the shader, as opposed to importing several image files to map onto each shader attribute separately. This, of course, requires a modest knowledge of Photoshop and some experience with Maya shading. As you learn how to shade with Maya, you'll come to appreciate the enhancements inherent in using Photoshop networks.

Try This

You'll create a single Photoshop file that will shade this sphere with color as well as transparency and a bump. Again, you're doing this instead of creating three different image files (such as TIFFs) for each of those shading attributes.

1. Create a poly sphere in a new scene and assign a new Lambert shader to it through the Hypershade. This creates a new shader and assigns it to the selection, in this case, your sphere.

2. Select the sphere and in the Rendering menu set (F6), choose Texturing ➢ Create PSD Network. In the option box that opens, select Color, Transparency, and Bump from the list of attributes on the left side and click the right arrow to move them to the Selected Attributes list on the right, as shown in Figure 7.33.

3. Select a location and filename for the PSD image's location. By default, Maya places the PSD file it generates in the Sourceimages folder of your current project, named after the surface to which it applies. Click Create.

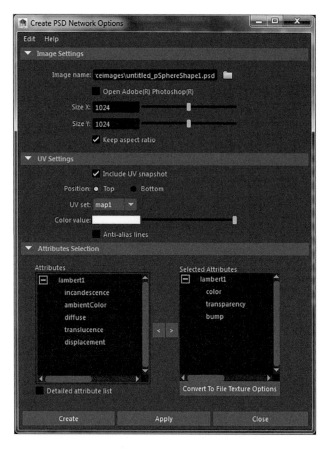

FIGURE 7.33   The Create PSD Network Options window.

4. In Photoshop, open the newly created PSD file. You see three layers grouped under three folders named after the shader attributes you selected when creating the PSD file. There are folders for lambert2.bump, lambert2.transparency, and lambert2.color, as well as a layer called UVSnapShot.

   The UVSnapShot layer gives you a wireframe layout of the UVs on the sphere as a guideline to paint your textures. Because the sphere is an easy model, you don't need this layer, so turn it off. You'll use UV SnapShot later in this chapter when texturing a model.

   You can now paint whatever image you want into each of the layers to create maps for each of the shader attributes, all in one convenient file. Save the PSD file. You can save over it or create a new filename for the painted file.

5. In Maya, open the Hypershade, and open the Attribute Editor for the Lambert shader assigned to the sphere (in this case, Lambert2). If you graph the connections to the Lambert shader in the Hypershade window's work panel, you see that the PSD file you generated is already connected to the Color, Bump, and Transparency attributes of the shader, with the proper layering set for you, as shown in Figure 7.34. Note however, the icons for the PSD layers (Color, Bump, and Transparency) all display the topmost layer of the PSD, in this case, the Bump. This is normal, however irritating.

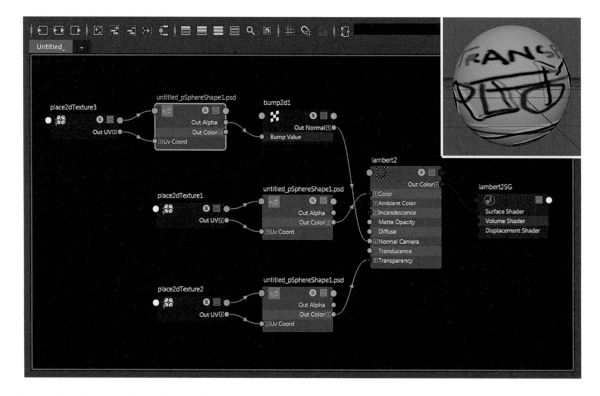

FIGURE 7.34   The PSD network for the Lambert shader in the Hypershade shows the connections to Color, Bump, and Transparency. The image inset (upper right) shows the sphere with the different PSD layers applied appropriately in Maya's viewport 2.0.

6. Open the file nodes for the shader and replace the PSD file with your new painted PSD file. If you saved your PSD file with the same name, all you need to do is click the Reload button to update the psdFile node.

If you decide you need to add another attribute to the PSD file's layering or if you need to remove an attribute, you can edit the PSD network. Select the shader in the Hypershade and choose Edit ➢ Edit PSD Network. In the option box, select new attributes to assign to the PSD file or remove existing attributes and their corresponding Photoshop layer groups. When you click Apply or Edit, Maya saves over the PSD file with the new layout.

3D and Environment Textures

3D textures are projected within a 3D space. These textures are great for objects that need to reflect an environment, for example.

Instead of simply applying the texture to the plane of the surface as 2D textures do, 3D textures create an area in which the shader is affected. As an object moves through a scene with a 3D placement node, its shader looks as if it swims, unless that placement node is parented or constrained to that object. (For more on constraints, see Chapter 9, "More Animation!")

Disconnecting a Texture

Sometimes, the texture you've applied to an object isn't what you want, and you need to remove it from the shader. To do so, double-click the shader in the Hypershade to open its Attribute Editor.

You can then disconnect an image file or any other texture node from the shader's attribute by RMB+clicking the attribute's name in the Attribute Editor and choosing Break Connection from the context menu, as shown in Figure 7.35.

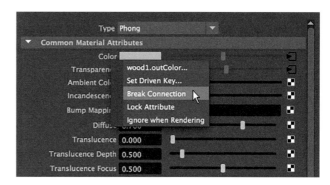

FIGURE 7.35   RMB+clicking a shader's attribute allows you to disconnect a texture node from the shader.

Textures and UVs for the Red Wagon

Now you'll assign shaders to a child's red wagon toy model. Figure 7.36 shows the real wagon. If you are reading a digital copy of this book, you can see the colors in Figure 7.36 easily. Otherwise, you can download the `ColorWagon.tif` photo from the book's website. The wagon is fairly simple; it will need a few colored shaders (Red, Black, Blue, and White) for the body, along with a few texture maps for the decals—which is where the real fun begins. The wagon will also require some more intricate work on the shaders and textures for the wood railings and silver metal screws, bolts, and handlebar; these will be a good foray into image maps and UVs.

This exercise is a prime example of how lighting and shading go hand in hand.

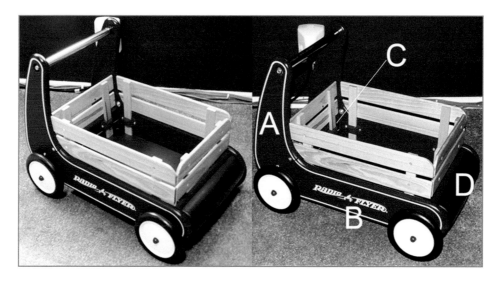

FIGURE 7.36   The red wagon and its named parts.

Assigning Shaders

Load the file `RedWagonModel.ma` from the Scenes folder of the RedWagon project to begin shading the model of the wagon.

> *Shading* is the common term for adding shaders to an object.

Study the color images of the wagon and see how light reflects off its plastic, metal, and wood surfaces. Blinn shaders will be perfect for nearly all the parts of the wagon. Follow these steps:

1. Open the Hypershade window and create four Blinn shaders.
2. Assign the following HSV values to the Color attribute of each Blinn shader and name them, as shown

in Table 7.2 and Figure 7.37. You'll create the shaders for chrome and wood later.

Initial Assignments

Look at the color image of the wagon from the book's web page (or in the e-edition of the book). The bullnose and tires are black, the wheel rims are white, the floor is blue, the screws and bolts and handlebar are chrome metal, the railings are

TABLE 7.2

HSV Color Values for the Wagon's Colors

Wagon Color	Shader Name	H Value	S Value	V Value
Red	Red	355	0.910	0.570
Black	Black	0	0	0
White	White	0	0	1
Blue	Blue	233	0.910	0.650

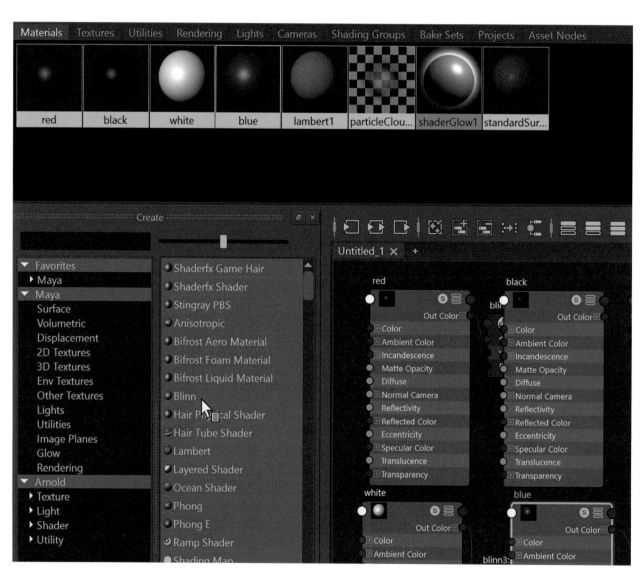

FIGURE 7.37 Create the four colored Blinn shaders.

wood, and the main body is red. Assign shaders to the wagon according to the color photo and the following steps:

1. In the viewport, select the side panels (the A and B panels, without the screws and bolts) and the wheel rim caps, as shown in Figure 7.38, and assign the Red Blinn shader to them. Press 6 to enter Texture Display mode.

2. Select the wheelMesh objects for all four wheels and assign them the White shader. The tires also turn white, but you'll fix that shortly; don't worry about it now (see Figure 7.39).

3. Select the bullnose (the rounded cylinder in front of the wagon) and assign it the Black Blinn.

4. Select the wagonFloor object and assign it the Red shader, as shown in Figure 7.40. You'll notice that the front and back bodies of the wagon turn red

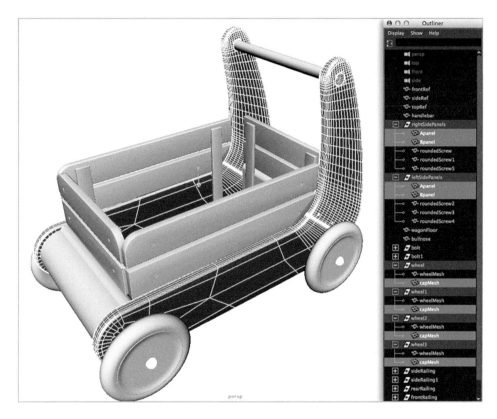

FIGURE 7.38   Assign the Red shader.

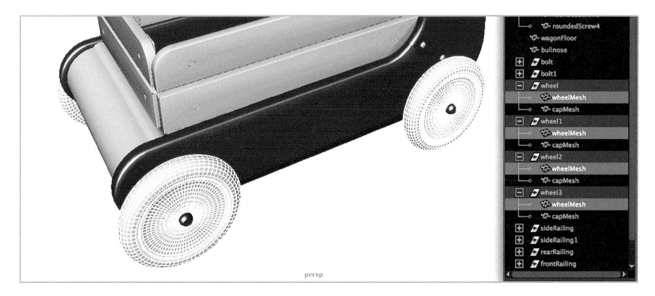

FIGURE 7.39   Assign the White shader.

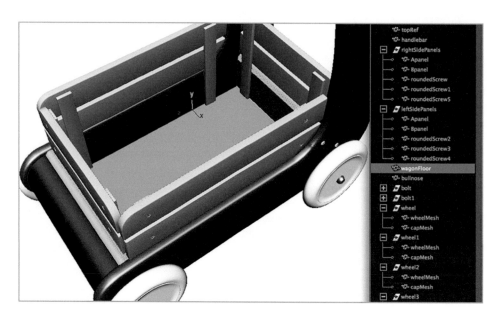

FIGURE 7.40 Assigning the Blue shader to the floor also changes the front and back.

like they're supposed to, but so does the floor of the wagon, which should be blue according to the photo. If you try to assign the Blue shader to the wagon floor mesh, the floor will be correct, but then the front and back of the wagon will be blue and not red as seen in Figure 7.40, so keep it with the red shader for now. You'll add the blue floor later.

Now you have initial assignments for the basic colors of the wagon's body. Let's tweak these shaders' colors next.

Creating a Shading Network for the Wheels

Refer to Figure 7.41 to observe how the materials are different for the rim and the tire of the wheel. The rim is glossier and

FIGURE 7.41 The tire on the wagon.

has a tighter, sharper specular, whereas the tire has a diffuse specular and is quite bumpy. You'll create a Layered shader for the wheels with white feeding into the rim portion and black into the tire portion.

Coloring the Wheel

First, you need to determine where the white ends and the black starts on the surface of the wheel mesh.

1. Select the White shader in the Hypershade window.

   Click the Map icon ( ) next to the Color attribute. RMB+click the Ramp Texture icon and select Create Texture. The wheel's color turns to a black-to-white gradient clockwise around the wheel (Figure 7.42 top), which is the wrong direction; you need the gradient to run from the center to the edge. In the ramp texture's Property Editor, set Type to U Ramp, as shown in Figure 7.42 (bottom).

   If the ramp doesn't show up in your viewports, make sure you press 6 to enter Texture Display mode. If the colors and ramp texture still don't display, make sure Use Default Material isn't checked in the viewport's Shading menu.

2. Now the gradient is running black from the center to light gray on the outside edge through to white on the reverse side of the wheel. Select the round handle for the black color and change Selected Color to white. Then select the round white handle on the right side of the ramp and change Selected Color to black.

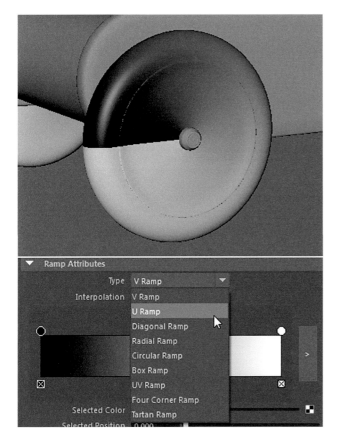

FIGURE 7.42 The Ramp direction is wrong (top). Set the ramp to a U Ramp type (bottom).

3. Click in the middle of the ramp to create a new color, which will be gray. Set that color to black. Move that new black handle in the ramp until its Selected Position value is about 0.6, as shown in Figure 7.43. Note that I am using the Attribute Editor to adjust the ramp in this figure, though you can use the Property Editor as well.

4. Set the Interpolation attribute (found above the ramp color) to None so you get clean transitions from white to black, instead of a soft linear gradient where the black slowly grades to white. Name this ramp **wheelPositionRamp**.

5. The backs of the wheels are solid black. In the wheel-PositionRamp, move the round handle for the black color all the way at the right of the ramp and set that color to white; set its position to about **0.920** to place white behind the wheels, keeping the black only where the tire is (see Figure 7.44).

   Now that you've pinpointed where the white rim ends and the black tire begins, you'll use this ramp as a transparency texture to place the Tire shader on top of the Rim shader in a Layered shader that you'll create later. This will allow you to have two different materials on your tire, a smooth white plastic and a rough black plastic.

6. You don't need this Ramp shader on the color of the shader anymore—you only did this so you could easily see the ramp positions on the wheel in the viewports. We will be using that ramp texture to control a layered shader for the wheel and the tire. In the Hypershade, select the White shader and click the Input And Output Connections icon ( ) to graph the shader in the work area, as shown in Figure 7.45.

7. In the Property Editor, RMB+click the Color attribute and select Break Connection from the context menu to disconnect the ramp from the color. Set the Color back to white. Notice that the rubber band link connecting the ramp texture node to the White shader node disappears in the Hypershade window.

8. Create a Layered shader. MMB+drag the White shader from the Hypershade to the top of the Layered Shader Attributes window, as shown in Figure 7.46. Delete the default Green shader in the Attribute Editor by clicking the checked box below its swatch.

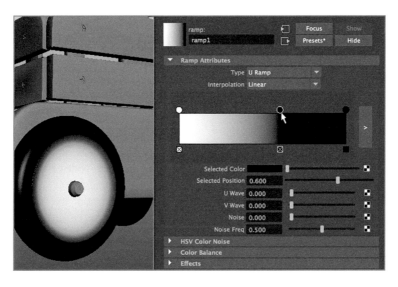

FIGURE 7.43 Move the new black handle.

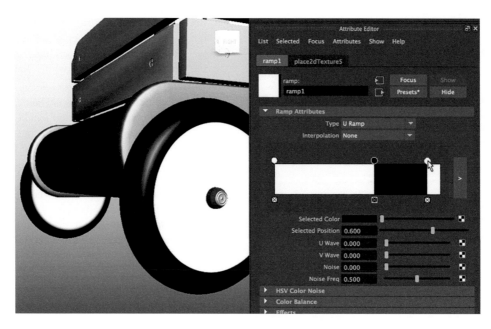

FIGURE 7.44   Setting the tire location using a ramp.

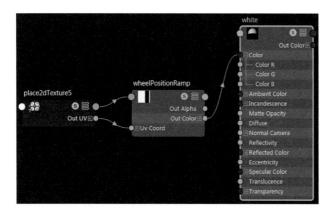

FIGURE 7.45   The White shader has the ramp attached as color.

9. Create a new Blinn shader and set its color to black. Name the shader **tireShader**. Select the Layered shader and then MMB+drag the new tireShader from the Hypershade to the Layered shader's Attribute Editor (or Property Editor in the Hypershade) and then place it to the left of the White shader, as shown in Figure 7.47. Name the Layered shader **wheelShader**.

10. Select the wheels and assign the wheelShader Layered shader to them. The wheels should appear all white (yours may turn all black). This is where the ramp you created earlier (wheelPositionRamp) will come into play in the next steps.

11. Select the wheelShader and click Input And Output Connections to graph the network in the Work Area of the Hypershade window. In the top panel of the Hypershade, click the Texture tab to display the texture nodes in the scene so you can see wheelPosition-Ramp's node.

FIGURE 7.46   Drag the White shader to the Layered shader and delete the default Green shader from it.

12. In the wheelShader's Attribute Editor, click the tire-Shader swatch on the left. MMB+drag the wheel-PositionRamp node to the Transparency attribute, as shown in Figure 7.48.

13. When you attach the ramp, the wheelShader icon turns white on top and black on the bottom. Render a frame in the persp viewport to make sure the black tires line up properly, as shown in Figure 7.49. Note that the scene file you're using has already been set to render with Maya Software native rendering. The wheel coloring is complete!

FIGURE 7.47 Add the black tireShader.

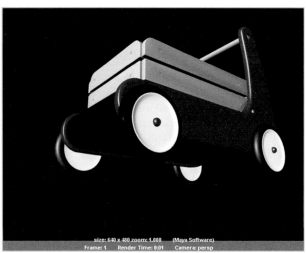

FIGURE 7.49 The tires are done!

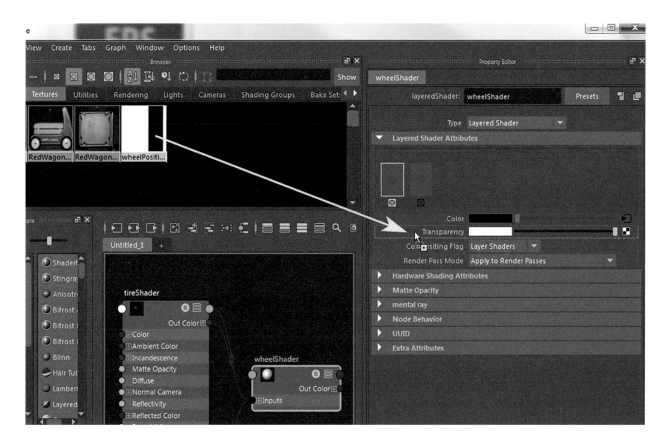

FIGURE 7.48 Attach the ramp to the Transparency attribute of the tireShader in the wheelShader by MMB dragging.

**HEY, HOLD ON A MINUTE:
WHY TWO SHADERS?**

Why did you go through a Layered shader with two different shaders (one white and one black) when you could more easily use one shader and assign the same black-to-white ramp to its color? You did this because the white rim and the black tire are different materials, and you need to use two different shaders to properly show that in renders.

Setting the Feel for the Materials and Adding a Bump Map

Because the material look and feel on the real wheels differs quite a bit between the rim and the tire, you'll further tweak the white rim and the black tire shaders. The rim is a smooth, glossy white, and the tire is a bumpy black with a broad specular. Follow these steps:

1. Let's set up a good angle of view for your test renders. Position your persp viewport to resemble the view in Figure 7.50. Render a frame with Maya Software rendering.

2. Select the White shader and set Eccentricity to **0.05** and Specular Roll Off to **0.5**. Doing so sharpens the specular highlight on the rim.

3. Select the black tireShader and set Eccentricity to **0.375** and Specular Roll Off to **0.6** to make the highlight more diffuse across the tire. Set Reflectivity to **0.05**. Render a frame; refer to Figure 7.51 to see how the specular highlight is broader and less glossy than in Figure 7.50.

FIGURE 7.51   Setting specular levels.

4. Open the Attribute Editor for the tireShader and click the Map icon ( ) in the Bump Mapping section. In the Create Render Node window, click to create a fractal texture map. Notice that the entire wheelShader icon becomes bumpy. Render a frame, and you'll see that the entire wheel is bumpy—not just the tire (see Figure 7.52), argh!

5. You have to use the wheelPositionRamp to prevent the bump from showing on the white rim. Select the wheelShader and click the Input And Output Connections icon ( ) in the Hypershade to graph its network (Figure 7.53).

6. Select the fractal to display it in the Attribute Editor and MMB+drag the wheelPositionRamp from the

FIGURE 7.50   Set your view to this angle and render a frame.

FIGURE 7.52   The whole wheel becomes bumpy!

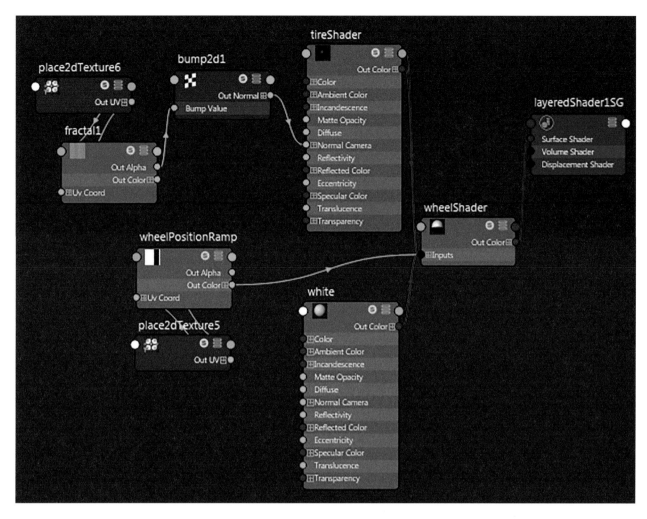

FIGURE 7.53 Graph the wheelShader network.

Notice the single green connecting line between the fractal1 node's OutAlpha output socket and the bump2d1 node's BumpValue input socket in the Hypershade. This means the alpha channel of the fractal feeds the amount of bump that is rendered on the tireShader. You have to alter the alpha coming out of the fractal node with the positioning ramp to block the rim from having any bump. The white areas of the ramp allow the bump map from the fractal to show on the tire, whereas the black area of the ramp keeps any bump from appearing. Because you already used this ramp to position the Rim shader and the Tire shader on the wheel, it will work perfectly for the bump position as well.

Hypershade to the Alpha Gain attribute for the fractal, as shown in Figure 7.54.

7. Render a frame, and you see that now the tire has no bump and the rim is bumpy (Figure 7.55).

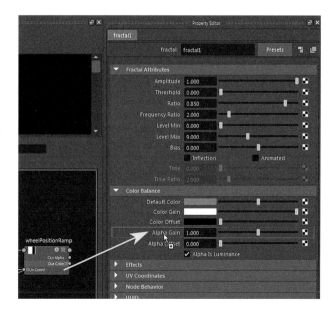

FIGURE 7.54 MMB+drag the ramp to the Alpha Gain attribute of the fractal.

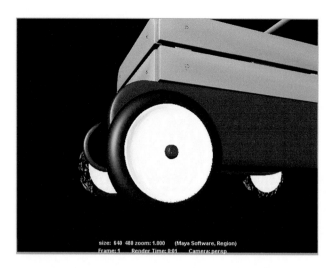

FIGURE 7.55 The tire is smooth, and now the rim is bumpy.

8. This is easy enough to fix. All you need to do is reverse the ramp and then feed that reversal into the Alpha Gain attribute of the fractal so that the tire is bumpy and the rim is smooth. In the Hypershade, in the Create pane on the left, type "reverse" into the text filter box and click on Reverse icon to create a reverse node in the Hypershade window's Utilities tab (see Figure 7.56). Make sure to delete the word "reverse" from the filter. This new Reverse node appears in the work area.

9. In the Hypershade, click+drag the OutColor socket of the wheelPositionRamp node onto the Input socket of the Reverse node and release the mouse button. This connects the output of the ramp to the reverse node, which will then reverse the effect of

the ramp on the fractal when you connect it in the next step (Figure 7.57 top).

10. On the fractal1 node's upper right, click the node display size icon ( ) until the three slots are filled white ( ). This expands the fractal1 icon to display more input and output sockets. In the upper-right corner of the reverse1 node, click the plus symbol next to Output (**Output**⊞●) to display Output X, Output Y, and Output Z sockets, as shown in Figure 7.57 (bottom).

11. Drag the Output X socket from the reverse1 node to the Alpha Gain input socket on the fractal1 node.

12. Open the Render Settings window by choosing Windows ➢ Rendering Editors ➢ Render Settings (or click the Render Settings icon [ ] in the status bar at the top of the UI). Make sure Render Using is set to Maya Software and then click the Maya Software tab and set Quality to Production

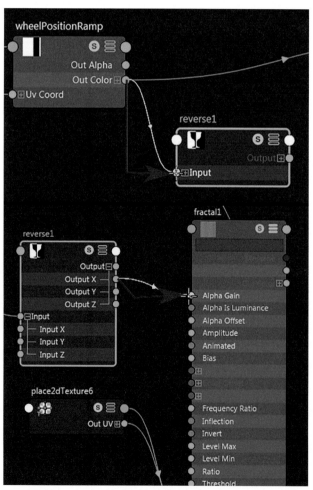

FIGURE 7.57 First connect the ramp to the Reverse node (top image). Then connect the Reverse node to the Fractal node (bottom image).

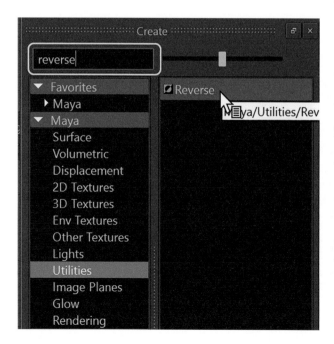

FIGURE 7.56 Create a reverse node.

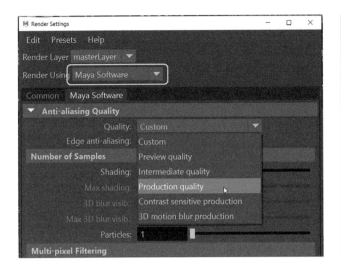

FIGURE 7.58   Set Quality to Production Quality.

FIGURE 7.61   The wheel looks pretty good.

be called something like *place2dTexture6*), and in the Property Editor, set the Repeat UV values to **18** and **48**, as shown in Figure 7.60. Doing so makes the fractal pattern finely speckled on the tire.

14. Render a frame; the fractal's scale on the bumpy tire looks too strong. Double-click the bump2d node in the Hypershade, and in the Property Editor, set Bump Depth to **0.04**. Render and check your frame against Figure 7.61. The bump looks much better, if not a little strong from this angle; you can finesse it to taste from here.

Tire Summary

Congratulations! You've made your first somewhat complex shading network, as shown in Figure 7.62. By now, you should have a pretty good idea of how to get around the Hypershade and create shading networks. To recap, you're using a ramp to place the two different (Tire and Rim) shaders on the wheel, as well as using it to place the bump map on just the tire part by using a reverse node. The more times you make shading networks, the easier they will become to create.

This type of shading is called *procedural shading* because you used nothing but stock Maya texture nodes to accomplish what you needed for the wheels. In the following sections,

FIGURE 7.59   Now you have the bump where you need it.

Quality in the pull-down menu (see Figure 7.58). Render a frame; you finally have a bump on the tire and a smooth rim (see Figure 7.59).

13. It's not a convincing bump yet, so select the fractal node and set Ratio to **0.85**. In the Hypershade, click the purple Placement node icon for the fractal (it should

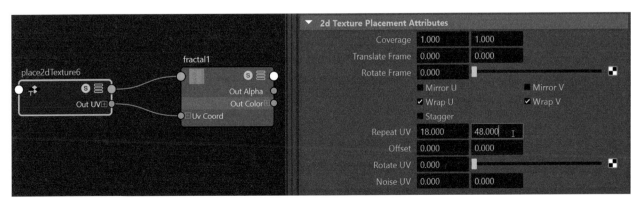

FIGURE 7.60   Set the Repeat UV values for the fractal map.

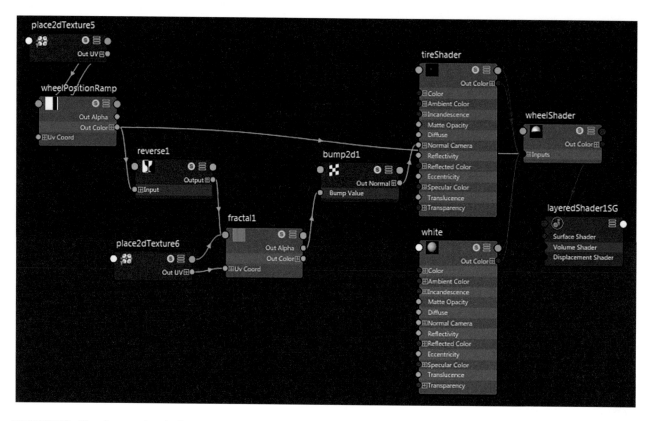

FIGURE 7.62 Your first complex shading network.

you'll make good use of image mapping to create the decals for the wagon body as well as the wood for the railings.

You can load the file `RedWagonTexture _ v01.ma` from the Scenes folder of the RedWagon project to check your work or skip to this point.

Putting Decals on the Body

Figure 7.63 shows you the decals that need to go onto the body of the wagon. They include the wagon's logo, which you'll replace with your own graphic design, and the white stripe that lines the side panels.

FIGURE 7.63 You need to add the body decals.

Instead of trying to make a procedural texture as you did with the wheel, you'll create an image map that will texture the side panels' white stripe. The stripe is far too difficult to create otherwise. You'll create an image file using Photoshop (or another image editor) to make sure the white stripe (and later the red wagon logo) lines up correctly.

Working with UVs

Mapping polygons usually involve the task of defining UV coordinates for them so that you can more easily paint an image map for the mesh. UVs again are a way to define where and how on a polygon mesh an image is mapped. You must either edit or create your own UV coordinates on a polygonal surface to get a clean layout on which to paint in Photoshop. When poly models are created, especially from primitives, they have UV coordinates; however, these coordinates may not be laid out in the best way for texture-image manipulation, especially after adjusting the mesh with extrusions and other poly modeling tools. It's always best to see what a mesh's UV layout is, and then decide on how best to lay them out for use as a template on which to paint in Photoshop. Figure 7.64 shows the default UV layout for a poly cube primitive in the UV Editor window (Windows ➢ UV Editor). As you can see, the UV layout looks like the box has been cut open at the sides and laid out flat. These outer seams are shown in bold white. Selecting a face on the cube also highlights its UV position in the UV Editor.

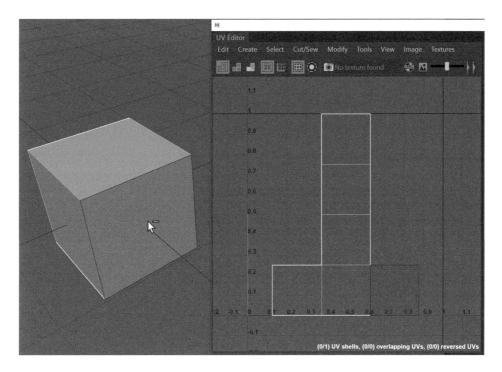

FIGURE 7.64   The default UV layout for a poly primitive cube.

Working with the A Panels

Let's look at how the UVs are laid out for the A panel of the wagon model. Use Figure 7.36 earlier in this chapter to remind yourself where the A panel is.

1. Using the scene file RedWagonTexture _ v01. ma from the Scenes folder of the RedWagon project, select the A panel on one side of the wagon and

choose Windows ➢ UV Editor, as shown in Figure 7.65. It is roughly in the same upside-down T shape, we saw in Figure 7.64. This is because the A panel was originally modeled from a poly cube. But as you can see in Figure 7.65, these UV shapes (called UV Shells) are not representative of the actual shape of the model, and that's what we need. We need to lay out the UVs to better match the shape of

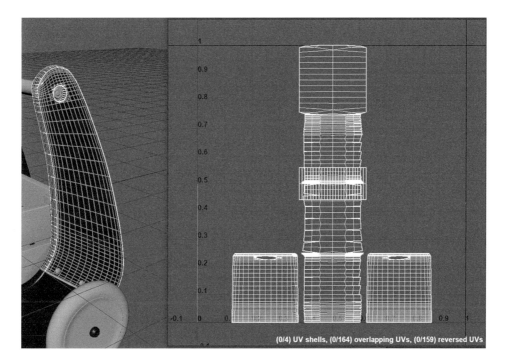

FIGURE 7.65   The A panel in the UV Editor.

the A panel model itself to make texturing the stripe much easier and cleaner.

This section assumes you have some working knowledge of Adobe Photoshop. You can skip the creation of the maps and use the maps already on the companion web page, which are called out in the text later in the exercise.

The UV Editor works almost like any other viewport. You may navigate the window and zoom in and out using the familiar Alt+mouse button combinations.

2. RMB+click any part of the wireframe UV layout in the UV Editor window and select UV Shell to enter the UV Shell selection (Figure 7.66 top). Select the UV Shell at the lower right, as shown in Figure 7.66 (bottom). Notice that the shell turns red on the model as well.

3. A UV Shell is one shape made up of UV points. In the UV Editor, right-click on the UV layout and this time choose UV, as seen in Figure 7.67 (top). Then click and drag to marquee and select that entire shell, as shown in Figure 7.67 (bottom), to see the UV

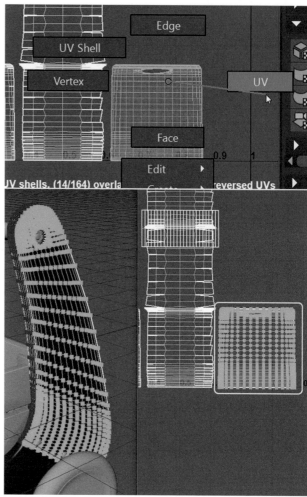

FIGURE 7.67 Choose to select UVs instead (top) and select the UVs shown (bottom).

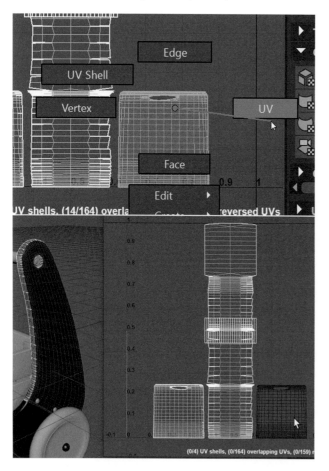

FIGURE 7.66 Enter UV Shell selection (top image) and then select the UV Shell on this part of the A panel mesh (bottom image).

points selected. You will see the UV points selected on the model as well.

As a matter of fact, feel free to select other UV Shells or UV points in the UV Editor to see what corresponding shells or points appear on the mesh in the persp viewport. This helps orient you as to how the UV layout works on this mesh, as well as getting your head around how UVs work in general.

4. Ok, let's start by better laying out this shell of the wagon's UVs. Select the A panel's shell, as shown in Figure 7.66 (top image), again (not its UV points). This selects the faces of that part of the model as well, which is what we need to create a new layout for that shell.

5. With that shell selected, in the UV Editor window, choose Create ➢ UV ➢ Planar ❏. In the option box, set the Project From option to X-Axis, check the Keep Image Width/Height Ratio option, and then click Project (see Figure 7.68). The UV Editor shows the front A panel face.

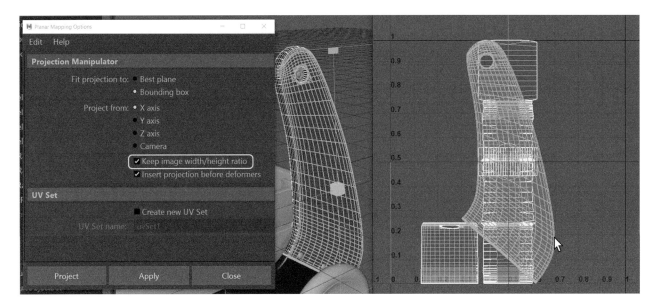

FIGURE 7.68 Create a planar projection for the UV layout.

6. Now the front face has a much simpler UV layout from which to paint. However, it's centered in the UV Editor and will overlap the other UVs of the same mesh. When UVs overlap, the image will not properly map on to the mesh, and will repeat in areas of overlap. Therefore, you should move and size it to fit into its original corner, more or less, to make sure no UVs double up on each other. First, double-click the Move tool icon to open its options and make sure that Symmetry is turned off (or check the Symmetry drop-down menu in the Status Bar at the top of the main UI (▼ Symmetry: Off)). If Symmetry is enabled for the Move tool, this and the following steps will not work for you.

7. In the UV Editor, RMB+click on the wireframe and select Shell to enter Shell selection. Click to select that new shell.

8. Press W for the Move tool and move the selected UV shell to the side of the UV Editor. Press R for the Scale tool and scale the shell down a bit to fit into the corner, as shown in Figure 7.69. Since the A panel model is mostly red and has a graphic stripe on just this front side that needs a good UV layout, we are done with the UV layout and can move on to painting the stripe in Photoshop.

9. Earlier in this chapter, you saw how to write out a PSD file with a UV snapshot as one of its layers. You'll use a similar technique to paint the decal for the panel. Click an empty area of the UV Editor to deselect everything. Then, in Object Selection mode (press F8 if you need to exit Component Selection), select the A panel mesh in the persp viewport in the main Maya UI.

10. In the UV Editor window, select Image ➢ UV Snapshot to open the option box. Set both Size X and

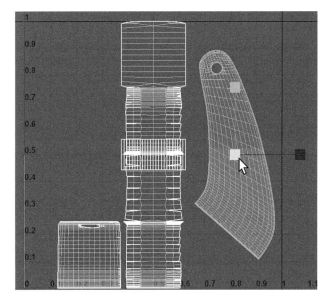

FIGURE 7.69 Position this UV Shell to make sure they don't overlap the rest of the A panel mesh's UVs.

Size Y to **1024**. Change the image format to TIFF, click the Browse button at the top next to the File Name field, and navigate to the RedWagon project's Sourceimages folder on your hard drive. Name the file `ApanelUV_mine.tif`, and click Save. Note that the Sourceimages folder already has an `ApanelUV.tif` for your convenience, which is why you add "_mine" to the filename. Leave the UV Area set to Tiles, and click OK (see Figure 7.70).

Working in Photoshop

Next, you'll go into Photoshop to paint your map according to the UV layout you just output.

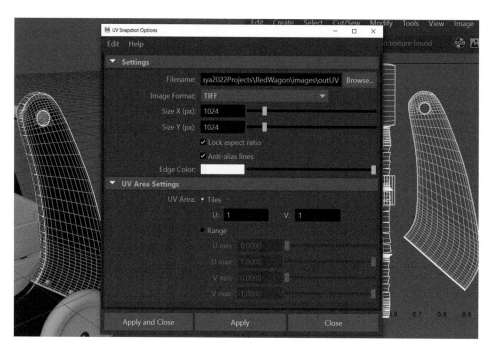

FIGURE 7.70 Settings for the UV snapshot of the A panel.

1. In your OS file browser, navigate to the RedWagon project's Sourceimages folder and open the file `ApanelUV.tif` in Photoshop, or the one you created in the previous steps. Figure 7.71 shows the layout of the UVs that you'll use to create the white stripe for the front of the A panel.

2. In Photoshop, create a new layer on top of the background layer that is the UV layout (white on black, as shown). Using the Paint Bucket tool, fill that new layer with the same red you used on the shader in your scene. To do so, click the foreground color swatch in Photoshop and set H to **357**, S to **100**%, and B to **80**%, as shown in Figure 7.72, to better match the red we created in Maya earlier click OK.

3. Using the Paint Bucket tool, click to fill the entire image with the red you just created. The trouble is that now you can't see the UV layout. Set the Opacity value of the red layer in Photoshop to **50**%, as shown in Figure 7.73.

4. Set Photoshop's foreground color to white. Using the Line and Brush tools set to a width of about 6 pixels, draw a stripe following the UV layout lines, as shown in Figure 7.74. Doing so places that white stripe along the A panel's outer edge because the UV lines you're following correspond to that area of the mesh. The rest will be left red.

5. You may have drawn directly on the red layer in Photoshop or created a new layer for the stripe. In either case, set the Opacity value of the red layer back to **100**% so you can no longer see the UV layout. Your image file should look like the one in Figure 7.75. Save the image as `ApanelStripeMine.tif` in the Sourceimages folder of your RedWagon project. You can keep the layers in the TIFF file, or

you can choose to flatten the image or merge the layers. It may be best to keep the stripe and red on separate layers so that you can go back into Photoshop and edit the stripe as needed.

> You may create your own image using Photoshop (`Apanel StripeMine.tif`) and use the `ApanelStripe.tif` image file in the Sourceimages folder of the RedWagon project on the companion web page instead.

Creating and Assigning the Shader

Now, let's create the shader and get it assigned to the geometry.

1. In Maya, open the Hypershade and select the Red shader. Duplicate it by choosing Edit ➤ Duplicate ➤ Shading Network in the Hypershade window, as shown in Figure 7.76.

2. Rename the newly duplicated shader (currently called red1) to **ApanelStripe**. In the Property Editor, click the Map icon ( ) next to Color and choose File. In the Attribute Editor, click the Folder icon next to the Image Name field. Navigate to your Sourceimages folder and select your image `ApanelStripeMine. tif` (or use the one provided—`ApanelStripe. tif`), as shown in Figure 7.77.

3. In the Hypershade, you may see that the Shader icon may turn somewhat transparent. Maya may automatically map the Transparency attribute of the shader as well as the color since you are using a TIFF (which

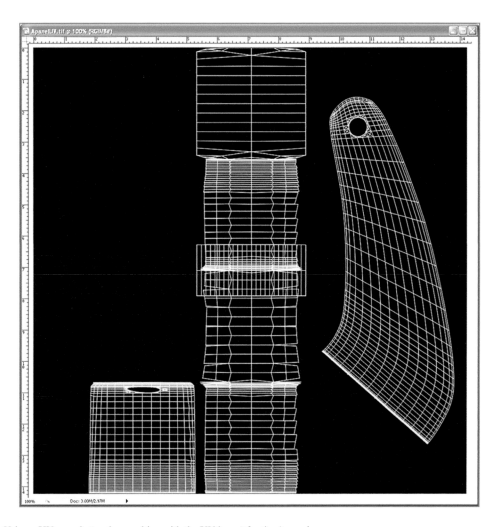

FIGURE 7.71 Using a UV snapshot makes working with the UV layout for the A panel easy.

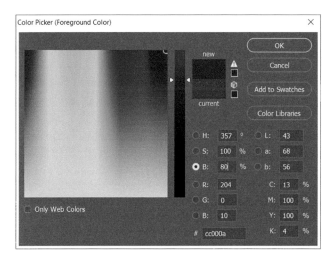

FIGURE 7.72 In Photoshop's Color Picker, create the same red you used for the wagon.

FIGURE 7.73 Set the opacity for the red layer in Photoshop so you can see the UV layout on the layer below.

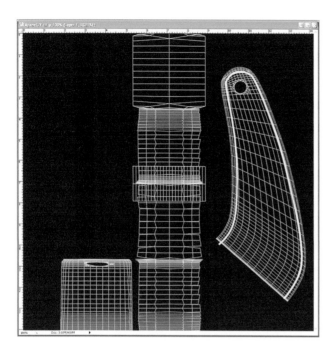

FIGURE 7.74   Follow the UV lines to draw the white stripe.

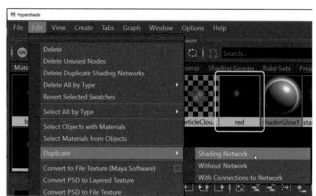

FIGURE 7.76   Duplicate the original Red shader.

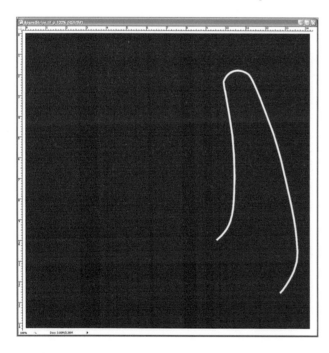

FIGURE 7.75   The striped image file.

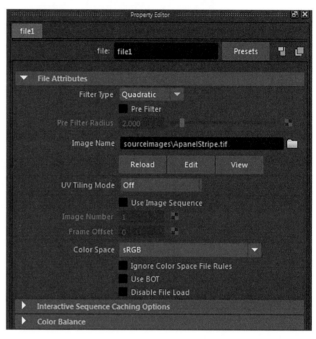

FIGURE 7.77   Select `ApanelStripe.tif` or your own `Apanel-StripeMine.tif` file.

may contain an alpha channel). In the Property Editor, RMB+click Transparency, and select Break Connection from the context window if there is a connection. Now your shader is set to the same red you used earlier, but now it gives you a stripe along the side A panel.

4. Assign the new ApanelStripe shader to the A panel mesh and press 6 for Texture Display mode in the persp viewport (see Figure 7.78). The stripe lines up well. Don't worry if the red on the A panel may

not match with the red in the rest of the wagon in the view panels. This is due to color space and is automatically adjusted when rendering; the reds will match better in the rendered image vs. the view panel.

Copying UVs

You need to put the stripe on the other side's A panel. Select the other A panel and assign the ApanelStripe shader to it. You'll notice that no stripe appears (see Figure 7.79). This is because the UV layout for this A panel hasn't been set up yet. Don't worry; you don't have to redo everything you did for the first A panel. You can essentially copy the UVs from the first A panel mesh to this one.

FIGURE 7.78 The stripe.

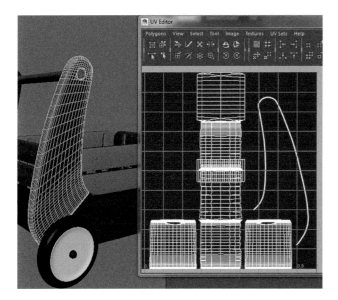

FIGURE 7.79 Assign the ApanelStripe shader to the other side's A panel.

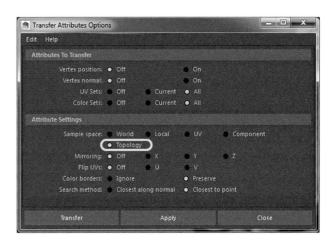

FIGURE 7.80 The Transfer Attributes settings.

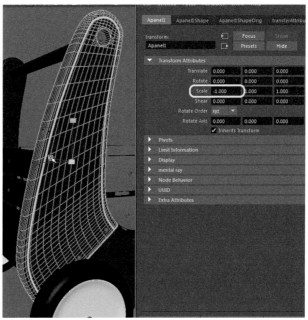

FIGURE 7.81 The stripe is on the correct side now.

1. Select the first A panel (with the stripe) and then shift-select the second panel (without the stripe). In the Modeling menu set, choose Mesh ➢ Transfer Attributes ❐. In the option box, set Sample Space to Topology, as shown in Figure 7.80, and click Transfer.

2. The stripe appears on the inside of the back A panel, not on the outside as you need. Select that A panel and choose Modify ➢ Center Pivot.

3. In the Channel Box, enter a value of **−1.0** for Scale X. The stripe flips to the correct side, as shown in Figure 7.81.

4. With that A panel still selected, choose Modify ➢ Freeze Transformations. This sets the current transformations (move, rotate, and scale) as the new default for this mesh.

   You can load the file `RedWagonTexture_v02.ma` from the Scenes folder of the RedWagon project to check your work or skip to this point.

The file texture you'll use for the panels was painted in Photoshop to place the stripes and logo properly on the wagon using their UV layouts. Study the image file and see how it fits on the mesh of the wagon. Try adjusting the image file with your own artwork to see how your image map affects the placement on the mesh.

Working with the B Panels

With the A panels done, you'll move on to the horizontal B panels (Figure 7.36 earlier in this chapter) and use much the same methodology you did with the A panels. To begin, follow these steps:

1. Select one of the B panels, shown in Figure 7.82 (top), and open the UV Editor window.

2. The B panel does not have a convenient shell for the front side as you had with the A panel before. For the B panel, select the UV points on the lower-right side of the layout in the UV Editor, as shown in Figure 7.82 (bottom), to isolate the front face of the B panel.

3. Since we only have UVs selected this time and not a shell, we need to convert the selection to select the faces on the model. In the UV Editor, choose Select ➤ Convert Selection ➤ To Faces. You've isolated the front face of the B panel, and a little bit on the left side that we don't need. Press and hold Ctrl and click and drag to unselect the unneeded faces, as shown in Figure 7.83.

4. In the UV Editor, choose Create ➤ Planar ❐. In the option box, set the Project From option to X-Axis, and make sure the Keep Image Width/Height Ratio option is still checked on, just as before. Your B panel shows up nicely laid out in the UV Editor (see Figure 7.84).

5. This action has created another shell, making it easier to work with the front side of the B panel. RMB+click the wireframe in the UV Editor and choose Shell. Make sure that Symmetry is not turned

on for the Move tool before proceeding. Select the new shell shape and use Move (W), Scale (R), and Rotate (E) to position the UV layout for that front face, as shown in Figure 7.85.

6. Press F8 to enter Object Selection, and select the B panel mesh itself in the main Maya UI. In the UV

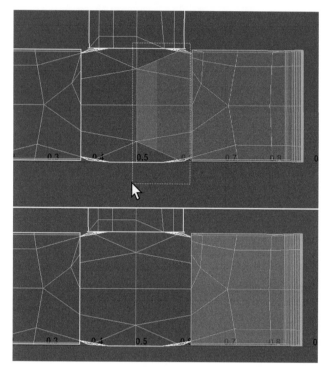

FIGURE 7.83 Deselect the extra faces on the side (top image) to only have these faces selected (bottom image).

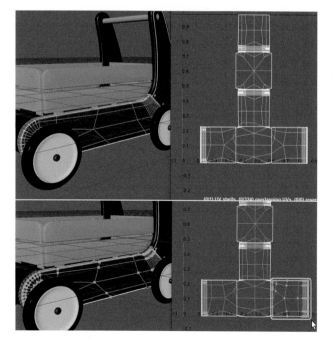

FIGURE 7.82 Starting on the B panels (top image) and selecting the UV points for the front side of the panel (bottom image).

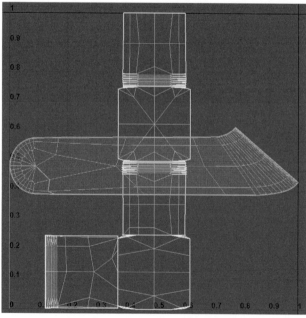

FIGURE 7.84 The planar projection creates a nice UV layout for the front faces of the B panel.

Editor, save a UV snapshot called `BpanelUV.tif` to the Sourceimages folder of the RedWagon project.

7. Open the `BpanelUV.tif` image or use your own image from the previous step in Photoshop and follow the same steps as you did for the A panel to lay down a red layer and paint a stripe along the layout, as shown in Figure 7.86. It's best to save the stripe on its own layer in Photoshop because you'll probably need to edit and reposition the stripe to make sure it lines up with the A panel stripe after you assign the shader.

FIGURE 7.87   Create a logo in Photoshop.

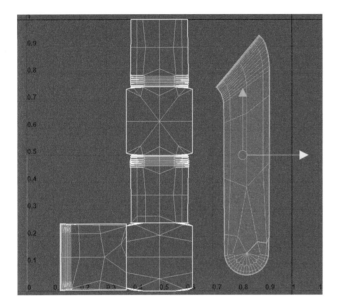

FIGURE 7.85   Put the front face UV shell on the side.

8. Create your own logo to place in the middle of panel B and place it in the Photoshop image file, as shown in Figure 7.87. Save the image file as `Bpanel-StripeMine.tif` into the Sourceimages folder, so as not to overwrite the one provided for you.

You can skip the image creation in Photoshop and use the `BpanelStripe.tif` image file in the Sourceimages folder of the RedWagon project on the companion web page.

9. Duplicate another Red shader and, as you did previously, assign the `BpanelStripeMine.tif` (or use the file provided, which is `BpanelStripe.tif`) as its color map. If necessary, disconnect the transparency from the shader as you did with the A panel's shader. Name the shader **BpanelStripe**.

10. Assign the BpanelStripe shader to the B panel model, as shown in Figure 7.88.

Creating the Other B Panel Texture

Finally, you need to create the shader for the other side's B panel. Assign the BpanelStripe shader to the other B panel. Nothing happens, because the UVs for the second B panel aren't set up yet.

However, because there is a logo with text, setting up its UVs won't be as simple as copying the UVs from the first B panel and then mirroring the mesh, as you did with the A panel with a Scale X value of −1.0. Doing so will make the logo and

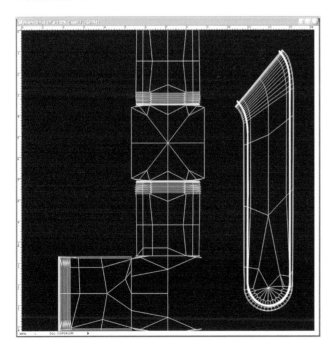

FIGURE 7.86   Create the B panel's stripe in Photoshop using the UV snapshot.

FIGURE 7.88   The B panel has its decals.

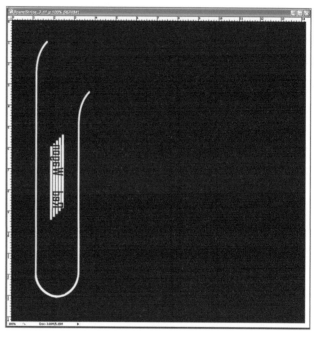

FIGURE 7.90   Flip the original image horizontally to fit the new UV layout of the second B panel.

text read backward. First, you'll copy and flip the UVs to the other B panel.

1. Select the first B panel with the correct texture; then select the other side's B panel and choose Mesh ➢ Transfer Attributes ❐. Make sure Sample Space is still set to Topology and set Flip UVs to U. Click Transfer to copy the UVs, flipping them over, as you can see in Figure 7.89.

2. You have to go back to Photoshop and create a second BpanelStripe.tif image file with a mirrored logo. In Photoshop, create a marquee around

the logo and mirror or flip the canvas horizontally (see Figure 7.90).

3. Select the logo portion of the image and flip that vertically, as shown in Figure 7.91. Save the image as BpanelStripeMine_2.tif. You may instead use the image provided—BpanelStripe_2.tif.

4. Duplicate the BpanelStripe shader in the Hypershade by selecting the shader and choosing Edit ➢

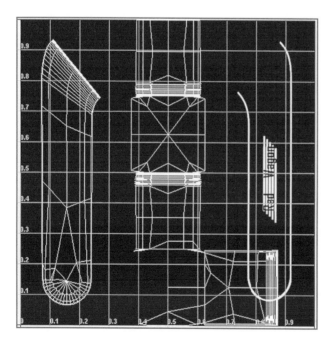

FIGURE 7.89   Copying and flipping the UVs to the other B panel.

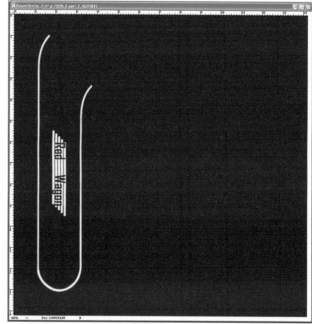

FIGURE 7.91   Flip the logo vertically and save the image as its own file.

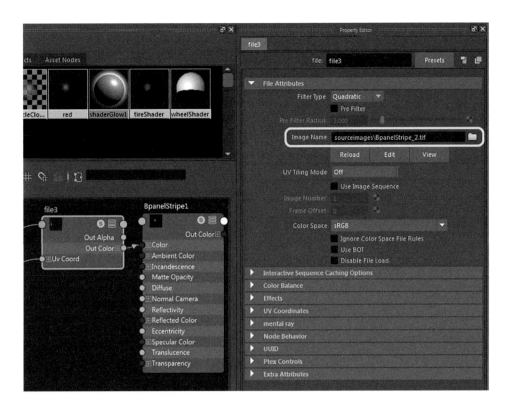

FIGURE 7.92 Assign the new image file to the new BpanelStripe1 shader.

Duplicate ➤ Shading Network. The copy is called BpanelStripe1.

5. Select the newly copied BpanelStripe1 shader and graph its input and output connections (![icon]) in the Hypershade. Notice that this copied material also copied the File node that points to the original B panel image. Select that file node to view it in the Property Editor. Click the Folder icon to select a new image file and then select the `BpanelStripeMine _ 2. tif` (or the provided `BpanelStripe _ 2.tif`) you just created in the Sourceimages folder (see Figure 7.92). This only changes the image for the second B panel since we made a new material by copying the first one.

6. The stripe and logo displayed on the wrong side of the B panel. Select the mesh and center its pivot.

7. Set the Scale X attribute for the B panel to **−1.0** to mirror it. The stripe and logo decals now show up on the correct side of the panel. Select the mesh and freeze its transforms. Figure 7.93 shows the wagon so far.

Texturing the Floor

Right now, the floor of the wagon is red, like the rest of its body. However, the real wagon has a blue floor! If you select the mesh for the wagon's floor (named wagonFloor) and assign the Blue shader you created, the whole body of the wagon turns blue, and that isn't what you want. You need only the

FIGURE 7.93 The wagon has decals on both sides.

inside and bottom of the floor to be blue, not the front and back sides of the wagon's body.

You'll make a face assignment instead of dealing with UVs and image files. RMB+click the wagon floor mesh and select Face from the marking menu. Select the two faces for the floor, as shown in Figure 7.94.

With the faces selected, assign the Blue shader from the Hypershade window, and you're finished! You have a blue floor. All that remains now are the screws, bolts, handles, and wood railings.

FIGURE 7.94 Select the floor faces.

You can load the file `RedWagonTexture _ v03.ma` from the Scenes folder of the RedWagon project to check your work or skip to this point.

Shading the Wood Railings

You'll use procedural shading to use the Wood texture available in Maya to create the wood railings. Begin here:

1. In the Hypershade, create a new Phong material.

2. Click the Color attribute's Map icon () and choose the Wood texture from the 3D Textures heading in the Create pane in the Hypershade, or enter "wood" in the text filter box to find it easier.

3. In the Attribute Editor for the Wood texture, set the Filler Color and Vein Color attributes according to Table 7.3.

4. Set Vein Spread to **0.5**, Layer Size to **0.5**, Randomness to **1.0**, Age to **10.0**, and Grain Contrast to **0.33**. In the Noise Attributes heading, set Amplitude X to **0.2** and Amplitude Y to **0.1**, as shown in Figure 7.95. Name the shader **Wood**.

5. Select all the wood railings and posts and assign the Wood shader to them. Render a frame and compare it to Figure 7.96. Notice a green cube called place3d-Texture node is now in your scene (see Figure 7.97).

TABLE 7.3

Filler Color and Vein Color Attributes

Attribute	H Value	S Value	V Value
Filler color	43	0.25	1.0
Vein color	10.7	0.315	0.9

FIGURE 7.95 Setting the Wood texture.

FIGURE 7.96 Assign the Wood shader.

6. The side wood railings look fine; however, the wavy pattern on the front and back wood railings looks a bit odd. In the Hypershade, duplicate the shading network for the Wood shader and call the new shader **woodFront**.

7. Assign that shader to the front and back railings and posts. Graph the network on the new woodFront shader in the Hypershade window's work area.

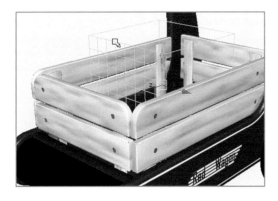

FIGURE 7.97   The place3dTexture node for the wood texture.

8. In the Hypershade, select the place3dTexture2 node (Figure 7.98), and its green cube in the viewports is also selected.

9. Rotate that placement node in the persp viewport 90° to the right or left. Render a frame, and compare it to Figure 7.99. The wood should no longer have that awkward wavy pattern.

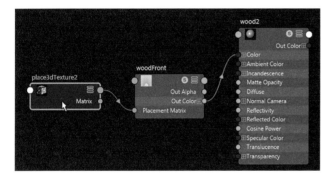

FIGURE 7.98   Select the placement node for the second wood texture.

The wood railings are finished. Now, for some extra challenge, you can use pictures of real wood to map onto the railings for a more detailed look. The procedural Wood texture can give you only so much realism. If you create your own wood maps, use your experience with the side panels to create UV layouts for the railings so you can paint realistic wood textures using Photoshop. You'll use custom photos and texture-image maps next to simulate the rich wood in the decorative box later in this chapter.

Finishing the Wagon

Now that the railings are done and you have test renders, there are only two parts left to texture: the bullnose front of the wagon and the metal handle and screws. From here, take your time and create a bump map based on a fractal, as you did for the tires, and apply it to the bullnose's black shader. Figure 7.100 shows a nice subtle bump map on the bullnose.

And last, you'll need a metal shader for the screws, bolts, and handlebar for the wagon. Use a Phong shader with a blue-gray color and a low diffuse value and assign it to all the metal parts of the wagon, as shown in Figure 7.101. You can then add an environment map to the reflection color as you did for the table lamp stem earlier in this chapter to give the metal a reflective look.

Because metal is a tricky material to render and a lot of a metal's look is derived from reflections, you'll experiment with creating a better metal shader in Chapter 11 using Arnold and its own materials.

Figure 7.102 shows the wagon with all its parts assigned to shaders. Figure 7.103 shows a quick render of the wagon as it is now.

You can load the file `RedWagonTexture _ v04.ma` from the Scenes folder of the RedWagon project to check your work or skip to this point.

FIGURE 7.99   The wood on the front and back railings looks better.

FIGURE 7.100   A nice bump for the bullnose.

FIGURE 7.101   Select all the metal screws, the bolts, and the handlebar and assign the Metal shader to them.

FIGURE 7.103   A current render of the wagon.

Photo-Real Mapping: The Decorative Box

With all the references you can find to any given object on the Internet, why not use real photos to create the textures for a model? That's exactly what you'll do next, with the decorative box you modeled in Chapter 3, using pictures of the real box.

You'll take this texturing exercise one important step further in Chapter 11 and experience how you can add detail to an object through displacement mapping, after you assign the color maps in this chapter. This will allow you to add finer detail to a model without modeling those details.

Setting Up UVs

The UVs on the decorative box aren't too badly laid out by default, as you can see in Figure 7.104. The only parts of the box that are missing in the UV layout are the feet. That is a common issue when extruding polygons: their UVs are rarely laid out automatically as you extrude them. Frequently, they're bunched up together in a flat layout that is difficult, if not impossible, to see in the UV Editor.

Set your project to the Decorative_Box project that you've downloaded from the companion web page. Open the file `boxModel07.mb` in the Scenes folder or continue with your own finished model from earlier.

First, you have to make room for the feet UVs.

1. Select all the UV shells for the box in the UV Editor. Press R for the Scale tool and scale everything down uniformly to gain some space in the normalized UV space, shown in Figure 7.105.

2. Now you have to create new UVs for the 4 feet and then move them to where they should be in the

FIGURE 7.102   The wagon in the Perspective panel.

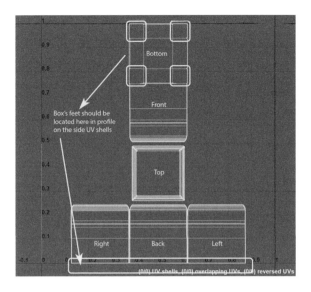

FIGURE 7.104 The feet UVs are missing from the box model, especially in the side shells.

full box's UV layout. Go into Component mode and select all poly faces for the 4 feet, as shown in Figure 7.106.

3. With the faces selected, in the UV Editor, select Create ➢ Automatic. The feet now have UV shells that are selected (Figure 7.107). However, they're large and overlapping the rest of the box's UVs.

4. With the shells still selected, scale them down and move them to the side, as shown in Figure 7.108.

Select all the feet UVs in the UV Editor and scale them all down uniformly together. You want to scale them all so that one of the squares fits into one of the corners of the top shell, as shown in Figure 7.109 (top). Then move them all together off to the side, as shown in Figure 7.109 (bottom). You'll position and scale them to fit properly soon.

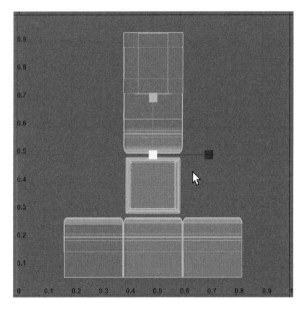

FIGURE 7.105 Scale all the UVs down a bit.

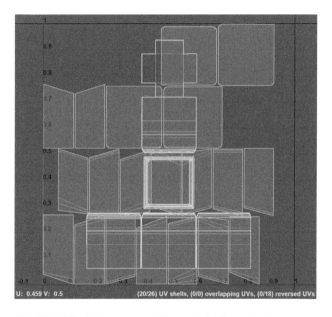

FIGURE 7.107 The automatic UV creation is simple, but lays out the UV shells.

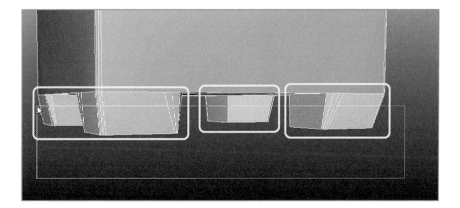

FIGURE 7.106 Select all the faces for the 4 feet.

Although it's recommended that you follow along with this exercise to lay out UVs for the box (because doing so will give you more practice and experience with UVs), you can skip straight to color-mapping the box in the next section by downloading the file boxTexture01.mb in the Scenes folder of the Decorative_Box project on the companion web page.

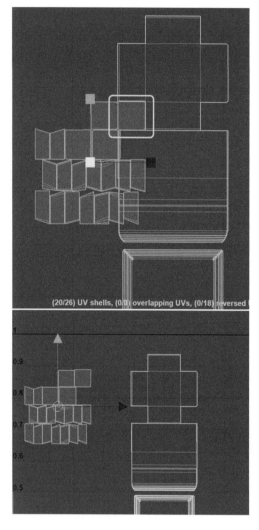

FIGURE 7.108 Scale the feet UVs to fit the size of the rest of the box's UVs (top). Then move the feet UVs to the side of the UV editor (bottom).

5. Now comes the task of figuring out where which foot UV fits. In the UV Editor window, select the edges shown in Figure 7.109 by Shift+single-clicking them. Do not use a marquee selection to make sure you select only the single edges you need. Notice that as you select each edge, they become selected in the model as well as the feet UVs off on the side of the UV Editor window. These are the edges where the outside sides of the feet meet the box. If you find it easier, you can select those edges from the model itself instead of the UV Editor.

6. With those edges selected, in the UV Editor's menu bar choose Cut/Sew ➤ Move and Sew (Figure 7.110). This will snap the UVs for the outside sides of the feet to their respective sides on the box. If you did not scale the feet UVs in step 4 well enough, you will notice that the feet will stick out from the sides of the box's UVs, as shown in Figure 7.110 (left). If that is the case, it's easier to return to step 4 (press Z for undo until you reach step 4 again) and scale those feet UVs more accurately. This can have a little bit of a back-and-forth. As long as you are within reasonable size, you will be fine. Figure 7.110 (right) shows a better matching scale of the feet after the UVs are sewn together.

7. RMB+click in the UV Editor and select Shell from the marking menu. Select all the Shells together, including the feet shells on the side, and scale everything smaller slightly to better fit in the UV space allotted, and then move them together to re-center the layout, as shown in Figure 7.111 (left). Then select the shell for the bottom of the box and move it up away from the back-side of the box, as shown in Figure 7.111 (right).

8. Figure 7.111 (right) also shows the remaining feet UVs off on the left side of the UV Editor window. The four square shapes are the bottoms of the feet. Select one of the square shells and move it to fit to the bottom UVs of the box, as shown in Figure 7.112.

9. Repeat step 8 to place all the feet bottom shapes (they will be square shaped) around the UV shell of the box's bottom, as shown in Figure 7.113.

10. Then select the shells of the remaining feet UVs on the side of the UV Editor, and line them up to the side of the box's bottom as also shown in Figure 7.113. Those remaining feet UV shells are the inside faces of the feet and share the same generic wood texture as the bottom of the box, so aligning and sewing them together as you did for the outside faces of the feet in steps 5 and 6 is not necessary (Figure 7.114).

MOVING UV SHELLS

Before you begin trying to move UVs and UV shells, make sure that Symmetry is turned off for the Move tool through its options.

When you've finished, your UV Editor should resemble the one shown in Figure 7.115. Because the box's decorations are seamless from the top of the box down to the four sides, let's

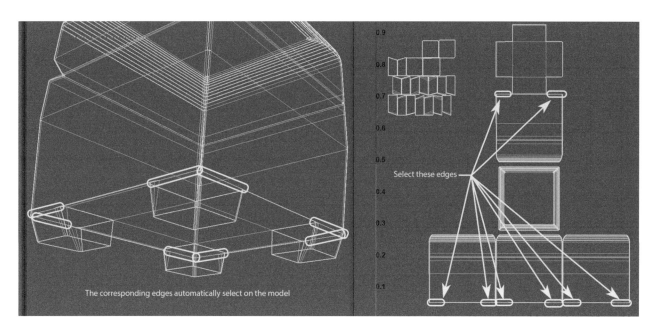

FIGURE 7.109 Select these individual edges either in the model view or in the UV Editor.

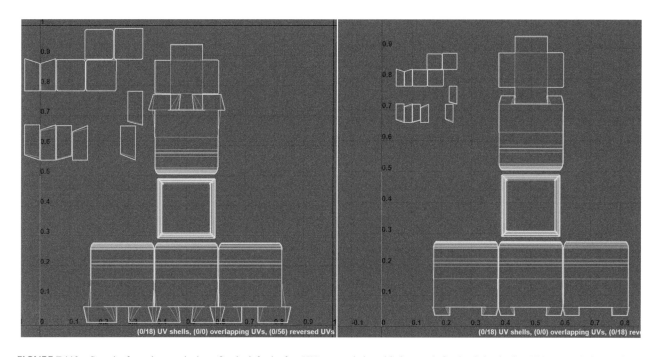

FIGURE 7.110 Sew the feet edges to the box. On the left, the feet UVs are scaled too big in step 4. On the right, the feet UVs are scaled properly.

lay out the UVs to make painting and editing in Photoshop easier.

In the UV Editor, select the box top's edges, as shown in Figure 7.116 (left). Then in the UV Editor menu, choose Cut/ Sew ➢ Move and Sew and your UV layout should match Figure 7.116 (right). The top and sides of the box are all one UV shell now.

A good UV layout is essential for good texturing and is a cornerstone to a good look in rendering. You can check your work against the file `boxTexture01.ma` in the Scenes

folder of the Decorative_Box project on the companion web page. You can also take a much-needed breather. I hope you've been saving your work with File ➢ Increment and Save!

Color-Mapping the Box

Now that you have a good UV layout, you can output a UV snapshot and get to work editing your photos of the box to make the color maps. Start with the following steps:

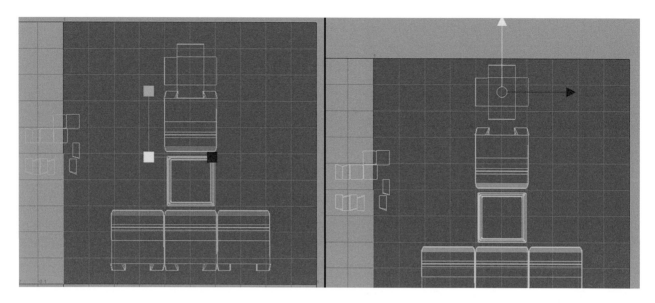

FIGURE 7.111   Scale down and re-center the UV layout (left); then select the shell and move the bottom UVs up in the UV Editor (right).

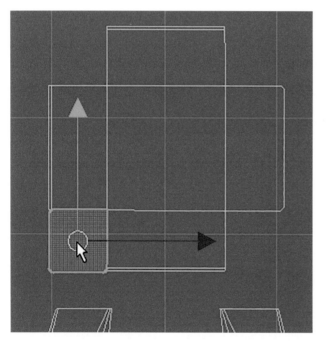

FIGURE 7.112   Select one square UV shell and move it to fit the box bottom UV shape.

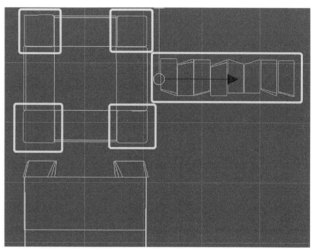

FIGURE 7.113   Place the feet bottoms to the box bottom and then line up the remaining feet UVs to the side.

1. Select the box and open the UV Editor window. From the UV Editor menu, select Image ➤ UV Snapshot. In the UV Snapshot window, set Size X and Y to **2,048**. Change Image Format to TIFF.

    Click the Browse button and select a location for your UV snapshot image. Generally, the project's Sourceimages folder is the best place for it. Make sure you don't write over the UV snapshot already created for you. Type in a name for your UV snapshot and click OK to create the image. Figure 7.117 shows the option box, and Figure 7.118 shows the UV snapshot image.

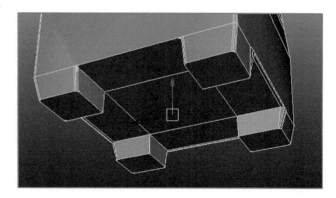

FIGURE 7.114   These faces will have a generic wood texture like the bottom of the box and do not need to be carefully lined up.

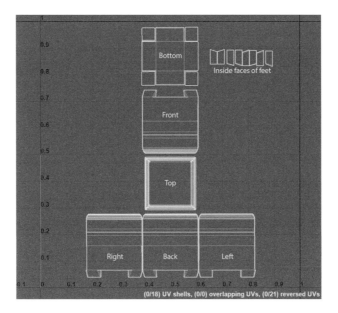

FIGURE 7.115   Finally, you're finished with the feet UVs.

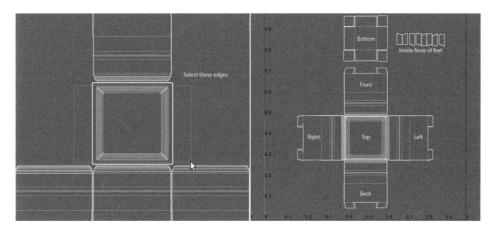

FIGURE 7.116   Select the box-top edges (left) and sew them together (right).

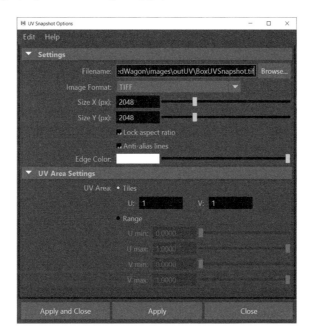

FIGURE 7.117   Setting the UV Snapshot options.

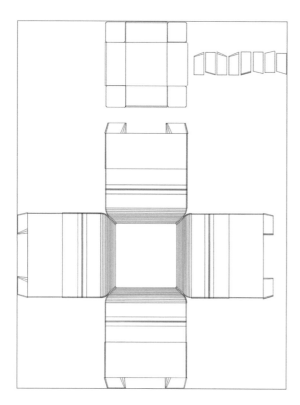

FIGURE 7.118 The UV snapshot for the decorative box, shown as black lines on white. You may see white lines on black in Photoshop.

2. Open the UV snapshot image in Photoshop or your favorite image editor and set it as its own layer. Rename the layer to **UV Snapshot**. I've done the heavy lifting for you and have prepared five photos of the decorative box that you can use to map the model. Figure 7.119 shows the photos of the box. This image file is included as `lineup.jpg` in the Sourceimages folder in the Decorative_Box project on the companion web page.

3. As you've probably guessed, you need to copy and paste the photos to their respective views over the UV Snapshot layer. Open the `lineup.jpg` file in Photoshop alongside the UV snapshot. Marquee+select a box around the top image (the one at the left in Figure 7.119) and copy it (Ctrl+C or Edit ➢ Copy in Photoshop).

4. Go to the UV snapshot image in Photoshop and paste the image on top. Rename the new layer to **Box Top** and set the layer's Opacity to 50% so you can still see the UV layout, as shown in Figure 7.120.

5. Use the Scale function in Photoshop (Edit ➢ Transform ➢ Scale) to move and scale the top image to fit over the top of the UV layout, as shown in Figure 7.121. Make sure you scale the box-top image uniformly to keep it from distorting.

   These photo images of the box have been retouched and painted to create an overlap. This means that parts of the sides of the box are shown in the top image. As you can see in Figure 7.121, the top image extends slightly all around the four sides. This allows the different parts of the texture map (top and four sides) to overlap and blend with each other better when put on the model.

   Save your work as `boxColorMap01.psd` in the project's Sourceimages folder. Saving as a Photoshop file will preserve the layers for easier editing.

6. Marquee+select the right-side image of the box (immediately to the right of the top image in `lineup.jpg`) and copy it. Paste it into `boxColorMap01.psd` in Photoshop. Do your best to align the right-side image with the top image, using the features of the box to line them up, as you can see in Figure 7.122. You can fix this later by adjusting both the map and the UVs on the box for a tighter fit. For now, be fairly accurate and leave the finesse for later. Save the file.

7. Use the same procedures in Photoshop to line up the other sides of the box, as shown in Figure 7.123. Set the box-top image to be the topmost layer, make sure all the layers are at 100% opacity, and then turn off the UV Snapshot layer so it's not visible.

8. And finally, open the file `boxBottomAndFeet.jpg` from the Sourceimages folder of the project. Select the entire image and copy and paste it into your `boxColorMap01.psd` file. Position and place the image to fit the bottom UVs of the box in your map in Photoshop. Just get close; you will fine-tune the placement of the image to UV later.

9. Save the final Photoshop file. Then, resave the file as a JPEG called `boxColorMap01.jpg`. This is the file you'll map (see Figure 7.124).

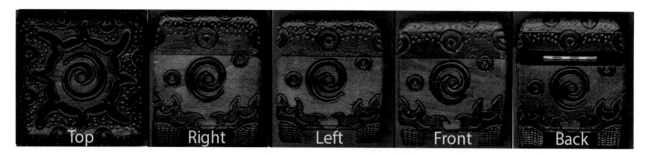

FIGURE 7.119 Photos of the box.

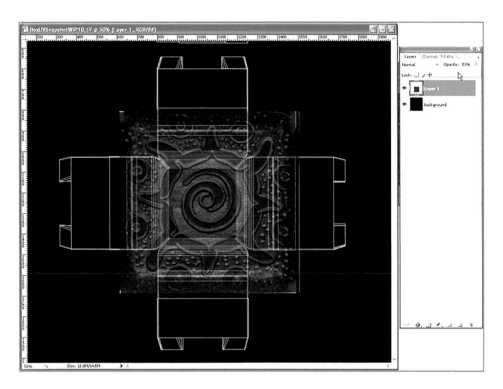

FIGURE 7.120   Paste the top image onto the UV snapshot image.

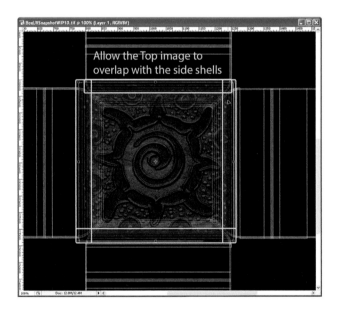

FIGURE 7.121   Position and scale the top image in Photoshop to line up with the UVs of the top of the model. Notice the overlap of the Top image over the side shells.

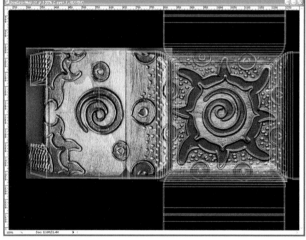

FIGURE 7.122   Align the right-side image with the right-side UVs.

Mapping the Box

Let's map this color image to the box and see how it fits. Based on rendering the box, you can make adjustments to the UVs and the image map to get everything to line up. This, of course, requires more Photoshop and/or image-editing experience, which could be a series of books of its own. If you don't have enough image-editing experience, have no fear: the images have been created for you so you can get the experience of mapping them and learn about the underlying workflow that this sort of texturing requires. Follow these steps:

1. In Maya, open the Hypershade window and create a new Phong shader. In the Property Editor, click the Map icon (■) next to the Color attribute and select File.

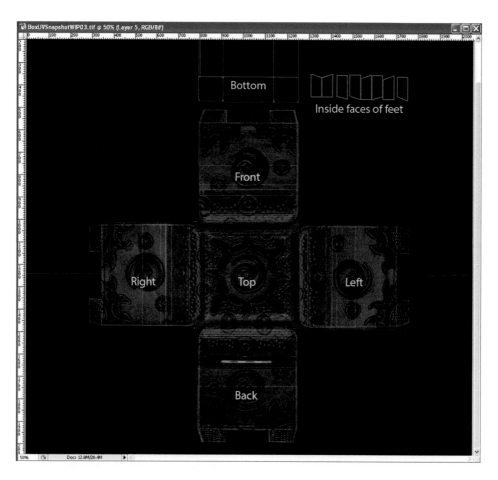

FIGURE 7.123 Copy, paste, and line up the box sides and the back to their respective UV areas.

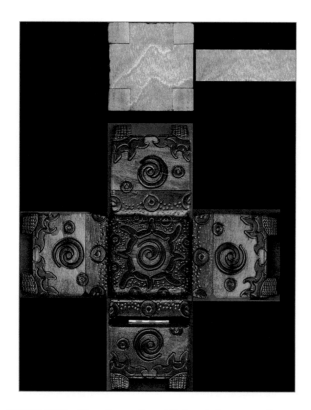

FIGURE 7.124 The color map layout file boxColorMap01.jpg.

2. In the Property Editor for the File icon, click the Folder icon next to the Image Name attribute, navigate to the Sourceimages folder for the project, and select the boxColorMap01.jpg file (not the PSD file). Graph the Input and Output Connections (⬛) on the new Phong into the work area (see Figure 7.125).

3. Select the file1 node and in the Property Editor rename it to **boxColorMap** (see Figure 7.126).

4. Select the box and assign the Phong shader to it. Rename the Phong to **boxShader**. In the persp viewport, press 6 for Texture view. The color map is fairly well aligned on the model. Not bad! (see Figure 7.127).

5. Render a frame to see how the box looks. Notice that there are small alignment issues at the edges where the sides meet and where the top meets the sides. Save your Maya scene.

This gives you a pretty good place to work from. You need to adjust the color map image to be more seamless. The scene file boxTexture02.ma in the Scenes folder of the Decorative_ Box project on the companion web page will catch you up to this point.

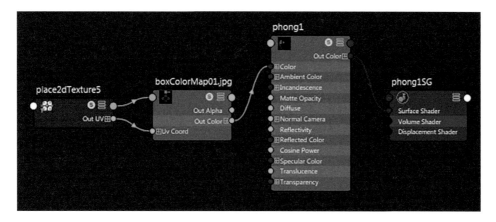

FIGURE 7.125   The color map's file node.

FIGURE 7.126   The icon is named properly.

FIGURE 7.128   Use masks to feather the transitions between the different parts of the box.

FIGURE 7.127   The color map fits pretty well already, but there are a few alignment issues at the edges.

Photoshop Work

This is where the image-editing experience is valuable. Here, it's all about working in Photoshop to further line up the sides to the top and the sides to each other to minimize alignment issues and yield a seamless texture map. Although I won't get into the minutia of photo editing here, I'll show the progression of the images and the general workflow used in Photoshop to make the color map's different sides and top line up or merge better. The images have already been created and are on the companion web page in the Sourceimages folder for this project.

For example, using masking in Photoshop, spend some time feathering the intersection of the box's sides in boxColor-Map01.psd so there is no hard line between the different sides and the top. Figure 7.128 shows a smoother transition between the different parts. This image has been created for you; it's boxColorMap02.jpg in the Sourceimages folder. Make sure you don't overwrite that file if you're painting your own.

In Maya, double-click the boxColorMap node in the Hypershade and in the Attribute Editor replace the original boxColorMap01.jpg file with the boxColorMap02.jpg file from the Sourceimages folder (or your own retouched image file). Render and compare the difference. The top and front should merge a little better. In the persp viewport, orbit around the box in Texture View mode (press 6) to identify any other alignment issues. In some cases, as you can see in Figure 7.129, gray or black is mapped onto the box on its right side, and there is a warped area. Also, the crease where the lid meets the box is lower than you've modeled.

The blank areas on the box are outside the bounds of the image in the Photoshop image and can be fixed by adjusting the UVs in Maya. The same goes for the distorted areas on the side of the box—you just need to adjust the UVs in Maya.

1. Select the box and open the UV Editor window. The image shows in the UV Editor under the UV wireframes. Figure 7.130 shows some primary areas for you to work on.

2. In the UV Editor, select the UVs (RMB+click and choose UV) shown in Figure 7.131 on the left. Press W for the Move tool and realign the UVs to

the seam where the lid meets the box, as shown in Figure 7.131, on the right. As you make the changes in the UV Editor, you should immediately notice them in the Perspective window (as long as you're in Texture View mode).

3. Look at the image on top in Figure 7.132. Move the appropriate UVs to align the edge of the UV layout to the image for the right side of the box, as shown on the bottom of Figure 7.132.

4. The distortion is getting better, and the texture fits nicer. But notice in the image on the left of Figure 7.133 that the right side of the box and the back of the box don't line up well. There are some other instances of the textures not lining up well all around the box. Using the Texture View mode (press

FIGURE 7.129   There are blank areas on the box as well as a little distortion.

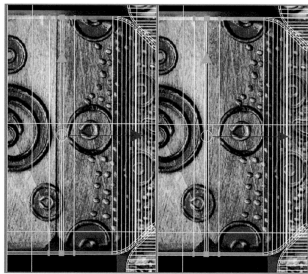

FIGURE 7.131   Move the UVs.

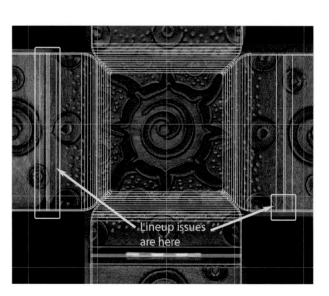

FIGURE 7.130   Here are the main problems to fix.

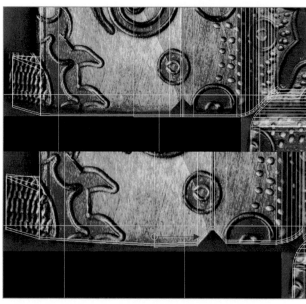

FIGURE 7.132   Line up the UVs to the image for the right side of the box.

FIGURE 7.133   Line up the UVs for the right-side/back-side edge of the box.

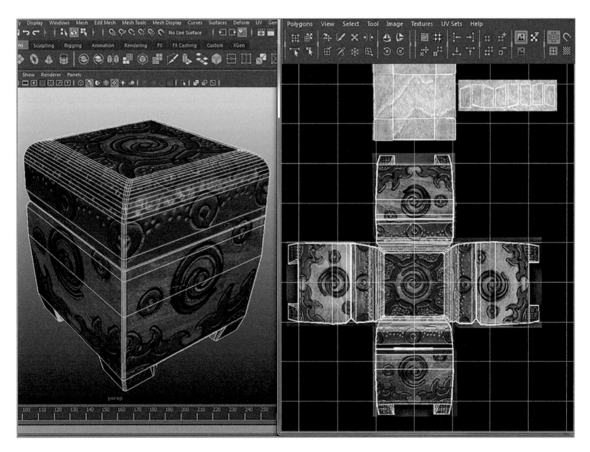

FIGURE 7.134   The UVs laid out for the decorative box.

6) in the Perspective window and the UV Editor, go around the box in its entirety and adjust the UVs, point by point as needed, so that they all line up with the image in the UV Editor. Make sure that the sides line up at the edges of the box as well as you can. The image on the right of Figure 7.133 shows correctly aligned UVs for the right side/back side of the box. Don't forget to line up the bottom of the box and feet, too. That part should be much easier.

This part of tweaking the UVs takes time and patience. The key is to keep looking back and forth between the UV Editor and the persp panel to see how the textures are lining up as you move the UVs. Figure 7.134 shows the UV Editor and a persp view of the box with UVs lined up and reasonably ready to go. You can compare your work to the scene file `boxTexture03.ma` in the Scenes folder of the Decorative_Box project on the companion web page. Render a few different views to take in all the hard work. In Chapter 10, you'll light the box and prepare it for rendering, and in Chapter 11, you'll use displacement maps created from these photos to detail the indentations and carvings that are in the actual box. You've had enough excitement for one chapter.

Toon Shading

Not everything needs to be textured to look real. Maya has a neat shading system that gives you a cartoon look using clever shaders and a powerful feature called Paint Effects, which you will look at a bit more in Chapter 12. The toon-shading system makes your scenes and animations render more like traditional cartoons with flat colors and outlines. Next, you'll take a quick look at how to apply toon shading to the wagon you textured earlier in this chapter to make it render more like a cartoon.

Try This

Set your project to the RedWagon project and open the `RedWagonModel.ma` scene file from the Scenes folder.

1. You'll see the wagon in a 3/4 view in the persp viewport. Select all the parts of the body of the wagon without the railings or wheels, as shown in Figure 7.135.

2. Switch to the Rendering menu set (F6) and select Toon ➤ Assign Fill Shader ➤ Shaded Brightness

FIGURE 7.135　Select the main body of the wagon, without the wheels or the rails.

Two Tone. There is a new Ramp shader added to the scene in the Hypershade's Materials tab. Select and graph it into the work area, as shown in Figure 7.136.

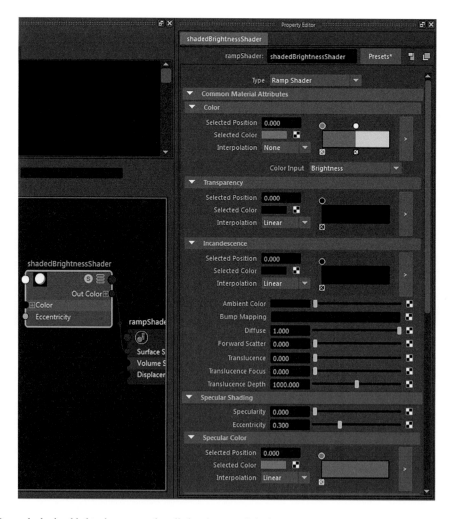

FIGURE 7.136　A Ramp shader is added to the scene and applied to the wagon's body.

FIGURE 7.137   The wagon now has a toon-shaded body. The front side of the wagon is a darker red than the front because of the lighting in the scene.

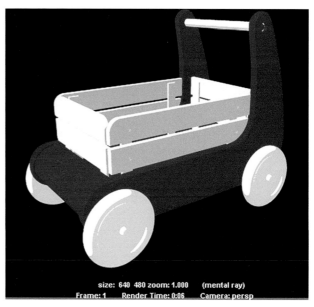

FIGURE 7.138   The wagon has Toon shaders for the fill color applied.

FIGURE 7.139   The black outlines are applied, but they're too thick.

3. Under the Color heading, set the color of the gray part of the ramp to a dark red and set the white part of the ramp to a bright red. Your wagon should turn red in the persp viewport if you're in Shaded or Texture view. Render a frame, and you should see the wagon in only two tones of red but with gray railings and wheels (shown in grayscale in Figure 7.137).

4. Select the rail objects and select Toon ➤ Assign Fill Shader ➤ Shaded Brightness Two Tone to create another Toon shader. Set the colors to a dark tan and a bright tan color in the Color ramp.

5. Select the handlebar and all four wheels and create another two-tone fill shader with a gray and white Color ramp (which is the default).

6. The frame, railings, and wheels now have a Toon shader as well. Notice the wheels in Figure 7.138 and how cool they look when toon-shaded. Of course, adjust any of the colors to your liking.

7. Now for the toon outlines. Select all the parts of the wagon and select Toon ➤ Assign Outline ➤ Add New Toon Outline. A black outline appears around the outside of the wagon's parts, and a new node called pfxToon1 appears in the Outliner or Hypergraph. The outlining is accomplished with Paint Effects.

8. Before you render a frame, set the background to white to make the black toon outlines pop. To do so, select the persp camera and open the Attribute Editor. Under the Environment heading, set Background Color to white.

9. Open the Render Settings window and make sure that the renderer is set to Maya Software. Render a frame and compare your work to Figure 7.139. The outlines are too thick!

10. Select the pfxToon1 node in the Outliner and open the Attribute Editor window. Click the pfxToon-Shape1 tab to open the attributes for the outlines. Set the Line Width attribute to **0.03** and render a frame. Compare your work to Figure 7.140.

Adjust the toon outline thickness the way you like and have some fun playing with the toon outline's attributes to see how they affect the toon rendering of the wagon. You can check your work with the RedWagonToon_v01.ma file in the Scenes folder of the RedWagon project. As you can see, there are a lot of attributes for the toon outlines. Paint Effects is quite a complex system, but after you experiment with the toon outlines, it'll make much more sense. You will return to Paint Effects in Chapter 12 for another quick look at that wonderful system.

Feel free to adjust the colors and the ramps of the fill shader to suit your tastes, and you can easily try the other Fill shader types, such as a three-tone shader to get a bit more detail in the

FIGURE 7.140 The cartoon wagon.

coloring of the wagon. This is just a quick primer to get you into toon shading. The rest, as always, is up to you. With some playing and experimenting, you'll be rendering some pretty nifty cartoon scenes in no time.

For Further Study

For a challenge and more experience, create new image maps for the wagon and try your own decal designs with more traditional (non-toon) renders. You can even change the textures for the decorative box and make your own design. As previously suggested, you can try to create more realistic wood maps for the wagon's railings. In Chapter 10, you'll begin to see how shading and rendering go hand in hand; you'll adjust many of the shader attributes you created in this chapter to render the toy plane and decorative box in Chapter 11.

Summary

In this chapter, you learned about the types of shaders and how they work. Each shader has a set of attributes that give material definition, and each attribute has a different effect on how a model looks.

To gain practice, you textured the toy plane scene using a couple of shaders and texture nodes.

Next, you learned about the methods you can use to project textures onto a surface, and you learned about the Maya texture nodes, including PSD networks and the basics of UVs, and how to use them to place images onto your wagon and decorative box models in detailed exercises exposing you to manipulating UVs and using Photoshop to create maps. And finally, you took a quick look at toon shading and created a cartoonish render of the wagon.

Texturing a scene is never an isolated process. Making textures work involves render settings, lighting, and even geometry manipulation and creation. Your work in this chapter will be expanded in Chapters 10 and 11 with discussions of lighting and rendering.

The single best weapon in your texturing arsenal, and indeed in all aspects of CG art, is your eye, specifically, your observations of the world around you and how they relate to the world you're creating in CG.

8

Introduction to Animation

Learning Outcomes

In this chapter, you will be able to

Set keyframes to establish the movement scheme for an object

Import objects into a scene

Create the feeling of weight and mass for an animated object using scale animation

Read animation curves in the Graph Editor

Differentiate among different animation principles such as squash, stretch, anticipation, and follow-through

Set up a hierarchy for better animation control

Transfer animation between objects

Create text

Create motion trails and animate objects along a path

Set up models for animation

Use selection handles to speed up workflow

Animate objects in time with each other

Keyframe Animation: Bouncing a Ball

No matter where you study animation, you'll always find the classic animation exercise of creating a bouncing ball. Although it's a straightforward exercise and you've probably seen it a hundred times on the Web and in other books, the bouncing ball is a perfect exercise with which to begin animating. You can imbue the ball with so much character that the possibilities are almost endless, so try to run this exercise as many times as you can handle. You'll improve with every attempt.

First, you'll create a rubber ball and create a simple animation hierarchy for it. Then, you'll add cartoonish movement to accentuate some principles of the animation techniques discussed at the end of the ultra-fabulous Chapter 1, "Introduction to Computer Graphics and 3D." This exercise also serves to reinforce hierarchies in animation.

Visit the book's web page for a video tutorial on this ball animation exercise.

Creating a Cartoon Ball

First, you need to create the ball, as well as the project for this exercise. Follow these steps:

1. In a new scene, make sure you have turned off Interactive Creation. Begin by creating a poly sphere and then create a poly plane. Scale the plane up to be a ground.

2. Press 5 for Shaded mode.

3. Move the sphere 1.0 unit up in the Y-axis so that it's resting on the ground and not halfway through it, as shown in Figure 8.1.

4. Choose Modify ➤ Freeze Transformations to set the ball's resting height to **0**, as opposed to 1. This action sets the ball's Translate attribute to 0, effectively resetting the object's values. This is called *freezing the transforms*. This is useful when you position, scale, and orient an object and need to set its new location, orientation, and size as the beginning state.

5. Choose File ➤ Project Window to create a new project. Call the project **Bouncing_Ball** and place it in the same parent folder as your Solar_System project folder. Choose Edit ➤ Reset Settings to create the necessary folders in your project and then click Accept. Save the scene file into that project.

Setting Up the Hierarchy

First, you'll set up the ball with three null nodes above it, listed here from the top parent node down: translate, scale, rotate. All the animation will be placed on these three nodes and not the sphere itself. This allows you to easily animate the ball bouncing, squashing, stretching, and moving forward in space.

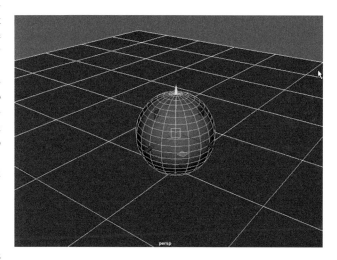

FIGURE 8.1   Place the ball on the ground.

DOI: 10.1201/9780429490958-9

1. Select the sphere and press Ctrl+G to create the first group (or Edit ➤ Group). In the Outliner, call this new group **rotate**.
2. With the rotate node selected, press Ctrl+G to create the **scale** group and name it **scale**.
3. With the scale group selected, press Ctrl+G one last time to create the **translate** group and name it **translate**. Figure 8.2 shows the hierarchy.

As you animate, you'll quickly see why you've set up a hierarchy for the ball, instead of just putting keys directly on the sphere.

Animating the Ball

Your next step is to keyframe the positions of the ball using the nodes above the sphere. You'll start with the *gross animation*, which is to say the overall movement scheme, a.k.a. *blocking*. You'll move the ball up and down to begin its choreography in these steps:

1. Press W to open the Translate tool, select the translate group node, and move it up to the top of the frame, say about 10 units up in the Y-axis and 8 units back in the X-axis at (−8, 10, 0). Place the camera so that you'll have some room to work in the frame.
2. Instead of selecting the Translate attributes in the Channel Box and RMB+clicking for the Key Selected command, you'll use hotkeys this time.
   Press Shift+W to set keyframes on Translate X, Translate Y, and Translate Z at frame 1 for the top node of the ball (named translate). Maya is by default set to animate at 24 fps, which is preferred. However, let's see how to change frame rates with this

FIGURE 8.2 The ball's hierarchy.

exercise. Choose Windows ➤ Settings/Preferences ➤ Preferences to open the Preferences window or by clicking the Animation Preferences button ( ) next to the Auto Keyframe button. In the Settings category of the Preferences window, set Time to NTSC (30 fps). A frame range of 1–120 is good for now. Figure 8.3 shows the ball's start position. Feel free to change the frame rate back to 24 fps for other projects.

3. In the lower-right corner of the user interface (UI), click the Auto Keyframe button ( ) to turn it on; it turns red. Auto Keyframe automatically sets a keyframe at the current time for any attribute that has changed since its last keyframe for the selected object or node.

> For the Auto Keyframe feature to work, you first have to set an initial keyframe manually for each of the attributes you want to animate.

4. Disregarding any specific timing, go to frame 10 and move the ball down in the Y-axis until it's about one-quarter through the ground plane. Since you'll be creating squash and stretch for this cartoon ball (see Chapter 1 for a brief explanation), you need to send the ball through the ground a little bit. Then, move the ball about 3 units to the right, to about (−5, −0.4, 0). The Auto Keyframe feature sets a keyframe in the X- and Y-axes at frame 10. Remember, this is all on the translate node, not the sphere geometry itself.
5. Move to frame 20 and raise the ball back up to about half of its original height and to the right about 2.5 units (−2.5, 4, 0). Auto Keyframe sets X and Y Translation keyframes at frame 20 and will continue to set keyframes for the ball as you animate.
6. At frame 30, place the ball back down a little less than one-quarter of the way through the ground and about 2 units to the right, at about (−0.5, −0.3, 0).
7. At frame 40, place the ball back up in the air in the Y-axis at a fraction of its original height and to the right about 1.5 units, at about (1.1, 1.85, 0).
8. Repeat this procedure every 10 frames to about frame 110 so that you bounce the ball a few more times up and down and to the right (positive in the X-axis). Make sure you decrease the ball's height and travel in X with each successive bounce and decrease how much the ball passes through the ground with every landing until it rests on top of the ground plane. Open the Graph Editor for a peek into the ball's animation curves (see Figure 8.4). (Choose Windows ➤ Animation Editors ➤ Graph Editor.)

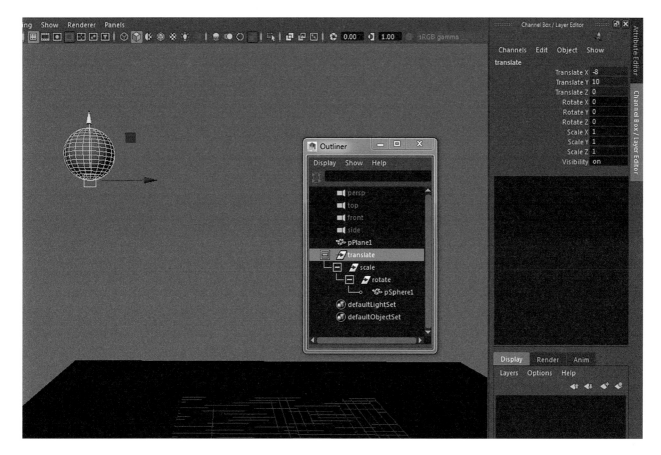

FIGURE 8.3   Start the ball here and set a keyframe on the translate node.

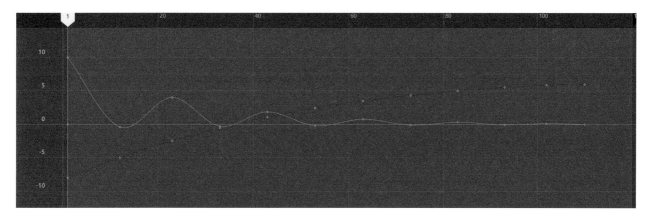

FIGURE 8.4   The Graph Editor curves for the ball's translate node.

By holding down the Shift key as you pressed W in step 2, you set a keyframe for Translate. Likewise, you can keyframe Rotation and Scale with hotkeys. Here's a summary of the keystrokes for setting keyframes:

Shift + W
Sets a keyframe for the selection's position in all three axes at the current time.

Shift + E
Sets a keyframe for the selection's rotation in all three axes at the current time.

Shift + R
Sets a keyframe for the selection's scale in all three axes at the current time.

You'll resume this exercise after a look at the Graph Editor.

Using the Graph Editor

To use the Maya Graph Editor, select Windows ➤ Animation Editors ➤ Graph Editor. It's an unbelievably powerful tool for the animator (see Figure 8.5) to edit keyframes in animation.

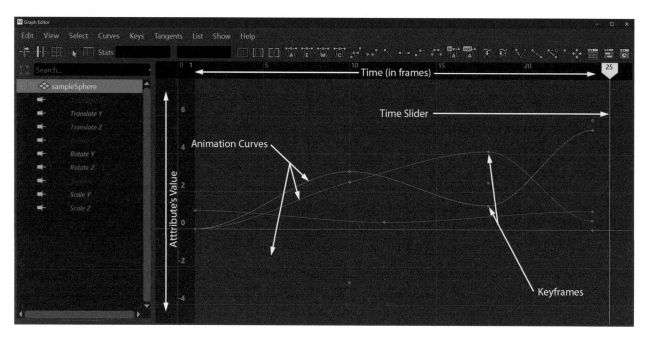

FIGURE 8.5 The Graph Editor.

Every movement that is set in Maya generates a graph of value versus time, and the Graph Editor gives you direct access to those curves for fine-tuning your animation. The Graph Editor displays animation curves as value versus time, with value running vertically and time horizontally. Keyframes are represented on the curves as points that can be freely moved to adjust timing or value. This window is truly an animator's best friend. Move a keyframe in time to the right (to be later in the timeline), for example, to slow the action. Move the same keyframe to the left (to be earlier in the timeline) to speed up the action.

The Graph Editor is divided into two sections. The left column, much like the Outliner, displays the selected object(s) and their hierarchy with a listing of any animated channels or attributes. By default, all of an object's keyframed channels are displayed as colored curves in the display to the right of the list. However, by selecting an object's attribute(s) in the list in the left side column, you can isolate only those animation curves.

Reading the Curves in the Graph Editor

Using the Graph Editor to *read animation curves*, you can judge an object's direction, speed, acceleration, and timing. You'll invariably come across problems and issues with your animation that require a careful review of their curves. Here are a couple of key concepts to keep in mind.

The curves in the Graph Editor are like the NURBS curves you've modeled so far. This time, points on an animation curve represent keyframes, and you can control the curvature with their *tangency handles*. By grabbing one end of a key's handle and dragging it up or down, you adjust the curvature. You will see the tangent when you select a keyframe.

The vertical part of the graph is a representation of the object attribute's position (or rotation or scale or other animated

attribute), while time is represented by the horizontal part of the graph. Not only does the placement of the keys on the curve make a big difference but so does the shape of the curve itself. Here is a quick primer on how to read a curve in the Graph Editor and, hence, how to edit it.

In Figure 8.6, the object's Translate Y attribute is being animated. In the beginning, the curve slowly begins to move positively, which means that the object is going up in space. The object then turns sharply (linear tangent) to go back down, coming to an *ease-out*, where it decelerates to a stop and then turns to go back up, easing to a final stop at the highest of its travel. The stop is signified by the flat part of the curve at the last keyframe at frame 24.

Consider a single object in motion. The shape of the curve in the Graph Editor defines how the object moves. The object shown in Figure 8.7 is moving in a steady manner in one direction.

Figure 8.8 shows the object slowly accelerating toward frame 24, where it suddenly comes to a stop. If there is nothing beyond the end of the curve, there is no motion. The one exception deals with the *infinity* of curves, which is discussed shortly.

The object in Figure 8.9 begins moving immediately and comes to a slow stop by frame 24, where the curve first becomes flat.

Animating a Cartoon Ball

Now, let's apply what you've learned about the Graph Editor to the bouncing ball. Follow these steps:

1. Select the ball's position group node in the Outliner and in the Graph Editor, look at the animation curves. They should be similar to the curves shown earlier in Figure 8.4.

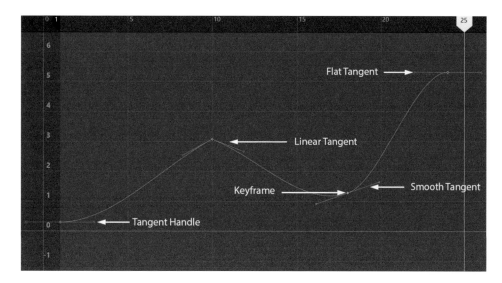

FIGURE 8.6 An animation curve.

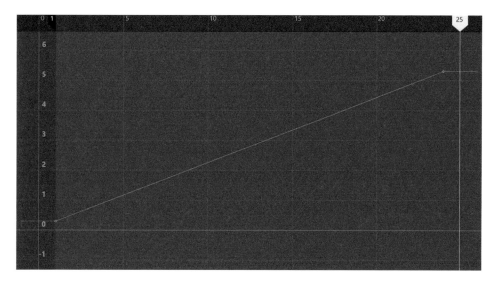

FIGURE 8.7 Linear movement.

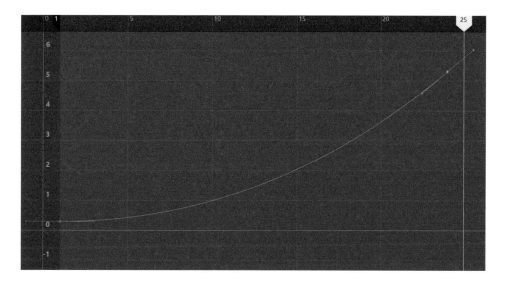

FIGURE 8.8 Acceleration (ease-in).

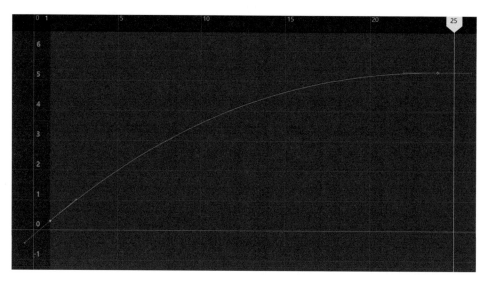

FIGURE 8.9 Deceleration (ease-out).

2. Notice how only the X- and Y-axes' translates have curves, and yet Translate Z has a single keyframe but no curve. It's from the initial position keyframe you set at frame 1. Because you've moved the sphere only in the X- and Y-axes, Auto Keyframe hasn't set any keys in the Z-axis.

3. Play back the animation and see how it feels. Be sure to open the Animation Preferences window. Click the Animation Preferences icon ( ) to set the playback speed to Real-Time (30 fps). You'll find this icon in the Playback section in the Time Slider category.

4. Timing is the main issue now, so you want to focus on how fast the ball bounces and then move keyframes to tweak the animation. To move a keyframe, select it in the Graph Editor, then press W for the Move tool, and then MMB+click to move it. But before you move any keys, do the following:

   • Watch the motion, and you'll see that the ball is falling too fast initially, although the second and third bounces should look fine.

   • To fix the timing, move the keyframes in the Graph Editor. For the X- and Y-axes, select the keyframes at frame 10 and all the others beyond on both curves. Move them all back to two frames (see Figure 8.10). Press and hold the Shift key while moving using the MMB_click to keep the keys moving only in axis (left-right or up-down) so that you only change the time and don't accidentally change the value of the key, too.

Currently, as the ball's bounce decays over time, it goes up less in the animation, but still takes the same amount of time (10 frames) to go up the lesser distance. For better timing, adjust the last few bounces to occur faster. Select the keys on the last three bounces and move them, one by one, a frame or two to the left to decrease the time for these last few bounces to speed them up (see Figure 8.11).

> To move a key in the Graph Editor, press W to enter the Move tool, MMB+click, and drag the cursor in the Graph Editor window. Press the Shift key and drag the cursor left and right or up and down to lock the movement to either horizontal or vertical to make it easier to control.

Understanding Timing

In animation, timing is all about getting the keyframes in the proper order. Judging the speed of an object in animation is critical to getting it to look right, and that comes down to timing. Download the file `ball_v1.ma` from the Bouncing_Ball project on the companion web page, to get to this point.

When you playback the animation, it seems unrealistic, as though the ball is rising and falling on a wave or a rubber band, rather than hitting the ground and bouncing back up. The problem with the animation is that the ball eases in and out as it rises and falls. By default, setting a key in Maya sets the keyframes to have an ease-in and ease-out in their curves, meaning their curves are smooth like a NURBS curve. In this case, for a more natural motion, you need to accelerate the ball as it falls with a sharp valley in the curve, and you need to decelerate it as it rises with smooth, rounded peaks. Follow these steps:

1. In the Graph Editor, select the Translate Y entry for the ball's translate group node in the left panel of the window to isolate your view to just that curve in the editor panel on the right. Select all the landing keyframes (the ones in the valleys of the curve) and change their interpolation from smooth to linear by clicking the Linear Tangents button ( ).

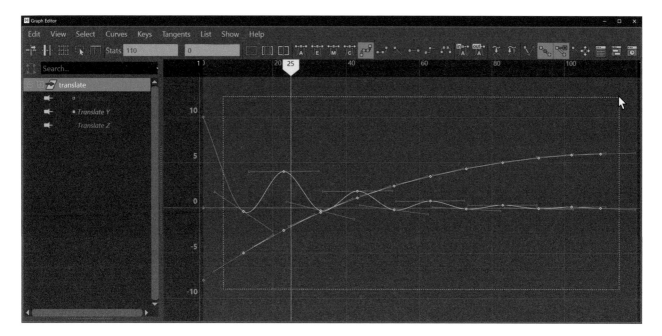

FIGURE 8.10 Move all the selected keyframes for both curves to the right to slow the initial fall by two frames, but leave the timing the same for the rest.

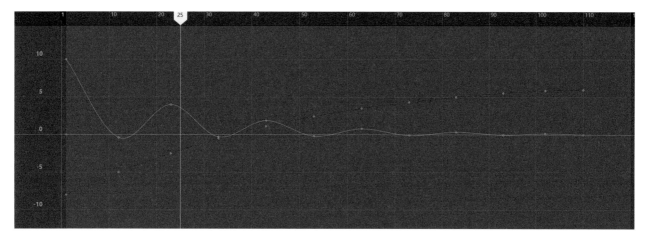

FIGURE 8.11 Move keys to make the final short bounces quicker and the bounce height feel right.

2. Likewise, select all the peak keyframes at the ball's rise and change their tangents to flat by clicking the Flat Tangents icon ( ) to make the animation curve like the one shown in Figure 8.12.

3. When you play back the animation, the ball seems to be moving more realistically. If you need to, adjust the keys a bit more to get the timing to feel right to you, before you move on to squash and stretch and rotation.

Squashing and Stretching the Ball

The concept of *squash and stretch* has been an animation staple for as long as animation has existed. It's a way to convey the weight of an object by deforming it to react (usually in an exaggerated way) to gravity and motion. You can do this by scaling your object.

Download the file `ball_v2.ma` from the Bouncing_Ball project on the book's web page and follow these steps to make sure the timings used below work for you:

1. Select the scale group node (not the sphere itself!) and select Modify ➤ Center Pivot. This places the scale pivot point in the middle of the ball.

2. At frame 9, press Shift+R to set initial scale keyframes on the scale node of the ball, a few frames before the ball impacts the ground.

3. To initiate squash and stretch, go to frame 12, where the ball hits the floor the first time. With the scale node selected, press R to open the Scale tool; scale the ball down in the Y-axis until it no longer goes

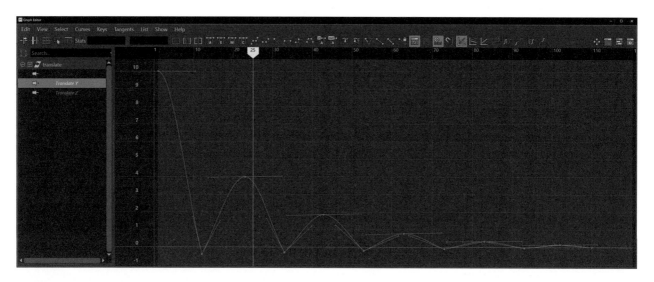

FIGURE 8.12 The adjusted timing of the bounce.

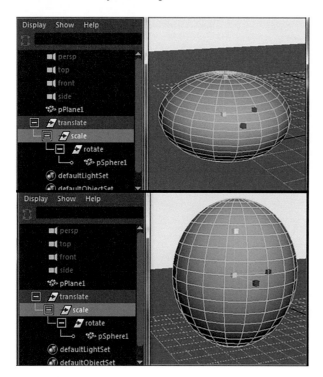

FIGURE 8.13 Squashing and stretching the ball to react to bouncing on the floor.

through the floor (about **0.6**), as shown in the image on the top in Figure 8.13. Set a keyframe for scale by pressing Shift+R.

4. Move ahead in the animation about three frames to frame 15. Scale the ball up in the Y-axis slightly past normal to stretch it up (about **1.15**) immediately after its bounce, as shown in the image on the bottom in Figure 8.13. Three frames later, at frame 18, set the Y-axis scale back to **1** to return the ball to its regular shape.

5. Scrub your animation, and you should see the ball begin stretching even before it hits the ground. That's a bit too much exaggeration, so open the Graph Editor

and move the Y-axis scale key from 9 to 11. Now, the ball squashes when it hits the floor and stretches as it bounces up.

6. Repeat this procedure for the remaining bounces, squashing the ball as it hits the floor and stretching it as it bounces up. Remember to decay the scale factor as the ball's bouncing decays to a stop; the final bounce or two should have very little squash and stretch, if any.

Download the file `ball_v3.ma` from the Bouncing_Ball project on the book's web page to get to this point.

Rolling the Ball

Let's add some roll to the ball in the following steps:

1. Select the ball's rotate node and select Modify ➤ Center Pivot to set that node's pivot at the center of the ball.

2. At frame 1, press Shift+E to set keys for rotation at (**0, 0, 0**).

3. Scrub to the end of your animation (frame 100 in this example) and set a value of **−480** for Rotate Z in the Channel Box.

4. Open the Graph Editor to see the rotation curve on the ball's rotate group node. It's a linear (straight) line angled down from 0 to −480. You need the rotation to slow to a stop at the end of the animation, so select the final keyframe and click to make it a flat tangent, as shown in Figure 8.14.

Load the file `ball_v4.ma` from the Bouncing_Ball project from the companion web page to see an example of the finished bouncing ball. Although the bouncing of this ball looks okay, it could definitely use some finesse, a little timing change, and so on. Open the file, open the Graph Editor, and edit the file to get a feel for animating it in your own style.

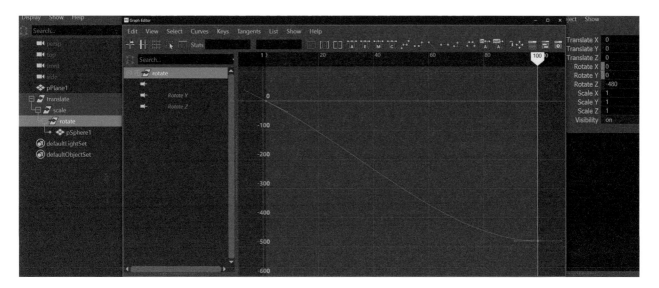

FIGURE 8.14   Setting a roll for the ball.

The ball's hierarchy (grouping) was set up this way to allow the movement, scale, and roll animations of the ball to remain discrete. This way the ball squashes and stretches properly, whereas if all those animations were put on the sphere geometry itself without these group nodes, the ball would not squash and stretch properly and would look it would weird. Frequently in animation production, objects are given controllers (such as these group nodes) so that keyframes are placed on these controls, as opposed to the geometry itself for maximum flexibility and best outcome.

Throwing an Axe

This next project will exercise your use of hierarchies and introduce you to creating and refining motion to achieve proper animation for a more complex scene than the bouncing ball. The workflow is simple but standard for properly setting up a scene for animation, also known as *rigging*. First, you'll model an axe and its target, and then you'll set up the grouping and pivots for how you want to animate. Then you'll throw your axe!

The Preproduction Process

To begin the animation right away, you'll use a basic axe and bull's-eye target to focus on animation and technique.

Create a new project by choosing File ➢ Project Window and clicking the New button, or copy the project folders provided on the book's companion web page. Place this project in the same folder or drive as your other projects, call it **Axe**, and click Accept. Click the Animation Preferences button and make sure that the frames per second is 24 fps.

What separates good animation from bad animation is the feeling of weight that the audience infers from the animation. People instinctively understand how nature works in motion. You see an object in motion, how it moves, and how it affects its surroundings. From that, you can feel the essence of its motion, with its weight making a distinct impression on you. As it pertains to animation, that essence is simply called *weight*. A good feeling of weight in animation depends on timing and follow-through, which require practice.

It's a good idea first to try an action you want to animate. It may upset the cat if you grab a real axe and start throwing it around your house, but you can take a pen, remove its cap, and lob it across the room. Notice how it arcs through the air, how it spins around its center of balance, and how it hits its mark. Just try not to take out anyone's eye with the pen. According to some Internet research, the perfect axe throw should contain as few spins as possible.

Animating the Axe: Keyframing Gross Animation

The first step is to keyframe the positions of the axe, starting with its *gross animation*—that is, the movement from one end of the axe's trajectory to the other.

Setting Initial Keyframes

Load the scene file axe _ v1.mb in the Scenes folder of the Axe project from the companion web page and follow these steps:

1. Select the axe's top group node called axe. To make selecting groups such as this easier, display the object's selection handle. To do so, select the axe's top node and choose Display ➢ Transform Display ➢ Selection Handles. Doing this displays a small cross, called a *selection handle* (   ), at the axe's pivot point. You need only select this selection handle in the viewport now to select the top node of the axe, instead of selecting the group node in the Outliner.

You can turn on selection handles for practically any object in Maya—no matter where it is in a group's hierarchy—whether it's a child or a parent.

2. With the axe top node selected, go to frame 1 and set a keyframe for the rotation and translation.

3. Hold down the Shift key, press W for the axe's translation keyframes and then press E for the axe's rotation keyframes for its start position.

Creating Anticipation

Instead of the axe just flying through the air toward the target, you'll animate the axe moving back first to create *anticipation*, as if an invisible arm were pulling the axe back before throwing it. Follow these steps:

1. Go to frame 12.

2. Move the axe back in the X-axis about 8 units and rotate it counterclockwise about 45°.

3. The Auto Keyframe feature sets keyframes for the position and new rotation at frame 12.

Because you've moved the axe back only in the X-axis and made the rotation only on the Z-axis, Auto Keyframe sets keyframes only for Translate X and Rotate Z. Take note that the other position and rotation axes aren't auto-keyframed because their values didn't change.

4. Scrub through the animation and notice how the axe moves back in anticipation.

Auto Keyframe inserts a keyframe at the current time for the selected object's changed attributes only.

5. Go to frame 32 and place the axe (via its top group node) so that the blade cuts into the center of the target.

Notice that you have to move the axe in the X- and Y-axes, whereas before you had to move it back only in the X-axis to create anticipation. This is because the axis of motion for the axe rotates along with the axe. This is an example of the *Object Axis*. The Local axis for any given object shifts according to the object's orientation. Because you angled the axe back about 45°, its Object Axis rotated back the same amount.

The file `axe_v2.mb` in the Scenes folder of the Axe project from the companion web page will catch you up to this point in the animation.

This last step reveals a problem with the animation. If you scrub your animation now, you'll notice that the axe's

movement back is different from before, setting a keyframe at frame 32. Why intentionally create a problem like this? Troubleshooting problems in a scene is vital to getting good as a CG animator, so the more you learn how to diagnose problems, the easier production will become.

The problem is caused by the Auto Keyframe feature. At frame 1, you set an initial keyframe for the X-, Y-, and Z-axes of translation and rotation. Then, at frame 12, you moved the axe back in the X-axis only (in addition to rotating it in the Z-axis only).

Auto Keyframe has automatically set a keyframe for Translate X at frame 12. At frame 32, you moved the axe in *both* the X- and Y-axes to strike the target. Auto Keyframe has set keyframes at 32 for Translate X and Translate Y. Because the last keyframe for Translate Y was set at 1 and not at 12, as in the case of Translate X, there is now a bobble in the Y position of the axe between frames 1 and 12.

With the axe selected, open the Graph Editor (choose Windows ➤ Animation Editors ➤ Graph Editor) to see what's happening. You should see red, green, and blue line segments running up and down and left and right. You'll probably have to zoom your view to something more intelligible. By using the Alt key (or the Alt/Option key on a Mac) and mouse-button combinations, you can navigate the Graph Editor much as you can any of the modeling windows.

The hotkeys A and F also work in the Graph Editor. Click anywhere in the Graph Editor window to make sure it's the active window and press A to zoom all your curves into view. Your window should look something like Figure 8.15.

The curves in the Graph Editor represent the values of the axe's position and rotation at any given time. The X-, Y-, Z-axes are in their representative red, green, or blue color, and the specific attributes are listed much like they are in the Outliner in the left column. Selecting an object or an attribute on the left displays its curves on the right.

You should also notice that the curves are all at different scales. The three rotate curves range in value (vertical part of the graph) from about –45 to 45, the Translate Y curve ranges from about 15 to 5, and Translate Z looks flat in the Graph Editor. It's tough to edit a curve with low values and still be able to see the timings of a larger value curve at the same time.

You can select the specific attribute and zoom in on its curve to see it better, or you can *normalize* the curves so that you can see them all in one view. Click the Normalized View icon in

the top icon bar of the Graph Editor ( ) toward the right (Figure 8.16). The values don't change, but the curves now display in a better scale in relation to each other so you can see them all together.

Figure 8.16 also shows the Graph Editor from Figure 8.15 with the same curves but now in a normalized view. Keep in mind that this doesn't change the animation in the slightest. All it does is allow you to see all the curves and their relative motion. You can denormalize the view by clicking back to the

Absolute View icon in the Graph Editor ( ).

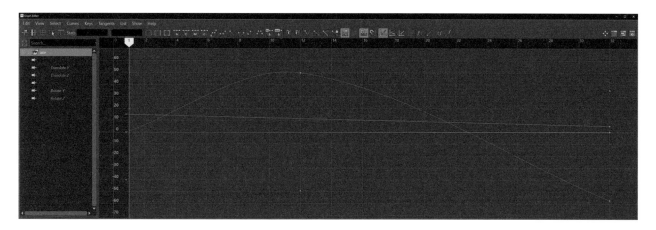

FIGURE 8.15 The Graph Editor displays the axe's animation curves.

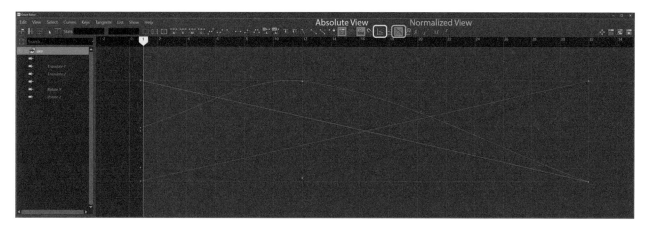

FIGURE 8.16 The normalized view in the Graph Editor lets you see all the curves of an animation together in the same scale.

Notice that the curve for Translate Y has keyframes only at frames 1 and 32. The animation dips in the first 15 frames because there is no keyframe at frame 12 like there is for Translate Z. That dip wasn't there before you set the end keyframe at frame 32.

Continue the exercise by fixing this issue:

1. Move the first keyframe of Translate Y from frame 1 to frame 12 to fix the dip.

   • Press W to activate the Move tool in Maya and select the first Translate Y keyframe. Now, we just want to move the key left-right, and not up-down, which would also change its value. To do that, you could press and hold Shift as you MMB+click to move the key, but this time,

   use the constrained movement (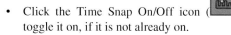) icon in the Graph Editor at the very top right for sideways-only movement of the keyframe (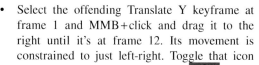).

• Click the Time Snap On/Off icon ( ) to toggle it on, if it is not already on.

• Select the offending Translate Y keyframe at frame 1 and MMB+click and drag it to the right until it's at frame 12. Its movement is constrained to just left-right. Toggle that icon

back to unconstrained movement ( ) when done. As stated before, you could have instead used Shift to constrain a key's movement as you MMB+click move it.

Scrub your animation, and the backward movement looks like it did before.

The axe now needs an arc on its way to the target.

2. Go to the middle of the axe's flight, frame 24.

3. Move the axe up in the Y-axis in the view panel by using the green handle of the Tool manipulator.

If the axe is slightly rotated in frame, Auto Keyframe can set a key for both Translate Y and

Translate X, although you were perhaps expecting only a key in Translate Y. Because the Move tool is on the axe's Object Axis and because the axe was slightly rotated at frame 27, there is a change in the Y and the X positions in the World axis, which is the axis represented in the Graph Editor.

4. Select the new Translate X key at frame 24, if one was created, and press Delete in the Graph Editor to delete it.

5. Now you'll add a full spin to the axe to give the animation more reality and life. You can spin it in one of two ways.

   • Go to frame 32, select the axe, and rotate it clockwise a full 360° positive. Auto Keyframe enters a new rotation value at frame 32, overwriting the old value. You should see the Rotate Z curve angle down steeply as soon as you let go of the Rotate manipulator.

   • In the Graph Editor, make sure you're at frame 32, grab the last keyframe on the Rotate Z curve, and MMB+click and drag it down, probably past the lower limit of the window. If you keep the middle mouse button pressed as you move the mouse, the keyframe keeps moving as you move the mouse, even if the keyframe has left the visible bounds of the Graph Editor.

If you hold down Shift as you MMB+click and drag the keyframe to move it in the Graph Editor, the keyframe will move in only one axis (up or down, left or right).

By moving the keyframe down, you change the Rotate Z value to a lower number, which spins the axe clockwise. Before you try that, though, move your Graph Editor window so you can see the axe in the Perspective window. As you move the Rotate Z keyframe down in the Graph Editor, you see the axe rotate interactively. Move the keyframe down until the axe does a full spin.

6. Play back the animation by clicking the Play button in the playback controls. If your animation looks blazingly fast, open the Animation Preferences window by clicking its icon in the lower right of the

   main Maya UI (⬚) and set Playback Speed to Real-Time (24 fps).

   Now, when you play back the animation, it should look slow. Maya is playing the scene back in real time, but even at 24 fps, the scene plays back slowly, which means that the animation of the axe is too slow.

7. All you need to do is tinker in the Graph Editor a bit to get the right timing. For a good result in timing, move the first set of keyframes from 12 to 10. Then, grab the Translate Y keyframe at frame 24 and move it to 15. Finally, grab the keyframes at frame 32 and move them all back to frame 20. Play back the scene.

Changing the playback speed of an animation through the Animation Preferences window doesn't alter the timing of your animation. It only changes the speed at which Maya plays the animation back to you in its windows. To change the playback speed, choose Windows ➤ Setting/Preferences ➤ Preferences to open the Preferences window, choose Settings ➤ Working Units, and select the proper setting.

Adding Follow-Through

Load the `axe_v3.mb` file from the Axe project on the book's web page or continue with your own file.

The axe is missing weight. You can add some finesse to the scene using follow-through and secondary motion to give more weight to the scene.

In the axe scene, follow-through motion is the axe blade driving farther into the target a little beyond its initial impact. Secondary motion is the recoil in the target as the momentum of the axe transfers into it. As you increase the amount of follow-through and secondary motion, you increase the axe's implied weight. You must, however, walk a fine line; you don't want to go too far with follow-through or secondary motion. Follow these steps:

1. Select the axe in the scene using its selection handle and open the Graph Editor.

2. Because you'll add three frames to the end of this animation for follow-through, go to frame 23 (20 is the end of the current animation).

3. In the Perspective window, rotate the axe clockwise another 1.5° or so in the Z-axis.

4. Rotating the axe in step 3 effectively moves the axe's blade down a bit in the Y-axis. To bring the axe back up close to where it was before the extra rotation, move the axe up slightly using the Translate Y manipulator handle. This also digs the axe into the target a little more. You'll see a keyframe for Translate Y and most probably for Translate X, as well as for Rotate Z.

   If you play back the animation, the follow-through doesn't look good. The axe hits the target and then digs into it as if the action were done in two separate moves by two different animators who never talked to each other. You need to smooth out the transition from the axe strike and its follow-through in the Graph Editor.

5. Highlight the Rotate Z attribute in the Graph Editor to not see the other curves in the window. Figure 8.17 shows the Rotate Z curve of the axe after the follow-through animation is added.

6. Focus on the last three frames of the curve and zoom into that range only. The curve, as it is now, dips down past where it should and recoils back up a small amount.

   When you set keyframes for the axe, you create Bézier splines animation curves in the Graph Editor.

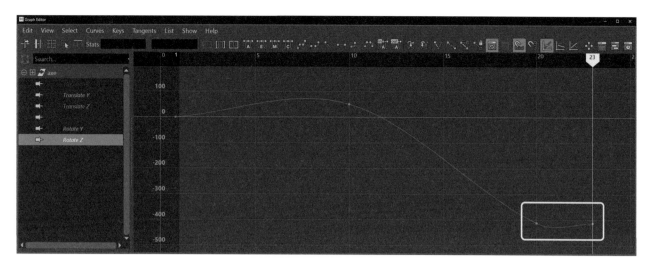

FIGURE 8.17 The Rotate Z curve of the axe after the follow-through animation.

These curves stay as smooth as possible from beginning to end. When you set the new keyframe, rotating the axe about 1.5 more degrees for follow-through, the animation curve responds by creating a dip, as shown in Figure 8.17, to keep the whole curve as smooth as possible.

SECONDARY MOTION AND FOLLOW-THROUGH

Secondary motion in animation comprises all the little things in a scene that move because something else in the scene is moving. For example, when a superhero jumps from a tall building and his or her cape flutters in the wind, the cape's undulation is secondary motion.

Follow-through is the action in animation that immediately follows an object's or a character's main action. For example, after the superhero lands from their jump, his or her knees buckle a little, and the superhero bends at the waist, reacting to his or her weight as it settles, creating follow-through.

The axe needs to hit the target with force and dig its way in, slowly coming to a stop. You need to adjust the curvature of the keyframes at frame 25 by using the keyframe's tangents. *Tangents* as you've seen are handles that change the amount of curvature influence of a point on a b-spline (Bézier spline). Selecting the keyframe in question reveals its tangents, as shown in Figure 8.18.

7. Select the Out tangent (handle on the right side of the key) for the Rotate Z attribute's key at frame 25 and MMB+click and drag it up to get rid of the dip. Notice that the tangency for the In tangent (handle on the left side of the key) also changes.

8. Press Z to undo your change. You need to break the tangent handles so that one doesn't disturb the other.

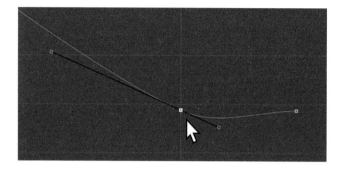

FIGURE 8.18 The tangent handles of a keyframe. The handle to the left of the keyframe is the In tangent, and the handle to the right is its Out tangent.

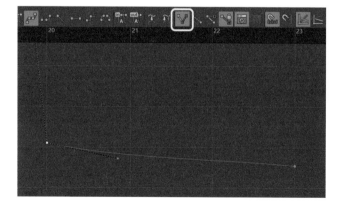

FIGURE 8.19 Zoomed into the end segment of the Rotate Z animation curve after the dip is fixed.

9. Select the Out handle and click the Break Tangents icon ( ) to break the tangent (Figure 8.19).

10. Move the handle up to get rid of the dip so that the curve segment from frame 25 to frame 28 is a straight line, angled down. Figure 8.19 is zoomed into this segment of the curve after it's been fixed and also shows where the Break Tangents icon is.

Now, to get the axe to stop slowly as it digs into the target, you need to curve that end segment of the Rotate Z curve to flatten it out.

11. Grab the last frame to reveal its handles. You can manually move the In handle to make it horizontal, or you can click the Flat Tangents icon (⬛▬⬛) on the left side of the icon bar, under the menus in the Graph Editor (Figure 8.20).

    The curve's final segment for Rotate Z should now look like Figure 8.20.

12. Adjust the keyframe tangents similarly for the axe's Translate Y and Translate X curves, as shown in Figure 8.21.

13. Play back the animation, and you should see the axe impact the target and sink into it a bit for its follow-through.

    Now, you need to polish things up more.

Adding Secondary Motion

Load `axe_v4.mb` from the Axe project from the book's web page or continue with your own scene file. For secondary

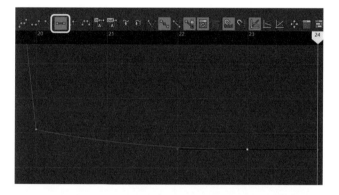

FIGURE 8.20 Zoomed into the end segment of the Rotate Z animation curve. Notice how the curve now smoothly comes to a stop by flattening out.

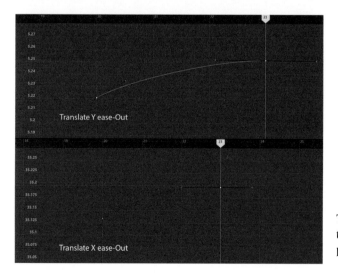

FIGURE 8.21 Smoothed translate curves to ease out the motion.

motion, you'll move the target in reaction to the impact from the axe's momentum.

An object in motion has momentum. Momentum is calculated by multiplying the mass of an object by its velocity. So, the heavier and faster an object is, the more momentum it has. When two objects collide, some or all momentum transfers from one object to the other.

In the axe scene's impact, the axe lodges in the target, and its momentum is almost fully transferred to the target. But because the target is more massive than the axe, the target moves only slightly in reaction. The more you make the target recoil, the heavier the axe will seem.

First, group the axe's parent node under the target's parent node by grouping the axe under the target; when you move the target to recoil, it will keep the axe lodged in it. You will use the Hypergraph instead of the Outliner, so let's take a quick look at its interface first.

Continuing the Axe

First, you need to reset the target node's Translate and Rotate attributes to **0** and its Scale attributes to **1**.

1. Go to frame 1 in the timeline. To freeze the transforms, select the target's group node (Target) and then choose Modify ➤ Freeze Transformations (Figure 8.22).

2. In the Outliner, MMB+click and drag the axe node to the target to group the axe node under the target node.

3. Go to frame 20, the moment of impact, and set Translate and Rotate keyframes on Target using Shift+W and Shift+E, respectively.

4. Go to frame 24, rotate the target node in the Z-axis about –2.5° (clockwise), and move it up and back slightly in the Y- and X-axes, as shown in Figure 8.23.

5. Go to frame 27. Rotate the target node back to 0 in the Z-axis, move it down to 0 in the Y-axis, and move it back a bit more in the X-axis.

> If you don't freeze the transforms on the target's parent node before grouping the axe under it, the axe's animation will change and yield undesirable results.

6. Go to frame 30 and repeat step 4, but move it only half as much in Rotate Z, Translate X, and Translate Y.

7. Go to frame 32 and repeat step 5 to put it back down on the ground, but move Target back only slightly in the X-axis.

The preceding steps should give you an animation similar to `axe_v5.mb` in the Axe project from the companion web page.

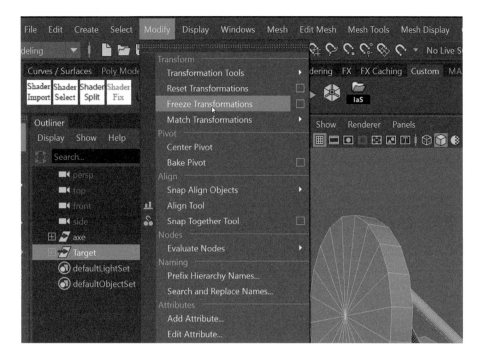

FIGURE 8.22 Freezing the Transformations of the Target group node.

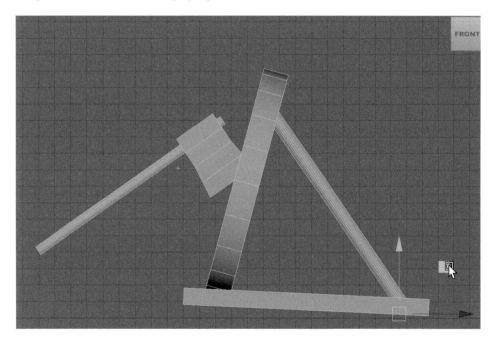

FIGURE 8.23 The front-view panel display of the target reacting to the impact of the axe.

Animating along a Path

As an alternative to keyframing the position of the axe, you can animate it along a path. Path animation allows you to assign an object to move along the course of a curve, called a *path*.

Load `axe_v6.mb` from the Axe project from the companion web page. This is the finished axe animation, but the translation keys have been deleted from the axe, though the rotation keys and everything else are intact. You'll replace the translation keyframes with a motion path instead. There is an arched curve in this scene called pathCurve that was already created for you using the CV curve tool. Look how nice I am to you!

1. Once you open the scene (`axe_v6.mb`), scrub the animation and you'll see that the axe spins around; it and the target recoil at the moment of impact, but the axe doesn't actually move. There is also a curve in the scene that represents the eventual motion of the axe.

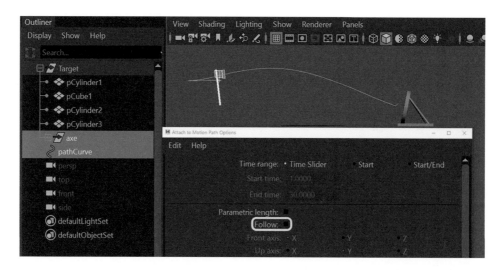

FIGURE 8.24   Select the Axe project's group node and the curve.

2. Go to frame 1 in the timeline and select the axe group node in the Outliner and then Shift+select the path curve (Figure 8.24). In the Animation menu set, choose Constrain ➤ Motion Paths ➤ Attach To Motion Path ❑.

3. In the option box, turn off the Follow check box.

The Follow feature orients the object on the path so that its front always points in the direction of travel. This will interfere with the axe's motion, so you'll leave it off. Click Apply, and now the axe will follow the line from end to end between frame 1 and frame 48. Of course, you have to adjust the timing to fit better, as with the original axe animation.

The file `axe_path_v1.mb` in the Axe project will bring you up to this point.

4. Select the axe node and open the Graph Editor to see the axe's curves. There is a violet-colored curve called motionPath1.U Value curve that now controls the translation. On the left side of the Graph Editor, select any of the motionPath1.U Value curve entries to display only that animation curve on the right of the editor. Zoom into the graph curve by pressing A to view all.

5. The curve is an ease-in and ease-out curve from 1 to 48. You need the axe to hit at frame 20, so move the end of that curve to frame 20 from frame 48. Then use the tangent handle to shape the end of the curve to be more like Figure 8.25. This will add acceleration to the end of the curve for more of a punch on the hit.

6. Scrub the animation until the axe moves all the way back (about frame 6). You'll add a keyframe here to help retime the backward movement. Select the purple U Value animation curve and then select the Insert Keys tool (▮▮) in the top-left corner of the Graph Editor. MMB+click the curve to create a key at frame 6. (You can MMB+click and then drag the

cursor to place the key precisely at frame 4 before releasing the mouse button.)

7. Move this new keyframe to frame 4. Scrub the animation, and the timing is just about right. You'll have to adjust the tangents a bit to make the axe move more like before, but the movement is essentially there with path animation.

The file `axe_path_v2.mb` in the Axe project will bring you up to this point.

Path animation is extremely useful, especially for animating an object along a particular course. By adjusting the resulting animation curve in the Graph Editor, you can easily readjust the timing of the path animation, and you can always adjust the shape of the path curve itself to change the motion of the object. A good path animation exercise is to reanimate the Solar_System exercise with paths instead of the keyframes that you set on the rotations.

Replacing an Object

It's common practice to animate a *proxy* object—a simple stand-in model that you later replace. The next exercise will show you one way how you can replace the axe you already animated with a fancier model of an axe and how to copy an animation from one object to another.

Replacing the Axe

Load the scene file `axe_v5.mb` from the book's web page. Now, follow these steps:

1. Choose File ➤ Import.

2. Locate and import the `Axe_Replace.ma` scene file from the Scenes folder of the Axe project from the companion web page. The new axe appears at the origin in your scene.

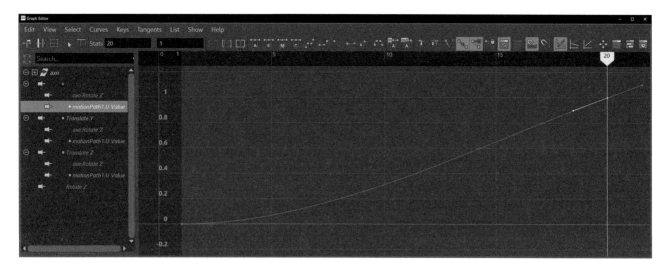

FIGURE 8.25 Set the last key to frame 20 and reshape the curve at the end.

Transferring Animation

Transferring all the properties and actions of the original axe to a new axe requires some setup. Follow these steps:

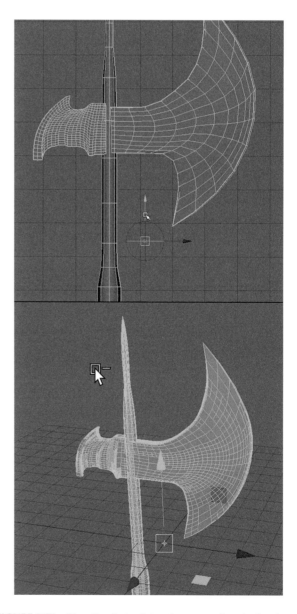

1. Move the pivot on the new axe's top node (called either new_Axe or Axe_Replacement:new_Axe) to the same relative position as the pivot on the original animated axe (up toward the top and a little out front of the handle, just under the blade). This ensures that the new axe has the same spin as the old axe. Otherwise, the animation won't look right when transferred to the new axe. Figure 8.26 shows the pivot's location for the new axe (top image).

2. Use grid snap to place the top node of the new axe at the origin (as seen in Figure 8.26 in the bottom image).

3. Choose Display ➤ Transform Display ➤ Selection Handles to turn on the selection handle of the new axe.

4. Go to frame 1. Select the original axe's axe node, open the Graph Editor, and in the Graph Editor's menu bar (not the main Maya menu), choose Edit ➤ Copy. This copies the original axe's animation to the clipboard.

5. Select the new axe to display its curves in the Graph Editor. It has no curves to display yet. With the new_Axe node selected in the Graph Editor menu bar, choose Edit ➤ Paste. As shown in Figure 8.27, the new axe is slightly offset from the original axe.

6. You have to move the new axe to match the original, but because it's already animated, you'll move it using the curves in the Graph Editor. With the new axe selected, in the Graph Editor select the Translate Y curve; move the curve down in the Graph Editor to match the height of the original axe in the view panel.

FIGURE 8.26 Place the pivot point on the new axe here (top) and snap the axe's position to the origin (bottom).

When you copy and paste curves in the Graph Editor, make sure you're on the first frame of the animation. Pasting curves places them at the current frame. Because the animation of the original axe started at frame 1, make sure you're at frame 1 when you paste the curves to the new axe.

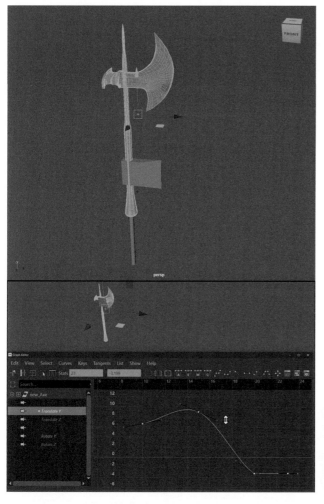

FIGURE 8.27   The new axe is now next to the original (top). Adjust the animation curve to line up the axes (bottom).

7. Scrub the animation to see that the new axe has the same animation except at the end when it hits the target. Remember that you grouped the original axe under the target node for follow-through animation. Place the new axe under this node as well.

   The file `axe_v7.mb` in the Axe project from the book's web page has the new axe imported and all the animation copied to get you caught up to this point.

8. After you scrub the animation and make sure the new axe animates properly, select the original axe's node and delete it.

Animating Flying Text

It's inevitable. Sooner or later, you will need to animate a flying logo or flying text. Animating flying text—at least, the way you'll do it here—can show you how to animate pretty much anything that has to twist, wind, and bend along a path; this technique isn't just for text.

You'll need to create the text, so follow these steps:

1. In a new scene, select Create ➤ Type. An abject spelling out "3D TYPE" appears in your scene. In the Attribute Editor, select the Type1 tab, enter your text, and select a font to use (see Figure 8.28). In this case, Times New Roman. Maya's Type tool has a huge array of options to customize the look of the geometry text organized into tabs as shown in Figure 8.28. The Type tab controls the text itself. The Geometry tab controls how the text geometry itself is created. Experiment with some of the Geometry tab settings to make the text thicker or thinner under the Extrusion heading. The geometry will be updated as you make the changes.

2. When you are happy with the text, you need to create a curve for it to animate along. Using either the CV or EP Curve tool, create a winding curve like a rollercoaster for the logo, as shown with the text in Figure 8.29.

4. Just as you did with the motion path axe exercise, you'll assign the text object to this curve as its motion path. Set your frame range to 1–100. Select the text, Shift+select the curve, and, in the Animation menu

FIGURE 8.28   The Type tool.

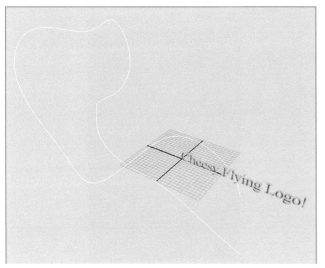

FIGURE 8.29 Create a curve path for the text to follow.

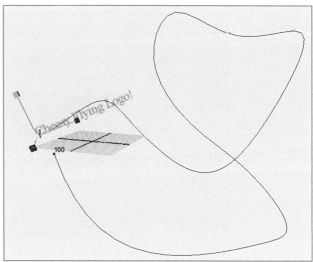

FIGURE 8.31 The text is on the path.

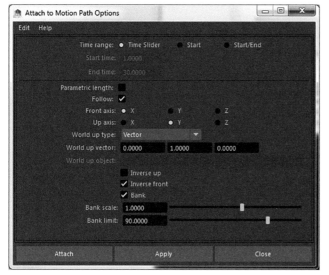

FIGURE 8.30 The Attach To Motion Path Options box.

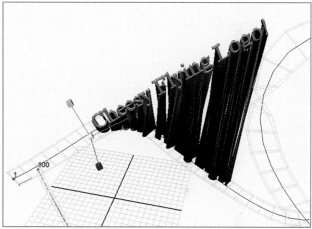

FIGURE 8.32 The geometry doesn't fit the lattice well. Ouch!

set, choose Constrain ➤ Motion Paths ➤ Attach To Motion Path ❐. Check the Follow box to turn it on. Set Front Axis to X and Up Axis to Y and select the Bank check box, as shown in Figure 8.30.

Depending on how you create your curve and text, you may need to experiment with the Front Axis and Up Axis attributes to get the text to fly the way you want.

5. Orbit the camera around to the other side, and you can see the text on the path, as shown in Figure 8.31. In the Attribute Editor for the motion path, notice the U Value attribute; this is the position of the text along the curve from 0 to 1. Scrub the animation, and the text should glide along the curve.

6. The text isn't bending along with the curve at all yet. To accomplish this, you need to add a lattice that bends the text to the curvature of the path. Select the text object, and choose Constrain ➤ Motion Paths ➤ Flow Path Object ❐.

7. In the option box for the Flow Path Object, set Divisions: Front to **120**, Up to **2**, and Side to **2**, and select Curve. Make sure the Local Effect box is unchecked. Doing so creates a lattice that follows the curve, giving it 120 segments along the path. This lattice deforms the text as it travels along the path to the curvature of the path.

8. Scrub your animation, and you see a fairly strange result; parts of the text explode out from the lattice, as shown in Figure 8.32.

9. The geometry is going outside the influence of the lattice. To fix the situation, select the lattice and base node; then scale up the lattice *and* its base node together to create a larger size of influence around the path (see Figure 8.33).

Scrub your animation to check the frame range and how well the text flies through the lattice. When the lattice and its base are large enough to handle the text along all of the path's corners and turns, *voilà*—Cheesy Flying Logo! (see Figure 8.34).

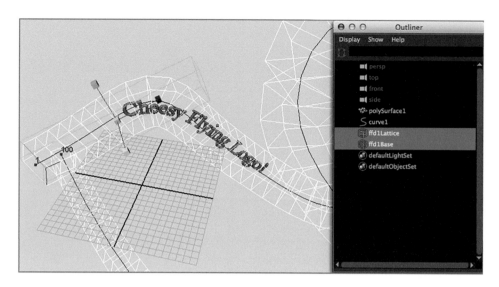

FIGURE 8.33   Scale the lattice and its base node to accommodate the flying text.

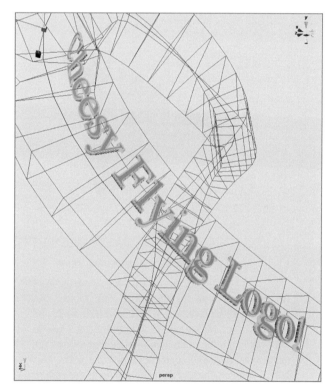

FIGURE 8.34   Cheesy Flying Logo! makes a nice turn.

Animating the Catapult

As a further exercise in animating a system of objects, you'll now animate the catapult from Chapter 4, "Beginning Polygonal Modeling." You'll turn its winch to bend back the catapult arm, which shoots the projectiles, and then you'll fire and watch the arm fly up.

Let's get acquainted with the scene file and make sure its pivots and hierarchies are set up properly. The scene file `catapult_anim_v1.mb` in the Catapult_Anim project from the companion web page has everything in order, although it's always good to make sure. Figure 8.35 shows the catapult with its winch selected and ready to animate.

Get a sense of timing for the winch first, and use that to pull back the arm to fire. Follow these steps:

1. Select the Winch group with its selection handle. At frame 1, set a keyframe for rotation. If the selection handle isn't turned on, select Winch from the Outliner and turn on the selection handle by choosing Display ➤ Transform Display ➤ Selection Handles. To keep it clean as you go along, instead of pressing Shift+E to set a key for all three axes of rotation, select only the Rotate X attribute in the Channel Box, right-click to open the context menu, and choose Key Selected. There only needs to be rotation in X for the winch.

2. Jump to frame 60. Rotate the winch backward a few times or enter **−400** or so for the Rotate X attribute.

3. Open the Graph Editor, ease in the curve a bit, and ease out the curve a lot so that the rotation starts casually but grinds to a stop as the arm becomes more difficult to pull back.

   Because animating a rope is a fairly advanced task, the catapult is animated without its rope; however, the principle of an imaginary rope pulling the arm down to create tension in the arm drives the animation.

4. To accentuate the more difficult winding at the end, add a key to the X-axis rotation through the Graph Editor. To do so, select the curve and click the Insert Keys Tool icon (■) in the upper-left corner of the Graph Editor.

5. Click and drag to place a new keyframe positioned at frame 42. It may help to turn on the key snapping first (see Figure 8.36).

6. Move that keyframe down to create a stronger ease-out for the winch. Be careful not to let the curve dip down so that the winch switches directions.

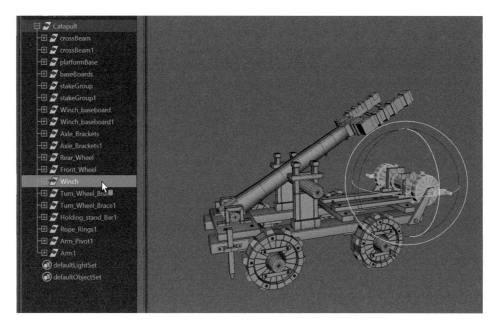

FIGURE 8.35 The catapult's winch is ready to animate.

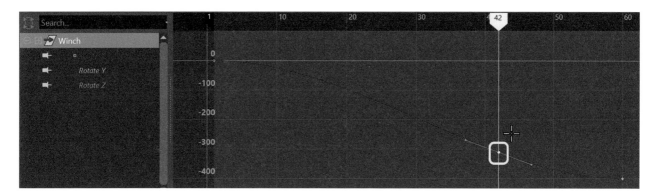

FIGURE 8.36 Insert a keyframe at frame 42.

Adjust the handles to smooth the curve. You can also add a little recoil to the winch by inserting a new keyframe through the Graph Editor at frame 70, and creating a slight dip in the curve with the last keyframe's tangent handle (see Figure 8.37).

Animating with Deformers

It's time to animate the arm coiling back, using the winch's timing as it's driving the arm. Because the catapult's arm is supported by a brace and the whole idea of a catapult is based on tension, you have to bend the arm back as the winch pulls it.

You'll use a nonlinear deformer, just as you did in the axe head exercise in Chapter 5, but this time, you'll animate the deformer to create the bending of the catapult arm. Follow these steps:

1. Switch to the Modeling menu set. Select the Arm1 group and choose Deform ➢ Nonlinear ➢ Bend to create a Bend deformer that is currently

perpendicular to the arm. Select the deformer and rotate it to line it up with the arm, as shown in Figure 8.38.
2. With the Bend deformer selected, look in the Channel Box for bend1 under the Inputs section, and click it to expand its attributes. Try entering **0.5** for Curvature. More than likely, the catapult arm will bend sideways. Rotate the deformer so that the arm is bending back and down instead, as shown in Figure 8.39.
3. You don't want the arm's base to bend back, just the basket side. You want it to bend at the brace point, not in the middle where it is now. Move the deformer down the length of the arm until the middle lines up with the arm's support brace.
4. To prevent the bottom of the arm from bending, change the Low Bound attribute to **0**. To keep the basket from bending, set the High Bound attribute to about **0.9**.
5. Instead of trying to match the speed, ease-in, and ease-out of the winch, set the gross keyframes for the arm pulling back first. Reset Curvature to **0** and set a

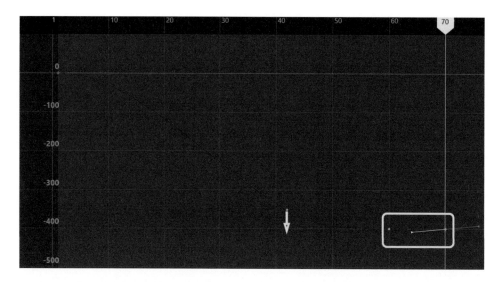

FIGURE 8.37   Creating a greater ease-out and adding a little recoil at the end.

FIGURE 8.38   Align the Bend deformer with the catapult arm.

key for Curvature at frame 1. (Select bend1's Curvature in the Channel Box, right-click, and choose Key Selected from the context menu.)

The Low Bound and High Bound attributes control how far up and down the deformer the object is affected. The Envelope attribute for a deformer governs how much the object is affected overall, with 0 not affecting the geometry at all.

6. Go to frame 60 and set Curvature to −50. If Auto Keyframe is turned on, this sets a keyframe; otherwise, set a key manually (see Figure 8.40).

7. If you play back the animation, notice that the way the winch winds back and the way the arm bends don't match. In the Graph Editor, you can adjust the animation curve on the Bend deformer to match the winch's curve.

8. Insert a key on the Curvature curve at frame 42 and move it up to match the curvature you created for the winch.

9. Insert a new key at frame 70 and make the arm bend back up slightly as the winch recoils. Set Curvature to about −49 from −50.

10. Go to frame 90 and set a key again for Curvature at −49. Set a key at −51 for frame 97 to create anticipation in the arm and then keyframe at frame 103 to

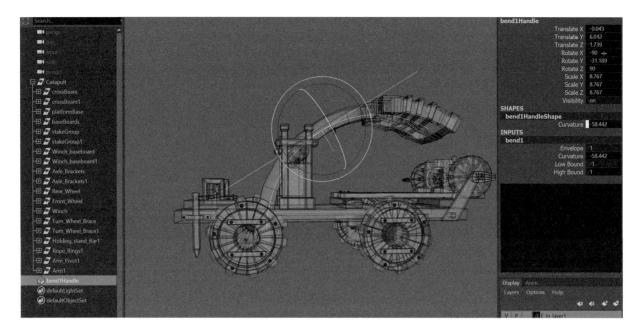

FIGURE 8.39 Orient the Bend deformer to bend the arm back and down.

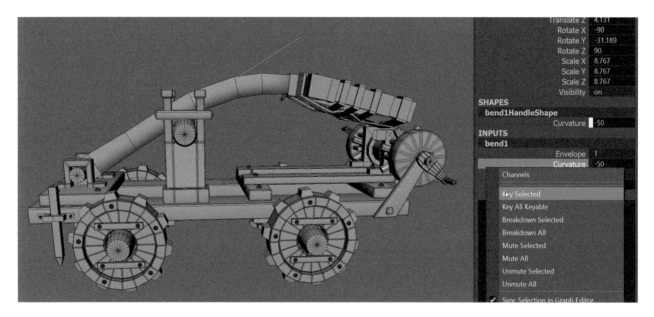

FIGURE 8.40 Bend the arm back at frame 60 and set a keyframe.

release the arm and fire the imaginary payload with a Curvature of **0**.

11. Add some rotation to the arm for dramatic effect. At about frame 100, during the release, the arm is almost straight. Select the Arm1 group and set a rotation key on the X-axis. Go to frame 105 and rotate the arm 45° to the left in the X-axis. If the starting rotation of the arm is at about 30 (as it is in the sample file), set an X-axis rotation key of **75** at frame 105.

12. Notice that the arm is bending strangely now that it's being rotated. It's moving off the deformer, so its influence is changing for the worse. To fix this, go back to frame 100 and parent the deformer node (called

bend1Handle) under the Arm1 group (MMB+drag the bend1Handle to the Arm1 group in the Outline), as shown in Figure 8.41. Now it rotates along with the arm, adding its own bending influence.

13. Work on setting keyframes on the deformer and the arm's rotation so that the arm falls back down onto the support brace and quivers until it becomes straight again. The animation curve for the Bend deformer should look like Figure 8.42. The rotation of the arm should look like Figure 8.43. Remember to make the tangents flat on the keys where the arm bounces off the brace and at the peaks, like the ball's bounce from earlier in this chapter.

FIGURE 8.41   Group the deformer node under the Arm1 group node.

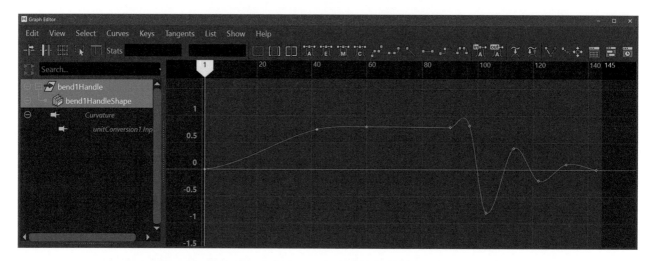

FIGURE 8.42   The animation curve for the arm's vibration back and forth as it comes to a rest.

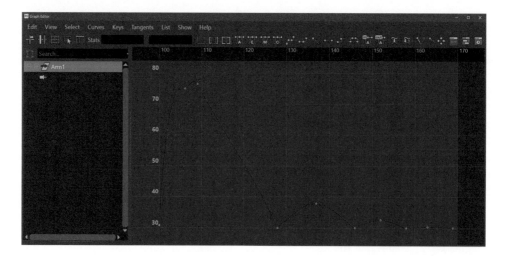

FIGURE 8.43   The animation curve for the arm's rotation as it heaves up and falls back down, coming to an easy rest on the brace.

The file `catapult_anim_v2.mb` will give you a good reference to check out the timing of the arm bend and rotation. Here are some items you can animate to make this a complete animation:

- Spin the winch around as the arm releases, as if its rope is being yanked away from it.
- Animate the entire catapult rocking forward and backward as the arm releases, similar to the way a car rocks when you jump onto the hood.
- Move the catapult forward on a road, spinning its wheels as best you can to match the distance it travels.
- Design and build your own catapult and animate it along the same lines.

Summary

In this chapter, you began to learn the fundamentals of animating a scene. Starting with a bouncing ball, you learned how to work in the Graph Editor to set up and adjust timing as well as how to add squash and stretch to the animation. The next exercise, throwing an axe, expanded on your experience of creating timing in the Graph Editor and showed you how to add anticipation, follow-through, and secondary motion to your scene. You then learned how to animate the axe throw using path animation. You went on to learn how to replace a proxy object that is already animated with a different finished model and how to transfer the animation. Finally, you used the catapult to animate with deformers and further your experience in the Graph Editor.

Animating a "complex" system, such as a catapult, involves creating layers of animation based on facets of the mechanics of the system's movement. With the catapult, you tackled the individual parts separately and then worked to unify the animations. You'll use rigging concepts in the next chapter to automate some of that process for a locomotive. The same is true of the Bouncing_Ball and Axe_Throwing exercises. The different needs of the animation were addressed one by one, starting with the gross animation and ending with finishing touches to add weight.

Animation is the art of observation, interpretation, and implementation. Learning to see how things move, deciphering why they move as they do, and then applying all that to your Maya scene is what animation is all about.

9

More Animation!

Learning Outcomes

In this chapter, you will be able to

Use hierarchies in animation tasks

Create and manipulate a skeleton system for animation and group models to bones

Create a walk cycle using forward kinematics for pose animation

Discern the two ways—smooth and interactive—to bind a mesh to a skeleton in Maya

Use inverse kinematics in a rig of a simple character

Create a walk cycle using IK animation

Use constraints to automate animation

Create set-driven keys for animation rigging

Rig a locomotive for automated animation

Rig a simple character for basic character animation

Skeletons and Kinematics

In your body, your muscles move the bones of your skeleton, and as your bones move, parts of your body move. In computer graphics (CG) animation, a *skeleton* is an armature built into a three-dimensional (3D) model that drives the geometry when the bones are moved. You insert a skeleton into a CG model and attach or bind it to the geometry. The skeleton's bones are animated, which in turn move the parts of the geometry to which they're attached. By using a skeleton, the Autodesk® Maya® software allows you to bend and deform the attached geometry at the skeleton's *joints*. A skeleton is useful for character work, but skeletons have many other uses. Any time you need to drive the geometry of a model with an internal system, such as a fly-fishing line or a tree bending in the wind, you can use skeletons. You'll use skeletons to drive locomotive wheels and a simple character later in this chapter.

Skeletons and Hierarchy

Skeletons rely on hierarchies (see Figure 9.1). Bones are created in a hierarchical manner, resulting in a *root joint* that is the parent of all the joints beneath it in the hierarchy. For example, a hip joint can be the root joint of a leg skeleton system in which the *knee joint* is the leg's child, the *ankle joint* belongs to the knee, and the five *toe joints* are the ankle's children.

Geometry need not deform to be attached to a bone system; objects can be grouped with or under joints. They move

under their parent joint and rotate around that joint's pivot as opposed to their own pivot point.

A skeleton is essentially just a collection of grouped and properly positioned pivot points called *joints* that you use to move your geometry. A *bone* is the length between each joint; bones show you only the skeletal system and are not actual geometry.

Inverse kinematics (IK) and *forward kinematics* (FK) are the methods you use to animate a skeletal system. FK rotates the bones directly at their top joint to assume poses. This method resembles *stop-motion animation*, in which you pose a puppet, along with its underlying armature, frame by frame. With FK, the animator moves the character into position by rotating the joints that run the geometry.

Rotating a joint affects the position of the bones and joints beneath it in the hierarchy (see Figure 9.2). If you rotate the hip up, the knee and ankle swing up as if the character is kicking.

IK uses a more complex, but often easier, system of *IK handles* that are attached to the tip of a joint system. The corresponding base of the IK system is attached farther up the skeleton hierarchy to a joint determined as the root of that IK segment. It need not be the root joint of the entire skeleton, though.

The bones and joints in the IK chain are affected only by movement of the IK handle. When the handle moves, an *IK solver* figures out how to rotate all the joints to accommodate the new position of the IK handle.

The effect is as if someone grabbed your hand and moved it. The person holding your hand is similar to an IK handle. Moving your hand causes the bones in your arm to rotate

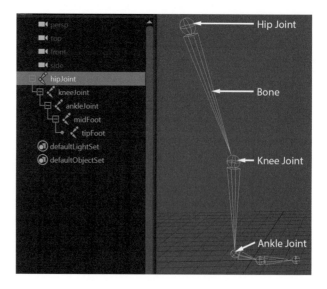

FIGURE 9.1   A leg skeleton and its hierarchy.

DOI: 10.1201/9780429490958-10

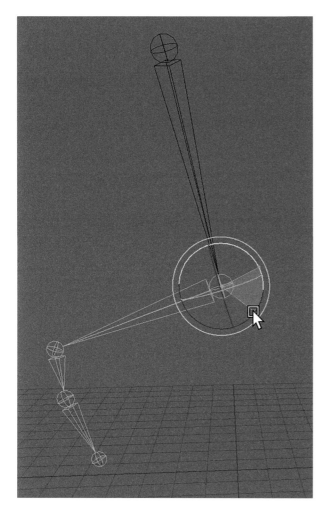

FIGURE 9.2 In forward kinematics, the joints are rotated directly.

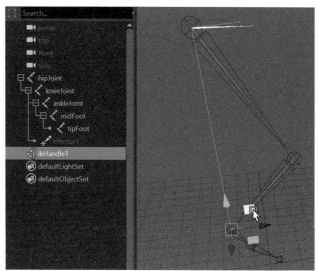

FIGURE 9.3 In inverse kinematics, the joints rotate in response to the IK handle's position.

around the shoulder, elbow, and wrist. As you can see in Figure 9.3, the animation flows up the hierarchy and is therefore called inverse kinematics.

Forward Kinematics: The Block Man

To understand skeletal hierarchy, look at Figure 9.4, which shows a simple biped (two-legged) character made of primitive blocks. He's called the Block Man. (Clever!) Each block represents part of the body, with gaps between the blocks representing points where the body pivots.

The pivot of each block is placed to represent the appropriate joint location. For example, the shin's pivot is located at the knee. Each block is grouped up the chain so that the foot moves with the shin, which moves with the thigh, which moves with the pelvis.

The hands are grouped under the arms, which are grouped under the shoulders, and so forth, down the spine to the pelvis. The head groups under the first neck block and so on down the spine to the pelvis. The pelvis is the center of the body, which is known as the *root* of the figure.

The way this figure is grouped (see Figure 9.5) represents how the hierarchy of a character basically works. Each body part is attached and becomes the child of the part above it in the chain.

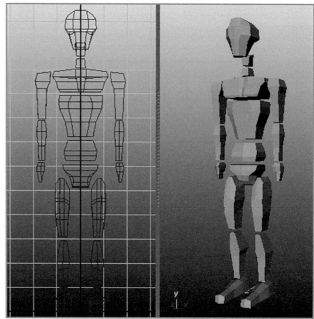

FIGURE 9.4 The Block Man's cubes arranged.

Load the file `block_man_v02.ma` from the Block_Man project folder on the book's web page, for a good reference of the grouping structure. This file shows you what a skeleton hierarchy essentially does in how the body parts are organized in the hierarchy.

Creating the Skeleton

The basis of how the Block Man is laid out and grouped is what skeletons are all about. Skeletons make character animation easier by automating, at the least, the hierarchy and pivot placement described earlier.

THE PELVIS AS ROOT

Traditionally, the pelvis is the basis of all biped setups. The root of any skeletal system (whether using bones or geometry as the example) is the character's pivot point—the center of balance. Because a biped character centers itself on 2 feet, its pelvis becomes the root of its skeletal system. In CG, the pelvis becomes the parent node of the whole system and is the node used to move or orient the entire character. In a skeleton system, this would be the root joint.

The root is then the top parent of the system below it and runs the entire chain. Therefore, selecting character parts straight from the Outliner or the Hypergraph is sometimes easier. You can see that a good naming convention is always important with character setups.

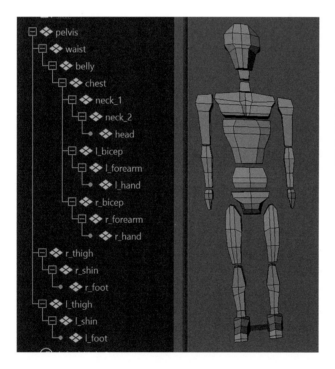

FIGURE 9.5 Pivot placements and grouping.

You'll use the Block Man to create a simple skeleton. Load `block_man_v01.ma` from the Block_Man project. This is the same as `block_man_v02.ma`, but this version isn't grouped.

1. Maximize the front view window. Switch to the Rigging menu set by using the drop-down menu or by pressing F3.
2. Activate the Joint tool by choosing Skeleton ➤ Create Joints. Your cursor turns into a cross.
3. Click in the middle of the pelvis to place the first joint, which is the root joint of the skeleton.

4. Shift+click up to the space between the pelvis and the waist.

The joint display sizes in your Maya window may not match those shown in the book. This isn't a problem; however, you can change the joint sizes by clicking Display ➤ Animation ➤ Joint Size.

By pressing Shift as you click, you create a joint in a straight line from the last joint placement. A bone is created between the two joints as a visual guide to the skeleton. The placement of the joints depends on the active view.

5. Click more joints up the spine at the gaps between the body parts, as shown in Figure 9.6. Place the second-to-last joint at the base of the skull, as shown in the side view in Figure 9.6. Place the last joint at the top of the head. Then press Enter to exit Create Joints. Select the top joint at the head and, in a side view, move that joint toward the forehead as shown to make the angle in Figure 9.6.

Pressing the Up arrow key takes you up one node in a hierarchy (a.k.a. *pick-walking*). Pressing the Down arrow key takes you down one node in a hierarchy. This approach also applies to skeletons because they're hierarchies.

6. Use Figure 9.6 as a guide to name your joints to keep them organized. Now you need to start a new branch of joints leading into the legs and arms. Begin with the arms.
7. Activate Create Joints (Skeleton ➤ Create Joints). In the front view, click to place a new joint at the top-left side of the upper chest just to the side of the joints you've already placed (see Figure 9.7, left); then click to place a second connected joint in the bicep at the shoulder. Click down to create joints at the elbow, the wrist, and the tip of the character's right hand (which is on the left side of your screen). Press Enter to complete that part of the skeleton.
8. Reenter Create Joints and repeat the previous step to create joints for the other arm, as shown in Figure 9.7 (right). Name your joints!
9. You'll notice that the arms are not part of the main skeleton yet. You need to connect them to the main skeleton. Open the Outliner and select the lt_clavicle joint. MMB+drag it to the chest node to group it to the chest (see Figure 9.8). Notice that a new bone appears between these two joints. Group the rt_clavicle to the chest as well. Figure 9.9 shows the arms are now part of the main skeleton.
10. To start another string of joints in the first leg, enter Create Joints. Then click the pelvis joint,

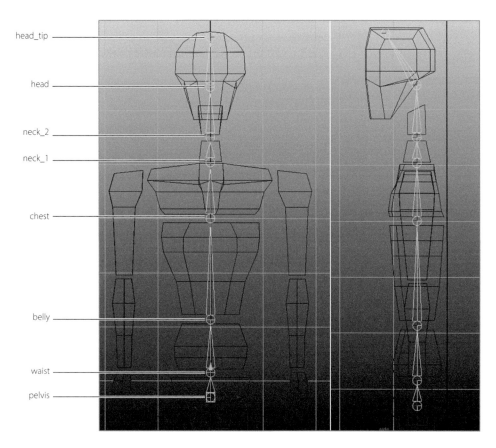

FIGURE 9.6 Place spine joints straight up the middle of the body and offset the last joint in the head.

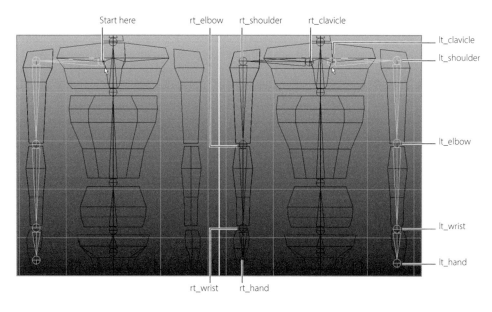

FIGURE 9.7 Place joints for the arm.

selecting it. In the front view, place the first leg joint at the top of the screen-left thigh (the character's right thigh). Place the next joint between the thigh and knee and then another at the top of the foot where it meets the ankle. Do not exit Create Joints yet!

11. Switch to the side view and place another joint at the ankle, another in the middle bottom of the foot, and the last joint at the tip of the foot. Press Enter to exit Create Joints, and you'll see that your leg is already attached to the pelvis; there's no need to group in the Outliner this time like with the clavicles.

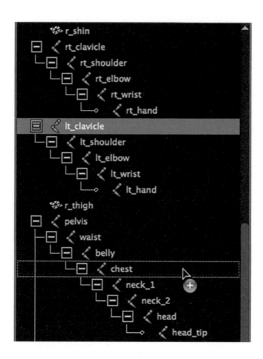

FIGURE 9.8   Group the lt_clavicle to the chest.

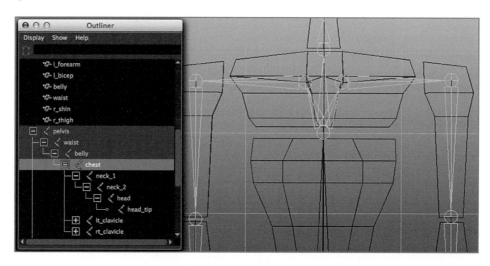

FIGURE 9.9   The arms are grouped to the chest, and the joints are connected with new bones.

12. In the side view, select the knee joint, and enter Pivot mode by pressing and holding the D key. Very slightly move the knee joint away from the front of the character, out toward the toe. This slight bend will be needed later when you continue the character rig. Using Pivot mode, make sure your joints are placed properly for the leg and foot using Figure 9.10 as a guide. Name your joints!

13. Select the rt_hip joint and press Ctrl+D to duplicate the hip and the joints beneath it. In the front view, move the new rt_hip1 joint to the other leg and place it as shown in Figure 9.11 (left). Rename those new joints as shown.

You're all done! You'll be adding to this later in this chapter as you create a more well-rounded rig for the character, but for now, check your work against Figure 9.11 (right) and the `block_man_skeleton_v01.ma` file from the Block_Man project.

Attaching to the Skeleton

You now have a full skeleton for your character. To attach the geometry, all you need to do is parent the body parts under their appropriate joints. Before you get to that, take a few minutes and make sure all your joints are named in the Outliner to make the scene easier to manage. You can use Figure 9.12 as a naming reference.

You can also load the `block_man_skeleton_v01.ma` file from the Block_Man project to get to this point.

To parent the Block Man's geometry to the skeleton, follow these steps:

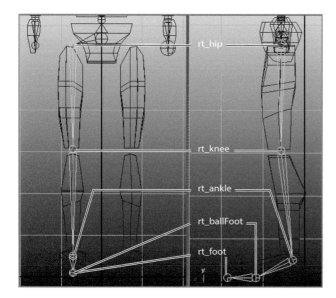

FIGURE 9.10 Place the leg joints and name them.

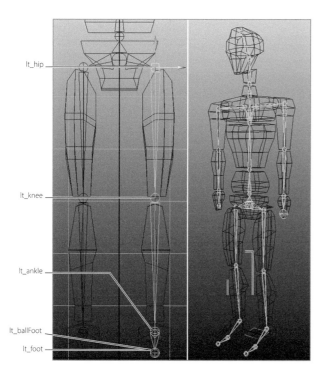

FIGURE 9.11 Duplicate the leg joints, move them to the other leg, and name the new joints (left). The skeleton is complete (right).

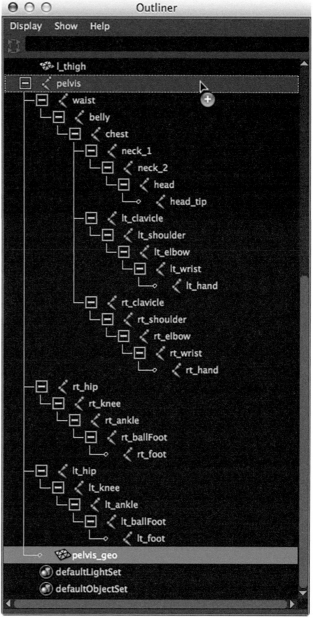

FIGURE 9.12 After you check your naming, you'll parent the pelvis geometry under the pelvis joint.

1. Starting with the pelvis, parent it under the pelvis joint by MMB+clicking and dragging it to the pelvis joint. Once it's in the group, MMB+drag the pelvis_ geom again and place it between the pelvis and waist joints, as shown in Figure 9.12.

2. Continue the MMB+dragging process in the Outliner to place everything but the feet geometry in its proper place in the skeleton using the following list and Figure 9.13 as guides. You will deal with the feet a little differently. Figure 9.13 shows the finished hierarchy in the Outliner and Hypergraph.

   - Shins under the knees; thighs under the hips
   - Hands under the wrists; forearms under the elbows
   - Biceps under the shoulder joints
   - Head under the head joint (not the head_tip joint)
   - Top neck geometry (neck_2) under neck_2 joint
   - Bottom neck geometry (neck_1) under the neck_1 joint
   - Chest under the chest joint
   - Belly under the belly joint
   - Waist under the waist joint

3. Now you'll bind the feet to the foot joints, instead of grouping them. Since there is a joint in the middle of the foot, you'll want to bend the foot. You will explore binding in more detail later in this chapter, but for

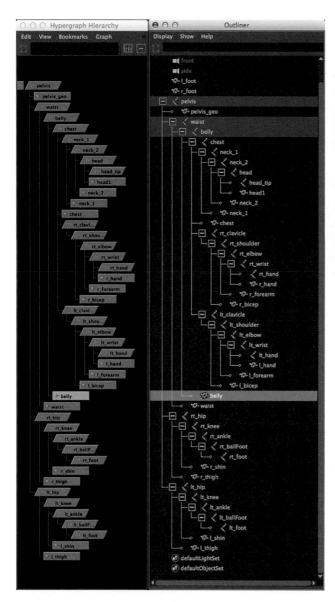

FIGURE 9.13 Parent all the geometry except the feet into its proper place in the skeleton. The finished hierarchy is shown in the Hypergraph and Outliner side-by-side.

now, select the l_foot geometry in the Outliner; then press Ctrl and select all three foot joints (lt_ankle, lt_ballFoot, and lt_foot) in the Outliner as well (see Figure 9.14, bottom image).

4. Select Skin ➤ Bind Skin ❑, set Bind To to Selected Joints and Bind Method to Heat Map, and click the Bind Skin button. This will bind (a.k.a. skin) the foot geometry to the joints so you can then bend, or deform, the foot.

5. To test the bind, select the middle foot joint (lt_ball-Foot) and rotate it; the tip of the foot should move. Select the ankle and rotate it, and the whole foot should move. Undo your rotations or set the rotations back to 0 so that the foot is at its rest pose (a.k.a. *bind pose*) again. Just don't undo the binding unless you need to redo steps 3 and 4 (see Figure 9.14, top image).

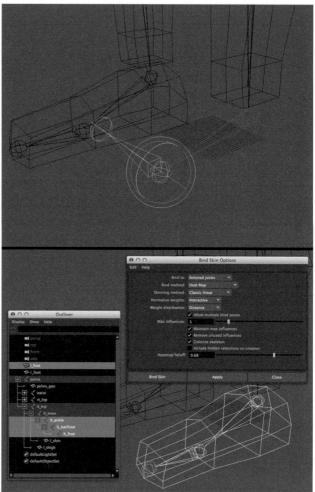

FIGURE 9.14 Bind Skin Options: the left foot geometry and the left foot joints selected (bottom image). Bind and test the left foot (top image).

6. Repeat steps 3 and 4 for the other foot to bind the geometry and test its movement. Just remember to undo your rotations to return to the bind pose.

The Block Man is now set up with a skeleton that you'll use to make a simple walk cycle. This exercise will help get you more familiar and comfortable with animating a character. You will do more to this setup to make a better animation rig for the Block Man character later in this chapter.

The Block Man: FK Walk Cycle

This is a basic exercise to *merely introduce* the concepts behind bi-ped character movement with a walk cycle animation. A *walk cycle* is an animation that takes the character through a few steps that can be repeated many times so that the character seems to be taking numerous steps. In a cycle, make sure the position of the first frame matches the position of the last frame so that when the animation sequence is cycled, no "pop" occurs in the motion at that point.

Now, try animating this character's walk cycle using FK on the skeleton. You'll find the workflow straightforward, as if you were adjusting positions on a doll.

Load the `block_man_skeleton_v02.ma` file from the Block_Man project from the companion web page for the properly grouped and bound model and skeleton. In this file, the right arm and leg have drawing overrides enabled; this makes their wireframe display white to make it easier to distinguish between the right and left sides while working.

Use the key poses in the following figures to guide you in animating the body as it walks. You'll key at five-frame intervals to lay down the gross animation. You can go back and adjust the timing of the joint rotations in the Graph Editor to make the animation better later. The white leg and arm are behind the body, farther from the camera.

This type of animation is also called *pose animation* because you're posing the character from keyframe to keyframe.

Starting Out: Frames 1 and 5

Figure 9.15 shows the character's starting position. Here, you'll set a key for this position and then begin the walk cycle by moving the joints into their second position and keyframing that.

1. At frame 1, set a key for the rotation of all the joints. The easiest way is to select all the joints (and only the joints) in the Outliner or the Hypergraph. With pose animation, you have to make sure that all the joints are keyframed at every step, even if Auto Keyframe is turned on. Also, set a position keyframe for just the pelvis joint.

2. Go to frame 5. Rotate the back leg back (the Block Man's right, white leg), rotate the rt_ballFoot joint to bend the foot, and bend the ankle to make the ball of the foot level again. Lower the body (select and move the pelvis joint) to line up the back heel with the ground. This will keep the man on the ground as he goes through the walk cycle, although he won't actually move forward yet.

3. Rotate the near leg (the man's left blue wireframe leg) forward, bend the knee, and pivot the foot up a bit.

SELECTING ONLY JOINTS IN THE OUTLINER

A quick way to select all the joints, and only the joints, is to filter the Outliner view to show only joints. In the Outliner, choose Show ➤ Objects ➤ Joints. To reset the Outliner, choose Show ➤ Show All.

4. Rotate the back white wireframe arm forward and rotate the near arm back (opposite from the legs). Bend the arms at the elbows.

5. Bend the man forward at the waist, bend neck_1 forward, and tilt the head back up to compensate a little. Figure 9.16 shows the pose at this point.

6. Select all the joints in the Outliner and set a rotation key. You're setting a pose for all the joints, which will ensure that all the body parts are in sync.

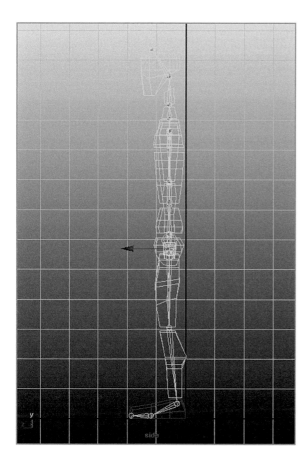

FIGURE 9.15 The character's starting position.

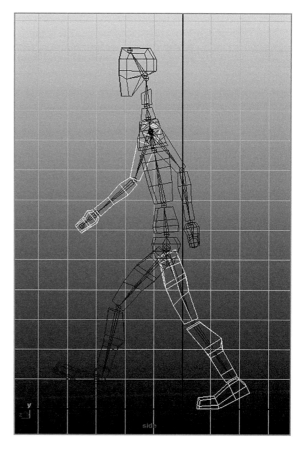

FIGURE 9.16 The second pose (frame 5).

If you don't key everything every step of the way, some parts of the body won't key with Auto Keyframe properly because the last time they moved may have been two steps previous. This may cause confusion, so it's best to key every joint at every step until you feel more comfortable editing character animation.

Frame 10

Figure 9.17 shows the position you'll keyframe at frame 10; it's approximately midstride for the first leg.

1. Go to frame 10. Rotate the back leg out further and level the foot. Lower the body to place the man on the ground.
2. Rotate the front leg out, straighten the knee, and flatten the foot to place it on the ground. This is midstride. Swing the arms in their current direction a touch more. Bend the torso forward some more. Make sure you set a key for all the joints.

Frame 15

Figure 9.18 shows the position you'll keyframe at frame 15. At this point, the character begins to shift his weight to the front

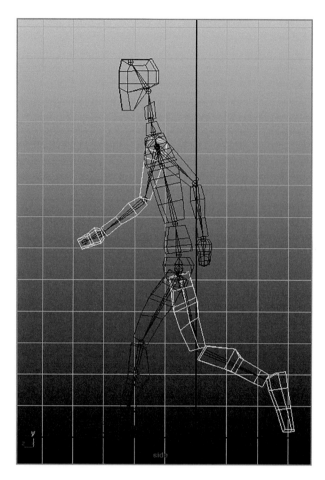

FIGURE 9.18   The fourth pose (frame 15).

leg as it plants on the ground, and the character also begins lifting the back leg.

1. Go to frame 15. Rotate the front leg back toward the body and raise the body as the man steps to keep the front foot flat on the ground. Rotate the back knee up to lift the foot and rotate the foot down to make him push off the toe.
2. Start swinging the arms in the opposite direction. Start straightening the torso back up, but bend the head forward a bit.

Frame 20

At frame 20, the man will shift all his weight onto the front leg and move his body over that leg, lifting his rear leg to begin its swing out front to finish the stride. Figure 9.19 shows the pose.
Follow these steps:

1. Rotate the front leg almost straight under the man and lift up the body to keep the front foot on the ground. Lift the rear leg and swing it forward.
2. Straighten the torso and keep the arms swinging in their new direction. Key all the joints.

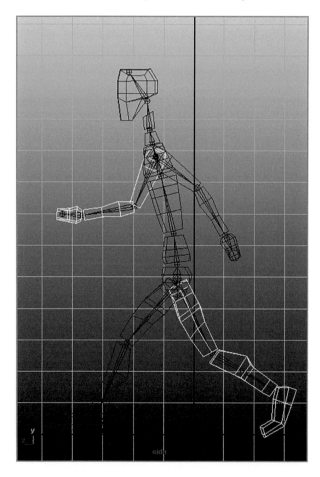

FIGURE 9.17   The third pose (frame 10).

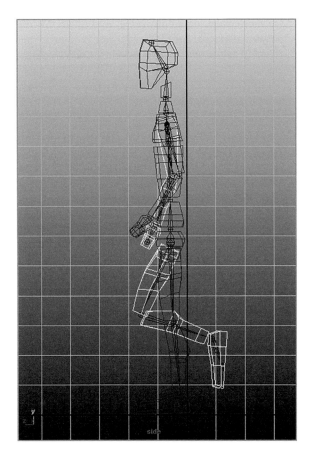

FIGURE 9.19   The fifth pose (frame 20).

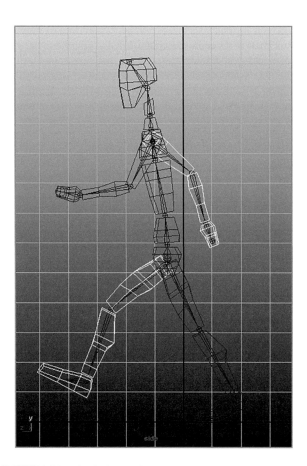

FIGURE 9.20   The sixth pose (frame 25).

Frame 25

Now, the man will swing his whole body forward, pivoting on the left leg (the dark one) to put himself off-center and ready to fall forward into the next step. Figure 9.20 shows the pose.

Here are the steps:

1. Go to frame 25.
2. Rotate the front (dark) leg back behind the man and swing the white leg up and ready to take the next step. Lower the body to keep the now rear foot (the dark one) on the ground.

Frame 30

Use Figure 9.21 as a guide for creating the next pose. Notice that it's similar to the pose at frame 10. As a matter of fact, the only major differences are which leg and arm are in front. Everything else should be about the same. You'll want some variety in the exact positions to make the animation more interesting, but the poses are similar.

Completing the First Steps

You've finished a set of poses for the character's first step. You animated the left leg taking a step forward in the first series of poses. The next series of poses has to do with the right leg. The pose at frame 35 corresponds to the pose at frame 15. Frame 40 matches frame 20. You will copy keyframes in the Graph Editor to make more steps, but first, let's retime these initial keys before continuing.

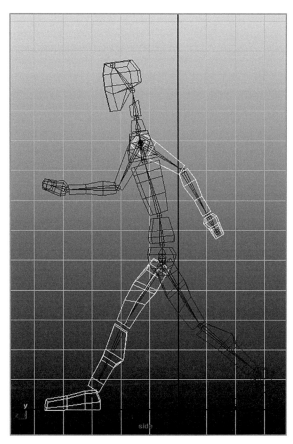

FIGURE 9.21   The seventh pose (frame 30).

When a 30-frame section is complete, you need to return to the animation through the Graph Editor. Adjust all the keyframes that you initially set at these five-frame intervals to make the animation more realistic. Right now, you have only the gross keyframes in place, so the timing is off. Timing the frames properly is ultimately a matter of how the animation looks to you.

Logistically speaking, some poses take a little less time to achieve than the evenly spaced five frames you used. For example, achieving the second pose from the start position should take four frames. The third pose (see Figure 9.17, earlier in this chapter) from frame 5 to frame 10 should take four frames. The next frame section, originally from frame 10 to 15 (the fourth pose; see Figure 9.18, earlier in this chapter), should take only three frames. To accomplish this easily, follow these steps:

1. Select the top node of the skeleton (the pelvis) and open the Graph Editor. On the pelvis node in the left side of the Graph Editor, Shift+click the plus sign to open the entire tree of nodes beneath the pelvis. All the animated channels show their curves, as shown in Figure 9.22 (top).

2. Marquee-select all the keyframes on the curves beyond frame 1, not including those at frame 1. Press the W key to activate the Translate tool. Shift+MMB+click in the Graph Editor (so you can move in only one axis) and drag the keys horizontally to move them all 1 unit (frame) to the left. All the keyframes move, and the second pose now goes from frame 5 to frame 4.

3. Deselect the keys now at frame 4 by holding down the Ctrl key (you also use the Ctrl key on a Mac) and marquee-deselecting all those keys at frame 4. Shift+MMB+click and drag the remaining selected keys 1 unit to the left again. The third pose goes from being at frame 9 to frame 8.

4. Deselect the keys now at frame 8 and Shift+click and drag the other selected keys to the left two frames so that the fourth pose animates between frame 8 and frame 11. Deselect the frame 11 keys and move the rest over two frames to the left again so that the next section runs from frame 11 to frame 14. The following section should go from frame 14 to frame 18. The final section should go from frame 18 to frame 22. Figure 9.22 (bottom) shows the new layout for the curves.

5. Continue to set and adjust keys for another cycle or two of the walk. The majority of time spent in animating something like this involves using the Graph Editor to time out the keyframes to make the animation look believable. Also, try offsetting some of the arm rotations a frame to the left or right to break up the monotony that arises from having everything keyed on the same frame.

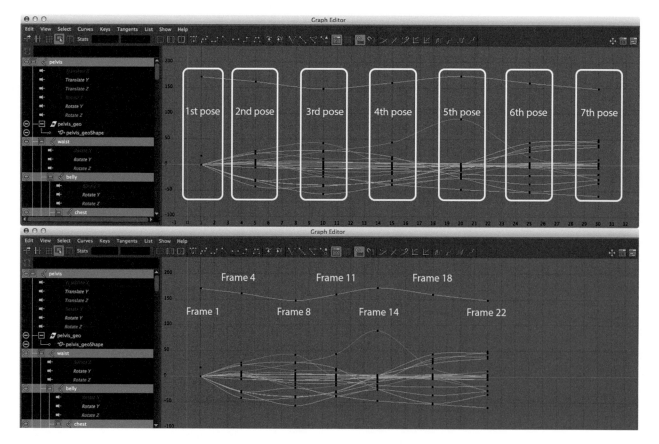

FIGURE 9.22 The Graph Editor shows the walk animation curves (top). The curves are retimed (bottom).

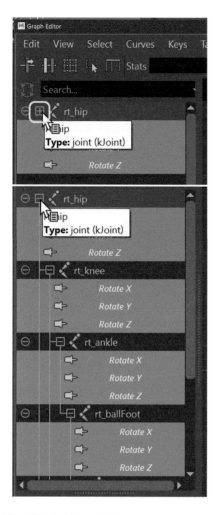

FIGURE 9.23 Click the plus symbol (top) to expand the entire hierarchy below (bottom).

Load the file `block_walk_v01.mov` or `block_walk_v01.avi` of this walk cycle from the Images folder of the Block_Man project on the companion web page to see the animation in motion. It's a rough cycle, and you have to keep adjusting the character's height to keep the feet on the ground. This is where IK comes in handy, as you'll see later in this chapter. Also, the file `block_man_skeleton_walk_v01.ma` in the Block_Man project has the keyframed steps for you to play with and continue animating.

Copy and Paste Keyframes

Now that you have a base to work with, you'll copy and paste keyframes to extend the animation. This process can get a little tricky, so take it slow if you're not comfortable with the Graph Editor yet. Open the file `block_man_skeleton_walk_v01.ma` to follow along with these steps:

1. Extend the Time Range slider to 18 frames and open the Graph Editor. Select the back (white) leg at the `rt_hip` joint.

2. In the Graph Editor, Shift+click the plus sign next to the rt_hip entry (Figure 9.23 top) to see all the joints and all their curves beneath it in the hierarchy (Figure 9.23 bottom).

3. Marquee-select all the keys from frame 4 to frame 22. In the Graph Editor window, select Edit ➤ Copy.

4. Move the Time slider to frame 30 and, in the Graph Editor window, select Edit ➤ Paste ❒. In the option box, set the Paste method to Merge. This setting is important; otherwise, the curves will not paste properly for your use! Click Apply to paste the keys at frame 30. Figure 9.24 shows the pasted frames in the Graph Editor and the Paste options.

5. Select the other leg (lt_hip) and repeat steps 2–4 to copy all the keys from frames 4 through 22. Go to frame 30 and paste (with the Merge option as in step 3) the keys for this leg. Don't forget to Shift+click to expand all the joints beneath the hip joint in the Graph Editor to see, copy, and paste all the joints' keys as you did in step 1.

6. Repeat steps 2–4 for each of the two arms (rt_shoulder and lt_shoulder) to copy and paste their keys as well (copying keys from frame 4 through 22 and pasting at frame 30). Again, don't forget to Shift+click them in the Graph Editor (step 2)!

7. If you scrub your animation in the Timeline all the way to frame 48, you can verify that the animation copied properly for the arms and legs.

8. The body is not moving yet, so let's copy and paste those keys now. In the Outliner, Ctrl+select the waist, belly, chest, neck_1, neck_2, and head joints.

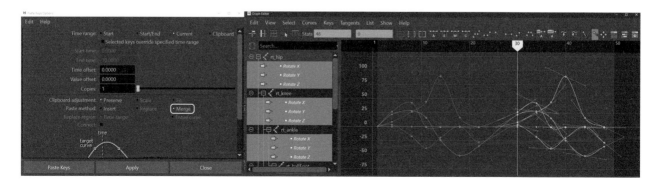

FIGURE 9.24 Copy and paste keys for the white leg.

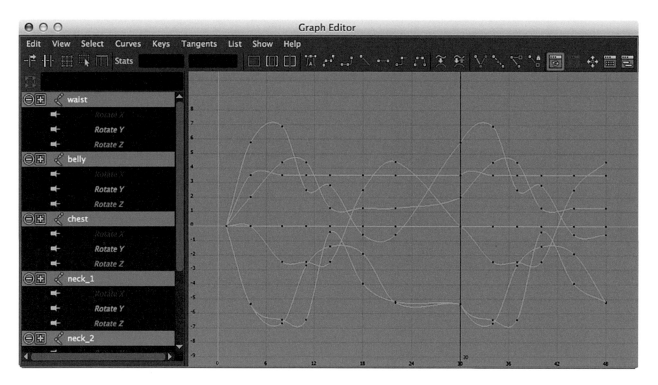

FIGURE 9.25   Copy and paste keys for the body movement.

9. Repeat steps 3 and 4 to copy and paste keys from frames 4 through 22 to frame 30 as you did with the legs and arms. There is no need to Shift+click any of the joints in the Graph Editor (step 2) this time since you individually selected each of the joints you need. Figure 9.25 shows the pasted frames for the body movement.

10. Scrub your animation, and you'll see you need to copy and paste keys for the pelvis next. Select the pelvis joint.

11. In the Graph Editor, select all the keys from frame 1 to frame 22. This time, go to frame 27 and paste (with the Merge option as before!) the keys.

12. Scrub your animation, and everything should be working great! But around frame 25, you should see the character dip down too far. Simply raise him up and key the pelvis position at frame 25 to compensate, and you're done! The Block Man is walking for a full 48-frame clip now.

Open the file `block_man_skeleton_walk_v02.ma` from the Block_Man project to check your work to this point.

Walk Cycle Wrap-Up

This walk cycle animation is about getting comfortable with keyframing and skeletons and not about creating great walk animation. The character rig is a simple example, with many great rigs available on the Internet for you to practice animating with. Character animation takes a lot of time and patience,

and I encourage you to keep tweaking this animation and even create different walks of your own. Several great books and resources are devoted to character rigging and animation alone, and you can easily research the field for ways to become more proficient. However, keep in mind that movement and timing are what make animation good, and this serves as merely an introduction to these concepts, with an entire world of character animation still left to explore.

Skeletons: The Hand

For another foray into a skeletal system, you can give yourself a hand—literally. You'll create a basic skeleton to deform geometry and animate a very simplistic hand rig, and see how it attaches to the geometry of the hand. Again, this is meant purely as a primer into these concepts to make further research and exploration easier.

Load the file `poly_hand_skeleton_v01.ma` from the Poly_Hand_Anim project from the companion web page. The hand is shown in Figure 9.26 (top).

You'll use it to create a bone structure to make the hand animate. This process is called *rigging.*

Rigging the Hand

To create the first bones of the hand, follow these steps:

1. Maximize the top view window. Switch to the Rigging menu set by using the drop-down menu.

2. Activate Create Joints by choosing Skeleton ➤ Create Joints. Your cursor turns into a cross.

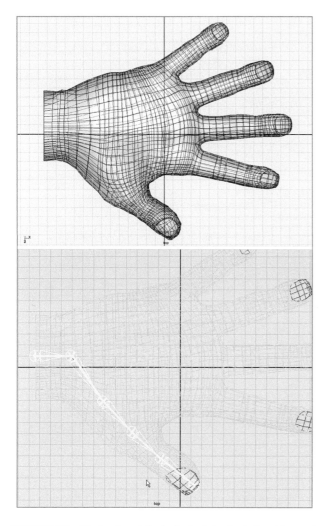

FIGURE 9.26 The hand mesh (top); placing joints in the hand (bottom).

3. Click at the base of the wrist to place the first joint. This will be the root joint of the hand.

4. Shift+click the bottom part of the palm.

5. Place joints down through the thumb from this second joint, according to the corresponding bones in Figure 9.26 (bottom).

6. To start another string of joints into the palm, press the Up arrow key four times until you're at the second joint at the base of the palm.

7. The next joint you place will be a branch from this joint. Place that joint in the middle of the palm. Place another joint up further along the palm and then branch it out to the index finger. Press the Up arrow key to return to that upper palm joint and start a new branch into the middle finger.

Repeat this procedure to place joints for the remaining fingers, as shown in Figure 9.27. With these joints placed, you have a simple skeleton rig for the hand. This rig allows you quite a bit of hand and finger movement.

Check the other views (see Figure 9.28) to see where you need to tweak your joint positions to fit the hand. Ideally, you want the joints to be set inside your intended geometry in the same way that real bones are laid out.

Positioning the Joints

To position the joints, you can use either of two Maya tools: Move or Move Pivot. First, you'll try the Move tool.

1. Select the tip joint for the pinky. It needs to be lowered into the pinky itself.

2. Select the Move tool (press W) and move it down into the tip of the pinky.

3. Now, move on to the top pinky knuckle. Notice that if you move the knuckle, the tip moves as well. That's not such a great idea.

Instead, it's best to move joints as pivots. Because joints are nothing more than pivots, go into Move Pivot mode (hold down the D key to activate Move Pivot or press the Ins key on Windows or the fn+Home key on a Mac) to move joints.

1. Select the top pinky-knuckle joint, and move it with Move Pivot instead. Only the joint moves, and the bones adjust to the new position.

2. Set the positions on the remaining joints to be inside the hand properly, as shown in Figures 9.29 and 9.30.

Binding to Geometry

An integral part of rigging a character or an object with a skeleton is *binding*, also known as *skinning*. Binding is another way to attach geometry to a skeletal system. With the Block Man, you directly attach the whole pieces of geometry to the bones through parenting, whereas binding involves attaching *clusters*, or groups of vertices or control vertices (CVs), of the geometry to the skeleton to allow the skeleton to deform the model. This is typically how skeletons are used in character animation work. (For more on grouping and parenting, refer to the solar system exercise in Chapter 2, "Jumping into Basic Animation Headfirst.")

The basic technique of binding a character is easy. However, Maya gives you tremendous control over how your geometry deforms.

Binding Overview

Binding is, in theory, identical to the Lattice deformer you saw in Chapter 5, "Modeling with NURBS Surfaces and Deformers." A lattice attached to an object exerts influence over parts of the model according to the sections of the lattice. Each section affects the CVs of a NURBS surface or the vertices of a polygon surface within its borders—and as a section of the lattice moves, it takes those points of the model with it.

Skeletal binding does much the same thing. It attaches the model's points to the bones, and as the bones pivot around their joints, the section of the model that is attached follows.

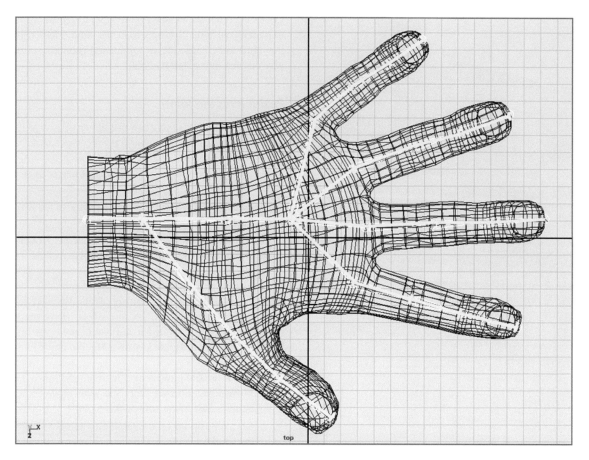

FIGURE 9.27   The joints in the hand.

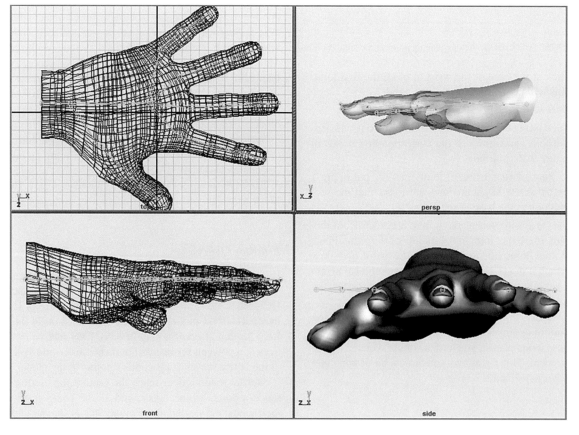

FIGURE 9.28   Four views of the hand with initial placement of the joints.

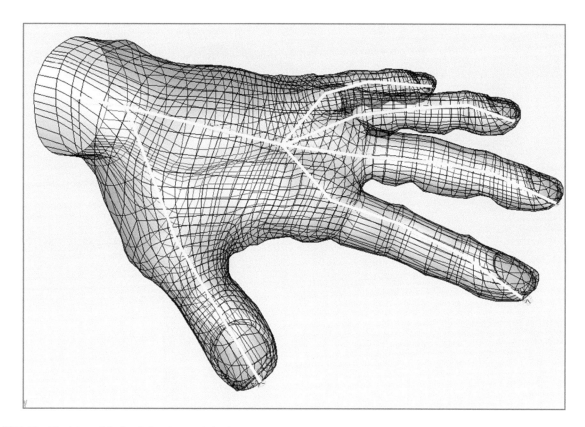

FIGURE 9.29 The joints of the hand placed properly in the geometry.

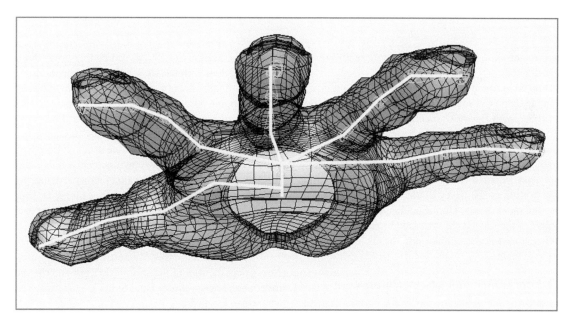

FIGURE 9.30 Second view of the hand's skeleton.

By attaching vertices or CVs (depending on your geometry) to a skeleton, you can bend or distort the geometry. When a bone moves or rotates about its joint, it pulls with it the points that are attached to it. The geometry then deforms to fit the new configuration of the bones bound to it.

You can bind geometry to a skeleton in two ways: using Bind Skin and using Interactive Bind Skin. Figure 9.31 shows a cylinder with a Bind Skin. An Interactive Bind Skin will yield similar results to the regular bind. The only real difference between the two methods is the editing capabilities while

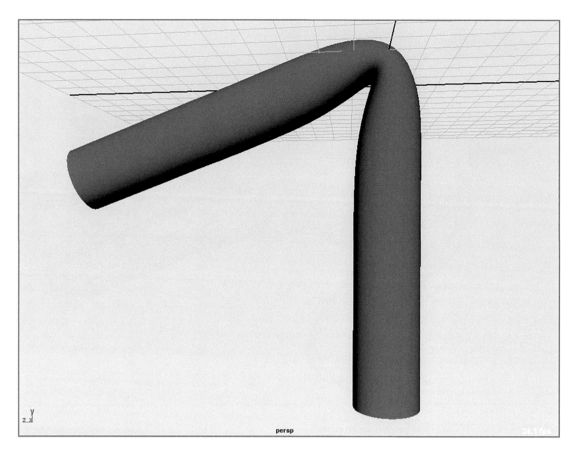

FIGURE 9.31   Bind Skin with a cylinder. The crease is fairly smooth. You may expect this result from the interactive Bind Skin as well.

you are binding the skin. You'll take a look at these differences later in this chapter.

With a Bind Skin, there are two common binding methods that I'll compare here: Closest Distance and Heat Map. Create a polygon cylinder, with Height Divisions of 16. The more spans you have in the deformable model, the better it will bend. Scale the cylinder in Y to a scale of 5 to make it tall. Duplicate the cylinder and move it over in your window in the X-axis. Now, in the front view, create a four-bone (five-joint) skeleton that starts at the bottom of the first cylinder and goes straight up the middle, ending at the tip. Duplicate the skeleton and move it to the center of the second cylinder (see Figure 9.32). Check in your different viewports to make sure the skeleton is in the middle of the cylinders.

Creating a Smooth Bind with Closest Distance

To create a smooth bind, select the root of the first skeleton and its cylinder and choose Skin ➢ Bind Skin ❑.

In the option box, you'll find the Bind To parameter at the top, set to the default of Joint Hierarchy (set it to Joint Hierarchy if it is different). You'll also find, under the Bind Method drop-down menu, the options Closest Distance, Closest In Hierarchy, Heat Map, and Geodesic Voxel. Closest Distance disregards a joint's position in the hierarchy of the skeleton and assigns influences according to how far the point is from the joint. The Heat Map method uses a "heat diffusion" technique to create influence falloff radiating out from the joint and is arguably the most commonly used for character work because it assigns skin weights best suited for character

movement, giving you creases at bending areas that are more believable than with the Closest Distance method.

Max Influences sets a limit on how many joints can affect a single point. Dropoff Rate determines how a joint's influence diminishes on points farther from it. For example, with Smooth Bind, one shoulder joint can influence, to varying degrees, points stretching down the arm and into the chest and belly. By limiting these two parameters, you can control how much of your model is pulled along by a particular joint.

Set Bind Method to Closest Distance and click Bind Skin in the option box window to bind your first cylinder to the bones using Closest Distance (the default).

Creating a Smooth Bind with Heat Map

Now select the root of the second skeleton and the second cylinder and choose Skin ➢ Bind Skin ❑. This time, set the Bind Method to Heat Map.

Bend both cylinders to get a feel for how each creases at the bending joints. Figure 9.33 shows the difference. The Heat Map binding on the right shows more defined creases at the joints, much like fingers, while the Closest Distance binding on the left creates a smoother arc over the entire cylinder.

Interactive Skin Bind is practically the same as Smooth Bind and yields similar results to the smooth binding using Closest Distance shown in Figure 9.33, but the editing of the influences is slightly different than for Smooth Bind. You will explore Interactive Skin Bind with the hand model later in this chapter.

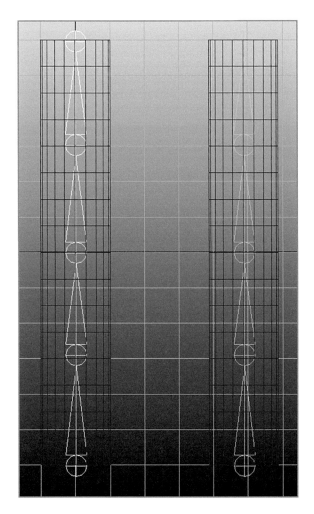

FIGURE 9.32 Make two cylinders with skeletons in them.

Detaching a Skeleton

If you want to do away with your binding, select the skeleton

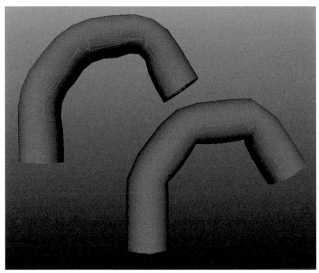

FIGURE 9.33 Closest Distance and Heat Map-Smooth-bound cylinders. The cylinder on the left is Closest Distance bound, and the one on the right is Heat Map bound.

and its geometry, and choose Skin ➤ Unbind Skin. The model will snap to the shape it had before the bind was applied and the joints were rotated. It's common to bind and detach skeletons several times on the same model as you try to figure out the exact configuration that works best for you and your animation.

If you need to go back to the initial position of the skeleton at the point of binding it to the model, you can automatically set the skeleton back to the bind pose after any rotations have been applied to any of its joints. Simply select the skeleton and choose Skin ➤ Go To Bind Pose to snap the skeleton and model into the position they were when you bound them together. It's also best to set your skeleton to the bind pose whenever you edit your binding weights.

Binding the Hand: Closest Distance Method

Try skinning the hand with Bind Skin.

Load your own hand or the `poly_hand_skeleton_v02.ma` file from the Poly_Hand_Anim project from the web page. You can also access a video tutorial to help you with this exercise from the author's website (`www.koosh3d.com`). Now, follow these steps to smooth-bind the hand:

1. Select the skeleton's root at the wrist and Shift+click the hand as shown in Figure 9.34. Choose Skin ➤ Bind Skin ❐. Make sure Bind Method is set to Closest Distance and click Bind Skin.

2. Try rotating some of the knuckle joints to see how the fingers respond. Go back to the bind pose when you're finished.

3. Rotate the middle knuckle of the index finger down. Notice how the knuckle gets thinner the more you bend the finger there. Go to the top knuckle of the index finger and rotate that joint. Notice that part of the hand moves with the finger. Figure 9.35 shows the result of bending at the index finger.

Editing a Bind

You usually edit a bind by *painting skin weights*. Because points on the model are influenced by multiple joints in a smooth bind, you need to adjust just how much influence is exerted by these joints on the same points.

1. Make sure you're in Shaded mode (press 5). Select the hand and then choose Skin ➤ Paint Skin Weights ❐.

You paint skin weights on the affected geometry and not on the joints themselves, so you need to select the model and not the skeleton before invoking this tool.

2. Your hand should turn black, with a bit of light gray at the wrist (or perhaps at the index finger if that joint is selected). The option box appears, listing the joints that are connected to the hand, as shown in Figure 9.36.

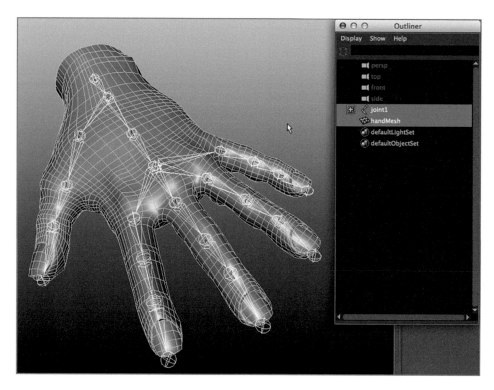

FIGURE 9.34   Select the root joint as well as the top node of the hand.

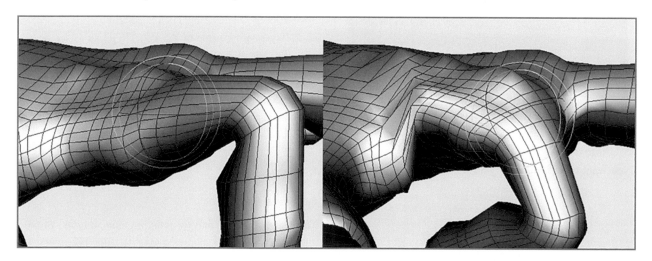

FIGURE 9.35   Bending at the index finger causes some unwanted deformation.

3. The color value (between white and black) determines how much binding influence the selected joint in the option box is exerting on that part of the geometry. It's best to name your joints properly so that selecting from this window is easier and more intuitive. If you loaded the file from the web page, you need to name the joints yourself to organize the scene and make working with it easier.

4. In the option box, select joint 9, the index finger's top knuckle, and make sure the Paint Operation button under the Influence section is set to Replace. Change the Value slider to 0. In the Stroke section, Radius(U) and Radius(L) govern the size of your brush. In the Influence section, make sure the Opacity slider is set to 1.

To change the size of your Artisan Brush while you're painting weights, you can hold down the B key and drag the mouse left or right to adjust the radius of the brush interactively.

FIGURE 9.36 The option box for the Paint Skin Weights tool.

return to regular Shaded mode. Try bending the rest of the fingers and painting their influences; then, animate the hand, making gestures or grabbing an object using FK animation to set keys on the rotations.

When you paint weights on polygons, keep in mind that you're painting using the UVs. You may need to re-create the UVs of a polygonal mesh with a UV projection map for the Paint Weights tool to function properly, especially when you're importing and exporting the weight maps from one mesh to another (a procedure you won't encounter until later in your Maya experience).

The scene `poly_hand_skeleton_v03.ma` from the Poly_Hand_Anim project from the companion web page has the hand smooth-bound with painted weights on just the index finger for your reference. Try painting the other knuckles as needed for your animation.

Rigging work is essential for getting a good animation from your model. In a professional shop, it usually falls under the domain of a technical director (TD) who oversees the setup of characters and may also model their geometry. The more time I spent rigging scenes for the animators when I was a TD on the television show *South Park*, the easier and faster they were able to accomplish their animations.

Binding the Hand: Heat Map Method

Now let's try the same exercise using a Heat Map binding method instead of Closest Distance.

Load your own hand model before it was bound or the `poly_hand_skeleton_v02.ma` file from the Poly_Hand_Anim project from the web page. Now, follow these steps to smooth-bind the hand with the Heat Map method to compare to the previous method you tried:

1. Select the skeleton's root at the wrist and the hand mesh and choose Skin ➤ Bind Skin ❐. Change Bind Method to Heat Map and click Bind Skin.
2. Rotate the middle knuckle of the index finger down. Go to the top knuckle of the index finger and rotate that joint as well. Notice that the bending is cleaner than before. Not much of the hand moves when you bend the index finger joints as it did in the previous exercise using Closest Method. Figure 9.39 shows the result of bending at the index finger having used the Heat Map method of the Smooth Bind.
3. Select the hand mesh and choose Skin ➤ Paint Skin Weights ❐. Just as before, the hand turns black except for white areas on the mesh corresponding to the selected joint (shown in Figure 9.40 with the index finger's joint 9 selected).

5. Click and paint a black color around parts of the hand and palm that shouldn't be affected by the index finger bending at its top knuckle (joint 9), as shown in Figure 9.37.
6. Smooth out the area where it goes from white to black. In the option box, in the Influence section, set Paint Operation to Smooth. Right-click to smooth the area around the knuckle for a cleaner deformation, as shown in Figure 9.38. Your index knuckle should now bend beautifully.

Skin weights must always be normalized in a smooth bind, meaning the values have to add up to 1. When you reduce the influence of a joint on an area of the surface, the influence amount is automatically shifted to other joints in the hierarchy that have influence over that area; those joints are now more responsible for its movement.

You can exit the Paint Skin Weights tool by selecting another tool (press W for Translate, for example), and your view will

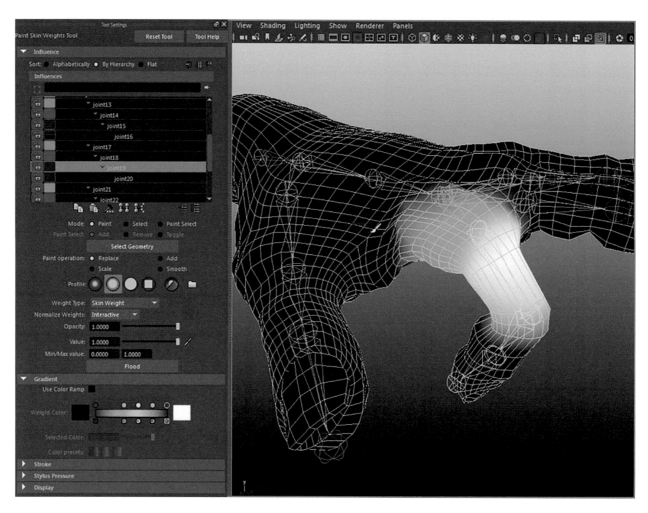

FIGURE 9.37   Paint the new weights to avoid unwanted deformations in the hand.

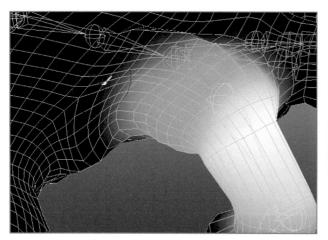

FIGURE 9.38   Smoothing out the bend at the index finger.

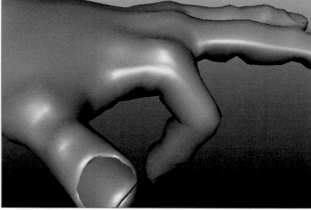

FIGURE 9.39   The index finger seems to bend more cleanly than before.

4. Paint weights on this hand, and you'll notice that it is a little easier now that you've used Heat Map instead of Closest Distance.

The Heat Map method gives you cleaner creases and bends at the knuckles, where Closest Point was a bit more soft, often deforming parts of the hand that shouldn't be affected much by a bending finger. There's still some painting to be done to make the fingers bend perfectly even when using the Heat Map method. The `poly_hand_skeleton_v04.ma` file from the Poly_Hand_Anim project has the hand with the index finger with painted weights as a reference for you.

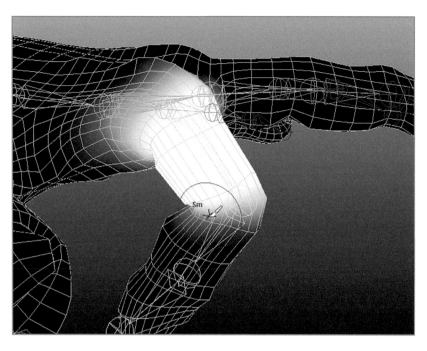

FIGURE 9.40 Painting skin weights on the Heat Map method bound hand.

Binding the Hand: Interactive Bind

Now, try skinning the hand with Interactive Bind.

Load your own hand or the `poly_hand_skeleton_v02.ma` file from the Poly_Hand_Anim project from the web page.

The Interactive Bind method is a bit easier to control when compared to the painting of the Smooth Bind weights.

1. Select the root joint at the wrist and the handMesh object and choose Skin ➤ Interactive Bind Skin. Figure 9.41 shows the color scheme of a Volume manipulator that allows you to set the initial skin weights of the hand easily.

2. In the Outliner, select the different joints of the hand to see how the interactive binding shows the volume influences. Then select the top knuckle of the index finger (joint9). Figure 9.42 shows the influence. Select the red circle at the end of the Volume manipulator and size it down to reduce the influence on the middle finger, as shown in Figure 9.43.

3. Grab the green spherical end, and you can see that you can move that in or out to lengthen or shorten the Volume manipulator. You can use the move or rotate handles to move the volume as well. Make adjustments to the finger to remove influences on the middle finger and other undesired areas of the hand, as shown in Figure 9.44.

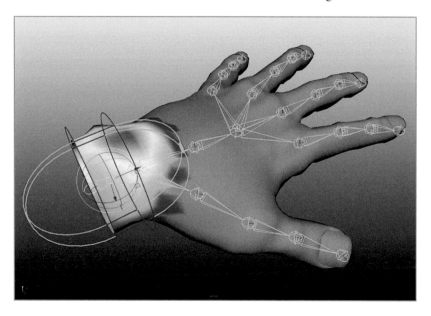

FIGURE 9.41 The Volume manipulator shows the influence of the selected joint at the wrist.

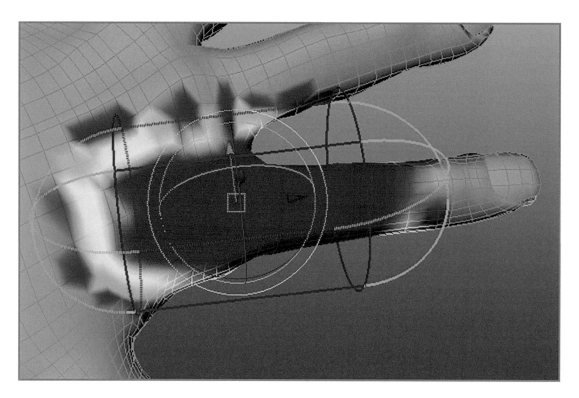

FIGURE 9.42   The index finger's first knuckle influences the middle finger, too.

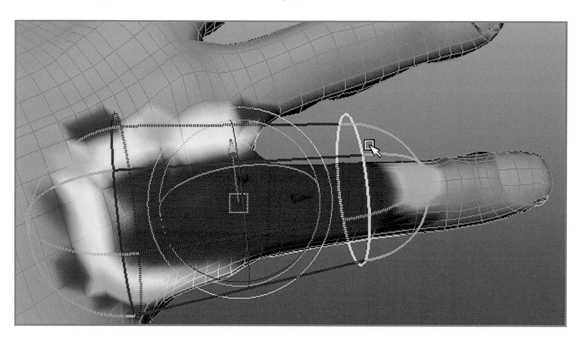

FIGURE 9.43   Use the Volume manipulator to reduce the influence on the middle finger.

Editing the interactive skin bind, as you can see, is easy using the Volume manipulators. If you exited the tool when you first created the bind and no longer see the Volume manipulators, you can access them by choosing Skin ➤ Interactive Bind Skin Tool. When you access this tool, the Volume manipulators appear again, and you're able to adjust your skin's influences.

When you are happy with the proper level of influence, keep picking the other joints in the index finger to make sure your binding is proper. Then continue to the other fingers to set up the binding on the hand properly. Though this method is easier than painting weights as we did before, it is not as easy to control. Test the bind by bending the joints. Here you are using a more interactive way to bind a mesh than Smooth Bind, which may be more or less effective depending on the model you are binding. It does, however, use the Closest Distance method by default, and the Heat Map method is not available for the Interactive Bind. In addition, you can paint skin weights when you use Interactive Bind, just as you did with the regular Bind Skin.

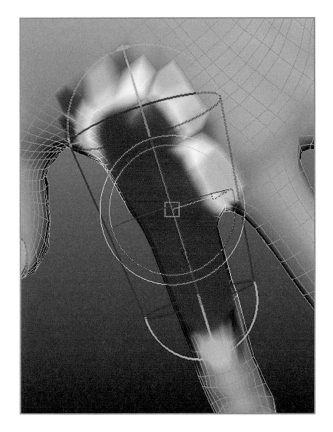

FIGURE 9.44   Set the influences by adjusting the Volume manipulator.

In the case of this hand and skeleton setup, the most-effective binding has been using a Smooth Bind with the Heat Map method, with some subsequent skin weight painting.

This process is pretty handy. Now, try your hand at creating a skeleton and binding it to your cartoon hand model from earlier in the book. When you're done, congratulations, give yourself a hand!

Inverse Kinematics

With IK, you have tools that let you plant a foot where it needs to be so you're not always moving the skeleton or model to compensate and keep the heel in place.

For legs, IK is nothing short of a blessing. There is no clearly preferable workflow to suggest for dealing with rigging arms and hands, however. Many people use IK on hands as well, but it can be better to animate the legs with IK and animate every other part of the body with FK. IK is best used when parts of the body (such as the feet) need to be planted at times. Planting the hands isn't necessary for a walk cycle, and having IK handles on the arms may create additional work while you are animating them. You will create a more well-rounded character rig that uses IK and easy-to-use character controls at the end of this chapter. First, let's get familiar with how IK works.

Rigging IK Legs

Let's go back to the Block Man. Switch to that project and load your version or the `block_man_skeleton_v02.ma` file from the Block_Man project from the companion web page.

You'll create an IK chain from the hip to the ankle on each foot. Creating the IK from the hip to the toe won't work.

Because IK automatically bends the joints in its chain according to where its end effector, or IK handle, is located, it has to choose which way to bend at a particular joint. This is why you created the legs slightly bent in the Block Man rig earlier in this chapter.

If you did not do this or your setup has straight legs for whatever reason, select the two knee joints and, in Pivot mode (hold down the D key), move the knees forward a bit over the feet to create a slight crook in the legs. Don't go too far; a slight amount is enough. This lets the IK solver know which way those joints are supposed to go.

Now, on to creating the IK:

1. In the Rigging menu set, open the IK Handle tool by choosing Skeleton ➤ Create IK Handle. Your cursor changes to a cross.
2. Select the start joint for the IK chain. This will be the root of this chain. Click the left thigh joint and then pick your end effector at the ankle joint. The bones in the IK chain turn brown. Repeat this procedure for the other leg. Figure 9.45 shows handles on both ankles.

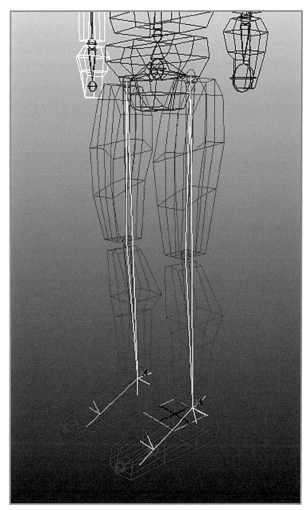

FIGURE 9.45   IK handles on both ankles with the roots at the hip joints.

If for some reason you can't manage to pick a joint for the IK tool, make sure Show ➤ Pivots is turned on in your view panel. Also, if you have difficulty seeing the handles, you can increase their size by choosing Display ➤ Animation ➤ IK Handle Size.

3. Move the IK handles around to see how the legs react. When you're finished, reset the IK handle positions.

4. Grab the top joint of the skeleton, which is the pelvis joint. Move the joint, and the entire body moves with it. Deselect the pelvis and then select the two ankle IK handles and set a translation key for them (press Shift+W). Grab the pelvis joint again and move it. The feet stick to their positions on the ground. Move the pelvis down, and the legs bend at the knees. Notice how the feet bend into the ground, though (see Figure 9.46, left).

5. Move the pelvis back to the origin. You can create an IK handle for the foot so that the foot stays flat on the ground. Open the IK Handle tool. For the start joint, select the first ankle; for the end effector, select the joint in the middle of that foot (lt_ballFoot or rt_ballFoot). Repeat for the other foot.

You can invoke the last tool you used by pressing Y.

6. Set a translate key for the foot IK handles. Move the pelvis down; the legs bend at the knees and the ankle, keeping the feet flush on the ground (see Figure 9.46, right).

Creating an IK Walk Animation

Because the Block Man's feet will stick to the ground, creating a walk cycle with IK animation is far easier than using FK ("Why didn't you tell me that before?"). Making the animation look good is still a tough job that requires a lot of practice, though.

Load the scene file `block_man_IK_v01.ma` from the Block_Man project from the companion web page or use your own IK-rigged Block Man with handles at the ankles and feet. The white leg and arm are, again, on the far side of the character. You'll set keys every five frames again for the gross animation. To keep this short, I'll just discuss setting poses with the feet. You can always return to the scene to add animation to the upper body with FK, as you did earlier in this chapter. Follow these steps:

1. On frame 1, set translate keys on the pelvis joint and all four IK handles for their start position.

2. Go to frame 5 and move the pelvis forward about 1 unit. The legs and feet lift off the ground a bit and strain to keep their position, but they stay back. Lower the pelvis to get the feet flat on the ground again. Set a key for the pelvis. Because Auto Keyframe is turned on, all keys are set for this animation. (With the FK animation, you set keys for everything at every pose.)

3. Grab both near IK handles for the ankle and foot (blue leg) and move them forward and up to match the pose shown in Figure 9.47.

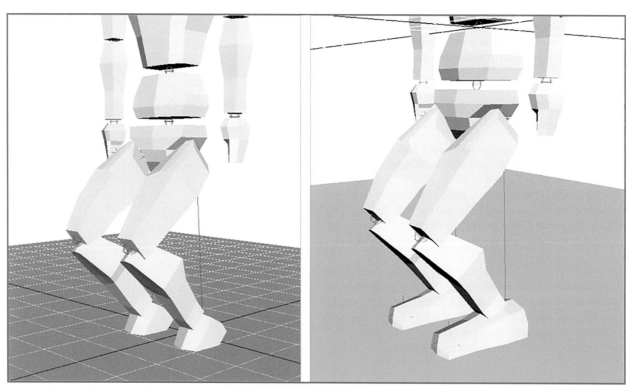

FIGURE 9.46 Creating another IK chain from the ankle to the tip of the foot and setting keyframes makes the feet stay on the ground (right) and not rotate into the ground (left).

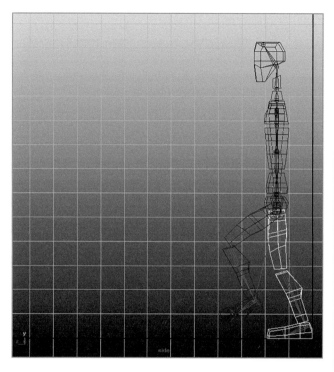

FIGURE 9.47 Step 3's pose (frame 5).

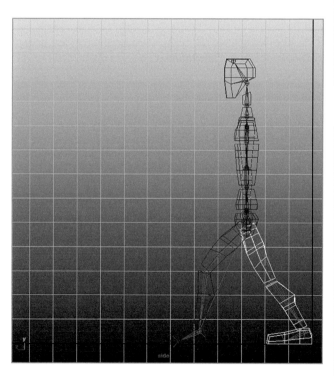

FIGURE 9.48 Step 4's pose (frame 10).

5. Go to frame 15. Move the pelvis another 2 units to center the body over the front foot. Lift the rear ankle and foot IK handles up to bend the knee and bring the knee up a bit. Match the pose shown in Figure 9.49.
6. Go to frame 20. Move the pelvis forward 1 unit and swing the white leg forward as in the pose shown in Figure 9.50.

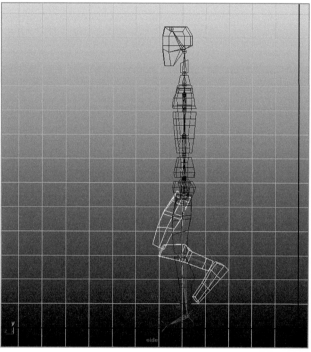

FIGURE 9.49 Step 5's pose (frame 15).

4. Go to frame 10. Move the front foot forward and plant it on the ground. Move the pelvis another three-fourths of a unit. Set translation keys for the rear ankle and foot handles where they are. Be sure to place the pelvis so that the rear foot is almost flat on the ground. Match the pose shown in Figure 9.48.

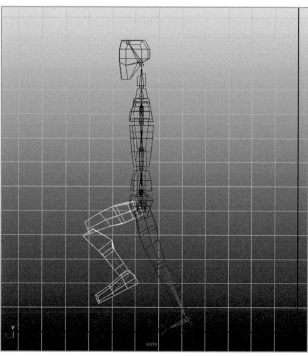

FIGURE 9.50 Step 6's pose (frame 20).

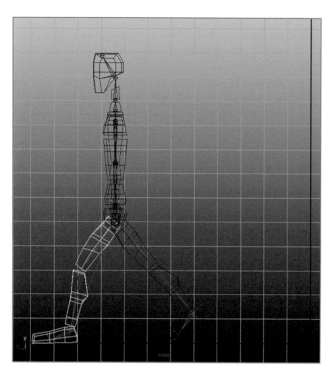

FIGURE 9.51 Step 7's pose (frame 25).

7. Move the pelvis three-fourths of a unit forward and plant the front leg down. Set keys for the rear leg and foot where they stand. Match the pose shown in Figure 9.51.

The next pose should match the pose in frame 10, although with the other leg. Continue the cycle, with each successive pose matching the one 15 frames before it on the opposite side.

At the end of this chapter, you'll take this process one step further and create a simple character animation rig for the entire Block Man so you can have a nicely functioning character for animation.

Further Uses for IK Chains

Many animators use IK chains more often in effects animation than in character work. IK chains can drive whips and ropes, flutter flags, bounce ponytails, and pump pistons as well as move legs and arms. For example, you can use a different type of IK chain, the *spline* IK chain, to control the shape of your bone chain with a NURBS spline. This IK chain is great for snakes and other long, deforming objects.

To create a spline IK chain, choose Skeleton ➤ Create IK Spline Handle and then select your top joint and end effector. Maya creates a spline running the length of the bone chain. Adjusting the curvature of the spline in turn drives the bones, which in turn drive the geometry bound to them. Figure 9.52 shows a spline curve affecting the curvature of the bones in its spline IK chain.

Basic Relationships: Constraints

As you know, Maya is all about the relationships between object nodes. You can create animation on one object based on the animation of another object by setting up a relationship between the objects. The simplest way to do that (outside of grouping) is to create a *constraint*. For example, you can "glue" one object to another's position or rotation through a constraint.

A constraint creates a direct relationship between the source and the target object's Translate, Rotate, or Scale attributes. This section explores six types of constraints: point, orient, scale, aim, geometry, and normal.

The Point Constraint

To attach a source object to a target object but have the source follow only the position of the target, use a *point constraint*. A point constraint connects only the Translate attributes of the source to the target. To use this method, select the target objects and then Shift+click the source object. In either the

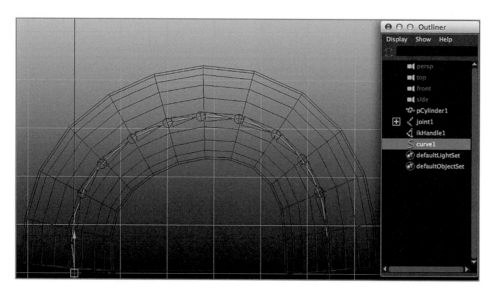

FIGURE 9.52 A spline IK chain is driven by the curvature of a NURBS spline. Adjusting the curve's CVs moves the joints.

Animation menu set (F4) or the Rigging menu set (F3), choose Constrain ➤ Point ❑.

Constraints are based on the pivots of the objects, so a point constraint snaps the source at its pivot point to the pivot point of the target and keeps it there, even in animation. However, the options allow you to set an offset that creates a gap between the source and the target.

You can constrain the same source to more than one target object. The source then takes up the average position between the multiple targets. By setting the Weight slider in the option box, you can create more of an influence on the source by any of the targets.

In Figure 9.53, a cone has been point-constrained to a sphere. Wherever the sphere goes, the cone follows. This is different from parenting the cone to the sphere in that only its translations are affected by the sphere. If you rotate or scale the sphere, the cone won't rotate or scale with it.

Although you can blend keyframe animation with constraint animation, as a beginner to Maya, consider that after you set a point constraint like that shown in Figure 9.53, you're unable to control the cone's Translate attributes because they're being driven by the sphere's translations.

Point constraints are perfect to animate a character carrying a cane or a sword, for example. The rotations on the sword are still free to animate, but the sword is attached to the character's belt and follows the character throughout the scene.

The Orient Constraint

An *orient constraint* attaches the source's Rotation attributes to the target's Rotation attributes. Select the target object or objects first, then Shift+click the source object, and then choose Constrain ➤ Orient ❑.

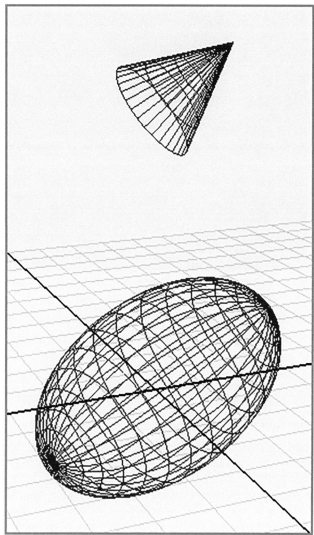

FIGURE 9.54   The cone's rotations match the sphere's rotations.

The Offset parameter allows you to set an offset in any axis. Otherwise, the source assumes the exact orientation of the target. In the case of multiple targets, the source uses the average of their orientations. Figure 9.54 shows the cone's orientation following an elongated sphere (the target).

A rotation constraint saves a lot of hassle when you have to animate an object to keep rotating in the same direction as another object. For example, you can use the rotation of one wheel of a locomotive to drive the rotation of all the other wheels.

The Point on Poly Constraint

A *point on poly constraint* attaches a source object to a vertex of a mesh. Select the target object's vertex first and then Shift+click the object you want to place at that point (see Figure 9.55, left). In the Animation or Rigging menu set, choose Constrain ➤ Point On Poly ❑.

The object is snapped to the vertex of the target at its pivot point. Even if the target object is animated and deforming, like a character, the object will stay on that vertex. Figure 9.55

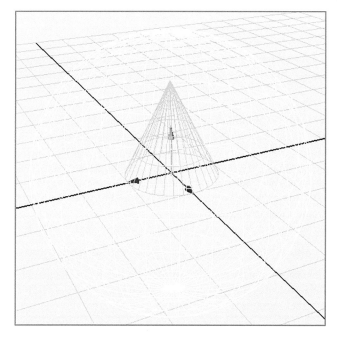

FIGURE 9.53   A cone point that is constrained to a sphere follows that sphere's position.

Selected vertex

FIGURE 9.55   The red ball is placed on the tree branch like a fruit with a point on poly constraint.

(right) shows the sphere pinned to the branch at the selected vertex location.

The point on poly constraint is good for pinning objects together, such as leaves on a branch.

The Aim Constraint

The *aim constraint* adjusts the source's rotations so that the source always points to the target object. Select the target objects first and then Shift+click the source object. In the Animation or Rigging menu set, choose Constrain ➢ Aim ❏.

The aim constraint has more options than the other constraints because you need to specify which axis of the source is to point to the target. You do so using the Aim Vector and Up Vector settings.

The Aim Vector setting specifies which axis of the source is the "front" and points to the target. In the cone and sphere examples, you set the Aim Vector option of the cone to (**0**, **1**, **0**) to make the Y-axis the front so that the cone's point aims at the sphere. If Aim Vector is set to (**1**, **0**, **0**), for example, the cone's side points to the sphere. Figure 9.56 shows the cone pointing to the sphere with an Aim Vector setting of (0, 1, 0).

The Offset values create an offset on the source's Rotation attributes, tilting it one way or another. The Up Vector setting specifies which way the cone faces when it's pointing to the sphere.

Aim constraints are perfect for animating cameras to follow a subject, such as a car at a racetrack.

Geometry and Normal Constraints

The *geometry* and *normal constraints* constrain the source object to the surface of the target object (as long as it's a NURBS or poly mesh).

With a geometry constraint, the source object attaches, at its pivot point, to the surface of the target. It tries to keep its own position as best it can, shifting as its target surface changes beneath it. Again, select the target, select the source object, and choose Constrain ➢ Geometry.

A geometry constraint is useful when you want to keep an object on a deforming surface, such as a floating boat on a lake. Figure 9.57 shows the cone after it has been geometry-constrained to a NURBS plane that is being deformed by a Wave deformer (in the Rigging menu, set choose Deform ➢ Nonlinear ➢ Wave). The cone sits on the surface as the waves ripple through, but it doesn't rock back and forth to stay oriented with the surface.

To get the cone to orient itself so that it truly floats on the surface, you need to use a normal constraint. Using a normal constraint rotates the cone to follow the surface's normals, keeping it perpendicular to the surface.

> A *surface normal* is an imaginary perpendicular tangent line that emanates from all surfaces to give the surface direction.

The normal constraint is similar to the aim constraint, and its options are similar. Using the Aim Vector setting, you specify which way is up for the object to define the orientation that the source should maintain. However, this setting doesn't constrain the location of the source to the target. If you want a floating effect, use geometry and a normal constraint to get the cone to bob up and down and roll back and forth as the waves ripple along (see Figure 9.58).

Scale, Parent, Tangent, and Pole Vector Constraints

Four more constraints are possible in Maya: the scale, parent, tangent, and pole vector constraints. Simply, a *scale constraint* attaches the source's Scale attributes to the target's Scale attributes. A *parent constraint* constrains an object's translation and rotation to another object by mimicking a parent–child relationship without actually parenting the objects. This keeps objects aligned without worrying about any grouping issues.

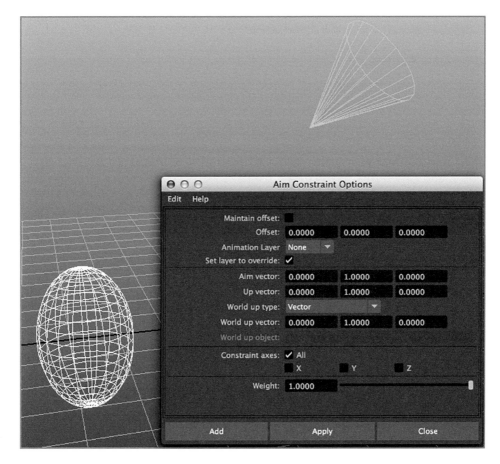

FIGURE 9.56 The cone aiming at the sphere.

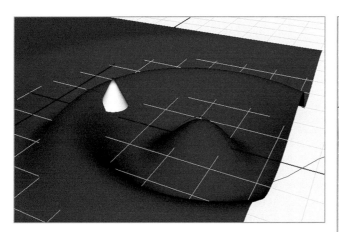

FIGURE 9.57 With a geometry constraint, the cone sits on the deforming surface.

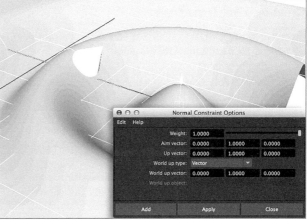

FIGURE 9.58 The cone now animates to float on the water surface, using both geometry and normal constraints.

You'll have a firsthand look at this in the exercise where you rig the locomotive later in this chapter. Lucky you!

A *tangent constraint* keeps an object's orientation so that the object always points along a curve's direction. This constraint is usually used with a geometry constraint or path animation to keep the object traveling along a curve pointed in the right direction, no matter the direction of the curve. A point on poly constraint allows you to select a vertex on a poly mesh and constrain an object to that vertex. *Pole vector constraints* are used extensively in character animation rigs to keep IK joints from flipping beyond 180° of motion.

Basic Relationships: Set-Driven Keys

A great feature for animation riggers (a.k.a. Technical Animators) is the *set-driven key* (SDK). An SDK establishes a relationship for objects that lets you create controls that drive certain features of a character or an object in a scene.

Before you can use an SDK, you must create extra attributes and attach them to a character's top node. These new attributes

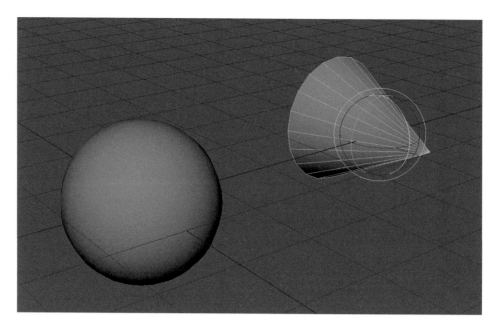

FIGURE 9.59 Lay out a cone and a sphere.

drive part of the character's animation. The term *character* is used broadly here. For example, you can set up a vehicle so that an SDK turns its wheels.

Let's start with a simple SDK relationship between two objects. You'll create a relationship between a ball and a cone. As the ball moves up in the Y-axis, the cone spins in the X-axis. As the ball descends, the cone spins back. You'll then revisit the hand and set up an SDK on the skeleton that animates the model.

Creating a Set-Driven Key

To create a simple SDK to make a sphere control the animation of a cone's rotation, follow these steps:

1. Create a Poly sphere and a poly cone in a new scene. Move the cone to the side of the sphere and lay it on its side, as shown in Figure 9.59.

2. Select the sphere and, in the Animation menu set, choose Key ➢ Set Driven Key ➢ Set. The Set Driven Key window opens with the pSphere1 object selected in the lower half of the window (the Driven section). Its attributes are listed on the right, as shown in Figure 9.60 (left).

3. You want the sphere to drive the animation of the cone, so you need to switch the sphere to be the driver

and not what's driven. With the sphere selected, click the Load Driver button to also list the sphere in the top half of the window.

4. Select the cone and click the Load Driven button to now display the cone's attributes in the bottom half of the window.

5. In the Driver section, highlight the sphere's Translate Y attribute. In the Driven section, highlight the cone's Rotate X attribute as shown in Figure 9.60 (middle left).

6. Click the Key button to set an SDK that essentially says that when the sphere is on the ground (Y=0), the cone's X rotation is 0 because both attributes are currently 0. The cone's Rotate X attribute turns blue in the Channel Box, meaning a driven key has been set.

7. Select the sphere and raise it in Y to a height of **5**. Select the cone and rotate it in X to **1,800** to make it spin properly. Click the Key button in the Set Driven Key window to specify that when the sphere is at a height of **5**, the cone's Rotate X attribute is **1,800°**. As the sphere's height increases from 0 to 5, the cone spins from 0 to 1,800 in X. Two images in Figure 9.60 (middle right and right) show the cone rotating as the sphere is lowered.

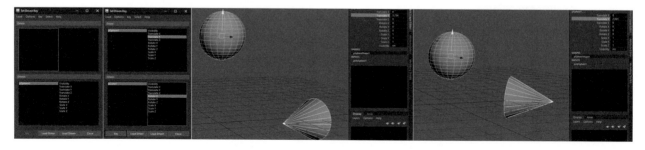

FIGURE 9.60 The initial Set Driven Key window (left). Correct settings (right).

An Advanced Set-Driven Key: The Hand

Automating some animations on a character is indispensable to an animator. This can't be truer than when setting up an SDK for hand control. After you model and bind a hand to a skeleton, you're ready for an SDK.

Open the scene `poly_hand_skeleton_v05.ma` from the Poly_Hand_Anim project from the companion web page or use your own file that has the hand and its skeleton and is bound to the skin. Your file shouldn't have animation, though. Set your hand to the bind pose before you begin.

Creating a New Attribute

First, you'll create a new attribute called index_pull to control a contracting finger.

1. Select the hand. In the handMesh tab of the Attribute Editor, click the Extra Attributes section. For now, at least, this section is empty.

2. In the Attribute Editor's menu bar, choose Attributes ➤ Add Attributes to open the Add Attribute window, which is shown in Figure 9.61. In the Long Name field, enter **index_pull**. Maya will automatically display that attribute as Index Pull in the user interface. Make sure the Make Attribute Keyable option is selected and that the Float option is selected in the Data Type section. In the Numeric Attribute Properties section, set Minimum to **0**, Maximum to **10**, and Default to **0**. Click OK.

After you click OK, the Index_Pull slider appears in the Attribute Editor and the Channel Box when you select the handMesh object. This attribute alone will control the entire index finger.

Assigning the Set-Driven Key

To set up the relationships with the SDK, follow these steps:

1. Make sure you're in the Animation menu set. With the handMesh selected, open the Set Driven Key window (choose Key ➤ Set Driven Key ➤ Set). Click Load Driver to specify that the hand should drive the animation.

2. Because you're animating the index finger pulling back, you want to drive the rotations of the top three knuckles. Deselect the hand, and then Shift+click all three knuckles on the index finger to select them. Click the Load Driven button. All three knuckles appear on the bottom.

3. Select the hand's Index Pull attribute (although you named the attribute index_pull, Maya will display it as Index Pull in the Set Driven Key window and a few other places like the Channel Box) and the three knuckles' Rotate Y attributes, as shown in Figure 9.62.

4. With the rotations of the knuckles at 0 and the Index Pull attribute at 0 as well, click the Key button to set the first relationship. When Index Pull is at 0, the finger is extended.

5. Select the handMesh node and set the Index Pull attribute to **5**.

FIGURE 9.61 The Add Attribute window.

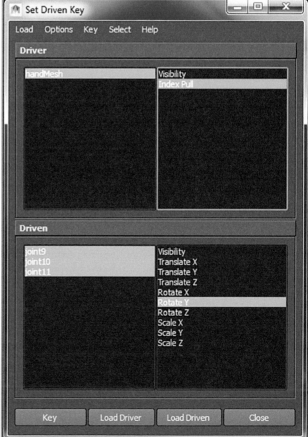

FIGURE 9.62 The Set Driven Key window for the hand.

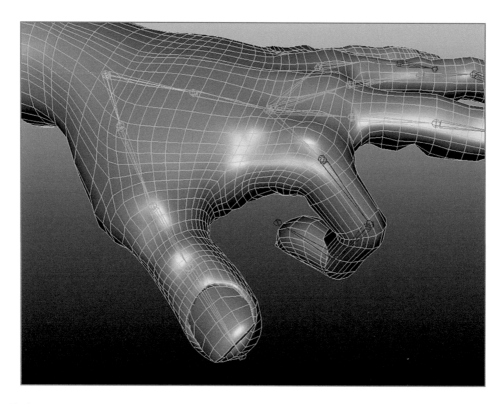

FIGURE 9.63   The bent index finger.

6. Select the fingertip's knuckle (joint11 in the web page file) and rotate it in Y to **20**. Select the next joint up the chain (the middle knuckle, joint10) and rotate it to **35** in the Y-axis. Select the final index knuckle (joint9) and rotate it in the Y-axis to **5**.

7. In the Set Driven Key window, select the three joints' Rotate Y and the handMesh Index Pull attribute and click the Key button. When the Index Pull attribute is at 5, the finger assumes this bent position.

8. Select the handMesh and set Index Pull to **10**.

9. Set the tip knuckle (joint11) to rotate to **65** in Y. Set the middle knuckle (joint10) to **60**. Set the last knuckle (joint9) to **50**. Click the Key button to see the result shown in Figure 9.63.

Select the handMesh node and change the value of the `Index Pull` attribute to curl your index finger. All you need to do to animate the finger is to set keys on that one attribute! Furthermore, you can set up a single SDK to control the bending of all the fingers at once, or you can set up one SDK for each finger for more control.

Open the scene `poly_hand_skeleton_v06.ma` from the Poly_Hand_Anim project available on the companion web page to see the hand with the SDK set up on the index finger.

Rigging the Locomotive

In this section, you'll use a locomotive to put your new animation skills to use. Download the file `fancy_locomotive_anim_v1.mb` from the Scenes folder of the Locomotive project from the book's web page; this scene is shown in Figure 9.64. Notice in this scene there are small plus signs near the wheels. These are selection handles, allowing you to more easily select objects or groups of objects. They have been enabled for some of the objects on the locomotive to make it easier to work with. To toggle selection handles on or off for any node in Maya, select Display ➢ Transform Display ➢ Selection Handles.

After selection handles for the locomotive's wheels and drive arms are turned on, only the objects that have selection handles will be selected when you make a marquee selection that covers the entire locomotive.

Setting Up Wheel Control

Your goal here is to rig the scene to animate all the secondary movements automatically based on some simple controls, as you did for the hand earlier in this chapter. In reality, the locomotive's steam pump drives the arms that then turn the wheels on the locomotive. You'll work backward, however, and use one wheel to drive the animation of everything else.

As a challenge, you can also try this exercise of rigging the locomotive wheels to rotate in unison by using rotation constraints instead of the Connection Editor.

Because all the large wheels have the same diameter, they rotate the same as the locomotive moves. In this case, you'll use the Connection Editor to attach the X Rotation on all the wheels to your main control wheel. You'll pick the middle

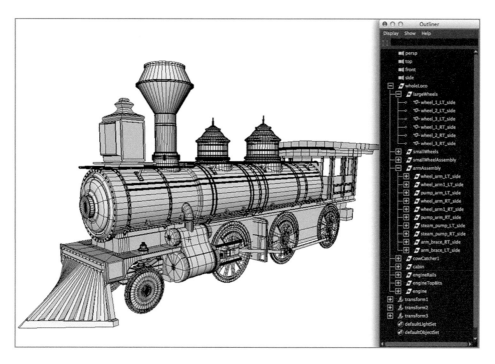

FIGURE 9.64 The fancy locomotive model.

wheel to be the control. To set up the locomotive, follow these steps:

1. Select the middle wheel on the left side of the locomotive (node wheel_2_LT_side), as shown in Figure 9.65. Open the Connection Editor (choose Windows ➤ General Editors ➤ Connection Editor). Click the Reload Left button to load the attributes of the selected middle wheel. Now, select the front wheel on the left side and click the Reload Right button.
2. Scroll down in the Connection Editor until you find Rotate in both columns. Click to highlight Rotate in the left column and then click to highlight Rotate in

the right column. Doing so connects the two rotations so that they both rotate at the same time, effectively letting you drive the animation of both wheels from just the center wheel. Figure 9.66 shows the Connection Editor.

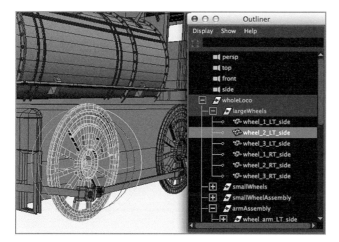

FIGURE 9.65 Select the middle wheel.

FIGURE 9.66 Connect the rotations of the two wheels.

3. Select the back wheel on the left side (wheel_3_ LT_side). Click the Reload Right button in the Connection Editor. Connect the Rotate attribute for the middle and back wheels. Close the Connection Editor and select just the middle wheel. When you rotate the wheel, all three wheels rotate together.

4. Repeat this procedure to connect the rotations of the three wheels on the other side to this middle wheel as well. Now all six wheels rotate in sync with the one control wheel. When you select that left-side middle wheel (the control wheel), the other five wheels turn magenta, signifying a connection between these objects.

If you get strange results when you connect the rotations of objects (for example, if the wheels flip over or rotate in the opposite direction of the control wheel), try disconnecting all the connections, freezing transforms, and reconnecting the attributes.

Controlling the Wheel Arms

You've now automated the animation of the wheels. Next, you'll figure out how to connect the wheel arms to the wheels and drive their motion as well. To do so, follow these steps:

1. Create a single joint that lines up with the first wheel arm. The root joint is placed where the wheel arm meets the middle wheel (control wheel), and the end joint is placed where the wheel arm meets the pump arm, as shown in Figure 9.67. The pump arm has been templated in this graphic (displayed in a light gray wireframe) to show you the entire wheel arm and joint.

2. Group the joint under the control wheel's node, as shown in the Outliner, earlier in Figure 9.65. Then, group the wheel arm under the top joint. This way, the joint rotates with the control wheel, also shown in Figure 9.68, albeit incorrectly for the pump arm.

3. As you saw in Figure 9.68, the joint isn't rotating properly to make the pump arm work right. The other end of it needs to attach to the pump arm in front of the front wheel, not fly up in space. You can use an IK handle for this. Make sure the rotation of the control wheel and the joint/wheel arm are set back to **0** to place them in the original position. In the Rigging menu set, choose Skeleton ➤ Create IK Handle. Make sure the settings are reset for the tool. Select the root joint as the start joint for the IK handle. Select the other tip of the bone as the end effector. You now have an IK handle at the tip where the wheel arm connects to the pump arm, as shown in Figure 9.69.

4. If you rotate the control wheel now, the wheel arm still separates from the pump arm. This is because the IK handle you just created needs a keyframe to keep it in position—that is, attached to the pump arm. Select the IK handle and, at frame 1, set a position keyframe. Now, if you rotate the control wheel, the joint and wheel arm pump back and forth.

5. Group the IK handle (ikHandle1) under the top node of the locomotive (wholeLoco), as shown in Figure 9.70.

FIGURE 9.67   Create a joint from the middle wheel to the pump arm at the first wheel.

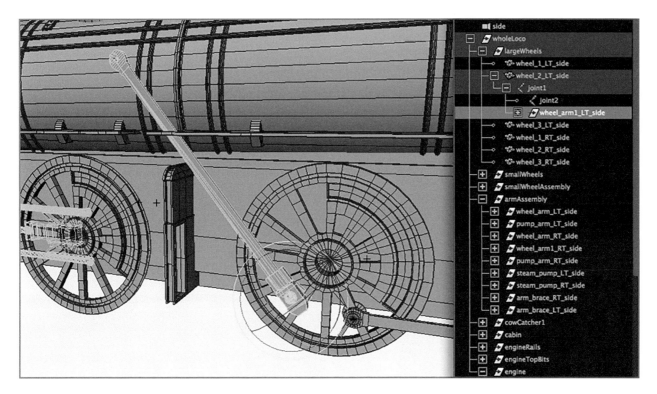

FIGURE 9.68 Group the top joint under the wheel and then group the wheel arm under the top joint.

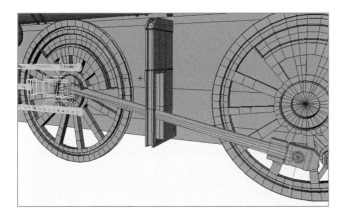

FIGURE 9.69 Place the end effector where the pump arm and the first wheel connect.

Controlling the Pump Arm

Next, you need to attach the pump arm to the wheel arm so that it pumps back and forth as the control wheel turns. If you simply group the pump arm with the end joint of the wheel arm's bone, the pump arm will float up and down as it pumps back and forth. You need to use a constraint to force the pump arm to move back and forth only in the Z-axis.

1. Make sure the control wheel is set back to 0 rotation. Select the pump arm, templated in Figure 9.71 so that you can see through to the wheel arm and joint, and line up its pivot with the end joint of the wheel arm bone.

2. Select the end joint (called joint2), Ctrl+click (or Cmd+click on a Mac) the pump arm group in the Outliner (called pump_arm_LT_side), and in the Rigging menu set choose Constrain ➤ Point ❐. In the option box, under Constraint Axes, select only Z to constrain the pump arm only in the Z-axis and click the Add button. Now if you rotate the control wheel, you see the pump arm and wheel arm connected. The pump arm pumps back and forth, although you'll immediately notice a need to adjust the model to make the piece fit when it animates. Figure 9.72 shows that the pump arm's geometry isn't yet quite right for animation. This is normal for this process and luckily needs only a quick fix.

3. To fix the pump arm, select the vertices on the ends of the cylinders and extend them to make them longer, as shown in Figure 9.73. Now the pump arm won't pull out of the steam pump assembly.

4. Adjust the pump arm so that the geometry fits when the pump pushes in as well.

The scene file `fancy_locomotive_anim_v2.mb` will catch you up to this point. Compare it to your work.

Controlling the Back Wheel

All that remains is to control the animation of the back wheel and its wheel arm. To set up the wheel arm animation, follow these steps:

FIGURE 9.70   Group the IK handle under the locomotive's top node.

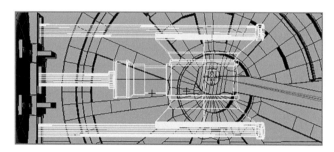

FIGURE 9.71   Line up the pivot of the pump arm with the end joint of the wheel arm joint.

1. Using the methods described in the steps in the "Controlling the Wheel Arms" section, create a joint to follow along the wheel arm between the middle control wheel and the back wheel. The root of the joint is set at the control wheel, as shown in Figure 9.74.

2. As before, create an IK handle for the end joint of this new bone, where it meets the back wheel, as shown in Figure 9.75. Make sure the handle is at the back wheel, not the middle control wheel.

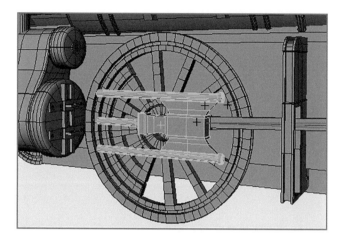

FIGURE 9.72   The pump arm is too short!

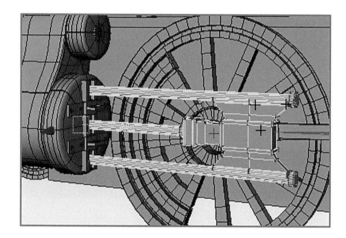

FIGURE 9.73   Use vertices to extend the pump arm.

3. Group the new joint under the master wheel and then group the wheel arm under this new joint. If you rotate the control wheel, the wheel arm rotates with the joint and wheel but doesn't connect to the back wheel yet. You need to attach the IK handle you just created for that joint to the back wheel.

   If you group the IK handle, as shown earlier in Figure 9.70, you'll run into a problem when you animate. Let's try it. Group the IK handle (ikHandle2) under the end back wheel, as shown in Figure 9.76, and then rotate the control wheel. The wheel arm pumps back and forth along with the back wheel, but every now and then the wheel arm geometry flips over backward. This isn't good.

   Fixing this is easy. The grouping of the IK handle to the back wheel is causing the issue. Although that is pretty much what you want to do, parenting the IK handle under the wheel is problematic. Here is where the parent constraint becomes extremely helpful. It gives you the desired result without the geometry flipping.

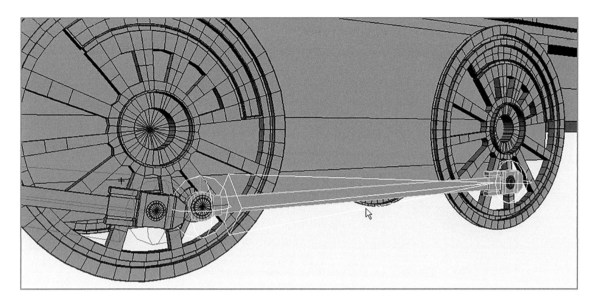

FIGURE 9.74 Create a joint to control the back wheel arm.

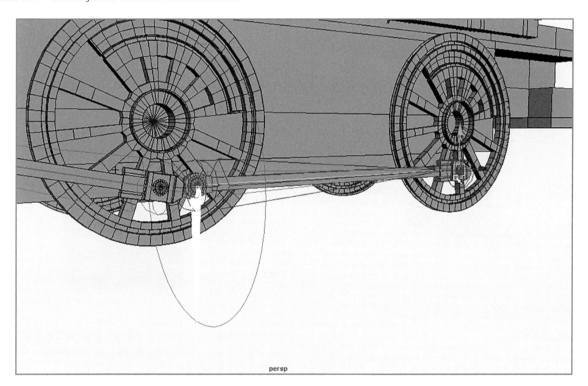

FIGURE 9.75 Create an IK handle to attach the wheel arm and the back wheel to the control wheel.

4. Make sure your control wheel is back to **0** rotation first. MMB+click in the Outliner and place the IK handle outside the hierarchy of the locomotive to remove the IK handle from under the back wheel's node. You may also undo your past actions to the point before you grouped the IK handle (ikHandle2) under the back wheel. (You have to love Undo!)

5. Select the back wheel, Shift+click the IK handle (ikHandle2), and choose Constrain ➢ Parent. Now, if you rotate the control wheel, everything works great.

6. Group the IK handle (ikHandle2) under the top node of the locomotive (wholeLoco).

You can use `fancy_locomotive_anim_v3.mb` to compare your work.

Again, seeing procedures go slightly awry, like when the wheel arm flipped over, is important. Doing so gives you a taste of trouble and a chance to fix it. Troubleshooting is an integral skill for a good CG artist.

FIGURE 9.76   The wheel arm geometry flips over if you group the IK handle under the back wheel.

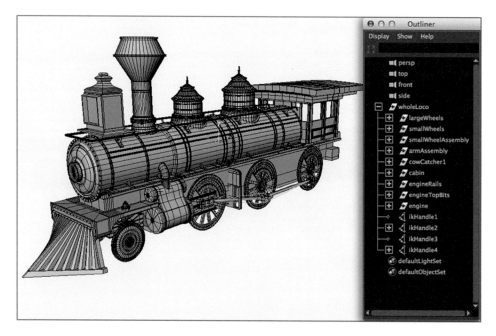

FIGURE 9.77   The rigged fancy locomotive.

Finishing the Rig

You're almost home free with the locomotive wheel rigging. Everything works great when you rotate the control wheel. If you select the top node of the locomotive and translate the train back and forth, everything should work perfectly. Repeat the steps in the previous few sections to connect the wheel arms and wheels on the other side of the locomotive, and you're finished! Figure 9.77 shows the completed and rigged locomotive.

Creating a Simple Character Rig

In this section, you will revisit the Block Man setup to create a more well-rounded character rig with controls. This rig was created by Maks Naporowski, a fellow professor at USC and CG animator/rigger, as a fairly simple biped rig for animation. Bear in mind that character rigging is an involved process, and

you are starting to scratch the surface here. When you are done with this rig, you will have a simple two-legged character that you can easily animate using the controls you will set up based on what you've already accomplished throughout this chapter.

Creating Control Shapes

Animators hardly ever manipulate and keyframe IK handles or joints directly when a good rig is available to them, and that's what you should keep in mind for the following rig:

1. Open the scene file `block_man_skeleton_v02.ma` from the Block_Man project.

2. In the Rigging menu set, choose Skeleton ➤ Create IK Handle ◻. In the option box, set the Current solver attribute to Rotate-Plane Solver. Click one of the hip joints and then click the ankle joint. This makes an

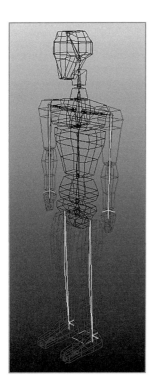

FIGURE 9.78 Create IK handles for the arms and legs.

IK chain for the leg. Repeat for the other leg. Name them **lt_ikHandle** and **rt_ikHandle**.

3. Create an IK chain for the arms, from the shoulder to the wrist, also making sure to use the Rotate-Plane Solver. Name them as well. Figure 9.78 shows all four IK handles created.

4. Create a circle (Create ➢ NURBS Primitives ➢ Circle). Scale it up and center it around the left wrist. Name this circle **lt_arm_CNTRL**. Duplicate the circle, move the copy to the center on the right wrist, and name it **rt_arm_CNTRL**. Refer to Figure 9.79 for placement.

5. In the Channel Box/Layer Editor, click the Display tab in the Layer Editor and create two new layers: **lt_cntrls** (make it blue) and **rt_cntrls** (make it red). Assign the left wrist circle to lt_cntrls and the right

wrist circle to rt_cntrls. This makes it easier to visualize and control (see Figure 9.79).

6. Select both circles and select Modify ➢ Freeze Transformations. This will zero out their positions. Name the left wrist circle **lt_arm_CNTRL** and the right wrist circle **rt_arm_CNTRL**.

7. Create two more circles and adjust their CVs to make them oval to fit around the feet. Size and place them around the feet as shown in Figure 9.80. Assign each foot oval to the appropriate lt_cntrls or rt_cntrls display layers and name the ovals **lt_foot_CNTRL** and **rt_foot_CNTRL**, respectively.

8. Create a large circle and center it around the pelvis joint (name it **body_CNTRL**). Make another large square shape and place it on the floor around the feet (name it **main_CNTRL**). Assign these two shapes to a new display layer called **cn_cntrls** and make it green.

These shapes will be the primary controllers for the animation of the character. They are easy to select and manipulate and make animation much easier.

Setting Up the Controls

Now comes the tough part of rigging it all to work! You'll group the shapes and create relationships to the skeleton here:

1. Parent the body_CNTRL under the main_CNTRL shape.

2. Parent the two arm controllers (rt_arm_CNTRL and lt_arm_CNTRL) under the main_CNTRL shape as well.

3. Parent each of the two wrist IK handles under each respective circle shape, as shown in Figure 9.81.

4. Select the left wrist circle and the lt_wrist joint and choose Constrain ➢ Orient ❑. In the option box, turn on Maintain Offset and click Add.

This allows you to control the hand's rotation with the circle, as well as the hand's position. Select the wrist circle and move and rotate it around to see how the arm reacts. The elbow can swing around a little much, so you'll add a control for the twist of the arm.

FIGURE 9.79 Create circles for the wrists, place them, and assign them to their own display layers.

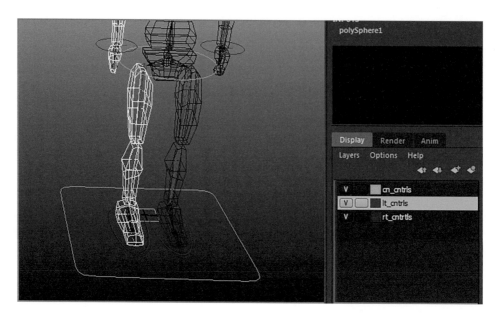

FIGURE 9.80   Create control shapes for the feet, pelvis, and body.

FIGURE 9.81   Grouping the controllers and IK handles.

5. Select the left wrist circle and open the Attribute Editor. Choose Attributes ➤ Add Attribute. Enter the name **twist** to the wrist circle and keep the options at their default (Data Type: Float).

6. Now you'll connect it to the IK handle. Select the left wrist's IK handle and also its circle controller and choose Windows ➤ Node Editor. You will see two nodes in the Node Editor (see Figure 9.82, top). Click once on the View Mode icon ( ) on the right of

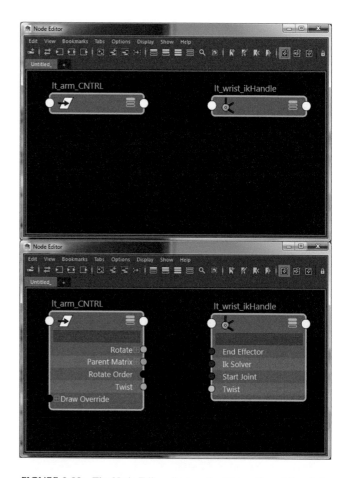

FIGURE 9.82   The Node Editor displays the IK handle and the circle control shape in compact display (top). The nodes with expanded display show attributes (bottom).

each node to expand its view, as shown in Figure 9.82 (bottom). The white and colored circles on either side of the nodes are input and output sockets.

THE NODE EDITOR

The Node Editor gives you an easy way to create and manage connections between objects or nodes. You can navigate it easily with Alt+mouse combinations like other Maya windows, and you can arrange the display of nodes, however, you want.

7. Click the output socket of the lt_arm_CNTRL node (the green circle on the right) next to the Twist attribute and drag the cursor to reveal a yellow rubber band attached to your cursor. Drag the mouse to the input socket of the lt_wrist_ikHandle node's Twist attribute (the light blue circle on the left) and release the mouse button. This connects these two attributes; however, the Node Editor doesn't show the connection immediately. To see the actual connection, click the lt_arm_CNTRL node in the Node Editor and

   click the Input And Output Connections icon ( ) at the top of the window. You'll now see the connection is made through an intermediate node (unitConversion1), as in Figure 9.83.

   You can ignore this extra node, but rest assured that the connection is made. Clicking the Input And

   Output Connections icon ( ) is always a good idea to check your connections in the Node Editor.

8. Now if you select the wrist circle and adjust the twist value, the arm will twist. If nothing happens, check your node connection and make sure you used the ikRPsolver when you created the IK handles in the previous section.

9. Repeat steps 4–8 for the right hand.

10. Now let's do the same for the feet for the Twist attribute. Select the left foot's control oval and add a new attribute called **twist**. Select the oval and the ankle joint (lt_ikHandle1) and open the Node Editor and

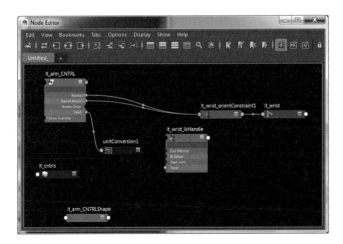

FIGURE 9.83 You've connected the Twist attributes, though you can't see it until you click Input And Output Connections icon, which is kind of silly.

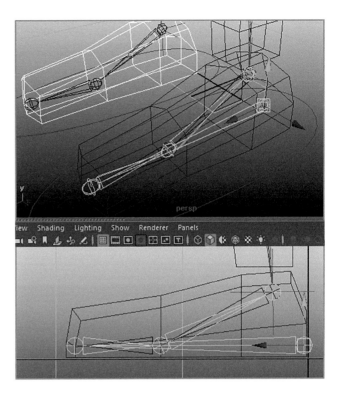

FIGURE 9.84 Create a reverse joint chain for the left foot.

connect the Twist attributes as you did in step 7 for the arm. Repeat for the right leg.

11. Select the pelvis joint and parent that under the body_CNTRL circle.

Setting Up Heel Controls

Now let's move on to creating some nice foot controls to allow the character to stand on his tiptoes or his heels easily. For that, you will need to build a reverse joint chain to control the foot from the heel to supplement the existing leg joints.

1. In the side view, choose Skeleton ➤ Create Joints and place a joint at the back of the left heel, as shown in Figure 9.84. Place the second joint exactly on the existing toe joint (lt_foot). Hold down V for point snaps when you create the joint so you can snap it exactly to that toe joint. Snap the third joint to the existing lt_ballFoot joint; finally, snap the fourth joint to the existing lt_ankle joint.

2. Grab the top joint of this reverse chain and parent it under the lt_foot_CNTRL oval. Name the joints as noted in Figure 9.85. Finally, parent the left ankle's IK handle (lt_ihHandle1) under the lt_rev_ankle joint as shown. Repeat for the other foot.

3. Next, parent both the foot control ovals under the main_CNTRL square (see Figure 9.86).

4. Select the main_CNTRL square and move the rig around. The character moves along with it. Select the body_CNTRL circle. When you move the body

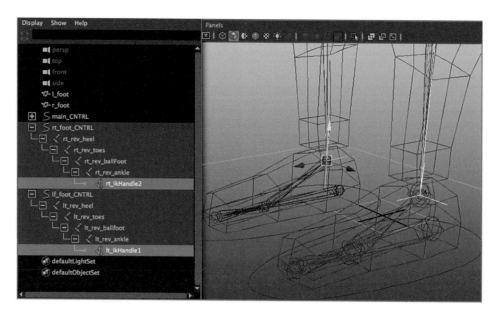

FIGURE 9.85   Parent the heel joints and ankle IK handles.

FIGURE 9.86   Parent the foot controls.

control, the feet and hands stay because of IK (see Figure 9.87), and that's how you want it. Undo your moves.

5. Create a display layer called **rigging**. Select the lt_rev_heel and rt_rev_heel joints you just created and parented and assign them to the new rigging display layer. This will make it easy to hide these extra reverse joints to keep them out of the way later.

6. Select the lt_rev_toes joint first and then the lt_ballfoot joint (see Figure 9.88 for the selections)

and choose Constrain ➤ Orient ❑. Make sure Maintain Offset is checked and click Apply. The constraint node should appear under the lt_ball-Foot node, as shown in the Outliner in Figure 9.88 (left image).

7. Select the lt_rev_ballFoot joint and then the lt_ankle joint and create an aim constraint like in the previous step.

8. Repeat steps 6 and 7 for the right foot.

9. When you're done, your Outliner should be similar to the one shown in Figure 9.88 (right image). If your constraint nodes are not in the right places, check to make sure you selected the nodes in order in steps 6 and 7 when you made the aim constraint.

Set-Driven Keys: Heel Controls

Now let's set up some fancy heel controls.

1. Select the left foot control oval and add a new attribute to it called **heel**. In the options, change Data Type to Float, but give it a Minimum of **−5** and a Maximum of **10** (see Figure 9.89). Repeat for the right foot.

   You need to set up an SDK to raise or lower the heel based on the value of the Heel attribute.

2. Select the left foot control oval and choose Key ➤ Set Driven Key ➤ Set from the Animation menu set. Click Load Driver to load the control oval as the driver of this SDK.

3. Select lt_rev_heel and click Load Driven in the SDK window.

4. In the SDK window, select Heel as the driver attribute on the oval and the RotateZ attribute on the driven joint (see Figure 9.90).

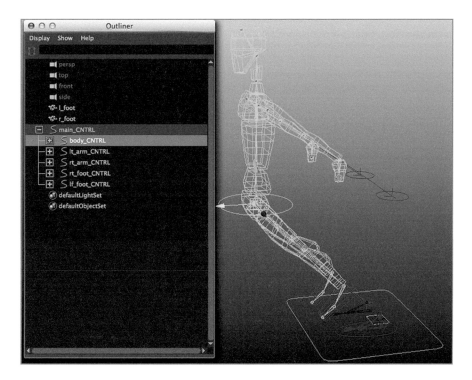

FIGURE 9.87 Moving the body control and the main control works perfectly.

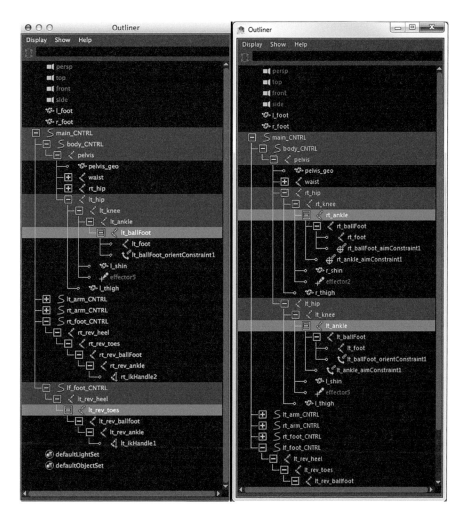

FIGURE 9.88 Aim constrain the two joints together.

FIGURE 9.89 Create a new attribute for the foot control oval.

5. Make sure the Heel attribute is set to **0** and the Rotate Z for the lt_rev_heel joint is also **0**. Click Key in the SDK window.

6. Set the Heel attribute to **−5** and rotate the lt_rev_heel **45°** up in Z. Click Key in the SDK window. If you now select the foot control oval and change the Heel attribute to between **−5** and **0**, the heel will raise and lower. Make sure to set it back to **0** when you're done testing.

7. Select the lt_rev_ballFoot joint and click Load Driven in the SDK window. Keep lf_foot_CNTRL's Heel as the driver. Select the RotateZ attribute for the driven joint (see Figure 9.91.)

8. Set Heel to **0** and rotate in Z for the rev_ballFoot to **0**. Click Key in the SDK window.

9. Set Heel to **5** and rotate in Z for the rev_ballFoot to **45°**. Click Key in the SDK window.

10. Set Heel to **10** and rotate in Z for the rev_ballFoot back to **0**. Click Key in the SDK window.

11. Test the Heel slider by sliding it to a value of 5, and you should see the back of the foot moving up, as shown in Figure 9.92. Set Heel to **10**, and the heel comes back down.

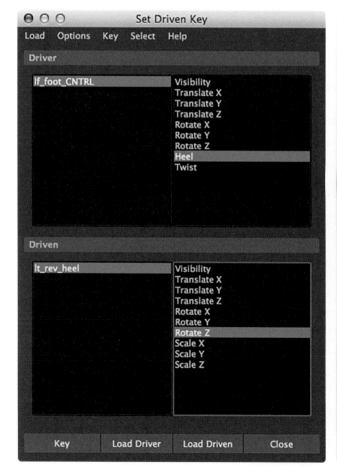

FIGURE 9.90 The first SDK relationship for the reverse heel joint.

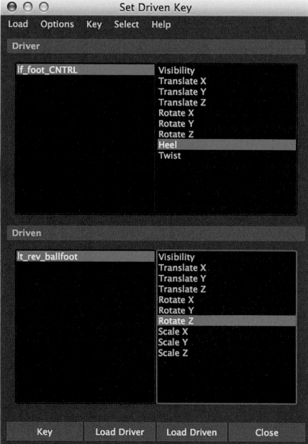

FIGURE 9.91 The next SDK relationship for the reverse ballFoot joint.

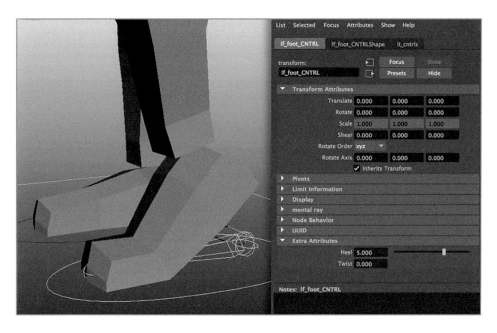

FIGURE 9.92 When the Heel attribute is at 5, the heel should raise up like shown.

12. Finally, select lt_rev_toes and click Load Driven in the SDK window. Keep lf_foot_CNTRL's Heel as the driver. Select Rotate Z as the driven channel for the lt_rev_toes joint in the SDK window. Figure 9.93 shows the SDK relationship.

13. Set Heel to **5** and make sure the lt_rev_toes joint's Rotate Z is **0**. Click Key in the SDK window.

14. Set Heel to **10** and rotate in Z the lt_rev_toes joint to **45°**. Click Key in the SDK window.

15. Test the Heel slider, and you'll see at a value of 10 that the foot is up and the toes are on the ground (see Figure 9.94).

16. Repeat steps 1–15 for the right foot. This time, you will use the rt_ nodes in place of the lt_ nodes you used earlier.

Make sure you're saving your progress as you go! When you're done, your rig should have some pretty handy controls. You will move the entire character using the main_CNTRL node. You can move the body itself while keeping sticky IK hands and feet by using the body_CNTRL node. And, of course, you control the arms/hands and legs/feet using the respective arm_CNTRL and foot_CNTRL nodes. All keyframes and animation should happen on these nodes only; you should not have to manipulate the joints or the IK handles directly at all. And that, in a somewhat long-winded nutshell, is the purpose of a character rig.

You can load the file `character_rig_v01.ma` from the Block_Man project to check your work or just to use it as a rigged character for some animation fun!

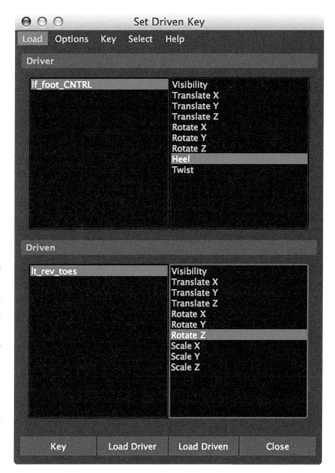

FIGURE 9.93 The final SDK relationship for the reverse toe joint.

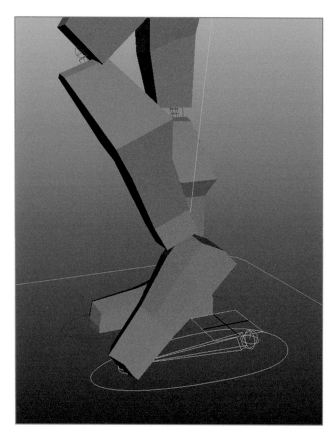

FIGURE 9.94   The foot position when Heel is set to 10.

For Further Study

Animation is as much a sport as it is an art, meaning practice makes you better. Use the rigged character from the end of this chapter to redo the walk animations from the beginning of this chapter. Also, try different types and moods of walk.

Can you animate a simple walk that looks happy and enthusiastic? Can you make that walk sad and lonely? Being able to convey emotion in your movement is key, and the more you try, the better you get.

Summary

In this chapter, you extended your experience with animation and learned about rigging techniques and automation. Starting with the simple Block Man, you learned how to set up a hierarchy for forward kinematics animation to create a walk cycle. Then, you used a skeleton to rig a hand for animation. Next, you learned how to bind the geometry of the hand to the skeleton using two different methods of smooth bind and also the interactive bind, as well as how to edit the binding. You also learned how to create an IK system to drive the joints in the Block Man for an IK walk cycle animation. After that, you learned how constraints can be used in rigging and how to set up SDKs to create easy controls to animate the hand. Then, you put all these rigging tricks together to rig the wheels of the locomotive to automate the animation of that complex system with a single control based on the middle wheel. And finally, you tackled a pretty tough rigging assignment in rigging the Block Man even further to have some nice options for movement using controllers.

The true work in animation comes from recognizing what to do in the face of certain challenges and how to approach their solutions. Maya offers a large animation toolset, and the more familiar you become with the tools, the better you'll be able to judge which tools to use in your work. Don't stop with this chapter; experiment with the features not covered here to see what happens.

Animation is about observation and interpretation. The animator's duty is to understand how and why something moves and to translate that into their medium without losing the movement's fidelity, tenacity, or honesty.

10

Autodesk® Maya® Lighting

Learning Outcomes

In this chapter, you will be able to

Understand basic concepts for setting up CG lighting

Choose the appropriate Autodesk® Maya® or Arnold light for a scene based on light attributes

Control which lights illuminate certain objects through light linking

Illuminate and render a scene with Arnold Physical Sky

Produce special lighting effects with a volumetric lighting effect

Practice setting up a basic lighting solution for the toy airplane, glass candle holder, and decorative box

Animate the attributes of a light

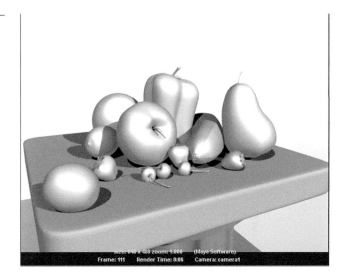

FIGURE 10.1 An overlit still life.

Basic Lighting Concepts

It's no surprise that lighting in Maya resembles direct-lighting techniques used in photography and filmmaking. Lights of various types are placed around a scene to illuminate the subjects as they would be for a still life or a portrait. Your scene and what's in it dictate, to some degree at least, which lights you put where.

Although it's easy to insert and configure lights, it's *how* you light that will make or break your scene. Knowing how to do that really comes only with a good deal of experience and experimentation, as well as a good eye and patience.

This chapter will familiarize you with the basic techniques of lighting a scene in Maya and start you on the road to finding out more.

What Your Scene Needs

Ideally, your scene needs areas of highlight and shadow. *Overlighting* a scene flattens everything and diminishes details. Figure 10.1 shows a still life with too many bright lights.

Similarly, *underlighting* your scene makes it muddy and lifeless, and it flattens the entire frame. Figure 10.2 shows the still life underlit. The bumps and curves of the mesh are hardly noticeable.

Like a good photographer, you want your image to have the full range of exposure. As shown in Figure 10.3, light and shadow complement each other and work to show the features of your surface.

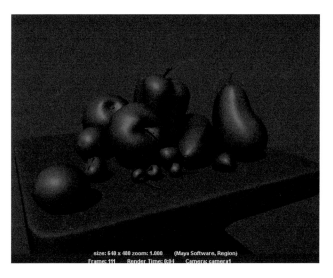

FIGURE 10.2 An underlit still life.

Three-Point Lighting

The traditional filmmaking and television approach to lighting is called *three-point lighting*. Three distinct roles are used to light the subject of a shot. More than one light can be used for each of the three roles, but the scene should seem to have only one primary (or *key*) light, a softer light to fill the scene, and a back light to pop the subject out from the background.

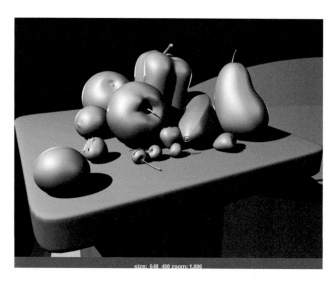

FIGURE 10.3   Balanced lighting creates a more interesting picture.

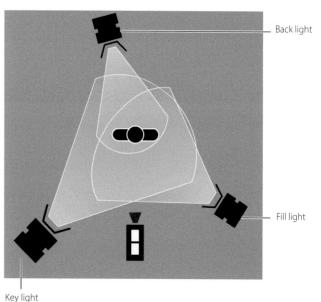

FIGURE 10.4   A three-point lighting schematic.

Three-point lighting ensures that the primary subject's features aren't just illuminated but featured with highlights and shadow. Using three directions and qualities of light creates the best level of depth. Figure 10.4 shows a schematic of a basic three-point setup.

Key Light

A *key light* is placed in front of the subject and off to the side of the camera to provide the principal light on the subject. Because it's usually off-center, the key light creates one side of brighter light, increasing the depth of the shot. This light also provides the primary shadows and gives the important sense of lighting direction in the shot.

Although it's possible for several lights to fulfill the role of key light in a scene—for example, three ceiling lights

overhead—one light should dominate, creating a definitive direction. Figure 10.5 (left) shows the subject being lit by only a key light, although it's physically composed of two lights.

The direction of the two lights remains the same, and one takes intensity precedence over the other and casts shadows. The effect creates a single key light, which produces a moody still life.

Try This

1. Set your project to the Lighting project downloaded from the book's website. Open the scene file still_life_v01.ma from the Scenes folder.

2. In the camera1 viewport panel, press 7 for lighting mode. It should turn black; there are no lights.

3. Click Create ➤ Lights ➤ Point Light and, in the persp window, place it as your key light (Figure 10.5, right). Use the camera1 viewport to gauge how the lighting composition is working for optimum placement of the Point light.

Fill Light

A more diffused light than the key light, the *fill light* seems directionless and evenly spread across the subject's dark side. This fills the rest of the subject with light and decreases the dark area caused by the key light.

The fill light isn't usually meant to cast any shadows onto the subject or background itself and is actually used to help soften the shadows created by the key light. Figure 10.6 shows the still life with an added fill light. Notice how it softens the shadows and illuminates the dark areas the key light misses.

Typically, you place the fill light in front of the subject and aim it so that it comes from the opposite side of the key light to target the dark side of the subject. Even though the still life in Figure 10.6 is still a fairly moody composition, much more is visible than with only the key light in the previous figure.

Try This

1. In the existing scene that you started with a single Point light, choose Create ➤ Lights ➤ Directional Light. Where you place the light doesn't matter, but how you rotate it does.

2. Rotate the light so you get a lighting direction opposite to the direction of the key light from the Point light already in the scene.

3. With the Directional light selected, change its Intensity attribute in the Channel Box or the Attribute Editor from 1.0 to **0.5**. Use the camera1 viewport to see how the fill light is working.

Back Light

The *back light*, or rim light, is placed behind the subject to create a bit of a halo, which helps pop the subject out in the shot. Therefore, the subject has more presence against its background. Figure 10.7 shows how helpful a back light can be.

FIGURE 10.5   Key light only.

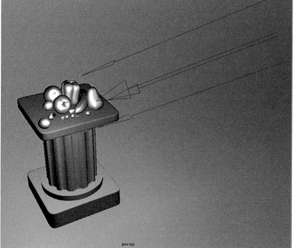

FIGURE 10.6   A fill light is now included.

The back light brings the fruit in this still life out from the background and adds some highlights to the edges, giving the composition more focus on the fruit.

Don't confuse the back light with the background light, which is used to light the environment itself.

Try This

1. In your current scene with the two lights, create a third light to be a Spot light.
2. You can use Move and Rotate to position the light to shine from behind the fruit, or you can use the special manipulator. To use that, press T with the Spot light selected. You will see two Move manipulators, one for the source of the light and one for the target.

3. Move the target to the front of the column stand and move the target behind and slightly above the fruit (Figure 10.7, right). Use the camera1 viewport to see how the back light should be placed.

Using Three-Point Lighting

The three-point lighting system is used for the primary subject of the scene. Because it's based on the position and angle of the subject to the camera, a new setup is needed when the camera is moved for a different shot in the same scene. Three-point lighting is, therefore, not scene-specific but shot-specific, as long as it does not break the overall continuity of the scene.

After the lighting is set up for the subject of a shot, the background must be lit. Use a directed primary light source that

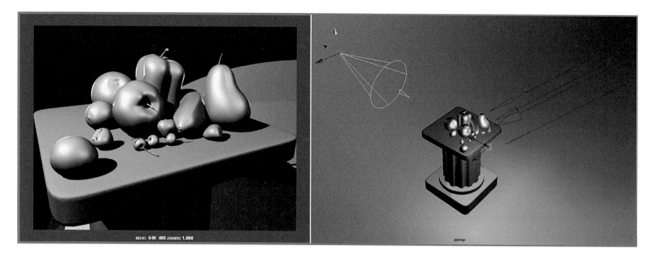

FIGURE 10.7   A back light makes the subject pop right out.

matches the direction of the key light for the main light, and use a softer fill light to illuminate the rest of the scene and soften the primary shadows.

Maya Native Lights

Lighting in Maya is dependent on how you wish to render. There are several renderers that plug into Maya, including Arnold, which is included in Maya's installation. Other renderers include V-Ray and Red Shift that can be purchased to plug into Maya. Other renderers often come with their own set of lights. The base Maya lights should work in other renderers but are seldom used anymore since a renderer's own lights give a better outcome. Nonetheless, Maya's native lights can be useful, so let's take a look at these stock lights before moving on to Arnold lights, which give a much better look when rendered through Arnold, which is the default renderer with Maya currently.

To see how to switch from one renderer to another, open the Render Settings window by choosing Windows ➢ Rendering Editors ➢ Render Settings. At the top of the Render Settings window, you can select among the installed renderers, as shown here.

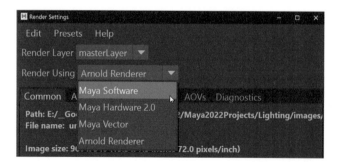

We will start by discussing lights used primarily with Maya Software render, and then move on to the more powerful Arnold lights.

Six types of light are available in Maya: Ambient, Directional, Point, Spot, Area, and Volume. How you use each light dictates whether they become key, fill, or rim lights. Each light can fill any of those roles, although some are better for certain jobs than others. All of these Maya lights render in Maya rendering, and most, but not all, will work with other renderers as well.

To create each native light, choose Create ➢ Lights and click the light type; that light will appear at the origin of your scene.

Common Light Attributes

All lights in Maya are treated like any other object. They can be transformed, rotated, scaled, duplicated, deleted, and so forth, and they are visible as nodes in the Outliner alongside other objects in the scene. Like any other node, lights have attributes that govern how they function. Figure 10.8 shows the Attribute Editor for a typical Maya native light.

When you select any light type and then open the Attribute Editor, you'll see the following attributes and options:

Type
    This drop-down menu sets the type of light. You can change from one light type to another (for instance, from Spot to Point).

Color
    This controls the color cast by the light. The darker the color, the dimmer the light will be. You can use Color in conjunction with Intensity to govern brightness, although it's best to set the brightness of a light using Intensity only. You can keyframe Color by simply RMB+clicking the attribute name Color in the Attribute Editor or Channel Box and choosing Set Key (Attribute Editor) or Key Selected (Channel Box).

Intensity
    This attribute specifies how much light is cast. The higher the intensity, the brighter the illumination will be. You can keyframe intensity by RMB+clicking the attribute just as with Color.

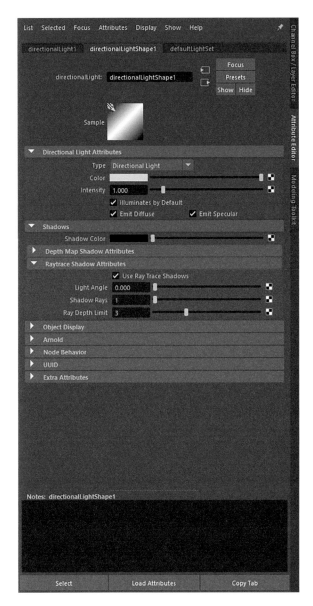

FIGURE 10.8 A typical Maya light's Attribute Editor.

Illuminates By Default check box

This check box deals with *light linking*, or the ability to illuminate specific objects with specific lights. Clearing this check box causes the light not to illuminate all objects by default, requiring you to manually link the light to objects you do want it to light. Keep this check box checked unless you're linking lights to specific objects. This chapter will briefly touch on light linking later.

Emit Diffuse and Emit Specular check boxes

For all light types, except the Ambient light type, these check boxes toggle on or off the ability to cast diffuse lighting or specular highlights on an object (see Figure 10.9). This is useful for creating specific lighting effects. For example, if lighting an object makes it too shiny, you can disable the specular emission from one or more of the lights on that object to reduce the glare.

Native Light Types

Maya native lights are not used much anymore, especially rendering with Arnold. Just the same, Maya native lights can be useful in some cases, so let's take a quick look at them.

Beyond the common light attributes, each light type carries its own attributes that govern its particular settings. In the following section, open the scene file `still _ life _ v01. ma` from the Lighting project and create each light being described to see firsthand how that particular light affects the scene. This scene file is already set to render using Maya Software Renderer, as opposed to Maya's current default of Arnold rendering, which will produce different results than what is described here.

Ambient Lights

Ambient lights cast an even light across the entire scene. These lights are used for creating a quick, even illumination in a scene; but, as you can see in Figure 10.10, they flatten the composition. They're perhaps best used sparingly and at low

Full render　　　　　Diffuse only render　　　　　Specular only render

FIGURE 10.9 Lights can render diffuse or specular components if needed.

FIGURE 10.10   Ambient light.

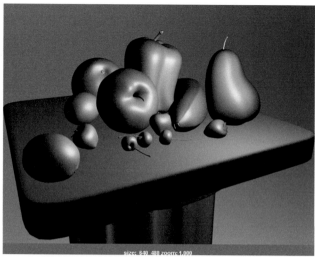

FIGURE 10.12   A Point light placed in the front right of frame.

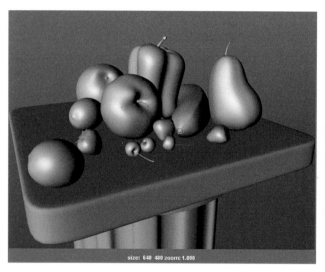

FIGURE 10.11   Directional light.

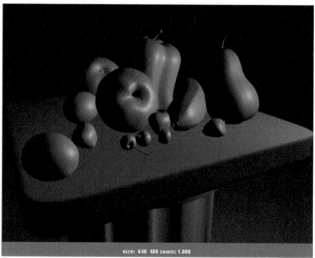

FIGURE 10.13   A Point light with a Decay Rate set.

intensities as fill lights or background lights, or for stylized looks. However, Ambient Lights do not work in Arnold.

Directional Lights

Directional lights cast a light in one general direction evenly across the scene (see Figure 10.11). These lights are pretty good for sunlight or general outdoor lighting, and for fill and back lights. They give an accurate sense of direction without having to emanate from a specific source.

Point Lights

A *Point light* casts light from a single specific point in space, similar to a bare lightbulb. Its light is spread out evenly from the single point (see Figure 10.12).

Using the Decay Rate drop-down menu in the Attribute Editor, you can set how a Point light's intensity diminishes over distance. With No Decay, the Point light illuminates an

object far away as evenly as it does up close, which gives an unnatural result.

Setting Decay Rate to Linear, Quadratic, or Cubic requires you to increase the intensity level considerably to compensate for the decay. In reality, lights have decay rates, so using them in CG creates a more natural falloff for light, as shown in Figure 10.13. Modern renderers, including Arnold, already take decay into account with their own lights, so if you choose to use Maya native lights while rendering with Arnold (or other renderer), using the decay rate setting on these lights will be advisable.

Spot Lights

Spot lights are useful lights in Maya because they can be used for keys, fills, or rims, and give a spot of light easily.

Similar to Directional lights, Spot lights emphasize direction. But these lights emit from a specific point and radiate out in a cone. As such, Spot lights can create a circular focus of light on the geometry much like a flashlight on a wall. Figure 10.14 shows a Spot light on the still life.

The following attributes govern the behavior of Spot lights:

Decay Rate
Specifies how the light's intensity falls off with distance. Again, the intensity needs to increase considerably to account for any decay.

Cone Angle
Sets the width of the cone of light emitted by the Spot light, thereby affecting the size of the spot itself.

Penumbra Angle
Specifies how much the intensity at the edges of the circular focus dissipates.

Dropoff
Similar to Decay Rate, Dropoff specifies how much light is decayed along the distance of the cone. The higher the dropoff, the dimmer the light gets farther along the length of the cone.

For example, a desk lamp's light can be simulated with a Spot light. Remember, with a Spot light, you can press T for the special manipulator, allowing you to move the source and target of the Spot light easily to orient and place the light in your scene. Spotlights are probably the most used Maya native light when rendering with the likes of Arnold.

Area Lights

Area lights emit light from a flat rectangular shape (see Figure 10.15). This type of light is the go-to light for most renderers including Arnold, though Arnold has its own area light that is preferred to use.

Because you can control the size of the area of light being emitted, these lights are also very good for creating effects such as a sliver of light falling onto an object from a crack in a door (as in Figure 10.18 later), overhead skylights, or the simulation of large, diffused lighting fixtures such as overhead office lights.

In addition, Area lights give off a softer feel the larger they are. Often area lights give the best photographic light quality compared to the other light types, and they create the most accurate-looking shadows. As mentioned before, Arnold has its own version of an area light, as we will see later in this chapter.

Volume Lights

Volume lights emit light from a specific 3D volumetric area as opposed to an Area light's flat rectangle (see Figure 10.16). Proximity is important for a Volume light, as is its scale, though these lights will not work with Arnold.

Volume lights are not to be confused with *volumetric lighting*, such as the effect of a flashlight in smoke or headlights driving through fog. For volumetric effects, see the section "Volumetric Lighting" later in this chapter.

Any of these aforementioned lights will work with Maya Software rendering and some with Arnold. It's good to know

FIGURE 10.14   Using a Spot light.

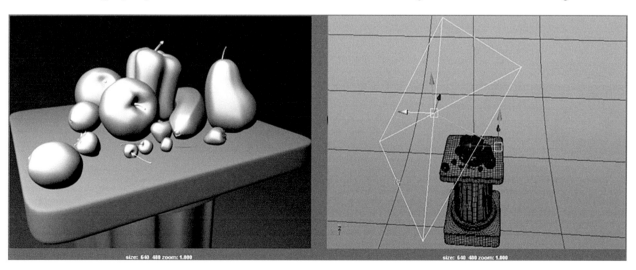

FIGURE 10.15   An Area light and its placement.

FIGURE 10.16   A Volume light and placement.

how to use these native lights as they could give support when rendering with advanced renderers like Arnold (which we will get to very soon).

Shadows and Raytracing

Don't be too quick to create an over-abundance of light in your scene to show off your models and textures. Shrouding objects in darkness and shadow is just as important as revealing them in light. A careful balance of light and dark is important for a better composition. As Figure 10.17 shows, the mood of a scene is greatly increased with the simple addition of well-placed shadows. Don't be afraid of the dark. Use it liberally but in balance.

But when you create a native Maya light and render with Maya Software, you will not see any shadows! This is not a big deal since Maya Software rendering is all-but-defunct. But turning on shadows is good to know in case you need to render with Maya Software. To see shadows in your Maya Software rendering, you need to enable raytracing in the renderer itself (which also turns on reflections). Open the Render Settings window by choosing Windows ➤ Rendering Editors ➤ Render

Settings or by clicking the Render Settings icon (   ) in the Status line; then enable the Raytracing check box under the Raytracing Quality heading. Let's take a quick look in the following steps:

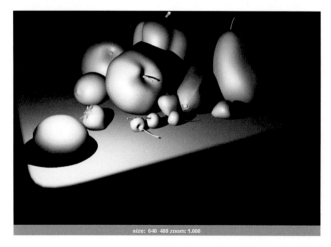

FIGURE 10.17   Darkness and shadow help add a sense of depth and mood to an otherwise simple still life.

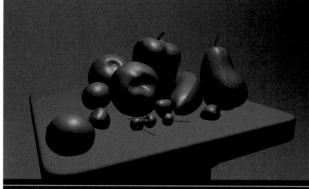

FIGURE 10.18   No shadows from the point light above (top). Shadows add a lot to the scene (bottom).

1. Using the file `still_life_v01.mb` from the Lighting project, create a Point light and place it above the fruit. Ender a frame through camera1 and you won't see any shadows (Figure 10.18, top). This scene is rendering with Maya Software.

2. Select the point light and in the Attribute Editor, and make sure Use Ray Trace Shadows is enabled under the Shadows ➤ Raytrace Shadow Attributes heading, as shown in Figure 10.19 (left). That check box should be checked on by default, but always good to make sure.

3. Open the Render Settings window and in the Maya Software tab, under Raytracing Quality, enable Raytracing (Figure 10.19, left).

4. Render a frame, and you'll see the scene looks more natural now with shadows (Figure 10.18, bottom). Note that turning on raytracing has also enabled reflections in the fruit.

Controlling Shadows per Object

To better control your lighting, you can specify whether an object can cast and receive shadows in Maya. For example, if you have geometry casting light in front of a shadow but you don't want it to cast a shadow, you can manually turn off that feature for that object only. This feature works the same with Maya Software as well as Arnold rendering.

To turn off shadow casting for an object, follow these steps:

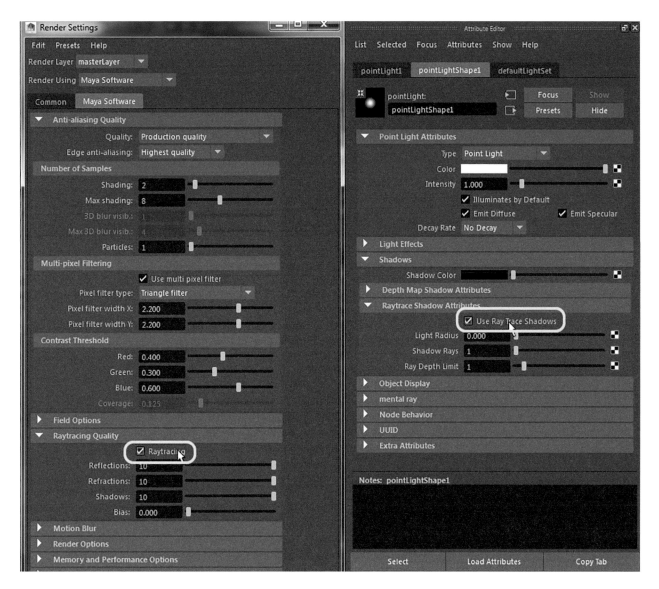

FIGURE 10.19 Make sure Use Ray Trace Shadows is checked on for the light (right) and enable Raytracing for the Maya Software renderer in the Render Settings window (left).

1. Open the `still_life_linking_v01.ma` scene from the Lighting project folders and render a frame through the camera1 view. Everything has shadows. Remember, to switch any view panel's view, choose the Panels menu at the top of the view panel, and choose the desired view (camera1, as shown here).

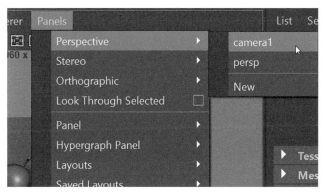

2. Select the foreground lemon and open the Attribute Editor. In the Render Stats section is a group of check boxes that control the render properties of the object, as shown in Figure 10.20 (right). Clear the Casts Shadows check box. If you don't want the object to receive shadows, clear the Receive Shadows check box as well.

3. Render a frame, and you'll see that the lemon has no shadows on the column's tabletop whereas the other fruits still do.

Light Linking

Similar to controlling which objects cast shadows as we saw earlier, you can also control which lights illuminate specific objects by using Maya *light linking*. By default, lights created

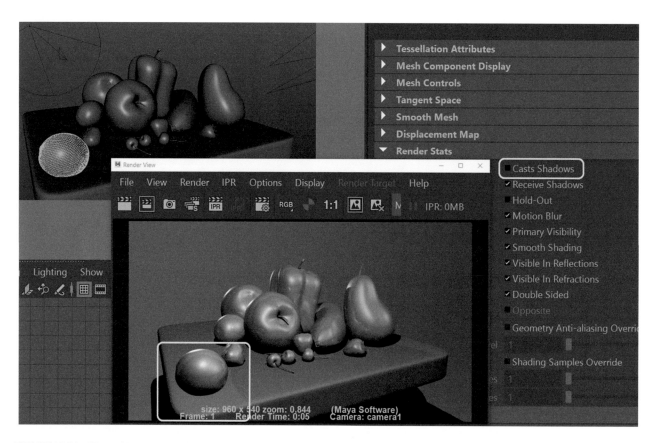

FIGURE 10.20 You easily can set whether an object casts or receives shadows in the Attribute Editor (right). The lemon does not cast a shadow (left).

in your scene illuminate all objects in the scene. The easiest way to create an exclusive lighting relationship is first to create a light and then to turn off the attribute Illuminates By Default in that light's Attribute Editor. This ensures that this light won't cast light on any object unless specifically made to do so through light linking.

1. Open the scene file `still_life_linking_v01.ma` from the Lighting project. Click the Render button

   (![button]) in the Status line to render a frame and you'll see all the objects illuminated by the three lights already in the scene.

2. Create a new Directional light and, in the Attribute Editor, turn off the check box Illuminates By Default (it's right below the Intensity slider, as shown in Figure 10.21). Set Intensity to **2** or more. You can also see the placement of the light in Figure 10.21 (right).

3. Render a frame, and you won't see any change. Adding a new light with Illuminates By Default disabled won't increase the overall light level in the scene until it is linked to objects in the scene.

4. To assign your new light to the objects you want to illuminate exclusively, choose Windows ➤ Relationship Editors ➤ Light Linking ➤ Light-Centric. This opens

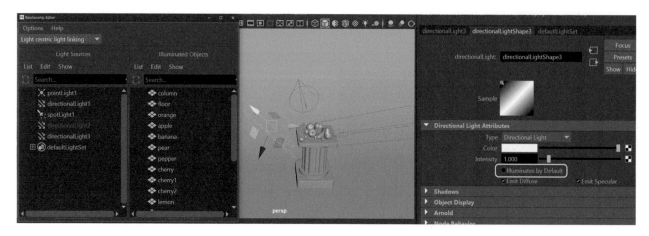

FIGURE 10.21 The Light Linking window and the newly added Directional light.

the Relationship Editor and sets it for light linking. Light-Centric means the lights are featured in the left side of the panel, as shown in Figure 10.21, and the objects in your scene that will be lit are on the right.

5. Now, select the light you want to link (in this case, the directionalLight2 you just created) and the objects in the scene you'd like to link to (in this case, the apple and the pepper, as shown in Figure 10.22). Notice that no other objects on the right side of the Relationship Editor are selected; this means they will receive no illumination from this specific light source.

6. Render a frame, and you'll see that only the two objects (apple and pepper) you linked are lit by the new light. In this case, the apple and the pepper are brighter than the other fruit in the still life (see Figure 10.23).

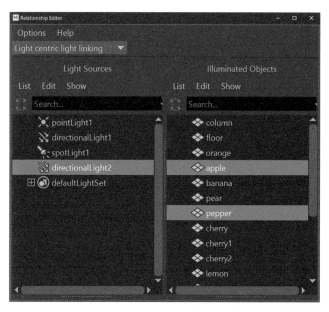

FIGURE 10.22 Select the scene objects to link to the new Directional light.

FIGURE 10.23 A linked light creates extra light for only the apple and the pepper behind it. The other objects aren't illuminated by that light.

When you're in Lighted mode (press 7 in the viewport), linked lights aren't taken into account in the display. Linked lights work with both Maya Software rendering and Arnold rendering.

Arnold Lighting

Arnold lighting and rendering open up a large range of possibilities within Maya. As with all rendering, lighting plays a primary role. I'll cover Arnold rendering more in the next chapter; however, because rendering and lighting go hand in hand, it's tough to ignore it in this chapter. This section is a primer on Arnold light functionality.

> Open the Render Settings window by choosing Windows ➤ Rendering Editors ➤ Render Settings. If you don't see the Arnold option in the Render Using drop-down menu, you need to load the plug-in. Choose Windows ➤ Settings/Preferences ➤ Plug-in Manager to open the Plug-in Manager. Make sure `mtoa.mll` (or `mtoa.bundle` on a Mac) is checked for Loaded as well as for Auto Load to ensure that it loads by default.

Arnold is an advanced, physically based renderer (a.k.a. PBR) that considers the physical properties of light and materials, including the fact that light life bounces in real. In CG, this is called *Global illumination (GI)*—the effect of light reflecting from one object to another.

For example, if you place colored spheres inside a gray box and shine a light (in this case an area light) pointed only at the ceiling of the box, the light will bounce inside the box to illuminate the spheres, as shown in Figure 10.24 (top), when rendering with Arnold, but the same scene rendered in Maya Software (which does not calculate Global Illumination, a.k.a. GI) will be quite wrong, as seen in Figure 10.24 (bottom).

We will continue with Arnold lighting through the rest of the book, starting with a rundown of the Arnold lights available in Maya.

Area Light

Arnold lights live in their own menu heading in Maya and are not found in the Create menu. Choose Arnold ➤ Lights to access the submenu for creating Arnold lights. As shown in Figure 10.25, Arnold has six lights available. We will start perhaps with the most commonly used: the Area light.

In the following steps, we will set up an existing scene with the Area light. This is the go-to light for most lighting needs. Just like Maya's native Area light, Arnold's version is a light that emits from a rectangle or disc shape, giving natural highlights, reflections, and shadowing when rendering with Arnold.

Before we begin, set your project is still set to the Lighting project from the book's web page.

size: 960 x 540 zoom: 1.000   (Arnold Renderer)
emory: 2094Mb   Sampling: [3/2/2/2/2/2]   Render Time: 0:04   Camera: /persp1/perspShape1   Layer

size: 960 x 540 zoom: 1.000   (Maya Software)
Frame: 1   Render Time: 0:02   Camera: persp1

FIGURE 10.24 Arnold results in a more accurate lighting (top) while Maya Software renders with no bounced light (bottom).

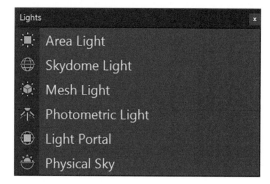

FIGURE 10.25 Arnold lights.

1. Open the scene file `still_life_v01.ma` from the Lighting project.
2. Switch to Arnold rendering by choosing Windows ➢ Rendering Editors ➢ Render Settings or the

   (![icon]) icon in the Status Bar at the top of the Maya user interface (Figure 10.26).
3. Focus on the *camera1* viewport and render a frame and it will be all black, since there are no lights in the scene. Now, every time we make a change, for example, by creating a light, we would need to re-render that camera view. Instead, let's use interactive

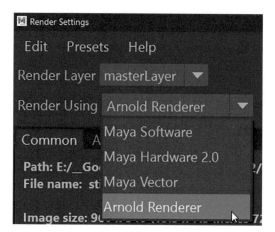

FIGURE 10.26 Switch to rendering with Arnold.

rendering with Arnold by choosing Arnold ➢ Open Arnold RenderView.

4. The Arnold RenderView window (Figure 10.27, left) pops open and is very similar to Maya's Render View window, but would be blank for now. You can close Maya's native Render View window and keep this one open.
5. Choose Arnold ➢ Lights ➢ Area Light to create an Arnold Area Light. Place it in the scene as shown in Figure 10.27 (right).
6. Set the camera to *cameraShape1* in the RenderView as shown in Figure 10.27 (left) and then click the red Play symbol in the RenderView window to start an interactive rendering of the scene. You will see a nice, but dim result.
7. Frequently, Arnold lights will start off being dim, or even completely unnoticeable in your scene. With the Area Light selected, set the Intensity higher to 25 or higher by typing in the value (as opposed to moving the slider, since the slider may only go to 10 at first) and you will get a nicer result. The interactive render will update as you change Intensity, making it much easier to adjust to find the right illumination in the scene (Figure 10.28).

It is common to see Arnold lights reaching Intensity values in the tens, hundreds, and even the thousands in value, so don't be shy with the Intensity setting. While the slider may only go up to a value of *10* at first, simply type in the values you need, and the slider will update its range.

Furthermore, the fruit looks very glassy and shiny. This is because of their shaders, or materials. In this scene, the fruit all have a simple Blinn material. But Arnold's own materials will give a much more physically accurate and nuanced result. We will cover Arnold's materials in a later chapter.

Skydome Light

Now let's introduce the next commonly used Arnold light in the following steps:

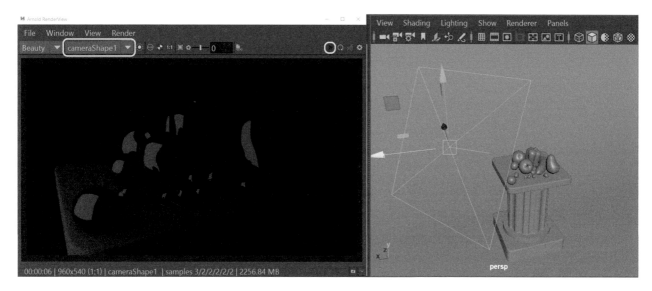

FIGURE 10.27 Arnold RenderView can speed up lighting workflow by interactively rendering.

1. In the same scene, with the Area Light still there and RenderView still rendering interactively, choose Arnold ➤ Lights ➤ Skydome Light. This creates a dome that surrounds the scene with an even illumination (Figure 10.29).

2. There is now a great fill light in the scene and brightens the entire image and knocks back the harshness of the shadows from Figure 10.28.

FIGURE 10.28 Finding a better illumination level.

FIGURE 10.29 Adding a Skydome Light.

3. Perhaps the scene may be too bright. With the Skydome selected, reduce the Intensity to 0.4 and reduce the Area Light Intensity to about 20. You can find the values that you prefer, and all the time the RenderView will give you instant updates.

4. Experiment with some different colors to create some interesting looks for the still-life scene.

5. Add another Area Light as you see fit to experiment with finding a nice lighting for the shot. Remember, you need to set Intensity values much higher, as the initial Intensity setting of 1.0 may not give you any noticeable light in the scene. However, try not to have more than one Skydome Light in a scene, at least for now.

Arnold Physical Sky

While the Skydome light gives you an even illumination around your scene, using Arnold's Physical Sky mimics an open-air sunlit environment. Let's try this out in another scene.

Make sure your project is still set to the Lighting project from the web page and use the scene file `WagonSunlight_v01.ma` from the Scenes folder to follow along with these steps:

1. The perspective camera for this scene is already set up in the persp viewport. Open the Render Settings window and check to make sure we are already in Arnold in the Render Using pull-down menu at the top of the window, as shown earlier.

2. Select Arnold ➤ Open Arnold RenderView and select the play symbol to start an interactive render of the *persp* view. It will be black as there are no lights yet.

3. Select Arnold ➤ Lights ➤ Physical Sky to create the Physical Sky in the scene. The RenderView will show the toy wagon, with a blue sky in the background, as shown in Figure 10.30. You can see glints of the sun in the parts of the wagon, which is using basic Maya native shaders.

FIGURE 10.30 Adding the Physical Sky.

4. In the persp panel, move the camera as the RenderView updates the render. If you zoom out quite a bit, you can see the Physical Sky object is a giant sphere surrounding the scene. This is actually a Skydome light as we have used before, except its color attribute is connected to a new node called the *aiPhysicalSky*, which controls all the sun and sky settings.

5. Zoom back to the wagon. You can see sharp sun-shadows and a slight warm color to the light on the gray ground. Rotate the camera up to see the sky more, and you'll notice a gradient of blue in the sky and (at the proper angle) a small disc for the sun itself, as shown in Figure 10.31.

6. Put the camera back on the wagon. Select the Physical Sky's Skydome and rotate it in just the Y-axis to change the direction of the sun (Figure 10.32).

7. With the Physical Sky's Skydome still selected, go into the Attribute Editor. It has the same attributes that we saw earlier with the Skydome light, as shown in Figure 10.33 (left), except now the *Color* seems to be black. Actually, it is not black but is connected to the Physical Sky. Click the black arrow icon next to the *Color* attribute's slider to access the Physical Sky settings, as shown in Figure 10.33 (right).

8. With the interactive render still playing in the RenderView, change the *Turbidity*. This sets the pollution in the air, changing the coloration of the sunlight as well as how hazy the sky looks.

9. The *Ground Albedo* is the color of the "ground." Since the sky is a 360° dome, the top half is the blue gradient of the sky and the bottom half of the dome is the ground coloration. In this scene, we also have a polygon plane as a floor where we can see shadows of the wagon. The *Ground Albedo* will change the coloration of the ground in the dome which will affect the overall illumination in the scene, but it will not change the color of the gray polygon floor we have in the scene.

10. Next, the *Elevation* slider will set the position of the sun itself and consequently the light direction. Set it to 90 and the daylight makes it noon where the sun is directly above. Set it back down to a lower number

FIGURE 10.31 The sky has a slight gradient to its blue and the sun appears as a bright dot with a soft yellow gradient.

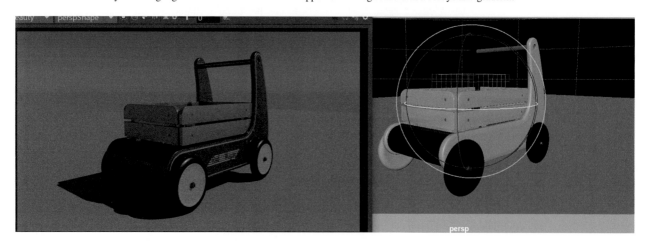

FIGURE 10.32 Rotate the Physical Sky dome in the Y-axis only to change the angle of the sun.

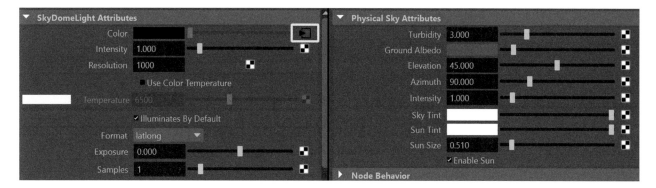

FIGURE 10.33 Getting to the Physical Sky attributes (left) and the Physical Sky settings themselves (right).

FIGURE 10.34 A low Elevation gives a sunset look with long shadows (left). Use the Azimuth attribute slider to change the direction of the sun.

to bring the sun down toward the horizon creating longer shadows. The lower the Elevation, the more like a sunset/sunrise the scene will look, as shown in Figure 10.34 (top). It changes the color as well as the relative intensity of the lighting.

11. Set the Elevation to about 30. Then use the Azimuth slider to change the direction of the setting sun, as shown in Figure 10.34 (bottom).

12. Lastly, to brighten or darken the scene, simply adjust the *Intensity* slider to a higher or lower value. It is advised to set the *Intensity* in the Physical Sky node, as opposed to the *Intensity* of the Skydome light itself, they are controlled separately.

More on the Area Light!

You can add additional Arnold lights to a scene lit with the Physical Sky; you aren't limited to just the Physical Sky's results. Let's make this wagon scene into a darker sunset, and then add a street lamp in the following steps.

1. In the same scene with the Physical Sky from the previous steps, set the Elevation to 2.0 and the Azimuth to 250 to place the sun behind the wagon. Start an interactive render in the RenderView by selecting the red play symbol in the upper right.

2. Set the Sun Size to 1.0 for a bigger sun ball. The scene is nice and dark, and the sun is setting behind the wagon.

3. Create an Area light and place it above and in front of the wagon, as shown in Figure 10.35 (top). Set the Intensity of the Area light to 120. Figure 10.35 (bottom) shows the RenderView result. This helps define the front of the wagon, hinting that there is another light source, perhaps a street light behind the camera.

4. Notice also that we can see the sunball behind the wagon, and its size can be adjusted using the *Sun Size* attribute in the Physical Sky attributes. The sun in Figure 10.35 (bottom) is set to 1.0.

5. The front light on the wagon doesn't look like a street lamp yet. Select the Area light. Click the *Use Color Temperature* check box and set the *Temperature* attribute to 3,400 to create a very warm light. You could also use *Color* instead of *Temperature* if you prefer, just make sure to uncheck *Use Color Temperature*.

6. The light is too wide to be a street lamp; we want more of a spot light effect. In the Area light's attributes, set the *Spread* slider down to 0.2 to focus the light more. Notice the light seems brighter when it's focused more using *Spread*. You may need to adjust the orientation of the Area light to point more on the wagon directly (Figure 10.36).

The Physical Sky system can get you some fairly nice and natural illumination results quickly. Keep experimenting with different settings for the attributes for the system to see what results you can get for your scene. Add Area lights to create areas of interest in your scene.

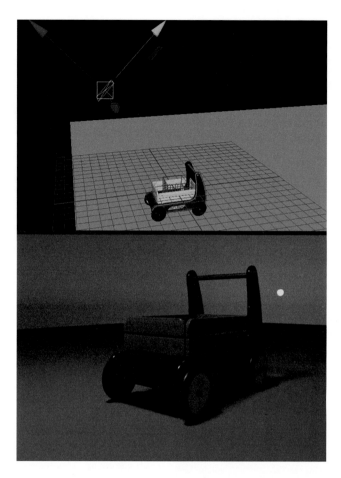

FIGURE 10.35 Adding an area light to illuminate the front of the wagon in this sunset scene (left). Making the Area light more like a spotlight (right).

FIGURE 10.36 Now we have a street lamp! Mom's gonna be mad, it's getting late!

This is the perfect time for a break, so save your work (as if I have to tell you that at this point!), go grab some iced tea, and rest your eyes for a bit.

Mesh Light

A very interesting way to create a light that needs a custom shape is to use Arnold's Mesh Light. This allows you to turn almost any polygonal mesh into a truly light-emitting object. There are performance issues to consider, as mesh lights use more resources than standard lighting, causing the render to take longer at times, so keep this in mind as you experiment with this Arnold light. Let's take a look at the following steps using the original wagon scene we started for the Physical Sky lighting from earlier in this chapter.

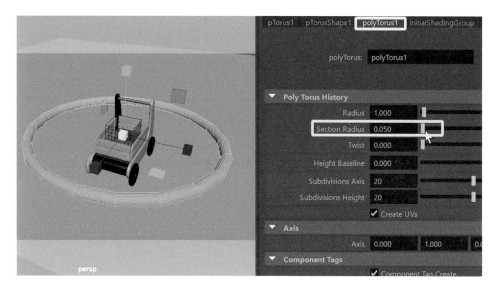

FIGURE 10.37   Making a thin torus to surround the wagon.

1. Make sure your project is still set to the Lighting project from the web page and use the original scene file `WagonSunlight_v01.ma` from the Scenes, without any of the lights we made earlier in this chapter.

2. Choose Create ➤ Polygon Primitives ➤ Torus to create a donut in the middle of the scene. Scale the torus to 7 in all three axes to surround the wagon.

3. With the torus selected, in the Attribute Editor, click on the *polytorus* tab for its Creation Node. There, set Section Radius to 0.05 to make the torus much thinner, as shown in Figure 10.37.

4. Open the Arnold RenderView and click the red "play" icon in the upper right to begin an interactive render. It will be black as there are no lights in the scene.

5. With the torus selected, choose Arnold ➤ Lights ➤ Mesh Light to turn the thin donut shape into a light. The torus turns from solid to wireframe in the Maya viewports. The Attribute Editor now shows light controls and the RenderView will still be black. Set the *Intensity* to 400 and you will see a ring of light illuminating the wagon, and reflecting in the sides of the wagon, as shown in Figure 10.38.

6. Experiment with adjusting the torus' position, rotation, and size to see how the light affects the scene's lighting.

7. If you wish to see the light itself in the render, in the Attribute Editor check the Light Visible box and the torus will appear in the render around the wagon. This is helpful for creating light shapes such as neon lights, fluorescent tubes, and other interesting lighting effects.

Volumetric Lighting

How do you create an effect such as a flashlight beam shining through fog? This lighting effect is called *volumetric*

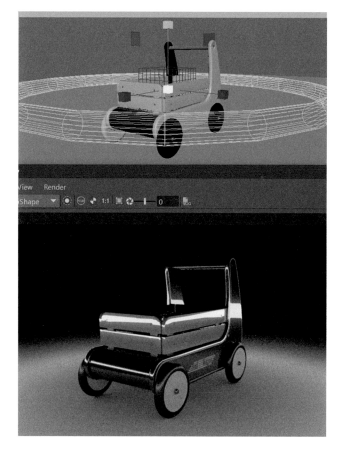

FIGURE 10.38   The torus is now illuminating the wagon!

lighting, and you can use it to create some stunning results that can sometimes be time-consuming to render. Let's add a little ambience to the wagon scene from earlier in this chapter where we added a street lamp. Use your file from that section, or use the scene file `WagonSunlight_v02.ma` from the Scenes folder of the Lighting project.

1. Open the Arnold RenderView and start an interactive render. You will see the wagon with the sun setting behind it as well as a street lamp spot-lighting the wagon using an Area Light.

2. To add a bit of atmosphere (like fog, for example) to the scene, open the Render Settings and click on the Arnold Renderer tab. Scroll down and open the Environment section and select the mapping icon (![icon]) next to Atmosphere, as shown in Figure 10.39, and choose *Create aiAtmosphereVolume*.

3. Your interactive render in the RenderView will remain unchanged, but now you can see the atmosphere volume's attributes in the Attribute Editor. Set the *Density* to 0.1 and the street lamp will show a golden fog glow (a.k.a. volumetric lighting effect) shining down on the wagon, sometimes referred to as a god ray (Figure 10.40).

4. The settings of the light such as Intensity directly affect how the volumetric effects look, so experiment with adjusting the light's properties as well as its position and orientation in the scene for the desired effect.

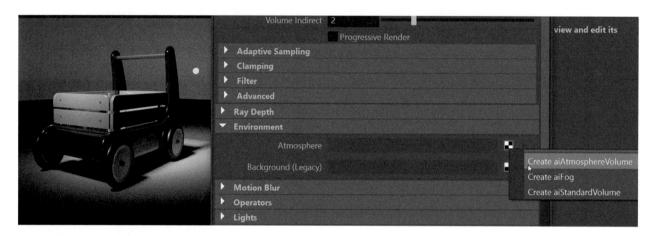

FIGURE 10.39   Creating atmosphere in the scene.

FIGURE 10.40   Creating a volumetric lighting effect shining down on the wagon.

Assembling and Lighting a Scene

In this section, you'll set up and light a simple scene with the toy plane and the decorative box so that you can render them together. Furthermore, in the next chapter, you'll start using displacement maps for detail on the box, and you'll use a high dynamic range image (HDRI) to get the most from lighting and rendering. The lighting you'll start with will be basic for now. In the following exercise, you'll create a basic lighting setup for the scene and get a direct lighting solution first. In the next chapter, you'll expand on this lighting using mental ray and HDRI.

Set your current project to the Plane project, which you should have already downloaded from the book's web page. This is important to make sure Maya finds all the project files it needs, so it bears repeating: Set your project to Plane! Did you set your project yet?

How about now?

Assembling the Scene

To begin lighting, open the `planeLightingScene _ v01. ma` scene file from the Scenes folder of the project. This is a simple scene with a camera in place and a corner made up of a redwood tabletop and two white walls that will show you how to bring in other scenes to assemble a shot using Import as well as Reference:

1. Let's start with importing the toy plane. Select File ➢ Import and, in the Options section on the right of the Import dialog window, turn off Use Namespaces, set Resolve to Clashing Nodes, and leave With set to the file name. This makes sure that Maya doesn't append any additional names to the original objects being imported from this file. Choose `planeShad- ing _ v01.ma` from the Scenes folder.

2. Open the Outliner and select the top node of the toy plane (planeGroup). Go into the four-view layout so you can see all four viewports. Select one of the viewports and select Panels ➢ Perspective ➢ render-Cam. This way you can work in the persp viewport and see how it affects the camera view from which you'll be rendering.

   Next, you will bring in the decorative box from the previous chapters. This time, instead of import-ing, you will use referencing. This allows you to import a file into your current scene. However, with a reference, any time you adjust the original file, it will automatically update that model in the scene in which it has been referenced. You'll see this in action in the next chapter.

3. Choose File ➢ Create Reference. On the right side of the Reference dialog window, check the Use Namespaces box to turn it on. This will place the filename you are referencing in front of the object names in the Outliner.

4. Still in the Plane project, in the Scenes folder, select `boxDetail01.ma` to bring in the latest decora-tive box scene from Chapter 7, "Autodesk® Maya® Shading and Texturing," as a Maya reference. This file is actually the same scene file as `boxTex- tures03.mb` in the Decorative_Box project that you completed in Chapter 7, but cleaned up a bit and placed in the Plane project folders for simplic-ity's sake. The texture files you need for the box are already in the Plane project's Sourceimages folder, also for simplicity's sake.

5. Rotate the box to 200° in the Y-axis and position the box next to the toy plane to match Figure 10.41.

6. You'll now import the glass candle holder you cre-ated in Chapter 5 using NURBS techniques. There's no need to use a reference as you did with the deco-rative box, so select File ➢ Import and turn off Use Namespaces, set Resolve to Clashing Nodes, and leave With set to the filename, just like in step 1.

7. Navigate to the candleholder project and, in the Scenes folder, select and import the `candle- Model _ v03.mb` file.

8. In the Outliner, select the candle's top node (candle-Group) and move it to the front side of the toy plane, near to the camera. You will also have to scale the candleGroup to **0.65** to match the position and size in Figure 10.42. Don't worry, the candle holder is all gray for now. Save!

Creating the Lights

Save your file and compare it to `planeLightingScene _ v02.ma` or skip to the following section. Here you will lay out lighting using the three-point lighting system discussed earlier.

1. In the renderCam viewport, press 6 for Texture mode and then 7 to add lighted display mode. Using the persp viewport, create an Area Light; in the Attribute Editor, set Spread to **0.25** and Intensity to **5,000**. Place and orient the Area Light to be the key light, matching the position and orientation shown in Figure 10.43.

2. Create another Area Light and place that as shown in Figure 10.44. Set its scale to 3 in all axes, Spread to 1.0 and Intensity to **3,000**. Try not to place it behind the back wall because the wall will shadow the light. If you ever need to, you can disable shadows for a light in the light's Attribute Editor by unchecking the Cast Shadows box.

3. Create a rim light with a third Area Light with a scale of 3 in all axes, a Spread of 0.8, and an Intensity value set to **6,000**; place it as shown in Figure 10.45 just above the back wall.

FIGURE 10.41 Orient and place the decorative box next to the plane to match this position.

4. The view panels in lighted mode will seem a bit bright with these settings, but if you open the Arnold RenderView and start a render of the renderCam viewport, you should see something like what is shown in Figure 10.46. You need to create a simple glass shader for the candle, and plane and decorative box look very shiny with a gray candle holder, but it's a start. The reflections are coming from raytracing, which is always on in Arnold.

Adjusting the Materials

Save your file and compare it to `planeLightingScene_v03.ma` to bring you up to this point. Up to this point, we have been using Maya's native shaders (a.k.a. materials) like Blinn on your models, even when rendering in Arnold. As you can see in Figure 10.46, the toy airplane looks very shiny and not like plastic, and we lose most of the speckle of the Noise texture that we had added earlier. Let's make that a little nicer looking.

1. Select the body of the plane in the persp viewport and open the Hypershade window. In the Hypershade, click the Graph Materials On Selected Objects icon

( ) to bring up the plane's yellow Blinn shader in the Work Area.

2. Click the yellow shader and, in the Property Editor, under the Specular Shading section, set Eccentricity to **0.425**, Specular Roll Off to **0.525**, and Reflectivity to **0.25**.

3. Select the gray Blinn shader and repeat the same attribute values as step 7.

4. In the Hypershade, click the phongFloor shader and set its Cosine Power to **30** and Reflectivity to **0.15**. Look at a render in the Arnold RenderView and your frame should look more like Figure 10.47, with improvement to the look of both the yellow and gray plastics.

You can see that those simple changes to the Maya native shaders helped the plastic look of the plane. We will replace those with Arnold's own shader called the aiStandardSurface material in the next chapter for an even better result.

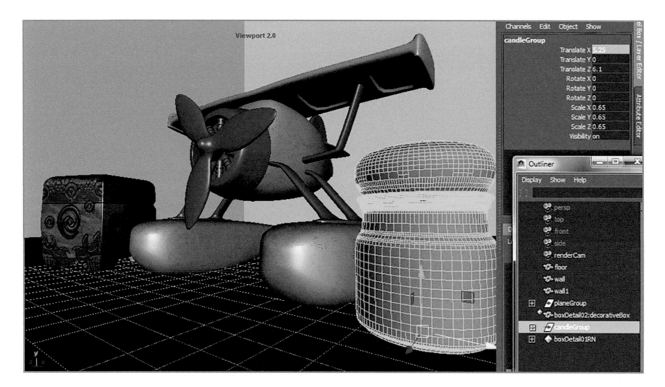

FIGURE 10.42   Import and place the candle to match this layout.

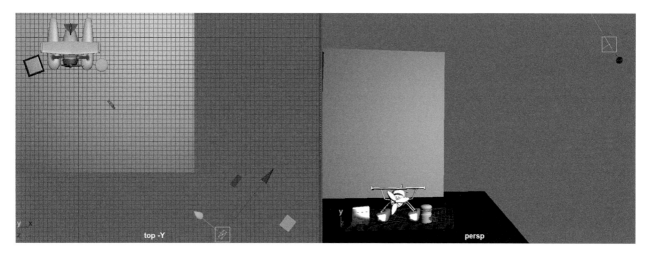

FIGURE 10.43   Create an Area Light and place it as shown.

Making a Quick Glass

Now turn your attention to the glass candle holder and the candle inside. You can continue with your own scene or load the scene file `planeLightingScene _ v04.ma` to skip to this point. You will create a glass shader and a simple shader for the candle in the following steps:

1. In the Hypershade, create a new Phong shader and name it **candleGlass**.
2. Open the Outliner. Shift+click the plus sign to the left of the candleGroup node to expand all the child nodes beneath it. Select the glassJar and glassLid objects; in the Hypershade, RMB+click the new candleGlass Phong shader and choose Assign Material To Selection.
3. Start an interactive render in the Arnold RenderView and the candle appears as a solid, shiny gray object. In the candleGlass shader, move the Transparency slider so that the black color swatch turns almost pure white. This will make the shader almost entirely transparent.
4. Set Cosine Power to **60** to make the specular highlights tighter and more glossy looking. In the RenderView you'll notice the jar is now clear glass with a gray candle inside. You may also notice some strange vertical bars between the glass and the gray candle (Figure 10.48).

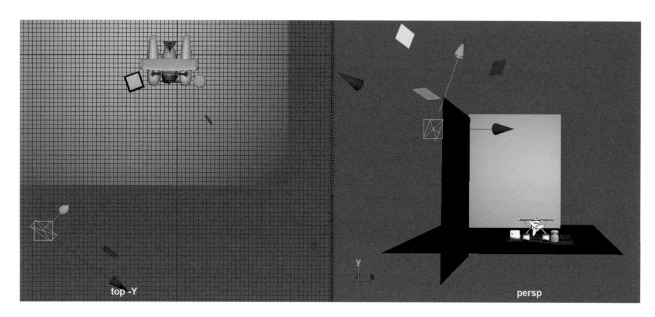

FIGURE 10.44   Create and place a Directional light as shown here.

FIGURE 10.45   Create a Spot light for a rim light and place it as shown here.

FIGURE 10.46   A simple render of the plane scene.

FIGURE 10.47   Reducing the glossy look of the plastic toy plane and the wooden tabletop.

FIGURE 10.48 Rendering a glass look for the candle jar shows a little bit of penetration with the gray candle inside. That's okay for now.

This render artifact occurs when two surfaces penetrate each other. Since Maya interprets the geometry of the glass and the candle inside slightly differently during render time, this penetration may occur. You can simply reduce the size of the candle inside ever so slightly. However, you will address this issue when you return to this scene in the next chapter when we convert to using Arnold's own materials, so you can leave it be for now.

5. There is a gray ring inside the lid of the jar that should be white plastic (it is the plasticSealer object in the Outliner grouped under jarLid). In the Hypershade, create a new Blinn and give it a white color. Set Reflectivity to **0.1**. Call this shader **whitePlastic**.

6. In the Outliner, select the plasticSealer object under the jarLid group and assign it to the whitePlastic shader.

7. Make another Blinn shader and give it a dark red color. Set Eccentricity to **0.125**, Specular Roll Off to **0.85**, and Reflectivity to **0.1**. Name it **candleWax**.

8. In the Outliner, select the candle object grouped under the jarCandle group and assign it to the candle-Wax shader.

9. Finally, create a dark gray Lambert called blackWick and assign it to the wick object in the Outliner.

10. In the RenderView with an interactive render running, the candle is looking nicer, but the glass is still missing something. To get a much better-looking glass, we will use Arnold materials in the next chapter.

The render is not looking too shabby, but when you tackle this scene again with Arnold materials in the next chapter, you will see how powerful Arnold can be. In Chapter 11, you'll add more texture maps to add carving detail to the decorative box, create Arnold-specific shaders for the objects in the scene, experiment with metallic materials, and use an HDRI to light the scene to take it to a new level. Woo!

You can check your work against the scene file `plane-LightingScene _ v05.ma` in the Scenes folder of the Plane project.

Further Lighting Practice

CG lighting professionals are called on to find the most efficient way to light a scene and bring it to the peak of its beauty. Again, this comes only from experience. The best way to become a crackerjack lighting artist is to spend years honing your eye and practicing the latest procedures, such as high dynamic range (HDR) lighting, as well as developing an understanding of traditional photography.

The file `still_life _v01.ma` in the Lighting project on the web page contains the scene of the still life with no lights, so you can play with lighting and shadow methods as well as light linking to create some extra focus on some parts of the frame. The file `still_life_v02.mb` contains the same scene but with three-point lighting already set up.

Notice in the `still_life_v02.ma` file that two lights make up the key light (spotLight1 and spotLight2). One light makes up the fill light (directionalLight1), and two lights (spot-Light3 and spotLight4) make up the back light. How would the scene look using all Arnold Area Lights instead of Maya native lights, as we did with the toy plane scene?

For practice, download some models from the Internet and arrange them into your own still-life scenes to gain more lighting experience. Set up scenes, time the rendering process, and try to achieve the same lighting look using faster lighting setups that may not be as taxing on the renderer. Also, try taking pictures of situations and trying to match the lighting in the photo.

Try setting up simple scenes. Start with an indoor location that is lit by a single lightbulb. Then, try the same scene in the following locations to expand your lighting repertoire:

- A photography studio
- Outside in the morning on a bright summer day
- Outside at dusk in the fall
- Outside at night under a street lamp
- Inside on a window ledge
- At the bottom of a closet lit by a nearby hallway light

Tips for Using and Animating Lights

When you're lighting a scene, invoking a lighting mode in your perspective or camera viewport will give you great feedback regarding the relative brightness and direction of your lights. Most consumer graphics cards can handle a maximum of eight lights in Lighted mode; some professional cards can handle more.

As you've seen, you invoke Lighted mode by pressing 7 on your keyboard (not through the number pad on the side). You must first be in Shaded mode (press 5) or Texture mode (press 6) to be able to press 7 for Lighted mode. Remember that Lighted mode displays linked lights as if they're lighting the entire scene. This can cause some confusion, so it's wise to take notes on any light linking in your scene.

Animating a Light

Any attribute of a light can be animated in the same way that you animate any other object attribute. You cannot, however, animate a light's type. To edit a light's animation, you need only select the light and open the Graph Editor to access its keyframes. You can set keyframes on Intensity, Penumbra Angle, Color, and so on, within the Channel Box or the Attribute Editor. RMB+click the name of the attribute and choose Key Selected from the context menu.

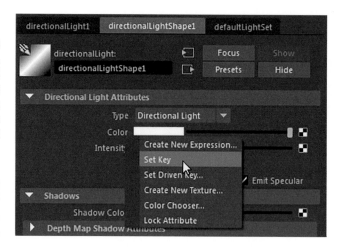

FIGURE 10.49   Set a key for the light.

> By animating a light's intensity, you can simulate the real-world appearance of a light turning on or off. To turn on a light, create a quickly increasing curve so that its brightness arcs up slowly at first before climbing to full brightness. This animation mimics the way real lights turn on and off better than simply enabling or disabling them in your scene.

When you animate the color of a light or a shader, you set keyframes for the color's RGB values as three separate keyframes. The Graph Editor shows a separate curve for the red, green, and blue channels of color when you animate a light's color. You can set all three keys at once by RMB+clicking the Color attribute in the Attribute Editor and choosing Set Key from the context menu, as shown in Figure 10.49.

In addition, lights can be animated to be moved, scaled, and rotated like any other object. For further study, try animating the lighting for the simple scenes you set up to practice lighting from the previous section. Try creating animated lights to simulate a candle illuminating your scene, a campfire, or the flashing emergency lights you would find in your average space-station airlock.

Summary

This chapter explored lighting in Maya, beginning with basic concepts that included the three-point lighting technique. You then learned about the different native lights in Maya, how they work, and how you can use light linking to control your scene better. We then looked at the Arnold lights: Area and Skydome Lights, followed by a quick exploration of the Physical Sky system with Arnold and then the volumetric lighting effect. You then created simple lighting for the toy plane, candle holder, and decorative box for a still rendering, adjusting the existing Maya materials along the way. Finally, you learned how to begin animating lights for your scenes.

Lighting is truly the linchpin of CG; it can make or break a scene. As you'll see in the next chapter, lighting goes hand in hand with rendering and shading, and the more you understand about all three functions together, the better your scenes will look. Don't be afraid to experiment with lighting and shading schemes on all your projects.

11

Autodesk® Maya® and Arnold Rendering

In this chapter, you will be able to

Set up your scenes for output through rendering

Choose resolutions, image formats, and other settings for rendering

Create and edit cameras

Render with motion blur and differentiate between the types of motion blur

Set up and use Arnold materials for various looks including metal and glass

Render in AOV layers and compose them back together

Apply an HDRI map as a reflection source

Apply a displacement map to create finer detail in a model

Rendering Setup

When your lighting scene from the previous chapter is complete, you've had a celebration smoothie for your hard work, and you're ready to start a render, you'll need to set up how you want it rendered. Although this is the last part of the CG process, from now on you should be thinking about rendering throughout your production. When you create models and textures with the final image in mind and you gear the lighting toward showing off the scene elegantly, the final touches are relatively easy to set up.

Decide which of the render engines included with Maya you'll use: Maya Software, Maya Hardware 2.0, Arnold (the most popular of the renderers that comes standard with Maya 2017 and beyond), or Maya Vector. Each engine has its own particular workflow and can yield entirely different results. The choice of a rendering method depends on the final look you want and sometimes on the number of machines and licenses with which you can render. Maya Software rendering comes with an unlimited number of licenses, which means you can render on any machine you have (with Maya installed), although you can work with the Maya application only on as many machines for which you have licenses. Arnold on the other hand only allows one license to render, without purchasing more. There are also third-party developers in the CG field that have created other render engines that plug right into Maya, such as V-Ray® for Maya, Red Shift®, and Pixar's RenderMan® for Maya.

No matter which renderer you use, the lighting and general setup are fairly common across the board, though you may use different lights accordingly. Therefore, it's a very good idea to choose your render engine when creating your scene. It's best to begin with basic Arnold to pick up the fundamentals of lighting, texturing, and rendering before you venture into other plug-in renderers.

Regardless of the type of render, you need to specify a set of common attributes in the Render Settings window. Choose Windows ➤ Rendering Editors ➤ Render Settings to open the Render Settings window. Figure 11.1 shows the Render Settings window for the Maya Software renderer and its tabs: the Common tab and the Maya Software tab. You use the options in this window's Common tab to set up all your rendering preferences, including the resolution, file type, frame range, and so forth.

The Common tab contains the settings common to all the rendering methods, such as image size. When in Maya Software rendering, the Maya Software tab gives you access to render-specific attributes, such as quality settings, raytracing settings, motion blur, and so on.

If you need to switch the Render Using pull-down menu from Maya Software to Arnold Renderer, you'll notice several tabs: Common, Arnold Renderer, System, AOVs,(which stands for Arbitrary Output Variables), and Diagnostics. These tabs give you access to all the settings for the powerful Arnold renderer.

You may notice that some of the render engines like Arnold may not show up in the Render Settings window right away. In this case, the renderers' respective plug-ins must be loaded first. I'll discuss this further later in this chapter.

Choosing a Filename

Renderings are almost always output as image file sequences, as opposed to video files. Rendered images are identified by a filename, a frame number, and an extension, in the form *name.#.ext*. This is an example: `stillife.0234.tif`.

The File Name Prefix text box is where to define the image sequence name. If you don't enter anything in this text box, Maya automatically names your rendered images after your scene file (`stillife` in the example). This is strongly the preferred naming convention—using the scene name as the image filename; this way you can immediately identify the scene file from which a particular image file was rendered. So, you can leave that at its default of: *(not set; using scene name)*.

In the Frame/Animation Ext drop-down list box, select *name.#.ext* to render out a sequence of files. If you leave this setting at the default of `name.ext`, only a single frame will render, no matter what the animation range is in the Time slider.

`Name.#.ext` is perhaps the most commonly used convention, as opposed to `name.ext.#` or `name.#`, because it allows you to identify the file type easily in Windows. Although Mac OS X isn't as picky about the order of the number and extension, most Mac compositing software applications (such as After Effects and Shake) want filenames that end in the three-letter extension. Therefore, it's best for both Mac and Windows users to employ the `name.#.ext` format.

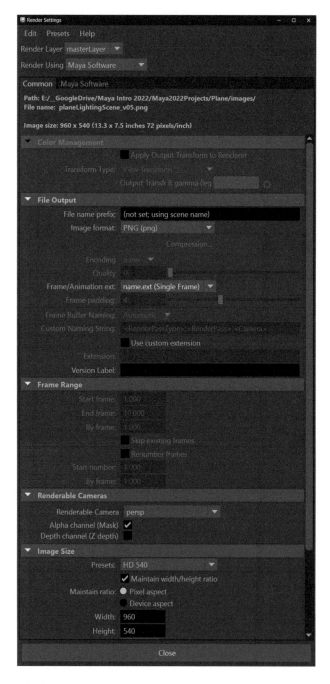

FIGURE 11.1   The Render Settings window.

The extension portion of the image name is a three-letter abbreviation for the type of file you're writing to disk to ensure that you can identify the file type.

Image Format

In the Image Format drop-down list box, select the type of image file you want to render. Maya will add the appropriate extension to the filename.

The image format you choose depends on your own preference and your output needs. For example, JPEG (or JPG) files may be great for the small file sizes preferred on the Internet, but their color compression and lack of alpha channel (a feature discussed later in this chapter) make them undesirable for most CG work beyond test renders.

It's best to render a sequence of images rather than a movie file for two reasons. First, you want your renders to be their best quality with little or no image compression. Second, if a render fails during a movie render, you must re-render the entire sequence. With an image sequence, however, you can pick up where the last frame left off.

For test renders, JPG and PNG are great, but arguably, the best file type format to render to is EXR (OpenEXR). This format enjoys universal support, has little to no compression, and supports an alpha channel as well as any number of additional channels. Almost all image-editing and compositing packages can read EXR-formatted files. For more on image formats, see Chapter 1, "Introduction to Computer Graphics and 3D."

Frame Range

Maya defaults to the frame range 1–10, which you may likely need to change to render your entire sequence. You must choose a naming convention other than Name (Single Frame) to access the frame range. Enter the Start Frame and End Frame attributes for part of the sequence or the entire sequence.

The By Frame attribute specifies the intervals at which the sequence will render. For example, if you want to render only the odd-numbered frames, set the Start Frame attribute to 1, and set the By Frame attribute to 2. If you want to render only even-numbered frames, set Start Frame to 2, set By Frame to 2, and so on. Typically, you leave By Frame set to 1 so that Maya renders each frame.

The Frame Padding attribute and slider deal with how an operating system, such as Windows or Mac OS X, orders its files by inserting leading zeros in the frame number. For example, if Frame Padding is set to 4, the filename contains three leading zeros; therefore, frame 8 is `name.0008.tif` as opposed to `name.8.tif` (which is set to a padding of 1).

Large sequences of files are easier to organize if they all have a frame padding of at least 3. Figure 11.2 shows an image sequence without padding and with padding. The files without padding aren't shown in numeric order.

Camera and Channels

Under the Renderable Cameras heading, you choose the camera to render and enable the Alpha and Depth channels.

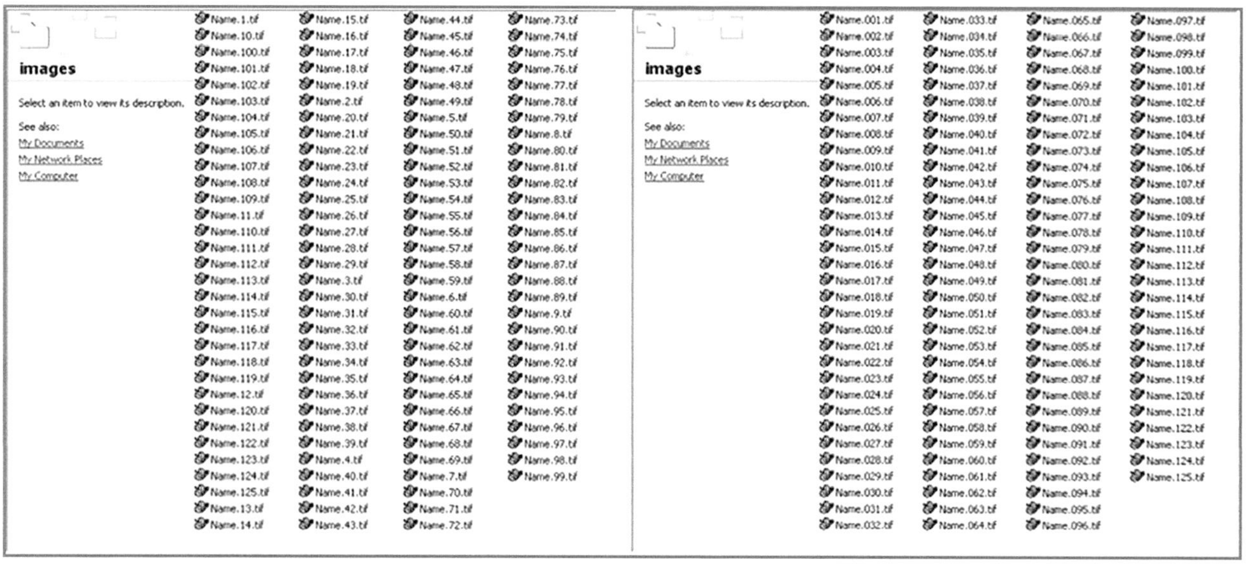

FIGURE 11.2   Images rendered without frame padding (left). Frame padding makes file sequences easier to organize (right).

Image files are composed of red, green, and blue channels. Each channel specifies the amount of the primary additive color (red, green, or blue, respectively) in the pixels of the image. (See Chapter 1 for more on how computers define color.) Most file formats save a fourth channel, called the *alpha channel*. This channel defines the image's transparency level. Just as the red channel defines how much red is in an area of the image, the alpha channel defines how transparent the image is when layered or composited on another image. If the alpha channel is black, the image is perfectly see-through. If the alpha channel is white, the image is solid and opaque. The alpha channel is also known as the *matte*. An object with some transparency like tinted glass will render with a gray alpha channel, as shown in Figure 11.3.

The alpha channel can be displayed in the Render View window as well as Arnold RenderView. As discussed later in this chapter, your test renders also display in either of these windows, though we have been relying mostly on Arnold RenderView.

To view an image's alpha channel in the Maya Render View or Arnold RenderView, click the Display Alpha Channel icon (). To reset the view to RGB (full-color view), click the Display RGB Channels icon () found at the top of both windows.

Most renders already have the alpha channels selected in the Render Settings window, so leave the Alpha Channel (Mask) check box selected at all times, as shown in Figure 11.4. Note, however, that JPEG, Graphics Interchange Format (GIF), and Windows bitmap files don't support alpha channels, regardless of whether the Alpha Channel (Mask) check box is selected.

Setting Resolution

The Width and Height attributes set the pixel size of the image to be rendered, a.k.a. the image *resolution*. In the Image Size section of the Render Settings window, you can select a resolution from the Presets drop-down list. The commonly used resolution for professional broadcast is 1,920×1,080 High Definition, which appears as HD 1,080 in the Presets list. To composite Maya CG into a standard definition (SD) home-shot digital video (DV) movie, you use the standard DV resolution of 720×480 to render your scene, but you must enter that resolution manually in the Width and Height fields. (For more on resolutions, see Chapter 1.)

The Device Aspect Ratio and Pixel Aspect Ratio attributes adjust the width of the image to accommodate certain professional output needs; you do not need to adjust them here.

Make sure your Pixel Aspect Ratio attribute is set to 1 before you render, especially HD resolutions; otherwise, your image may look squeezed or widened compared to any live-action footage you use to composite against.

The higher your resolution, the longer the scene will take to render. With large frame sequences, it's advisable to render tests at half the resolution of the final output or less to save time. In addition to turning down the resolution for a test, you can use a lower-quality render.

FIGURE 11.3   This wine bottle's transparency renders with a gray alpha channel.

FIGURE 11.4   Output an alpha channel.

Selecting a Render Engine

Maya allows you to select a render engine in the Render Settings window. Although Arnold is most commonly used currently, the other rendering methods give you flexibility in choosing a final look for your project.

Maya Software

Maya Software, the default software rendering method, can capture just about everything you want in your scene, from reflections to motion blur and transparencies. You can use the software rendering method in a couple of ways, and even though it is largely replaced with Arnold, it is good to know how Maya Software works.

Using Raytracing

Raytracing, a topic introduced in Chapter 10, "Autodesk® Maya® Lighting," is used to incorporate two optical effects into a rendering that the default software rendering method can't handle. *Raytracing* traces rays of light from each light source to every object in the shot and then traces the light's reflection from the object to the camera's lens. This allows

true *reflections* and *refractions* to appear in the render as well as highly defined shadows (for more on shadows, see Chapter 10). This is always on when rendering with Arnold, but not with Maya Software, as you've already seen earlier in the book.

True Reflections

True reflections occur when every object in the scene is viewed in a reflective surface, as a reflection, of course. You can also have objects with reflections explicitly turned off through the Render Stats section in the Attribute Editor in case you don't want a particular reflection, which is common. Although it's possible to simulate reflections in Maya Software using *reflection maps*, true reflections can be generated only through raytracing.

Refractions

Refractions occur when light bends as it passes through one medium into another medium of different density. For example, a pencil in a glass of water appears to be broken. Refraction can also be turned on or off explicitly through Render Stats for objects that you don't want to see refracting through another clear object.

You saw in the previous chapter that raytracing is also a vital component of Arnold.

As soon as raytracing is enabled in Maya Software (or implicitly with Arnold), any reflective surface receives a true reflection of the objects and environment in the scene. Even objects with reflection maps reflect other objects in addition to their reflection maps. For more on reflection maps, see the section "Reflections and Refractions" later in this chapter.

Render Quality

With software rendering, the render quality depends most noticeably on *anti-aliasing*. Anti-aliasing is the effect produced when pixels appear to blur together to soften a jagged edge on an angled line. Increasing the anti-aliasing level of a render produces an image that has smoother angles and curves. The Render Settings window contains presets that specify this level and a few others to set the quality of your render. Follow these steps:

1. In the Render Settings window, make sure Maya Software is selected in the Render Using drop-down list and click the Maya Software tab.
2. In the Anti-aliasing Quality section, select either Preview Quality or Production Quality from the Quality preset drop-down list.

Figure 11.5 shows the fruit still life from Chapter 10 rendered with the Preview Quality preset and the same image with the Production Quality preset. Of course, the higher the quality, the longer the render will take.

We will explore anti-aliasing quality settings for Arnold later in this chapter.

Maya Hardware 2.0

The hardware rendering method uses your graphic card's processor to render the scene. Maya Hardware renders are similar to what you may see when you play a 3D video game and closely resemble what you already see in the view panels.

This method results in faster render times, but it lacks a lot of the features and quality you get from a software render. In recent years, hardware renderers (a.k.a. GPU rendering) have incorporated raytracing and can give amazing results. Arnold has a GPU mode, for example, that offloads the rendering tasks to the video card.

To use the Maya Hardware renderer, in the Render Settings window, make sure Maya Hardware 2.0 is selected in the Render Using drop-down list. To specify hardware quality, select a level from the Number Of Samples drop-down list on the Maya Hardware tab.

Arnold

Arnold has become a standard for rendering through Maya, supplanting the Maya Software renderer because of its stability and quality results. Arnold emulates the behavior of light much more realistically than Maya Software, even with raytracing enabled.

The Arnold renderer can be an advanced and intricate rendering language with shaders and procedures all its own. This chapter covers Arnold rendering using Arnold materials for the best effect, as well as introducing using high dynamic range (HDR) image-based lighting. To use Arnold, you still need to be experienced at least a little with the basics of lighting and rendering with Maya Software, even though it's often best to just use Arnold throughout. We'll be getting deeper into Arnold soon.

Maya Vector

Vector rendering is an older rendering scheme that lets you render your objects with an illustrated or cartoon look, though this has been much improved with Toon Shading, a process we looked at earlier in the book. You can render "ink" outlines of your characters to composite over flat-color passes. Figure 11.6 shows the fruit still life rendered with Maya Vector.

If Maya Vector is not available in the Render Using drop-down at the top of the Render Settings window alongside Maya Software and Arnold Renderer, you need to enable its plug-in by choosing Windows ➤ Settings/Preferences ➤ Plug-in Manager. At the top of the Plug-in Manager window, search for VectorRenderer and enable it.

Maya Vector can output animated files in Adobe Flash format for direct use in web pages and animations, as well as Adobe Illustrator files and the usual list of image formats.

FIGURE 11.5 With Preview Quality (left), the edges of the fruit are jagged. With Production Quality (right), the jaggedness is gone.

FIGURE 11.6   The fruit still life as a vector render.

To specify the attribute settings for Maya Vector, you use the Maya Vector tab in the Render Settings window (see Figure 11.7).

In the Fill Options section, click the Fill Objects check box, and select the number of colors for each object to set the look of the render. If you want the renderer to include an outline of the edges of your geometry, in the Edge Options section, click the Include Edges check box and set the line weights. But most recent renders may have their own methods for rendering outlines like these, commonly known as Toon Shading, something we covered briefly for Maya Software rendering in Chapter 7.

Previewing Your Render: The Two Common Render View Windows

The Maya Render View window automatically opens when you test-render a frame, as you've already seen in your work through this book. To open it manually, choose Windows ➣ Rendering Editors ➣ Render View. This is Maya's native render view window, which also shows Arnold as well. However, you have more power with Arnold's own RenderView window, as we've already seen, especially when using interactive rendering. Figure 11.8 shows the names of the icons in this window compared to those of the Arnold RenderView, and the following list highlights what the more important ones do.

Maya Render View icons explained:

Render the current frame
Renders the last-rendered viewport.

Render Region
Renders only the selected portion of an image. To select a portion of an image, click within the image

FIGURE 11.7   The Maya Vector rendering settings.

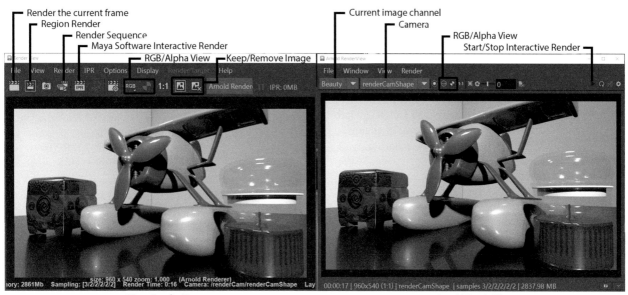

FIGURE 11.8 The Maya and Arnold Render View windows compared.

in the Render View window and drag a red box around a region.

Render Sequence

Begins rendering the scene's animation using the frame range set in the Render Settings window.

RGB/Alpha View

Toggles between the full color of the image and its alpha channel (transparency).

Render Using Pull-Down Menu

(Not called out in Figure 11.9) Lets you select the rendering method. This is the same as selecting it in the Render Settings window. Currently shown as Arnold Renderer in Figure 11.9.

Information Readout

At the bottom of the Render View window is a readout of information about the frame rendered. This information tells you the resolution, renderer used, frame number, render time, and camera used to render. This readout is a huge help in comparing different render settings and different frames as you

FIGURE 11.9 IPR rendering lets you fine-tune your textures and lighting with near-real-time feedback.

progress in your work, especially when you keep images in the buffer (as explained later).

Arnold RenderView icons explained:

Current Image Channel

Usually shown as Beauty, this allows you to view the various channels available in an Anrold render. By default, these are simply Beauty (a.k.a. RGB) and Alpha. When AOVs are enabled, these AOV channels will be viewable here. AOV, in short, is the ability to render an image into multiple passes that separate the different components of a render such as color, shadows, reflections, refractions, etc. to allow for greater control in compositing. This is an advanced rendering workflow that is not covered in this book.

Camera

Displays the camera that is currently rendering in the RenderView. This drop-down allows you to switch to another camera for the render.

RGB/Alpha view

Toggles between the full color of the image and its alpha channel (transparency).

Start/Stop Interactive Render

Starts or stops interactive rendering with Arnold.

Information Readout

At the bottom of the Arnold RenderView window is also a readout of information. This information tells you the render time, resolution, camera, samples (render quality), and memory used.

Saving/Loading an Image

Although you typically use either of these Render View windows to test a scene, you can also use them to save single frames by choosing File ➢ Save Image to save in any image formats supported in Maya in either window. Likewise, choose File ➢ Open Image to display any previously rendered image file in either window. If your task in Maya is to create a single frame, this is the best way to render and save it.

Keep/Remove Image

The Maya Render View window is a prime place to see adjustments to various parts of your scene. You can store images in its buffer by clicking the Keep Image icon. When you do, a scroll bar appears at the bottom of the window, and you can scroll through any saved images. This is handy for making a change, rendering it, and scrolling back and forth between the old saved image and the new render to make sure the change is to your liking. You can store a number of images in the buffer.

Similarly in the Arnold RenderView, you can keep and compare images (called snapshots) by choosing View ➢ Store Snapshot. However, in the Arnold RenderView instead of a simple scroll bar, you are given thumbnails to browse for comparison to previously stored snapshots.

IPR Rendering and Arnold RenderView Interactive Rendering

As you saw in previous chapters, a fast way to preview changes to your scene is to use interactive rendering in the Arnold RenderView window. You also have something similar in Maya Software rendering called IPR (Interactive Photorealistic Rendering) by clicking the IPR button ( ) in the status bar or at the top of the Maya Render View. After you IPR-render a viewport, specify the region you want to tune by dragging a box around that area of the image in the Render View window. Maya updates that region every time you make a shader or lighting change to the scene. Figure 11.9 shows the plan scene as an IPR render as the color and specular levels are being fine-tuned against a snapshot of the model.

IPR is perfect for finding just the right lighting and specular levels, and even though IPR will work with Arnold rendering, it is better replaced by Arnold RenderView and its interactive rendering capability.

Setting the Default Renderer

By default, whenever you launch Maya, it should set Arnold as the renderer of choice. To change this default behavior to another renderer (such as Maya Software, or an installed and licensed plug-in such as Red Shift or V-Ray), in the main menu bar select Windows ➢ Settings/Preferences ➢ Preferences. In the Preferences window, select Rendering in the list on the left side, and set the Preferred renderer drop-down menu to your desired renderer and click Save. From here on, new scenes will default to using that renderer.

Reflections and Refractions

With raytracing, Maya (with raytracing enabled) or Arnold reflects any objects in the scene that fall in the proper line of sight. All you need to do is use shaders that have reflection attributes such as Phong or Blinn. Note that Lambert shader does not reflect. Environmental reflections play an important role in photorealistic rendering, especially with materials such as metal and glass. This is one place where HDR image-based rendering is a huge help. More on this later.

Raytraced Reflections

Rendering reflections using Arnold is simple. Just assign shaders to your objects that have a Reflection attribute such as Phong or Blinn, or Arnold's own materials. If you need to use Maya Software, however, you must enable raytraced reflections. First, make sure to use a material that has a Reflections attribute (for example, Phong or Blinn). Then, open the Render Settings window and choose Maya Software as your renderer.

On the Maya Software tab, click the Raytracing check box in the Raytracing Quality section (see Figure 11.10).

The sliders control the quality of the render by specifying how many times to reflect or refract for any given object. Setting Reflections to 2, for example, enables an object's reflection in a second object to appear as part of its reflection in a third object.

The first image in Figure 11.11 shows the still life reflecting onto the surface of its table. In this case, Reflections is set to 1. If you increase Reflections to 2, however, you'll see the reflections of the pieces of fruit in each other also reflecting in the surface of the table.

Notice the difference in the reflections of the fruit in the table between the two renders.

You can control the number of reflections on a per-object basis through its shader as opposed to setting limits on the entire scene through the Render Settings window. To access a shader's reflection limits, select the shader in the Hypershade. In the Raytrace Options section of the Property Editor or the Attribute Editor, drag the Reflection Limit slider to set the maximum number of reflections for that shader. The lower value (either this value or the Reflections value in the Render Settings window) dictates how many reflections are rendered for every object attached to that shader. The default shader reflection limit is 1, so make sure you change the Reflections value as well as each shader's value if you want more than one level of reflection.

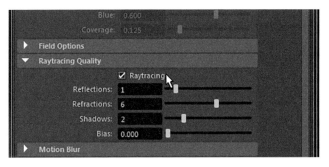

FIGURE 11.10 Enabling raytracing in Maya Software rendering.

Furthermore, you may not want some objects to cast reflections in a scene with raytraced reflections. To specify that an object doesn't cast reflections, select the object in a Maya panel and open the Attribute Editor. In the Render Stats section, clear the Visible In Reflections check box. This trick applies to Maya Software as well as Arnold and most other renderers in Maya.

Rendering Refractions (Maya Software)

Refractions are also a raytraced-only ability. Refractions require that an object be semitransparent so that you can see through it to the object (or objects) behind it being refracted. To control refractions, use the shader.

To enable refractions in Maya Software, select an appropriate shader in the Hypershade. In the Raytrace Options section of the Property Editor (or Attribute Editor), click the Refractions check box. Now you need to set a refractive index for the shader and a refraction limit, similar to the reflection limit.

The refractive index must be greater or less than 1 to cause a visible refraction. Typically, a number within 0.2 of 1 is perfect for most refractive effects. The first image in Figure 11.12 is raytraced with a refractive index of 1.2 on the wine bottle and glasses; the second image has a refractive index of 0.8 on both bottle and glasses.

You can specify whether an object is visible in a refracting object by clicking or clearing the Visible In Refractions check box in the Render Stats section of the object's Attribute Editor.

When rendering refractions, make sure the Refractions attribute under Raytracing Quality in the Maya Software tab of the Render Settings is set to at least 2 or higher; otherwise, your refraction may not appear properly.

Making Glass in Arnold

Now that we have covered basic refraction in glass just in case you need to use Maya Software rendering, let's see how a much more powerful renderer handles refractions through glass.

FIGURE 11.11 Reflections set to 1 (left); Reflections set to 2 (right).

FIGURE 11.12 Refractive index of 1.2 (left top render); refractive index of 0.8 (left bottom render).

FIGURE 11.13 Basic render of the scene with Maya materials. The glass does not look good.

Graph Materials icon ( ) to display its material. It's a simple PhongE shader.

3. In the Hypershade's search box (Figure 11.14), start to type in aiStandardSurface and the Create panel will filter only those materials. Click on aiStandard-Surface. This is the go-to material in Arnold for creating a wide range of materials from plastic to wood to glass to metal and more. Name this material arnoldGlass.

The Arnold Standard Surface Material

If you select the aiStandardSurface material you just made in the Hypershade to see its attributes, you will notice that it is fairly different than the attributes of the Maya native materials like the Blinn. Figure 11.15 shows these attributes, with explanations following below. We will try them all hands-on after the descriptions.

In the Base section are attributes to control the base color of the surface. The base Color attribute of course sets the base, primary color of the object. The base Weight controls the amount of that color that is allowed to bounce back to the eye. A weight of 0 will always lead to a black base color. The Metalness slider controls how the surface reflects to make it appear metallic to varying degrees. A setting of 1.0 will result in a pure metal surface, which we will explore later in this chapter.

The Specular section gives you access to the material's reflection properties. The specular Color controls the color of the reflection. The brighter the color, the brighter the reflection, with black creating no reflections at all. The specular Amount controls the amount of reflection, alongside the brightness of the specular Color. A value of 0 kills all reflections, just like a specular Color of black would.

Specular Roughness slider controls the glossiness of the surface. The lower this Roughness value, the glossier, the sharper the reflections will appear. The higher the specular Roughness value, the less apparent the reflections will appear since they will be diffused (essentially blurred) the rougher the surface is.

The IOR value (a.k.a. Index of Refraction) controls the way reflections are calculated. This is sometimes referred to as

1. Set your project to the Lighting project down-loaded from the book's website. Open the scene file `still_life_Arnold_v01.ma` from the Scenes folder. Open the Arnold RenderView and start an interactive render for the camera1 view panel (or select cameraShape1 from the RenderViews camera drop-down menu (Figure 11.13)). You will notice basic Maya shaders on the objects, including the wine glasses and bottle.

2. With Arnold, refraction will occur through its own materials, most notably the aiStandardSurface, which we will switch to using now. Select one of the wine glasses and open the Hypershade. Select the

FIGURE 11.14   Search for the aiStandardSurface in the Hypershade.

the Fresnel Effect. It essentially controls how well reflections are at any given angle of the target surface. In other words, a reflection can appear stronger in parts of a surface that angle away from the camera, where the same reflection is somewhat muted in parts of the surface that more directly face the camera. This value also controls how much refraction is visible through a transparent surface. It is best to leave this value at its default of 1.5 while first learning rendering with Arnold.

The Anisotropy value allows you to stretch the reflections in the surface simulating surfaces like brushed metal and creating interesting highlights, while Rotation allows you to set the angle of that stretching effect. Let's see how these attributes work on the wine bottle and glasses scene.

1. In the scene you just loaded, you just created a new aiStandardSurface material and called it arnold-Glass. Select the three wine glasses in the scene and assign them to arnoldGlass.
2. Start an interactive render in the Arnold RenderView and the wine glasses are a basic gray solid surface. Select the arnoldGlass material in the Hypershade and in the Specular section, set the specular Roughness to 0 for a glassy reflection, though it will be hard to see due to the bright lighting.
3. Open the Transmission section in the material and set the transmission Weight up to 1.0. This creates

a transparency in the surface like glass and water. It creates refraction through the surface, which is controlled by the IOR value in the Specular section of the Attribute Editor. The RenderView will immediately show a much nicer-looking glass than before as shown in Figure 11.16.

Note that when making a glass object, it is important to model a glass object like a wine glass or bottle with a thickness to the walls of the surface, if it is not completely solid like a marble. This will create more accurate refractions than if the wine glass's sides did not have a thickness to the geometry. If you examine the wine glasses and bottle in this scene, you will see they all have been modeled to have such a thickness to their glass.

4. With the interactive render running in the RenderView, experiment with the arnoldGlass material's IOR to see how IOR affects the refraction inside the glass. Then set it back to the default of 1.5.
5. Now for the bottle. Make another aiStandardSurface material and name it arnoldBottle. Assign it to the bottle model.
6. For the bottle's material, set the specular Roughness to 0 to get glossy reflections, and then set the

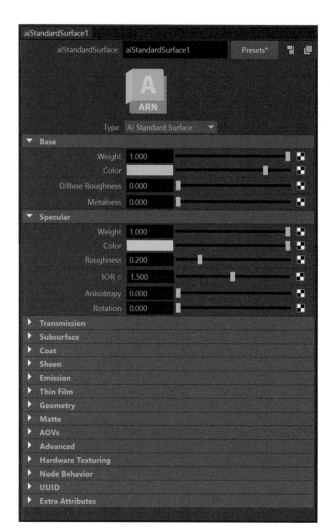

FIGURE 11.15   Attributes for the aiStandardSurface.

FIGURE 11.16   The glasses look like they're made out of glass!

transmission Weight to 1.0 and the bottle will look like a clear glass bottle.

7. But the bottle should be green! In the Transmission section, set the transmission Color to a somewhat bright green to tint the glass green. Figure 11.17.

FIGURE 11.17   Attributes for the aiStandardSurface.

8. Now, in the Specular section, set the specular Roughness to 0.2, and now the bottle looks like a frosted glass bottle. As you can see the specular Roughness affects not just the glossiness of the reflection, but also of the refraction as well. Too bad the wine bottle is empty!

Now save your work. You can compare it to `still_life_ Arnold_v02.ma` from the Scenes folder of the Lighting project. The aiStandardSurface is incredibly powerful and can mimic so many different real-world materials just with adjustments to the specular Roughness. Experiment with this attribute to see what else you can get your surfaces to look like.

Making Plastic and Metal in Arnold

Now that we've played around a bit in making glass with Arnold, let's make some other materials like plastic and metal. Continue here with your scene file from the previous section, or load the file `still_life_Arnold_v02.ma` from the Scenes folder of the Lighting project.

1. Start an interactive render. Select the apple in the scene and confirm that it, as well as all the other fruit, are assigned to a Blinn material (blinn1) and look pretty glossy. Create an aiStandardSurface material and name it arnoldFruit. Assign the new material to just the apple for now.

2. In the RenderView, it looks bright. Darken the base Color to a dark-gray tone. Figure 11.18 shows the difference between the Blinn and the new aiStandardSurface on the apple. The reflections look more realistic, giving us a nicer plastic look. Experiment with the specular Roughness to dial in a somewhat dull plastic sheen. Figure 11.18 shows a specular Roughness of 0.30.

3. Once you are happy with the general plastic look, assign that material to the other fruit.

4. Now let's make the table out of metal! Select the table and it is assigned to a phongE material called Table. Create a new aiStandardSurface and

FIGURE 11.18   The apple looks more like plastic than the other fruit.

call it arnoldTable. Assign it to the table object (Figure 11.19).

5. In the attribute editor for the new arnoldTable material, set the specular Roughness to 0.0 and in the Base section, set the Metalness slider to 1.0. The table is now chrome silver by making the reflections perfectly visible in all angles of the table. The silver seems a little dark, so set the base Color up to pure white and it should brighten the chrome silver noticeably.

6. Now set the base Color to a bright orange and the table is now made of polished gold! Play with the specular Roughness to reduce the polish on the gold. Figure 11.20 shows the specular Roughness at 0.3 for a brushed-metal gold look. If it were only that easy to make actual gold.

Save your work! You can compare your results with the scene file `still_life_Arnold_v03.ma` from the Scenes folder. The aiStandardSurface is the Swiss Army knife of

FIGURE 11.19   The table with a default aiStanardSurface applied.

FIGURE 11.20   Look, the table is made out of gold. We're rich!

materials in Arnold. And we're just scratching the surface. Pun intended.

Using Cameras

Let's take a break from the Arnold materials and move on to another important part of the rendering process: cameras! Cameras capture all the animation fun in the scene. The more you know about photography, the easier these concepts are to understand.

The term *camera*, in essence, refers to any perspective view. You can have as many cameras in the scene as you want, but it's wise to have a camera you're planning to render with placed to frame the shot and a different camera acting as the perspective work view so you can move around your scene as you work. The original persp viewport fits that latter role well, although it can be used as a render camera just as easily.

You can also render any of your work windows to test-render orthogonal views of your model the same way you render a perspective view.

Creating a Camera

The simplest way to create a new camera is to choose Panels ➢ Perspective ➢ New, as you've seen in a previous exercise. This creates a new camera node in Maya and sets that active panel to that view. Cameras will work in any renderer, though some renderers such as Arnold or VRay may provide their own specialized cameras or camera attributes.

You can see and select a camera in another viewport and transform it (move it, rotate it, and scale it) just as you would select and transform any other object in Maya to be animated or positioned. Furthermore, you are actually moving and rotating a camera when using the Alt/Option key and mouse button combinations to move your view in a panel.

For example, click inside a new Maya Scene Perspective window to make it active. Select that view's camera by choosing View ➢ Select Camera. The camera's attributes appear in the Channel Box. Try moving the view around using the Alt/ Option key and mouse button combinations. Notice how the attributes change to reflect the new position and rotation of the camera. You can animate the camera—for example, zoom in or out or pan across the scene—by setting keyframes on any of these attributes.

Camera Types

You can create three types of nonstereo cameras for your scene: Camera; Camera And Aim; and Camera, Aim, And Up (also known as single-node, two-node, and three-node cameras, respectively). To create any of these cameras, choose Create ➤ Cameras. You can also change the type of these cameras at any time through the Attribute Editor. The other two options for creating cameras are Stereo Camera and Multi Stereo Rig to allow for a stereoscopic effect, although they aren't covered in this book.

The single-node camera (Camera) is the most common (see Figure 11.21). This camera consists of a single camera node that you move and rotate as you would any other object for proper positioning. The persp viewport's camera is a single-node camera.

The two-node camera (Camera And Aim) consists of the camera node and an aim node. You use the aim node to point the camera as opposed to rotating it to orient it properly. This is useful for animating a camera following an object. You

animate the movement of the aim node to follow your object much as you'd follow a car around a racetrack. The camera pivots to follow its aim point and, hence, the object (see Figure 11.22).

The three-node camera (Camera, Aim, And Up) has a camera node, an aim node, and an up node. The additional up node is to orient the camera's up direction. This gives you the ability to animate the side-to-side rotation of the camera as well as its aim direction (see Figure 11.23).

Camera Attributes

As an example, use the scene file `still_life_Arnold_v03.ma` from the Lighting project, or continue on with your scene from the previous section making the gold table. Set one of your view panels to the *persp* view and another to the *camera1* view as seen in Figure 11.24.

If you open the Arnold RenderView and start an interactive render, you probably will notice that what you see in the view panel in Maya and what you see in the render are slightly different, with the render most likely cropping some of the view, as also shown in Figure 11.24. This is perfectly normal. But to better gauge your final frame in your Maya view, go to the

camera1 view panel and click the Resolution Gate icon ( ) to see dark green lines show you the extents of what you will be rendering.

You'll also the resolution at the top as it is set in the Render Settings (960×540, which is half HD resolution) and the name of the camera (camera1) at the bottom.

Special attributes control the function of camera nodes. To set these attributes, follow these steps:

1. Select the *camera1* camera through the Outliner and open the Attribute Editor (Ctrl+A), or click the

   Camera Attributes icon ( ) at the top of the *camera1's* view panel.

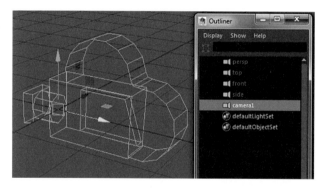

FIGURE 11.21   A single-node camera.

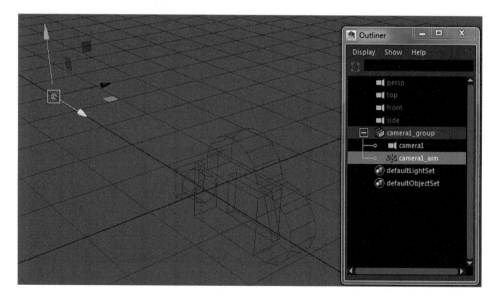

FIGURE 11.22   A two-node camera.

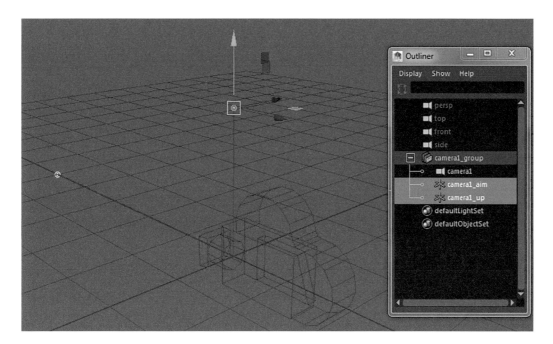

FIGURE 11.23 A three-node camera.

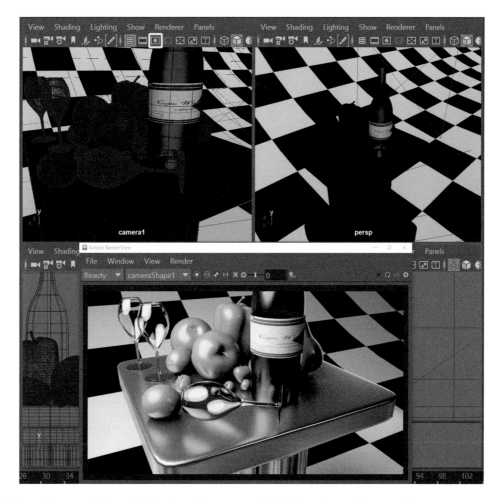

FIGURE 11.24 The render crops a little and is wider than what we can see in the Maya view panel for camera1.

2. At the top of the Attribute Editor window, select the type of camera controls you want. The Controls attribute sets the type of camera from single- to two- to three-control nodes that we explored previously. Figure 11.25 shows the Attribute Editor for the *camera1* camera.

Focal Length

The Focal Length attribute specifies the length of the lens. The lower the focal length (a.k.a. short lens), the wider the view. At very low numbers, however, the image is distorted, as you can see in the comparison in Figure 11.26. The higher the focal length, the closer the subject appears to the camera.

Although adjusting the Focal Length attribute of a camera zooms in and out, it isn't the same as moving the camera closer to your subject using the Alt+RMB+click procedure to zoom in viewports (which is called *trucking* the camera). Focal length zooming can create optical distortions, such as

FIGURE 11.26 Different focal lengths on the same camera from 12 mm (top) to 35 mm (middle) to 65 mm (bottom).

can be created with a fish-eye lens. And longer lenses (higher focal lengths) will flatten the perspective of a shot.

Clipping Planes

All cameras in Maya have clipping planes that restrict the amount of information that needs to be processed (seen) through them. The clipping plane is defined by the Near Clip Plane and Far Clip Plane attributes. These set the minimum and maximum distances, respectively, of the clipping plane. Any object or portion of an object that passes beyond these distances won't show in the window and should not render.

If you notice objects disappearing as you move your camera and create a scene, it may be because of the clipping plane. Increase the Far Clip Plane attribute, and the objects should reappear in the view. You can display the near and far clipping planes of any camera with the check boxes in the Frustum Display Controls section, as well as viewing your angle of view by turning on Display Frustum.

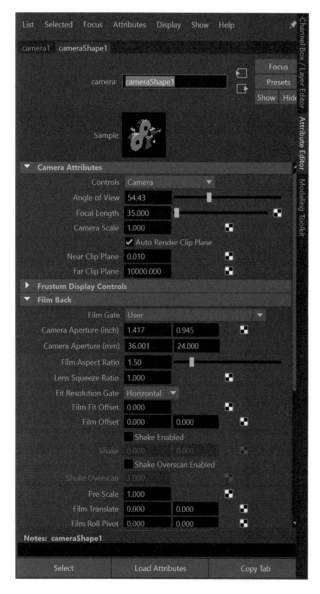

FIGURE 11.25 The Attribute Editor for the camera1 camera.

Film Back

The Film Back attributes concern the type of output you'll be dealing with after your renders are finished and you're ready to put your animation on tape, DVD, film, or what have you.

Film Gate

Defines the aspect ratio of your camera's view. Images that are output to HD television have an aspect ratio of 1:1.78, which aggravatingly enough does not have a preset in the Film Gate drop-down list. For an HD camera output, simply set Film Aspect Ratio to **1.78**. (For more on aspect ratios, see Chapter 1.)

Fit Resolution Gate

Allows you to align footage you may have imported as a camera image plane to match up CG properly to live action.

Overscan

Found in the Display Options section for the camera's Attribute Editor, Overscan lets you resize the view without changing the film gate that will render. For example, the scene on the top in Figure 11.27 is set up with an Overscan setting of 1.3, allowing you to see more than what will render, which is defined by the outline box. The scene on the bottom in Figure 11.27 is set up with an Overscan setting of 2, which increases even more how much you see in the camera1 panel but doesn't change the view when rendered.

You can turn the green box in the camera's viewport on and off through the camera's Attribute Editor in the Display Options section where you will also find Overscan (Figure 11.28), or with the Resolution Gate icon ( ) at the top of the view panel itself.

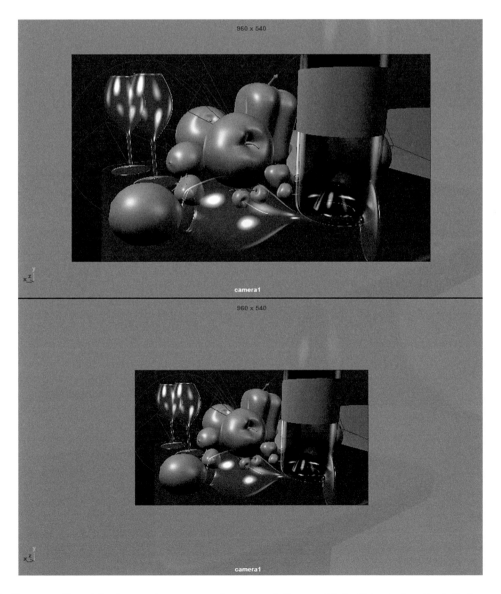

FIGURE 11.27   Overscan settings define how much you can see of your scene in the camera but not how much renders in the image.

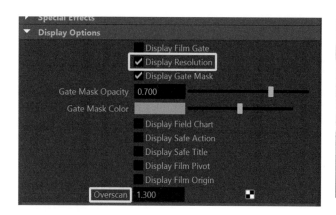

FIGURE 11.28   Camera display options.

FIGURE 11.29   Adjusting the camera's environment and creating camera image planes.

FIGURE 11.30   An HD image to import as a camera image plane.

Environment

In the Environment section, you'll find attributes to adjust the background color that renders behind any scene objects and to create a camera image plane, as shown in Figure 11.29.

If you want to use a solid color as the camera's background when you render, click the color swatch next to Background Color to change the background color in your renders using the Color Chooser. The slider allows you to control the value, or brightness, of the current color. Neither changes the background color of your viewports, however.

Camera Image Planes

A camera image plane isn't like the reference planes you used for modeling the red wagon in Chapter 6, "Practical Experience." In this case, an image plane is created to be a background specific for that particular camera or viewport, but it's typically also used as a reference that is locked to the

view of that one camera and is meant for lining up CG with live-action elements shot in a photo or footage. Camera image planes are useful when you're matching your scene to existing footage or an image. For example, if you need to animate a little unidentified flying object (UFO) landing next to a cat in the snowy mountains, you would import the video as an image sequence into Maya as a camera image plane through a perspective camera to be able to line up your UFO properly on the road next to the cat.

You can import an image plane by clicking the Create button in the Environment section of the Attribute Editor (see Figure 11.29) or directly through a viewport's menu, as you'll see in the next exercise.

You can find the file cat _ UFO.jpg in the Sourceimages folder of the Lighting project, shown in Figure 11.30. In the following steps, we will import an image plane as a background for a camera.

Follow these steps:

1. Choose File ≻ New Scene. Pick the top view panel and select Panels ≻ Perspective ≻ New to make a new camera in that view panel (Figure 11.31).

2. Import the photo of the cat into Maya as a camera image plane for the new camera (persp1) by selecting the *persp1* camera and in the Attribute Editor, open the Environment section and click on the Create button next to the Image Plane attribute (Figure 11.32).

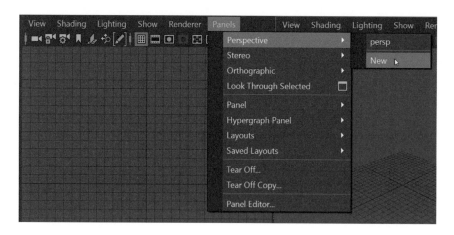

FIGURE 11.31   Create a new camera in the Top view panel.

FIGURE 11.32   Click the Create button.

3. Navigate to the Sourceimages folder of the Lighting project, and choose the `Cat _ UFO.jpg` image. The photo now displayed in the persp1 view panel as shown in Figure 11.33. You can see the image as a background for persp1, but you can also see the persp1 camera itself with this attached cat image in the persp view panel as well. If you move the persp1 camera in any way, the background image will go along with it. You can see the Image Plane's attributes in Figure 11.34.

If you can't see the image plane, click Show in the viewport's menu bar and make sure Image Planes is checked.

Image Plane Sequence

A movie file or a sequence of files can also be brought in to animate or to track motion (a.k.a. *matchmoving*) as a camera image plane. It's generally best to use a frame sequence, however. When you bring in an image for an image plane, check the Use Image Sequence box in the image plane's Attribute Editor window, as shown in Figure 11.34. Maya will automatically load the image to correspond to the frame number in the scene. For example, at frame 29 in your Maya animation, Maya loads frame 29 of your image sequence. But your image file sequence must be numbered correctly (such as `filename.###.tif`). You can import an image plane into any perspective view in the same way.

If the clutter of seeing a camera image plane in the other windows bothers you, under Image Plane Attributes in the Attribute Editor, change the radio button selection next to Display from In All Views to Looking Through Camera. This setting removes the image plane from the other windows.

Motion Blur

Motion blur is an optical phenomenon that occurs when an object moves quickly in front of a camera; the object looks blurred as it crosses the frame. Maya Software rendering renders motion blur in two ways— 2D blur or 3D blur—although neither will render as reflections.

- In the 2D blur process, Maya calculates after the frame is rendered. Any objects moving in the frame are blurred with a 2D filter effect. The 2D blur is effective for most applications and faster than 3D blur.

- The 3D blur process is calculated while a frame of the sequence is rendering. Every motion blur-enabled object is blurred with typically better results than 2D blur but at the cost of a much longer render time.

I'll briefly cover motion blur in Arnold later in this chapter.

To enable motion blur for the Maya Software renderer, open the Render Settings window. In the Motion Blur section in the Maya Software tab, click the Motion Blur check box. Then, choose 2D or 3D blur.

Typically, you control the amount of blur rendered for 2D and 3D by setting the Blur By Frame attribute—the higher the number, the greater the blur. Using additional controls, however, you can increase or decrease the 2D blur effect in the render. The Blur Length attribute affects the streakiness of the blur to further increase or decrease the amount of motion blur set with the Blur By Frame attribute.

Setting a camera's Shutter Angle attribute (in the camera's Attribute Editor in the Special Effects section) also affects the amount of blur rendered—the higher the number, the greater the blur.

Batch Rendering

So far, you've used single-frame rendering numerous times to see a scene in the Render View window. But how do you start rendering an animation sequence to disk? There are two options, with the first called *batch rendering*, whichever

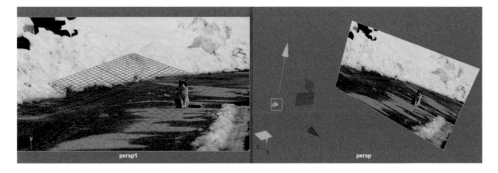

FIGURE 11.33   Seeing the image plane in persp1 camera view.

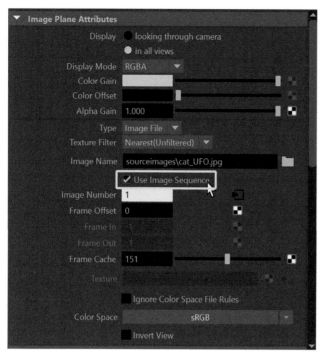

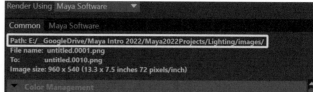

FIGURE 11.35 The Render Settings window shows you where the images will be rendered.

You can see progress updates of the render in the Command line at the bottom of your Maya screen and in the Script Editor window if you open it.

To see a frame as the batch render progresses, choose Render ➤ Show Batch Render. To cancel a batch render, choose Render ➤ Cancel Batch Render.

When you batch render, your image files are written to the images folder of the current project. Make sure your project is properly set before starting the render; otherwise, your files will end up in an unexpected folder. You can always see the render path and the image name at the top of the Render Settings window, as shown in Figure 11.35.

FIGURE 11.34 Importing a sequence of image files as a camera image plane.

renderer you use, as long as it is licensed. To batch-render an animation with Maya Software, follow these steps:

1. Open the Render Settings window and choose Maya Software to use to render. On the Common tab, in the File Output section, set Frame/Animation Ext to name.#.ext to enable rendering an animation. Otherwise, Maya will render only a single frame.

2. Next, enter the start and end frames of your animation and select your image format. Select your quality and resolution settings. Finally, set the camera you want to render in the Renderable Camera attribute.

> Be sure to select name.#.ext in the Frame/Animation Ext drop-down list to render a sequence of files. Remember, if you leave the default setting, which is name.ext, only a single frame renders.

3. In the main Maya window under the Rendering menu set, choose Render ➤ Batch Render to set off the render. Maya will render in the background the frame sequence specified in the Render Settings with the Start and End frame values. If you click on the options box ❏ for Batch Render, you will be able to select the number of processor cores to dedicate to the background rendering process, if you wish to continue working in Maya as it renders.

Rendering the Wine Bottle

In this section, you'll set up and render an animated camera to move over 25 frames of a wine bottle still life using Maya Software rendering at first.

Set your current project to the Lighting project downloaded from the book's web page and then load still_life_render_v01.ma. You'll also adjust your render settings and some shader properties to make the wine bottle look more like glass.

Selecting Render Settings Options

Set your resolution and quality settings in the Render Settings window.

1. Open the Render Settings window and select Maya Software. Click the Maya Software tab.

2. From the Quality drop-down list, select Production Quality. Doing so presets the appropriate settings to produce a high-quality render.

3. Click the Common tab. Set Frame/Animation Ext to name.#.ext, set Start Frame to **1**, set End Frame to **25**, and set Frame Padding to **2**.

4. From the Image Format drop-down list, select TIFF.

5. Make sure Renderable Camera is set to camera1. In the Image Size section, set Presets to HD 540.

Setting Up the Scene

Now, set up some of the objects in the scene. The wine bottle has been imported into the still life scene, and three wine glasses have been added. All the lights are in place, as is the camera.

Start by setting up this scene to raytrace to get true reflections and refractions.

1. Turn on refractions for the Glass shaders. In the Hypershade, select the Glasses material and in the Property Editor or the Attribute Editor, under the Raytrace Options section, click the Refractions check box and set Refractive Index to **1.2**. Set Reflection Limit to **2**. Select the Wine_Bottle material and repeat the previous steps.

2. You need to change your lights' shadows to raytraced shadows. Semitransparent objects cast solid shadows unless shadows are raytraced when in Maya Software rendering, so the glasses and wine bottle will cast shadows as if they were solid and not glass. In the Outliner, select spotLight1. In the Attribute Editor, in the Shadows section, enable Use Ray Trace Shadows. Repeat these steps for the remaining two shadow-casting lights: spotLight4 and spotLight3. Figure 11.36 shows the three shadow-casting lights in the scene in white.

3. Open the Render Settings window and turn on raytracing in the Raytracing Quality section. Set Reflections to **2**.

You can't select all three lights at once to turn on raytraced shadows in the Attribute Editor. Any adjustments you make in the Attribute Editor affect only the most recently selected object, not multiple selections.

Setting Up the Camera

Next, you'll set up the camera to render the scene.

1. Make sure you are looking through the camera1 camera. Open the camera's Attribute Editor through the camera1 viewport menu (choose View ➢ Camera Attribute Editor or click the Camera Attributes icon) ( ).

2. Select the Display Film Gate option in the Display Options section to turn on a dashed green box in the camera1 viewport. Enable the Display Resolution option. Notice that the two boxes aren't aligned.

3. Because the resolution is 960 × 540, you'll need a 1.78 aspect ratio. Enter **1.78** for the Film Aspect Ratio under the Film Back section of the Render Settings. The two green boxes now align. Although it's not absolutely necessary to match the resolution with the film gate, it's definitely good practice to do so, especially if you'll later insert CG in live-action videos.

4. As soon as you change the film gate, the framing of the scene changes. You may need to move the camera out to frame the entire still life. If you try to use the Alt key and mouse button combinations to zoom out, you'll notice that you can't move the camera in this scene; the movement attributes for the camera have been locked to prevent accidental movement that would disrupt the shot.

5. To unlock the camera, you can click the Lock Camera icon in the view panel's icon bar shown in Figure 11.37. You can also choose View ➢ Select

FIGURE 11.36   Shadow lights.

FIGURE 11.37 Seeing the image plane in persp1 camera view.

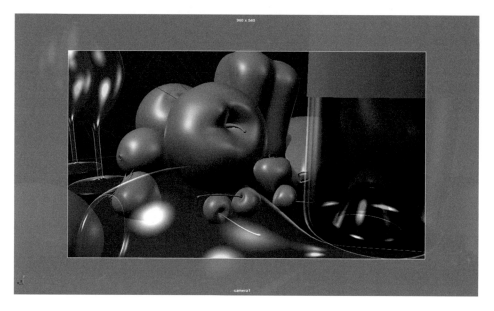

FIGURE 11.38 The camera view at the beginning of the animation.

Camera. The camera's attributes appear in the Channel Box. Some are grayed out, signifying that they're locked and can't be changed. Highlight the locked attributes and RMB+click Unlock Selected in the Channel Box.

6. Create an animated camera move to pull out and reveal the still life slowly over 25 frames. Set your Range slider to 1–25 frames. Go to frame 1. The camera1 view should be similar to that shown in Figure 11.38. Select all three Translate and Rotate channels in the Channel Box and RMB+click Key Selected to set keyframes for the first camera position. You can also use the hotkey Shift+W to key all three Translate axes and Shift+E to key all three Rotate axes.

7. Move (actually, truck) the camera out by pressing Alt+RMB+click to a wider framing to reveal the entire still life. Highlight the Translate and Rotate channels again in the Channel Box and set keyframes for them (see Figure 11.39).

Scrub your animation, and you'll see a pullout revealing the full scene.

You can lock the camera to prevent accidentally moving the view after you set your keyframes, especially if Auto Keyframe is on. Use the Lock Camera icon in the camera's view panel ( ), or select the camera and then highlight Translate and Rotate attributes in the Channel Box, RMB+click, and choose Lock Selected.

Batch Rendering and Playing Back the Sequence

Now, you're ready to render the 25-frame sequence. Choose Render ➤ Batch Render.

Because you're raytracing this scene at full resolution, this render could take 10 minutes or longer. To chart the progress of the render, open the Script Editor by clicking its icon on the Help line in the bottom right corner of the Maya window ( ), or by choosing Windows ➤ General Editors ➤ Script Editor.

To see the frames play back, you'll need a program that can load the images in sequence and play them back for you. You can also import the image sequence into a compositing or

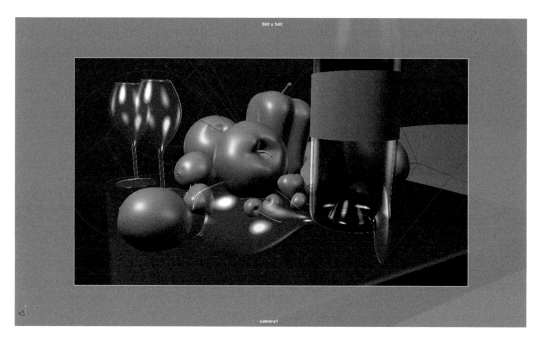

FIGURE 11.39 Pull out the camera.

FIGURE 11.40 FCheck, shown here with a sample image, plays back your rendered sequence.

editing program, such as Adobe After Effects or Premiere, to play back as a clip and edit as you like.

You can also use FCheck, a frame viewer that is included with Maya. This small and surprisingly powerful program plays back your images in real-time so that you can judge your finished animation. To use FCheck, follow these steps:

1. In Windows, open the Start menu and navigate down to the Autodesk Maya 2023 folder. Then choose FCheck to open the FCheck window, as shown in Figure 11.40.

2. Choose File ≻ Open Animation.

3. In the file browser, find your images folder in your project and click the first frame of the sequence you want to play back. FCheck loads the images frame by frame into RAM and then plays them back in real-time. Just set your playback speed and use the playback controls to play back your sequence.

Some More Arnold

You had some experience with Arnold rendering in the previous chapters as you lighted using Physical Sky as well as turning a table into gold earlier in this chapter. In this part of this chapter, I'll discuss Arnold options to begin to further scratch the surface of this powerful renderer.

First, if you haven't done so already, be sure that Arnold is loaded. When you first start up, Maya occasionally may not load Arnold's plug-in. Choose Windows ≻ Settings/Preferences ≻ Plug-in Manager to open the Plug-in Manager, as we did in the previous chapter. At the top, enter "mtoa" in the Search box to filter Arnold's plug-in, and then make sure both the Loaded and Auto Load check boxes for `mtoa.mll` (or `mtoa.bundle` for Mac users) are checked so that Arnold loads by default.

To render with Arnold, open the Render Settings window and change the Render Using drop-down menu selection to Arnold Renderer if it isn't already, as shown in Figure 11.41 (shown with the Arnold Renderer tab selected). The Render Settings window now has the Common tab along with four other Arnold-specific tabs: Arnold, System, AOVs, and Diagnostics.

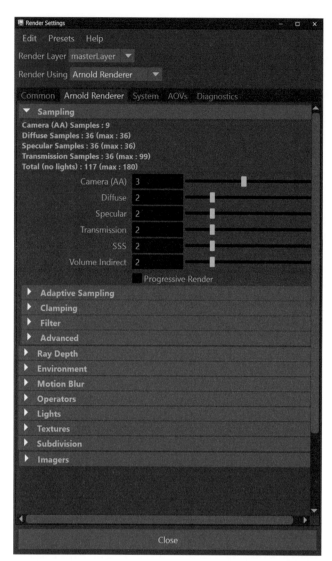

FIGURE 11.41 The Render Settings window for Arnold, showing the Arnold Renderer tab.

Arnold Image Quality Settings

Rendering an image takes time. The more time a renderer spends rendering an image, the less noisy the image will appear through the process of sampling. With lower-sampling renders, the image will appear to have grain, or noise. Increasing sampling values will help reduce this noise. As with the Maya Software renderer, the primary quality settings for the Arnold renderer center on sampling (or anti-aliasing). However, Arnold offers you much finer control over how you set the quality levels through the Arnold Renderer tab (shown in Figure 11.41), where you'll find settings to control the sampling in a number of specific ways under the Sampling heading:

Camera (AA) controls the overall image sampling (anti-aliasing) and is usually the first and only setting to increase to improve the quality of a render, though at the cost of increased rendering time per frame. This, as well as all of the other sampling values, are exponential, so it is advised to increase the sampling values slowly while checking the results to find

your acceptable quality level where the image is not as grainy. This value considers all of the other sampling values discussed below. If increasing the Camera (AA) sampling improves most of the image, but you still find unacceptable levels of noise in parts of the image, you can fine-tune them with the following sampling values without forcing higher sampling over the entire image causing even longer render times when using only Camera (AA).

Diffuse controls the noise found specifically in surfaces that are not reflective, or in the surface beneath its reflection.

Specular controls the noise found in reflections and glossy surfaces. This is the most commonly found noise, and so adjusting this value to account for reflective noise is more efficient than solely using Camera (AA).

Transmission controls noise found in refractive surfaces such as glass.

SSS adjusts the noise levels found in surfaces using SubSurface Scattering effects, which is a material effect we will experiment with a little later in this chapter.

Volume Indirect addresses noise found specifically in volume lighting effects such as god-rays and fog.

Render Settings in Action!

In this section, you'll look at how the sampling values work to determine the quality of the render of a toy wagon. You can find the scene (still _ life _ Arnold _ v03.ma) to render in the Lighting project on the book's web page. Make sure to set your project to Lighting.

Open the Render Settings window, making sure you are set to Arnold, and open the Arnold Renderer tab. The sampling values are set to their default values. Open the Arnold RenderView and start an interactive render. Notice at the bottom the RenderView in the information display, is a readout of the sampling values as well as a progress bar for the current render, as shown in Figure 11.42. Even though this is an interactive render, meaning it continuously renders the image, Arnold will stop improving the image once the sampling levels are reached, at 100% in the progress bar, which then disappears leaving the render time to show in the left corner of the information display.

FIGURE 11.42 Arnold RenderView shows sampling levels as well as the current render's progress.

When the render reaches 100% in the RenderView, you will see some grain/noise in the image, particularly in the gold metal table and the wine bottle. This frame took 13 seconds to render on my PC as shown in Figure 11.43 (top). In the Arnold Renderer tab of the Render Settings window, first increase the Camera (AA) value from 3 to 4 and the interactive render will restart the render and continue until it reaches 100%. Now you should notice an improvement in the overall noise, especially

in the gold table and bottle. This render, however, took 21 seconds, a 61%-time increase.

Now, set the Camera (AA) value back to 3 and set the Specular value from 2 to 3 instead. The interactive render will re-render the frame taking only 19 seconds as shown in Figure 11.43 (middle). This time the noise in the gold table and the bottle are improved just like before with the increase to Camera (AA), but we saved 2 seconds on the render with no discernable loss in quality anywhere else in the image. Even though 2 seconds is not a big deal, it could be a great time saver with larger more complicated renders, especially when rendering hundreds of frames in an animation. Figure 11.43 (bottom) shows an enlarged portion of the render to try and show the difference in noise levels when increasing sampling values.

You have to decide in your own images how far to set sampling values for the best result in the shortest render times. Simply cranking up the Camera (AA) will result in overall improvements, but potentially more inefficient render times. Your results as you render the scene on your own computer will be more noticeable than the images shown here.

Motion Blur with Arnold

Now that you have a primer on quality settings in Arnold, you'll learn how its motion blur works.

1. Set your project to the Solar_System project. Load the `Planets _ motionBlur.ma` scene file from the Solar_System project on the web page. This is an animated scene of the solar system with just the first few planets and moons, as shown in Figure 11.44. A blast from the past!

2. Open the Render Settings window. The scene should already be set to render with Arnold. If your scene isn't, make sure the Arnold plug-in is loaded and set the scene to render with Arnold Renderer.

3. On the Common tab, set Frame/Animation Ext to `name.#.ext`, Frame Padding to **4**, Start Frame to **1**, and End Frame to **100**.

4. Set Image Size to HD 540 and leave the renderable camera to persp.

5. Go to frame 75 and start an interactive render of the persp viewport in the Arnold RenderView. Figure 11.45 shows the result.

6. In Render Settings' Arnold Renderer tab, open the Motion Blur heading and check the Enable check box to turn on motion blur. Your interactive render will update to show the planets with motion blur applied as shown in Figure 11.45 (middle). The speed of an object typically determines the length of the motion blur, however, you can exaggerate motion blur by increasing the Shutter Angle Length attribute as shown in Figure 11.45 (bottom) with a Length of 1.0 resulting in a 360° shutter angle and longer motion blur streaks in the planets.

FIGURE 11.43   Lower sampling values (top image) show more noise than higher sampling levels (bottom image)

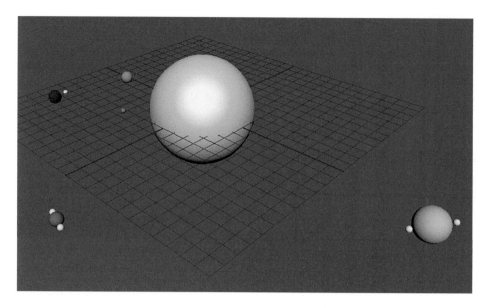

FIGURE 11.44 The Solar_System project is back!

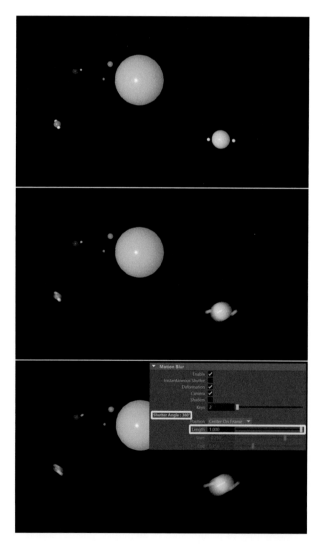

FIGURE 11.45 A render of frame 75 shows the planets in motion without motion blur (top); with motion blur (middle); and with a higher shutter angle (bottom).

7. Using motion blur adds to the noise of an image and can take longer to render. You can use Camera (AA) sampling values to increase the quality of the render.

Rendering in Layers and Arnold AOVs

Most of the time, it's best to composite different elements together to form a final CG image. Professional CG workflow almost always requires multiple render passes that are composited together later for the maximum efficiency and quality.

Maya does a great job of making rendering in layers much easier with render layers using the Render Setup window found in Windows ➢ Render Editors ➢ Render Setup. As you saw earlier in this book, using display layers helps a lot in keeping your scene organized. Render layers operate in basically the same way, although they function by separating different elements of the scene into separate renders. This is a fairly advanced and complicated workflow that will not be covered in this book but is mentioned for your information.

We will, however, cover basic Arnold AOV rendering, which breaks out a render into its different image components, such as isolating just the reflections for example. AOV stands for Arbitrary Output Variables, which is quite likely one of the least artist-friendly and confusing name for anything in the CG world. Autodesk, call me…

Creating AOVs

With AOVs, we are able to isolate the different components, or layers if you will, of an image to be able to re-assemble in an image editor like Adobe Photoshop or in a compositing application such as Adobe After Effects. This allows an artist to carefully adjust the look of an image without needing to re-render it in many cases, for example, in adjusting how prominent a reflection shows in the image without needing to lower the Reflectivity of a material and re-rendering the image in Arnold from scratch.

To see how AOVs work, follow these steps:

1. Set your project to the Lighting project down-loaded from the book's website. Open the scene file `still_life_Arnold_v03.ma` from the Scenes folder of the Lighting project.

2. Choose the camera1 view panel and start an interactive render in the Arnold RenderView. The image you see is called the Beauty image and is what you typically expect to see with a render.

3. Open the Render Settings window and choose the AOV tab as shown in Figure 11.46.

4. In the AOV Browser, on the left side under Available AOVs, scroll down and double-click on diffuse to add it to the right side under Active AOVs. The interactive render will re-render the frame, though you will not see any changes to the render.

5. Select the drop-down menu in the top left of the RenderView, and change it from Beauty to diffuse, as shown in Figure 11.47.

6. The RenderView now shows just that component of the render, showing the fruit and the wine bottle label with no reflections and the wine glasses, the bottle, and the table as flat black. This is the diffuse lighting, and since glass uses refraction and the metal table is purely metallic and therefore relies solely on

FIGURE 11.47 The diffuse AOV.

reflections for its color, these objects are not represented at all in the diffuse AOV.

7. Now let's add more AOV layers. In the left-side panel of Available AOVs, double-click on specular and transmission to add them to the diffuse AOV already in the Active AOVs list.

8. Your interactive render will update the image and make the new AOVs available in the pull-down menu. Select specular from the list and you will see the reflections in the glasses and the bottle, as well as the color of the gold metal table, as shown in Figure 11.48 (top). Select transmission from the drop-down menu to see the refractions in the wine glasses and bottle as shown in Figure 11.48 (bottom).

Compositing AOVs

When these AOV layers are saved as their own image files, they can be put back together to re-form the beauty image with an image-editing or compositing application, as mentioned before. Let's take a look at that process using these AOVs with Photoshop in the following steps:

1. Save the AOVs as image files by first selecting the AOV to view in the RenderView drop-down menu. Start with the diffuse by selecting it in the drop-down, and then in the RenderView menu bar select File ➤ Save Image. Navigate to the images folder of the Lighting project (if your project is set properly, it will take you there directly) and save the diffuse AOV as diffuseAOV.png. Make sure not to forget the ".png" in the name to tell RenderView to save it as a PNG image.

2. Select the specular AOV and repeat the above step to save it as specularAOV.png.

3. Select the transmission AOV and save it as transmissionAOV.png.

4. In Photoshop, open the diffuseAOV.png to begin the composition, as shown in Figure 11.49. You can alternatively use the images already provided in the images folder of the Lighting project called sampleDiffuse.png, sampleSpecular.png, and sampleTransmission.png.

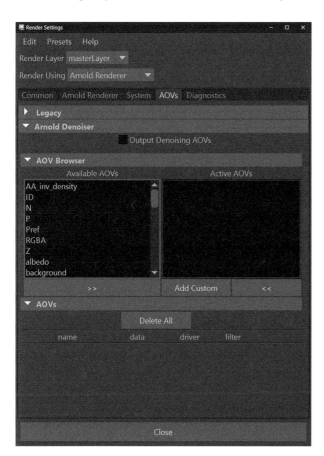

FIGURE 11.46 The AOV tab of the Render Settings window.

FIGURE 11.48 The specular AOV (top) and transmission AOV (bottom).

5. Now drag the specularAOV.png file from your file browser directly into and on top of the diffuseAOV.png image already open in Photoshop. This will create a new layer with the specular AOV on top, completely overtaking the diffuse image, as shown in Figure 11.50 (top).

6. We need to adjust the layering type so that this layer doesn't overtake the previous layer but adds on to it instead. In Photoshop's Layers tab in the lower right side of the interface, click to select Layer 1. Click on the Blending Mode drop-down menu as shown in Figure 11.51 and select Screen. Now the specular layer is properly composited on top of the diffuse layer as shown in Figure 11.50 (bottom).

7. Repeat steps 5 and 6 to bring in the transmissionAOV.png image and layer on top of the other two layers with a Blending Mode of Screen to result in a composited image that matches the beauty render from the RenderView in Maya as shown in Figure 11.52.

In this case, we manually saved each AOV as its own image file, but when batch rendering or, as we shall see in the next section, when sequence rendering, Maya and Arnold will output the AOVs in your scene as their own image sequences into the project's images folder.

This process of AOV rendering and compositing is shown in one of its simplest forms. As you create more intricate renders using more complex materials and lighting, rendering in AOVs becomes a more complex and intricate process, but is the foundation of professional rendering in many studio workflows.

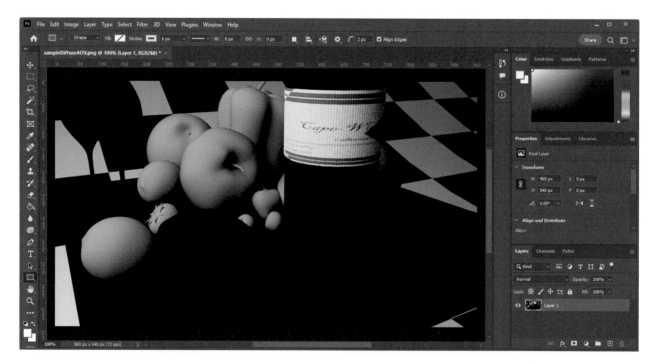

FIGURE 11.49 The diffuse AOV open in Photoshop.

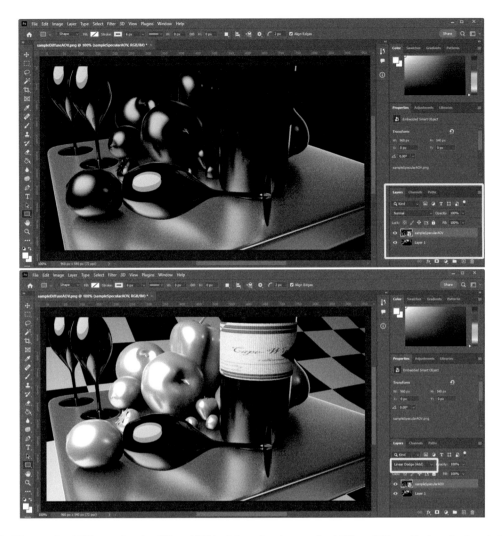

FIGURE 11.50   The specular AOV overtakes the diffuse AOV (top). Layering the specular AOV as additive adds the reflections to the diffuse layer underneath (bottom).

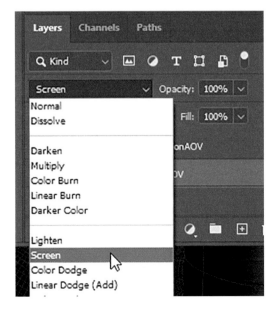

FIGURE 11.51   Change the Blending Mode in Photoshop.

Batch and Sequence Rendering with Arnold

Now that we have saved the AOV passes manually through the RenderView, let's render a short sequence of frames from the same scene. Feel free to use your own scene from the previous AOV exercise and add a slight camera movement from frame 1 to 12. You can also open the scene file still_life_Arnold_v04. mb from the scenes folder of the Lighting project. This file has the AOV setup from the previous exercise (with diffuse, specular, and transmission AOVs active) as well as a short 12-frame camera movement on camera1. Make sure you are set to the Lighting project before opening the scene to render out an image sequence in the following steps:

1. Open the Render Settings and choose the AOV tab. Make sure diffuse, specular, and transmission are in the Active AOVs list and that they are checked as shown in Figure 11.53.

2. In the Common tab, set the Frame/Animation ext: to name.#.ext. Set the Start frame to 1 and the End frame to 12. And set the Renderable Camera to camera1, as shown in Figure 11.54. Notice at the top of

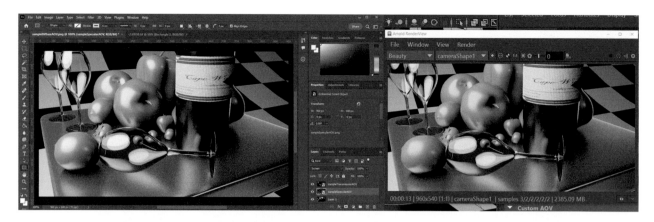

FIGURE 11.52   The re-assembled composite image in Photoshop (left) compared to the original Beauty image in the RenderView window (right).

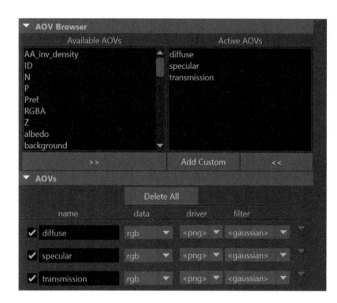

FIGURE 11.53   Make sure the AOVs are active.

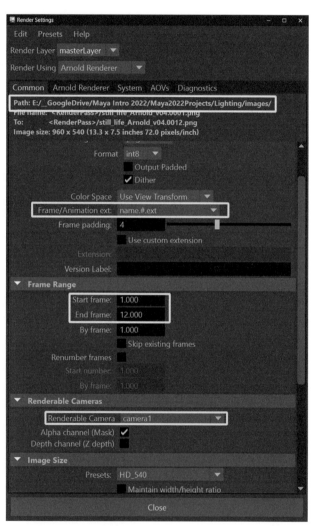

FIGURE 11.54   Choosing the proper settings.

the Render Settings where your images will go when rendered to verify that you've set your project properly before opening the scene.

3. This render will take a few minutes to complete. Go ahead and batch render as we did before. Open the Script Editor to monitor the render progress, as shown in Figure 11.55.

4. Once the render is complete, in a file browser, navigate to the images folder of the Lighting project and you will see four new folders, each for the beauty render and the three AOV passes that we activated.

As you can see, batch rendering the scene automatically organized the AOV passes and saved them into folders. In some older versions of Maya, however, batch rendering an Arnold scene may not work as expected. Due to licensing issues with previous Maya versions before Maya 2022, when batch rendering an Arnold scene produced a watermark on the rendered images. If this is the case, there is a second method of rendering a sequence called Render Sequence. This methodology outputs exactly the same as a batch render but bypasses

the licensing bug that watermarked renders in older Maya versions.

To use Render Sequence, you go through all the usual steps of setting up the render in the Render Settings, as we did in the previous example. But instead of choosing Render ➢ Batch Render as we did before, you would instead choose Render ➢ Render Sequence ❐ to open its options (Figure 11.56).

FIGURE 11.55 The Script Editor shows the render progress during a batch render.

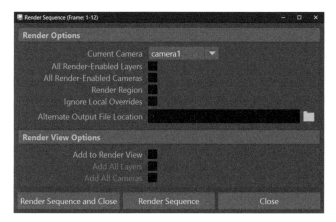

FIGURE 11.56 Render Sequence options

The Render Sequence options give you the ability to redirect where the rendered images are saved to, as well as camera choice to override what is selected in the Render Settings. Everything will be the same as before including the AOV folders, but this time, instead of working in the background as Batch Render does, this will render frame after frame directly in Maya's Render View window, letting you see each frame as it renders.

Canceling a Render Sequence is a bit annoying, however, and requires you to press the Escape key several times to skip each upcoming frame, or even force quitting Maya altogether. Therefore, and for many other reasons, it is always advisable to save your scene before starting any rendering, be it with batch or sequence rendering commands.

I have only begun to scratch the surface here. When you get the hang of rendering and as your CG needs begin to grow, you'll find a plethora of options when rendering with layers and rendering with AOVs through Arnold.

HDRI

An HDRI stands for high dynamic range imagery and is a term for an image that has an extended range of color and brightness information. Several photos at varying exposures are taken of the same subject; they range from very dark (low exposure), highlighting only the brightest parts of the scene, and go all the way up to very bright (overexposure), capturing the absolute darkest parts of the scene. When these images (usually five or seven images) are compiled into an HDR image, you get a fantastic range of bright to dark for that one subject all in one image file, more than what a typical image can hold.

How does this help you light? With image-based lighting (IBL), you can use real-world photography to create a fake environment in your scene. In Arnold, you use a Skydome light to that effect, on which you assign an image, most usually an HDRI. That environment sphere, much like the white dome of an Arnold Skydome light we used earlier in the book, uses the brightness and color values of its image to cast light in your Maya scene. And when a properly taken and calibrated HDRI is used, those values generate enough energy to light the scene as if that CG object were really in that photographed environment.

The best type of image to capture for IBL is sometimes called a *light probe*. This is a picture of an environment, such as the office reflected in a chrome ball shown on the left of Figure 11.57 or the stitched-together panoramic stills compiled into a map shown on the right of Figure 11.57. The stitched panoramic on the right of Figure 11.57 was photographed at four 90° angles using a fish-eye camera lens capable of capturing a field of view of close to 180° using a panoramic tripod attachment.

Figure 11.57 shows the middle exposure of five exposures taken of the office and one of the four angles of the living room. Figure 11.58 shows five images in the range from underexposed (dark) to overexposed (bright) photos that were used to compile the HDRIs shown here. You will use an HDRI made from the living-room panoramic photos to light the decorative box in the next section.

The living-room photos are taken at 90° intervals inside the living room and then stitched and compiled into an HDRI file using a photographic software package (shown in Figure 11.59). The HDRI file is called `livingRoomPanoramic.hdr` and is in the sourceimages folder of the Plane project from the book's web page for the next section's HDR

FIGURE 11.57 A light-probe photo of a desk is taken with a chrome ball (left) and a panoramic stitch (right).

FIGURE 11.58 Five exposures make up the HDRI of a desk using a chrome ball (left); and a living room using a panoramic stitch (right), which is to be used in the next section.

lighting exercise. You won't be able to see the extensive range of the HDR because most computer displays are limited to a display of 8-bit color.

The HDR will eventually be mapped onto an IBL sphere. This is a large sphere that surrounds the environment in your Maya scene, which in Arnold is usually a Skydome Light. The individual photos first need to be stitched together and converted to a rectangular image file, as shown in Figure 11.59. The full spherical panorama space captured in these photos and stitched together is laid out into a rectangular format that

is suitable to project onto a sphere in Maya, just as if a geographic map on a school room globe was unwrapped into a rectangular sheet of paper.

Software such as HDRShop, available online for free, allows you to combine multiple images into an HDR. The app PTGui (available for a demo online at `www.ptgui.com`), stitches panoramas and merges HDR images I won't get into the details of creating an HDRI because it's an advanced topic using Adobe Photoshop, PTGui, and/or other software; however, it's good to know the origins of HDR images and how they come to be used in an IBL.

And of course, if you haven't already searched the Internet for free HDRI, please have a go. There are resources such Poly Haven at https://polyhaven.com/hdris offer an assortment of HDR images that you can use in your renders. Finding a good environment is crucial to a lovely render, especially when a lot of reflections are expected, such as glass and metal.

You will use an HDRI to light a scene later in this chapter. And boy is it going to be fun.

Going Deeper into Arnold: Bump and Displacement Mapping

Before continuing with the lighting and rendering for the lamp and decorative box, let's first address a need for detailing just the box by itself. As we saw in Chapter 7, bump mapping can add surface detail to an otherwise flat surface. Look at the actual photo of the box in Chapter 3 (Figure 3.21) and compare it to the renders of the box in Chapter 10 (Figure 10.65); both are compared in Figure 11.60. You'll see that the carved details in the CG box need such surface detail. Let's start by taking a closer look at the box by itself.

1. Make sure your project is set to the Plane project. Open the file `planeLightingScene _ v05.ma` from the Plane project. An error may come up saying that the reference file cannot be found (if so, it will look like Figure 11.61). If that is the case, simply click Browse and navigate to where you have saved the Decorative_Box project's scenes folder, where you will find the scene file `boxDetail01.ma`. Otherwise, the scene should open with no issues. There is a copy of the `boxDetail01.ma` file in the scenes folder for the plane project as well. These things tend to happen and throw you for a loop, especially when first beginning CG. Try to keep your files

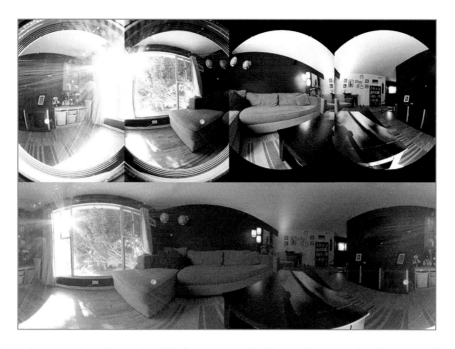

FIGURE 11.59   Fish-eye photos are taken at four angles of the living room, each with several exposures from light to dark (above). The fish-eye photos are then warped and stitched together using the handy software package PTGui and merged into an HDR image file (bottom).

organized (and backed up) and well-named, and that effort will greatly benefit your process.

2. Select the top node of the toy plane (planeGroup) and create a new display layer called **planeLayer**. Turn off visibility for the planeLayer.

3. In the Render Settings window, confirm you are using Arnold Renderer.

4. Use the persp camera (not the renderCam, it is locked) and the Arnold RenderView to line up a view of the box to match the box render shown in Figure 11.62.

5. In the render, please note the lack of definition in the box when compared to the real photo of the box.

6. Save your work!

In the current render, the grooves are flat and shiny, whereas, in the real box, they're carved into the wood and aren't as glossy as the rest of the box. In addition, the material seems flat. You will add definition to the model through textures next.

You can use the scene file `planeLightingScene_v06.ma` to catch up to this point or compare your camera angles.

Bump Mapping

Since we will be in Arnold, let's first assign an Arnold material to the box to replace the current Phong material.

1. With the RenderView interactive render running, select the box model and open the Hypershade. Click the Graph Materials icon ( ) and the `boxDetail02 phong1` material node that comes up. There is an image map connected to the Color of the phong material.

FIGURE 11.60   Comparing photo of the decorative box (top) to the latest render (bottom).

FIGURE 11.61   Oh no! Reference file not found!

FIGURE 11.62   The decorative box's current look when you finished the lighting in Chapter 10.

2. Move these icons to the side of the work area and create a new aiStandardSurface material. Arrange the nodes as shown in Figure 11.63 and then click+drag from the texture map boxColorMap02.jpg Out Color slot over to the aiStandardSurface's Base Color input slot.

3. Name the new material *box_aiStandard*. Move the hypershade to be side-by-side to the Arnold Renderview and with one eye, assign the *box_aiStandard* to the box mode, and with the other eye, watch the results in the RenderView. Bam! It should

immediately pop. That's not to say you couldn't get the old Phong material to look more like this (shout-out to the old school). It just means the aiStandardSurface is calibrated at a better starting point. A huge difference is the addition of the Fresnel effect on the surface; whereby the reflections in the box are more complex than those in the Phong render (Figure 11.64).

4. Rotate the persp view to look around the box in the RenderView and settle looking up at the front corner of the box as shown in Figure 11.65, so that one of the area lights glares across the surface (a.k.a. specular reflection).

5. Notice that the surface of the box appears flat and evenly reflective. Select the box_aiStandard material and in the Hypershade, tighten the reflections by decreasing the specular Roughness to 0.1 and the IOR to 1.3.

6. We need to add surface definition to the carvings by trying a texture map that isolates just the carvings, as shown in Figure 11.66, which shows the box's color map side-by-side with a black-and-white map that shows only the carved regions of the box. This map was created with elbow grease and hard work to

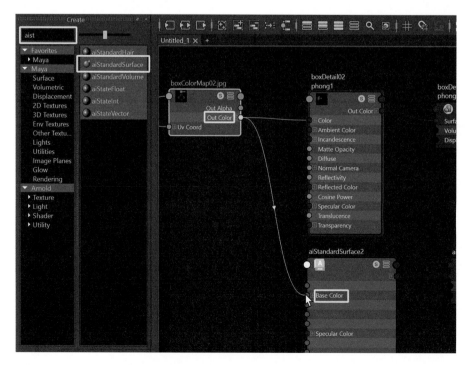

FIGURE 11.63   Connect the box's texture image to the new Arnold material.

FIGURE 11.64 The aiStandardSurface already looks better.

FIGURE 11.65 The surface of the box looks flat.

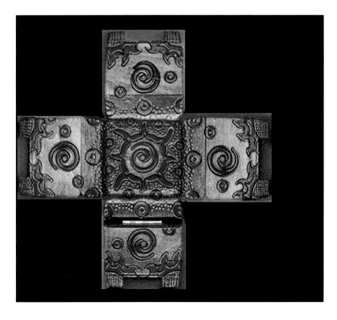 

FIGURE 11.66 The black-and-white map on the right shows only the carved areas of the box.

manually isolate just the carved areas of the box in Photoshop. See how much I do for you?

7. Import the black-and-white carving map by selecting the file `boxCarvings.jpg` in the sourceimages folder of the Plane project in your file browser, and then drag it into the Hypershade directly. Maya creates a File texture node and imports the map.

8. Select the box_aiStandard in the Hypershade, open the Geometry section in the Property Editor, and use the MMB to drag the boxCarvings.jpg file texture node to the Bump Mapping attribute, as shown in Figure 11.67. This creates an intermediary node (bump2d1) which controls the bump, as we've seen in Chapter 7. It also creates a rubber-band connection in the Hypershade to the box_aiStandard icon's Normal Camera input socket.

9. Check your RenderView interactive render and you will see carvings in the surface, but they don't look

good and show artifacts and noise. The bump is too much. Select the bump2d1 node and reduce the Bump Depth to a very low 0.02, and the carvings will look much nicer, but perhaps a bit too glossy (Figure 11.68).

10. Experiment with the specular Roughness a little bit now that we have further surface definition. A value around 0.2 works well.

One thing that doesn't look perfect is the silhouette of the decorative box. The bump map, while looks pretty good at a fairly close distance, the outside silhouette of the box does not look carved. Figure 11.69 shows an edge of the box, and the carvings are still flat. Bump maps do not alter the surface of a geometry, they only *appear* to do so, as we discussed in Chapter 7. Instead, we need to use a displacement map for that added layer of detail.

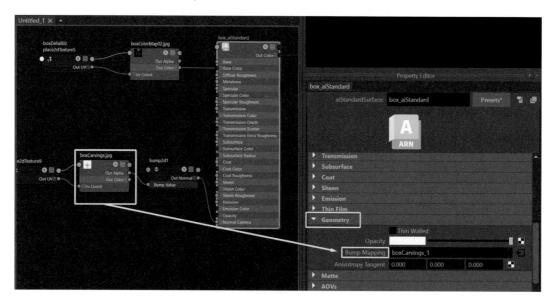

FIGURE 11.67 MMB drag the boxCarving file node to the Bump Mapping attribute.

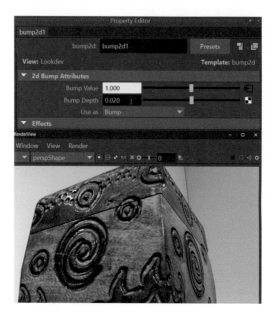

FIGURE 11.68 The carvings are looking nicer.

HYPERSHADE

Keep in mind that you are primarily using the Hypershade's Property Editor in Attribute Editor mode and not Lookdev mode. Lookdev mode (on the left in the following image) shows only some of the attributes for the selected node in the Hypershade, while the Attribute Editor mode (on the right in the following image) shows all of the node's attributes almost exactly like the Attribute Editor itself. See Chapter 3 for more on the Hypershade.

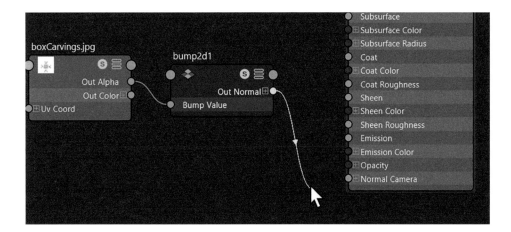

FIGURE 11.69   Disconnect the bump map.

Displacement Mapping

Now that we've seen how the bump map looks, you'll use the same image map to create displacements in the box instead of the bump, to better sink the carvings into the box. Isn't that convenient?

1. Disconnect the `bump2d1` node by clicking and dragging the connective rubber-band away from the Normal Camera input socket as shown in Figure 11.69 or by deleting the node itself.

2. Connected to the right of the box_aiStandard material is the Shading Group node called `aiStandardSurface2SG` (yours may be named slightly differently, such as with `1SG`). Select this node to access the displacement mapping for the box's material. If you don't see any such Shading Group node, select the `box _ aiStandard` material and click

   the Input and Output Connections icon (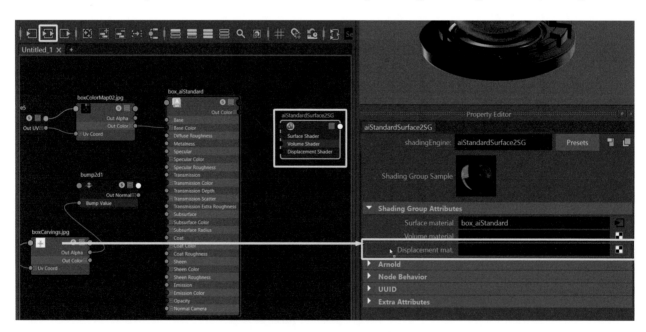) in the Hypershade as shown in Figure 11.70. Maya creates a new node called displacementShader1 in the Hypershade to control the displacement map.

3. Your interactive render in the RenderView will explode the box. The displacement map is too much. Select the new node `displacementShader1` and reduce the Scale to 0.05. The box looks bloated and larger than before. This is because the white parts of a displacement map cause displacement while black areas do not. Our carvings map is white on the flat surface and black in the carvings.

4. We need to invert the carving map to have white inside the carvings and black where the surface of the box is flat. Select the `boxCarvings.jpg` node in the Hypershade and in its Property Editor, check to make sure you are not in Lookdev mode.

If you are, click the toggle ( ) icon as shown in Figure 11.71.

5. Scroll down and open the Effects section and check the Invert checkbox to invert this map to white carvings on black background. The box will return to normal size in the RenderView, but the carvings will stick out instead of carving into the surface (Figure 11.72).

6. Select the `displacementShader1` node and set the Scale to −0.03 and the box looks better with proper carvings in the wood that will affect the geometry and the silhouette of the object, where the bump map could not. The negative number causes the white areas of the map (the carvings) to displace the surface geometry inward instead of outward (Figure 11.73).

Occasionally when you click to view the input and output of a shader as you did in step 3, the Hypershade will put some nodes on top of others. If you don't see any of the nodes, try clicking and dragging some of the nodes around in the Hypershade to see whether there are any accidentally hidden nodes. These little touches make Maya extra fun!

Save your work and compare it to the `planeLightingScene _ v07.ma` scene file. All the work we just did on the decorative box in the Plane's lighting scene applies to the box in just this scene. Since the box is being referenced into the scene, it will override the original material settings in the box's original Maya file that we referenced into the scene. This is one of the great strengths of using references, the original model

FIGURE 11.70 MMB drag the map to the Displacement mat. for the Shading Group node.

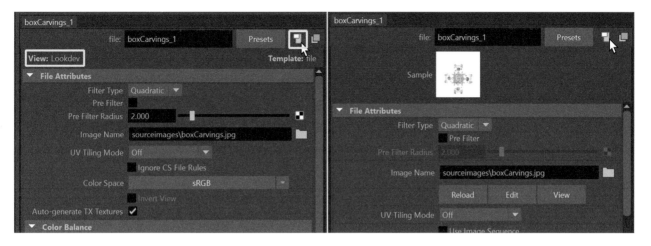

FIGURE 11.71 Toggle out of Lookdev mode, which can omit certain properties of a material or texture node and cause confusion. Autodesk, call me.

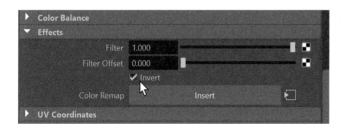

FIGURE 11.72 Invert the carvings map.

FIGURE 11.73 The box's carvings are now from the displacement mapping.

Rendering the Scene with Arnold

You're all grown up and ready to light a full scene using some advanced materials, an HDRI, and regular lights to get the best bang for your buck out of Arnold rendering. In the previous chapter, you quickly lit the plane, candle, and decorative box with key, fill, and rim lights (the three-point lighting system). In this exercise, you'll take this concept a few steps further and change the scene to best use Arnold, so take a deep breath, call your mother and tell her you love her, and let's get started!

Continue with your own scene file, or make sure your project is set to the Plane project and open the `planeLighting-Scene _ v07.ma` file from the scenes folder. Remember that you turned off the plane's display layer earlier and focused the persp camera on the box, so the plane will not be seen when you load this file. Turn on the `planeLayer` display layer to see the toy plane. This scene has the lights created in Chapter 10 and is set to render through Arnold already.

Render a frame from the renderCam camera view in the Arnold RenderView (Figure 11.74).

We can't just leave the box with improved materials. In the following steps, we will replace the plane's and candle's materials with the aiStandardSurface.

file remains untouched, so if it is also being used elsewhere, it will continue to have its original Phong material without any of this mapping. However, whenever you open this plane lighting scene file, it will apply these changes to the box model being referenced in.

You can open the original scene file `boxDetail01.ma` in the scenes folder of the Decorative_Box or Plane projects to check, they are untouched. If, however, you want this box to always be imported or referenced into any scene with the box_aiStandard and the displacement map, you would need to make these changes to the original scene file for the decorative box `boxDetail01.ma`.

You'll next add an HDR image you saw earlier in this chapter to the scene next.

FIGURE 11.74 The plane scene with the improved box.

1. Select the yellow body of the plane and display its material in the HyperShade with the Graph Materials icon ( ). It is a Blinn from the olden days named `yellow` using a yellow noise texture map for its color.

2. Create a new aiStandardSurface and name it `yellow_aiStandard`. Connect the Out Color from the noiseYellow texture to the `yellow_aiStandard` Base Color input socket as shown in Figure 11.75.

3. Since the original `yellow` Blinn material is assigned to several objects in the scene, you can either select all of the geometry for the yellow plane manually or right-click on the yellow Blinn material and choose Select Objects with Materials from the marking menu, as shown in Figure 11.76.

4. With all those yellow plastic parts selected, assign them to the new material by right-clicking on the `yellow_aiStandard` material and selecting Assign Material to Viewport Selection. Make sure you right-click on the material and not left-click as that will select the material and unselect all the plane's yellow parts that we selected in the previous step.

5. Your interactive render will show a nicer yellow plastic already. Select the `yellow_aiStandard` material and set the specular Roughness to 0.4 and the specular Weight to 0.7 for a less glossy plastic.

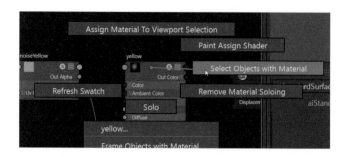

FIGURE 11.76 Selecting all the geometry assigned to this yellow Blinn material.

6. Select one of the gray parts of the plane and graph its materials in the Hypershade as we did in step 1 to see the `gray` Blinn.

7. Repeat steps 2–4 for a new gray Arnold shader we'll name `gray_aiStandard` to assign to all the plane's gray parts.

8. Set the specular Weight of the gray_aiStandard to 0.8 and the specular Roughness to 0.25 for a slightly shinier gray plastic than the yellow plastic. Feel free to experiment and settle for your own values for these plastic materials.

9. Repeat the process in steps 2–4 to create an aiStandardSurface material for the desk with a specular Roughness of 0.1 to make a nice, polished table top. Figure 11.77 shows the results of our work so far. If you compare with earlier renders of the scene (such as Figure 10.48 in Chapter 10), the plastic will look more natural.

Materials for the Candle

And now for the candle. We'll start with the glass in the following steps. Start an interactive render in the Arnold RenderView.

1. Select the glass lid for the candle jar and show its material (a Phong called `candleGlass`) in the Hypershade. There are no maps to worry about.

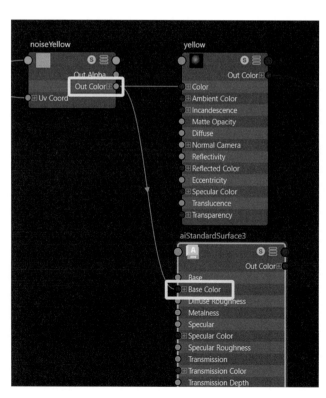

FIGURE 11.75 Connect the yellow texture to the new Arnold material.

FIGURE 11.77 We have replaced the plastic and table top materials with aiStandardSurface materials.

FIGURE 11.78 The glass jar looks so much nicer.

2. Create a new aiStandardSurface and name it glass_aiStandard, and assign it to the glass parts of the jar. Set the specular Roughness to 0.05.

3. In the Transmission section, set the transmission Weight to 1.0. The glass immediately looks much nicer than before in the RenderView.

4. Create a new aiStandardSurface and name it white_aiStandard. Select the solid white plastic insert inside the glass lid and assign the new material to it.

5. In the white_aiStandard properties, set the transmission Weight to 0.95 and the specular Roughness to 0.4 for a sheer white soft plastic look. Figure 11.78 shows the progress so far.

6. In Figure 11.78, notice that the white soft plastic ring inside the glass lid has a lot of noise in it. Open the Render Settings window and in the Arnold Renderer tab, turn up the Transmission samples from 2 to 3.

The render will take longer to resolve to final quality, but will look much nicer for the jar. Feel free to set Transmission samples back to 2 or lower to speed up your interactive render tests until you're ready for a final render.

Subsurface Scattering

Subsurface Scattering is when light penetrates into and/or through an object's material, bounces around inside (scattering), and comes back out the surface, like shining a flashlight through your finger reveals a bright red glow inside your finger.

1. Select the wax candle object itself. It has a dark red Blinn assigned. Replaced it with a new aiStandardSurface with a similar shade of red on the base Color and call the material wax_aiStandard.

2. Wax materials in CG can benefit from having Subsurface properties. Select the wax_aiStandard material and in the Hypershade's Property Editor, at the top, click on Presets*, select wax ➤ Replace.

3. This will set up the material to have subsurface properties by adjusting various Transmission values including Weight, Color, and Scatter as well as adjusting the base color values for Color and Weight as well. It has turned the candle pink, but the RenderView should show a more natural wax.

4. To augment any subsurface effect, it's not a bad idea to backlight that object. Using the persp window, insert a new Arnold Area light with an Intensity of 75 behind the candle as shown in Figure 11.79.

FIGURE 11.79 The candle has turned pink!

5. Let's see what the wax preset changed and get the candle closer to its original red color without losing the subtle effect of the subsurface scattering. Select the `wax _ aiStandard` material. The Base Color is now pink. Change that color to a darker red as we originally had. One cool trick with Subsurface effects is to have a contrast between the Base Color (dark red) and the Transmission Color and Transmission Scatter colors (both pink). Notice in Figure 11.80 that the right side of the candle wax is more pink than the left side, due to the backlighting from the new area light from the previous step.

6. Candle wax looks nice. Feel free to experiment with the Transmission Color and Transmission Scatter Color to find a coloration you prefer.

7. Now that we have the wax looking nice, let's add a subtlety to the jar's glass. Select the glass_aiStandard, and in the Transmission section, set the Dispersion Abbe* to 5. The glass of the jar now has a little rainbow effect in some of its parts as the refraction is now being dispersed, creating a chromatic aberration. Note, however, that your render times increase appreciably. Compare Figure 11.80 with Figure 11.81.

Lastly, there are still slight vertical stripes in the render where the wax meets the glass of the jar. The two geometries are

FIGURE 11.81 The jar's glass has a slight rainbow effect due to chromatic aberration in the refraction.

FIGURE 11.80 The wax looks great with the backlighting!

matched exactly, the outside of the wax perfectly meets the inside of the glass. To get a great look with an object inside a glass vessel like a wax candle in a jar or drink inside a glass, it's best to have that inside geometry be ever-so-slightly larger inside the glass container. This way the outside of the wax penetrates the inside of the glass jar very slightly, creating a much nicer refraction.

Select the wax object and scale it to 1.005 in all three axes. Compare the render shown in Figure 11.81 with Figure 11.82 where the wax object is slightly larger, penetrating slightly into the glass jar's geometry, creating a more realistic refraction.

You can compare your work to the `planeLighting-Scene _ v08.ma` scene file from the Scenes folder of the Plane project.

Adding an HDR

Here's where things get fun. You'll add an HDR image to the scene to give the scene more of an environment to reflect.

1. In your own scene or the `planeLightingS-cene _ v08.ma` scene, start an interactive render in the Arnold RenderView. This scene has the Transmission Sampling turned down to 2 (from 3 before) for a faster rendering).

FIGURE 11.82 Creating a better refraction of the wax inside the glass jar.

2. Choose Arnold ➤ Lights ➤ Skydome Light to create a skydome light in the scene. Your render will get very bright.

3. With the Skydome selected, click the mapping icon next to Color as shown in Figure 11.83 and choose File in the Create Render Node window that pops up.

4. The Attribute Editor shows the new file node created. Click the folder icon ( ) next to Image Name and navigate to the sourceimages folder of the Plane project on your system and select the file living-RoomPanoramic.hdr.

5. Notice the lighting comes down from the bright render before and now you can see new reflections in the table and glass. Experiment with rotating the Skydome light to position the reflections to taste, as shown in Figure 11.84.

Figure 11.85 shows the rendering of this scene with higher sampling rates. Look, you're done!

If you need to prevent the HDR image from showing up in the background of your renders, select the Skydome light, and, in the Attribute Editor under the Visibility heading, set the Camera value to 0.0, and the HDR image will not render in the background of your scene.

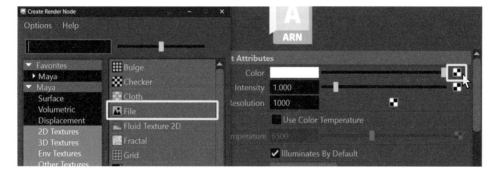

FIGURE 11.83 Click to create a map for the Skydome's Color.

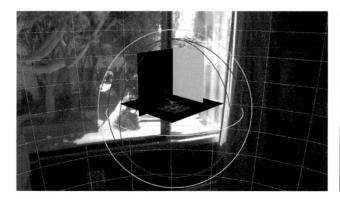

FIGURE 11.84 The Skydome light with an HDR image applied.

FIGURE 11.85 Rendering of the completed plane scene!

Adding Depth of Field

Wait, did I say we completed the plane lighting scene? Well, maybe not. Such a liar! One last item of interest is adding a depth of field (DOF) to the image. This effect adds blur to the render for the areas of the image that may be out of the lens's focal depth. It can greatly add to the photorealism of a rendered image.

Select the renderCam and open the Attribute Editor. In the Arnold heading, check the Enable DOF attribute. Set Focus Distance to **12** (the number of units from the camera to where you want the camera to focus) and set Aperture Size to **0.25**. The Aperture Size setting, like a real lens, sets how much is in focus around the focal distance. With a higher value, the focus runs deeper than with a low value. As you adjust your Focus Distance attribute, you can see the blurriness in the Arnold RenderView.

To determine what the Focus Distance should be, you can count the number of units from the front of the camera to the object to be in focus, or to be more precise, you can use Maya's Distance Tool.

1. In the scene, choose Create ➤ Measure Tools ➤ Distance Tool. Your cursor changes to a plus symbol.

2. Click on Snap to Points as shown in Figure 11.86 (top) and click on the front of the camera to snap a locator to the camera's lens.

3. Next, click on the front of the propeller to snap a second locator to the propeller of the plane. A distance is then shown between the two locators, as shown in Figure 11.86 (bottom). This verifies that a Focus Distance of 12 for the camera is good for showing the propeller in focus.

4. Experiment with the Aperture Size attribute to change how strong the out-of-focus areas appear in the render.

Figure 11.87 shows the final render of the scene with DOF enabled. Your render times will be longer and if you want a better render than this one, which has some grain, especially in the glass candle jar, you'll need to increase your Camera (AA) and Specular sampling values in the Render Setting's Arnold Renderer tab. This render can take quite some time, though, especially with Depth of Field and chromatic aberration in the glass. Figure 11.87 took 50 minutes to render on a top-tier 12th-generation Intel i9-based workstation PC at half HD resolution, but with a noise in the depth of field on the candle, so it had quite high sampling rates, which warmed up my office by about 10°!

The scene `planeLightingScene _ v09.ma` from the scenes folder in the Plane project will take you to this point.

Notice from the render that the back of the toy plane is thrown out of focus, along with the candle, decorative box, and back walls. Experiment with varying focus distance and Aperture Size values to try different looks for your scene.

Lighting, rendering, and shading all go hand in hand, and as you can see from the previous exercise, you have to go back and forth to best achieve the look you want.

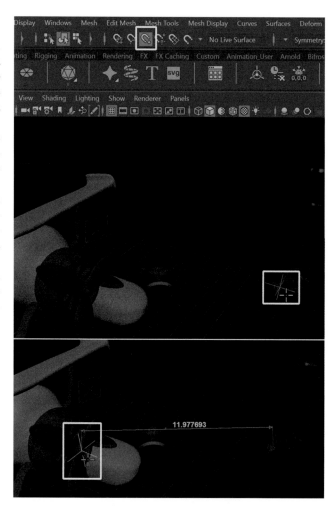

FIGURE 11.86 Snap a locator to the front of the camera.

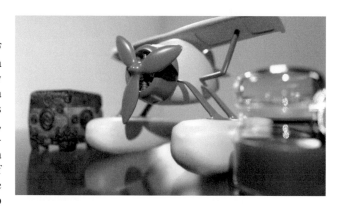

FIGURE 11.87 The propeller is in focus! Now you're finished!

Depending on the need and the size of the render, you'll have to set the sampling levels to suit your needs—but be warned that your rendering times will dramatically increase, easily tripling depending on the quality settings. There are several ways to create DOF in a render that are faster or more controllable than what I've covered here. You can render out a depth pass to use with a lens filter in a compositing package such as Nuke or After Effects to keep render times down.

For an interesting challenge, take a photo in your house; render the plane, candle, and box to match the lighting in the photo; and then composite the render against your photo.

Summary

In this chapter, you learned how to set up your scene for rendering. Starting with the Render Settings window and moving on to the different render engines available, you learn how to render your scene for a particular look. Then, I covered how to preview your render and how to use the Arnold RenderView for fast scene feedback. I moved on to cover how to render reflections and refractions, how to create and use cameras, and how to render with motion blur. You tested your skill on a wine bottle scene, and to batch-render it out into a sequence of images, you checked it in a program like FCheck. You also used Arnold AOVs to make your renders easier to control in compositing. Finally, you applied this knowledge to rendering the toy plane, a glass candle holder, and the decorative box using Arnold and an HDR of a living room.

Getting to this point in a scene can take some work, but when you see the results playing back on your screen, all the work seems more than worth it. Always allow enough time to ensure that your animations render properly and at their best quality. Most beginners seriously underestimate the time needed to complete this step properly in CG production.

After you create numerous scenes and render them, you'll begin to understand how to construct your next scenes so that they render better and faster. Be sure to keep on top of your file management—rendering can produce an awful lot of files, and you don't want to have them scattered all over the place.

12

Autodesk® Maya® Dynamics and Effects

Learning Outcomes

In this chapter, you will be able to

Create rigid body dynamic objects and create forces to act upon them

Keyframe animated passive rigid bodies to act on active rigid bodies

Bake out simulations to keyframes and simplify animation curves

Understand nParticle workflow

Emit nParticles and have them move and render to simulate steam

Draw Paint Effects strokes

Create and manipulate an nCloth object

Collide nObjects and add forces and dynamic constraints

Cache your nDynamics to disk

Customize the Maya interface

An Overview of Maya Dynamics

Dynamics is simulating motion by applying the principles of physics. Rather than assigning keyframes to objects to animate them, with Maya dynamics you assign physical characteristics that define how an object behaves in a simulated world. You create the objects as usual in Maya, and then you convert them to *nCloth* objects, which can be rigid objects or soft objects like cloth. Rigid dynamics, where the surface of a dynamic object does not deform, are fairly easy to set up and play around with in Maya, especially when using the Legacy Rigid Body Dynamics system that Maya retains. You will take a quick look at that later in this chapter.

Dynamic objects, whether particles or objects that are rigid or deforming (like cloth), are affected by external forces called *fields*, which exert a force on them to create motion. Fields can range from wind forces to gravity and can have their own specific effects on dynamic bodies.

In Maya, dynamic objects are categorized as nCloth, nParticles, nHair, Legacy Rigid Bodies, Maya Fluids, and Bifrost liquid simulation. nCloth are meshes created in Maya that have varying degrees of rigidity, so you can create solid objects (and hence avoid using Legacy Rigid Bodies) as well as cloth objects. *nParticles* are points in space that have renderable properties and are used for numerous effects, such as fire and smoke. I'll cover nParticle basics in the latter half of this chapter. *nHair* consists of curves that behave dynamically, such as strings. *Fluids* are, in

essence, volumetric particles that can exhibit surface properties. You can use fluid dynamics for natural effects such as billowing clouds or plumes of smoke. Bifrost is a liquid simulation that allows you to create animations such as pouring water.

Nucleus is a stable and interactive engine for calculating dynamic simulations in Maya and is the basis for all the nDynamic objects mentioned earlier (except for Bifrost).

I'll introduce nCloth and nParticles later in this chapter; however, soft bodies, nHair, Bifrost, and fluid dynamics are advanced topics and won't be covered in this book.

Rigid Bodies

Rigid bodies are now a legacy feature in Maya that deal with the dynamics of solid objects, such as a pair of dice or a baseball. Fields and collisions affect the entire object and move it accordingly. I will provide a brief look into them because this legacy system is still a little simpler to implement than using nCloth for rigid objects, at least in my view.

Creating Active and Passive Rigid Body Objects

Any surface geometry in Maya can be converted to a rigid body. After it's converted, that surface can respond to the effects of fields and take part in collisions. Sounds like fun, eh?

The two types of legacy rigid bodies are active and passive. An *active rigid body* is affected by collisions and fields. A *passive rigid body* isn't affected by fields and remains still when it collides with another object. A passive rigid body is used as a surface against which active rigid bodies collide.

As an example, let's create a bouncing ball using Maya rigid bodies. Switch to the FX menu set and follow these steps:

1. Create a polygonal plane and scale it to be a ground surface.

2. Create a poly sphere and position it a number of units above the ground, as shown in Figure 12.1.

3. Make sure you're in the FX menu set (choose FX from the Status line's drop-down bar). Select the poly sphere and choose Fields/Solvers ➤ Create Active Rigid Body. The sphere's Translate and Rotate attributes turn yellow. There will be a dynamic input for those attributes, so you can't set keyframes on any of them.

4. Select the ground plane and choose Fields/Solvers ➤ Create Passive Rigid Body. Doing so sets the poly plane as the floor. For this exercise, stick with the default settings and ignore the various creation options and Rigid Body attributes.

DOI: 10.1201/9780429490958-13

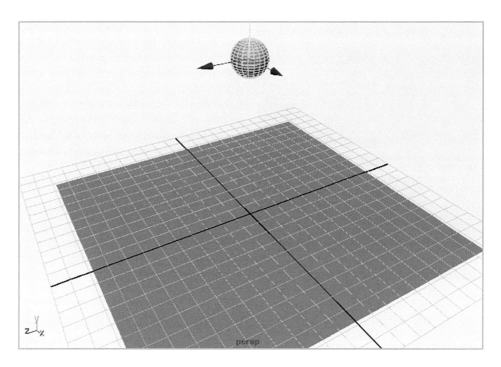

FIGURE 12.1   Place a poly sphere a few units above a poly plane ground surface.

5. To put the ball into motion, you need to create a field to affect it. Select the sphere and choose Fields/Solvers ➤ Gravity. By selecting the active rigid objects while you create the field, you connect that field to the objects automatically. Fields affect only the active rigid bodies to which they're connected. If you hadn't established this connection initially, you could still do so later, through the Dynamic Relationships Editor. You'll find out more about this process later in this chapter.

If you try to scrub the timeline, you'll notice that the animation doesn't run properly. Because dynamics simulates physics, no keyframes are set. You must play the scene from start to finish for the calculations to execute properly. You must also play the scene using the Play Every Frame option. Click the Animation Preferences button to the right of the Range slider, or choose Windows ➤ Settings/Preferences ➤ Preferences. In the Preferences window, choose Time Slider under the Settings header. Choose Play Every Frame from the Playback Speed menu. You can also set the maximum frames per second that your scene will play back by setting the Max Playback Speed attribute.

To play back the simulation, set your frame range from 1 to at least 240. Go to frame 1 and click Play. Make sure you have the proper Playback Speed settings in your Preferences window; otherwise, the simulation won't play properly.

When the simulation plays, you'll notice that the sphere begins to fall after a few frames and collides with the ground plane, bouncing back up.

As an experiment, try turning the passive body plane into an active body using the following steps:

1. Select the plane and open the Attribute Editor.
2. In the rigidBody2 tab, select the Active check box. This switches the plane from a passive body to an active body.
3. Play the simulation. The ball falls to hit the plane and knock it away. Because the plane is now an active body, it's moved by collisions. But because it isn't connected to the gravity field, it doesn't fall with the ball.

To connect the now-active body plane to the gravity field, open the Dynamic Relationships Editor window, shown in Figure 12.2 (choose Windows ➤ Relationship Editors ➤ Dynamic Relationships).

On the left is an Outliner list of the objects in your scene. On the right is a list from which you can choose a category of objects to list: Fields (default), Collisions, Emitters, or All. Select the geometry (pPlane1) on the left side and then connect it to the gravity field by selecting the gravityField1 node on the right.

When you connect the gravity field to the plane and run the simulation, you'll see the plane fall away with the ball. Because the two fall at the same rate (the rate set by the single gravity field), they don't collide. To disconnect the plane from the gravity field, deselect the gravity field in the right panel.

FIGURE 12.2 The Dynamic Relationships Editor window.

You can also connect a dynamic object to a field by selecting the dynamic object or objects and then the desired field and choosing Fields/Solvers ➤ Assign To Selected. This method is more useful for connecting multiple dynamic objects to a field.

Turning the active body plane back to a passive floor is as simple as returning to frame 1, the beginning of the simulation, and clearing the Active attribute in the Attribute Editor. By turning the active body back to a passive body, you regain an immovable floor upon which the ball can collide and bounce.

RELATIONSHIP EDITORS

The relationship editors, such as the Dynamic Relationships Editor window, let you connect two nodes to create a special relationship. With the Dynamic Relationships Editor window, you connect dynamic attributes so that fields, particles, and rigid bodies can interact in a simulation. Another example of a relationship editor is the Light Linking window mentioned in Chapter 10, "Autodesk® Maya® Lighting," which allows you to connect lights to geometry so that they light only a specific object or objects. These are fairly advanced topics; however, as you learn more about Maya, their use will become integral in your workflow.

Moving a Rigid Body

Because the Maya dynamics engine controls the movement of any active rigid bodies, you can't set keyframes on their translation or rotation. With a passive object, however, you can set keyframes on translation and rotation as you can with any other Maya object. You can also easily keyframe an object to turn either active or passive. For instance, in the earlier

bouncing ball example, you could animate the rotation of the passive body ground plane to roll the ball around on it.

Any movement that the passive body has through regular keyframe animation is translated into momentum, which is passed on to any active rigid bodies with which the passive body collides. Think of a baseball bat that strikes a baseball. The bat is a passive rigid body that you have keyframed to swing. The baseball is an active rigid body that is hit by (collides with) the bat as it swings. The momentum of the bat is transferred to the ball, and the ball is sent flying into the stadium stands. You'll see an example of this in action in the next exercise.

Rigid Body Attributes

Here is a rundown of the more important attributes for both passive and active rigid bodies as they pertain to collisions:

Mass
Sets the relative mass of the rigid body. Set on active or passive rigid bodies, *mass* is a factor in how much momentum is transferred from one object to another. A more massive object pushes a less massive one with less effort and is itself less prone to movement when hit. Mass is relative, so if all rigid bodies have the same mass value, there is no difference in the simulation.

Static and Dynamic Friction Sliders
Set how much friction the rigid body has while at rest (static) and while in motion (dynamic). *Friction* specifies how much the object resists moving or being moved. A friction of 0 makes the rigid body move freely, as if on ice.

Bounciness
Specifies how resilient the body is upon collision. The higher the *bounciness* value, the more bounce the object has upon collision.

Damping
Creates a drag on the object in dynamic motion so that it slows down over time. The higher the *damping*, the more the body's motion diminishes.

Initial Velocity
Gives the rigid body an initial push to move it in the corresponding axis.

Initial Spin
Gives the rigid body object an initial twist to start the rotation of the object in that axis.

Impulse Position
Gives the object a constant push in that axis. The effect is cumulative; the object will accelerate if the impulse isn't turned off.

Spin Impulse

Rotates the object constantly in the desired axis. The spin will accelerate if the impulse isn't turned off.

Center of Mass (0, 0, 0)

Places the center of the object's mass at its pivot point, typically at its geometric center. This value offsets the center of mass, so the rigid body object behaves as if its center of balance is offset, like trick dice or a top-weighted ball.

Creating animation with legacy rigid bodies is straightforward and can go a long way toward creating natural-looking motion for your scene. Integrating such animation into a final project can become fairly complicated, though, so it's prudent to become familiar with the workings of rigid body dynamics before relying on that sort of workflow for an animated project.

Here are a few suggestions for scenes using rigid body dynamics:

Bowling Lane

The bowling ball is keyframed as a passive object until it hits the active rigid pins at the end of the lane. This scene is simple to create and manipulate.

Dice

Active rigid dice are thrown into a passive rigid craps table. This exercise challenges your dynamics abilities as well as your modeling skills if you create an accurate craps table.

Game of Marbles

This scene challenges your texturing and rendering abilities as well as your dynamics abilities as you animate marbles rolling into each other.

Rigid Body Dynamics: Shoot the Catapult!

Now for a fun exercise—you'll use rigid body dynamics to shoot a projectile with the already animated catapult from Chapter 8. Open the scene file `catapult_anim_v2.mb` from the Catapult_Anim project downloaded from the companion website.

1. For the projectile, create a polygon sphere and place it above the basket, as shown in Figure 12.3.

   Since dynamics takes a lot of calculations, to make things easier you will create an invisible object to be the passive rigid body collider instead of the existing geometry of the basket itself. This is a frequent workflow in dynamics, where proxy geometry (often hidden) is used to alleviate calculations and speed up the scene.

2. Create another poly sphere with Axis Divisions and Height Divisions both set to **40**.

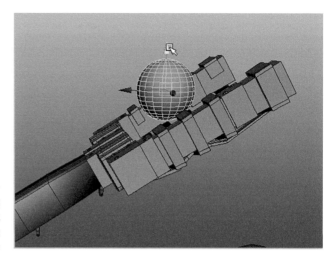

FIGURE 12.3 Place a sphere over the basket.

FIGURE 12.4 It puts the sphere in the basket, or else it gets the hose again.

3. Select the top-half faces of the sphere and delete them to create a bowl and place it over the catapult basket, as shown in Figure 12.4. Use the D key along with Point Snaps to place the bowl's pivot point on the top rim of the bowl, also shown in Figure 12.4.

   The animation of the catapult arm is driven by a Bend deformer, so simply placing and grouping the bowl to the basket will not work. You will use a point on poly constraint to rivet the bowl to a vertex on the arm.

4. Select the vertex shown in Figure 12.5; then Shift+select the bowl object. In the Animation menu set, choose Constrain ➢ Point On Poly. The bowl will snap to the arm, as shown in Figure 12.6.

5. Select the bowl and, in the Channel Box, click the pSphere2_pointOnPolyConstraint1 node. Set Offset Rotate Y to **−90** and Offset Rotate X to **8** to place the bowl in the basket better (Figure 12.7).

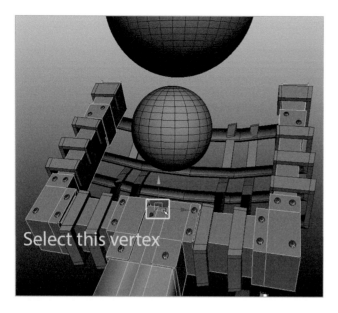

FIGURE 12.5 Select the vertex.

FIGURE 12.6 The bowl snaps to the arm at a weird angle.

FIGURE 12.7 Set offsets to place the bowl properly in the basket.

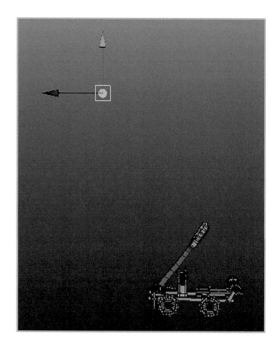

FIGURE 12.8 The ball shoots!

6. Go into the FX menu set. Select the projectile sphere and at frame 1 of the animation choose Fields/ Solvers ➤ Gravity. The ball will instantly become an active rigid body and will have a gravity attached. If you play back your scene, the ball will simply fall through the bowl and catapult.

7. Select the bowl object and choose Fields/Solvers ➤ Create Passive Rigid Body to make the bowl a collision surface for the projectile ball. Play back your scene and *bam*! The projectile will bounce into the bowl as the catapult arm bends back, and the catapult will shoot the ball out, as shown in Figure 12.8.

8. Select the bowl object and press Ctrl+H to hide it. Now when you play back your scene, the ball looks like it rests inside the catapult basket. The scene file `catapult _ dynamics _ v1.mb` will catch you up to this point.

If you play back the scene frame by frame, you'll notice that the arm and basket will briefly pass through the projectile ball for a few frames as the arm shoots back up around frames 102–104. Increasing the subdivisions of the ball and the bowl before making them rigid bodies will help the collisions, but for a fun exercise, this works great. Play with the placement of the ball at the start of the scene, as well as the gravity and any other fields you care to experiment with, to try to land the projectile in different places in the scene.

Baking Out a Simulation

Frequently, you create a dynamic simulation to fit into another scene, perhaps to interact with other objects. In such cases, you want to exchange the dynamic properties of the dynamic body

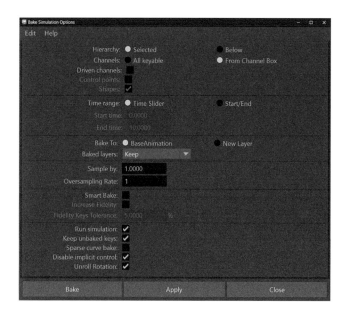

FIGURE 12.9 The Bake Simulation Options window.

you have set up in a simulation for regular, old-fashioned animation curves that you can more easily edit. You can easily take a simulation that you've created and bake it out to curves. As much fun as it is to think of cupcakes, *baking* is a somewhat catchall term used to describe converting one type of action or procedure into another; in this case, you're baking dynamics into keyframes.

You'll take the simulation you set up earlier with the catapult and turn it into keyframes. Keep in mind that you can use this introduction as a foundation for your own explorations.

To bake out the rigid body simulation of the catapult projectile, follow these steps:

1. Open the scene file `catapult _ dynamics _ v1.mb` from the Catapult_Anim project on the web page, or if you prefer, open your own scene from the previous exercise.

2. Select the projectile ball (pSphere1) and choose Edit ➢ Keys ➢ Bake Simulation ☐. In the option box,

shown in Figure 12.9, set Time Range to Time Slider (which should be set to 1–240). This, of course, sets the range you would like to bake into curves.

3. Set Hierarchy to Selected and set Channels to From Channel Box. This ensures you have control over which keys are created. Make sure Keep Unbaked Keys and Disable Implicit Control are checked and that Sparse Curve Bake is turned off. Before clicking the Bake or Apply button, select the Translate and Rotate channels in the Channel Box. Click Bake.

4. Maya runs through the simulation. Scrub the timeline back and forth. Notice how the projectile shoots as if the dynamic simulation were running—except that you can scrub in the timeline, which you can't do with a dynamics simulation. With the projectile selected, open the Graph Editor; you'll see something similar to Figure 12.10.

   The curves are crowded; they have keyframes at every frame. A typical dynamics bake gives results like this. But you can set the Bake command to sparse the curves for you; that is, it can take out keyframes at frames that have values within a certain tolerance so that a minor change in the ball's position or rotation need not have a keyframe on the curve.

5. Let's go back in time and try this again. Press Z (Undo) until you back up to right before you bake out the simulation to curves. You can also close this scene and reopen it from the original project, if necessary. This time, select the projectile sphere and choose Edit ➢ Keys ➢ Bake Simulation ☐. In the option box, turn on the Sparse Curve Bake setting and set Sample By to **5**. Select the Translate and Rotate channels in the Channel Box and click Bake.

   Maya runs through the simulation again and bakes everything out to curves. This time it makes a sparser animation curve for each channel because it's setting keyframes only at five-frame intervals, as shown in Figure 12.11. If you open the Graph Editor, you'll notice that the curves are much friendlier to look at and edit.

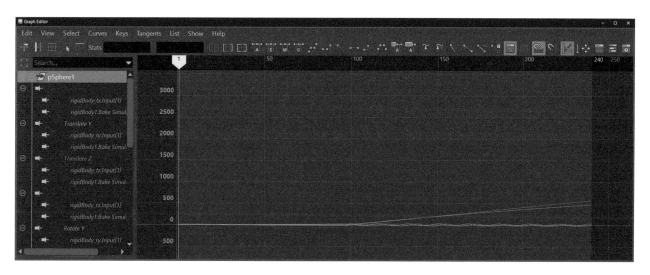

FIGURE 12.10 The projectile has animation curves.

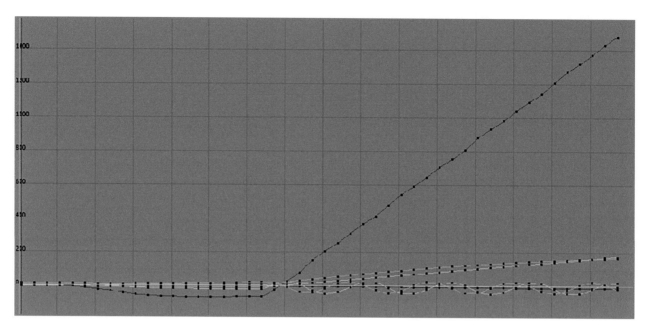

FIGURE 12.11   Sampling by fives makes a cleaner curve.

Sampling by fives may give you an easier curve to edit, but it may also oversimplify the animation of your objects; make sure you use the best Sampling setting for your simulation when you need to convert it to curves for editing.

Simplifying Animation Curves

Despite a higher Sampling setting when you bake out the simulation, you can still be left with a lot of keyframes to deal with, especially if you have to modify the animation extensively from here. One last trick you can use is to simplify the curve further through the Graph Editor. You have to work with curves of the same relative size, so you'll start with the rotation

curves because they have larger values. To simplify the curve in the Graph Editor, follow these steps:

1. Select the projectile and open the Graph Editor. In the left Outliner side, select Rotate X, Rotate Y, and Rotate Z to display only these curves in the graph view. Figure 12.12 shows the curves.

2. In the left panel of the Graph Editor, select the rigid-Body_rx.Input[1], rigidBodyry.Input[1], and rigid-Body rz.Input[1] nodes displayed under the Rotate X, Y, and Z entries for all three curves, as shown in Figure 12.13. In the Graph Editor menu, choose Curves ➤ Simplify Curve ☐. In the option box, set

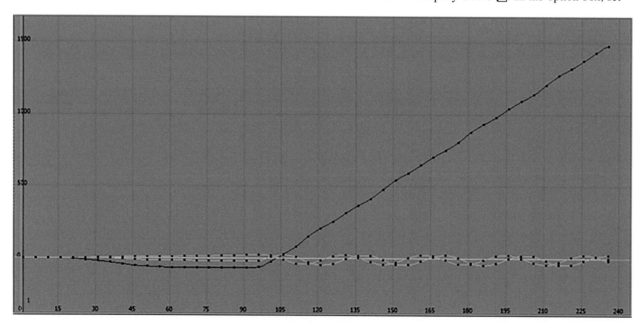

FIGURE 12.12   The Graph Editor displays the rotation curves of the projectile ball.

FIGURE 12.13   Select the curves to simplify them.

Time Range to All, set Simplify Method to Classic, set Time Tolerance to **10**, and set Value Tolerance to **1.0**. These are fairly high values, but because you're dealing with rotation of the projectile, the degree values are high enough. For more intricate values such as Translation, you would use much lower tolerances when simplifying a curve.

3. Click Simplify, and you see that the curves retain their basic shapes but lose some of their keyframes. Figure 12.14 shows the simplified curves, which

differ perhaps a little from the original curve that had keys at every five frames.

Simplifying curves is a handy way to convert a dynamic simulation to curves. Keep in mind that you may lose fidelity to the original animation after you simplify a curve, so use this technique with care. The curve simplification works with good old-fashioned keyframed curves as well; if you inherit a scene from another animator and need to simplify the curves, do it just as you did here.

nParticle Dynamics

Like legacy rigid body objects, particles are moved dynamically using collisions and fields. In short, a *particle* is a point in space that is given renderable properties—that is, it can render out. When particles are used en masse, they can create effects such as smoke, a swarm of insects, fireworks, and so on. nParticles implement particles through the Maya Nucleus solver, which provides better and easier simulations than traditional Maya particles.

Although nParticles can be an advanced and involved aspect of Maya, it's important to have some exposure to them as you begin to learn Maya.

It's important to think of particle animation as manipulating a larger system rather than as controlling every single particle. nParticles are most often used together in large numbers so that the entirety is rendered out to create an effect. You control fields and dynamic attributes to govern the motion of the system as a whole.

Emitting nParticles

A typical workflow for creating an nParticle effect in Maya breaks out into two parts: motion and rendering. First, you create and define the behavior of particles through emission. An *emitter* is a Maya object that creates the particles. After you create fields and adjust particle behavior within a dynamic simulation, much as you would do with rigid body motion, you

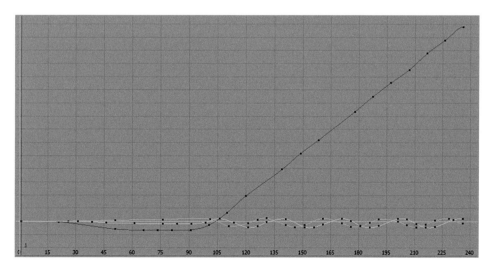

FIGURE 12.14   A simplified curve for the rotations of the eight ball.

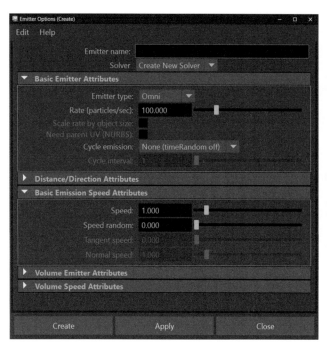

FIGURE 12.15   Creation options for an nParticle emitter.

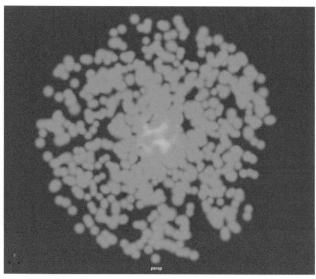

FIGURE 12.16   An Omni emitter emits a swarm of cloud particles in all directions.

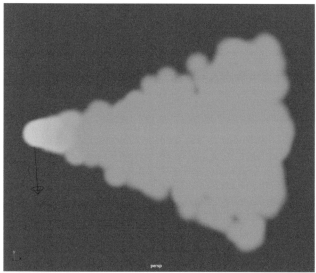

FIGURE 12.17   Cloud nParticles are sprayed in a specific direction.

give the particles renderable qualities to define how they look. This second aspect of the workflow defines how the particles come together to create the desired effect, such as steam. You'll make a locomotive pump emit steam later in this chapter.

To create a nParticle system, follow these steps:

1. Make sure you're in the FX menu set, choose nParticles ➤ Create Options, and select Cloud. Then choose nParticles ➤ Create Emitter ☐. The option box gives you various creation options for the nParticle emitter, as shown in Figure 12.15.

   The default settings create an Omni emitter with a rate of 100 particles per second and a speed of 1.0. Click Create. A small round object (the emitter) appears at the origin.

2. Set your time range to 1–240 frames. Click the Play button to play the scene. As with rigid body dynamics, you must also play back the scene using the Play Every Frame option. You can't scrub or reverse-play particles unless you create a cache file. You'll learn how to create a particle disk cache later in this chapter.

You'll notice a mass of circles streaming out of the emitter in all directions (see Figure 12.16). These are the nParticles.

Emitter Attributes

You can control how particles are created and behave by changing the type of emitter and adjusting its attributes. Here are the most often-used emitters:

Omni
   Emits particles in all directions.

Directional
   Emits a spray of particles in a specific direction, as shown in Figure 12.17.

Volume
   Emits particles from within a specified volume, as shown in Figure 12.18. The volume can be a cube, a sphere, a cylinder, a cone, or a torus. By default, the particles can leave the perimeter of the volume.

After you create an emitter, its attributes govern how the particles are released into the scene. Every emitter has the following attributes to control the emission:

Rate
   Governs how many particles are emitted per second.

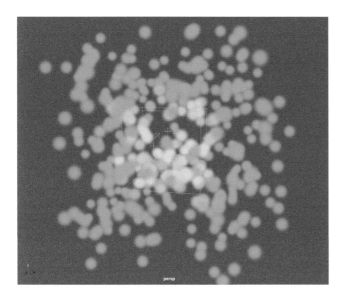

FIGURE 12.18 Cloud nParticles emit from anywhere inside the emitter's volume.

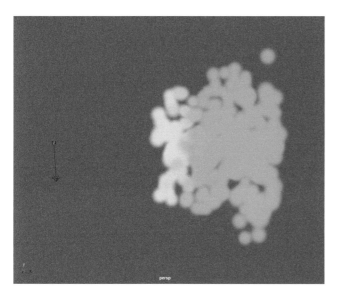

FIGURE 12.19 An emitter with Min Distance and Max Distance settings of 3 emits cloud nParticles 3 units from itself.

Speed

Specifies how fast the particles move out from the emitter.

Speed Random

Randomizes the speed of the particles as they're emitted, for a more natural look.

Min and Max Distance

Emits particles within an offset distance from the emitter. You enter values for the Min and Max Distance settings. Figure 12.19 shows a Directional emitter with Min Distance and Max Distance settings of 3.

nParticle Attributes

After being created, or born, and set into motion by an emitter, nParticles rely on their own attributes and any fields or collisions in the scene to govern their motion, just like rigid body objects.

In Figure 12.20, the Attribute Editor shows a number of tabs for the selected particle object. nParticle1 is the particle object node. This has the familiar Translate, Rotate, and Scale attributes, like most other object nodes. But the shape node, nParticleShape1, is where all the important attributes are for a particle, and it's displayed by default when you select a particle object. The third tab in the Attribute Editor is the emitter1

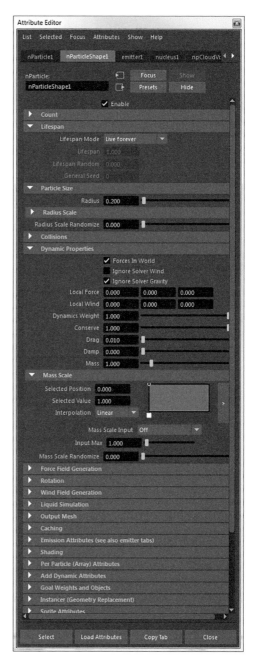

FIGURE 12.20 nParticle attributes.

node that belongs to the particle's emitter. This makes it easier to toggle back and forth to adjust emitter and particle settings.

The Lifespan Attributes

When any particle is born, you can give it a *lifespan*, which allows the particle to die when it reaches a certain point in time. As you'll see with the steam locomotive later in this chapter, a particle that has a lifespan can change over that lifespan. For example, a particle may start out as white and fade away at the end of its life. A lifespan also helps keep the total number of particles in a scene to a minimum, which helps the scene run more efficiently.

You use the Lifespan mode to select the type of lifespan for the nParticle.

Live Forever

The particles in the scene can exist indefinitely.

Constant

All particles die when their Lifespan value is reached. Lifespan is measured in seconds, so upon emission, a particle with a Lifespan of 1.0 will exist for 30 frames (in a scene set up at 30 fps) before it disappears.

Random Range

This type sets a lifespan in Constant mode but assigns a range value via the Lifespan Random attribute to allow some particles to live longer than others for a more natural effect.

LifespanPP Only

This mode is used in conjunction with expressions that are programmed into the particle with Maya Embedded Language (MEL). Expressions are an advanced Maya concept and aren't used in this book.

The Shading Attributes

The Shading attributes determine how your particles look and how they will render. Two types of particle rendering are used in Maya: software and hardware. *Hardware particles* are typically rendered out separately from anything else in the scene and are then composited with the rest of the scene. Because of the compound workflow for hardware particles, this book will introduce you to a software particle type called *Cloud*. Cloud, like other *software particles*, can be rendered with the rest of a scene through the software renderer.

With your particles selected, open the Attribute Editor. In the Shading section, you'll find the Particle Render Type drop-down menu (see Figure 12.21).

The three render types listed with the (s/w) suffix are software-rendered particles. All the other types can be rendered only through the Maya Hardware renderer. Select your render type, and Maya adds the proper attributes you'll need for the render type you selected.

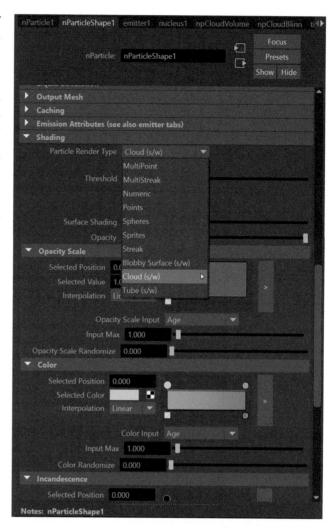

FIGURE 12.21   The Particle Render Type drop-down menu.

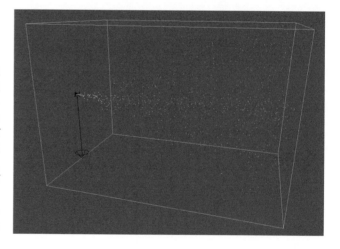

FIGURE 12.22   Dots on the screen represent point particles.

For example, if you select the Points render type from the menu, your particles change from circles on the screen to dots, as shown in Figure 12.22.

Several new attributes that control the look of the particles appear when you switch the Particle Render Type setting. Each Particle Render Type setting has its own set of render attributes. Set your nParticles back to the Cloud type. The Cloud particle type attributes are Threshold, Surface Shading, and Opacity (see Figure 12.23).

In the Shading heading for the cloud nParticles, shown in Figure 12.24, are controls for the Opacity Scale, Color, and Incandescence attributes. They control how the particles look when simulated and rendered. Notice how each of these controls is based on ramps.

nParticles are already set up to allow you to control the color, opacity, and incandescence during the life of the particle.

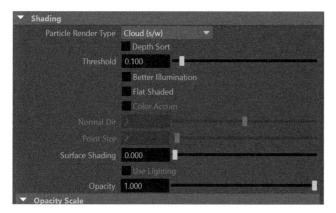

FIGURE 12.23 Each Particle Render Type setting displays its own set of attributes.

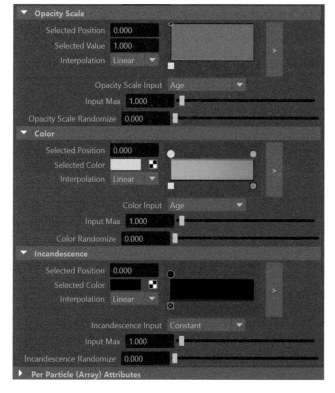

FIGURE 12.24 Controls for the Opacity Scale, Color, and Incandescence attributes.

For example, by default, the Color attribute is set up with a white-to-cyan ramp. This means that each of the particles will begin life white in color and will gradually turn cyan toward the end of its lifespan, or Age setting.

Likewise, the Particle Size heading in the Attribute Editor contains a ramp for Radius Scale that works much the same way as the Color attribute just described. In this case, you use the Radius Scale ramp to increase or decrease the size of the particle along its Age setting.

nCaching Particles

It would be nice to turn particles into money cash, but I can show you only how to turn your particles into a disk cache. You may have noticed that when you playback a dynamic particle scene, Maya automatically caches the particles so you can play them back faster, as well as scrub the animation in the timeline, but you have to let Maya finish playing the scene to cache it all. Once you make changes, Maya automatically re-caches the scene, signified by a thin orange bar in the timeline under the frame number tick marks.

Although this automatic memory caching is generally faster than disk caching, creating a disk cache lets you cache all the particles as they exist throughout their duration in your scene and ensures that the particles are rendered correctly, especially if you're rendering on multiple computers or across a network. You usually create a particle disk cache before rendering.

If you make changes to your particle simulation but you don't see the changes reflected when you play back the scene, make sure you've turned off any memory or deleted any disk cache from previous versions of the simulation.

Creating an nCache on Disk

After you've created a particle scene and you want to be able to scrub the timeline back and forth to see your particle motion and how it acts in the scene, you can create a particle nCache to disk. This lets you play back the entire scene as you like, without running the simulation from the start and by every frame.

To create an nCache, make sure to be in the FX menu set, select the nParticle object in your view panel or Outliner, and choose nCache ➢ Create New Cache ➢ nObject. Maya will run the simulation according to the timeline and save the position of all the particle systems in the scene to cache files in your current project's Data/Cache folder. You can then play or scrub your animation back and forth, and the particles will run properly.

If you make any dynamic changes to the particles, such as emission rate or speed, you'll need to detach the cache file from the scene for the changes to take effect. Choose nCache ➢ Delete Cache. You can open the option box to select whether you want to delete the cache files physically or merely detach them from the current nParticles.

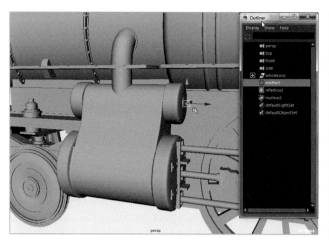

FIGURE 12.25   Place the emitter at the end of the pump.

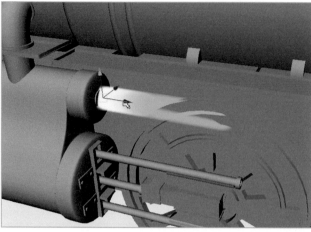

FIGURE 12.26   Cloud nParticles emit in a straight line from the pump.

Now that you understand the basics of particle dynamics, it's time to see for yourself how they work.

Animating a Particle Effect: Locomotive Steam

You'll create a spray of steam puffing out of a pump on the side of a locomotive that drives the wheels that you rigged previously. You'll use the scene `fancy_locomotive_anim_v3.ma` from Chapter 9, "More Animation!"

Emitting the nParticles

The first step is to create an emitter to spray from the steam pump and to set up the motion and behavior of the nParticles.

1. In the FX menu set, make sure nParticles ➤ Create Options ➤ Cloud is still checked and then choose nParticles ➤ Create Emitter ☐. Make sure you select the first entry of Create Emitter in the menu under the Emit section, and not the second listing of Create Emitter under the Legacy Particles section of the menu at the bottom. Set Emitter Type to Directional and click Create. Place the emitter at the end of the pump, as shown in Figure 12.25.

2. To set up the emission in the proper direction, adjust the attributes of the emitter. In the Distance/Direction Attributes section, set Direction Y to **0**, Direction X to **0**, and Direction Z to **1**. This emits the particles straight out of the pump over the first large wheel and toward the back of the engine.

3. Play back your scene. The cloud nParticles emit in a straight line from the engine, as shown in Figure 12.26.

The Direction attributes are relative. Entering a value of **1** for Direction X and a value of **2** for Direction Y makes the particles spray at twice the height (Y) of their lateral distance (X).

FIGURE 12.27   The emitter's Spread attribute widens the spray of particles.

You can load the file `locomotive_steam_v1.ma` from the Locomotive project on the web page to check your work.

4. To change the particle emission to more of a spray, adjust the Spread attribute for the emitter. Click the emitter1 tab in the particle's Attribute Editor (or select the emitter to focus the Attribute Editor on it instead) and change Spread from 0 to **0.30**. Figure 12.27 shows the new cloud spray.

The Spread attribute sets the cone angle for a directional emission. A value of 0 results in a thin line of particles. A value of 1 emits particles in a 180° arc.

5. The emission is rather slow for hot steam being pumped out as the locomotive drives the wheels, so change the Speed setting for the emitter from 1 to **2.0** and change Speed Random from 0 to **1**. Doing

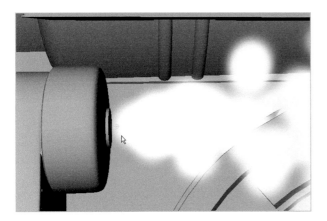

FIGURE 12.28   A range of offset between 0 and 0.3 units creates a more believable emission.

so creates a random speed range between 1 and 3 for each particle. These two attributes are found in the emitter's Attribute Editor in the Basic Emission Speed Attributes section.

6. So that all the steam doesn't emit from the same point, keep the emitter's Min Distance at 0, but set its Max Distance to **0.3**. This creates a range of offset between 0 and 0.3 units for the particles to emit from, as shown in Figure 12.28.

Setting nParticle Attributes

It's always good to get the particles moving as closely to what you need as possible before you tend to their look. Now that you have the particles emitting properly from the steam pump, you'll adjust the nParticle attributes. Start by setting a lifespan for them and then add rendering attributes.

1. Select the nParticle object and open the Attribute Editor. In the Lifespan section, set Lifespan Mode to Random Range. Set Lifespan to **2** and Lifespan Random to **1**. This creates a range of 1–3 for each particle's lifespan. (This is based on a lifespan of 2, plus or minus a random value from 0 to 1.)

2. You can control the radius of the particles as they're emitted from the pump. Under the Particle Size heading in the Attribute Editor, set a Radius attribute of **0.50**. Set the Radius Scale Randomize attribute to

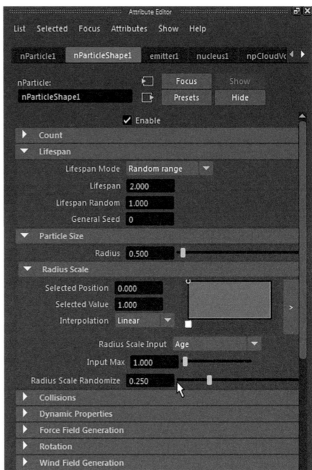

FIGURE 12.29   The initial radius settings for the steam nParticles.

0.25. This allows you to have particles that emit with a radius range between 0.25 and 0.75. Figure 12.29 shows the attributes.

3. If you play back the simulation, you'll see the particles are quite large initially. Because steam expands as it travels, you need to adjust the size (radius) of your nParticles to make them smaller at birth; they will grow larger over their lifespan and produce a good look for your steam.

4. In the Radius Scale heading in the Attribute Editor, click the arrow to the right of the ramp to open a larger view of the ramp, as shown in Figure 12.30.

FIGURE 12.30   Open the Radius Scale ramp.

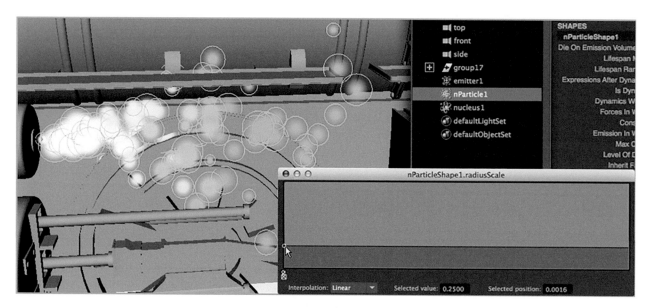

FIGURE 12.31 Decrease the radius of the nParticles using the Radius Scale ramp.

5. Click and drag the ramp's first and only handle (an open circle at the upper-left corner of the Ramp window) down to a value of about 0.25, as shown in Figure 12.31. The particles get smaller as you adjust the ramp value.

6. To allow the particles to grow in size, add a second handle to the scale curve by clicking anywhere on that line and drag to a value of 1.0 and the position shown in Figure 12.32. The particles toward the end of the spray get larger.

7. You can set up collisions so the nParticle steam doesn't travel right through the mesh of the locomotive. Select the meshes shown in Figure 12.33 and choose nCloth ➤ Create Passive Collider.

8. In the Outliner, select the three nRigid nodes that were just created and set the Friction attribute in the Channel Box to **0.0** from the default of 0.10. Play back your scene, and your particles now collide with the surface of the locomotive (see Figure 12.34).

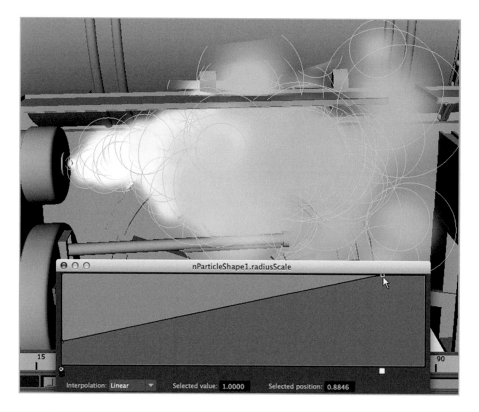

FIGURE 12.32 Adjust the Radius Scale ramp to grow the particles.

FIGURE 12.33 Select the meshes with which the nParticles will collide.

FIGURE 12.34 The particles now react nicely against the side of the locomotive.

If you want to check your work, download the file `locomotive_steam_v2.ma` from the Locomotive project on the web page.

Setting Rendering Attributes

After you define the nParticle movement to your liking, you can create the proper look for the nParticles. This means setting and adjusting their rendering parameters.

PARTICLE TYPE

Because Maya has several types of particles, the particles are set up according to their type; the workflow in this section applies only to the Cloud particle type.

1. Select the nParticle object and open the Attribute Editor. Expand the Shading heading and look at the Color ramp. By default, the particles go from white to light blue in color. Click the cyan color's circle handle on top of the ramp. The Selected Color attribute next to the ramp shows the cyan color. Click in the swatch to open the Color Chooser and change the color to a light gray.

2. Click the arrow bar to the right of the Opacity Scale ramp to open a larger ramp view. Grab the first handle in the upper-left corner and drag it down to a value of **0.12**.

3. The steam needs to be less opaque at its birth, grow more opaque toward the middle of its life, and fade completely away at the end of the particle's life. Click to create new handles to create a curve for the ramp, as shown in Figure 12.35. The values for the five ramp handles shown from left to right are 0.12, 0.30, 0.20, 0.08, and 0.

4. In the Render Settings window make sure you are using Maya Software rendering and not the Arnold Renderer, set Image Size to 960×540. On the Maya Software tab, set Quality to Intermediate Quality. Run the animation, and stop it when some steam has been emitted. Render a frame. It should look like Figure 12.36. The steam doesn't travel far enough along the engine; it disappears too soon.

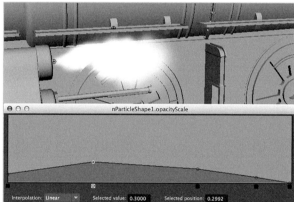

FIGURE 12.35 Creating an Opacity ramp for the steam.

FIGURE 12.36 The steam seems too short and small.

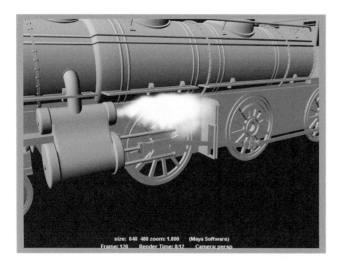

FIGURE 12.37   A better emission but a bit too solid.

> With the steam nParticles selected, open the Attribute Editor; in the Radius Scale, under the Particle Size heading, change the first handle's value from 0.25 to **0.35** to make the steam particles a bit larger. Below the Opacity Scale ramp is the Input Max slider; set that value to **1.6**.

5. Select the emitter1 tab, and change the Spread value for the emitter to **0.2**. Change Rate (Particles/Sec) to **200** and Speed to **3.0**. Play back the simulation, and render a frame to compare to Figure 12.37.

6. The Color ramp in the nParticle's Attribute Editor controls the color of the steam, and a shader is assigned to the particles. In the view panel, select the steam nParticle object and open the Hypershade window. In the Hypershade, click the Graph Materials On Selected Objects icon (![icon]) to show the particle's shader, as shown in Figure 12.38.

7. In the Hypershade, select the npCloudVolume shader. Notice in the Hypershade's Property Editor (or in the Attribute Editor) that the attributes in the Common Material Attributes section all have connections (they display this icon: ![icon]). The ramp controls in the nParticle Attribute Editor are controlling the attributes in this Particle Cloud shader.

8. Under the Transparency heading in the Attribute Editor for the shader, set Density to **0.35**. Try a render; the steam should look better (see Figure 12.39).

Batch-render a 200-frame sequence of the scene, to see how the particles look as they animate. (Check the frames with FCheck. Refer to Chapter 11, "Autodesk® Maya® Rendering," for more on FCheck.)

Open the file `locomotive_steam_v3.ma` from the Locomotive project on the web page to check your work.

Experiment with the steam by animating the Rate attribute of the emitter to make the steam pump out in time with the wheel arm. Also, try animating the Speed values and playing with different values in the Radius and Opacity ramps.

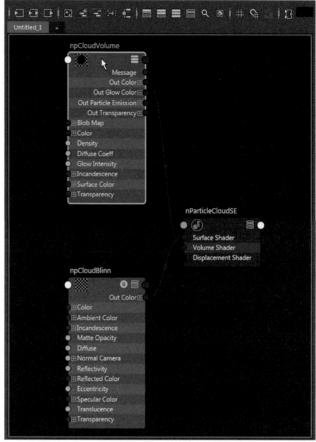

FIGURE 12.38   The shaders assigned to the cloud nParticle.

The steam you'll get in this tutorial looks pretty good, but it isn't as lifelike as it could be. Particle animators are always learning new tricks and expanding their skills, and that comes from always trying new things and retrying the same effects with different methods.

When you feel comfortable with the steam exercise, try using the cloud nParticle to create steam for a mug of coffee. That steam moves much more slowly and is less defined than the blowing steam of the locomotive, and it should pose a new challenge. Also try your hand at creating a smoke trail for a rocket ship, a wafting stream of cigarette smoke, or even the billowing smoke coming from the engine's chimney.

Cloud nParticles are the perfect particle type with which to begin. As you feel more comfortable animating with clouds, experiment with the other render types. The more you experiment with all the types of nParticles, the easier they will be to harness.

Introduction to Paint Effects

One tool in the Maya effects arsenal, Paint Effects, lets you create results such as a field of grass rippling in the wind, a head of hair or feathers, or even a colorful aurora in the sky. Paint Effects is a rendering effect found in the Modeling menu set under the Generate menu. It has incredible dynamic properties that can make leaves rustle or trees sway in a storm.

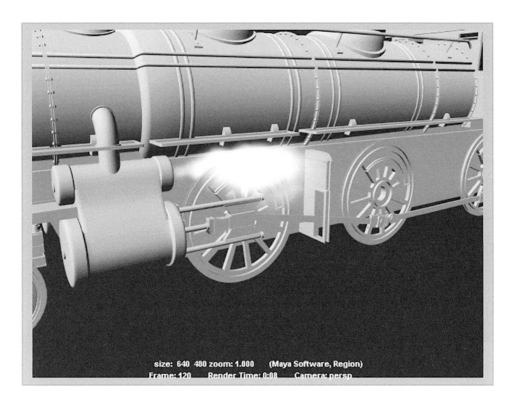

FIGURE 12.39 The steam is less flat and solid.

Paint Effects uses its own dynamics calculations to create natural motion. It's one of the most powerful tools in Maya, with features that go far beyond the scope of this introductory book. Here you'll learn how to create a Paint Effects scene and how to access all the preset brushes to create your own effects.

Paint Effects uses brushes to paint effects into your three-dimensional (3D) scene. The brushes create strokes on a surface or in the Maya modeling views that produce tubes, which render out through the Maya Software renderer. These Paint Effects tubes have dynamic properties, which means they can move according to their own forces. Therefore, you can easily create a field of blowing grass.

Try This

Create a field of blowing grass and flowers; it will take you all of 5 minutes.

1. Start with a new scene file. Maximize the perspective view. (Press the spacebar with the Persp window active.)

2. Switch to the Modeling menu set (press F2). Choose Generate ➤ Get Brush under the Paint Effects section of the menu to open the Visor window. The Visor window displays all the preset Paint Effects brushes that automatically create certain effects. Select the Grasses folder in the Visor's left panel to display the grass brushes available (see Figure 12.40). You can navigate the Visor window as you would navigate any other Maya window, using the Alt key and the mouse buttons.

3. Click the `grassWindWide.mel` brush to activate the Paint Effects tool and set it to this grass brush. Your cursor changes to a Pencil icon.

4. In the Persp window, click and drag two lines across the grid, as shown in Figure 12.41, to create two Paint Effects strokes of blowing grass. If you can't see the grass in your view panel, increase Global Scale in the Paint Effects Brush Settings in either the Attribute Editor or the Channel Box to see the grass being drawn onto the screen.

5. To change your brush so you can add some flowers between the grass, choose Generate ➤ Get Brush and select the Flowers folder. Select the `dandelion_Yellow.mel` brush. Your Paint Effects tool is now set to paint yellow flowers.

6. Click and drag a new stroke between the strokes of grass, as shown in Figure 12.42.

7. Position your camera, and render a frame. Make sure you're using Maya Software and not mental ray® to render through the Render Settings window and that you use a large enough resolution, such as 640×480, so that you can see the details. Render out a 120-frame sequence to see how the grass animates in the wind. Figure 12.43 shows a scene filled with grass strokes as well as a number of different flowers.

After you create a Paint Effects stroke, you can edit the look and movement of the effect through the Attribute Editor. You'll notice, however, that there are a large number of attributes to edit with Paint Effects. The next section introduces the attributes that are most useful to the beginning Maya user.

Paint Effects Attributes

It's best to create a single stroke of Paint Effects in a blank scene and experiment with adjusting the various attributes to

FIGURE 12.40   The preset grass brushes in the Visor window.

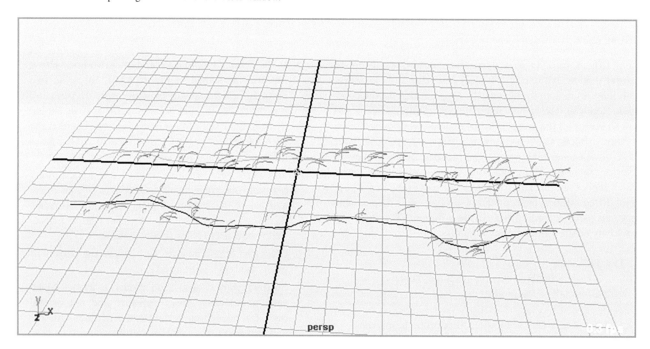

FIGURE 12.41   Click and drag two lines across the grid.

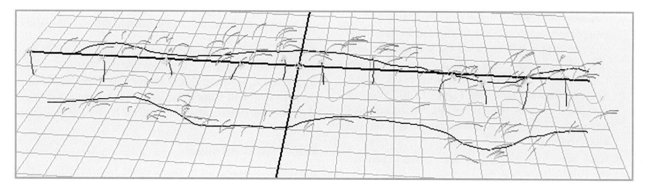

FIGURE 12.42   Add new strokes to add flowers to the grass.

FIGURE 12.43   Paint Effects can add flowers and grass to any scene.

see how they affect the strokes. Select the stroke and open the Attribute Editor. Switch to the stroke's tab to access the attributes. For example, for an African Lily Paint Effects stroke, the Attribute Editor tab is called africanLily1.

Each Paint Effects stroke produces tubes that render to create the desired effect. Each tube (you can think of a tube as a stalk) can grow to have branches, twigs, leaves, flowers, and buds. Each section of a tube has its own controls to give you the greatest flexibility in creating your effect. As you experiment with Paint Effects, you'll begin to understand how each attribute contributes to the final look of the effect.

Here is a summary of some Paint Effects attributes:

Brush Profile

Gives you control over how the tubes are generated from the stroke; this is done with the Brush Width attribute. This attribute makes tubes emit from a wider breadth from the stroke to cover more of an area.

Shading and Tube Shading

Gives you access to the color controls for the tubes on a stroke.

Color 1 and Color 2
From bottom to top, graduates from Color 1 to Color 2 along the stalk only. The leaves and branches have their own color attributes, which you can display by choosing Tubes ➢ Growth.

Incandescence 1 and 2
Adds a gradient self-illumination to the tubes.

Transparency 1 and 2
Adds a gradient transparency to each tube.

Hue/Sat/Value Rand
Adds some randomness to the color of the tubes.

In the Tubes section, you'll find all the attributes to control the growth of the Paint Effects effect. In the Creation subsection, you can access the following:

Tubes Per Step

Controls the number of tubes along the stroke. For example, this setting increases or decreases the number of flowers for the africanLily1 stroke.

Length Min/Max

Controls the height of the tubes to make taller flowers or grass (or other effects).

Tube Width 1 and Width 2

Controls the width of the tubes (the stalks of the flowers).

In the Growth subsection, you can access controls for branches, twigs, leaves, flowers, and buds for the Paint Effects strokes. Each attribute in these sections controls the number, size, and shape of those elements. Although not all strokes in Paint Effects create flowers, all strokes contain these headings.

The Behavior subsection contains the controls for the dynamic forces affecting the tubes in a Paint Effects stroke. Adjust these attributes if you want your flowers to blow more in the wind.

Paint Effects are rendered as a *postprocess*, which means they won't render in reflections or refractions as is and they will not render in mental ray without conversion to polygons. They're processed and rendered after every other object in the scene is rendered out in Maya Software rendering only.

To render Paint Effects in Arnold, you can convert Paint Effects to polygonal surfaces. They will then render in the scene along with any other objects so that they can take part in reflections and refractions. To convert a Paint Effects stroke to polygons, select the stroke and choose Modify ➢ Convert ➢ Paint Effects To Polygons. The polygon Paint Effects tubes can still be edited by most of the Paint Effects attributes mentioned so far; however, some, such as color, don't affect the poly tubes. Instead, the color information is converted into a shader that is assigned to the polygons. It's best to finalize your Paint Effects strokes before converting to polygons to avoid any confusion.

Paint Effects is a strong Maya tool, and you can use it to create complex effects such as a field of blowing flowers. A large number of controls to create a variety of effects come with that complexity. Fortunately, Maya comes with a generous sampling of preset brushes. Experiment with a few brushes and their attributes to see what kinds of effects and strange plants you can create.

Getting Started with nCloth

nCloth, part of the nucleus dynamics in Autodesk Maya, is a simple yet powerful way to create cloth simulations in your scene. From complex clothing on a moving character to a simple flag, nCloth dynamics can create stunning movement, albeit with some serious setup. I will briefly touch on the nCloth workflow here to give you a taste for it and familiarize you with the basics of getting started.

Making a Tablecloth

Switch to the FX menu set. The nCloth menu is where you need to start to drape a simple tablecloth on a round table in the following steps:

1. Create a flat disc with a poly cylinder to make the basic table. Set the Y scale to **.175** and the X and Z scales to **5.25**. Set Subdivisions Axis to **36** for more segments to make the cylinder smoother.

2. Create a poly plane with a scale of **20** to be larger than the cylinder. Set both Subdivisions Width and Subdivisions Height to **40** for extra detail in the mesh. Place the square a few units above the cylinder, as shown in Figure 12.44.

3. Now you'll set the plane to be a cloth object. Select the plane and choose nCloth ➢ Create nCloth. The plane will turn purple, and a pair of new nodes is added to the scene: nucleus1 and nCloth1.

4. Set your frame range to **1–240** and click Play. The plane falls down and through the cylinder object. The nucleus engine has already set up the nCloth plane to have gravity.

5. Now let's define the cylinder as a collision object to make it the tabletop for the tablecloth. Select the cylinder and choose nCloth ➢ Create Passive Collider. That's it! Click Play, and watch the cloth fall onto the table and take shape around it (see Figure 12.45).

Well, as easy as that was, there's a lot more to it to achieve the specific effect you may need. But you're on the road already. The first thing to understand is that the higher the resolution of the poly mesh, the better the look and movement of the cloth,

at the cost of speed. At 40 subdivisions on the plane, the simulation runs pretty well, but you can see jagged areas of the tablecloth, so you would need to start with a much higher mesh for a smoother result.

Select the tablecloth and open the Attribute Editor. A wide range of attributes can be adjusted for different cloth settings; however, you can choose from a number of built-in presets to make life easier. In the Attribute Editor, choose Presets*, as shown in Figure 12.46. Select Silk ➢ Replace. As you can see, several Blend options appear in the submenu, allowing you to blend your current settings with the preset settings.

In this case, you've chosen Replace to set the tablecloth object to simulate silk. It will be lighter and airier than before. Figure 12.47 (left) shows the tablecloth at frame 200 with the silk preset. Now, in the Attribute Editor, choose Presets ➢ thickLeather ➢ Replace for a heavier cloth simulation (Figure 12.47, right). Notice the playback for the heavy leather was slower as well.

As a beginner to Maya, you may find it most helpful to go through the range of presets and see how the attributes for the nCloth change. Here is a preliminary rundown of some of the nCloth attributes found under the Dynamic Properties heading in the Attribute Editor. Try changing some of these values to see how your tablecloth reacts, and you'll gain a finer appreciation for the mechanics of nCloth.

Stretch Resistance
Controls how easily the nCloth will stretch. The lower this value, the more rubbery and elastic the cloth will behave.

Bend Resistance
Controls how well the mesh will bend in reaction to external dynamic forces and collisions. The higher this value, the stiffer the cloth.

Rigidity
Sets the stiffness of the cloth object. Even a small value will have a stiffening impact on the simulation.

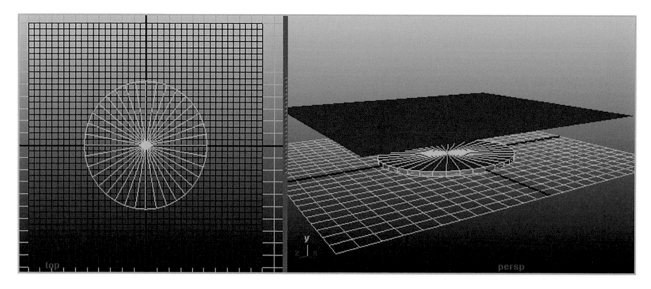

FIGURE 12.44   Place a square plane above a flat cylinder.

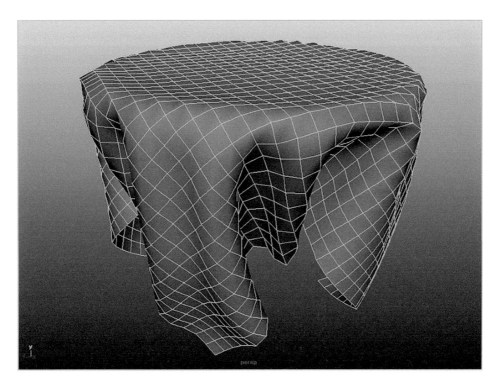

FIGURE 12.45   The cloth is working already!

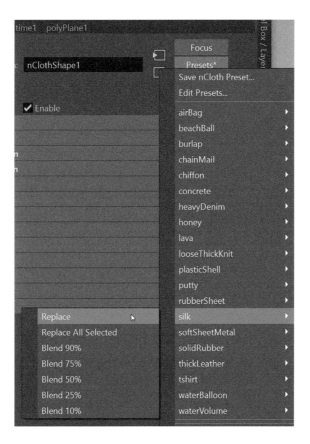

FIGURE 12.46   The built-in nCloth presets.

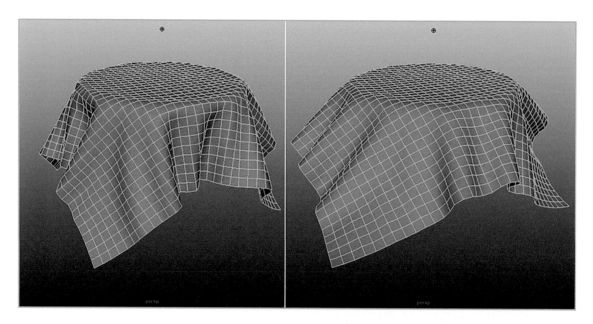

FIGURE 12.47 The silk cloth simulation is lighter (left); the leather simulation is heavier and runs slower.

Input Mesh Attract

Compels the cloth mesh to reassume its original shape before the cloth simulation, which in this case is a flat square plane. At a value of 1, the cloth may not move at all. Using some Input Mesh Attract will also give the cloth object a stiffer and more resilient/rubbery appearance.

Making a Flag

Now let's make a quick flag simulation to get familiar with nConstraints.

1. Make a rectangular polygon plane that is scaled to (20, 14, 14) and with subdivisions of **40** in width and height. Orient and place it above the home grid, as shown in Figure 12.48.

2. With the flag selected, choose nCloth ➢ Create nCloth. Set your frame range to **1–240** and click Play. The flag falls straight down. You need to keep one end from falling to simulate the flag being attached to a pole.

3. Select the edge vertices on the left side of the flag, as shown in Figure 12.49, and choose nConstraint ➢ Transform Constraint. The vertices you selected turn green, and a locator appears at the side of the flag. Now click Play, and the flag falls, while one end is tethered as if on a pole (see Figure 12.50).

4. Now you'll add wind to make the flag wave. Select the flag and open the Attribute Editor. Click the nucleus1 tab, and under the Gravity and Wind heading, set the Wind Speed attribute to **16**. Figure 12.51 shows the flag flapping in the wind.

Adjust the Air Density, Wind Speed, Wind Direction, and Wind Noise attributes to adjust how the flag waves. You can

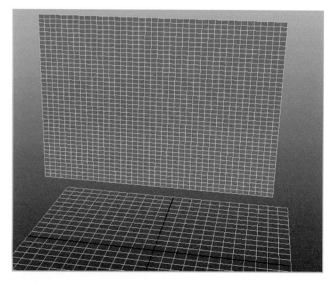

FIGURE 12.48 Create the mesh for the flag.

Select these vertices

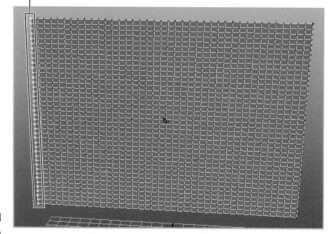

FIGURE 12.49 Select the vertices for the nConstraint.

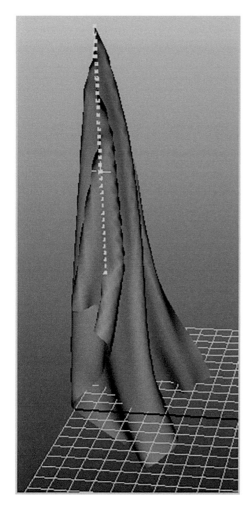

FIGURE 12.50   The flag is tethered to an imaginary pole now.

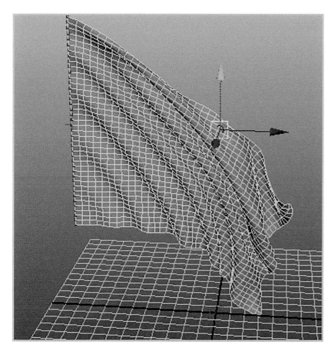

FIGURE 12.51   Wave the flag.

use a similar workflow to create drapes blowing in an open window, for instance.

Caching an nCloth

Making a disk cache for a cloth simulation is important for better playback in your scene. Also, if you are rendering, it's always a good idea to cache your simulation to avoid any issues. Caching an nCloth is simple. Select the cloth object, such as the flag from the previous example, and in the main menu bar, choose nCache ➤ Create New Cache ➤ nObject ☐. Figure 12.52 shows the options for the nCache. Here you can specify where the cache files are saved as well as the frame range for the cache. Once you create the cache, you will be able to scrub your playback back and forth.

If you need to change your simulation, you must first remove the cache before changing nCloth or nucleus attributes. To do so, select the cloth object and choose nCache ➤ Delete Cache ☐. In the option box, you can select whether you want to delete the cache files or just disconnect them from the nCloth object.

You can reattach an existing cache file by selecting the nCloth object and choosing nCache ➤ Attach Cache. The existing cache must be from that object or one with the same topology.

Customizing Maya

One of the most endearing features of Maya is its almost infinite customizability. Everyone has different tastes, and everyone works in their own way. Simply put, for everything you can do in Maya, you have several ways of doing it. There are always a couple of ways to access the Maya tools, features, and functions as well.

This flexibility may be confusing at first, but you'll discover that in the long run it's advantageous. The ability to customize enables the greatest flexibility in individual workflow.

It's best to use Maya at its defaults as you first learn. However, when you feel comfortable enough with your progress, you can use this section to change some of the interface elements in Maya to better suit how you like to work.

User Preferences

All the customization features are found under Windows ➤ Settings/Preferences, which displays the window shown in Figure 12.53.

The Preferences window (see Figure 12.54) lets you make changes to the look of the program as well as to toolset defaults by selecting from the categories listed in the left pane of the window.

The Preferences window is separated into categories that define different aspects of the program. Interface and Display deal with options to change the look of the program. Interface affects the main user interface, whereas Display affects how objects are displayed in the workspace.

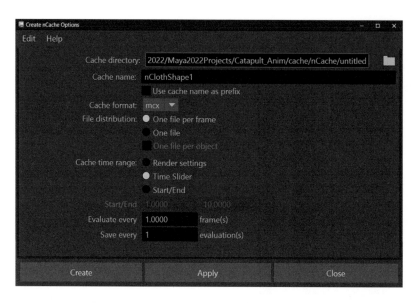

FIGURE 12.52 Create nCache Options dialog box.

FIGURE 12.53 The Settings/Preferences menu.

The Settings category lets you change the default values of several tools and their general operation. An essential aspect of this category is Working Units; these options set the working parameters of your scene (in particular, the Time setting).

By adjusting the Time setting, you tell Maya your frame rate of animation. If you're working in film, you use a frame rate of 24 frames per second (fps). If you're working in NTSC video (the standard video/television format in the Americas), you use the frame rate of 30 fps.

The Applications category lets you specify which applications you want Maya to start automatically when a function is called. For example, while looking at the Attribute Editor for a texture image, you can click a single button to open that image in your favorite image editor, which you specify here.

> In the Settings section, click the Undo header and set Undo Queue to Infinite. Doing so allows you to undo as many actions as have occurred since you loaded the file. This feature is unbelievably handy, especially when you're first learning Maya.

Shelves

Under the Shelf Editor command (Windows ≻ Settings/Preferences ≻ Shelf Editor) lurks a window that manages your shelves (see Figure 12.55). You can create or delete shelves or manage the items on the Shelf with this function. This is handy when you create your own workflow for a project. Simply click the Shelves tab to display the icons on that Shelf in the Shelf Editor window. Click in the Shelf Contents section to edit the icons and where they reside on that selected Shelf. Clicking the Command tab gives you access to the MEL command for that icon when it is single-clicked in the Shelf. Click the Double Click Command tab for the MEL command for the icon when it is double-clicked in the Shelf.

You can also edit Shelf icons from within the user interface without the Shelf Editor window. To add a menu command to the current Shelf, hold down Ctrl+Alt+Shift and click the function or command directly from its menu. Items from the Tool Box, pull-down menus, or the Script Editor can be added to any Shelf.

- To add an item from the Tool Box, MMB+drag its icon from the Tool Box into the appropriate Shelf.

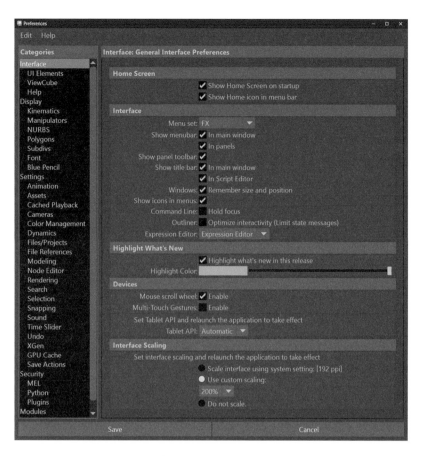

FIGURE 12.54   The Preferences window.

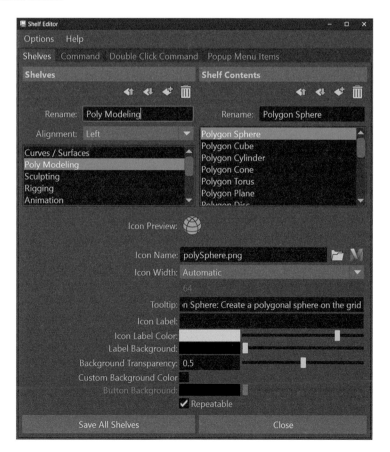

FIGURE 12.55   The Shelf Editor.

- To add an item from a menu to the current Shelf, hold down the Ctrl+Alt+Shift keys while selecting the item from the menu.

- To add an item (a MEL command) from the Script Editor, highlight the text of the MEL command in the Script Editor and MMB+drag it onto the Shelf. A MEL icon will be created that will run the command when you click it.

- To remove an item from a Shelf, MMB+drag its icon to the Garbage Can icon at the end of the Shelf or use Windows ➤ Settings/Preferences ➤ Shelf Editor.

Hotkeys

Hotkeys are keyboard shortcuts that can access almost any Maya tool or command. You've already encountered a few in your exploration of the interface and in the solar system exercise in Chapter 2, "Jumping into Basic Animation Headfirst." What fun! You can create even more hotkeys, as well as reassign existing hotkeys, through the Hotkey Editor, shown in Figure 12.56 (Windows ➤ Settings/Preferences ➤ Hotkey Editor).

Through this monolith of a window, you can set a key combination to be used as a shortcut to virtually any command in Maya. This is the last customization you want to touch. Because so many tools have hotkeys assigned by default, it's important to get to know them first before you start changing things to suit how you work.

Every menu command is represented on the left of the window when you select menu items from the drop-down menu, as shown in Figure 12.56. Menu categories are on the left, and as you select each command, its current hotkey (if any) appears in the Hotkey column. Simply enter the key combination you

want to assign to the selected command under the Hotkey column. The keyboard on the right side of the window simply shows the existing assigned keys; it's not used to assign keys.

Keep in mind that Maya is *case sensitive*, meaning that it differentiates between uppercase and lowercase letters. For example, one of my personal hotkeys is Ctrl+H to hide the selected object from view; pressing Shift+Ctrl+H unhides it.

Color Settings

You can set the colors for almost any part of the interface to your liking through the Colors window shown in Figure 12.57 (Windows ➤ Settings/Preferences ➤ Color Settings).

The window is separated into different aspects of the Maya interface by headings. The 3D Views heading lets you change the color of all the panels' backgrounds. For example, color settings give you a chance to set the interface to complement your office's decor as well as make certain items easier to read.

Customizing Maya is important. However—and this can't be stressed enough—it's important to get your bearings with default Maya settings before you venture out and change hotkeys and such. When you're ready, this chapter will still be here for your reference.

> The important things to focus on right now are discovering how to use the tools to accomplish the tasks you need to perform and establishing a basic workflow. Toward that end, I strongly suggest learning Maya in its default configuration and using only the menu structure and default shelves to access all your commands at first, with the exception of the most basic hotkeys.

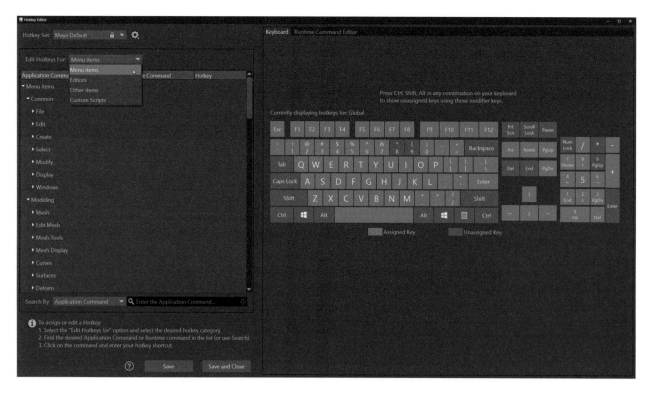

FIGURE 12.56   The Hotkey Editor.

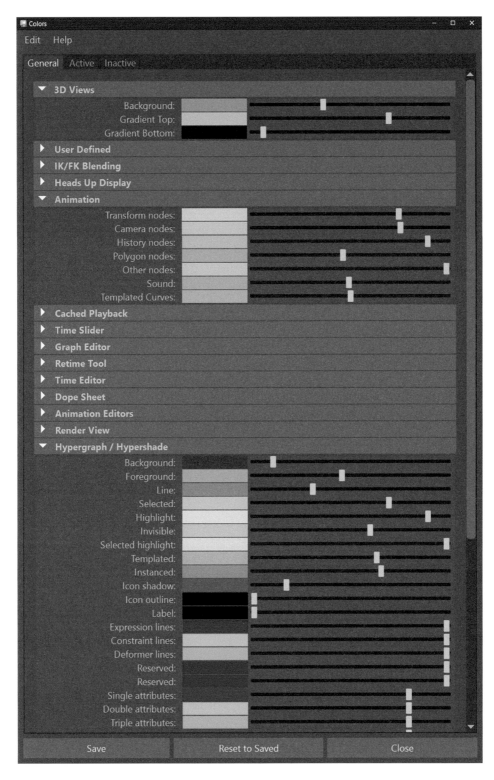

FIGURE 12.57 Changing the interface colors is simple.

Summary

In this chapter, you learned how to create dynamic objects and create simulations. Beginning with rigid body dynamics, you had a quick, fun exercise where you shot a projectile with the catapult, and then you learned how to bake that simulation into animation curves for fine-tuning. Next, you learned about particle effects by creating a steam effect for a locomotive using nParticles. Then, you learned a little about the Maya Paint Effects tool and how you can easily use it to create various effects such as grass and flowers. Then you learned how to create cloth effects using nCloth to make a tablecloth and a flag, and finally, you learned how to customize Maya to suit your own preferences.

To further your learning, try creating a scene on a grassy hillside with train tracks running through. Animate the locomotive, steam and all, driving through the scene and blowing the grass as it passes. You can also create a train whistle and a steam effect when the whistle blows, and you can create various other trails of smoke and steam as the locomotive drives through.

The best way to be exposed to Maya dynamics is simply to experiment once you're familiar with the general workflow in Maya. You'll find that the workflow in dynamics is more iterative than other Maya workflows because you're required to experiment frequently with different values to see how they affect the final simulation. With time, you'll develop a strong intuition, and you'll accomplish more complex simulations faster and with greater effect.

Where Do You Go from Here?

It's so hard to say goodbye! But this is really a "hello" to learning more about animation and 3D!

Please explore other resources and tutorials to expand your working knowledge of Maya. Several websites contain numerous tips, tricks, and tutorials for all aspects of Maya; my own resources and instructional videos and links are online at `http://koosh3d.com/` and on Facebook at `facebook.com/IntroMaya`, and you can contact or follow me through Twitter at `@Koosh3d`.

Of course, `www.autodesk.com/maya` has a wide range of learning tools. Now that you've gained your all-important first exposure, you'll be better equipped to forge ahead confidently.

The most important thing you should have learned from this book is that proficiency and competence with Maya come with practice, but even more so from your own artistic exploration. Treat this text and your experience with its information as a formal introduction to a new language and way of working for yourself; doing so is imperative. The rest of it—the gorgeous still frames and eloquent animations—come with furthering your study of your own art, working diligently to achieve your vision, and having fun along the way.

Thank you so very kindly for your time and attention, and for using my book as a resource to help you start on your journey with Maya. Enjoy, and good luck.

Index

Note: **Bold** page numbers refer to tables and *italic* page numbers refer to figures.